WORKBOOK Wie, bitte?

INTRODUCTORY GERMAN
FOR PROFICIENCY

STUDY TEXT

William B. Fischer

Portland State University

Peter N. Richardson

Linfield College

WILEY

JOHN WILEY & SONS
New York   Chichester   Brisbane   Toronto   Singapore

Table of Contents

You no doubt realize by now that *Wie, bitte?* is a different sort of language program. Because it is different, we want to tell you something about what you will be asked to do every day as you become more and more familiar with German.

LISTENING • *HÖREN*

Adults spend the largest portion of their "linguistic day" listening, and the development of good listening skills is crucial to your progress in German. The tape exercises have been designed with this in mind. (We strongly urge you to use headphones so that you hear better and do not disturb those nearby.)

There are three levels of tape exercises. Level "A" presents the complete dialogs in the **Class Text** chapters. The level "B" exercises are variations of the level "A" dialogs, but without a printed text to guide you; here you must rely solely on your listening skills. In level "C" you will hear selections from authentic German radio broadcasts. As the course progresses, you will return several times to most of the selections on the broadcast tapes.

Be sure to follow these directions for all tape exercises:

- First listen to the entire tape segment before undertaking any of the exercises. It is important that you hear German in its natural context, that you become used to hearing large blocks of language, much or most of which you will not understand. Remember that we often do not understand 100% of what we hear every day, even in our native language.
- Then note your task. The **Study Text** will ask you to listen for specific information on the tapes, and you must train yourself to disregard material that you think is extraneous. You may have to listen to the tape segment several times in order to complete your task.
- Now go on to the next task, and listen just as you did before. Do not try to perform more than one task at a time. Most of the tape segments are short, and each time you hear one you are training your ear and your mind to be receptive to the new sounds and forms. Use your common sense, too: You will find that your knowledge of the world around you is a big help in understanding each tape segment.
- Note-taking is an important skill. Frequently you will be asked to make a chart to help you with a listening exercise. This is a simple, but essential, part of developing your listening skills.
- Above all, do not be impatient with all the unfamiliar words you hear. As you progress

this year, you will understand more and more of each tape segment. Remember that you would understand very little of what you heard if you went to a German-speaking country right now.

SPEAKING • *SPRECHEN*

Before you begin your speaking exercises, be sure that you have studied carefully the *Gespräche*, or dialogs, in the **Class Text**. They provide you with the patterns you will be working with. In the **Class Text** (*Situationen* 1 and 2) the speaking roles are clearly prescribed, and you will be working with at least one other person. The speaking exercises in the Study Text, on the other hand, give you things to do on your own. These are not translation drills, and we have worded the tasks in such a way as to discourage you from equating English with German. You are asked to say what would be required of you in various situations. For example, in the situation "A person enters your train compartment. It is 9 a.m." you are not required to know the word for "compartment" or "enters," but simply to say what one is expected to say in that situation: "Guten Morgen." In fact, a variety of responses or reactions is possible for many of the situations. In language work, as in most areas of human activity, there is often more than one "right answer".

READING • *LESEN*

Wie, bitte? exposes you to a good deal more German than you might expect at the elementary level. The reading selections were not devised by German professors as classroom exercises. Every bit of reading material was produced by native speakers of German for other native speakers of German in everyday environments, and appears here in its original typographical form. The variety of printed materials (*Drucksachen*) represents the broad range of human activities you are likely to encounter during even a brief stay in a German-speaking environment. As a stranger to the language, you are asked to look for information within written texts. You are not required to translate anything. Each reading exercise asks you to look for specific information, and you should disregard the rest. In the course of the book, you will be returning again and again to the *Drucksachen*, each time looking for more detailed information. Students who have learned to read this way become fearless readers. They assume that if something is printed in German, they can understand what they need to. We want you to be fearless too, though you should not expect to understand everything you see in German,

even after a year's study. After a year with *Wie, bitte?*, you can reasonably expect to understand the facts in personal communications, advertising, familiar news sources, and information about cultural or entertainment events — that is, the sorts of things you would need to read during an extended stay in a German-speaking environment.

While you should not worry about all the words you do not understand in your *Drucksachen*, you will probably find a small dictionary helpful this year.

WRITING • *SCHREIBEN*

Writing is in many ways the least important of the four skills you will be practicing this year, because during your initial stay in a German-speaking country the chances are that most of your writing would be in letters home — in English. But we also expect that you would be called upon to perform certain specific writing tasks in a German-speaking environment.

The *Wie, bitte?* writing exercises were designed accordingly. At first, many consist of making lists, filling out forms, taking notes, and writing short messages to people telling them about your plans. The writing tasks often require you to consult a printed text and to write something specific in reaction to what you see.

As you carry out these tasks, be sure to imagine yourself in the individual situations. If a situation begins, "You have to leave your apartment for a short time and decide to write a note to a friend . . ." then you will begin the text of your note not with the German for "You," but with *ich*, "I". Again, the task does not involve translation, but rather functioning within a certain situation — just like the speaking situations described above.

You should also know that writing something down helps you remember it, and not just because you can then read it. Writing, like speaking, is a creative skill, and the process of creation reinforces linguistic patterns and improves your fluency.

STRUCTURAL EXERCISES

The topics of the structural exercises at the end of each **Study Text** chapter correspond to the grammar explanations (*Struktur*) in the **Class Text**. Your teacher may want you to work on these exercises one by one as you proceed though each chapter, or you may be asked to hand in the entire set of exercises at one time. In either case, approach these written exercises as you do those in the rest of the Study Text: not as

meaningless mechanical paper exercises, but as real tasks requiring your careful thought and engagement. Because we believe that what you do with German each day is directly relevant to active use of the language in a German-speaking environment, we have tried to establish a believable context for each exercise in the book.

At all times we are concerned that you not just manipulate the forms of language for their own sake, but that you use them to express what you need to say. The exercises demand that you not lock yourself into predictable patterns, but that you think about what you are saying at all times. Above all, the exercises are intended to stress that grammar is the skeleton that holds the body of the language together. Without our skeletons we would not even resemble human beings; without a strong grammar base, your German will not be recognizable as German beyond a very primitive level.

Most **Class Text** *Struktur* sections include marginal references to specific paragraphs in the Reference Grammar, which is found in the **Study Text**. For example, on page 12 of the **Class Text** you are referred to "Pronouns §§ 1,4,9,10", four paragraphs of the Pronoun section in the Reference Grammar that expand on the information you are given in the **Class Text**. You should be sure to study these Reference Grammar paragraphs before you begin the Structural Exercises in each chapter.

LEARNING VOCABULARY

There are many different ways of learning vocabulary, and in *Wie, bitte?* we have tried to add to the ways you may already know. It has long been recognized that we learn words most effectively when they are presented in a context, and for that reason we have added the picture dictionary, or *Bildwörterbuch*, to the **Class Text** (pp. 284-309). When you practice speaking situations on your own or with a friend, turn to the pages of the *Bildwörterbuch* that deal with the topic — food, clothing, nature, and so on — and you will find that you will be doing less groping for words and images than you would without the pictures and vocabulary to help you. As far as learning the chapter vocabulary is concerned, the dialogs present those new words in a believable and manageable context. After you have worked through the dialogs carefully and in conjunction with their translations in this Study Text, you will probably find that you already know many of the words. The rest you can learn either from the lists in this text or from flash cards that you make yourself.

WHAT ABOUT PRONUNCIATION?

Reasonably accurate pronunciation is necessary for efficient communication, though you should not become obsessed wih developing a flawless accent in the first year. Our advice to you is simply to speak as much as possible, and to listen carefully, both to your teacher and to the tapes that accompany this text. No matter how much you may study lists of words with extensive pronunciation hints, the very best avenue to good pronunciation is through your ears and mouth. Do not just imitate, but mimic your teacher, who is your contact with German-speaking culture. Perhaps you are one of those people who delight in imitating public figures — politicians, entertainers, and so on. If so, you are a natural candidate for cultivating an excellent German accent. All you must do is have the courage to abandon your English sounds when you deal with this new language. It may seem facetious to say that German is spoken with a German accent, but it is true. Millions of native speakers of this language go through life without pronouncing it with an American accent, and you can, too.

One of the authors of *Wie, bitte?* tells his students the following anecdote about his own experience learning German in college: "I took German for three years in high school, but never really pronounced it well. When I was studying one evening in my college dorm, my roommate (who had taken Spanish in high school) asked me what German sounded like. I read a paragraph to him, and he said, 'That really sounds different.' Then I said, 'But here's how my German teacher would read it.' And I read it with the accent of my teacher, who was a native speaker. My roommate said, 'Boy, that's really different. It sounds neat.' All of a sudden I realized — as if a light bulb had been turned on over my head — that my teacher's pronunciation was the valid one. It was both an intellectual and an emotional realization. When it was my turn to read the next day in class, I read with my 'new' accent, and after class the teacher came up to me and said, 'You know, your Cherman is really very goot all of a zudden.' I couldn't summon the courage to tell him that it had finally dawned on stupid me that I had to trust my ears. (By the way, my roommate, who was a math major then, is now a professor of German.)"

HOW TO USE YOUR STUDY TIME

Certainly there is much that you will be able to do studying German on your own — working with the reading, listening, and writing exercises, certainly, but also speaking alone what you will later say in actual conversation. There is also much that you can and should plan to do with a classmate. The dialogs in the **Class Text** should be practiced thoroughly, both inside and outside of class, for they are the structural models on which the situations in both **Class Text** and **Study Text** are based. Because language involves communication between speakers, these exercises are ideal for one-on-one work in your room or in some other place where you needn't be ashamed of making funny noises. Write notes in German to your classmates, too: "When do you want to go eat?", "I'll see you at the gym at 7:00", "Can you bring that new tape over tonight?"

How much time should you spend studying on your own? Learner types and abilities vary greatly. We estimate, however, that the average time should be about 12 hours for each complete chapter — about two hours for each hour in class. We suggest that you try dividing the twelve hours as follows: two hours each for reading, writing, and speaking; three hours for listening (you will need some extra time to find the appropriate exercises on your tapes); and three hours for studying your Reference Grammar and writing the Structural Exercises. On the average, you should plan to spend about 30 minutes on each of the "Stages" in each **Study Text** chapter.

Preliminary Chapter 1
WIE, BITTE? WER? WAS?

LISTEN • HÖREN

The *Wie, bitte?* package includes three kinds of taped material:

A Performances of the **Class Text** dialogs (*Gespräche*). The Study Text listening exercises that use this material have labels that begin with **A**.

B Dialogs similar in content to the **Class Text** dialogs, but more complex in language. The listening exercises that use this material have labels that begin with **B**. Since these dialogs are intended for listening comprehension exercise only, you are not given transcripts of them.

C Authentic broadcast excerpts recorded directly from German radio. The corresponding listening exercises have labels that begin with **C**. These materials too are intended for listening comprehension exercise only.

There are 27 sixty-minute "Chapter" cassettes. The first contains the materials for Preliminary Chapter 1 (first side) and Preliminary Chapter 2 (second side). Each of the other 26 cassettes contains the materials for one of the 26 main chapters of the course. The **A**, **B**, and **C** recordings are presented in precisely the order that the exercises in this **Study Text** use them. An announcement in English precedes each item. You will likely want to keep on hand one or two cassettes onto which you have copied the materials from chapters you are currently studying or reviewing; you may then "recycle" the cassettes by replacing old materials with new.

There are also 2 sixty-minute **C** cassettes. They contain the authentic broadcast excerpts, but not in the order that they are used in the **Study Text** exercises. The segments are grouped instead according to theme, and then in general order of increasing difficulty; see the TABLE OF CONTENTS on the next page. Thus Tape 1, Side A begins with 17 different radio announcements giving the time of day. We offer the **C** materials in this auxiliary form so that you can listen to sets of similar materials, either in class with the help of your teacher, or when you study by yourself. You might want to make permanent copies of both tapes.

Before you begin your listening exercises, read the *Study Guide* at the front of this book. There you will find advice about how to get the most out of the time you spend listening. As you study, remember that the listening exercises have three important functions. Sometimes, as in the taped performances of the **Class Text** dialogs or *Gespräche*, you will be given models for your own speaking. Often, too, you will be aiming to comprehend specific information; that is particularly so with the listening exercises labeled **B** in this **Study Text**. But always you will be encouraged to develop confidence and stamina by hearing large quantities of German; that is one of the two main purposes of the authentic listening materials used in the **C** exercises.

Stage 1

A1 Just listen several times to the dialogs for Preliminary Chapter #1. Talk along if you like.

A2 Practice saying the dialog lines. Use your "pause" button if you have one.

A3 You will hear some of the dialog prompts in random order. Respond by talking about yourself.

B1 You will hear greetings, sometimes mixed with other material. List the greetings you hear.

B2 You will hear statements about people. List the sex, first name, and last name of each person.

B3 You will hear statements about people. List the name, sex, nationality, age, and city of origin of each person. If no information is given, mark X.

Stage 2

B4 1. You will hear a number in English, and then a name spelled out; write what you hear.

2. You will hear an official reciting a list of the names, ages, and passport numbers of a group of travelers. Write what you hear.

c   You will now hear an example of each major type or <u>section</u> of the authentic radio broadcast materials. First consult the TABLE OF CONTENTS on this page to see what kinds of materials are in the sections. Then do the exercises below.

You may find it useful to sketch out a chart for your listening, with space as well for other notes. There is, of course, nothing wrong with trying to understand more than you are asked to understand. In any case, you will hear most segments several times over the course of the book.

Broadcast Excerpts — TABLE OF CONTENTS

SECTION	TITLE	SETS	SEGMENTS (by Set)		LENGTH
	C Tape 1 — Side A				
1	Zeitangaben • *Time of Day*	5	17	(3/4/4/4/2)	3 :30
2	Das Programm • *Broadcast Schedule*	3	7	(3/2/2)	6
3	Glückwunschkonzert • *Music by Request*	2	4	(2/2)	8 :30
4	Verkehrsübersicht • *Traffic Report*	2	5	(2/3)	4 :30
5	Wetterbericht • *Weather Report*	2	11	(6/5)	7 :30
	C Tape 1 — Side B				
6	Werbung • *Commercials*	4	26	(9/7/7/3)	14
7	Börsenbericht • *Stock Market Report*	1	3		7
8	Lotto und Sport • *Lottery and Sports*	2	4	(2/2)	7
	C Tape 2 — Side A				
1	Nachrichten • *News*	4	17	(5/5/5/2)	13 :45
2	Leute • *People*	2	7	(4/3)	12 :15
3	Akzent und Dialekt • *Accent and Dialect*	1	4		2
	C Tape 2 — Side B				
4	Freizeit • *Leisure Time*	3	7	(2/3/2)	13 :45
5	Gesellschaft • *Society*	4	11	(1/4/3/3)	16

Exercises

<u>Section 1 — Set 1 — Segment 1</u> Which two numbers did you hear?

<u>Section 2 — Set 1 — Segment 1</u> List two topics that will be featured in upcoming broadcasts; of the several possibilities, one is a city and the other a leisure activity.

<u>Section 3 — Set 1 — Segment 1</u> What kind of radio program are you hearing?
   a) family health advice   **b)** birthday congratulations   **c)** news
   How might you have figured that out, other than by reading the table of contents above?

<u>Section 4 — Set 1 — Segment 1</u> How's the traffic right now? Can you hear a German word that is almost the same as an English one?

<u>Section 5 — Set 1 — Segment 1</u> What time is it? List the temperatures you hear. When in the day were they recorded, and are they highs or lows? Use the chart on the inside front cover of the **Class Text** to estimate equivalents in degrees Fahrenheit.

<u>Section 6 — Set 1 — Segment 1</u> Write down some of the words that appear in both this ad and the **Class Text** dialogs for this chapter.

<u>Section 7 — Set 1 — Segment 1</u> What are you hearing, and how can you be sure?
   a) mathematics lecture   **b)** sports scores   **c)** stock report   **d)** ads

<u>Section 8 — Set 1 — Segment 1</u> Listen for numbers that correspond to your age, your birthdate, or your automobile license plate — just in case you were betting on those.

(Do this <u>only</u> if you are using the **C** tapes, rather than the Chapter tapes: Using the TABLE OF CONTENTS above, locate and listen to the first segment of the first set of each of the sections on the first of the two tapes. The selections are preceded by identifications in English. If your tape player has a counter, you can note where each major <u>section</u> begins. You can then quickly locate the same material later by rewinding the tape to its start, zeroing the counter, and fast-forwarding to the proper number. Otherwise, you can use the timing indications in the TABLE OF CONTENTS to estimate where the materials are. As you locate each segment, do the exercises after the TABLE OF CONTENTS.)

SPEAK • SPRECHEN

NAMES Here are some names which might be either German or English, except perhaps for slight differences in spelling. Practice saying them both ways.

Richard	Peter	Marie	Ingrid	Christa
Robert	Elisabeth	Katherine	Fischer	Paul
Klein	Neumann	Einstein	Wiener	Schneider
Braun	Weyerhäuser	Anheuser	Busch	Biermann
Michael	Schmidt	Schoendienst	Assenmacher	Herzog
Martin	Luther	Georg	Hermann	Ruth

Only first and last names are common in German-speaking countries, though some people have double first names like Hans-Dieter or Annemarie. Even where there is a middle name it is seldom used; the practice of including a middle initial is rare. In encounters with strangers, adult Germans almost always offer and expect last names. If you offer your first name first, as many Americans customarily do when they speak to other Americans, a German speaker might consider you immature, or else infer that you are insisting on a degree of intimacy which is not yet appropriate.

TITLES Just as they prefer to use last names until they know people quite well, German speakers use the titles *Herr* Mr., *Frau* Mrs., and *Fräulein* Miss, more readily than do English speakers. Customs vary somewhat from country to country, but in general you should be prepared to be more formal in your speech than you are with English. People who have a doctorate of any kind are gratified to hear their title acknowledged: *Guten Morgen, Frau Dr. Hartmann!* or *Guten Morgen, Dr. Hartmann!* Less commonly, the title can also extend to the spouse, so that *Frau Dr. Hartmann* could be either a woman who earned the degree herself or one whose husband is *Dr. Hartmann*. When in doubt, use the title.

When does a *Fräulein* become a *Frau*? Upon marrying, of course. But young women are now commonly addressed as *Frau* at age 16, or at the beginning of the tenth grade. In some conservative areas, unmarried older women may still prefer the title *Fräulein*.

NUMBERS These numbers are read on your tape after the B exercises.

0 = null	10 = zehn	20 = zwanzig	100 =hundert
1 = eins	11 = elf	21 = einundzwanzig	101 = hunderteins
2 = zwei	12 = zwölf	22 = zweiundzwanzig	102 = hundertzwei
3 = drei	13 = dreizehn	30 = dreißig	110 = hundertzehn
4 = vier	14 = vierzehn	40 = vierzig	123 = hundertdreiundzwanzig
5 = fünf	15 = fünfzehn	50 = fünfzig	200 = zweihundert
6 = sechs	16 = sechzehn	60 = sechzig	700 = siebenhundert
7 = sieben	17 = siebzehn	70 = siebzig	999 = neunhundertneunundneunzig
8 = acht	18 = achtzehn	80 = achtzig	1000 = tausend
9 = neun	19 = neunzehn	90 = neunzig	2000 = zweitausend

Stage 1 (⊗ = your classmate or other counterpart in the conversation)

1. Open a short conversation by offering a greeting and introducing yourself.
2. It's 9 a.m. You greet ⊗.
3. You know ⊗'s last name but need to know the full name as well.
4. You'd like to know if ⊗ is from Canada.
5. ⊗ has found out your first name. Provide further information.
6. You need to know ⊗'s age.
7. You're curious about ⊗'s main field of study.
8. Identify yourself to the customs official.
9. ⊗ thinks you're from Kentucky. You are.
10. ⊗ thinks you're from New York. You aren't. Provide further information.
11. You're looking for accommodations at a youth hostel. Give your age and name; if your last name is not German in origin, or not spelled in its original German form, spell it out.
12. You haven't yet chosen a major, but rather are taking courses in several subjects. Provide information about your subjects of study.
13. Be prepared to ask anyone in class three questions about basic personal information. Can you adapt to unexpected responses? Example: "Are you American?" "No." "Oh, are you Canadian?"

COLLEGE MAJORS North American students typically take 1/3 of their courses in general education, 1/3 in electives, and 1/3 in a major field. At universities in German-speaking countries, first-year students begin to concentrate right away in a major area, with other courses in one or two minor fields. For example, a student might have a major (*das Hauptfach*) in history with a minor (*das Nebenfach*) in economics or English, or both. Few electives are chosen outside these fields. The question *Was studieren Sie?* therefore means "What is your major?" and could also ask for a listing of current courses. (For a list of academic subjects, see the *Bildwörterbuch* section on p. 291 of the **Class Text**. For more about universities, see Chapter 17, *Universität*.)

Stage 2 1. Be prepared for an initial encounter with someone who appears to be a student. Assume, for example, that lack of table space in a university cafeteria has led you to share a table with strangers. Silence on your part will be interpreted as lack of manners. (**greetings! names! subjects of study!**)

2. Assume that your name is either Emerson Lee, Kimberly Elton John, Lane Rose, or Kwang Kim. People at home are often confused about which name is your first name and which is your last; some first names may be either male or female. Many Germans are familiar with common naming customs of foreigners, but in your case there has been some understandable confusion. Straighten out the German speaker you are talking to.

Now carry out the previous task with these complications:

3. The person with whom you are speaking mistakes your nationality. For example, you are not English or Canadian, but rather American.

4. A poor telephone connection leads the person with whom you are speaking to mistake your sex.

READ • LESEN

Stage 1 <u>NOTE</u>: **Class Text = CT**; Page 5 of the **Class Text = CT 5**; **Study Text = ST**.

1. Look at the list on **CT 5**. Make 4 lists: 1) female specialists in internal medicine; 2) male specialists in internal medicine; 3) female dermatologists; 4) male dermatologists. Practice saying the names.

2. Read the Christmas card with the handwritten message in English on **CT 274**. Can you correct the English mistakes?

Stage 2 1. Look again at the list on **CT 5**, and at the maps on **CT 312-13**. You have just arrived in Freiburg, and are staying at a small hotel, the Gasthaus Deutscher Kaiser, near Goethestraße. On the train ride from Köln you looked out the open window for hours, and something got in your eye. You suspect a scratched cornea. Make a list of three eye specialists closest to you within a reasonable walking distance (= about 500 meters). Be sure to include the addresses. For extra practice, do the same thing again, but assume that your hotel is in the heart of the city, right near the Münsterplatz.

2. Now that your eye is feeling better, read the concert program on **CT 8**. You are interested in vocal music. List appropriate events, with the following information: 1) name of composer; 2) name of piece; 3) names of singers. Can you figure out the dates, days, and times of the performances? For extra practice: You detest vocal music, but you want to go to a concert. Make a list of composers, pieces, and performers. Can you figure out the names of the instruments?

3. Transcribe the names and addresses on the Christmas card and envelope on **CT 274**.

4. Your trip is tax deductible — or so you hope to claim. But the tax collector probably doesn't read German. Transcribe the restaurant receipts on **CT 9**. For help, see the chart below. Check the arithmetic. Watch the 1's and 7's — maybe the tax collector reads a little German.

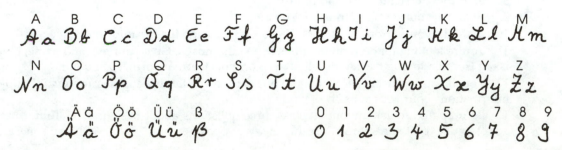

This alphabet is spoken after the numbers at the end of the tape for this unit.

WRITE • SCHREIBEN

Handwriting — Writing a neat hand is more important in the German-speaking countries than it is in the United States or Canada. Moreover, German has several special characters, and several letters and numbers are not written quite as they are in English. You need not adopt a completely German style of penmanship, but when writing as though it were for real you should use the German forms of the numerals "1" and "7". You must always pay attention to the "umlauts" — the two dots that may appear over *A/a*, *O/o*, and *U/u*; the umlauted vowels represent distinctly different sounds.

1.   Think about the lists of doctors' names and addresses you made. Would they have been legible to a passerby from whom you requested directions?

2.   Learn your major and write it where you will have it for ready reference. You might also wish to add the names of other academic subjects important to you. See the appropriate section of the *Bildwörterbuch* on **CT 291**.

3.   Fill out the hotel registration form below.

√ CHECK YOUR PROFICIENCY

SPEAKING — Can you:
__ produce — not by rote recitation, but rather when appropriate — all of the dialogs, using your own nationality, age, major?
__ ask the dialog questions that will induce someone else to carry out the preceding task?

LISTENING — Can you:
__ respond reasonably to the dialog questions in ways other than speaking — for example, by writing down your own name when asked in German to do so; by writing down, when spelled out, common personal names; by writing the digits for 0-100 when you hear them?

READING — Can you:
__ recognize the names and related nationalities of the major English-speaking countries?
__ recognize the words "Herren" and "Damen" (and symbols for them)?
__ distinguish between the numerals 1 and 7?
__ find your way through a form that asks you to fill in your birthdate and birthplace, country, place of residence, and nationality?

WRITING — Can you:
__ fill in a commonly-encountered personal data form, such as a hotel registration sheet, with handwriting legible to speakers of German?

LISTEN • HÖREN

Stage 1

A1 Just listen several times to the dialogs for Preliminary Unit #2. Talk along if you like.

A2 Practice saying the dialog lines. Use your "pause" button if you have one.

A3 Now you will hear some of the dialog prompts in random order. Respond. Where you can, adjust the content of the response by using different city names, times, days of the week, and prices.

B1 1.   You will hear names of cities read and then spelled. Write each one. See if you can write the name before it is spelled.

2.   Use the map on the inside front cover of the **Class Text**. You will hear the names of cities. Find each city on the map. Can you find each city before you hear the next one?

3.   You will hear statements which mention cities and sometimes their countries. If you do not hear the name of the country, that means that you should already know it, because speakers of German would not ordinarily supply it. Write the name of the city and then note the country in which it is located.

Stage 2

B2 1.   Write down the clock times you hear. Use digits — don't try to spell out the numbers in German.

2.   Write down the days you hear. Feel free to use the standard German abbreviations.

3.   You will hear statements which include mention of days of the week. For each item, note what day <u>today</u> is.

B3 You will hear remarks about concert, opera and ballet performances. Write the day and time of the performance next to its name. Then write the price of the tickets available.

C From now on short codes will be used to refer to the **C** materials. The codes, such as **1A:1.1.1**, show the location of the segments on the special **C** tapes, but right now you need not worry about that. When you work with the chapter tapes you will hear the code, and can then match it to the code printed in the margin of the **Study Text**. Since many segments will be re-used later, with ever greater challenges to comprehension, you may want to review earlier exercises that use the same materials. The appropriate information is provided in brackets at the end of a given exercise. Thus "[3]" means that the tape segment was used earlier, in Chapter 3; "P1" and "P2" refer to the preliminary chapters.

1A:1.1.1-3 What time is it? What station (*Programm*) are you listening to? Don't be upset if some segments lack the information you are being asked to listen for. Note its absence and proceed. [P1]

1A:1.2.1-4 The time indications in these segments are not precisely on the hour. On first listening try to figure out at least what approximate hour it is. The second time around you may well be able to get the exact time.

1A:1.3.4 Can you tell what day and date it is? Listen also for the greeting, the words *Damen und Herren*, and the time. If *Herren* means "Gentlemen", what does *Damen* mean?

1B:6.1.1-9 You will hear 9 radio commercials. All contain words that you have already learned, or words that are almost the same as English words. For each item, try to figure out the *kind* of product or service being advertised (examples: fast food, soft drinks, tires, wristwatches). For some you may also be able to list the brand name (examples: RC Cola, Goodyear, Timex). Finally, note any prices you hear.

1B:7.1.1-2 How is Volkswagen stock doing? What is the exchange rate for dollars to marks? As you may have noted when watching international sports events, in German the comma (*Komma*) is the equivalent of our decimal point.

1B:8.2.2 Concentrate on the first 35 seconds of this long sports report. You will hear the results of a soccer game. 1) During what part of the day was the report broadcast? 2) One of the teams was from the city of Bielefeld. What city was the other from? 3) Who won, and by what score? 4) How big was the crowd? 5) What other city is mentioned? (If you start hearing about a Danish soccer player in München, or basketball and volleyball reports, you have listened too long.)

If you listen to the rest of the sports report, note the following information: 1) names of sports — many are similar to English; 2) nationalities, countries, cities; 3) scores; 4) distinctions between men's and women's events; 5) at the end, the winning numbers in horse-racing and the lottery.

C tape coding system The code presents in order the tape number (1 or 2) and side (A or B), followed by numbers for the section, set and segment.

```
tape & side        section
          \     /
      1A:1.3.4 = tape 1, side A, section 1, set 3, segment 4
            /   \
        set        segment
NOTE: 1,2,5 = segments 1, 2, and 5; 1-5 = segments 1 through 5
```

SPEAK • SPRECHEN

Entschuldigung — Bitte

Say *Entschuldigung* to apologize for disturbing someone. The word serves two purposes:

It gains the listener's attention.

It requests forgiveness for slight personal offenses, such as unintended physical contact.

An appropriate reply in either instance is *Bitte*. But note the differences in intonation of both *Entschuldigung* and *Bitte* in their different functions.

Place Names

Study the maps of East and West Germany, Switzerland, and Austria, and use them when you do the workbook exercises.

Learn the German names of major countries, above all those in which German is an official language.

Learn the names of several major cities in each German-speaking country.

Learn the difference between West Germany and East Germany.

It is important to pronounce place names correctly. Certainly you want to be understood. You also don't want to offend people by mispronouncing the names of places dear to them. Recall how mispronunciation of place names like "Oregon" or "Worcester [Mass.]" can be annoying to the locals.

Many North American cities are named for German cities. Practice saying the American name and the German name. You might also locate the German city on your maps.

Frankfort, Ky. — Frankfurt	Berlin, Conn. — Berlin
Munster, Indiana — Münster	New Leipzig, ND — Leipzig
Stuttgart, Ark. — Stuttgart	Weimar, Texas — Weimar
Lake Lucerne, Wisc. — Luzern	Vienna, Ga — Wien

English-speaking NATO troops have long been stationed in West Germany, and of course North American tourists commonly travel to the Federal Republic, Switzerland, and Austria. We tend to anglicize the pronunciation of familiar cities in those countries. Practice genuine German pronunciation of these:

Heidelberg	Wiesbaden	Mainz	Bremen	Stuttgart	Würzburg
Garmisch	Hamburg	Hameln	Zermatt	Luzern	Basel
Salzburg	Kitzbühel	Innsbruck	Oberammergau		

Some larger cities have international or English names. Learn the German name and its pronunciation:

Köln (Cologne)	München (Munich)	Nürnberg (Nuremberg)
Braunschweig (Brunswick)	Zürich (Zurich)	Wien (Vienna)

Lastly, speakers of English often ignore umlauts. Practice on these:

Nürnberg	Schwäbisch Hall	München	Köln
Düsseldorf	Innsbruck	Saarbrücken	

(Did you notice that one of those words does <u>not</u> have an umlaut?)

Days of the week

<u>So</u>nntag   <u>Mo</u>ntag   <u>Di</u>enstag   <u>Mi</u>ttwoch   <u>Do</u>nnerstag   <u>Fr</u>eitag   <u>Sa</u>mstag

weekend=das Wochenende

Stage 1

1.   You have just bumped into someone by mistake.

2.   In a crowded bus someone steps on your foot. Wait expectantly for her to say something; after she does, you say something.

3.   You wonder what city the train is approaching. You suggest it's Aachen.

4.   Someone you've met is from Freudenstadt. You find out which of the German-speaking countries the city is in.

5.   Someone asks you for the time. You're not wearing a watch.

6.   Someone asks you for the time. You're not wearing a watch, but there's a clock 'way over there behind the person.

7.   You'd like to know if today is Thursday. Ordinarily you know what day it is, but you've had a long flight from Arizona. Try to add enough information that you won't appear foolish asking what day it is.

8.   You'd like to ask a stranger for some information — about time, city, date, etc. Begin the conversation.

Stage 2   1.   You are considering buying something in the display case, but you can't tell whether the price label is 16 or 76 marks.

2.   You are considering buying something in the display case, but you can't tell whether the price label applies to the item you are looking at or the one right below it.

3.   Point out where Köln is on your map.

4.   Point out where München is on someone else's map.

5.   Tell someone you're sorry today isn't Friday. Provide more information.

6.   You've stepped on an old woman's foot in the train. Apologize rapidly with two different expressions.

7.   What would you say if the old woman not only gracefully accepted your apology, but also struck up a conversation with you?

8.   What would you say if she turned out to be someone who had emigrated from Berlin to Milwaukee in 1947 and still spoke English with a heavy accent?

9.   The person you are talking to has said he's from a city called Chur. (How will you continue the conversation? What will you say if it turns out that you placed the city in the wrong country?)

10. Gently correct someone who has assumed that you are from, for example, Portland, Oregon, rather than Portland, Maine, or Decatur, Alabama, rather than Decatur, Georgia or Illinois, or Berlin, Germany rather than Berlin, Connecticut.

11. You are sitting in a window-seat on the train and need to go to the bathroom, which is located at the end of the corridor. The person next to you is engrossed in a newspaper. Say what you must.

12. Someone has asked you what time it is. It's 9:58. What do you say? (How exact do you have to be?)

13. Practice saying place names and numbers by reading the lists of phone numbers on **CT 136** and the hotel listing on **CT 320**. Say the numbers as strings of single digits.

14. Practice saying prices by reading the Jacobi menu on pp. 14-15 of the **ST** *Drucksachen*, which are located in the back of this book. Do only items whose prices are given in whole numbers.

READ • LESEN

Stage 1   1.   Look at the *Gaststättenverzeichnis*, or list of restaurants, for Mannheim on **CT 322**.

1.   Today is Monday; it's 5 p.m. You're hungry for Italian food. Can you get some right now? If so, where? If not, how long will you have to wait till someplace is open? How long will you have to wait to have a choice of Italian restaurants?

2.   It's 5 p.m. Sunday now. How many restaurants are open? How many different kinds of food do you have to choose from? Which restaurants seem to offer the greatest variety?

3.   It's Friday. Where can you be sure of getting fish for lunch?

4.   It's almost 3 p.m. Where can you go for a snack? What if it were almost 3 a.m.?

2.   Look at the list of Berlin hotel facilities on **CT 321**.

1.   List 15 words that would be understood by someone who knows no German.

2.   It's noon on Sunday and your tour group is leaving in half an hour. Do you have time to buy souvenirs? What if it were 6 o'clock? What if it were Saturday?

3.   It's midnight in Berlin and 3 p.m. earlier that same day on the West Coast of the U.S. Can you send a telex to Seattle from this hotel? Can you cash a traveler's check?

Stage 2

1.   Look at the Karlsruhe information on **CT 196-97**.

You'll be in this city from 2 to 9 July, but you have to work until 7 every evening on the weekdays. If you're willing to have just a quick bite for dinner, how many musical events do you have to choose from? How many sports events? What night <u>couldn't</u> you have a drink at Sam's?

2.   Consult the Mannheim *Tageskalender* on pp. 24-25 of the **ST** *Drucksachen*.

1.   Which Tuesday evening events would someone who knew no German be likely to attend?

2.   What is somewhat unusual about two of the musicians performing on Tuesday evening?

3.   What do you observe about ticket prices for children in Mannheim? If you think you can't do this one because you don't know the word for "children" yet, think about our English word "Kindergarten".

4.   Which of the many events listed would probably be most fun for a five-year-old?

5.   Say as much as you can about the event that takes place at 9:30 a.m. Thursday.

6.   How do they celebrate the Fourth of July in Mannheim?

WRITE • SCHREIBEN

Stage 1   1.   Look over the lists of restaurants you made in the reading exercises. Did you write the key letters and numerals in such a way that speakers (readers) of German would not be confused? Did you make your notes in German (*Montag*) or in English (Monday)? Did you use abbreviations?

2.   Sketch a calendar for the next two weeks. Label the days and dates, and then write in your class schedule. Abbreviate the German names for the days of the week, use the German names of your courses, and be sure to adjust your handwriting to German practices.

Stage 2   In the course of *Wie, bitte?* you will take an imaginary trip from Aachen to Köln (northwestern BRD), and then through Freiburg (southwestern BRD) to München (Bavaria). Locate those cities on your maps. You will also take some side trips to Switzerland, Austria and East Germany. In this exercise you will explore alternate routes. Use the *Zugbegleiter* (train brochures) for the IC 513 "Wetterstein" on pp. 2-5 of the **ST** *Drucksachen* and the IC 125 "Erasmus" on **CT 316-19**. Using the chart on the next page for a model, outline your plans for the trips described below. List main stops, with arrival and departure times. Perhaps you will want to outline alternatives, in case you decide to change your schedule underway. If so, use the three extra columns with the headings <u>Uhr/hours</u>.

1.   You want to go straight from Köln to München.

2.   You want to go from Köln to München, but you want to make some overnight stops along the way. You can't do it all, but here are some stops you might want to make: Koblenz for wine-tasting, Frankfurt to visit a business associate, Stuttgart to see the Mercedes factory, Würzburg to see a friend at the US military base, Nürnberg to take in the annual Toy Exhibition, and Mannheim to take in a concert.

Ihre Reiseverbindungen

Österreichische Bundesbahnen **Your travel-connections · Vos connections · I vostri collegamenti di viaggio**

Bahnhof / station gare / stazione		Uhr/hours heures ore	Uhr/hours heures ore	Uhr/hours heures ore	Uhr/hours heures ore	Bemerkungen remarks observations osservazioni
	ab/dp/pt					
	an/ar					
	ab/dp/pt					
	an/ar					
	ab/dp/pt					
	an/ar					
	ab/dp/pt					
	an/ar					
	ab/dp/pt					
	an/ar					

Auskunft ohne Gewähr · information without guarantee · information sous toutes réserves · informazioni con riserva.
W = an Werktagen · on weekdays · les jours ouvrables · nei giorni feriali.
S = an Sonn- und Feiertagen · on sundays and holidays ·   les dimanches et jours fériés · si effettuano nei giorni festivi.
X = umsteigen · change · changer de train · cambiare treno

Z 1322   Auskunftszettel - 150/105 mm - HD Wien - Auflagejahr (letzte Zahl maßgeblich): 1983.82 81

√ CHECK YOUR PROFICIENCY

CAN YOU:
__ identify yourself and say where you are from and what you are studying?
__ ask for clarification of things you don't understand?
__ say simple courtesy formulas?
__ count money?
__ name the days of the week?
__ ask questions about dates, times, and prices?
__ apologize?
__ locate and name major cities in the four German-speaking countries and immediately point to them on an unlabeled map of Europe?
__ respond by saying: "_____ . *Das ist in* _____." if you hear the name of a large city in a German-speaking country?

HÖREN

Stage 1

A1 Just listen several times to the dialogs for *Gespräche 1: Fahrkarten und Pässe, bitte*. Talk along if you like.

A2 Practice saying the dialog lines. Use your "pause" button if you have one.

B1 You will hear four brief conversations. On a chart, note for each one: **a)** the greetings and farewells you hear; **b)** the number of times you hear the word *bitte*; **c)** how many passengers there are; **d)** what the official wants.

B2 You will hear ten statements involving train passengers and their travel plans. List for each one the passengers and the cities involved, and write down the days and times of travel. Also write both the official and the casual clock time, if they differ.

Stage 2

B3 You will hear three conversations. Make a chart with four columns. Note for each conversation: **a)** how many passengers are involved; **b)** what greetings you hear; **c)** what cities are mentioned; **d)** what document the official wants. Now concentrate on the end of the <u>third</u> dialog, and on its <u>tone</u> more than its individual words. The official leaves, and then the passengers say something about him. What don't they like about his behavior, and what do they think causes it? **a)** loud voice — the uniform; **b)** pushy — he slept poorly; **c)** ugly — he didn't comb his hair.

B4 You will hear information about several different people. The first four introduce themselves; conversation #5 involves two people; conversation #6 deals with a person who is not present. On a chart with five columns for <u>first name</u>, <u>last name</u>, <u>age</u>, <u>major</u>, and <u>home town</u>, fill in the information you hear.

C1

1A:4.1.2 At what time is the traffic report being broadcast? Which city is mentioned most and might therefore be where the station and its listeners are located? There are traffic jams on two stretches of freeway (*Autobahn*). Fill in the chart below:

	STRETCH	ROAD #	LENGTH OF JAM (KM)
1)	Nürnberg-München	_____	_____
2)	Passau-München	_____	_____

1A:4.2.1 Another traffic report; fill in the chart below:

	STRETCH	ROAD #
1)	_____	_____
2)	Kempten-Ulm	_____

If you want to picture the locations in the reports, use the maps on **CT 158** or the inside covers of the **Class Text** and **Study Text**.

C2

1B:7.1.3 After 25 seconds of introductory information the stock market report offers a long list of company names with their current stock value and change from the previous trading session. Make a chart with columns headed <u>Company</u>, <u>Price</u>, and <u>Change (+/-)</u>. Then listen for information about the following companies whose products are well known world-wide: BASF, Bayer, BMW, Daimler-Benz, Löwenbräu, Lufthansa, Porsche, and Volkswagen. You are not expected to get all of the stock prices.

1B:8.2.1 Listen to the reports on the first three soccer games currently being played. Fill in the blanks below with cities and scores. Why do you think the announcer gives no numbers for the first game?

	LOCATION	TEAMS	SCORE
1)	_____	Saarbrücken - _____	_____
2)	_____	Mönchengladbach - _____	_____
3)	Schalke	Schalke 04 - Fortuna _____	_____

SPRECHEN

Stage 1   1.   The conductor would like to see your group's tickets.

2.   Your parents thank the person selling soft drinks on the train.

3.   It's 7 p.m. You greet the conductor.

4.   Bernd indicates that he'll be in Frankfurt at 9:00 p.m.

5.   You give your ticket to the conductor. Silence is not golden.

6.   The conductor accidentally lets your ticket fall to the floor.

7.   It's 8:15 a.m. The passport officer asks for your identification. Your I.D. seems to satisfy the passport officer.

8.   You didn't understand the conductor's question. Maybe you venture to guess what he wants.

9.   You tell the person in your compartment that you're from: **a)** Rome, Georgia — not Rome, Italy; **b)** Paris, Texas — not Paris, France; **c)** Moscow, Idaho — not the Russian city

10.   You'd like to know when the train gets to Aachen.

11.   You ask the woman sitting across from you whether the brown luggage is hers.

Stage 2   1.   You're leaving the compartment, suitcase in hand. You deny that the tattered green valise with socialist slogans is yours.

2.   ⊗ asks you something. You understand the question, but have no idea what the answer is. Can you say something to reassure ⊗ that you indeed understood the question?

3.   The boy next to you tells you that the train gets to Köln at 4:00 p.m.

4.   You suspect that the person next to the window is from Canada. You're curious, but do be polite.

5.   You ask your seatmate to show you where you are on the map. You ask her where her baggage is. She says she has no idea. You ask her whether you're in Köln or Aachen.

6.   You ask your other seatmate where his passport could be. You ask him whether he just might know if you'll be in Köln at 7:00.

7.   You tell the conductor that's not your ticket lying over there on the fold-out table by the window.

8.   You want to wake your friend and tell her you're in Köln.

LESEN

Stage 1   Look at the *Zugbegleiter* on **CT 316-19**. It provides information about the "Erasmus", a train that travels from Holland to Austria via Köln and München.

1.   Study the information given in both English and German before the actual timetable; look particularly at the *Zeichenerklärung* Explanation of Signs.

    1.   What is the first day of the week in German-speaking countries? In the U.S.?

    2.   What German words seem to be the equivalent of English 'train car', 'day', 'train', 'telephone', 'customs', 'station', and 'weekday'? What appears to be the literal meaning of the word for 'weekday'?

    3.   What is the most expensive train type? Why do you think it is so expensive? What is the abbreviation for the slowest train?

    4.   How many time zones are there in Europe? In North America?

2.   Now look at the timetable section, which lists cities along the route of the train.

    1.   The "Erasmus" leaves Amsterdam at 6:57 a.m. What are the German words for 'arrival' and 'departure'? Be sure to learn them: They are important.

    2.   If you boarded in Amsterdam, how long could you sleep before having to wake up to show someone your passport?

    3.   How many miles is it from Emmerich to Oberhausen? How long does the trip take? What is the approximate average train speed in km/h? In mph? If you thought you might like to get off in Oberhausen, how long would you have to make up your mind? (60 miles = 100 km)

4. In Duisburg you could take a train called the "Lötschberg". How long would you have between trains at the main station (*Hauptbahnhof*) in Duisburg? Where does the "Lötschberg" go? About when would you hear *"Die Pässe, bitte!"* on this train? How many of the cities it passes through can you find on your map? Where would you be when it is time for your 4:00 nap?

Stage 2   Using some of the explanatory information from the "Erasmus", now look at the schedule for trains from München to Köln on **CT 35**.

1. If you wanted to take the 7:57 Intercity to Köln, could you do so on Dec. 26th? If not, how long would you have to wait for the next train on that day?

2. Which train seems faster, the IC, the D, the FD, or the TEE?

3. If for some reason you wanted to travel only first class, which train would you take? How much would your ticket cost? Is there a discount for round-trip travel?

4. If you took the 10:57 train to Köln, how much would your one-way ticket cost?

SCHREIBEN

Stage 1   1. Check over your notes for the HÖREN and LESEN assignments. Did you pay attention to umlauts and capital letters? If a task was of the kind that might be encountered in real life, did you write in such a way that a speaker of German would not be confused by the difference between English and German characters?

2. Reread the *Struktur 1* section on nouns on **CT 12**, and the corresponding material in the *Reference Grammar*. Then read the introduction to the **Class Text** *Glossary* on **CT 350-51**. Be sure that you understand how noun plurals are formed and how the *Glossary* provides this information. Now look up and write down the plurals for the following nouns: *Name, Tag, Amerikaner, Kanadierin, Wurst*, and *Mathematik*.

Stage 2   1. Do the written grammar exercises on the appropriate forms at the end of the chapter.

2. Also at the end of the chapter, fill in the application for an entrance visa for East Germany.

IMBISS

HÖREN

Stage 1

A1   Just listen several times to the dialogs for *Gespräche 2: Imbiß*. Talk along if you like.

A2   Practice saying the dialog lines. Use your "pause" button if you have one.

B1   You will hear five conversations. On a chart, note for each one: **a**) food items and their prices; **b**) beverages and their prices; **c**) the total bill; **d**) the amount offered; **e**) the change returned.

B2   Listen to the tape of an Austrian tour group at an *Imbiß* in Klagenfurt. The tour leader is taking snack orders from the entire group. Note each person's name, and then write down the order of food and drink.

Stage 2

B3   The tour director from exercise **B2** above will now read the total order back to the group, with the prices in the local currency; write down the prices. He's made some mistakes in items and prices. Compare your list to his. Underline the items he will have to correct.

C1

2A:1.3.1-4 For each of the four news stories note the city or country in which the newsworthy event originated. Then listen to each report more carefully and do the following exercises — <u>Segment 1</u>: Note two words that are repeated several times; one is similar to an English word, while the other is a German word often used in English. Together they will tell you the major theme of the news story. <u>Segment 2</u>: How many children were just born (boys? girls?) and how are they doing? <u>Segment 3</u>: At what time is the story being broadcast? Where did the bomb go off? <u>Segment 4</u>: Listen for a word that sounds identical in German and English and describes a social problem.

C2

2A:2.1.1 During what part of the day and on which day(s) might this cheery broadcast be starting?

2A:2.1.2 The announcer has received a letter from some listeners. In what country are they located?

2A:3.1.1 The commercial for "Paulaner Salvator" beer is spoken in Bavarian dialect, but you can pick up certain important words. When does the speaker intend to go drink some Salvator? Complete the slogan: "_____, besser, Paulaner".

SPRECHEN

Stage 1

1. Your train has stopped at a station for 12 minutes, and you plan to dash out for a snack. Ask the man in your compartment if he would like some coffee, as long as you're going anyway.

2. The man doesn't want anything, but his wife would like a bottle of beer.

3. Your cup of tea costs DM 2,60. Give the person at the counter DM 5,00.

4. The person has only 10 and 50-pfennig pieces. Help her count out the change for that 5-mark piece.

5. Heinz and Barbara want to order two ice cream cups. Help them out.

6. The waiter asks Jürgen what he would like.

7. Frank tells Rainer he's drinking apple juice.

8. The waiter wants to know what Frau Karstens is eating. She says she'd like a sausage with a roll.

9. Elsa would like to order some coffee in a styrofoam cup to go.

10. The restaurant doesn't have any more Fanta. The waiter regrets this.

11. The waiter gives Martina her tea.

12. The restaurant manager says good-bye to two valued customers.

Stage 2

1. Ask Mrs. Kurz:
> what she has / what she would like / if she has her baggage

2. Ask Mr. and Mrs. Rümmel:
> what they would like / where your ticket is
> if they would like apple juice / what they have / what Brigitte has
> what Lars would like / what Lars and Brigitte would like
> where your passport is / where their tickets are

3. Tell Frank:
> you'd like a *Weißwurst* / you don't have any luggage
> you'd like a beer / Claudia and Hans would like a ticket to Freiburg

LESEN

Stage 1

1. Look at the Kirchheim menu on **CT 326-27**. Your expense allowance for meals (food and drink) is DM 35 per day. (Breakfast is included in the price of your room.) You want to splurge on lunch but still keep enough money to have a full dinner, and you want to have something to drink with both meals. List some possibilities.

2. Read and transcribe the handwriting on the restaurant photographs on **CT 25-26**.

Stage 2

1   Look at the newspaper excerpt on **CT 348**.

1.   Scan the two articles you see. In what country do you think the newspaper is produced? Why do you think so?

2.   On this page you will find the monthly subscription rate of the paper. What is it?

3.   Read the sub-headline beginning *"Mit . . . Kilowattstunden"* (upper left part of page). What general subject does this article seem to be about?

4.   List (and practice pronouncing) the personal names you find in the other article, headlined *"Festliche Jugendweihen"*.

2   Look at the pages from the guidebook reproduced on pages 20-21 of the **ST** *Drucksachen*.

1.   Practice saying the personal names you see on the left-hand page (p. 32 of the original).

2.   What city in what country is being described? How much evidence can you find for your answer?

3.   What is the *TiP*? When is it open?

4.   What countries are mentioned or implied on pp. 32 and 33 of the original pages?

3   Look at the circular sign on the front cover of the **CT**.

1.   Practice saying the numbers you see.

2.   What do you think the sign indicates?

SCHREIBEN

Stage 1   1.   First, go back and check what you wrote in the HÖREN and LESEN exercises. Would your handwriting be legible to speakers of German?

2.   Refer to one of your menus. Make a list of some meat dishes.

3.   Refer to your various menus. To afford a longer stay in Europe, you've taken a job in the food service business. Part of your job is to produce the friendly handwritten menus and the blackboard sign for outside, like those reproduced from photographs elsewhere in this chapter. Make up a list of today's specials. The restaurant is: **a)** a medium-priced tavern; **b)** an *Imbiß*; **c)** in a small but very respectable hotel.

Stage 2   You are the only German speaker in your group of four at the *Imbiß*, so you'll have to do the ordering for everybody. Make appropriate notes so you won't get caught in a lunch-hour rush with nothing to say. It wouldn't hurt to write in German style, in case you get in a real panic and just have to hand over your note.

STRUCTURAL EXERCISES

1   Insert the appropriate question word (*w___?*):

1.   _____ sind wir in Köln? _____, *bitte?*

2.   _____ Uhr ist es? *Neun Uhr.*

3.   _____ sind meine Tickets? *Hier sind Ihre Tickets.*

4.   _____ heißen Sie, bitte?

5.   _____ ist das? *Das ist Emilia.*

6.   Hamburg? _____ ist das? *In der BRD.*

7.   _____ ist der Name, bitte? *Holz. Arno Holz.*
Und _____ alt sind Sie? *25.*
Danke. Und _____ studieren Sie? *Physik.*

8.   _____ kostet das, bitte? _____, *bitte?*

9.   Ahem. _____ kostet mein Ticket? *Ach, ja. 16 Mark.*

10.   _____ spät ist es? *13 Uhr.*

2 Supply the correct form of the infinitive *sein*:

1. Wer _____ das? *Das _____ Rolf.*

2. Wie alt _____ Sie? *Ich _____ 22.*

3. Und wie alt _____ Richard? *Richard _____ 20.*

4. Und _____ Sie Amerikaner? *Nein, ich _____ Kanadier. Richard _____ auch Kanadier.*

5. Wo _____ Frankfurt? *Frankfurt _____ in der BRD.*

6. Wo _____ die Amerikaner? *Sie _____ heute in Aachen.*

7. _____ wir heute in Köln? *Nein, heute _____ wir in Aachen.*

8. Ach . . . Wann _____ wir in Köln? *Wie, bitte?*

9. _____ das Ihr Gepäck? *Nein, mein Gepäck _____ das nicht.*

10. _____ das Ihre Fahrkarten? *Ach, danke. Ja, das _____ meine Fahrkarten.*

11. Frau Schach, wo _____ Sie? *Hier _____ ich!*

12. Wo _____ Ihre Fahrkarten?
    Hier _____ meine Fahrkarten, und hier _____ auch mein Gepäck.

13. Was?! Ihr Gepäck? Nein, das _____ mein Gepäck!

14. Entschuldigung. Wie spät _____ es? *Es _____ 10 Uhr.*

15. _____ heute Donnerstag? *Ja, gestern _____ Mittwoch.*

16. Heute _____ Samstag, und morgen _____ Sonntag. *Ja, richtig. Gestern _____ Freitag.*

17. Heute _____ ich in Freiburg. *Gestern _____ ich in Aachen.*

18. Wie _____ Ihr Name, bitte? *Mein Name _____ Schulz.*
    Und wie alt _____ Sie, Herr Schulz? *Ich _____ 42.*
    Danke. Und wie alt _____ Herr Schmidt? Benno? *Ach, ich glaube, Benno _____ 47.*
    Und _____ Sie aus Kanada? *Ja, Benno und ich _____ Kanadier.*
    Aber Frau Schulz und Frau Schmidt _____ Amerikanerinnen?
    Ja und nein.
    Meine Frau _____ aus Amerika, aber heute _____ sie Kanadierin.
    Sie _____ Amerikanerin.

3 Insert appropriate verb and possessive pronoun forms:

1. Hier _____ mein____ Fahrkarte. Wo _____ Ihr____ Fahrkarte?

2. Was _____ das? *Das _____ mein____ Gepäck.*

3. Wo _____ mein____ Tickets? *Hier _____ Ihr____ Tickets.*

4. Und mein____ Paß? *Ja, hier _____ auch Ihr____ Paß.*

5. Wie _____ Ihr____ Name, bitte? *Henning _____ mein____ Name.*

6. Guten Abend, Herr und Frau Vollmer. Wie _____ Ihr____ Vornamen, bitte?

7. _____ das Ihr____ Pässe?

4 Complete the following postcard home with forms of the verb *sein*. Be sure to keep in mind the time relationships implied by *heute*, *gestern*, and *morgen*:

> Liebe Mama und Papa:
>
> Heute _____ ich noch nicht in Paris. Heute _____ Dienstag, und Erika und ich _____in Aachen. Gestern (Montag) _____ ich in Köln mit Karl und Heide, aus Österreich. Samstag _____ Heide in Innsbruck mit Konrad. Konrad sagte: "Wie _____ Ihr Vorname, Fräulein?" und Heide sagte: "Tut mir leid. Auf Wiedersehen." Heide und Karl _____ aber gute Freunde. Nun, morgen (Mittwoch) _____ wir alle in Paris zusammen.
>
> Herzliche Grüße
> Eure Annemarie

5 Imagine that the questioner in each instance is speaking to more than one person; rewrite the questions to fit:

Sind Sie Amerikaner?	Wie ist Ihr Vorname?	Wie heißen Sie, bitte?
Ihre Fahrkarte, bitte?	Ist das Ihr Paß?	Wie ist der Name, bitte?
Ist das mein Ticket?	Sind Sie Kanadierin?	

6   You overheard several exchanges of words in the train, but didn't catch absolutely every word. Use what you know to supply the missing forms.

    1.   Guten _____ . Die Pässe, bitte.

              _____ ?

              Paßkontrolle. Ze passports, pliz.

              Ach, ja. _____ .

              Danke _____ . _____ .

              Auf Wiedersehen.

    2.   Entschuldigung. _____ wir in Köln?

              Nein, _____ ist _____ Köln. _____ ist Karlsruhe.

              Hm. _____ _____ wir in Köln?

              _____ vierzehn _____ --also in zwei _____ .

    3.   Nein, ich _____ aus Dallas.

              Wie, _____ , Fräulein Schülke?

              Aus Dallas. Ich bin _____ .

              Was? Aus Amerika? Aber Sie sprechen _____ gut Deutsch.

              Ach, danke. Ja, meine Familie ist aus _____ .

              Aber ich bin in Amerika geboren.

              Und was studier____ Sie hier? Sie _____ Studentin, ja?

              Ja, in Köln. Ich studie____ Geschichte _____ Germanistik

7   Rearrange the scrambled sentence pairs, using your dialogs and grammar illustrations as models:

    1.   hier / Gepäck / das / Ihr / ist ?
         mein / nein, / ist / Gepäck / nicht / das.

    2.   in Köln / wir / sind / wann ?
         weiß / ich / nicht.

    3.   Kanadier / Sie / sind?
         Ja / komme / aus / ich / Kanada.

    4.   kostet / wieviel / bitte / das ?
         10 Mark / das / kostet.

    5.   Bratwurst / Kartoffelsalat / mit / und / ein / ich / bitte / möchte / Pils / eine .
         macht / bitte / drei / fünfzig / das / Mark / schön .

    6.   bitte / Bockwurst / frites / eine / Pommes / mit. Und / Tee / eine / Tasse.
         nicht / Tee / wir / haben. Kaffee / möchten / Sie?

    7.   kostet / Flasche / bitte / wieviel / eine / Mineralwasser?
         achtzig / zwei / das / Mark / kostet.

8   Write the cued verb forms according to what you have seen and heard in the dialogs:

    1.   Ich _____ eine Bratwurst, bitte. **(möchten)**

    2.   Also, ich _____ in Köln, und Hannes _____ in Bonn. Wir zwei _____ also in der BRD. **(studieren)**

    3.   Inge, die zwei Schweizer da _____ 15 Mark, und ich _____ 10. Zusammen _____ wir die 25 Mark für die Karten. **(haben)**

    4.   Gut. Und was _____ Sie, bitte?
         Ich _____ ein Pils, und mein Mann _____ eine Tasse Tee.
         (trinken — or maybe another verb)

    5.   Schön, Herr Wehner. Ich _____ den Kartoffelsalat und Sie _____ die Pommes frites, ja? Und Sie und ich _____ auch Currywurst. **(essen)**

    6.   Meine Karte nach Köln _____ 8 Mark, und Ihre Karte _____ nur 4. Zusammen _____ die Karten 12 Mark. **(kosten)**

    7.   Guten Tag. Ich _____ Beckmann, Jürgen Beckmann, und das ist meine Frau, Inge.
         Ach, Ihre Frau _____ Inge? Guten Tag, Frau Beckmann.
         Ich _____ auch Inge. Aber wir _____ nicht alle Beckmann.
         Mein Familienname ist Ingold. **(heißen)**

    8.   (on the phone) Guten Tag, hier _____ Frau Giesel.
         Ach, Frau Giesel, wo _____ Sie denn?
         Ich _____ hier in Köln. Und Manfred _____ auch hier.
         Gestern _____ wir in Aachen.
         Ach, schön. Und wie lange _____ Sie noch da?
         Ja, also heute ist Samstag. Wir _____ bis Dienstag hier. **(sein)**

Antrag auf Einreise in die DDR

Auszufüllen in Blockschrift!
Complete in block letters!
Remplir en majuscules!

Application for entry into the GDR / Demande d'entrée en R.D.A.

	1	2	3	4

Familienname / Family name / Nom de Famille: Geburtsname / Maiden name / Nom de jeune fille:

männlich* male Homme	weiblich* female Femme

Vorname / First name / Prénom:

Geburtsdatum und -ort / Date and place of birth / Date et lieu de naissance

Wohnanschrift einschl. Postleitzahl / Permanent address (incl. postal code) / Adresse complète:

Nr. des Passes und Ausstellungsbehörde:
Number of passport and issued by
No. du passeport et autorité délivrante

Staatsangehörigkeit:
Citizenship
Nationalité

Ausgeübte Tätigkeit:
Present occupation
Emploi actuel

Erlernter Beruf:
Occupation learned
Profession

Arbeitsstelle / Name and address of employer / Employé chez

Beabsichtigte Dauer des Aufenthaltes in der DDR / Duration of stay in the GDR / Durée du séjour en R.D.A.:
vom / from / du: bis / to / au: in / in / à:

Zweck der Reise*   dienstlich privat Touristik einmalig mehrmalig
Purpose of the journey   business   private tourism   once   several times
Motif du voyage   officiel   privé   touristique une entrée plusieurs entrées

Kennzeichen des Kfz / Registration number of vehicle / No. d'immatriculation du véhicule

Grenzübergangsstelle / Border crossing point / Point de passage:

Mitreisende Kinder bis 16 Jahre (Vorname, Alter):
Accompanying children under 16 years (first name, age)
Nom et âge des enfants de moins de 16 ans voyageant avec le requérant

* Zutreffendes ankreuzen / mark which is applicable / Marquer d'une croix les mentions utiles

---

Bei früherem Wohnsitz in der DDR letzte Wohnanschrift:
Last address if previous residence in GDR
Au cas ou vous auriez été domicilié en R.D.A., indiquez votre dernière adresse

Bei Privatreisen Angabe des Reisezieles in der DDR

For private journeys only, person(s) to be visited / En cas de voyage privé, donnez les
renseignements suivants sur la personne visitée

Familienname: Vorname: Personenkennzahl
Surname   First name
Nom de Famille   Prénom

Ausgeübte Tätigkeit   Arbeitsstelle:
Present occupation   Name and address
Emploi actuel   of employer / Employé chez

Wohnanschrift einschl. Postleitzahl:
Permanent address (incl. district)
Adresse complète

Verwandtschaftsverhältnis:
Degree of kinship
Degré de parenté

Weitere Reiseziele   (bei Dienst-/Geschäftsreisen Angabe der Namen u. Anschriften der Betriebe bzw. Institutionen):
Further destinations in GDR (for official/business trips names and addresses of institutions/firms to be visited)
Autres destinations en R.D.A. (pour voyages d'affaires: noms et adresses des usines ou institutions)

Ort / Datum / Place / date / lieu / date   den   19   Unterschrift / Signature

Raum für Bearbeitungsvermerke

A	B	C	D

PM 67 f/2

√ CHECK YOUR PROFICIENCY

CAN YOU:
__ make polite requests for information?
__ say greetings & farewells appropriate to specific times of the day?
__ ask for clarification of a statement?
__ ask questions about when, where, and how much?
__ order simple meals?
__ count money?
__ identify your possessions and those of a person or people you are talking with?

DO YOU REMEMBER HOW TO:
__ count from 0 to 100? Really count — not just recite numbers?
__ say the names of the days of the week?
__ identify yourself by name, age, major, and national origin?
__ identify major cities in all four German-speaking countries?
__ request and tell the time of day?

HÖREN

Stage 1

A1 Just listen several times to the dialogs for *Gespräche 1: Im Hotel*. Talk along if you like.

A2 Practice saying the dialog lines. Use your "pause" button if you have one.

B1 On a separate page make a chart with columns labeled as shown below. What are the hotel accommodations? Fill in the information from each of the three conversations you hear.

CONVERSATION #   SINGLE/DOUBLE   # OF NIGHTS   BATH/SHOWER   PRICE

Stage 2

B2 Listen to the 3 short conversations, then answer the questions below.

Conversation 1
  1. What clues tell you how many people are traveling?
  2. What does the room cost? What is included in the price?
  3. How long are the people staying?
  4. What time of year is it? How do you know?

Conversation 2
  1. How many people are asking for a room? How do you know?
  2. How long will the stay be? Why can't it be longer?
  3. Why would a traveler want to stay here longer?
  4. How much does the room cost? What kind of room is it?

Conversation 3
  1. How many people want rooms?
  2. Do you know where the rooms are? How do you know?
  3. What types of rooms do the people want?
  4. What is the difference in price between the two rooms?
  5. Who do you suppose will get the more expensive room? Why is it more expensive?

C1

1A:1.2.1-4 For each segment note the announced time. Where necessary, convert 24-hour time to am/pm time. In segment 4) Does the announcer speak <u>before</u> or <u>after</u> the announced time?

2A:1.1.3 What kind of building collapsed? What was its name? In what city was it?

2A:1.1.4 How many bottles of contaminated red wine were confiscated? Where was the wine probably produced? If you've had introductory chemistry you should be able to identify the toxic chemical.

C2

2A:2.2.1 You will improve your listening comprehension only by steady exercise with challenging material. One kind of challenge is extended speech where you attempt to comprehend only simple information of the kind you have already encountered. The skill to develop here is the ability to suppress panic, to quit demanding of yourself that you understand each and every word, and to wait for more information that might clear up what puzzled you earlier.

Here are some useful specific tactics: 1) Briefly attempt to determine what general kind of speech you are hearing, for example a news report, an interview, a technical discussion, a travel feature, or a music announcement. Often that overall information will tell you where to listen for more specific information. In a weather report, for instance, present or past temperatures will likely be given <u>before</u> forecast temperatures; in a news story about catastrophic drought the forecast might come instead <u>before</u> the summary of earlier weather. 2) Seize on any words that sound like English words; English is related to German, and many English words have become parts of other languages. 3) Listen for

place names, numbers, days and dates. 4) Note words that are repeated often. 5) Try to infer something about the identity, personality and mood of the speaker(s).

With that in mind, listen <u>without stopping</u> to the long (6 min.) interview with Vico Toriani, a European celebrity. As you listen, do the exercises below; except for general questions or those with several answers, the items are presented in the order in which you will encounter the desired information.

1.   What kind of celebrity is Toriani?

2.   How many other men speak during the broadcast, and what are their jobs?

3.   Where was the interview conducted?

4.   On what day is it being broadcast?

5.   How old is Toriani?

6.   List any cities, countries, and nationalities you can.

7.   What are Toriani's travel and work plans?

8.   In what year, at the latest, was the interview recorded?

SPRECHEN

Stage 1   1.   It's 6 p.m. You enter the hotel lobby. Don't try to sneak around.

2.   You tell the clerk you'd like a single room. The clerk needs to know how long you're planning to stay. You'd like a double with a shower.

3.   You'd like to know whether breakfast comes with the room.

4.   The clerk sounds surprised that you would ask that question. Breakfast is included, of course.

5.   You didn't hear what the clerk told you about the check-out time.

6.   You and your friend are staying four nights. You'd like two single rooms adjoining.

7.   You don't need a room with bath, but a shower would be nice.

8.   The clerk asks whether you'd like a single or a double. You're uncertain. Ask relevant questions, considering how many of you there are and how desperately you need a bath.

9.   You re-enter the hotel several hours later. The same clerk is there. Say something.

Stage 2   1.   The clerk has only a single with a shower left. That's fine with you: you're bushed.

2.   The clerk tells you that your room costs DM 85 per night. You think that's a little steep and ask about alternatives. Be polite.

3.   You don't have enough money for the opulent room the clerk suggested.

4.   You agree on the room and price.

5.   The clerk hands you your room key.

6.   The clerk asks you where your luggage is. You tell her.

7.   You already have a room for tonight, but need one for tomorrow night. The hotel you're staying in is too expensive; so was the one you had before that.

8.   Your bicycle touring club has just finished an 80km ride, and all seven of you are ready for a good scrubbing and a long night's rest. Arrange your rooms for the night with the hotel clerk. (You are the only one who speaks German.)

9.   You're going out. You're almost out the door when the clerk reminds you to leave your key at the desk. You're embarrassed.

10.   You're going out. This time you remember to hand the clerk your room key.

LESEN

Stage 1 Refer to the listing of Trier hotel facilities on page 6 of the **ST** *Drucksachen*.

1. Look at the quadrant designations for the Trier hotels and establish how the letters A-E and the numbers 1-5 would be arranged on the edges of the city map. (If Al is top left, where is A2? B1?)

2. According to the list of hotels, what is the least expensive place for a person to rent a room with a bath(room) in Trier? In what part of town is that hotel located? Does that seem to the the "low rent" district? Assuming the city map is the one reproduced on **CT 311**, is that the north or south part of town? What is the least expensive place without a bath(room)?

3. In what part of town (N, E, S, W) would you find a hotel offering the least expensive combination of room and full board?

4. You would like to do some wine-tasting during your stay in Trier. What hotel offers appropriate facilities?

Stage 2 Refer again to the Trier hotel listing on page 6 of the **ST** *Drucksachen*.

1. Twenty members of your hometown garden club, "The Bloomin' Idiots", want to stay in Trier for a fruit-growers' exhibition near the Nordbad. Can they all find reasonable accommodations in the same place? What is the cheapest per-person rate available there? What if they insisted on having pool and tanning facilities? Which hotel is closer to the center of town?

2. In what hotel would the 1100-member Eisenbähnlerverband Deutscher Nationen be likely to have their annual convention?

3. Assuming you are in Lübeck, what is the full telephone number you would have to dial to make room reservations at the Hotel Reichert in Trier? Why would the number be different if you were in Trier?

SCHREIBEN

Stage 1 A reminder about handwriting: Check your notes from the listening exercise **B1** and make sure that your handwriting would be legible to someone from Mannheim or Salzburg.

1. Fill out the Hotel Goldener Schlüssel registration form at the end of this chapter.

2. Make a copy of the room request form on **CT 150**, and then fill out your new copy. For class, be prepared to confirm orally how many people are in your party and how long they will be staying.

Stage 2

1 Consult the map of Trier on **CT 311**. You are making arrangements for your extended family to meet in Europe for a few days while you are there. You are studying in Trier, the oldest city in the Federal Republic, known in earlier days as "the Rome of the North" because of its thermal baths (*Thermen*) and its importance as a Roman colony. Your family consists of:

> Your parents, quite wealthy, who love to paint riverscapes. They are fastidious about their personal hygiene. Your mother is on a strict diet.
>
> Your father's brother Ted, a hypochondriac who believes he is in constant need of medication; he is a soccer fan and would probably enjoy the Moselstadion. He also loves television.
>
> Your sister Eva and her fiancé, Will, who your parents think are hopelessly radical; Eva and Will are studying philosophy and labor history in graduate school. Will is, frankly, rather unkempt; Eva doesn't care.

Referring to the map of Trier and to the list of hotels on p. 6 of the **ST** *Drucksachen*, find appropriate accommodations for them all. Write their names and the names of their hotels, including specifics.

2 Rewrite Rainer's order at the *Imbiß*. He has already written down what the four members of his group want to order, but they have suddenly become even more voracious:

1 Dose Pils	vier _____	
1 Kännchen Tee	zwei _____	
1 Bockwurst mit Senf	vier _____	
1 Brötchen mit Butter	drei _____	
1 Portion Käse	drei _____	
1 Scheibe Brot	sechs _____	
1 Tasse Kaffee	zwei _____	

RESTAURANT IM HOTEL

HÖREN

Stage 1

A1   Just listen several times to the dialogs for *Gespräche 2: Restaurant im Hotel*. Talk along if you like.

A2   Practice saying the dialog lines. Use your "pause" button if you have one.

B1   First study your various menus. Then listen to the two conversations that follow. Answer the questions below.

Conversation 1
1. Can you tell what time of day it is? What time could you probably eliminate?
2. What is the person ordering to drink? What is the cost of the drink order alone?
3. What color word do you hear? What others do you already know?
4. Write the substance the customer plans to pour into the beverage.

Conversation 2
1. What is going on here?
2. Where are these people?

Stage 2

B2   Listen to the conversations that follow. Answer the questions below.

Conversation 1
1. What green vegetables are mentioned?
2. What kinds of meat are mentioned?
3. Does the customer order potatoes?
4. The customer is: **a)** on a diet; **b)** splurging; **c)** having an ordinary meal.

Conversation 2
1. Is the conversation from the beginning or the end of a meal?
2. Could the conversation take place at an *Imbiß*?
3. What words describe the quality of the wine?
4. The people have drunk: **a)** none so far; **b)** 1 glass; **c)** 2 or more glasses.

Conversation 3
1. How many people are dining?
2. What kind of meat do you think *Forelle* is? What beverage is ordered with it?
3. List the foods you hear that would be good for a low-calorie diet.

C1

1B:6.1.2,4   In both commercials, listen for the word *schmecken*. How many sauces can you get for the Chicken McNuggets? What is in the <u>third</u> sauce? What kind of fish is in the fishsticks? The word for 'fish sticks' is *Fisch<u>stäbchen</u>*. Now go back to the McDonald's ad and find out what people can eat the chicken with. [P2]

C2

2B:4.1.1   The travel features gives information about several hiking trips. Note the phrase (after the second musical interlude) and chief feature: *"Zum Wandern ____ _____"*. Then note the details about the tour that begins in the town of Reutlingen: **a)** duration: ____ days; **b)** total distance to be hiked: __ km (How many miles a day would that be? Use the table on the inside front cover of the **Class Text**.); **c)** price of accommodations: DM____ per night with/without breakfast.

Feel free to take the same notes on the rest of the segment.

2B:4.1.2   What is the time of broadcast? The segment contains advice for vacationers. Listen closely to the second part of the segment, after the 3-tone break. Note a) the countries mentioned, and b) types and quantities of alcoholic beverages and tobacco products. (*Hochprozentiges* = high-proof liquor)

2B:5.1.1   You will hear the names of rivers and cities, followed by numbers. Use your map(s) of the BRD to identify at least 2 of the rivers; note some of the cities on them. Then concentrate on the cities on the Rhine. You should be able to recognize at least one city name immediately, without a map; others will be on your maps. In which order are the cities presented, going upstream or downstream? For the cities you know, record the numbers. What do you think they mean?

SPRECHEN

Stage 1   1.   You tell your guest you hope she enjoys her meal.

      2.   You're sitting at a table with strangers. Tell them you hope they enjoy their meal.

      3.   You call to a: a) 20-year-old waiter; b) 20-year-old waitress; c) 50-year-old waiter; d) 50-year-old waitress.

      4.   You raise your wine glass to that of your host.

      5.   You didn't understand the waiter's explanation of a seafood dish. You understand that the fish comes from the Ostsee, but you don't know whether it's from the BRD or the DDR.

      6.   You look at your watch and see that you have plenty of time. You and your friend decide you would both like another glass of red wine. Say what you must to a) the friend b) the waiter.

      7.   You ask Mr. and Mrs. Flaum what they would like to drink.

      8.   What would you say if the Flaums were both M.D.'s? Ph.D.'s?

      9.   Your broccoli really tastes terrific, but the meat is nothing to write home about.

      10.   You need a fork for your peas, and you'd also like to order a bit of dessert. Communicate this to the waitress, who has already brought you several things and seems to be getting impatient.

      11.   It's getting late. You'd like the check now.

      12.   You give the waiter a 50-mark bill for your meal, which cost DM 48. Be polite.

      13.   You want to pay for your meal, which cost 13 marks, but all you have is a 500 mark bill.

      14.   Your German acquaintances are reimbursing you for their share of the meal, which was DM 18.

      15.   You leave the restaurant. Don't forget that you're in Europe.

Stage 2   1.   You tell the waiter that isn't your wine. You think that's the wine that the Austrian lady at the next table ordered.

      2.   When the waiter brings you your wine, you realize you forgot to check the price. Ask whether he can't bring you just a glass of the wine instead. Apologize for the inconvenience.

      3.   You tell your friends you're eating supper at 6:00 p.m. today. Your friends tell you they're eating at 7:00. You're sorry about that.

      4.   ⊗ asks you whether you know what a word on the menu means. You don't, and suggest that you both ask the waiter to explain it.

      5.   You tell ⊗ you'll be in the hotel at 2:00. First you're going to have a first-class meal and see whether your other friends have arrived in town yet.

      6.   You take a place at a table where ⊗ is sitting. Introduce yourself and tell ⊗ what you think she would like to know about you. Ask her some discreet questions about herself as well.

      7.   Tell ⊗ you've left some things in the car: a) a personal possession; b) a gift; c) documents.

      8.   You see that your friend has ordered something you'd like instead of what the waitress has brought you. Without bothering the waitress or causing a commotion, see if you can negotiate a trade.

      9.   The other person at your table thinks you might know where Bern is. You tell him. From his terrible German accent and general nervous demeanor you think he is probably an American. Confirm your suspicion without letting on how you knew.

LESEN

Stage 1   Study the menu for the Motel-Center Kirchheim (**CT 326-27**).

1.   Does the restaurant serve meals for children? How do you know?

2.   Do you think many Americans eat there? Why?

3.   Look at menu item #23. What do you think *Käse* means? If you are unsure, look for the word elsewhere on the menu. What confirms the meaning for you? Now look up *Käse* in your dictionary and note its gender.

4.   Look at the right side of the right-hand page. What do you think *Getränke* means? Do you think it is a singular or plural word? Why? Now look up its gender.

5.   You are very thirsty. What beverage offers you the most liquid in one portion? You are also almost penniless. What beverage gives you the most liquid for your money? Can you order water here? What "water" on the menu is not really water?

6.   Look at item #20, the Chef's Special. With your English and the little German you have had, tell what its main items are.

7.   Look at the categories under which you find 1) menu item #09 and 2) espresso. What do you think *kalt* and *heiß* mean?

8.   How many kinds of non-alcoholic fruit drinks can you identify without a dictionary? With a dictionary?

9.   Do you get more beer per serving in a bottle (*die Flasche*) or on tap? Is a bottle of German beer bigger or smaller than a can of American beer?

10.   How many glasses of bitter lemon would it take to make about a quart? (You may need to consult the metric tables on the inside front cover of the **CT**.)

Stage 2   Look at the Kirchheim menu again.

1.   Look at menu items #69-73. What category of dish are they? Look up *süß* to see whether you guessed right.

2.   How many different flavors of ice cream can you identify in #69-73? Which flavors in #73 can you guess from another language? Which one can you guess just the second half of? Where is there another word related to this among the desserts? Guess what they mean, then look up the two words to see how close your guess was.

3.   How large is the piece of meat in #18? What fraction of a pound is that? How many different vegetables can you order with #16-19? From your own restaurant experience in this country, what do you think *Sc.* stands for?

4.   Which food item is listed twice on the menu? Why?

5.   Your stomach has been feeling queasy after a harrowing drive on the *Autobahn*. What do you order? Would #09 be a good choice? Why (not)? How about #13?

SCHREIBEN

Stage 1   1.   Consult the Motel-Center Kirchheim menu again (**CT 326-27**). The food was so good, you want to remember what you had. Write down your order.

2.   Consult the two menus, Motel-Center Kirchheim (**CT 326-27**), and Hotel Müller (**CT 22**). Write the different kinds of potato dishes you find.

3.   Consult just the Hotel Müller menu and:
   1.   Make a list of vegetables (other than potatoes). What is the most common vegetable?
   2.   Practice dividing the elements of the main dishes: First insert a mark to isolate the last element of the compound (**Example**: *Gulasch/suppe*), and then use the English equivalents to give you clues to other divisions.
   3.   Write the familiar elements — English words or those you have learned in this course — in ## 113, 155, 164, and 236.

Stage 2

1   Now consult the menu on **CT 95**.

   1.   You would like a hearty breakfast of sausage and eggs, with a roll and butter and jam. Write your selection of foods, with prices, and the total price.

   2.   What currency do you think **M** represents?

   3.   If you ordered a slice of liverwurst or roast beef with your meal, about how many ounces of meat would you get?

   4.   How many slices of Hungarian salami would weigh about the same as the one slice of roast beef?

   5.   If the management agreed, you might want to make you and your three friends some sandwiches (bread, butter, meat, cheese) for your afternoon walk in the Treptower Park, an attractive part of this capital city. Make a list of your sandwich materials.

   6.   One of your friends, a real skinflint, is on a diet — but he still wants a sandwich. What is the most modest and reasonably priced sandwich you could fix him? What sort of sandwich would you make for his kid sister, who won your state's junior shotput title?

2   Using your several menus, write up meal orders to fit the following circumstances:

   1.   Two not very adventurous adults.

   2.   Two adults and a picky seven-year-old child.

   3.   Five vegetarians. Three of them drink no alcohol.

STRUCTURAL EXERCISES

Insert appropriate forms of the indicated verbs as necessary:

   1.   Schön. Ich _____ heute, und Sie _____ morgen. (**zahlen**)

   2.   Wieviel _____ die Wurst? *Ich weiß nicht, aber die Wurst und der Kartoffelsalat _____ zusammen DM 5.* (**kosten**)

   3.   Bitte _____ Sie Ihr Schinkenbrot, und ich _____ mein Käsebrot. (**essen**)

   4.   Zweimal Tagesspezialität und eine Flasche Rotwein — das _____ DM 22. (**machen**)

   5.   Wie, bitte? Sie _____ Psychologie? Ach, _____ Sie Biologie, das ist interessanter. Ich _____ Philosophie. (**studieren**)

   6.   Ja, bitte, _____ Sie Ihr Pils, und dann _____ wir zusammen eine Flasche Alsterwasser. Ich _____ immer Alsterwasser, und Eberhart _____ das auch. (**trinken**)

   7.   Mm. Das _____ fantastisch. Die Weine aus Portugal _____ beide auch sehr gut. (**schmecken**)

   8.   Bitte, _____ Sie uns das gemischte Eis. (**bringen**)

   9.   Ja, guten Tag. Ich _____ ein Einzelzimmer, und der Herr und die Dame _____ ein Doppelzimmer für zwei Nächte. Wir _____ die Zimmer auch mit Dusche und WC, bitte. (**brauchen**)

   10. Das tut mir leid. Ein Einzelzimmer mit Bad und WC _____ ich nicht. Aber wir _____ es ohne Bad. Geht das? *Hm. _____ Sie es mit Dusche?* (**haben**)

   11. Und zum Trinken? Was _____ Sie, bitte? *Ich _____ Apfelsaft, bitte — nein, wir _____ beide Apfelsaft.* (**möchten**)

Name und Anschrift der Beherbergungsstätte

Meldeschein der Beherbergungsstätten

Ankunftstag	Abreisetag	Bitte Hinweise für das Ausfüllen beachten
Day of arrival / Date d'arrivée	Day of departure / Date de départ	**Please note directions on filling in**
		Avant de remplir la déclaration, lire attentivement les indications

Familienname (ggf. auch Geburtsname)	Vorname
Surname (if necessary also maiden name) / Nom de famille (évent. nom de naissance)	Christian Name / Prénom

Geburtsdatum	Geburtsort	Staatsangehörigkeit (bei Ausländern)
Date of birth	Place of birth / Lieu de naissance	Nationality (for foreigners) / Nationalité (pour les étrangers)
Date de naissance		

Postleitzahl, Wohnort	Straße, Hausnummer	Staat (b. Wohnort außerhalb d. Bundesgebiets)
Postal code, residence / Code postal. Domicile	Street, number / Rue, Numéro	State / Etat

Begleitender Ehegatte Accompanying spouse / Conjoint accompagnant

Familienname (ggf. auch Geburtsname)	Vorname	Geburtsdatum	Geburtsort	Anzahl der begl. Kinder
Surname (if necessary also maiden name)	Christian name / Prénom	Date of birth	Place of birth / Lieu de naissance	No. of accompanying children
Nom de famille (évent. nom de naissance)		Date de naissance		Nombre d'enfants accompagnants

WUHRMANN Fremdenmeldescheinbuch

Unterschrift des Gastes / Signature of guest / Signature du client

Unterschrift des Ehegatten / Signature of spouse / Signature du conjoint

---

√ CHECK YOUR PROFICIENCY

CAN YOU:
__ ask detailed questions?
__ find shelter and order meals?
__ make judgments and comparisons?
__ give simple orders to other people?
__ decipher compound nouns?
__ answer questions using negative forms?

DO YOU REMEMBER HOW TO:
__ ask for clarification?
__ count money and make change?
__ identify possessions of yours and others?
__ say appropriate greetings and farewells?
__ say you're sorry?
__ locate major cities in German-speaking countries?

HÖREN

Stage 1

A1 Just listen several times to the dialogs for *Gespräche 1: Fahrkartenschalter*. Talk along if you like.

A2 Practice saying the dialog lines. Use your "pause" button if you have one.

B1 Conversation 1
1. How many travelers are there?
2. What is the destination?
3. Is it one-way or round-trip?
4. What is the price per ticket?
5. How much money does the customer give the ticket agent?

Conversation 2
1. How many people are traveling? How do you know?
2. How much change should the ticket agent give for a 20-mark bill?

Conversation 3
1. Where is the traveler going?
2. What does the ticket cost?
3. Is it one-way or round-trip?
4. What time of day is it?

B2 Conversation 1
1. How many travelers are there?
2. What is their destination?
3. Is the train in the station yet?

Conversation 2
1. How many travelers are there?
2. What are their plans?
3. How much money does the traveler give the ticket agent?

Conversation 3
1. When does the train leave for Bonn?
2. When is it scheduled to arrive?
3. From which track does the train leave?

Conversation 4
1. What is the destination?
2. Is it round-trip or one-way?
3. Where is the person to find the train?
4. How much does the traveler give the ticket agent?

Stage 2

B3 Conversation 1
1. Write out the three clock times you hear.
2. How long will the travelers have in Mannheim?
3. What does the traveler say about the luggage?
4. What three city names do you hear? Locate them on your map.
5. Write the phrase that tells where the train is located.

Conversation 2
1. How many travelers are there?
2. How long is the layover in Frankfurt?
3. How much does each ticket cost?
4. Where is the traveler to find the track number? Write the phrase as well as you can.
5. How much change does he receive for his DM 50?

B4
1. Where is the traveler going?
2. What does the traveler want?
3. Does he find it here?
4. Is there much time before the train leaves?
5. What track number do you hear?

C1
1A:1.2.1-4
Listen to the time announcements <u>once only</u>, noting everything you can. You are making satisfactory progress if: **a**) you got all four times correct to the hour and minute; and **b**) you recognized one of the radio stations by name, city, or number.

1A:1.3.1-4
For each segment note the exact time. Which stations are you hearing in Segments 2 and 3? Is it 8 am or 8 pm in Segment 4? Can you figure out the German words for 'before' and 'after' in time expressions?

C2
1A:3.2.1
Part of listening proficiency concerns sheer stamina: the ability to deal with masses of items which, presented individually and at a slower pace, would not be above your current level.

With that in mind, listen to the long (almost 6 min.) excerpt from the music-by-request program that includes birthday congratulations for each age group. The celebrants are quite old; one is celebrating a 100th birthday. Assume you are doing an informal survey in which you seek to determine whether men or women live longer in the München area — a difficult question considering the greater maternal mortality in earlier times and the horrendous casualties — military and civilian — that Germany incurred in the First and Second World Wars (see **CT 235** for statistics). For each age group, note the numbers of men and women having birthdays. The lines in your chart will look something like this: "83 — 2 men — 5 women". How will you tell male from female? Some first names you will recognize, since English has similar names (*Elisabeth* — Elizabeth). Even more helpful will be the greater formality of German: you will hear *Herr* and *Frau* all over the place.

The birthday congratulations begin about 2 minutes into the segment. Before the birthday celebrants other people are congratulated. Can you figure out why?

C3
1A:4.2.3
After a 25-second introduction and a 7-tone beep signal, the announcer lists traffic problems on highways. City names rather than highway numbers are used to locate the tie-ups. List as many of the highway stretches as you can after listening <u>twice</u>. Maps of the southern BRD, especially the one of the München area on **CT 158**, may be useful. In some cases the announcer tells the lengths of traffic jams; where and how long are they?

SPRECHEN

Stage 1
1. You ask the price of a ticket to Aachen. You want your ticket round-trip, not one-way, and you give the ticket agent DM 10.

2. Tell the agent you want two tickets to Düsseldorf. She tells you the price of the tickets, and you say that's fine. You ask whether the train is leaving from gate 3.

3. It's 8:30 a.m. Begin the purchase of a train ticket. You tell ⊗ you want a one-way ticket to Trier.

4. You want the ticket agent to repeat the track number for you. You ask where track 9 is.

5. You need to find the rest room: 1) You are male; 2) You are female; 3) You are male, but it is your female companion who is in distress.

6. ⊗ tells you the ticket counter is around the corner. Repeat the directions.

7. You tell ⊗ it's 3:15 p.m. You're in the train station.

Stage 2   1.   You just disturbed an official on his lunch break. His counter is closed. However, you and your friend are in a hurry to buy round-trip tickets to Bonn and don't know where the ticket counter is. Apologize and ask for directions. Assume: 1) He doesn't look friendly; 2) It's <u>her</u> lunch break and <u>her</u> counter is closed; but she does look friendly and will probably help.

2.   Your friend pays you for the DM 22,40 ticket. Count her change from two 20-mark bills.

3.   While you are waiting for a train you strike up a conversation with an elderly lady. Tell her all about yourself and your travel plans, but don't just talk about yourself.

4.   You ask ⊗ how long the train will have a layover in Bremen.

5.   You ask whether the rest rooms are to the left or the right.

6.   You ask the ticket agent to give you two tens instead of a twenty. The agent apologizes for not being able to do that. You leave the ticket window after making your purchase.

7.   Tell the agent that you plan to go one-way from Köln to Trier, but also to stop for 3 hours in Bonn underway.

8.   ⊗ asks for directions, and you think you know the way. Tell ⊗ to go left about 50 yards. On second thought, you realize that you were confused for a moment and don't know the way after all.

LESEN

Stage 1   Look at the listing of tourist services in Hamburg on **CT 216-17**.

1.   What phone number(s) would you ask your German friends to call to find out about: **a)** general information about train travel? **b)** car rental in the city (not at the airport)?

2.   You have some time to see Hamburg and ask about renting a bicycle at the main tourist office. **a)** What seems to be the word for 'bicycle'? What is its plural? **b)** Could you arrange to rent a bike if it were 7:30 a.m.? 7:30 p.m.? Saturday at 4:00 p.m.? Sunday at 1:00 p.m.? **c)** What would it cost to rent a bike for a 2-hour ride? a 5-hour ride? What would you pay if you picked up the bike at closing time Friday and returned it early Monday? **d)** There are 5 true compound nouns in the bicycle text. What are they? How would you divide them? What are all their constituent words? Do you remember how to tell the gender of each one?

3.   In the rent-a-car information: **a)** what two words do you find that can mean 'street'? **b)** practice saying the street addresses of the rental agencies. Whoops! your German friend does not understand your pronunciation of the street names. Spell them for her. Now practice saying each 6-digit phone number, first as single digits and then in groups of two.

Stage 2   Now look at the banking information on **CT 216** and also at the train schedule on **CT 212**.

1.   Where are the banking hours more generous — in the train station or at the airport?

2.   It's Tuesday. You have just 20 minutes between trains, and your train to Copenhagen leaves at 11:10 p.m. Can you change DM to Danish kroner at the station, or must you wait until you are in Denmark?

3.   It's 10:00 Wednesday morning, just before your long trip from Hamburg to Brig. Do you have time to dash to the exchange window before your train, the "Mont-Blanc", departs? How long would you have to wait for the next train if you didn't make it back in time?

4.   You want to arrange for a berth on your long trip from Hamburg to Brig, but you want to take in the Hagenbeck zoo in the early afternoon before departing a bit later. What are the number and name of the train you will take? What symbol assures you that you'll be able to have a berth? (Assume they're not all taken yet.) Does it look like you will have to pay the Intercity surcharge? What country will you be in when you get to Brig? At what time of day or night do you arrive at the Swiss border? What would be your second-class fare if you went only as far as the Swiss capital?

5.   It's Saturday, 1/2 hour before the departure of your train, the "Italia-Express", at 4:02 p.m. Can you use the bank services to cash a traveler's check for the bike rental? Can you turn in your bike?

SCHREIBEN

Stage 1   1.   Look at the *Zugbegleiter* for the IC 125 "Erasmus" on **CT 316-19**. You are planning to travel from Oberhausen, where you have been visiting distant relatives, to Innsbruck, where you will be studying for a semester. Having found out when your train will leave, when it will arrive, how long the trip will take, what large cities you pass through, and where you cross the Austrian border, write a brief note to your contact in Innsbruck, Hans Reidl, to make sure he knows your travel plans.

2.   Using this information, write another note, this time to your parents' friend Fräulein Heym, who wants to see you off. Tell her when you're leaving the station; she might want to have breakfast with you in the *Bahnhofbuffet*. (Useful vocabulary: *essen / Kaffee / möchten / morgen / bitte / ein bißchen / beide / Frühstück / wunderbar*.)

> Liebes Fräulein Heym,
>
> . . . .

Stage 2   Consult the Vienna information on pages 16-17 of the **ST** *Drucksachen*. Now make a chart of activities you might want to undertake in the five hours between trains during your early November tour of Austria. Draw up a chart as shown below. Beside each entry, write whether you would (*ja*), or would not (*nein*) or could perhaps (*vielleicht*) visit the place or take part in the activity. You might want to call to confirm, so write down the phone number in each case. If there is no number listed, write *keine Nummer*. In the last column, write the name of each place so you can ask people for directions.

activity	ja/nein/vielleicht	phone #	name

It's late afternoon. Would you/Could you: take a boat ride on the Donau (Danube)? have a hot mineral bath? attend a Mormon religious service? hear a concert of the Vienna Choir Boys? take a sightseeing tour of the city? practice your tennis backhand? take a train out to the airport to have supper with a friend? call the police? change money? visit a Jewish temple? buy flowers? buy commemorative stamps?

REISEPROVIANT

HÖREN

Stage 1

A1   Just listen several times to the dialogs for *Gespräche 2: Reiseproviant*. Talk along if you like.

A2   Practice saying the dialog lines. Use your "pause" button if you have one.

B1   Conversation 1
  1.   What two things does the person order? What would be the dictionary entry for the first? What are two ingredients for the second? (write the dictionary entry for both)
  2.   What does the order cost?
  3.   Can you tell what time of day it is?

Conversation 2
  1.   Write down the order you hear, with quantities. About how many ounces of each would that be?
  2.   To what category of foods does the second belong? Can you name other types? (consult the menus from Chapter 2)
  3.   What do you suppose the third kind of food is? Confirm your guess.

Conversation 3
  1.   Write out the prices you hear. How is the seller's arithmetic?
  2.   What fruit (German name) is used to make the beverage named?
  3.   What beverage is made from the fruit named?

Conversation 4
1. What foods are mentioned? To what food groups do they belong?
2. How many travelers (not necessarily speakers) are there?
3. Where are they going? Does it sound like a long trip? How do you know?
4. Can you guess what a *Becher* is? What clues help you?

Stage 2

B2   Conversation 1
1. How many travelers are there?
2. Where do they plan to eat on the train? Do you know why?
3. Write down all the words for food and drink that you hear.
4. What words do you know that belong to the first category of food mentioned?

Conversation 2
1. What kind of cheese does the person order? Where do you think it is from?
2. What countries are mentioned? What foods are associated with these countries?
3. How much do oranges cost? What is the total price of oranges?
4. The speaker says *Trinkmilch* instead of *Milch*. What other kinds might there be in this culture? Why?
5. What does cheese cost per 100g?
6. What carbohydrates are chosen for the journey? How much do they all cost together?
7. What important part of the train station is mentioned? Why is it important?
8. What kind of food would you add if you were the traveler?
9. Unfortunately, another customer coughed and you didn't hear the total price of the purchase. Can you reconstruct it?

C

2B:5.2.1   The news item mentions two kinds of beverage: _____ and non-alcoholic (*alkoholfreie Getränke*). Write down the phrase in which the prices of the two are compared.

2B:5.3.3   The news item reports the outcome of a court trial. For each of the three persons described, note name, age, and length of sentence. Why are the three going to prison?

2B:5.4.1   Who does the speaker talk about? Count the number of male and female versions or nicknames that are derived from that person's name. About what time of the day was the segment broadcast?

SPRECHEN

Stage 1
1. You greet the storekeeper. It's 11 a.m. You'd like a bottle of some kind of soft drink.
2. You'd like three rolls and some chocolate, and the juicy oranges from Israel look tempting.
3. You'd like 200g of *Edamer* cheese. The salesperson gives you 180g. You say that's not enough.
4. You'd like a piece of *Landjäger*, a hard salami ideal for trips. The salesperson gives it to you, and you respond.
5. You ask the salesperson to wait just a second. Be polite.
6. You tell the salesperson that you love Swiss cheese.
7. ⊗ and ⊕, in line behind you, ask whether those are raisins. You tell them they're nuts.

Stage 2
1. You'd like about a quarter pound of Swiss cheese and 2 oranges.
2. You'd like 3 different kinds of fruit for 2 people for a 250km trip.
3. You're celebrating the end of your diet. Load up on carbohydrates for your trip.
4. The salesperson offers you 3 bananas, but you need more. You plan to eat your bananas not in the station, but rather in the compartment of the train.
5. You'd like 2 chocolate bars, one milk chocolate and one mocha.
6. You'd like to buy the bottle of Florida-Boy juice, but it's too expensive.
7. You'd also like a bottle of apple juice, but you've temporarily forgotten the word. Apologize to the people behind you while you thumb through your dictionary.

8. You don't know what *Mandeln* are, and ask for clarification.

9. You'd like 2 more packages of cookies.

10. You bump into someone, causing him to spill his Fanta.

11. You greet someone at 7:00 p.m.

12. The storekeeper hands you your purchases. You leave the store.

LESEN

Stage 1   You have bought a ticket on the "Alpen-Express", a train that serves, among other countries, Austria, Italy, and the BRD. Read the Buffet-Bar car menu on **CT 65** and answer the questions below.

1. What does the standard breakfast include?

2. Compare price lists. How does the value of the DM compare to that of the öS? Of the lire? How many lire do there appear to be in an öS?

3. What items listed on the Italian version of the menu are lacking in the German version?

4. What does the abbreviation *cl.* mean? About how many ounces is that? What do the fractions 1/4, 1/3, and 1/2 stand for?

5. You just have to have some chewing gum. What does it cost?

6. Does the lunch/dinner menu include drinks? What phrase tells you?

7. The full version of this menu is written in several languages. Which one do you think is the original? (Or: which one do you think is <u>not</u> the original? Hints: 1) Look at the general layout of the menu; 2) What could "Kaffee mit Milch oder Tee oder Schokolade" mean?)

Stage 2   Now look at the "Minibar" menu on p. 9 of the **ST** *Drucksachen*.

1. The menu lists six national currencies. In which country did the menu originate? Why do you think so? How do these prices compare to those on the "Alpen Express"?

2. The railway system in the DDR is called the *Deutsche Reichsbahn*. What items are prohibited for sale when the train car is passing through DDR territory?

3. It's April 30. Can you buy ice cream on this train?

4. If you were writing an English version of this menu, what word would you choose to render *Portion*? Why not "portion"?

SCHREIBEN

Stage 1   Refer again to the "Alpen-Express" train menu on **CT 65**.

1. Write out a club car snack order for yourself and 2 friends, complete with prices.

2. Write the various kinds of *Fruchtsäfte* you learned in chapters one and two. How does the price here compare to that on other menus?

Stage 2   Now consult the menu *Gute Reise und guten Appetit* on **CT 323**.

1. Write the names of the 6 countries represented on the menu. For each one, write its official language(s). How many different languages are represented by these 6 countries?

2. List the alcoholic and non-alcoholic beverages available. For which ones are you not given an exact quantity in liters?

STRUCTURAL EXERCISES

1   Give commands to the people indicated, using forms of *studieren, essen, trinken, bleiben, zahlen, finden, nehmen,* and *vergessen*:

    1. Englisch ist leicht; Russisch ist nicht leicht.
        Herr Behler, _____ lieber Englisch!

    2. Bier ist nicht gut für Frau Rohse.
        Frau Rohse, _____ kein Bier!

    3. Herr Ranzen hat Pommes frites, zwei Würstchen und einen halben Liter Bier.
        Herr Ranzen, _____ nicht zu viel!

    4. Herr und Frau Heyse fahren nach Wien.
        Herr und Frau Heyse, _____ den Zug, nicht Ihr Auto!

    5. Frau Hansen bleibt im Hotelzimmer. Herr Hansen ist im Taxi.
        Herr Hansen, _____ Ihre Frau nicht!

    6. Das Essen kostet 24 Mark, und Frl. Spieß hat 30 Mark.
        Frl. Spieß, ich habe nur ein bißchen. Bitte, _____für mich!

    7. Sie brauchen ein Einzelzimmer für eine Nacht.
        Bitte, Herr Steinke, _____ ein Einzelzimmer für mich!

2   You have already ordered one item for each of your traveling companions, and now they all want more. Because you are keeping track of expenses, complete the list you have already begun.

    Example —   Helene: eine Dose Bier   <u>zwei Dosen Bier</u>

                Annemarie: 1 Portion Kaffee   <u>zwei _____ _____</u>

                Irma: 1 Bockwurst mit Senf

                Uli: 1 Scheibe Brot mit Butter

                Karl: 1 Kännchen Schwarztee

                Sigi: 1 Tafel Schokolade

                Walter: 1 Becher Eiskrem

                Dagmar: 1 Päckchen Marmorkuchen

                Rüdiger: 1 Dose Pils

                Susanne: 1 Flasche Mineralwasser

3   Be more economical with what you're saying. Replace underlined forms with pronouns; be sure verbs and subjects match.

    1. <u>Hermann und ich</u> (_____) fahren nächste Woche nach Berlin.

    2. Im Oktober beginnen <u>Sie und Hans</u> (_____) Ihr Studium an der Universität.

    3. <u>Käthe und August</u> (_____) essen heute abend am Bahnhof.

    4. Nun? Was trinken <u>Sie und ich</u> (_____) heute abend?

    5. <u>Der Kartoffelsalat und eine Flasche Mineralwasser</u> (_____) kosten DM 5.

    6. Ich glaube, <u>mein Koffer</u> (_____) ist noch im Auto.

    7. <u>Erika, Liesel und Arthur</u> (_____) brauchen Karten nach Nürnberg.

    8. <u>Das Bier</u> (_____) ist ein bißchen zu kalt.

    9. <u>Die Frau am nächsten Schalter</u> (_____) kauft ein Ticket nach Ulm.

4   The indulgent Frau Reichmann wants to make sure her son's snack on the train is just right. Answer for him.

    Example: Wie schmeckt der Kuchen, Fritz? — *Er ist wirklich gut.*

    1. Ist der Tee heiß genug?

    2. Die Schokolade ist sehr süß, ja?

    3. Aber die Flasche Fanta ist zu groß, nicht?

    4. Ist der Eiskrembecher wirklich so gut?

    5. Und das Bier schmeckt fantastisch, nicht?

    6. Ach, das Päckchen Nüsse ist so klein!

5 The card below, from Frau Meßner to her employer, has some rain blotches on it, and some of the words are obscured. Reconstruct the original text:

> Liebe Frau Behr,
>
> Heute sind wir für 3 Tage _____ Freiburg, einer wunderschönen Stadt. Die Reise _____ Süddeutschland geht wirklich sehr gut; gestern waren wir _____ Baden-Baden, und Donnerstag fahren wir _____ Ulm, wo wir das Münster sehen. Ein Mann _____ Ulm ist auch hier und geht mit uns. Am 14. August fahre ich mit dem Zug wieder _____ Bremen.
>
> mit vielen Grüßen
Ihre   Elsa Meßner

6 You have struck up a conversation with a person in your train compartment. Formulate questions appropriate to his answers:

1. Hahn. Udo Hahn.
2. Ich? 24 — im April 25, ja, 25.
3. Morgen? Nach Salzburg.
4. In Bayern—ich habe ein Haus in Garmisch.
5. Das ist meine Frau Annegret.
6. Um 9 Uhr.
7. Mein Gepäck? Im Hotelzimmer.
8. Das? Das ist meine Gitarre—schön, nicht?
9. Ja, ich bleibe einen Tag hier, dann fahren wir alle nach Salzburg.

√ CHECK YOUR PROFICIENCY

CAN YOU:
__ give commands? With how many verbs?
__ ask questions relevant to train travel (directions, prices, times)?
__ express quantities of food and drink, including limited use of the metric system?
__ express simple clock time?
__ tell where you're from, where you are, and where you're going?
__ count money and make change with reasonable facility?

DO YOU REMEMBER HOW TO:
__ identify your possessions?
__ give appropriate greetings at different times of the day?
__ ask for clarification?
__ perform transactions involving money?
__ make polite requests?
__ ask detailed questions about shelter?
__ make up for gaps in your vocabulary?
__ make judgments and comparisons?
__ negate with *kein*?

HÖREN

A1   Just listen several times to the dialogs for *Gespräche 1: Im Zug*. Talk along if you like.

A2   Practice saying the dialog lines. Use your "pause" button if you have one.

B1   Conversation 1

        1. What time of day is it?
        2. How many families appear to be represented in the dialog?
        3. How many people are there in the larger family?
        4. Are there more males or more females in it?

    Conversation 2

        1. Write the names of the people you hear.
        2. Write the ages of the people named.
        3. Tell the destination of the family.
        4. Can you tell the destination of the other party? How?

    Conversation 3

        1. What time is it in the dialog?
        2. Is that time exact or an estimate?
        3. What is the destination?
        4. How long will it take to reach that city?

B2   Conversation 1

        1. Does the second speaker find a seat in this compartment? Why or why not?
        2. Is either of the speakers a tourist? How can you tell?
        3. What city are they talking about? How long is the second speaker staying there?
        4. What attraction will this person probably see first? Why do you think so?

    Conversation 2

        1. How many people seem to be in the compartment?
        2. Write the names of the cities you hear. Which ones are in the north? Which are in the south?
        3. What are the occupations of the two friends? How precise can you be?
        4. Where is the other person from? What words tell his opinion of that place? Is he there a lot?
        5. Does that person seem to be older or younger than the others? How do you know?

    Conversation 3

        1. How many people are there in the compartment?
        2. Where are they from?
        3. What does the North American do for a living?
        4. How does he happen to speak such good German?
        5. What do you know about that person's parents?

B3   1. What are the professions of the two people?
        2. What cities are mentioned?
        3. What does each person have to do with each city?
        4. How old is the person with an academic background?
        5. What does the other person find attractive about the city where the academic now lives?

B4   1. Where is the first speaker from?
        2. Where is the other speaker from?
        3. Does either have anything to do with Freiburg? Who? What?
        4. How does the second speaker contradict himself? How long does it take him to realize his mistake?

c

1A:2.1.3   The announcer passes on greetings to a traveler. Is the traveler a man or a woman? Note all you can about the children in the traveler's family. What day is "today" in the broadcast?

1A:3.1.1   The announcer passes on birthday congratulations to someone. Note what you can about the person and the family. You should be able to recognize terms for immediate family members; if you want to try more, consult the family tree on **CT 296**.

1A:3.1.2   Two people have requested that old favorite, "Listen! They're Playing Our Song." Take notes about the people who made the song requests and the people to whom the song is dedicated.

1A:3.2.2   The announcer reads a song-request postcard. From which country does the request come? Who wrote the card? To whom does he wish to dedicate the song? What is the title of the song? Observe the phrase *"eine wärmere Jahreszeit"* with its Chapter 4 vocabulary.

SPRECHEN

Study the *Bildwörterbuch* (pictorial vocabulary) pages entitled *People—Leute* (**CT 296**). Learn what you think you need to know right now.

Stage 1   1.   You ask if there is any room for you in the compartment. Thank the person who tells you there is.

2.   There's no room for you after all. Say you're sorry to have disturbed things. Then say good-bye.

3.   You wonder how late it might be, and finally summon the courage to ask — your train should be arriving at its destination any time now.

4.   You wonder whether the other person in the compartment is going to the same city you are. When you hear she is, you wonder whether she's a native of the city, and where she goes out to eat there.

5.   You are nearing Köln. Ask the person across from you whether he knows where the cathedral (*Dom*) is. Then ask when he thinks you might be arriving in the city.

6.   When the other person in the compartment stands up to get off the train, he mistakenly picks up your luggage. Enlighten him.

7.   A nice-looking young man enters the compartment and asks whether there might be room for him. There is. He then asks about additional places. There are three places empty.

Stage 2   1.   A person from Ireland boards the train and asks about room in your compartment. She assumes that you are German, and asks about what there is to see and do in Köln. Tell her.

2.   The passport official is a bit suspicious because you have had your feet on the seat and don't act like a European. By telling him where you're from, how old you are, where you study, and so on, do your best to convince him that you're a perfectly normal North American.

3.   Tell the person sitting with you on the train what your summer plans are. They include staying in one place for a while, then traveling to a few other places.

4.   You want to introduce your family — your mother, your father, and your siblings — to the nice person you have been talking with on the train. (They just returned from the dining car.)

5.   You just told someone the incorrect time because you mixed up your numbers. Set the record straight.

LESEN

Stage 1   Look at the pamphlet *Der Familien-Paß* on p. 40 of the **ST** *Drucksachen*. What does the family pass cost? Does it get you <u>unlimited</u> travel? Does it get you <u>free</u> travel? What kind of people, and how many, can use the pass? Could you get one if you were traveling alone? Hint: look at words that appear near a word you know: *Kinder*.

Stage 2   1.   You, your spouse, and two children (ages 6 and 8) would like to travel by train — second class, of course — from Hamburg to Freiburg and then return to Hamburg. How much money, if any, would you save if you bought the *Familien-Paß* , even if you used it for just this one trip? How about on a one-time-only one-way trip from Köln to Regensburg?

2.   Can you use the timetable on **CT 35** and the family-pass pamphlet together to figure out whether you and your spouse (no kids this time) might want to get the family pass for your round-trip train travel between Köln and München?

SCHREIBEN

Stage 1   1.   Look at the *Fahrplanauszug* or timetable for trains from München to Köln on **CT 35**. You're returning to Köln, and would like to stop for a day to visit acquaintances in Stuttgart. What can you do? Write out an itinerary for yourself, listing train number and departure/arrival times.

2.   Repeat the preceding exercise, but now under these conditions: You want to have lunch with a business contact in Mannheim. Moreover, you don't want to leave München before eating the breakfast that was included with your hotel room, and you'd like to get to Köln in time to find a hotel and rest up before having an early dinner. On which days and dates would you not be able to schedule your trip this way, and what would you do then?

Stage 2   Assume that you are going to make the trip from München to Köln, with the stopover to see acquaintances in either Mannheim or Stuttgart. Write a postcard note to the person you are going to visit, briefly telling your itinerary. You could play it safe and just reproduce your timetable. But you could also try to produce some genuine sentences and thus sound more personal. You can get a lot of use out of the verb *sein*, since in German the present tense can be used for future meaning — especially if you include a time phrase like "tomorrow", or "at 7 o'clock". Address the postcard in proper form — you can borrow an address from one of your hotel listings. Begin and close your note as follows:

        Lieber Herr _____ / Liebe Frau _____
        .....bis Montag (etc.)

WO IST DIE STRASSE?

HÖREN

Stage 1

A1   Just listen several times to the dialogs for *Gespräche 2: Wo ist die Straße?* Talk along if you like.

A2   Practice saying the dialog lines.

B1   Conversation 1
    1. Write the name of the hotel in question.
    2. How far is it?
    3. What two directions are mentioned?

    Conversation 2
    1. What building does the person want to find?
    2. How can one usually get there?
    3. Why is one of those ways impossible now?

    Conversation 3
    1. Where does the first person want to go?
    2. How far is it?
    3. Why will the trip be unsuccessful?

Stage 2

B2   Conversation 1
    1. Name the three landmarks in question (<u>not</u> the destinations).
    2. What is farther, the first mentioned or the second?
    3. How far is the third?
    4. How far is the second from the third?
    5. How does one get from the first to the second?

    Conversation 2
    1. What mode of transportation is mentioned?
    2. What mode of transportation is implied? By what word?
    3. How long does it take to get to the destination by bus?
    4. Which bus line goes there?

5. How many minutes ago did the last bus leave?

6. Would it be wise for the person to walk? Why (not)?

Conversation 3

1. What does the person want to find?

2. How far is it to that place?

3. What landmarks will the person see underway? Name them in order.

4. Is the traveler in his car or not? Why do you think that?

C1

1A:4.2.1

Use the maps of München on p. 1 of the **ST** *Drucksachen*, **CT 158**, **CT 166** and **CT 314-15** to follow the traffic report. Between München and what other city is there a traffic problem? Later on in the report the announcer focuses on streets within the city; listen for the words *Straße* and *Ring*. The second street she names is also a subway stop near the Olympic Center in the north of the city (see **CT 166**). The fourth and last street can be found in the upper right-hand corner of the map on **CT 315**. What might *stadteinwärts* and *stadtauswärts* mean? [1]

1A:4.2.2

What station are you listening to? Which *Autobahn* stretch is mentioned, and in which direction is the problem? Pinpoint the stretch by using the map of the München region on **CT 158**.

C2

2A:1.1.1

Which of the natural sciences are mentioned? Why are they in the news? If you want to expand your vocabulary of academic terms, consult the *Bildwörterbuch* display on **CT 291**.

SPRECHEN

Stage 1

1. Someone has asked you how to get to a landmark in the city. You don't know, but are eager to help out if you can. Make a reasonable suggestion.

2. You do know how to get from your hotel to the post office. The walk involves a distance of six or seven blocks, and several turns. Tell someone.

3. You have been asked about transportation across town. Considering both the weather and the condition of the person who is asking, recommend something.

4. You are giving directions. The desired destination is on the other side of town. List landmarks along the way, and estimate the distances in meters.

5. You are giving directions to a tourist attraction, such as a museum. It's pretty late already — You suspect the attraction is closed. Make an appropriate suggestion.

Stage 2

1. The taxi driver has misunderstood your destination. Fortunately, you discover that shortly after the drive begins.

2. The taxi driver has misunderstood your destination. Unfortunately, you discover that only after you arrive where you don't want to be.

3. You've been walking a long time, and wonder whether you're going the right direction. Stop someone and check.

4. You're sure you're going the right direction. Your companion isn't so sure. Prove your point.

5. You have a lot of baggage; defend your wish to use public transportation rather than walk.

6. You're preparing to take a taxi; you ask the driver about any extra charges for a large number of suitcases.

LESEN

Stage 1

1. Look at the LESEN exercises for Preliminary Units #1 and #2, particularly those you did not do earlier. Can you read fluently the street addresses, telephone numbers, and time indications — including such abbreviations as *-str.*?

2. Look at the map of Mannheim on **CT 310**. Locate one example each of the following types of paved area: *Straße, Ring, Platz, Promenade* and *Ufer*. Can you figure out what *Ufer* means without using a dictionary? Cite a name which incorporates the standard abbreviation for *Platz*. What do the abbreviations *WC, f., K., öffentl.,* and *Sch.* seem to mean? How many features are named for Germany's greatest cultural figure, Johann Wolfgang von Goethe (1749-1832)? Find two streets named for German philosophers. Find four streets named for German composers.

3. Look at the map of Mannheim on **CT 310** and the street map of Köln on **CT 85**. Can you find two or even three streets in Köln that have counterparts of the same name in Mannheim (hint: think composers and statesmen)? In Mannheim those streets are located close in, and are near streets named for other composers and statesmen; in Köln they are isolated at the left edge of the map. What does that suggest about the relative ages of the two cities?

Stage 2

1 Look again at the map of Mannheim on **CT 310** and the Mannheim restaurant list on **CT 322**, particularly the addresses and the remarks about location (*Lage*) and nearby features (*Umgebung*) in the right-hand columns.

1. Note that some of the restaurants have street addresses, while some have instead codes like *H7, 3* or *O7, 16*. How sure can you be that the codes in the list refer to the blocks with similar designations (but no second number) within the *Ring*?

2. Which of the restaurants listed are not on the map? Can you tell which direction you would go to search for them? What key words help you confirm quickly that a restaurant will be on the map?

3. The Mannheim map does not have a scale. How many different ways can you establish your own scale of distances? Hint: think about the size of the rivers.

4. It's Sunday. You'd like to spend the day in one of the parks along one of the rivers, and then try the local cuisine. Make a list of appropriate restaurants.

2 Look at pp. 20-21 in the **ST** *Drucksachen*, four pages from a guide to East Berlin.

1. List some heroes who have been memorialized in the names of city landmarks.

2. Wade through the background material and make a list of major landmarks: city squares, main streets, buildings, etc. Now begin constructing a map by drawing two circles big enough to label "Marx-Engels-Platz" and "Alexanderplatz". The circles should be separated by several diameters. Now, avoiding the historical and political verbiage, wade through the passages which guide the stranger through the heart of East Berlin. How well can you locate the streets and other landmarks on your map? You may find it helpful to read similar descriptions on **CT 186**, which shows detailed maps of smaller areas of a city. Further questions: Which buildings were built after World War II? When was the Berlin Cathedral built? What happened to it during World War II, at the end of which the Soviet Army surrounded and then conquered Berlin in a bitter battle?

SCHREIBEN

Stage 1 An acquaintance you have made doesn't speak German, but wants to travel across town to some special attraction. In handwriting legible to native speakers of German, write down the important points on the route, so that your acquaintance can show the paper to someone along the way. List also the name, address and telephone number of the destination. (Use any of your maps and lists as sources of material.)

Stage 2 Redo the immediately preceding situation, but under these two sets of circumstances:

1. You have been in city X long enough to learn your way around. An acquaintance — a native speaker of German — is coming to visit you, and will be arriving too late to pick up a map. Write a postcard giving directions from the train station to your hotel, which is quite far from the station. Certainly you will use the verb <u>sein</u> a lot, but *sehen* and *finden* will also be useful.

2. What if you were writing the postcard to an acquaintance in order to describe how someone else — an associate or relative of the acquaintance (*er* or *sie*) — should find your hotel?

STRUCTURAL EXERCISES

1 Complete the sentences with an appropriate form of the verb given in parentheses (___):

1. (**essen**)

Ach, Frau Klein, _____ Sie schon?

　　Nein, ich _____ noch nicht.

　　Mein Mann und ich _____

　　um 7 Uhr. Er _____ immer um 7 Uhr.

2. **(vergessen)**

Hm. Köln. Ich _____, wo das ist. Ist das in der DDR?

Nein. Warum _____ Sie das immer, Frau Mengel?

Ich weiß nicht. Aber meine Schwester _____ das auch immer.

Wir _____ immer unsere Geographie.

Hm. Schade, daß Sie das nicht wissen.

_____ Sie und Ihre Schwester denn auch immer Ihre Namen?

3. **(nehmen)**

Gut. Sie _____ mein Geld zum Fahrkartenschalter und kaufen eine Karte nach Aachen, einfach.

Schön. Ich _____ also das Geld und kaufe die Karte.

Und _____ Sie dann mein Gepäck zum Gleis, wo wir abfahren?

Ja, das mache ich. Aber schnell: wir _____ den Zug um 10 Uhr 46,

und wir haben nur 5 Minuten.

4. **(sehen)**

Was _____ Sie da? Ist das ein Imbiß?

Nein, ich _____ nur den Fahrkartenschalter.

Ach, ich bin so hungrig. Wo _____ wir denn endlich einen Wurststand?

Ich weiß nicht. Hm. Was _____ die Frau da?

Ich glaube, sie ist auch hungrig, und sie geht — sie geht — ja, sie

geht direkt zum Imbiß. Und jetzt gehen wir auch essen.

5. **(schlafen)**

Sehen Sie den Mann da? Er _____ zu viel, glaube ich.

Wie, bitte?

Ja, der Mann da. _____ er nicht zu viel?

Oh, ich glaube nicht. Ich _____ auch viel.

_____ Sie nicht auch viel?

Ich? Nein, ich nicht. Meine Schwestern _____ viel,

und mein kleiner Bruder _____ täglich 10 Stunden, aber ich nicht.

So, sehr interessant. Meine Familie _____ immer zu viel.

Wir _____ lange und fest zu Hause.

2   By inserting the indicated time phrase, tell more precisely and emphatically when your planned activities will take place.

Ich komme nach Köln.	**(im Sommer)**
Ich fahre mit dem Bus zur Jugendherberge.	**(zuerst)**
Ich bin da mit dem Gepäck.	**(in 10 Minuten)**
Ich finde das Hotel Stuttgarter Hof.	**(dann)**
Ich sehe auch eine Konditorei dort.	**(bald)**
Ich gehe zur Konditorei.	**(schnell)**
Die Konditorei ist aber geschlossen.	**(am Sonntag)**

3   Use the appropriate form of the verb *wissen* to complete the conversation:

HERR FRANK: Entschuldigen Sie, Herr Kurz, _____ Sie, wo die Theodulkirche ist?

HERR KURZ: Die Theodulkirche — nein, das _____ wir nicht. Tut mir leid.

HERR FRANK: Hm. Ihre Frau, vielleicht? _____ Sie, wo das ist, Frau Kurz?

FRAU KURZ: Die Theodulkirche — ja, ich glaube, ich _____ das.

HERR FRANK: Oh, schön. Wo ist sie denn?

FRAU KURZ: Das ist . . . Hm. Das ist hier rechts . . . .

HERR KURZ: Nein, nein, das ist die Elisabethkirche.

FRAU KURZ: Ach, ja. Aber fragen Sie die Frau da. Sie _____ ganz sicher.

HERR FRANK: Nein, sie _____ das nicht. Das ist nämlich meine Frau.

√ CHECK YOUR PROFICIENCY

CAN YOU:

__ arrange to get a seat on a train?

__ describe your family and friends?

__ ask and give directions in a city?

__ compare the quality and quantity of things?

DO YOU REMEMBER HOW TO:

__ order simple meals?

__ arrange for shelter for yourself and others?

__ count money?

__ tell time (official and casual)?

HÖREN

Stage 1

A1   Just listen several times to the dialogs for *Gespräche 1: Haltestelle*. Talk along if you like.

A2   Practice saying the dialog lines. Use your "pause" button if you have one.

B1   Conversation 1
1. Where does the person want to go?
2. Which bus goes there? How often does it run?
3. What time is it now? When did the last bus leave?
4. How long will the person have to wait for the next bus?

Conversation 2
1. Where does the person want to go?
2. Which bus should the person take?
3. How long will it be from now until the person has reached her destination?

Conversation 3
1. Where does the person want to go?
2. Does the person have a choice of buses? Explain.
3. Give the bus information you hear.
4. Does the person find out when the next bus is coming?

Stage 2

B2   Conversation 1
1. Where does the person want to go?
2. Will the person have to change buses?
3. How will the person be able to identify the destination?
4. What time of day is it?

Conversation 2
1. What modes of transportation are mentioned?
2. Which one must the traveler choose? What is another word for it?
3. What difficulties does the traveler encounter in asking for information?
4. Does the person giving the information know exactly how the traveler is to reach her destination? What are the directions?

Conversation 3
1. What buildings are mentioned? Where does the traveler want to go? Why?
2. Is it far to the bus stop? Why might it seem far to the traveler?
3. Which modes of transportation are mentioned? Which one is not mentioned, but only implied?
4. Give the reason(s) for the traveler's final decision.

C1

1A:5.1.1-6   Note the predicted low and high temperatures and the times of the reports.

1B:6.4.1   What does the woman in the commercial want? What worries her husband about what she wants? What kind of business is the ad for? Where is it located? What is its phone number?

1B:6.4.2   What kind(s) of transportation does Frau Schmidt use, and why? Use the maps of München on **ST** *Drucksachen* **DS-1**, **CT 158** and **CT 166** to find out where she went.

1B:6.4.3   How is this medicine supposed to help students?

C2

2A:3.1.1 Some special beers, like Paulaner's "Salvator" in this commercial or the "Animator" pictured on **CT 37**, are brewed and marketed only at certain times of the year. How long will the "Salvator" be available? What is the company slogan at the end of the commercial? [1]

2A:3.1.2 This commercial for tires is almost entirely in Bavarian dialect for the same reason that American ads for pickup trucks often use southern or western accents. One repeated word, common to English, German and several other languages, will tell you why this Bavarian buys his tires where he does: _____ . Now concentrate on the very last words, which are spoken in standard German by another man. How many stores do the Reifen Wagner folks have in Bavaria? _____

2A:3.1.3 Listen to the greeting to see what time of the day it is. This announcement, for a program of regional and dialect entertainment, is in *fränkisch* or Franconian dialect; *Franken* is located in northern Bavaria, around Nürnberg. A notable feature is the stretching of the 'a'-sounds; listen again as the announcer speaks the words *Abend, war, hab', achtzig,* and *Jahr'*. Think how differently 'rather' is pronounced in America and Britain. Note too how, shortly after the word *"Familie"*, the phrase *"ich auch"* is clipped to *"i' aa' "*. But that sort of thing happens in English too.

SPRECHEN

Stage 1

1. You ask someone when the next bus to Hockenheim will be there.

2. You want to reach a destination within the city and ask someone whether the bus or the streetcar is faster.

3. You wonder whether you will have to ask for a transfer to get to the train station.

4. You ask someone about the best way to get to the hospital, and are properly thankful for the advice.

5. The bus isn't scheduled to come for another 20 minutes, and you have lots of luggage. Make a decision.

Stage 2

1. The person asking you for transportation advice will have to take a bus other than the one you're waiting for.

2. The person to whom you're giving directions has answered *"Wie, bitte?"* to each of your statements so far. State as simply as you can what he must do to get to the city hall. It will involve a change of buses.

3. Suggest to the other person at the bus stop that she consider alternative modes of transportation because of the weather and the time of day.

4. The other person is mistaken: The bus number she asks about doesn't exist. You suggest another number and tell her how long she will have to wait for the next one.

5. The other person at your bus stop will have to change buses twice to carry out his complicated plan. Explain how this is to be done, and then suggest two simpler alternatives.

LESEN

Stage 1

Compare the street map of downtown München on **CT 314-15** and the map of the München suburban region on **CT 158** with the transit map of the city on **CT 166**, which shows the routes for the subway (*die U-Bahn,* "U") and the streetcar system (*die S-Bahn,* "S").

1. Find the following landmarks in the city: der Hauptbahnhof, die Universität, das Olympiastadion, der Marienplatz, die Theresienwiese. If they are not on your street or suburban maps, note that fact.

2. Find on the transit map the public transportation that would take you to each of these from each of the others.

3. Now find a few of the locations in outlying districts: <u>Freising</u> to the north, site of a famous medieval Benedictine abbey; <u>Dachau</u> to the northwest, location of an infamous Nazi concentration camp; <u>Starnberg</u> to the southwest, where one can find excellent fish specialties fresh from the Starnberger See; <u>Siemenswerke</u> to the south, site of the giant Siemens electrical concern; and <u>Riem</u> to the east of the city, where you are meeting your parents' flight from San Francisco.

Stage 2   1.   Familiarize yourself with the routes taken by the *S-Bahn* and the *U-Bahn* by starting at one end of each line and following the line to its other terminus. For example, follow S3 from Ismaning to Maisach. Practice saying the name of each terminus, and of stations in between.

2.   Can you tell which is the the shortest line? The longest?

3.   If you wanted to get through the center of the city without passing through the congestion at the <u>Hauptbahnhof</u>, which line would you have to take?

4.   How many ways could you get from the Hauptbahnhof to the Olympiazentrum using public transit?

SCHREIBEN

Stage 1   Return to your Stage 1 reading exercise above.

1.   You want to meet a business acquaintance for lunch near the Universität, and have agreed to leave her a note at the information desk at the Hauptbahnhof. Because she is a stranger to München, make sure you give her explicit instructions for taking the subway, and tell her exactly when you expect to see her.

> Liebe Frau X,
>
> . . .
>
>   Ihr(e) Y

2.   Now change the note to conform to the other destinations in the reading exercise.

3.   Now rewrite the note, assuming she is taking public transportation not from the Hauptbahnhof, but rather from the Olympiastadion.

HOTEL — BAD ODER DUSCHE?

HÖREN

Stage 1

A1   Just listen several times to the dialogs for *Gespräche 2: Bad oder Dusche?* Talk along if you like.

A2   Practice saying the dialog lines. Use your "pause" button if you have one.

B1   Conversation 1
   1.   How many people are looking for a room?
   2.   For how many days is the room requested?
   3.   What time of day is it?
   4.   Is this an expensive room? Why (not)?

Conversation 2
   1.   Do you know how many people are looking for a room?
   2.   What amenities does the requested room come with?
   3.   What floor is the room on?
   4.   What does the room cost?
   5.   How much is breakfast? Where is the breakfast room?

Stage 2

B2   Conversation 1
   1.   What room has been rented?
   2.   Does the room have a shower?
   3.   What floor is the room on?
   4.   Why is the customer a bit disappointed?

Conversation 2
1. Does this appear to be a modern hotel or an old-fashioned one?
2. How many people will be occupying the room?
3. What "extra" is found in this hotel?
4. How many nights is the room to be occupied by this party?

B3 The tour guide is reading a list of travelers and the rooms they have requested for the night. Draw up a chart with the following columns: _Name_, _Zimmer_ (Doppel-/Einzel-), _Bad_ (mit/ohne), _Dusche_ (mit/ohne). Under the Name column, put the following names: Herr/Frau Metz, Herr Falkenstein, Fräulein Bieder, Herr/Frau Braune, Frau Melk, Herr Melk, Herr Ortenburg, Fräulein Caspar. Insert check marks in the appropriate places to confirm the guide's list.

C1

1B:6.1.8 Fill in the blanks with words from recent vocabulary: "Der _____ _____ fertig. _____ frisch _____ ___ _____." Note particularly the use (and spelling!) of the singular form of _müssen_.

1B:6.1.9 The commercial is for Langnese honey, but it talks a lot about coffee. How is the coffee described? What do you do with the honey?

1B:6.2.1 The ad is for a women's tabloid newspaper. If you listen to the headline about new diets you can tell in which season the broadcast occurred. The same word occurs twice later. Which colors are in fashion in that season during the broadcast year?

1B:6.3.1 The household product in the ad is sold in America also, under the same brand name: _____ . What is the repairman fixing? What word is used to describe the cost of repairs?

1B:6.3.4 What can you win in the soap-company contest? How much is it worth, and what do you have to do? Note the city and phone number. What month is it in the ad?

1B:6.3.5 The household product in the ad is sold in America also, under the same brand name: _____ .

C2

2B:4.1.1 The travel feature describes hiking vacations where your baggage is transported for you. Do for the three tours what you did for just one in Chapter 2: take notes on the duration of the trip, the distance to be covered (per day? in total?), and the price of accommodations / meals. The tours are for three areas in the west/southwest BRD: the Schwäbische Alb, the Eifel, and the Hunsrück . Can you figure out what extras the Hunsrück trip offers? [2]

SPRECHEN

Stage 1 1. You would like a single room with a shower for one night.

2. You'd like a double room from now until Thursday, and you'd prefer a shower and a bath.

3. You need a single room, and a shower in the room isn't absolutely necessary, as long as there's one nearby.

4. Your room has turned out to be a bit noisy, since it's so close to the street on the front of the hotel. See what you can do to change things.

5. Explain to a man from Hong Kong how the shower works.

Stage 2 1. Defend the absence of bath and shower in some hotel rooms.

2. Arrange for rooms for your parents and for yourself. Take the wishes of all into consideration. The rooms should be close together, but needn't be adjacent.

3. Two couples from Albuquerque have found out that you know some German and prevail upon you to arrange for rooms for them. They are used to lots of luxury, but there's only one double room with bath left. Do your best.

4. You haven't been able to sleep because the people next to you have been making so much noise. Arrange for a different room with the same facilities, and see whether the hotel might give you a little discount on the room.

5. You have a few special requests: You and your spouse need a room with a crib for the baby; you would also like to have your two young boys in a separate room adjacent to and accessible from yours; and you would like to have breakfast at 6 a.m., although the breakfast room doesn't open until 6:30.

LESEN

Stage 1   Consult the advertisement for the Hotel Drei Löwen on **CT 319**.

1.   Using the information in the ad, locate the hotel on your street map of München.
2.   What does the name mean? (Don't use your dictionary!)
3.   What suggests to you that this is not an ordinary hotel?
4.   Is it possible to get a room without bath and shower?
5.   If you were in München, what phone number would you dial for reservations at this hotel?
6.   What if you were not in München, but rather in Freiburg?

Stage 2

1   Look at the listing of *Privatzimmer* in Lindau on **CT 152**.

1.   Where is it possible to find accommodations with bath or shower?
2.   Where would you have difficulty parking your car? Why do you suppose that is?
3.   Do most rooms have baths and showers, or just warm water?
4.   Do most rooms have two beds or just one?
5.   Are more toilet facilities located inside or outside the rooms?
6.   Where would you be least likely to stay? Why?
7.   What do all the establishments offer their guests?

2   Consult **CT 321**, the page of services available from a hotel in a European city.

1.   What indicates that it is possible to do the following in this hotel? sun-bathe / dance late at night / leave your car out of the rain / cash traveler's checks / borrow an electric razor / arrange for hotel rooms at other hotels / have your laundry done (what information do you have to supply with the laundry?) / buy souvenirs at 8:00 on Sunday mornings / have a doctor summoned to your room / have a facial
2.   What European city is this hotel located in? How many hints can you find that point to this answer?

SCHREIBEN

Stage 1   1.   Do the appropriate written structural exercises at the end of this chapter.
2.   Referring to the list of *Privatzimmer* in Lindau on **CT 152**, pick one of the establishments and write a note to your acquaintances in Köln telling them as much as you can about where you are staying while you are vacationing on the Bodensee. Tell them the price, the facilities, the location, and even the telephone number in case they have to reach you.

>   Liebe Familie Tischler,
>   Jetzt bin ich in Lindau am Bodensee. Das Wetter ist wunderschön. Ich habe ein
>   Privatzimmer mit Balkon . . . .

Stage 2   Compare the *Privatzimmer* in Lindau on **CT 152** to the Trier hotel facilities on p. 6 of the **S T** *Drucksachen*. Choose a place in each city and write a note to your acquaintance, Frau Schmied, in Köln, comparing the two. On the basis of the comparison, choose the place where you intend to stay during your next free weekend. (Use adjectives with *-er* for at least part of your comparison.)

STRUCTURAL EXERCISES

1   You are giving directions to various travelers. Combine the sets of sentences with **und, oder** or **aber** (as appropriate) to make a less choppy impression:

1.   Steigen Sie in der Fuchsstraße aus. Nehmen Sie dort die Linie 5.
2.   Fahren Sie nach Brühl? Fahren Sie nach Deutz?
3.   Am Rathausplatz müssen Sie umsteigen. Sie müssen die Nummer 7 nehmen.
4.   Sie finden den Bus an der Haltestelle um die Ecke. Es ist 23 Uhr und vielleicht zu spät.
5.   Sie müssen zum Krankenhaus fahren. Dort steigen Sie in die Nummer 12 ein.

2   Unscramble the words to form coherent statements:
1. Uhr Bus um 43 kommt der 9.
2. Bitte zum Bus Bahnhof dieser fährt?
3. Sie die sehen rechts Haltestelle.
4. Ein Bahnhof besser nehmen Taxi zum Sie.
5. Ich zum wann Museum fahren muß?

3   Insert in the blanks appropriate modal verb forms.
1. Wir _____ zum Bahnhof fahren, aber wir _____ nicht.
2. Wann _____ Sie wieder nach Wien fahren?
3. Wieviel _____ er für das Doppelzimmer haben?
4. Nein, mein Gepäck _____ das nicht sein. Mein Gepäck ist braun.
5. _____ Sie ein Doppelzimmer haben? Oder _____ es ein Einzelzimmer sein?
6. Gertrud? Nein, sie _____ nicht mitkommen. Sie hat keine Karte.
7. _____ wir jetzt endlich gehen? Haben Sie alles?
8. DM 200? Das _____ doch nicht so viel kosten!
9. _____ das nur mit Dusche sein? — Nein, das _____ mit Bad und Dusche sein.
10. _____ Ihr Kind zum Zoo gehen? Oder _____ er zuerst ein bißchen schlafen?

4   Someone wonders just how bad your taste is. Complete the sentences with conviction.
<u>Example:</u>   Ist/Sind das **Ihr__** X?   Nein, nein, **mein__** X ist/sind das sicher nicht!

1. Mann	2. Restaurant	3. Gepäck	4. Straße
5. Weißwein	6. Fahrkarten	7. Vorname	8. Fisch
9. Familienname	10. Haltestelle	11. Autos	12. Adresse
13. Töchter	14. Hote	15. Frau	16. Zimmer
17. Familie	18. Glas	19. Kotelett	20. Pommes frites

5   Use forms of *essen, vergessen, nehmen, sehen, schlafen,* and *wissen* to complete this tale of woe:

Frau Kranzmeyer _____ nicht, was sie mit dem Sohn Erich machen soll. Er _____ immer, was sie sagt. Er _____ zu viel im Bett, er _____ zu viel Zeit, wenn er im Restaurant _____, er _____ auch nichts in der Physikklasse. Wenn er sein Auto fährt, _____ er die anderen Autos nicht. Sie findet das alles sehr schade — Erich ist ein guter Sohn, aber sie denkt, sie muß ihn zum Arzt bringen.

Und Erich _____ nicht, was er mit der Mutter und dem Vater machen soll. Sie _____ immer, was er sagt. Sie _____ zu viel im Bett, sie _____ zu viel Zeit, wenn sie im Restaurant _____, sie _____ auch nichts, wenn er sie fragt. (Vielleicht sind sie dumm.) Und wenn sie das Auto fahren, _____ sie die anderen Autos nicht. Das findet er alles sehr schade. Er denkt, sie sind gute Eltern, aber vielleicht muß er sie zum Arzt bringen.

6   Return to the reading and writing exercises in the first half of this chapter (*Haltestelle*).

You want to send your business acquaintance on the bus, so that she will get to know the city during her stay. For each of the routes you have chosen above, see whether bus transportation is available. If it is, tell her in another series of notes the things she will see underway. Be sure to use the patterns of speech illustrated in your chapter dialogs (*"Dann kommt das . . . und dann sehen Sie . . ."*).

√ CHECK YOUR PROFICIENCY

CAN YOU:
__ deal with public transportation?
__ discuss hotel facilities?
__ find out how things work?

DO YOU REMEMBER HOW TO:
__ ask for information?
__ ask for clarification and elicit details?
__ use the metric system?
__ describe your family and friends?

HÖREN

Stage 1

A1   Just listen several times to the dialogs for *Gespräche 1: Geldwechsel*. Talk along if you like.

A2   Practice saying the dialog lines. Use your "pause" button if you have one.

B1   Conversation 1
1. How much money will the person receive for his $100?
2. In what form is his American money?

        Conversation 2
1. What two currencies does the person have?
2. How much of each?
3. Write the DM equivalent of the first currency.
4. Write the DM equivalent of the second currency.

        Conversation 3
1. What total amount does the person receive in DM?
2. Where is the person to date the receipt?
3. What time of day is it <u>not</u>?

Stage 2

B2   Conversation 1
1. What country's currency is being purchased?
2. Do we know in what country the transaction is taking place?
3. How many bills does the person receive? What is the total amount?

        Conversation 2
1. What currency is this? What word indicates a kind of coin?
2. What is the total amount?

        Conversation 3
1. What is the total number of bills the person receives?
2. What is the total number of coins the person receives? (careful!)
3. What is the smallest coin the person receives?

C

1B:7.1.3

You have now learned about decimal or fractional numbers and the use of *"Komma"*. Listen again to the long stock market report, taking notes on a chart with columns headed <u>Company</u>, <u>Price</u>, and <u>Change (+/-)</u>. The list of stocks to listen for now includes some more of the major German corporations like those whose products you have been exposed to in recent units: BASF, Bayer, BMW, Daimler, Hacker-Pschorr, Löwenbräu, Paulaner, Porsche, and Volkswagen. You will likely have to listen to the stock report at least three times before your chart is close to complete. <u>We suggest that you NOT stop and replay every few words, but rather take notes over longer blocks of speech</u>.

After the stock prices come metals and currencies. What is the quotation for an ounce of gold in London?

Note the exchange rates for the major German- and English-speaking countries. When you read **CT 225** you will find out why the rate for East German marks is not given.

If you are feeling confident about what you have learned up to now, try this: Your nearby metropolitan newspaper likely quotes foreign currency exchange rates (in dollars, of course). Can you compare the exchange rates in the broadcast with those in your own present time? Of course you'll have to do all sorts of conversions, and by now you may feel that neither math nor German is your strong point. So use skills like those you've been reading about in the **CT** *Strategie* pages. Buy time by saying and repeating the obvious, and then do your calculations out loud at a nice, slow pace with plenty of expression: "OK. One dollar was 2.18 marks. . . ."

SPRECHEN

Stage 1   1.   You'd like to change both American and Canadian dollars.

2.   You've left your passport in your hotel room. Make apologies to the bank clerk and to those in line behind you.

3.   You need small coins for the streetcar ticket machine.

4.   You'd like to consolidate your small bills into a couple of large ones.

5.   You'd like to know the difference between the exchange rate for cash and that for traveler's checks. Don't forget to specify which currency you have.

Stage 2   1.   You change $200 into traveler's checks. Be sure to get a receipt.

2.   You realize your father has your passport in the car down the street, and the exchange booth is closing soon. Try to convince them to stay open long enough for you.

3.   You are rushing back to the bank, where a different employee is closing the doors. Try to talk your way inside.

4.   It didn't work. Ask the employee where else you can cash traveler's checks at this hour in this city. Be polite.

5.   You need coins for transportation and vending machines, and you have only American dollars. All the banks are closed, and you are at a small counter in the train station, where the exchange rate is not as good as it will be at the Dresdner Bank tomorrow morning at 8:00. Adjust your tone of voice appropriately.

LESEN

Stage 1   Look at the "Minibar" train menu on p. 9 of the **ST** *Drucksachen*.

1.   Identify the countries whose currencies are represented. Then find the individual currency whose basic unit is worth the most.

2.   A person traveling from one country to another must be able to adapt quickly to the new currency system, using approximate or "ball-park" estimates at first, then becoming more precise in calculating prices and values as time goes on. What ball-park ratio of currencies would a traveler establish who goes from the BRD to Austria? (i.e., 1:4? 4:1? 3:7? 2:3?)

3.   What approximate ratio would the traveler establish for the move from Austria to Switzerland? From Switzerland to the BRD? Is it easier to work with ratios or with percentages, adjusting currencies close in value by adding or subtracting a small percentage? Example: It is probably easier to compare U.S. dollars and Canadian dollars by using percentages rather than ratios.

Stage 2   Look at the picture of the currency-exchange board on **CT 68**. To the right of each country's name is the number of basic currency units (usually 100 here) that would be needed to buy the number of DM listed in the first column of numbers (*Verkauf*), or that one would receive from the West German bank if one presented for exchange the amount of West German currency listed in the second column (*Ankauf*). (Understandably, the banks buy foreign currency for less than they sell it for.)

1.   What <u>single</u> basic unit of currency yields the largest number of DM? What is the next most valuable single unit? What is the third?

2.   What mistakes do you find in the $ and £ lines? (Hint: check the decimal points in the two columns.) What different mistake do you find in the *dKr* line?

3.   If you were coming from Austria to the Federal Republic, how many DM could you buy for 100 schillings?

4.   If you were traveling from the BRD to Switzerland, how many DM would you have to spend to buy 100 Swiss Francs?

5.   If you were traveling from Switzerland to the BRD, how many DM would 100 Swiss francs buy?

SCHREIBEN

Stage 1 You've been to the bank to change money for your group of students, most of whom are not North Americans. Now you need to list names, currencies, and DM amounts so everyone can read the information. On a separate sheet of paper transcribe the names and foreign currency amounts / units listed below. Each line should end with a blank, in which you will enter the DM equivalent of the foreign currency each person has had you exchange. The exchange rate for the purchase of Deutsche Mark is provided in the photo on **CT 68**. Remember: Your handwriting should be legible to those for whom German is the common language.

Frl. Alvarez, 7000 Pts.	Herr Stranitzki, 1500 öS
Herr Jensen, 5000 dKr.	Hugh Smythe, £100
Frau Bierma, 250 hfl.	Signorina Cicciolina, L. 100 000

Stage 2 Your company has transferred you to West Germany, where you hold a middle-level executive position. You and several others are going on two-night business trips abroad this week, and will need various large amounts of foreign currency for hotel and meal allowances. One of the duties of a subordinate is to take care of the money-changing at the local bank, so that you executives will have local currency on hand even if you arrive at odd hours. You need to write a note to that person, specifying who is to receive what. Of course many on the office staff understand English, but your company, having learned from the policies of Japanese and German companies in America, wants its American executives to keep a low profile, and therefore urges them to use the local language.

Here are names and destinations: Herr Fritzsche, Rom; Herr Weiß, Kopenhagen; Frau Ebert und Frau Bodmer, Zürich; yourself, Wien. Arrange for a reasonable amount to cover the per diem expenses of each traveler. You can assume that lodging and meals will cost about the same as they do in West Germany; consult Chapters 1, 2, and 5 if you need to check prices.

You might try writing the note two ways. The first and easier way would be to offer a simple chart much like the one you made in Stage 1 immediately above. All you would need to add would be an initial salutation ("*Herr Braun —*") and perhaps "*Danke*" at the end. More effective would be a note with more complex phrases and even sentences; examples: "Mr. X needs ___;" "£125 for Ms. Y;" "We'd like ___."). Try to avoid repeating yourself and thereby sounding like a machine. Remember your manners.

KIOSK

HÖREN

Stage 1

A1 Just listen several times to the dialogs for *Gespräche 2: Kiosk*. Talk along if you like.

A2 Practice saying the dialog lines. Use your "pause" button if you have one.

B1 Conversation 1
1. How many items does the person buy?
2. What kind of chocolate does the person buy?

Conversation 2
1. What does the person buy?
2. What is the most expensive single item?

Conversation 3
1. What kind of fruit is mentioned? What other kinds do you know?
2. What is the total amount of the purchase?
3. What time of day is it?

Stage 2

B2 Conversation 1
1. What kind of ticket does the person buy? Why?

Conversation 2
1. How many individual items does the person buy?
2. Is the customer a tourist? Why do you think that?

Conversation 3
1. Does the person have good luck shopping? Explain.
2. What newspaper names do you hear? Which one is available?
3. What compromises must the customer make?
4. How much change should the customer receive for a DM 20 bill?

C1

1B:6.1.5   What are the day, date and month given in the ad? What do you do with a *"Bild"* ? (eat, drink, read, wear)

1B:6.1.6   Since the ad uses the word *lesen*, you already know that *Auto-Bild* is some kind of publication. Is it a magazine or a newspaper — or something else?

1B:6.2.1   What kind of publication is *Bild der Frau*? How much does it cost?

1B:6.2.4   Note the use of *Ich möchte*. Any idea why he wants a sombrero?

C2

2A:1.1.1   How much did the new science center cost in DM? What is that in dollars? Where is it located? [4]

2A:1.1.2   Note the dateline city, the age of the counterfeiter, and the denomination of the coins he was making.

2A:1.1.3   Observe the use of the verb *suchen* (from Chapter 4). How high was the hotel before it collapsed? When did the disaster occur (*MEZ = mitteleuropäische Zeit*)? What did the building look like as it collapsed? Try to estimate the casualties. [2]

SPRECHEN

Stage 1   1. You'd like some fruit for your train trip to Baden-Baden. Pick two varieties and complete the transaction.
2. You need a streetcar ticket, but don't know what kinds are available or how much they cost.
3. You don't find just what you want at the kiosk and decide to look for a grocery store. Be polite to the kiosk clerk, but do find out directions.
4. You need some stationery supplies and a snack before retiring to the city park to write to friends. You'll go from there to a mailbox to send off the letters and cards you write. Be complete.
5. An Australian couple wants to buy some souvenirs — mostly chocolate — at the kiosk where you are standing, but they speak no German. Help them out.

Stage 2   1. You want to buy a newspaper, and the clerk keeps trying out his English on you. Be polite, but firm: you're here to learn German and can handle yourself perfectly well.
2. Pick a number of different kinds of reading material from the Kiosk, inquire about the price, pay, and leave. Be polite.
3. The clerk at the kiosk would love to diminish her supply of apples, but you aren't very interested. You'd rather have an orange and a couple of pears for a snack with your friends.
4. You are asking for directions to the St.-Margarethen-Kirche and feel that you should thank the kiosk employee by buying something. Ask about something that it would not be tasteless to unfurl in the church.
5. You want to send letters to friends and acquaintances in various countries, and need stamps for them all. In addition, you want to buy something small to send them as a souvenir of your stay in Austria. Be imaginative.

LESEN

Stage 1

1   Look at the apple juice label on **CT 17**.
    1.   If you drink a big glass of juice every day, is this enough for a week?
    2.   Assuming that juice costs roughly the same in the U.S. and the BRD, what might a reasonable price be for the juice? DM 0,20 DM 2.000 DM 20,— DM 200,—   DM 2,—
    3.   How much natural juice is in the beverage?
    4.   Is the juice fresh or processed?

2   Look at the picture of the cigarette machine on **CT 66**.
    1.   What sales appeal do the <u>Sollfrank</u> people make? Bargain prices? The human touch? Many different brands? Low-tar/nicotine smokes?
    2.   Find the pun. Why would it be difficult to translate the play on words?

Stage 2

1   Look at the picture of the storefront at the top right of **CT 68**. Then reread the dialogs in Chapter 6 *Gespräche 2: Kiosk*. Which of the items mentioned in the dialogs might you expect to find in the store? How about the following items: matches; bathroom supplies; snack foods; pencils; postcards?

2   Look at the multilingual transit ticket on **CT 50**.
    1.   Can you use the ticket for subway transportation?
    2.   After what activity did the user of this ticket likely begin using it? lunch? concert? dinner? night-club visit?
    3.   Could the owner of the ticket use it for a shopping trip tomorrow morning?
    4.   What — don't head straight for your dictionary — does *entwerten* mean?

3   Now use what you learned from reading that ticket to help you decipher the long German-only ticket on **CT 51**.
    1.   Is this a family ticket? A long-term ticket?
    2.   How many times, if at all, can one transfer with the ticket?
    3.   Does it need to be signed or stamped?

SCHREIBEN

Stage 1   You and three friends are planning to spend a few hours in the park on the other side of town, resting and catching up on your postcards before you leave town early tomorrow morning. Make a list of what you want to pick up at the kiosk; you'll need transit tickets and light snacks. Pay particular attention to noun plurals and units of measurement.

Stage 2   The little store had only some of the items you were sent to fetch. Some of the items were temporarily unavailable, and some the store does not carry at all. The person you were to get them for has stepped out, and you have to leave right away. Can you write a note explaining what you did and did not pick up? Can you offer any suggestions about what to do now?

STRUCTURAL EXERCISES

1   The teller at the bank asks or tells you several things. Respond to each one, beginning with the suggested words.

      1.   *Haben Sie Ihren Paß?*
         Ja, ich _____
         Ja, mein___ Paß _____
         Nein, mein___ Paß _____
         Nein, d___ Paß _____

2. *Brauchen Sie große Scheine?*
   Ja, ich _____
   Nein, große _____

3. *Bitte, vergessen Sie das Datum nicht.*
   Gut, ich _____
   Ja. Das _____

4. *Möchten Sie einen 20-Mark-Schein und drei 10-Mark-Scheine?*
   Nein, ich _____
   Ja, d___ 20___ (_____) aber _____

5. *Wo ist denn Ihr Paß?*
   Mein Paß? D___ ist _____
   D___ habe ich _____
   Brauchen Sie _____?

2 Konrad does not have the following items, so he's writing a birthday wish list to his parents. Each time he says what he doesn't have, then uses a verb expressing <u>wanting</u> to underscore the pressing need.

> **Example**: Reiseschecks   Ich habe keine Reiseschecks. Ich will Reiseschecks haben.

1. Seife
2. Nüsse
3. Wein
4. Schokolade
5. Handtuch

3 Herr Gröning can't find various things, but the police are telling him that he has to. What do the police say to him?

> **Example**:   Koffer   Wo ist Ihr Koffer? Sie müssen ihren Koffer finden!

1. Platz
2. Kinder
3. Gepäck
4. Fahrkarte
5. Paß
6. Reiseschecks
7. Frau

4 The person at the kiosk is suggesting that Frau Krupp buy some items. She is so sure she doesn't need any of them that she answers in two different ways each time.

> **Example**: Rosinen   KIOSK PERSON: Brauchen/wollen Sie Rosinen?
> FRAU KRUPP: Nein, Rosinen brauche ich nicht. Ich brauche keine Rosinen.

ITEM	KIOSK PERSON	FRAU KRUPP
Schokolade		
eine Orange essen		
Nüsse		
Apfel		
die Zeitung lesen		
eine Fahrkarte kaufen		
die 24-Stundenkarte		

√ CHECK YOUR PROFICIENCY

CAN YOU:
__ exchange money?
__ make small purchases?
__ count change?
__ engage in small talk?

DO YOU REMEMBER HOW TO:
__ talk about hotel facilities?
__ describe your family and friends?
__ listen carefully for travel directions?
__ give directions for public transportation?

HÖREN

Stage 1

A1 Just listen several times to the dialogs for *Gespräche 1: Stadtrundfahrt*. Talk along if you like.

A2 Practice saying the dialog lines. Use your "pause" button if you have one.

B1 Conversation 1
1. How many people want to take part in the activity?
2. What does each ticket cost?
3. How old are the people?
4. What time of day is it?
5. When does the tour leave?

Conversation 2
1. How many members are in the family involved?
2. How old is the youngest?
3. How much does a children's ticket cost?
4. What time of day is it?
5. What time will the tour begin?

Conversation 3
1. How many people want to take the tour?
2. Which tour do they choose?
3. Which tour did they want?
4. How many tours are offered on this day?
5. What time of day is it?
6. How much does each ticket cost?

Stage 2

B2 Conversation 1
1. What are the woman's plans? Why?
2. What advice does she receive? Why?
3. What will the woman be doing the next day? With whom?

Conversation 2
1. What seems to be the problem?
2. How could it be solved?
3. Why is time an important factor?

Conversation 3
1. List the four main activities mentioned, by verb and other important words.
   <u>Example</u>: *im See fischen*
2. What seems to be the most important activity?
3. What time of day is it?
4. What is the last of these activities that will take place today?

C1 For each weather report note the time of the broadcast and the period the forecast covers — if indeed such information is given. Observe also the use of *bis* to indicate ranges of temperature. See how much you can guess about precipitation and other atmospheric conditions. The German and English words for 'rain', 'snow', 'frost', 'hail', 'wind', 'sun', and the compass directions are very similar. If you're having trouble consult the *Bildwörterbuch* display "*Natur* • Nature" on **CT 300-01**. [5]

1A:5.1.1-6

C2

2A:1.1.5   What kind of business did Mr. Nixdorf have? In what country did he live? How old was he when he died just a short time before the news broadcast?

2A:2.1.3   What kind of market does the announcer talk about? What two activities, services or commodities does it provide? On what day and at what time does it begin? How can you get in touch with other people using the market? Observe the many uses of *wenn*.

2A:2.1.4   What day and time is it? What holiday is mentioned, though not by name? What advice do the announcer and the song offer?

SPRECHEN

Stage 1   1.   You'd like to go on the latest city tour to leave in the morning. Inquire about schedules and prices.

2.   There's no room on the latest tour, but there is on an earlier one — or one in the afternoon. Make a decision.

3.   You're not sure you can make it to the next tour, which will leave in 15 minutes. Explain that the rest of your family isn't there yet, and that you'll buy the tickets when they all arrive.

4.   You have two errands to run before rejoining your group in front of the cathedral. Explain what you must do, how long it will take, and where you will see everyone again.

5.   You aren't feeling up to climbing to the top of the cathedral tower with the others. Tell them that you'll take care of lunch arrangements and see them when they return.

Stage 2   1.   You're tired after the morning walk and would like to forgo the group lunch, preferring to return to your room and put your feet up for an hour or so. Make appropriate excuses to the tour leader.

2.   Suggest an afternoon's activities to your friends, including seeing some sights in Köln, getting a bite to eat, and buying supplies to let the folks back home know how things are going.

3.   You are out of film, and your camera seems not to be functioning correctly. Tell the tour guide what the problem is and suggest what you plan to do about it.

4.   You want to take pictures inside the Dom, but there's a service beginning in 20 minutes. You might come back later, or you might find a way to take pictures without disturbing the service. Solicit suggestions from your tour leader.

5.   One of the other members of your tour group wasn't listening when the guide outlined the day's activities. The guide gave specific times for seeing various sights, including extended visits to the Dom, the Römisch-Germanisches Museum, the St. Gereon Kirche, and the Rheinpark. Be sure the other person understands just when you'll be doing each thing; don't forget when and where you'll be eating lunch.

LESEN

Stage 1   Compare the map of Trier on **CT 311** with the Trier information on pp. 18-19 and 37 of the **ST** *Drucksachen*. Eva and Will, for whom you reserved rooms in the city earlier, would like to know more about the Karl Marx archives and museum in Trier. Their German isn't as strong as it should be; will they be able to benefit from a visit to the museum anyway? If they wanted to undertake some serious study, would they be best advised to come in the summer or the winter? How about the Christmas holidays? How much would they have to pay to enter? Where in Trier would they be able to find out the most about Marx? Are you sure you reserved them a hotel room in the right place? For good measure, find out from the **CT** *Glossary* where Karl Marx is buried.

Stage 2   1.   Having grown up in the Willamette Valley, Eva has become very knowledgeable about wines. Inform yourself about what Trier has to offer her. Will her lack of German continue to be a handicap?

2.   In spite of his socialist ideals, Will is a true sybarite. He would probably enjoy a swim and a soak while Eva is off tramping through the vineyards. Find out where he might go. How many days per week could he indulge himself between 10 and 11 a.m.? Between 8 and 9 p.m.?

3.   You cannot forget your parents, who are funding your study abroad. In addition to their other interests, they are avid museum-goers. Consult the list of churches and museums, and figure out where they should go to see **a)** stained-glass windows; **b)** early Christian relics; **c)** the Gutenberg

Bible; **d)** documents relating to the city's history, including artistic treasures from the Middle Ages through the 19th Century; **e)** medieval manuscripts; **f)** the Roman baths; **g)** Roman coins.

SCHREIBEN

Stage 1   Now that you have familiarized yourself with what Trier has to offer, write a note to a friend at the university who will be meeting your relatives when they arrive. Say what you have found for Eva and Will to do while they are in town. Say what each one might like to do, what they can do together, what they absolutely must see, and so on. Be sure to give them an idea of where various things are located. Being attentive to the hours of each of the attractions, give a tentative schedule for their first day in Trier.

> Eva kann . . . und Will möchte wahrscheinlich . . . und sie müssen beide . . .

Stage 2   Now write another note, this one to a nice middle-aged couple you met in Blaubeuren who will be in Trier when your parents arrive and who would probably enjoy them. Suggest the same sort of first-day schedule for your parents' visit. Be sure to tell what can be seen and done, and do your best to say where things are. A ball-park estimate of distances would be helpful.

KONDITOREI

HÖREN

Stage 1

A1   Just listen several times to the dialogs for *Gespräche 2: Konditorei*. Talk along if you like.

A2   Practice saying the dialog lines. Use your "pause" button if you have one.

B1   First study the "Jansen Konditorei-Café" menu on **CT 324-25**. Then listen carefully to the conversations and answer the questions below.

    Conversation 1
1. Where do the people finally sit?
2. What do they decide to eat?
3. Why does the first person order what he does?

    Conversation 2
1. What do the two drinks have in common?
2. What portions do the people order to drink?
3. If the two people had to leave their table for 30 minutes, which dessert would still be recognizable when they came back?

    Conversation 3
1. Why is the first person so enthusiastic at first?
2. Why is the person suddenly sad?
3. What two drinks are ordered?
4. What drink quantity is specified?

Stage 2

B2   First study the "Wall Cafe" menu on pp. 10-13 of the **ST** *Drucksachen*. Then listen carefully to the three conversations and answer the questions below.

    Conversation 1
1. What do all the baked goods named have in common?
2. What does the customer order to eat and drink?
3. Does he have any special wishes?
4. What seems a bit odd about what he says?

Conversation 2

1. What does Herr Franzen order? Why?
2. What does he want to drink?
3. What does Frau Haenisch choose to drink?
4. Does she come here often? How do you know?
5. What does Frau Haenisch want to eat?

Conversation 3

1. What does the customer order to eat and drink?
2. How does this order differ from the ordinary?
3. Does the customer come here often? How do you know?
4. Why does the customer order the drink he does?

C1

1A:1.3.1-4   What time is it? Where two times are given, are they the same? [3]

1A:1.4.1-4   What time is it right now? Where two times are given, are they the same?

1A:1.5.1-2   What time is it right now? As in some earlier segments, the announcer does not give the current exact time, but rather the time that it will be after a convenient interval, so that you might prepare to set your watch.

C2

2B:5.1.1.   Note the river depth and change in level of the Rhine at the following major cities: Karlsruhe, Koblenz, Köln, Konstanz, Mainz, Mannheim. [2]

2B:5.3.1   What year is mentioned? How many tourists traveled to München in that year? What was the average attendance per day at the Oktoberfest?

SPRECHEN

Stage 1   1.   You are tired of tramping around in Bremen and suggest to your companion that you find a place to get a light snack.

2.   It's hot today, and you'd like something to help you cool off. Make a couple of suggestions to your companion.

3.   It's cold today, and you'd like something to help take the chill off. Make a couple of suggestions to your companion.

4.   You're hungry for an afternoon snack, but the menu in the *Konditorei* you find seems a bit limited. Ask the waiter about fixing something special for you.

5.   You enter a *Konditorei* with two friends, neither of whom speaks German. Order something for each to eat and drink, as well as something for yourself.

Stage 2   1.   The people you are with are diabetics, but you still want to find a *Konditorei* and treat them to something special during their stay in your city. Do the best you can.

2.   The waiter tells you that the tea you have ordered is not available, and suggests an alternative. You don't care for that suggestion and make one of your own.

3.   You don't see iced tea on the menu, but it would be perfect on this steamy afternoon. Describe to the waiter what you want, being careful not to order a cup of tea with a scoop of ice cream in it.

4.   The waiter misunderstands your order and brings you tea instead of coffee. When the coffee comes, it's just a cup instead of a pot. Iron out the difficulties as best you can.

5.   You and your friend are discussing the advantages and disadvantages of the fare available in the *Konditorei* where you are sitting. You decide on that day to turn over a new leaf and eat more healthful foods — after having a good snack, of course.

LESEN

Stage 1

1. Look again at the menu for the Jansen Konditorei-Café in Köln on **CT 324-25**.

2. Recalling the <u>second</u> Stage 1 conversation in HÖREN above, total the price of the two orders. What is the difference in price between the two? Which liquid drink is served in a larger portion?

3. Look at your notes from the <u>third</u> Stage 1 conversation. What will each speaker have to pay?

4. Not all the ice cream dishes are available year round. Which ones can one buy in the winter?

5. What is the price of the most modest breakfast at the Jansen Konditorei-Café? What would that breakfast cost if you wanted to add some meat? What advantages are apparent in ordering the most expensive breakfast instead? What would be more expensive — the least expensive breakfast with a side order of meat, or the most expensive breakfast with a boiled egg?

6. It's 4 p.m. Can you successfully order a mushroom omelet? Oxtail soup?

7. How many different kinds of fruit drink are available at this *Konditorei*? How many different alcoholic drinks are listed with the fruit drinks? Why are they here and not on the next pages?

Stage 2

1. Look again at the menu for the Wall Cafe in Bremen.

2. Recalling your notes from the <u>second Stage 2</u> listening exercise, tell how much Herr Franzen will have to pay for his order. How much will Frau Haenisch have to pay? Assuming that a 15% tip is included in the menu prices, and that one of the customers will pay for both, what West German bank note will cover both orders?

3. Compare the words in the semicircle at the top of each menu page with those uttered by Johann Pezzl in 1786 and printed on the last page. Does the Wall Cafe, which calls itself *"Bremens einziges Kaffeehaus"*, seem to be living up to its charge? Which of the foods and activities in the semicircle were probably unavailable to Johann Pezzl?

4. Are cigarettes available for sale in the dining area?

5. When does the Wall Cafe open in the morning? When does it close? Are the hours the same every day? How late in the day can one order breakfast? For how many people could one phone in a reservation to meet here to discuss the latest political issues?

6. Can anyone order the ice cream dish "Tutti-Frutti"?

7. A *Kaffeehaus* is good for activities other than drinking coffee. What cities' newspapers are available to the customers in the Wall Cafe? What publications are clearly from the north? What provision is made for listening to music? What else can one do here?

SCHREIBEN

Stage 1

On one of your walks around Köln in the afternoon, you and your three acquaintances are suddenly seized by an uncontrollable passion for ice cream. You visit the Jansen Konditorei-Café, which just happens to be nearby, and once you see the menu you realize that ice cream will be only the beginning. By this time your ability to read German has increased considerably, but you are still not so confident about your spoken German that you can carry out a large order of this sort. Therefore, write down the order for the four of you. Don't forget something to drink.

Stage 2

You have been staying with five other friends in the youth hostel in Dortmund. You have also been chosen to go into the city and find take-out desserts for everyone at a friendly *Konditorei*. Thankfully, your friends all wanted something other than ice cream. But the *Konditorei* didn't have exactly what they wanted: *Apfelstrudel, Erdbeertorte, Nußtorte, Marmorkuchen, Mandelhörnchen*, and an assortment of coffee and tea to drink. Now you have returned to the youth hostel, but find that they've all gone on a hike. Miffed, you resolve to go back to the Konditorei and gorge yourself without regard for them. Leave them a note of apology, though, telling them the things the *Konditorei* doesn't have and saying where you are.

> Liebe Freunde,
> Ich war in der Konditorei, aber sie haben kein__ . . . .

STRUCTURAL EXERCISES

1   Help the writer of this letter to acquaintances:

Lieber Herr Ehrismann, liebe Frau Ehrismann,

Seit gestern sind wir in Köln, einer wunderschönen Stadt. Hier gibt es so viel zu tun. Nach d___ Mittagessen waren wir in d___ St. Gereon-Kirche und auch i___ Dom. Und gestern abend waren wir auch i___ Rheinpark — sehr, sehr schön bei Nacht. D___ Rheinpark liegt direkt a___ Fluß mit d___ Tanzbrunnen zusammen.

Heute woll___ wir ein___ Taxi von unser___ Hotel zu___ Römerturm nehmen, und dann gehen wir zu Fuß vo___ Römerturm wieder zu___ St. Gereon-Kirche — die ist nämlich so schön mit ihren zwei großen Türmen. Von dort möchten wir zu___ mittelalterlichen Stadtmauer gehen. D___ alte Stadtmauer liegt a___ Hansaplatz. Und vo___ Hansaplatz nehmen wir wahrscheinlich ein___ Bus zurück z___ Hotel. D___ Mittagessen woll___ wir, glaube ich, irgendwo in d___ Stadtmitte finden, in ein___ Restaurant oder ein___ Konditorei. Und nach d___ Essen gehen wir ganz bestimmt z___ Dom. ___ ein oder zwei Uhr gibt es keinen Gottesdienst i___ Dom, also dürf___ wir mit den anderen Touristen i___ Dom sitzen, fotografieren u.s.w.

Später a___ Nachmittag komm___ d___ Zug von mein___ Schwester Nancy am Bahnhof an. D___ Bahnhof liegt direkt neben d___ Dom, das ist also gar nicht weit. Vor ein___ Woche war Nancy noch in Chicago, und gestern in Landquart, in d___ Schweiz, aber heute ist sie hier in Köln, und a___ Mittwoch reisen wir zusammen nach Bremerhaven.

Heute abend nach d___ Abendessen machen wir einen Spaziergang z___ Rheinufer. Dort ist d___ lange Rheinpromenade, und wir können stundenlang a___ Fluß sitzen oder spazieren. Morgen machen wir ein___ Abendfahrt auf d___ Rhein mit einem Dampfschiff. Aber noch vor d___ Essen heute abend möchte ich i___ Hotelzimmer ein bißchen schlafen, denn ich bin schon sehr müde.

Morgen wollen wir ein___ Oper sehen — ich glaube, "Der Rosenkavalier". D___ Opernhaus liegt gar nicht weit v___ Dom, nur 7 oder 8 Straßen; es ist auch gleich neben d___ Schauspielhaus. Hoffentlich können wir Karten bekommen!

Aber jetzt muß ich mein___ Brief fertigschreiben. Sie wissen jetzt etwas von d___ Stadt Köln, und ich möchte unten i___ Hotel frühstücken. Schöne Grüße an alle!

Ihre
Beverly Danuser

2   Rearrange the scrambled sentences.

1.   eine wollen einen Sie Becher Tüte oder?
und Rum Tasse möchte eine einen ich mit bitte Becher Tee
9,50 schön das danke zusammen macht

2.   zu Freunde immer zwei essen Konditorei Cafe in viel einer einem meine sitzen oder und
der schwimmen sie Abend in tanzen müssen oder Stadt am

3.   zwei wir Stadtrundfahrt für zweite Uhr haben 11 um noch Karten die
hole Frau vor ich um Gut! die meiner 11 Karten komme und mit Viertel
nicht möchten Karten Sie die reservieren?
mehr Viertel wir 11 haben vielleicht keine um vor Karten
weiß nicht ich / ich später vielleicht an Sie rufe

√ CHECK YOUR PROFICIENCY

CAN YOU:
__ inquire about ticket prices and schedules?
__ make plans for a day's activities?
__ order bakery goods?
__ ask advice about what to see and do?

DO YOU REMEMBER HOW TO:
__ change money?
__ ask for travel necessities at a Kiosk?
__ buy tickets for public transportation from a ticket machine?
__ arrange for an appropriate hotel room?
__ ask directions to various locations in a city?
__ order foods and beverages at a restaurant?

HÖREN

Stage 1

A1 Just listen several times to the dialogs for *Gespräche 1: Opernkasse*. Talk along if you like.

A2 Practice saying the dialog lines. Use your "pause" button if you have one.

B1 Conversation 1
1. What opera does the person want to see?
2. How many different performances are mentioned?
3. For which one(s) are tickets available?
4. Does it seem that the person will get to see the opera? Why (not)?

Conversation 2
1. When would the person like to see the opera?
2. Will that be possible?
3. How much does one ticket cost?
4. Where are the seats that are available?

Conversation 3
1. How many different performances of *Fidelio* are mentioned?
2. On what date is the third performance?
3. For which one does the customer want tickets?
4. Is he successful?
5. Why is he surprised?

Stage 2

B2 Conversation 1
1. What problem does the customer encounter?
2. What solution is suggested?
3. What does the customer do to have the best chance for a ticket?

Conversation 2
1. What opera does the person want to see?
2. For what evening are tickets available?
3. Where are the seats in the hall?
4. What do the tickets cost?
5. How many bills does the person use to pay with?

Conversation 3
1. For what day does the customer arrange to buy tickets?
2. Are they the tickets he wanted? (Why [not]?)
3. Where are the seats located?
4. How much do the tickets cost?

C1

2B:4.2.1 What day is "today" in the broadcast? How much are tickets to the open rehearsal? Find the location of the concert on your map of München on **CT 315**; it's in quadrant A9. If you wanted to go, would you have enough time between "now" and the concert to spend a few hours in a nearby museum and then still have an unhurried lunch? Would the Deutsches Museum (quadrant D 10-11) qualify as nearby? Try formulating a short speech offering your suggestions; begin *"Wir können . . . "* If you don't know much about Mozart look ahead to **CT 195**.

2B:4.2.2 What part of the day is it? When was the composer born and when and where did he die?

2B:4.2.3 The report describes a travelling art exhibition. In what city did it largely originate, and to what city is it travelling? How long will it be in the latter city? Where will it be, and for how long, when it returns?

C2 What was the final score of the soccer game? In which minutes of the game were the goals scored? **2B:4.3.1** The first player the sportscaster interviews after the game is in a hurry. Why? For help with sports vocabulary, see the *Bildwörterbuch* display on sports and hobbies, **CT 304-05**.

SPRECHEN

Stage 1 1.   Greet the person at the ticket counter. Arrange to buy tickets for yourself and your companion for tomorrow evening's performance of *Der Rosenkavalier*. Ask about prices and locations.

2.   You arrange to buy four tickets to *Aïda* for this evening. Make sure you get seats that have a good sight line to the stage.

3.   You want to buy tickets for three couples for the opera tomorrow evening. You want to have them all together if possible. You don't own any oil wells.

4.   You have arranged for tickets for the opera tonight, but realize you don't have any money with you. Convince the ticket clerk that you can be trusted to return as soon as you fetch your money from the hotel room. Be sure the tickets aren't sold in the meantime.

5.   The tickets you have been given to *Die Walküre* are for a matinee performance, but you'd rather go in the evening. Take them to the ticket office and try to exchange them.

Stage 2 1.   You are trying to work out ticket arrangements for next week, your last week in Köln. There are still tickets available for *Parsifal*, but they're not on an evening you have free. Tickets are still available for the following week, however. Suggest to your companion what you should do.

2.   You overhear the person in line in back of you say he needs tickets for the very performance for which you would like to return your extra tickets. The deal is struck, but then you realize that you should keep your tickets because a dear relative will be stopping in for a visit. Talk your way out of the mess.

3.   The ticket agent suggests various evenings for the concert you want to hear, but none is convenient for you. Ask about alternatives.

4.   You are trying to get tickets for yourself and for each of two other couples for performances this evening, tomorrow evening, and for the next evening as well. One of the other couples can't attend one of these performances.

5.   Explain to the person at the hotel desk that you have tickets to see *Porgy and Bess* at the opera house on the 21st. He suggests that you return your tickets and see the opera on another night because of a special concert in the Dom that evening. You're leaving the 22nd, but would like to see both. Discuss the possibilities with him.

LESEN

Stage 1 1.   In the **CT** *Glossary* you will find where many famous Germans are buried. Fourteen of these famous people were composers (*Komponisten*), many of whom wrote operas.

2.   In which European capital are more composers buried than in any other? How many German composers are buried in present-day European capital cities?

3.   Which German composers are not buried in Germany? Which one is buried in French-speaking territory?

4.   You would probably need a visa to visit the graves of three of the composers listed here. Which ones are they, and where are they buried?

Stage 2 1.   Good media reviews inspired patrons to see the musical *Cats* when it played in the Operettenhaus Hamburg. What two very positive phrases could you excerpt from the reviews on **CT 8** even if you knew no German? What sorts of media are represented here? If for some reason you wanted to see *Cats* twice on the same day (perhaps with two different groups of friends), what is the least you could spend to do so? What is the most you could spend?

2.   Look at a program from the Nationaltheater Mannheim on pp. 24-25 of the **ST** *Drucksachen*. The Nationaltheater can accommodate audiences in three different theaters. How many people could see productions at the same time in Mannheim? Are tickets available every day? Is it possible to buy tickets after the box office closes for the day, but just before a performance in the evening? Compare these ticket prices in Mannheim with those of a first-run musical in Hamburg. How long does the opera/ballet season appear to run in Mannheim? Which of the operas shown are not sung in German?

SCHREIBEN

Stage 1   You have been browsing in the Mannheim cultural events listings on pp. 24-25 of the **ST** *Drucksachen*, and have an idea for an activity for you and your German business associate. It is July 9, the day she is off at an afternoon wine-tasting with friends. Since you don't plan to be in later that afternoon, leave her a note at the hotel desk with your suggestions for the evening. Don't forget to explain fully what each of the events is, or to invite her for an after-theater/opera snack.

Stage 2   Choose a week in the schedule of the Deutsche Oper Berlin, shown on pp. 332-33 of the **ST** *Drucksachen*, then write a note to your German-speaking neighbor back home in Louisville, telling about all the things you're doing in Berlin. He might not be as knowledgeable about opera as you are, so be sure to tell him who wrote each of the operas you plan to see. Don't forget to say what you do just before and after each opera.

Example: "*Morgen abend sehe ich 'Lulu' von Alban Berg. . .*"

ALTSTADT

HÖREN

Stage 1

A1   Just listen several times to the dialogs for *Gespräche 2: Altstadt*. Talk along if you like.

A2   Practice saying the dialog lines. Use your "pause" button if you have one.

B1   Conversation 1
1. What time of day is it?
2. What is the second speaker's complaint?
3. What does he want to do now?
4. What are the first speaker's plans? What reason does he give for them?

Conversation 2
1. Where are the speakers?
2. What do they find so positive about this place?
3. What two places will they visit soon?
4. How will they get to the second one?
5. What time of day is it?

Conversation 3
1. What time of day is it?
2. Where are the people?
3. How does each propose getting across the Rhein?
4. What is the order of activities from now until later in the day?

Stage 2

B2   Listen carefully to the conversation between a tour guide and the various members of the group, who split up for an afternoon of exploring in Köln and then regrouped at the hotel in the evening to compare experiences. Each said where he intended to go, but not all stuck to their itineraries. Many of them elaborated about what they saw. <u>Task</u> - make up a chart with columns: <u>place(s) visited</u>, <u>remarks</u>; label the rows: <u>Frau Berger</u>, <u>Herr und Frau Fehling</u>, <u>Herr Leonhart</u>. Beside the people's names, write the places visited and anything that seems to have made their afternoon special.

C1   For both schedules of upcoming programs fill out a chart which shows what is being featured when
1A:2.2.1-2   on the the four channels B1, B2, B3, and B4. Note the time the schedule is being broadcast, if that information is given. Concentrate on the musical offering; if you don't like classical music, find out about sports events.

1B:8.2.1   Are you hearing final scores or updates on games in progress? If you are having trouble with this one, look again at the **Class Text** *Struktur* pages for this chapter. [1]

C2

2A:3.1.1   Until what date can you still get the special Paulaner Salvator beer? How long is that from the time of the broadcast? [1,5]

2A:3.1.2.   Write down and translate the slogan at the end of the ad for tires: *"Reifen Wagner . . . ."* [5]

SPRECHEN

Stage 1   1. You're delighted with Köln so far. Mention all the positive aspects of your visit.
2. You're disappointed with Köln so far. Tell why.
3. Tell your companion why you'd rather do something other than what he has planned.
4. Outline your plans for seeing and doing things during the afternoon. Don't forget a snack.

Stage 2   1. Someone has asked for directions from the Neumarkt to the Tanzbrunnen. Be as precise as you can.

2. Outline your plans for activities in Köln for the next three days. Be sure to mention dates and times. Don't forget cultural events in the evening.

3. Arrange to meet your business associate at the Jacobi Restaurant Café (*immer in Mode . . . mitten in Köln*) after the opera. Suggest an appropriate snack.

LESEN

Stage 1   It is not just the major cities that have some claim to age. Search through **CT 196**, the Karlsruhe *Tagesveranstaltungen*, for events commemorating a celebration for a town named Knielingen. What is the celebration all about? Make sure you know what is going on in each of the six events. This information will come in handy soon.

Stage 2   Consult *Freiburgs Stadtgeschichte leicht gemacht* on **CT 344-45**. The 1957 entry shows that the university celebrated its 500th anniversary. Can you find the name of the person who founded it? What seems odd about the rest of the information about the university, which is the "oldest" in some respect? The Freiburg map and accompanying text on **CT 313** show two university buildings. Which one is older? The text also mentions two other "oldest" entries, one being the oldest inn in West Germany. What is its name? The top of this particular map is not north, but west. In which part of town is this oldest inn located? The **CT 344-45** entry for the year 1258 mentions something named the "Hosanna". What is the "Hosanna", and where is it today? (It is also mentioned in the text on **CT 313**.)

SCHREIBEN

Stage 1   1. As your group's historian, imagine yourself in the first century A.D. Agrippina, the wife of the Roman emperor Claudius, was born here in Köln, and wants this to be a Roman city. In the year 50 A.D. Claudius grants her wish, and the Roman city is called *colonia*. Catholic bishops in Köln can be traced back to the year 313. Construction on the Dom begins in the 13th century, on the spot where a ninth-century church stood until 1248.

2. Now write complete notes to tell your group as much about "the old days" as you can. (You may use "*war*" in the first sentence to establish the historical context; then feel free to use present tense.)

Stage 2 Return now to the Karlsruhe *Tagesveranstaltungen* on **CT 196**. You have just attended the festivities for Knielingen, which have given you considerable insight into the ways people in small towns live their lives. Using the same writing strategy as in the exercise above (present tense / past tense), make diary entries for each of the festivities, telling what is going on and saying something about your reaction.

STRUCTURAL EXERCISES

1   Help Cornelia with a letter home. The larger blanks are for time phrases and personal pronouns.

Liebe Mama, lieber Papa,

Heute _____ , also schon um 8.25, waren wir im Hotel in Köln. Jetzt ist es ein

bißchen später — 9.30 — und wir sind fertig mit d___ Frühstück. Ich hoffe, das Frühstück

ist auch morgen _____ so gut. D___ heiße Schokolade war fantastisch. Um 10 Uhr

geht unser___ Gruppe durch d___ Altstadt, vo___ Dom zu___ römischen

Stadtmauer. Unterwegs muß ich zu___ Bank gehen: ich habe nur noch ein bißchen

Geld und brauche etwas für d___ Essen heute _____. Mit mein___ Freundinnen will

ich auch heute _____ im Kino d___ Film "Flucht vom Planeten der Affen"

sehen. D___ ist ein___ toller Film! Aber vor d___ Film gehen wir alle zu___ Rhein

hinunter. D___ Schiffe sind am Rheinauhafen und wir wollen _____ sehen. Und

dann fahren wir natürlich auch alle zu___ Zoo. Ich möchte so gern ein___ Tiger oder

zwei sehen! Und Monika sagt mir, ich muß auch d___ Elefanten besuchen.

Liebe Mama, lieber Papa, die Rheintour ist wirklich toll. Ich bin sehr begeistert. Aber

ohne mein____ Tiere ist d___ Tour nicht so gut, glaube ich. Ich vermisse mein___ zwei

Hunde und d___ Hamster. (Was machen _____ denn?) Nun, heute ist ja erst d___

fünft____, und a___ elft___ komme ich mit d___ Zug wieder nach Hause. Ich habe

noch sechs Tage. Morgen _____, das ist also d___ sechst____, sind wir um 15.30

Uhr in Bonn. Und a___ siebt____, acht___ und neunt___ fahren wir den Rhein hinauf

nach Koblenz, Mainz, Ludwigshafen und Karlsruhe. Dann geht's mit d___ Bus nach

d___ Schweiz weiter. Am zehnt___ sind wir in Basel, und dann haben wir ein___

ganzen Tag nur für d___ Stadt. Also sehen wir uns bald. Ich muß zu___ Bank.

Tschüß!
Cornelia, der Rhein-Fan

2   Cornelia is now in Bonn, assembling presents for her family and friends at home in Bremen. She has made a list of things and a list of people. Now she'll enter the chart in her diary in a less informal form. Complete the entries for her. Don't forget the accusative case!

example: (Ring   meine Mutter)   Ich kaufe einen Ring für meine Mutter.

GESCHENK	PERSON	
Krawatte	mein Vater	_____
Nußtorte	meine Schwester	_____
Zeitschrift	mein Englischlehrer	_____
2 Postkarten	meine Brüder (Idioten!)	_____
Päckchen Nüsse	meine Freundin Silvia	_____
5 Tafeln Schokolade	mein Freund Holger	_____
1 Bratwurst	der Hund	_____
Buch über Köln	die Eltern	_____
1 Flasche Heilwasser	der Onkel Rudolf	_____

3   Combine elements from all three columns in meaningful sentences about what you want to do. Use the "Let's . . ." form of the verb. There are many more than the ten possibilities implied below.

gehen	nach	der Rhein
spazieren	in	die Schweiz
schwimmen	durch	das Rathaus
springen	vor	das Fenster
schlafen	auf	die Oper
fahren	für	die Reiseführerin
arbeiten	neben	die Post
essen	ohne	der Zoo
baden	zu	die Dombesichtigung
bummeln	an	der Gottesdienst

√ CHECK YOUR PROFICIENCY

CAN YOU:
__ buy tickets to events?
__ make alternative arrangements?
__ plan a walk through a city?
__ express emotion?

DO YOU REMEMBER HOW TO:
__ ask for advice about what to see and do?
__ change money?
__ express different moods (must, want to, should) in a sentence?
__ point out things and people?

HÖREN

Stage 1

A1 Just listen several times to the dialogs for *Gespräche 1: Frühstück*. Talk along if you like.

A2 Practice saying the dialog lines. Use your "pause" button if you have one.

B1 Conversation 1
1. What does the customer order to drink, and in what quantity?
2. What drink is brought to the table?
3. How does the customer supplement the standard meal?
4. What seems to be the problem?
5. Is the utensil correct?

Conversation 2
1. How many people are finally sitting at the table?
2. Where is the last person who might be expected?
3. What is Herr Kampelmann drinking?
4. How does the service here differ from that at a normal meal?
5. What would Frau Reitmüller like to drink?

Conversation 3
1. What do we know about what the people are drinking?
2. What was last evening's activity?
3. How many of the people now at the table do we know were involved in that activity?
4. One of the people rejected tickets. Why?
5. How did that person finally get tickets, and what kind were they?

Stage 2

B2 Conversation 1
1. Look at the menus from the Wall Cafe on pp. 10-13 of the **ST** *Drucksachen* and the Jansen Konditorei-Café on **CT 324-25**. In which one does this conversation take place?
2. What extra does the person order? What does the entire breakfast cost?
3. Would you expect the person to order *"eine Scheibe Käse"* or *"zwei Scheiben Knäckebrot"* to go with the breakfast? Why (not)?

Conversation 2
1. Is the first person you hear ordering?
2. What cultural misunderstandings do you hear?
3. What is the reason for the second misunderstanding?
4. Person #1 seems surprised at something person #2 has done. What is it?
5. How many of the people present or mentioned in the conversation will be taking part in tomorrow's activity?

Conversation 3
1. What mistake was person #1 guilty of recently?
2. Did the mistake cause dire problems?
3. What additional problem was avoided because person #1 had some identification?
4. After person #1 has told her story, person #2 says something using the word *Ihnen* or *ihnen*. Which one is it? How do you know?
5. What misadventure does person #2 relate? Where was that?

C1
1A:2.1.2
Make a chart that imitates a broadcast schedule, perhaps with the channels going across from left to right and time indications on the left going down. Fill it in according to the broadcast; concentrate more on the time and channel indications rather than the details of the program items. What time is it "now"? The announcer doesn't say, but you can figure out fairly exactly within what range of time she must be speaking.

1B:6.1.7
At what time and during what activity should one enjoy butter, at least according to the ad? [P2]

1B:6.1.8
The ad tells you how much you can save (*sparen*) on a certain unit of weight (*pro _____*). The unit of measurement is not grams or kilograms, but rather a unit still used in Germany to weigh produce, meat, and even human beings. You can figure it out if you have grasped the relation between English and German sounds in 'penny' and *Pfennig*. Or you can find help in the table of weights and measures on the inside front cover of the **Class Text**. [P2, 5]

1B:6.1.9
How selective do the Langnese people claim to be about the honey they package? [P2, 5]

1B:6.4.1
Observe the following vocabulary and structures from recent chapters: *Naja* (6), *hätte gern* (9), *Wunsch* (9). Write down the slogan that is sung near the end: "*Norris Bank, die Bank . . .*" [5]

C2
2A:2.1.1
The Norris Bank, in the previous segment, claims to be the bank for everyone. How, then, does the announcer of the present segment envision the audience he greets so cheerily? What word from Chapter 9 *Frühstück* dialogs best describes his vacation? [1]

2A:2.2.1
After about 45 seconds of music and introductory remarks a radio reporter interviews the 65-year-old entertainer Vico Toriani. To gauge how much progress you have made, first redo the exercise with this same material in Chapter 2 (first half).

Concentrate next on Toriani's reply to the interviewer's question about how he manages to maintain his appeal (*Charme*): "*Ich glaube, . . . auch glaube.*"

Many of the remarks about Toriani concern his colorful past, but there is much talk too about his present and future, since he can't stand to hear the word "retirement". Can you hear the differences between time frames? Sometimes you can get that information from time phrases like *gestern*, *heute* and *morgen*. But often you must pay attention to verb forms. Observe the many instances of forms like *war-*, *hatte-*, *wollte-*, *mußte-*.

SPRECHEN

Stage 1
1.   You are in the Wall Cafe and would like just a very small breakfast. Describe it.

2.   You have just had your small breakfast and would like to order a couple of extras. Don't forget something else to drink, since there are no "bottomless" cups of coffee in Europe.

3.   The waiter has brought the wrong drink, and the wrong quantity. Straighten things out, but be polite.

4.   You are sitting at a table with a total stranger. Muster the courage to ask for two things out of your reach, and then finish the job.

5.   You and the total stranger strike up a conversation, and you ask him what he ordered for breakfast, since there are a couple of things for which you think you don't have the vocabulary.

Stage 2
1.   Your brother is visiting from Nevada, where he took Spanish instead of German. Order a hearty breakfast for him, bearing in mind that he probably won't find everything he's used to at home.

2.   The egg you ordered is not soft boiled, but hard boiled. Tell the waiter about it, and recommend a length of time for the replacement to be boiled.

3.   Your bus is leaving soon, and still no waiter has come to take your order. When you mention this to the person who is clearing the tables, he tells you it's a self-service breakfast and points to the trays of delicious food under the window. Say what you feel you must, but bear in mind the late hour and see whether you might take something with you.

4.   You have dropped your knife on the floor by mistake and need another. All the places are taken, so you can't swipe a knife from another table. Hail a waiter and say what is appropriate.

5.   For some reason, there are no seasonings on your table. When the waiter comes by, tell him about it. Also, order another roll for yourself and a couple of kinds of meat and cheese for your companion, who has gone off to the rest room for a moment.

LESEN

Stage 1   1.   Look at the Jansen Konditorei-Café menu on **CT 324-25**. Compare the prices of various breakfasts, then tell how much more a pot of coffee, tea, or hot chocolate costs than simply a cup.

2.   It's 8 a.m. You and two friends from Manitoba want to order breakfast here, but they have some extraordinary wishes. You want simply a modest breakfast with a cup of tea, but one of them — as yet unused to European ways — insists on fried eggs with ham and toast, while the other would like a mushroom omelet. They each want a pot of coffee. Will you have to find another restaurant, or do you think Jansen can fill the bill?

Stage 2   1.   Now consult the Wall Cafe menu again, on pp. 10-13 of the **ST** *Drucksachen*. It's 8 a.m. Will you be able to have breakfast yet? At 9:30? Is breakfast still available at 10:30? 3 p.m.? 10:30 p.m.? The Wall Cafe offers an extensive variety of entertainment, as you saw in Chapter 7. Is that reflected in the price of the breakfasts? What breakfast is available here that is not at the Jansen Konditorei-Café? What kind of bread is available here but not at Jansen? How would your Manitoba friends fare at the Wall Cafe? How would the price of the breakfast differ? Can you tell how much more a pot of coffee would cost than just a cup? Does the word *Portion* signify a specific quantity? How can you tell?

2.   The Jacobi menu on pp. 14-15 of the **ST** *Drucksachen* offers your Manitoba friends a different kind of egg dish. What is it? What would they probably not order as part of their standard North American breakfast? How do *belegte Brötchen* differ from normal *Brötchen*? What does tea come in?

3.   Find the Interhotel menu from East Berlin on **CT 95**. Now look at column 3, *Unsere Empfehlung ab 9.00 Uhr*. What do you suppose a *Katerfrühstück* is? What about it doesn't sound very appetizing to a North American palate? Now compare the price of the continental breakfast from the door hanger menu on **CT 94** with its equivalent in the Interhotel.

SCHREIBEN

Stage 1   You are a bit embarrassed by your Manitoba friends' logging-camp appetites and don't really want to order the large meal at the Jansen Konditorei-Café. You plan to excuse yourself for a few minutes, but before you do, write down the order for one of them to give the waitress when she comes. Order for all three of you.

Stage 2   You are staying at the Frankfurt Sheraton, where you are carrying out an assignment for your newspaper back home. Because the Sheraton is a first-class hotel, you have the possibility of room service. You have ordered breakfast from the door hanger menu on **CT 94**, and now the work for your paper begins. Once you have eaten your breakfast in the room, write a paragraph comparing this breakfast to the one you enjoyed in either the Wall Cafe or the Jansen Konditorei-Café. If appropriate, tell about things you wanted to eat, things you ate, or things you were required to eat. A note about the room service would be appropriate.

WAS EMPFEHLEN SIE?

HÖREN

Stage 1

A1   Just listen several times to the dialogs for *Gespräche 2: Was empfehlen Sie?* Talk along if you like.

A2   Practice saying the dialog lines. Use your "pause" button if you have one.

B1   Conversation 1
              1. What time of day is it?
              2. Where will the suggested activity take place?
              3. Which does it involve — art, music, or drama?
              4. What alternative activity do the people have in mind? Why?
              5. Is there a conflict between the two?
            Conversation 2
              1. Write the name of the destination you hear.
              2. Write the location, including the section of the city.
              3. How are the people to reach the destination?
              4. Where is definitive information to be found?
            Conversation 3
              1. How many blocks away is the UNICEF building?
              2. How many of the buildings named in the dialog are probably several hundred years old?
              3. Which streets named run perpendicular to Komödienstraße?
              4. Which buildings named are probably not of historical significance?

Stage 2

B2   Listen to the organizational meeting of a group of music lovers, who have met in Zürich and are planning an evening of concerts. They have all chosen to hear different events and will then regroup afterwards at a coffee house for a gala session comparing the concerts. Make a chart with the following columns: _Name_, _Anlaß_, _wo?/wann?_, _sonstige Information_. Label the rows: Herr Merker, Frau Eisler, Herr Knopp, Fräulein Giesel, Herr Hoffmann, Frau Gellert. Opposite the name of each participant in the chart, fill in the appropriate activity, including location, time, and whatever other information seems interesting to the group.

C1

1A:4.1.2   How is the weather affecting driving conditions? [1]

1A:5.2.1-5   For the 5 weather reports make and fill in a chart that covers the following categories: time of broadcast, period forecast covers, precipitation, atmospheric conditions, temperatures. If you have difficulties with this exercise, review the similar one in Chapter 7 (first half), which uses segments IA5.1.1-6.

C2
2B:4.1.1   Check yourself. Three hiking trips are described. Can you get the following information about them on one listening? — length of tour, distance to be hiked per day, price per night (is it with/without breakfast?).

SPRECHEN

Stage 1   1. You want to find out from your business associate how yesterday's activities went. Be sure to say something polite as he begins his meal.

2. You didn't understand everything he said, probably because he was talking with his mouth full and you were paying attention to something else. Ask him to repeat, especially the part where he told you what he wanted to do, but couldn't.

3. On the basis of your conversation so far, find out what he'd like to do after you've finished your business for the day. Suggest some exercise if he comes up empty-handed.

4. The evening promises to be a long one if you don't think of something exciting to do. Excuse yourself from the table for a moment, then approach the waiter and ask him for suggestions.

5. Tell the business associate that you've just had a wonderful idea, one he's sure to like. It involves a short trip on public transportation, a nice walk, and some entertainment at a popular place.

Stage 2   1. You have solicited and received from the hotel clerk a suggestion that your family take time out from a busy schedule and spend an afternoon at the zoo, a popular attraction to the north of the city center. Tell your spouse about this.

2. Your spouse had other plans. Say why you think the zoo is a better idea.

3.   Tell your acquaintances that the art gallery they're looking for is on Wallraf-Platz, near the Dom-Hotel, and that the Lengfeld'sche Buchhandlung is right next to the St. Kolumba-Kirche.

4.   You're not sure whether either one is open now at this late hour.

5.   The guide at the Dom has suggested that you try out a *Konditorei* near the university, but you don't know how to get there. Ask someone for specific directions.

6.   Following someone's advice, you have boarded a bus to visit the Stadtwald on the outskirts of the city. When you return to the bus stop, you realize that you have no money to buy a return ticket from the ticket machine. Perhaps a passing taxi could take you back to your hotel, then wait for you to go to your room and find your money; or perhaps not . . . . Be honest with the cab driver, and explain the situation before you get into the cab.

LESEN

Stage 1   1.   Look at the *Tagesveranstaltungen* from Karlsruhe on **CT 196**. What event(s) would be especially interesting to a 12-year-old? What non-musical event(s) would probably induce the 12-year-old to sleep? What events have to do with neither music nor theater?

2.   Look at the restaurant list on **CT 322**. It's Saturday, July 5. You want to attend some event in Karlsruhe before you leave on the train for Mannheim in time to meet friends for supper at the "Goldener Drache" as soon as it opens for the evening. Counting the walks to and from train stations, you'll need to plan for an hour and a half between the two cities. What event do you choose? Are you sure the restaurant is open today? Would the event be appropriate for your sister's two children, who are visiting you?

Stage 2   1.   Consult the Wetterstein *Zugbegleiter* on p. 2 of the **ST** *Drucksachen* for the ad placed by the city of Bielefeld. What activities does it suggest having to do with music? What outdoor activities are available? What does "*4.800 ha Wald*" mean? What words and phrases are intended to appeal to those who don't like to follow the crowd? Find the Teutoburger Wald on your map. (For an indication of the importance of this area for German history, see *Strategie — Kultur und Sprache* in the next chapter.)

2.   Add to what you already know about Trier by reading the *"Kurze Geschichte der ältesten Stadt Deutschlands"* and *"Trier heute"* on p. 37 of the **ST** *Drucksachen*. Read the page through without looking up any unfamiliar vocabulary. Then go back through it more carefully and guess the meaning of the following words: *Kaiserresidenz, Erzbischöfe, Besitz, Wirtschaftsmittelpunkt, Hafenstadt, Moselschiffahrtsweg, Weinhandelszentrum, Einwohner.*

When were the first human settlements in Trier? In what year was Roman Trier founded? When did Trier become the capital of this part of the Roman Empire? In what respect is Trier an important city today?

Consult what sources you must to find out what the *karolingische Reichsteilung* in 870 was all about.

SCHREIBEN

Stage 1   The Bielefeld information in on p. 2 of the **ST** *Drucksachen* so interested you that you want to follow up with a formal inquiry to the city chamber of commerce. Pick two activities and write a note to the *Verkehrsverein*, whose address you will find in the advertisement. Tell them what you think is interesting in the ad, and ask them to send you more information about (*über* with accusative) those activities. After you write down the address, begin your note *"Sehr geehrte Herren"*, even though you suspect not all the people in the office are gentlemen.

Stage 2   The Graunings of Regensburg would like to hear how you're getting along. Tell them about the latest activities you have undertaken in Köln: what you wanted to do, what you were able to do, and what you had to do. You can even tell them what you ate (use *haben*) if you want.

> Liebe Familie Grauning,
>> Heute bin ich wieder in Köln. Gestern (Dienstag) . . .

STRUCTURAL EXERCISES

1   Things have changed radically from yesterday to today. Write what yesterday's facts were. (Review **CT 68** , #2 first!)

Example: Heute habe ich kein Geld. <u>Gestern hatte ich (viel) Geld.</u>

    1.   Heute muß ich nicht viel schlafen.
    2.   Ingrid will heute nicht mit mir tanzen.
    3.   Heute morgen haben wir Kaffee zum Frühstück.
    4.   Heute abend können wir kein gutes Restaurant finden.
    5.   Heute muß Udo zur Bank gehen.
    6.   Heute mittag kann Ingrid in Frieden essen. Ihr Bruder ist weg.
    7.   Zum Rheinpark? Heute ist das eine gute Idee.
    8.   Herr und Frau Schröder haben heute keine Zeit für mich.
    9.   Wollen Sie heute abend am Rhein spazieren?
    10. Warum sind Sie heute im Hotelzimmer?

2   Sentences 1 through 8 in exercise 1 can be used to express your optimistic hopes about tomorrow as well. Because you're an optimist, begin your sentences with "*Hoffentlich . . .*", which means "I hope that . . ." Pick the more optimistic sentence in each pair.

Example: Heute habe ich kein Geld. <u>Gestern hatte ich (viel) Geld.</u>
Sentence #2 is more optimistic, so: <u>Hoffentlich habe ich morgen (viel) Geld.</u>

3   You have some complaints about your breakfast and ask the waiter to come to your table. Ask him to bring you various things, defining each with the word in parentheses at the end of your statement.

Example: Ich habe kein Messer. (**scharf**)   <u>Bitte, bringen Sie mir ein scharfes Messer.</u>

    1.   Ich habe kein Ei. (**weichgekocht**)
    2.   Mein Stück Brot ist hart. (**weich**)
    3.   Meine Serviette ist weg. (**neu**)
    4.   Meine Tasse ist schmutzig. (**sauber**)
    5.   Ich glaube, mein Kännchen Kakao ist leer. (**voll**)
    6.   Meine Omelette schmeckt nicht gut. (**besser**)
    7.   Mein Glas Orangensaft ist leer. (**voll**)
    8.   Meine Zitrone ist faul. (**frisch**)
    9.   Mein Schinken ist roh. (**gekocht**)
    10. Meine Rühreier sind kalt. (**heiß**)

4   Now you're speaking on behalf of others. Change your request accordingly.

Example: Mein Freund hat kein Messer. (**scharf**)   <u>Bitte, bringen Sie ihm ein scharfes Messer.</u>

    1.   Meine Tochter hat kein Ei. (**hartgekocht**)
    2.   Die Brötchen von meiner Schwester sind hart. (**weich**)
    3.   Die Tasse von meinem Sohn ist schmutzig. (**sauber**)
    4.   Die Omeletten von meinen Eltern schmecken nicht gut. (**besser**)
    5.   Unsere Zitronen sind faul. (**frisch**)
    6.   Die Spiegeleier von Herrn Braun sind kalt. (**heiß**)
    7.   Die Serviette von meiner Frau ist weg. (**neu**)
    8.   Unsere Würstchen sind zu kurz. (**lang**)
    9.   Die Sektflasche von meinem Vater ist zu klein. (**groß**)
    10. Der Apfel von meiner Mutter ist zu weich. (**frisch**)

√ CHECK YOUR PROFICIENCY

CAN YOU:
__ say in some detail what you would like to eat and drink for breakfast?
__ tell what you did recently and what you are planning to do next?
__ ask for advice about what to see and do?
__ deal with sometimes difficult directions in a city?

DO YOU REMEMBER HOW TO:
__ exchange money and make small purchases?
__ arrange for a city tour?
__ deal wih public transportation?
__ arrange for lodging, even if what you want is not available?

HÖREN

Stage 1

A1   Just listen several times to the dialogs for *Gespräche 1: Dom*. Talk along if you like.

A2   Practice saying the dialog lines. Use your "pause" button if you have one.

B1   Conversation 1
1. What time of day is it? What are the clues?
2. What is the second person buying film for?
3. Why does the first person want to undertake the activity?
4. Why is the second person a bit apprehensive about their plans?
5. What do you think *fit* and *Lift* mean?

Conversation 2
1. What do you think the profession of the first speaker is?
2. What does this person tell us about the Dom?
3. Why was that necessary?
4. What is the second speaker's reaction?

Conversation 3
1. What is the relationship between the first two speakers?
2. From the context, what do think a *Fernglas* is?
3. Where are these people?
4. What does the third person say about the Middle Ages?
5. In what year were the towers of the Dom completed?
6. What two adjectives are geographical terms?

Stage 2

B2   A member of the Köln city council happens to be up on the Dom tower, pointing out the sights to a trade delegation of brewers from South Korea. You overhear him giving the names of the seven bridges that cross the Rhine from Köln and its environs. Make note of the names, disregarding for the time being other information you hear.

B3   Consult the maps of Köln and environs on **CT 46** and **85**. Listen to the city council member's bridge tour again, this time paying attention to the names of the various parts of the city. Write down the names you recognize from the maps, following the bridge tour from north to south. Which name does not appear on the maps? Is it on the west or east side of the Rhine?

Now listen to the descriptions of the second and sixth bridges.
1. What is a *Hafen*? Which one(s) is/are on the east side? Which one(s) is/are on the west side?
2. What adjectives are used to describe the fifth bridge?
3. Over which two bridges do trains travel?
4. How is the word *Lastwagen* explained?
5. What do you think an *Autobahnkreuz* is?
6. Are there any women in the brewers' delegation?

B4   Now, while you are still looking at your Köln map, listen to the city council member as he explains where the Köln breweries are. How many breweries are there? Are there more on the east side or the west side of the Rhine? Can you associate each one with a specific part of the city?
1. What does the word *Kölsch* denote?
2. What does the label of the Dom-Brauerei show?
3. For the visitors, what is special about the Reißdorf brewery?
4. Write the slogan for the last brewery mentioned.

C1

1A:1.1.2   The segment announces a religious broadcast. Which religious faith is mentioned, what time is it, and is it a.m. or p.m.? [P2]

1A:1.4.1-4   You should be able to note, with only one listening, the exact time and, where it is given, the station. [7]

1B:6.1.6   How much does *Auto-Bild* cost? Where and when can you get the new issue? [6]

1B:6.2.4   What kind of product is being advertised? What is its relation to soccer? To figure out what *"WM"* means, look through the list on the upper right part of the *Bildwörterbuch* display on sports, **CT 305**. [6]

C2

2A:1.2.1   The report describes some young people who might be regarded as anything from political extremists to common delinquents. How many of them are there? Their street name, taken from what they wear, is _____, but now the authorities term them _____ .

2A:1.2.2   In what city does the fashion festival take place? How long does it last, and how many have there been before? How many of the exhibitors are from outside the country?

2A:1.2.3   How is the government going to commemorate the importance of women? When will the relevant meeting take place, and will the government official there be consulting with men or with women — or both?

SPRECHEN

Stage 1   1.   You tell your companion that the Dom tower is closed today because of the bad weather. Suggest an alternative plan until the weather improves.

2.   You tell the guide that you don't understand why just one person couldn't climb the tower to take just one little picture.

3.   Tell the person selling tickets for the *Dom-Aufstieg* that you especially want to see the towns on the other side of the Rhine, because that's where your grandparents emigrated from long ago.

4.   The person next to you didn't hear the guide tell how old the Hohenzollernbrücke is, or when the Dom was built. Tell him.

5.   You are astonished that Köln is as old as the guide says.

6.   You wonder how far it is from where you're standing, at the top of the cathedral, to the ground.

Stage 2   1.   You are very satisfied that you have learned a lot during your time up in the tower of the cathedral. But now it's time to think of some practical matters.

2.   You're in the photo store, buying supplies for your visit to the top of the cathedral. There may be special lighting difficulties up there — you don't know. In any case, your camera won't take pictures in extreme lighting circumstances, and you want good advice on film.

3.   The photo clerk asks why your camera has trouble with lighting — the light meter, perhaps? Tell her what you wanted to photograph last week, and why the picture didn't turn out.

4.   Your pictures have not turned out well. You're leaving Köln soon and want to find something to give you a professional-quality record of your trip. Suggest to your companion that you both go into a couple of stores on the Domplatz to find something fitting. Make suggestions about what stores those would be and what you hope to find.

LESEN

Stage 1   1.   In Chapter 8 you learned something about the history of the university in Freiburg, a city you will get to know better in Chapter 13. Return now to that document, *"Freiburgs Stadtgeschichte leicht gemacht"*, on **CT 344-45**. Is the Münster in Freiburg as old as the Kölner Dom? When was the Münster finished?

2.   What important person came to Freiburg in the wake of the Reformation? (You might want to consult the *Strategie* section of the **Class Text**.)

3.   What happened in Freiburg during the time of the Plague in the 16th century? Looking under the same year's entry, tell what at least some of the citizens of Freiburg found to explain the presence of the Plague in their city.

Stage 2   1.   Remembering the dates of the Thirty Years' War, tell what happened in the university during that time. Who were (and are) *Jesuiten*? Who invaded the city during that war?

2.   From what country did the next invaders of Freiburg come? How long did they stay? When did they return? How did the alliance between France and Austria come about? (Find out about Maria Theresia from the *Strategie* section.) What happened to the happy couple later in life? When did this invading country most recently occupy Freiburg?

3.   Other nations were represented in Freiburg during the Napoleonic Wars. Which ones?

4.   What happened in Freiburg during the First World War? When was that repeated? Who were the culprits?

5.   When was Freiburg's last major anniversary celebration?

SCHREIBEN

Stage 1   As your group's self-appointed historian, review for your traveling companions the summary of Freiburg's history that has fascinated you recently. In the form of an outline, write (where appropriate) either an exact date or simply a century to indicate when various events took place. Be sure to give more weight to those events that you find especially significant.

Stage 2   You have returned briefly to your home in Memphis to attend the wedding of your sister. While you are there, you visit your old high-school German teacher, who asks you to tell her class something about what you have learned in Europe in the eight months since you left home. You have a few slides, mostly of impressive buildings such as museums, cathedrals, and opera houses. You want to give the teen-age students some idea of the importance of history and religion in the Old World without boring them. The combination of slides and a summary of your observations and readings should do the trick. Write out your notes, keeping the German simple and avoiding vocabulary that is probably unfamiliar even to the German 4 students. Remember your strategy for telling about the past — beginning with a couple of past forms and then switching to the present tense. You can use past forms of *sein*, *haben*, and the modals to get off to a good start, of course. Aim for 10 sentences.

GESCHENKE

HÖREN

Stage 1

A1   Just listen several times to the dialogs for *Gespräche 2: Geschenke*. Talk along if you like.

A2   Practice saying the dialog lines. Use your "pause" button if you have one.

B1   Conversation 1
1. For how many individuals are the people buying presents?
2. Who is probably the youngest of them all?
3. Who is the oldest?
4. Are the presents "typical" male/female presents? (Suggest another, more interesting distribution of gifts.)

Conversation 2
1. How many people are shopping? What is their relationship? How do you know?
2. Who is Ingrid? What do we know about her?
3. What is Ingrid's hobby?

Conversation 3
1. How many people are shopping? For whom?
2. What are this other person's hobbies?
3. Are the gifts discussed for use in the summer or the winter — or both?
4. Does the salesperson's suggestion sound practical?
5. What do you think the shopper will finally buy? Why do you think so?

Stage 2

B2 Listen carefully to the gift plans, then make a chart with the following columns: Geschenk?, Wie viele?, Farbe?, Für wen?, Geburtstag am?. Number 6 rows, then fill in the chart.

C

2B:5.3.1 For what year does the report give statistics about tourism in München? How was the weather at the Oktoberfest in that year? To find out how good or bad the year was for tourism, listen for a word that sounds much the same in both languages. [7]

2B:5.4.1 If you didn't figure out in Chapter 3 who this "Joseph" is, listen for the word *stammen*. Which religious denomination is mentioned? What time is it, approximately? [3]

2B:5.4.2 What are the date, time (am?/pm?), and station? Which religious denomination is mentioned?

2B:5.4.3 To which religious denomination is this museum devoted? In which city or region is it located? About how many private museums are there in the area?

SPRECHEN

Stage 1 1. You'd like an attractive souvenir of your time in Köln — one for yourself and one for your twin. You've always had matching clothing; why stop now?

2. You're looking for an appropriate present to take to your little brother, who loves model boats and trains. Explain your preferences to the clerk. It can't cost you an arm and a leg, though.

3. You have been trying to find the toy department for 20 minutes and finally approach a clerk. Try to hide your disappointment when she tells you the store doesn't sell toys.

4. You've just bought a pretty scarf for your mother, whose birthday you'll celebrate as soon as you arrive home in a few days. Explain to the clerk that you won't have a chance to gift-wrap it, and ask whether that can be done there at the store.

5. Your grandfather is an inveterate pipe-smoker, but has enough pipes. Ask the clerk whether there are any other things pipe-smokers need.

Stage 2 1. You bought some presents for your sisters, but now realize that the size is too small. Tell the store clerk your problem and be sure to present your receipt for a refund.

2. Ask someone in your hotel where you might buy some records and tapes of local folk performances. Be sure to ask who the best groups might be and what sort of music is a part of local folk tradition.

3. The clerk shows you several things that might be good presents for your father, but nothing really strikes you. Ask about other colors and sizes, and then finally excuse yourself politely because you don't really see what you need.

4. You'd like to buy your family some Rhine wine, but wonder about shipping it home. Ask the storekeeper whether he can package it well enough to be sent. Keep insisting on just one more layer of packaging.

5. Now you realize that your family in Barboursville can buy Rhine wines for a ridiculously cheap price at the liquor store down the street. Tell the patient storekeeper that you've decided not to buy the wine after all. First, offer to pay him for his time and effort in packaging the wine; then say you'll simply take it along with you after all: you can share it with friends this evening.

LESEN

Stage 1   Look at the *Stadtrundgang* information on **CT 330-331**, which lists several aspects of commercial life in Hamburg. What words would excite people who are addicted to shopping? What are the names of the main shopping streets in Hamburg? What does the Hamburg chamber of commerce cite as a special European shopping attraction? What are normal business hours in the city? There is a pun in the phrase *Seh-Leute* used to describe certain people in what is a traditionally seafaring city. What is the source of the pun? Another example of chamber-of-commerce writing is the word *Kauf-Leute*, a new form of *Kaufleute* 'merchants'. Whom do they mean by their new form? What words of foreign origin are used to lend an especially cosmopolitan atmosphere to the Hamburg commercial scene?

SCHREIBEN

Stage 1   You have made a quick trip home to Hartford for an important family gathering, and have just sent a package full of presents to your eight friends back in Lübeck. Just to make sure they all know exactly what is intended for whom, send them a note with details by separate mail.

> **Example:**   Liebe Freunde,
>   Hier sind 8 Geschenke aus Amerika.
>   Das X ist für Y. Z bekommt den W . . .

STRUCTURAL EXERCISES

1   You are buying presents for people according to their interests Suggest to the person with you what you should give to whom, based on the cues.

Example: Jürgen raucht gern. (Pfeife - neu). <u>Kaufen wir ihm eine neue Pfeife</u>.

1. Hans spielt gern Tennis. (**Tennisschläger - billig**)
2. Wulf kocht gern. (**Kochlöffel - groß**)
3. Martina raucht gern. (**Zigarre - schwarz**)
4. Onkel Adolf trinkt gern Wein. (**Weingläser - 6, tschechisch**)
5. Theo reist gern im Süden. (**Sonnenbrille - modisch**)
6. Reinhard spielt gern Gitarre. (**Volksliedersammlung - amerikanisch**)
7. Petra schreibt gern politische Slogans. (**Kugelschreiber - grün**)
8. Dirk schnitzt gern Spielzeuge aus Holz für Kinder. (**Messer - scharf**)
9. Thomas joggt gern morgens. (**Wecker - gut**)
10. Elisabeth liest gern Romane. (**Taschenbuch - interessant**)

2   The gift-giving goes on. What hobbies do you suppose the various people have? Form the first statement, then invent a fitting conclusion.

Example: Emil / __ Computerprogramm.
<u>Ich kaufe Emil ein Computerprogramm. Er spielt gern im Zimmer</u>.

1. Eduard / dick___ Socken.
2. Monika / ___ Gitarre.
3. Hans und Fritz / neu___ Bücher.
4. Emilia / fest___ Arbeitshandschuhe.
5. Mein___ Frau / Pullover aus Wolle.
6. Unser___ Tochter / ___ Hündchen aus Ungarn.
7. Mädchen / toll___ Tonbandkassette.
8. Tante Beatrice / Agfa-Film mit 36 Aufnahmen.
9. Onkel Harald / acht Flaschen Bier.
10. D___ Großmutter / neu___ Spielkarten & ___ Aschenbecher.

3   Redo your first statements in #2 above, emphasizing the recipient of the gift.

Example: Emil / Computerprogramm.
<u>Emil kaufe ich ein Computerprogramm</u>.

4 Redo your first statements in #2 above, assuming you've already been talking about the individuals.

Example: Emil / Computerprogramm

　　Ich kaufe ihm ein Computerprogramm.

5 **Welch__ ? / Dies__** A: Complete your friend's questions, then B: tell which article you think you'll give to the person indicated.

Example: Welch__ Zeitung / Laurenz?

　　A:　　Welche Zeitung geben Sie Laurenz?

　　B:　　Ich glaube, ich gebe ihm diese Zeitung.

　　1.　Welch__ Flasche / d____ Großvater?
　　2.　Welch__ Schweizer Armeemesser / Ihr____ Sohn?
　　3.　Welch__ Arbeitshandschuhe / Ihr____ Großmutter?
　　4.　Welch__ Kochbuch / sein____ Eltern?
　　5.　Welch__ Kristallgläser / Ihr____ Mutter?
　　6.　Welch__ Hobbyzeitschrift / Ihr____ Bruder?
　　7.　Welch__ Puppe / Ihr____ Schwesterchen?
　　8.　Welch__ Fotos / Ihr____ zwei Tanten?
　　9.　Welch__ Tennisbälle / Ihr____ Tochter?
　　10. Welch__ Halskette / Ihr____ Freundin?

6 By analyzing the elements of the compound nouns, guess what their meaning might be within the context of each sentence.

　　1.　Auf der <u>Hochalpenstraße</u> sehen wir viele junge Leute auf Fahrrädern.
　　2.　In der Stadt muß Otto seinen Mercedes in einer <u>Tiefgarage</u> parken.
　　3.　Beim <u>Gebrauchtwagenhändler</u> wollten wir einen alten Opel kaufen.
　　4.　Nach der <u>Altstadtbesichtigung</u> können wir eine Konditorei finden.
　　5.　Der <u>Rheindampfschiffskapitän</u> schläft nicht gern auf seinem Schiff im Hafen.
　　6.　Sie dürfen bei einer <u>Hochwassergefahr</u> nicht auf dem Campingplatz am Fluß bleiben.
　　7.　Die <u>Erstbesteigung</u> von diesem Berg war im Jahre 1857.
　　8.　Die große Glocke hier gehört zur <u>tausendjährigen</u> Tradition in unserer Kirche.
　　9.　Die beste <u>Briefmarkenauswahl</u> haben Sie bestimmt bei der Post.
　　10. In den breiten <u>Verkaufsstraßen</u> Bremens konnte meine Tante nur teure Geschenke finden.

√ CHECK YOUR PROFICIENCY

CAN YOU:
__ discuss historical landmarks?
__ specify locations with some precision?
__ discuss concrete objects in considerable detail?
__ obtain things for other people?

DO YOU REMEMBER HOW TO:
__ talk about your family members?
__ deal with complex city directions?
__ inquire about tickets to events?
__ arrange for public transportation?

SW **Bitte nur 1 FILM pro Tasche – danke!** **SW**

			BETRAG
WEISS-HOCHGLANZ		WEISS-MATT	
Entwicklung und je 1 Bild	○ 9 x 9	○ 18 x 24	
Entwicklung und Kontaktbogen	○ 9 x 11,5 Pocket	○ 24 x 30	
○ Reportagestreifen	9 x 13	○ 30 x 40	

Chapter 11
ZOO

HÖREN

Stage 1

A1 Just listen several times to the dialogs for *Gespräche 1: Zoo*. Talk along if you like.

A2 Practice saying the dialog lines. Use your "pause" button if you have one.

B1 Conversation 1
   1. What animals are mentioned?
   2. Which ones are more active?

Conversation 2
   1. What is the relationship between the two people?
   2. What animals are mentioned?
   3. What is the relationship between the animals?
   4. What is the younger person's reaction to the animals?
   5. What is the older person's reaction to the younger person?

Conversation 3
   1. Is the child's first question reasonable?
   2. Is the child's second question reasonable?

Conversation 4
   1. Write down the infinitives of the verbs you hear.
   2. What is the probable relationship between the people?
   3. What animals are named?

Stage 2

B2 Conversation 1
   1. How many people are visiting the zoo?
   2. Why is the ticket seller suspicious? With good reason?

Conversation 2
   1. What do we know about the relationship between these people?
   2. Do they generally agree or disagree with each other's wishes?
   3. What is the man's name? Does he come here often or seldom?
   4. What does the man find so attractive about the monkeys?
   5. Why does he utter the last words that he does?

Conversation 3
   1. Who are these people?
   2. What specific warning is uttered?
   3. Why is that warning given?
   4. What activity brings about that warning?
   5. How does the one person tell the other not to worry?
   6. How many people appear to belong to the larger family circle?
   7. How did these two people probably get to the zoo? Why do you think that?

Conversation 4
   1. What animals are mentioned in the dialog?
   2. Who is addressed as *du* in the dialog?
   3. What do you think the meaning of the word before *bewegen* is?
   4. What questions are addressed to the animal?
   5. What activities are suggested after seeing this animal?
   6. Are these people here seldom or often? Why do you think so?

C1

2A:1.2.5   The news item describes a skiing accident. How old was the victim? Was the victim male or female? How serious were the victim's injuries?

2A:1.3.1   Note any numbers and any terms for family members. Try to guess the general theme of the news story. Is it sports? hobbies? politics? education? [1]

2A:1.3.2   Estimate the age of the mother. From the example given, construct at least the first part of the German words for 'quadruplets' and 'quintuplets'. Optional enrichment for math and English majors: Take a look at the section *"Formen und Gestalten"* in the *Bildwörterbuch* display on **CT 308**, and then figure out the German words for 'pentagon' and 'hexagon'. Compare them to the German words for 'quintuplets' and 'sextuplets'. Draw a conclusion about the two languages and try expressing it in simple German. [1]

2A:1.3.4   Note numbers, colors, and geographical terms. To what or whom do the numbers refer? [1]

C2
2B:4.3.2   What kind of animal is the focus of the story? When and where is the gathering? Note numbers for later reference. When the announcer talks about food, is it people food or animal food? Optional enrichment for biology and philosophy majors: The German word for 'leg' is *Bein*. Listen for the first part of a word for 'quadruped', and then guess how the German word for 'biped' might begin.

SPRECHEN

Stage 1   1. You tell your little brother that he's not allowed to feed the animals.

2. The 10-year-old next to you is afraid of the bears. Tell him there's nothing to be afraid of.

3. The camel is eyeing your straw hat. Say something to him.

4. Your companion would like to see smaller animals, but you're interested in larger ones. Arrange activities for the next two hours.

5. Ask your close friend if she would like to meet you back in front of the tigers at 3:00.

6. The weather has taken a turn for the worse. Make a suggestion to your companion.

Stage 2   1. Tell the people standing near you (whom you don't know) that the zoo has a number of houses for animals, each house notable for some reason: size, temperature, color, fame, and so on.

2. A young child near you has never seen live lions or tigers. Explain the differences between the animals in terms the child can understand.

3. Tell your niece what bears do all day.

4. Suggest to your companion that the two of you wait for the next feeding of the seals, then go see some mammals before you treat her to lunch.

4. You notice resemblances between the chimpanzees and a couple of members of your companion's family. Describe the similarities as well as you can without being offensive.

5. The 5-year-old you've been babysitting has been dawdling by the penguins. Tell him to forget the penguins and take your hand, then to eat his *Wurst* and come with you to where his parents are meeting you.

LESEN

Stage 1   Look at the menus in both of your texts. Make a list of the game dishes you find.

Stage 2   Now look on **CT 112** at the ad for the Wilhelma zoo in Stuttgart. How late is the zoo open daily in June? (Are you sure?) If you are planning to see both the fish and the other animals on Tuesday, and it's getting late, which should you probably see first? Looking under the prices for annual passes to the zoo, what bit of information might be insulting to a woman who would rather be known as something other than somebody's wife? Who are *Rentner*? *Schwerbeschädigte*?

SCHREIBEN

Stage 1   You're leaving your apartment for 2 weeks, and have arranged for the 8-year-old neighbor boy to feed and entertain your pets. Write him the necessary instructions.

> Lieber Bodo,
>
>   Du mußt / sollst / darfst (nicht) . . .

Stage 2   1.   Now look at the lists of animal names on **CT 114**. (This is your chance to load an ark and to get extra credit in your zoology course.) Make one list of the animals you would not be afraid to encounter face-to-face in the open. Now make another list of the **ten** you would <u>least</u> like to encounter in their native habitat. Beside each animal in the first list, write a word or two (probably an adjective) justifying its inclusion on the "not dangerous" list. (Example: Hamster — *lieb und süß*) Beside each animal in the second list, find a word or words that adequately express your fear of meeting it on its own terms.

2.   What large groups of animals (mammals, reptiles, birds, etc.) are represented on **CT 114**? What is the largest group?

ABENDFAHRT AUF DEM RHEIN

HÖREN

Stage 1

A1   Just listen several times to the dialogs for *Gespräche 2: Abendfahrt auf dem Rhein*. Talk along if you like.

A2   Practice saying the dialog lines. Use your "pause" button if you have one.

B1   Conversation 1
1. What seems to be the problem?
2. How is the problem solved?
3. What was the source of the problem?
4. What articles of clothing are mentioned?

Conversation 2
1. What do these people have on their agenda this evening?
2. What landmarks are mentioned?
3. How long will the first activity last?

Conversation 3
1. What comparisons are made in the dialog?
2. What adjectives are used in the comparisons?
3. What is the relationship between the speakers?
4. What reason is given for the lively comparisons?

B2   Conversation 1
1. Both *du* and *Sie* are used by the people in the dialog. Describe the relationships between them.
2. What activity is involved?
3. What are described as the positive aspects of the activity?
4. What has changed Eduard's evening, and apparently for the better?

Conversation 2
1. What words denote objects or phenomena from nature?
2. What prompts the last question?
3. List four inequalities mentioned.

Conversation 3
1. What is so special about this water excursion?
2. When does the excursion take place?
3. How long does it last?
4. Where is the lake that is mentioned?

C1

1A:3.1.2   What is the day and time of day? Observe the use of *du* in the song. [4]

1A:3.2.1   After an introduction, which lasts about a minute, the announcer lists those who are celebrating wedding anniversaries. Take notes on the <u>anniversary number</u>, the <u>people celebrating</u>, and the people <u>offering congratulations</u>. For additional exercise, continue the same note-taking with the birthday celebrants, perhaps noting as well the <u>locations</u>. Those celebrating birthdays 91 and 88 are particularly rewarding. The family tree in the *Bildwörterbuch* **CT 296** can help with vocabulary. When did the broadcast originate (day/month/year)? [3]

1A:3.2.2   Who is Peter's best friend? Why do he and his wife listen to the radio so much? What is his wife doing while they listen? [4]

C2
1A:5.1.1-6   Listen to the weather reports only <u>once</u>; take notes on the following: <u>time</u> of broadcast, forecast <u>period</u>, <u>low</u>/<u>high</u> temperatures, <u>precipitation</u>, <u>sky</u> conditions. Then write down all of segment 6 (10 words), and answer this question: Has it been foggy lately? [7]

2B:5.1.1   Your riverboat is cruising downstream all the way from Trier on the Mosel to Köln on the Rhein. You will see, in this logical order (but not that of the broadcast), the following cities: <u>Trier</u>, <u>Cochem</u>, <u>Koblenz</u>, and <u>Köln</u>. Can you note down the river measurements (depth and change) for each, listening only <u>once</u>? [2, 7]

2B:5.2.1   The Marksmen's Club has a new policy about which eating and drinking establishments may be chosen as meeting places for its youth groups. What do they demand? Could you explain briefly in German why a North American gun club would not even consider proposing — let alone accepting — such a policy? [3]

SPRECHEN

Stage 1
1. You indicate impatience about getting to the boat dock in time for an evening departure.

2. You want to make sure you and your companion have warm clothing for the evening's excursion.

3. You tell your companion that the boat trip from Mannheim to Rüdesheim takes 5 1/4 hours, and that you will be returning to Mannheim in buses at 7 in the evening after spending three hours at your destination.

4. You are planning a birthday celebration and want to arrange an evening cruise on the Rhein for your group of ten. Make sure there will be appropriate food and drink on board and ask about special activities during the cruise.

5. You ask the ticket agent whether the boat can make a special unscheduled stop at a town south of Köln.

Stage 2
1. You compare the temperature on the river in the evening to that in the city during the day.

2. Taking into account the evening temperature on the river and the activities on board the boat, make recommendations to your companion for clothing and other essentials needed during the excursion.

3. Compare the day's activities with the evening's activities: the physical environment, the location, the nature of your interests, and so on.

4. An elderly lady whose eye problems severely compromise her night vision is sitting next to you on the boat. Tell her what you see on the boat and from the boat, making comparisons where they are useful.

LESEN

Stage 1   1.   Look at the information about Rhine trips on **CT 116-117**. When does the trip *"Rhein in Flammen"* begin? Where? When do the passengers return? How? What seems to be the shortest time a passenger will spend on board and still see the fireworks?

2.   Is Rodenkirchen north or south of Köln? What word tells you? Could you go shopping and take a later boat back to Köln if you wanted?

3.   One of the sources lists price reductions for groups of people. At what age is one no longer considered a child? What discounts would the following groups get: **a)** a third-grade class of 35; **b)** a third-grade class of 15; **c)** a 90-member group from the Köln Rotary Club; **d)** three 19-year-old students in secretarial school?

Stage 2   1.   Where can one buy tickets on the <u>MS Domspatz</u>? What is the shortest trip that can be taken on this boat? How many times a week does the boat go to Porz? It's May. How many romantic evening cruises are available per week? Considering just the time spent on board, which is the better buy, the afternoon or evening cruise? What would the Monday afternoon cruise cost for a typical family of 5 (2 parents, children aged 3, 5, and 8) with a set of octogenarian grandparents?

2.   What historic structures do you see as you take the boat upriver from Heidelberg? What natural attractions are visible from the boat underway?

SCHREIBEN

Stage 1   Look at the information about Rhine trips on **CT 116-117**. List the positive words that are intended to lure passengers to the Rhine boats. What words appeal to the pocketbook? the stomach? the heart?

Stage 2   Make a list of key words you need to describe yesterday, when you went to the zoo and took the evening Rhine cruise. Then write a note to the Graunings, telling them what you were able to do yesterday. Don't forget the extra fun on the boat!

STRUCTURAL EXERCISES

1   Pronoun practice. Study the three diagrams below and see how the accompanying sentences relate to them. (First name: familiar; *Herr/Frau*: formal. ↔ means 'speak(s) with') Then perform the exercise with the ten sentences that follow the diagrams.

Examples:

ich ↔ Frank	*Ich spreche mit Frank. Ich sage "du" zu ihm.*
<u>ich Frank</u> ↔ Frau Kuhn.	*Frank und ich sprechen mit Frau Kuhn. Wir sagen "Sie" zu ihr.*
ich ↔ <u>Frau Kuhn Fräulein Bayer</u>	
	Ich spreche mit Frau Kuhn und Fräulein Bayer. Ich sage "Sie" zu ihnen.

1.   ich ↔ Hansjürgen.
2.   ich ↔ Frau Gebhart
3.   <u>ich Claudia</u> ↔ Robert
4.   <u>Frau Kunert Herr Gieseking</u> ↔ Hansjürgen
5.   <u>Hansjürgen Robert</u> ↔ Frau Kuhn
6.   Beatrice ↔ <u>Frau Holder Frau Klees</u>
7.   Robert ↔ Claudia
8.   Frank ↔ ich
9.   Thomas ↔ <u>Ernst ich</u>
10.   <u>Herr Neumann Fräulein Brutzer</u> ↔ <u>Frau Knigge Frau Nolte</u>

2   Rephrase the following sentences using another method of comparison.

example: Heute ist schöner als gestern.   *Gestern war nicht so schön wie heute.*

1.   Hermann ist nicht so alt wie Dorothea.
2.   Er ist auch nicht so klein wie sie.
3.   Aber sie ist nicht so faul wie er.

4. Hermann ist auch lauter als Dorothea.
5. Heute ist Dorothea müder als er.
6. Heute ist das Wetter nicht so schlecht wie gestern.
7. Gestern war es heißer als heute.
8. Und heute ist es kühler als gestern.
9. Die Berge sind nicht so trocken wie die Wüste.
10. Der Regen ist nicht so stark in den Bergen wie an der Küste.

3 Restate these comparisons, using the antonyms of the adjectives given.

example: Emilia ist häßlicher als Sieglinde. *Sieglinde ist schöner als Emilia.*

1. Deine Familie ist komplizerter als meine.
2. Und meine Familie ist interessanter als deine.
3. Aber meine Kinder sind lauter als deine.
4. Januartage sind kürzer als Julitage.
5. Sie sind auch kälter als Julitage.
6. Bei uns sind sie auch nässer als Julitage.
7. Im Januar sind die Straßen gefährlicher als im Juli.
8. Und im Juli ist der Boden weicher als im Januar.

4 You are arranging a meeting with your co-workers. With them gone right now, there is no one to take the message but the 15-year-old apprentice, Richard, who will also be at the meeting. Change the forms as necessary.

example: Herr Dahlke, kommen Sie bitte um 5 Uhr. *Richard, komm bitte um 5 Uhr.*

1. Treffen Sie mich am Rathausplatz.
2. Seien Sie bitte um 4.30 Uhr da.
3. Ich komme vielleicht etwas spät. Aber bitte warten Sie!
4. Nehmen Sie bitte diese Papiere mit.
5. Bringen Sie auch Ihre neuen Pläne.
6. Und vergessen Sie unsere Bücher nicht.
7. Sprechen Sie bitte mit den anderen. Die sollen auch kommen.
8. Nehmen Sie die Linie 4 zum Rathausplatz. Ich sehe Sie um 4.30 Uhr.

5 Rearrange the scrambled sentences:

1. sieht Deutschlehrer der im mein wie aus Zoo Tiger.
2. 20.18 der ab Zug Uhr nach nächste Heilbronn um fährt.
3. Büchern nach in schau alten den. du vielleicht findest etwas.
4. Onkel mit bitte alten Zoo nimm zum deinen.
5. nicht auf Sie so morgen stehen bitte früh.

√ CHECK YOUR PROFICIENCY

CAN YOU:
__ make detailed comparisons?
__ identify and describe various animals?
__ use *du* correctly?
__ handle formal introductions?

DO YOU REMEMBER HOW TO:
__ obtain things for other people?
__ give information about mass transit?
__ order food and drink items?
__ make alternate arrangements?

HÖREN

Stage 1

A1   Just listen several times to the dialogs for *Gespräche 1: Post*. Talk along if you like.

A2   Practice saying the dialog lines. Use your "pause" button if you have one.

B1   Conversation 1

1. How many things does the customer need to mail?
2. What are the destinations?
3. What is the total cost of the things for each destination?
4. In what country does the conversation take place?

Conversation 2

1. What sort of article does the person want to send?
2. Does the article qualify for sending by this postal rate? What would disqualify it?
3. The postal clerk says something the customer doesn't understand. What two questions does she use to get her message across? What was the original question?

Conversation 3

1. What is the destination of the articles to be mailed?
2. Make a simple chart of weights and prices for this kind of mailing.
3. What does the mailing weigh? How many kilos is that expressed in decimals?
4. What change would the customer receive for a 20 franc note?

Stage 2

B2   Conversation 1

1. What does the customer want to send?
2. Where does the customer find information about sending it?
3. Why does the postal employee not tell him herself?
4. Under what category is the information found?
5. What else is in this category?
5. At least how many items does the customer want to send today?

Conversation 2

1. What has cost so much?
2. What special request does the customer have for the clerk?
3. What else does the customer want?
4. How much change should the customer receive?

Conversation 3

1. What does the customer want to send? Where?
2. What words are used that describe packing material?
3. Where is such material available?

C1

2A:1.2.3   Which of the German-speaking countries will be issuing the stamps? (The answer "Germany" is not sufficient.) How many will be issued initially? Skim through the survey of history on **CT 104** and the list of Berlin political figures on **CT 224** to see whether you can find some reasonably eligible candidates for the series. [10]

2A:1.2.4   Which city is in the news? Which religious group is mentioned? As usual, note down any numbers for future reference.

2A:1.3.5   The news story reports a fatal hit-and-run accident. Listen for: **a)** the make, model and color of the car; **b)** the sex, age, and height of the victims. Convert metric units into English units.

C2

2A:2.1.2   The announcer has gotten some mail from the DDR. Is it a letter or a card? How often have the folks there written him? Write down and translate the title of the song they requested. [1]

2A:2.1.3   The segment lasts about 55 seconds. Toward the end, after the word *"Hobby"* and information about when this "Fleamarket of the Air" begins, the announcer gives the call-in number. She says the area code once, the rest of the number twice. That's fair warning. If now you can catch the fleamarket number on the fly, you're pretty good.

SPRECHEN

Stage 1   1.   You need stamps for two postcards to Mexico and four letters to New Mexico. Be sure to inquire about the rates.

2.   You would like to make a phone call to your parents in North Carolina, but you're unfamiliar with the equipment in the Austrian post office. Ask for help.

3.   You want to send most of your books home and inquire about appropriate packaging, maximum weight per package, and postage.

4.   You have bought fragile items — glasses, crystal dishes, and small pitchers — as gifts for your parents and grandparents in Montreal and Sacramento. Ask advice about packaging and postal rates. Weigh the advantages of surface mail and airmail.

5.   You have written letters to your siblings on stationery of various colors. Having given the letters to the postal clerk, you realize that you forgot to put return addresses on two of them. Identify the letters in question, ask for them back, and say why you need to have them again for a second.

Stage 2   1.   Your package of books is just a few grams overweight, and the clerk is reluctant to accept it for mailing. Do your best to convince him to take it.

2.   You have to call your family, but have no money with you on this bank holiday. A collect call is a possibility you should inquire about.

3.   You have brought four packages to the post office for mailing to various destinations in Europe and North America. Say where each one is going, and ask for the relevant forms to fill out.

4.   You would like a sheet of airmail stickers and a postal package large enough to carry 5 kg of clothing you're sending home. Make the appropriate inquiry at the post office.

5.   Someone has tried to barge in line in front of you, perhaps having sensed that you are a foreigner and thus easy prey. Be polite, but firm — you're in a hurry, too.

LESEN

Stage 1   1.   **CT 346** shows eight different special-issue Swiss stamps. What do the stamps *Schweizerische Landesausstellung*, *Die fünfte Schweiz*, and *Bundesverfassung* commemorate?

2.   The paragraph *Das Hoheitszeichen* describes the history of the Swiss flag. In 1815, when the Swiss Confederation reached its final form of 22 cantons (now 23), a special flag design symbolized the special nature of Swiss democracy. What did it look like? Where does today's name for the country come from? The last sentence describes another symbol that a large number of people all over the world see every day. What is it? What is its origin?

Stage 2   1.   Three Swiss cantons united in 1291, comprising the original unit around which the Swiss Confederation was formed in later centuries. Look at *Die Geschichte* on **CT 346** to determine:

1.   When the Swiss hallmarks of domestic peacefulness and neutrality toward other nations developed.

2.   How the Congress of Vienna affected Switzerland.

3.   (You will have to consult other sources in your library for this one) The name and location of the 23rd Swiss canton.

2.   Now look at the paragraph *Land und Leute*. Underline the words that have something to do with nature. Which sentence expresses both modesty and pride? What problems seem to confront the modern Swiss state? Are they unique to Switzerland?

3.   The Constitution of 1848 addressed the issue of linguistic pluralism. Two compound nouns in the *Vier Sprachen* text contain the word *Recht* 'law' and suggest how the Swiss viewed — and continue to view — the issue. What are the words, and what do they mean? Before dealing with the entire sentence that ends "*. . . wurde anerkannt*" look at **Adjectives & Adverbs §6**. Now read the sentence. What does it say about three languages? What happened to the fourth? (You'll have to consult an outside source.)

SCHREIBEN

Stage 1   Refer again to *Land und Leute* on **CT 346**. This paragraph gives you a thumbnail sketch of what one group of Swiss has chosen to say about the country. Make a list of the main words and phrases, a list from which you could give a short talk to your old German 4 class back in Ann Arbor. Using this list, write a short paragraph for the German Club Newsletter at home. Some of the words used in the *Land und Leute* article will not be known to the readers, so substitute freely where you think it necessary. The last two sentences are more difficult than the first ones, so reward the readership with an English version. Remember what you learned in **Adjectives & Adverbs §6**.

IM ABTEIL

HÖREN

Stage 1

A1   Just listen several times to the dialogs for *Gespräche 2: Im Abteil*. Talk along if you like.

A2   Practice saying the dialog lines. Use your "pause" button if you have one.

B1   Conversation 1
1. Was haben diese Personen gestern abend gemacht?
2. Was machen sie jetzt?
3. Vielleicht kommen sie nach dieser Stadt zurück. Warum?
4. Wo schlafen sie wahrscheinlich, wenn sie zurückkommen?

Conversation 2
1. Wo kann man in einem Zug übernachten?
2. Die zweite Person spricht von einer Möglichkeit. Wie teuer ist sie?
3. Was ist die positive Seite von einem Liegewagen?
4. Was ist die negative Seite davon?
5. Was ist "Bettzeug"?

Conversation 3
1. Welches Problem hat der Tourist?
2. Was muß er jetzt machen?
3. Muß er aussteigen? Warum (nicht)?

Stage 2

B2   Conversation 1
1. Sind diese Personen gute Freunde? Wie wissen Sie das?
2. Warum ist die eine Person so müde?
3. Wohin fahren die zwei?
4. Welche Jahreszeit ist es wohl <u>nicht</u>?

Conversation 2
1. Sind diese Personen gute Freunde oder nicht? Wie wissen Sie das?
2. Wie viele Brüder und Schwestern hat die Person mit dem Fotoalbum?
3. Ist diese Person verheiratet? Wie wissen Sie das?
4. Von wie vielen Personen hört man in dieser Diskussion?

    5. Wie viele Personen sieht man auf dem Familienfoto?

    5. Wer ist Monika? Wie viele Personen gibt es in ihrer Familie?

    6. Wer ist wahrscheinlich die älteste Person auf dem Foto?

    7. Wer ist Karli?

Conversation 3

    1. Was ist das Problem?

    2. Wo ist der Herr mit der Platzreservierung?

    3. Was hängt draußen neben der Tür?

    4. Gibt es am Ende immer noch ein Problem? Warum (nicht)?

C1

1B:6.1.1

Four times the person listening to the animals tries to communicate with them. Write down all four of his utterances. You might then read the section "How to Keep a Conversation Going" on the front flyleaf of the **Class Text** and ruminate a while. [P1, P2]

1B:6.1.2

How — claims the commercial — do the Chicken McNuggets Shanghai taste? What flavors are there in sauce #4? [P2, 2]

1B:6.3.3

How do you consume this product? List one of its ingredients.

C2

2B:4.1.2

In the first 30 seconds the announcer tells what will be covered in the upcoming features. What about the price of eggs at Eastertime? [2]

2B:4.3.1

After the play-by-play description of the soccer game the announcers start rapping and wrap it up. They use many of the verb forms that are described on **CT 128** and listed in the inside back covers of the **Class Text**. Don't take any notes; just think about patterns like *spielen / hat gespielt* and *sehen / hat gesehen*. [8]

2B:5.2.4

In a few words summarize the content of the broadcast. How many points or major divisions of his argument does the speaker list?

SPRECHEN

Stage 1

1. You cannot find your ticket to show to the conductor. Ask if he can't return later to give you time to look for it.

2. You find out that the other person in your compartment was just in Köln for a week. Ask what she found especially interesting there.

3. Now tell her what you thought was the high point of your own visit.

4. Continuing the conversation, compare four or five places in the city and say what you liked about each one.

5. You and the other person have enjoyed the conversation, and it is clear that you both enjoyed Köln. Say what you'll do when you return — if you have the time and money, that is.

Stage 2

1. You are just dozing off in your compartment when you notice that the suitcase you thought was yours does not belong to you after all. You must have picked up the wrong one in the station, or maybe the person who just got off took yours by mistake. When the conductor comes, explain what has happened and ask for advice.

2. The above situation is taking place in your compartment, but it involves someone else's suitcase, rather than yours. Tell the person what you think he might do: get off at the next station and return to the city he just left, perhaps, or call the information desk back at the station, or write a letter to the Österreichische Bundesbahn explaining what has happened.

3. You are showing a fellow passenger a picture of your family back in Freeport. There are three generations represented, with you belonging to the second. Identify all the people and say a little bit about each one.

4. You've been a student in Innsbruck for seven months now, and have made trips to each of the German-speaking countries. Tell the person in your compartment what you have seen and especially enjoyed in each country, and also say what you're studying and why.

5.   That other person in your compartment, a citizen of Basel, is planning a trip to North America, and is studying the page of his travel brochure (**CT 266**) that reads *"Vereinigte Staaten"*. He shows you the brochure and asks your opinion and advice about the sections entitled *Geschwindigkeitsbeschränkungen* and *Kulinarische Spezialitäten*. There is much to be discussed here. Take one topic at a time and do the best you can. Can you guess the meaning of the first section from context?

LESEN

Stage 1   Look at the *Milch* page of the Wall Cafe menu on pp. 10-11 of the **ST** *Drucksachen: Das gibt's, . . .daß . . .* Try to guess from context the meaning of the words *Ungerechtigkeiten, Ereignisse, ungeheuer,* and *nirgendwo.* What word seems to be the root word for *Ungerechtigkeiten?*

Stage 2   1.   Consult the *Checkliste vor der Abreise* on **CT 127**. Which of these boxes would you check if you were just leaving home for the weekend? For a week in another European country? For three months of work with the World Bank in Africa?

2.   Look on **CT 126**, at a brochure describing the "Glacier-Express", a narrow-gauge train that plies the high valleys of the Swiss Alps. What two towns does it connect? How far apart are they? How would a person journeying from Zürich connect with this train? How much does the trip cost one way? How long does it last? Where would passengers starting in St. Moritz have to change trains if they didn't want to go all the way to Zermatt, but rather on to Geneva? What features distinguish this trip from all others in the world? What unusual souvenirs of the trip are included in the fare?

SCHREIBEN

Stage 1   Look again at the *Milch* page of the Wall Cafe menu on pp. 10-11 of the **ST** *Drucksachen*. Now write a note to a friend in Graz, telling him about the wonderful place you've found in Bremen to undertake all sorts of activities. Begin with *"Wenn ich . . ."* Then be sure to invite your friend to come to Bremen and share in these activities with you.

Stage 2   Recalling your conversation with the Basel man who was planning a trip to North America, check your notes from that conversation and write him a short letter. You'll want to make sure he knows your opinion about the things that seemed questionable to him (**CT 266**). Begin your note *"Sehr geehrter Herr Burckhardt, . . ."*

STRUCTURAL EXERCISES

1   One way of indicating your approval of a plan is to say *"Es ist mir recht"*. That clause is often followed by *wenn*.

>   Gehen wir in die Oper?
>   *Ja, es ist mir recht, wenn wir in die Oper gehen.*

Of course, your response must take into account the entire situation, including your relationship with the other person.

>   Was meinen Sie? Soll ich hier bleiben?
>   *Ja, es ist mir recht, wenn Sie hier bleiben.*

>   Was meinst du? Soll ich hier bleiben?
>   *Ja, es ist mir recht, wenn du hier bleibst.*

>   Sollen wir deinen Vater besuchen?
>   *Ja, es ist mir recht, wenn wir meinen Vater besuchen.*

Now give your approval of the following evening plans:

>   1.   Essen wir in der Altstadt?
>   2.   Was meinen Sie? Soll ich um 6 Uhr vorbeikommen?
>   3.   Was willst du machen? Soll ich dich um halb acht abholen?
>   4.   Kaufen wir etwas Eis am Martinsplatz?
>   5.   Suchen wir Ihre Freunde bei der alten Stadtmauer?

      6.   Soll ich dich am Rathausplatz treffen?

      7.   Ich sehe dich am römischen Brunnen, ja?

      8.   Nach dem Konzert im Stadtpark bringe ich dich wieder nach Hause.

2   Little Lieselotte is at the Alpenzoo in Innsbruck, where she is writing a note to her friend back in Wiesbaden telling her about the zoo and its animals. Help her complete the message.

> Liebe Christiane,
>
>   Heute bin ich im Alpenzoo in Innsbruck. Zuerst habe ich das groß___ Aquarium und die schön___ Fische gesehen. Das war schon direkt am Eingang zum Zoo, mit dem WC. Dann habe ich die alt___ Eulen gefunden, und dann ein schmutzig___ Wildschwein. Pfui! Die wild___ Katze hat geschlafen und wollte nicht miauen — schade! Neben den Wildkatzen war ein fleißig___ Biber. Das braun___ Tier wollte nur seine Zweige fressen. Dann habe ich den klein___ Marder gesehen, und auch eine wunderschön___ Gemse. Wahrscheinlich war das klein___ Murmeltier in sein___ Loch — ich konnte es nicht sehen. Dann war auch ein groß___ Steinbock aus d___ Bergen da, und ein gefährlich___ Elch aus Norwegen. Natürlich mußte ich die lieb___ Hasen sehen, die sind doch so niedlich! So wie mein braun___ Hase zu Hause im Schlafzimmer. Aber du! Ich habe auch d___ haarig___ Wolf gesehen! Onkel Max hat mich ganz fest gehalten, und ich habe seine lang___ Zähne gesehen! (Nicht die Zähne vom Onkel Max — die vom bösen Wolf.) Da hatte ich wirklich Angst. Ich war auch froh, daß wir dann keine Zeit mehr für den Zoo hatten. Wir mußten wieder zur Oma.
>
>   Bald bin ich wieder zu Hause. Schöne Grüße!
>
>   Deine Lieselotte

3   You're checking your list of things to do before you board the train for Freiburg. As you suggest something, your companion says it's already been done. **Example:** *Müssen wir Eduard sehen? Nein, ich habe ihn schon gesehen.*

      1.   Mußt du deinen Rucksack finden?

      2.   Müssen wir dem Hausmeister den Schlüssel geben?

      3.   Mußt du deine Freundin am Tanzbrunnen treffen?

      4.   Mußt du noch einen Eisbecher essen?

      5.   Mußt du die Zeitung von heute lesen?

      6.   Müssen wir die Bücher zur Leihbibliothek nehmen?

      7.   Müssen wir das letzte Bier trinken?

      8.   Müssen wir das Gepäck zum Bahnhof bringen?

4   Another way of asking whether things have been done is to be more straightforward about it. Return to exercise #3 and change the questions according to this **Example:** *Müssen wir Eduard sehen? Hast du Eduard schon gesehen?*

√ CHECK YOUR PROFICIENCY

CAN YOU:

__ conduct postal transactions?

__ use the telephone?

__ ask for more precise information about trains?

__ talk about the past?

__ make plans for the future?

DO YOU REMEMBER HOW TO:

__ address children and close friends with *du?*

__ make detailed comparisons?

__ say the names of a variety of animals and articles of clothing?

__ specify locations?

__ obtain things for other people?

HÖREN

Stage 1

A1 Just listen several times to the dialogs for *Gespräche 1: Jugendherberge*. Talk along if you like.

A2 Practice saying the dialog lines. Use your "pause" button if you have one.

B1 Conversation 1
1. Warum ist die zweite Person so froh?
2. Wer hört besser, Person 1 oder Person 2?
3. Wie viele Gebäude gibt es in der Jugendherberge?

Conversation 2
1. What is the first person's attitude? Why?
2. How does the second person's attitude differ?

Conversation 3
1. What is the attraction in the youth hostel for the first person?
2. Why does the second person agree?
3. What is the second person's real reason for agreeing?

Conversation 4
1. What people are being discussed?
2. What phrases suggest that you might like to know them?
3. Which person do you know more about?

Stage 2

B2 Conversation 1
1. Welcher Aspekt vom Leben in der Jugendherberge war für die erste Person gut?
2. Welcher Aspekt vom Leben dort war nicht so gut?
3. Was will diese Person also jetzt machen?

Conversation 2
1. Wie lange war Person 1 in der Jugendherberge?
2. Wo war sie dann nachher?
3. Welche Wörter beschreiben das andere Zimmer?
4. Warum war das andere Zimmer besser für diese Person?

Conversation 3
1. Warum ist es nicht so ruhig auf der Hochalpenstraße?
2. Können Sie "Bergwiese" in diesem Kontext verstehen?
3. Warum ist Italien so attraktiv? (3 Gründe!)
4. Warum findet die zweite Person die Berge so schön?
5. Sind diese zwei Personen allein, oder haben sie auch Freunde dabei?

C

2A:2.2.1 1) What sorts of jobs has Vico Toriani had? They are listed several times, though with variation. 2) When talking about the past the speakers use forms of the following verbs, in this order: *schreiben, sagen, haben, machen, kommen, sehen, schlagen* ('hit', 'strike'), *lesen*. As you listen, write down the participles of these verbs (examples: *hören — gehört, trinken — getrunken*). Check your list against the **Class Text** *Glossary*. [2, 9]

2A:2.2.2 What is the title of the song, and who sang it? How long have Elisabeth and Franz been married?

2A:2.2.3 What day and part of the day is it? How long has the program lasted till now?

2A:3.1.4   Many Swiss speak standard German with a definite accent that you would not find too troublesome. Quite another thing is Swiss German, a true dialect rather than a mere accent. The difference between Swiss German and standard German (*Hochdeutsch*) is far greater than that between, say, American Black English and Australian English. Most citizens of the BRD or DDR, or even Austria, would find it quite difficult to get even the gist of simple speech in Swiss German. So listen to this excerpt from a comedy routine in which a famous Swiss skier is supposedly asked how he manages with his leg in a cast. The question is in standard German — you'll recognize some words; the answer is in Swiss German — you'll be baffled, as the German listeners were intended to be. Don't take any serious notes; just try to note the following words as they fly by, in this order: *so jung, nichts sagen, so schnell ich kann.*

SPRECHEN

Stage 1   1.   Tell your friends that you'll help with the dishes if they do a little cooking.

2.   You're planning to stay three days at the youth hostel. Make sure the *Herbergseltern* have room for you that long, and be sure to ask about bed linens.

3.   Tell the *Herbergsvater* that you won't be wanting to rise extra early tomorrow after all, because today was such a busy day.

4.   You'd like to attend an open-air concert tonight, but it will probably last past closing hour at the youth hostel. Do your best to arrange things with the *Herbergsmutter*.

5.   Ask your new-found friends what they'd like to do the next day. You're in Grindelwald, in the Swiss Alps, so all sorts of things are possible: a bike ride with picnic, some hiking, and maybe a relaxing guitar lesson in the evening.

Stage 2   1.   Tell your friends back in Köln all about the positive and negative aspects of your stay at the youth hostel in Maibrunn, not far from the Bayerischer Nationalpark.

2.   Out behind the youth hostel you discovered another young person who was breaking one of the hostel rules. Consult with your friends about whether to tell the *Herbergseltern*.

3.   You have asked the *Herbergseltern* to keep their eyes peeled for some items you are missing. Tell them what you were doing when you realized the things were lost. (You have been very active so far today, but the activities have been confined to the youth hostel.)

4.   You feel like biking for another hour or two before stopping for the evening, but your friends would like to stop at the attractive youth hostel up ahead. Give them good reasons for continuing instead of stopping.

5.   You are suddenly terribly low on cash, and have tried to phone your friends in Bremerhaven to have money sent through the postal service — but no one was home. Solicit funds from two of the friends you've been traveling with. Be sure to explain that you've already tried to get money through normal channels.

LESEN

Stage 1   Look at the map of Vienna with three accommodation listings on **CT 135**. What is the least expensive place to stay? How many months a year is it open? Where would your youth group of 45 probably choose to stay? Why would its distance from the city center seem not to be a disadvantage? Where would you stay if you wanted to do some hiking in the fabled Vienna Woods? Where would you be likely to have a fine view of the city skyline? Which way does the Danube flow? (Where is its source? How many countries does it touch before flowing into salt water?) From which train station would you depart for Hungary? Where would you arrive on the "Mozart" from Paris and München?

Stage 2   In your youth hostel guide you find the following suggestions for hiking gear:
   Stiefel mit Profilsohle; Hosen, die über die Knie reichen; Anorak (Windbluse); Reservehemd und -unterwäsche sowie warme Oberbekleidung (Pullover, Handschuhe, Kopfschutz); Regenschutz (Schirm); Rucksack (keine Akten- und Handtaschen oder Campingbeutel).

   Im Rucksack: u.a. Karte, Kompaß, Proviant, Feldflasche, Verbandszeug, Sonnenschutz (Brille und Creme).

What equipment is missing for an overnight hike? (Your dictionary will be helpful here.) Which of these items would be useful in **a)** cold, windy weather; **b)** hot, sunny weather; **c)** wet weather; **d)** medical emergencies; **e)** finding your way to safety?

SCHREIBEN

Stage 1   Consult **CT 135**. Your 20-member culinary club, the "Waist Nots", is interested in visiting Vienna for a week. You don't need anything fancy, and you'd also prefer to do your own cooking (and dishwashing!). Write a letter to the appropriate place, outlining your plans. Inquire whether there might be a discount for such a large group.

Stage 2   You are staying in the youth hostel in Vienna's seventh *Bezirk* (district), planning a surprise visit to your bosom pal from home who is spending the semester abroad with the Ranitzki family in the suburb of Hinterbrühl. Write a note to Mr. Ranitzki telling him about your plot and suggesting that the family lure your friend to the youth hostel for a surprise meeting. Remember to abide by the house rules. (Mr. Ranitzki might not know the way to the hostel.)

KRANKHEIT

HÖREN

Stage 1

A1   Just listen several times to the dialogs for *Gespräche 2: Krankheit*. Talk along if you like.

A2   Practice saying the dialog lines. Use your "pause" button if you have one.

B1   Conversation 1
1. Why is Erika impatient with the patient?
2. Why is his condition especially unfortunate?
3. What is her suggestion for his cure?
4. What is his reaction?
5. What words in the dialog refer to medication?

Conversation 2
1. What does the number in the dialog refer to?
2. How long has the person been sick?
3. What is supposed to help cure him?
4. What words and phrases identify the sickness?

Conversation 3
1. Why is the sick person uneasy about going to the doctor?
2. What word characterizes the other person's reaction to the patient's attitude?
3. How long has the patient been sick? How long will he have been sick before going to the doctor?

Stage 2

B2   Conversation 1
1. Whom are the two people talking about?
2. Name all the parts of the body you hear mentioned.
3. Which of these has/have not yet been affected by an accident?
4. What is the nature of the current accident?
5. What phrase expresses a generalization?

Conversation 2
1. What are the sick person's symptoms?
2. What seems to be the cause of the problem?
3. What is the sick person's husband doing?
4. What antidote does the sick person prescribe for herself?
5. How well does the sick person know the person she's talking to?

Conversation 3
1. Warum ist die kranke Person etwas barsch heute?
2. Ist die Person jetzt im Krankenhaus?
3. Wo kann die Person vielleicht wieder gesund werden?
4. Warum erscheint diese Möglichkeit besonders attraktiv?

C1

1A:1.4.1-4   Is the announcer giving upcoming time, current time, or time just past? Note verb tenses and words for 'now', 'just', etc. [10]

1A:1.5.1-2   How precisely can you determine what time it is right as the announcer speaks? [7]

1B:6.1.4   Observe how Captain Igloo uses the plural familiar form (*euch*) to address the kiddie chorus. [2]

1B:6.1.7   Transcribe the first line of the song ("*Wenn . . . macht*"), and then note which form of address (*du* or *Sie*) the singer uses in the next lines. How would you translate that first line without obscuring the different senses of 'you' that German can convey? [9]

1B:6.2.3   What symptoms does the medicine claims to combat, and where is it produced?

1B:6.2.7   The man who sneezes has: **a**) too much curry powder on his currywurst; **b**) a cold; **c**) a tickly mustache; **d**) hay fever. If you are doing <u>really</u> well, you can figure out whether the two men are using *du* or *Sie*. Try rereading **Class Text** *Struktur* 2 Section 3 on **CT 118**.

1B:6.3.5   How will the product make your house feel and look? Observe that the singer addresses the product in the *du*-form ("*O hilf mir*"). [5]

1B:6.3.6   How well do the man and woman know each other? Where is the event and for what days is it scheduled?

1B:6.4.3   Fill in the blanks at the start of the ad: "_____ _____ _____, *daß* _____ _____ _____ *Unkonzentriertheit, schlechtem Gedächtnis und bei Lernmüdigket* _____ _____ ?" Then divide *Lernmüdigkeit* into syllables and you'll see what medicine they're pushing. [5]

C2

2A:1.1.5   How long before the broadcast did Heinz Nixdorf die? Of what? The key word is in the Chapter 13 vocabulary, but for help you can consult the *Bildwörterbuch* display of body parts on **CT 294**. [7]

2A:1.3.2   When and where did the mother of the sextuplets die? Which internal organ failed? How are the children faring? [1, 11]

2A:1.3.3   A lot of people were in the disco when the bomb went off. Many were injured. Some were seriously injured. A few died. Listen for the numbers or similar information. [1]

2A:1.4.2   Note the day, time and station. For each of the 5 items reported briefly by the female announcer, try to copy down a few words or a phrase. Aim for enough that, if you were asked what was going on, you could provide — in English if not German — one general piece of information and one detail. Example from the previous segment (2A:2.3.3): "A bomb went off in a disco in Berlin and at least twice they said something about Americans."

SPRECHEN

Stage 1   1.   Your best friend is terribly sick. Express your sympathy to him and ask what you can do for him.

2.   Your friend refuses to seek any medical help, largely for financial reasons. Do your best to lend a hand, even if you have to dip into your own pocket to help out.

3.   A person on the train, with whom you have been discussing an obvious injury you have, has expressed keen interest in your health and advised you to seek medical assistance. Tell her that your religion forbids you to do so and reassure her that you are confident of a full and speedy recovery under your own power.

4.   An interested party in your youth hostel suggests that you should look to herbal medicine for help for your broken wrist, and begins to tell you the curative powers of various exotic plants. Tell him politely that your brother, whom you deeply respect, is a bone specialist.

Stage 2   1.   You have tripped and fallen getting onto a bus. Tell the helpful bus driver where it hurts and ask to be taken to an appropriate place.

2.   In the aftermath of a farewell celebration for one of your friends, you are not feeling at all well. Tell the person with you that the pains probably don't derive from the party *per se*, but perhaps from a fall you took on your way home. Ask advice, and be prepared for some cynicism.

3.   You and your traveling companion suddenly begin to feel logy and depressed, and are beginning to get on each other's nerves. A person in Innsbruck suggests that the cause of the maladies is probably *der Föhn*, a debilitating warm south wind. You aren't prepared to believe this explanation, so do your best to establish some other cause. When you have been convinced that the *Föhn* is indeed the culprit, suggest to your friend what you might do to escape it.

4.   You obviously need to see a doctor after your old toe problem suddenly reappeared, but now you're in Europe, where you do not know a doctor. In addition, you are philosophically opposed to "socialized medicine". Prepare to discuss the problem with the *Herbergseltern*, who are magnificent physical specimens.

LESEN

Stage 1   1.   You have just witnessed an accident in which someone has been badly injured. Rushing to a nearby phone booth, you find a page from the phone book that gives emergency numbers (**CT 136**). Which one do you dial for a) a doctor; b) an ambulance; c) the police; d) the Red Cross?

2.   What number would you dial if the little child next door had just swallowed a fistful of juniper berries?

Stage 2   1.   Consult p. 3 of the **ST** *Drucksachen*, the "Wetterstein" train schedule, which includes an advertisement for *Frischzellen*. What medical problems does the ad address? How is health restored to the afflicted?

2.   Now look at the advertisements for various curative programs on **CT 136**. In what country are they located? What aspects of physical and mental rehabilitation do they have in common? What seems to be the most important at the Kurmittelhaus Puchberg? Where is this place? What are the root words in the compounds *Schlaflosigkeit, Durchblutungsstörungen, Kreislauftherapie, heilklimatisch,* and *Kreislauferkrankungen*?

SCHREIBEN

Stage 1   After a close encounter with a streetcar in Freiburg, you decide that a week of rest and relaxation might be the best thing for your nerves. Because the Kurmittelhaus Puchberg (**CT 136**) caught your eye in the doctor's office, write to the institution asking for more information about their program and the charges involved. Be sure to tell them what happened to you and how long you have been in need of help, and ask whether their facilities are suited to your needs.

Stage 2   The second **Versuchen Sie doch** exercise at the end of this **Class Text** chapter describes a situation involving an auto accident. Imagine that you are not the messenger bearing the news of the tragedy, but one of the passengers in the back seat. You have been waiting for help to come, but few people pass by this remote area. Struggling to keep your composure, you decide to write a note to be given to medical personnel in case someone does come by soon. Tell how the accident took place and describe the nature of the injuries as well as you can. (Just as you finish writing and are feeling faint, a lone bicyclist appears, approaches the car, and says "Hi. I'm from Dayton. Can I help?")

STRUCTURAL EXERCISES

1   You have been having a wonderful time in the youth hostel in Bad Ischl, just east of Salzburg. You have also written a note to your friend Liesel back in Würzburg, asking her to join you in Austria for a couple of days. Suddenly you remember that Liesel's cousin, Verena, is visiting her, and that Verena would be hurt if your invitation didn't include her. Change the note as needed.

> Liebe Liesel <u>und Verena</u>,
>
> 1.   Ich bin seit Samstag hier in Bad Ischl. Möchtest Du auch kommen?
> 2.   Du kannst mit dem Intercity-Zug um 13.58 Uhr abfahren, und
> 3.   . . . um 16.25 bist Du in München. Dort mußt Du umsteigen.
> 4.   Um 17.20 Uhr nimmst Du den "Mozart" nach Salzburg.
> 5.   Du kommst um 18.56 Uhr in Salzburg an. Ich stehe dort am Bahnhof.
> 6.   Wir bleiben eine Stunde in Salzburg — nur Du und ich allein —
> 7.   — und dann nehmen wir den Zug nach Bad Ischl. Nun, was meinst Du?
> 8.   Hast Du Lust zu kommen? Darfst Du kommen? (Was sagen die Eltern?)

2   Various things are (or were) happening to Liesel's brother Michael at the same time. Show that the action was simultaneous.

> **example**:   Er schläft.   Er vergißt seine Probleme.
> **Beim Schlafen vergißt er seine Probleme.**
>
> 1.   Er ißt.   Er schreibt einen Brief an seine Mutter.
> 2.   Er hat gegessen.   Er hat einen Brief an seine Mutter geschrieben.
> 3.   Er trinkt Bier.   Er denkt an sein Liebchen zu Hause.
> 4.   Er wandert.   Er singt lustige Volkslieder.
> 5.   Er hat gesungen.   Er hat geweint.
> 6.   Er schwimmt.   Er wird fit.
> 7.   Er joggt.   Er verstaucht sein linkes Knie.
> 8.   Er fällt.   Er bricht sein linkes Fußgelenk.

3   Now make three original combinations of your own, using the elements in **2** above.

> 1.
>
> 2.
>
> 3.

4   Poor Michael is now in the hospital, recovering from his fall. Using the words suggested in parentheses, tell how long the various conditions or actions have persisted. Practice placing the time phrase at different points in the sentence.

> **example**:   Er liegt im Bett. (3 Wochen)   **Er liegt seit 3 Wochen im Bett.**
>   **Seit 3 Wochen liegt er im Bett.**
>
> 1.   Er liest keine Zeitungen mehr.   (2 Tage)
>
> 2.   Er sieht seine Freunde nicht mehr.   (1 Woche)
>
> 3.   Er schläft auf dem Rücken.   (20 Stunden)
>
> 4.   Er telefoniert mit seinen Eltern.   (15 Minuten)
>
> 5.   Er lacht nicht mehr.   (fast 1 Monat)

5 Michael's letters home are pitiful. He gives reasons for each aspect of his condition. His old writing skills are deserting him, though. He writes only short, choppy sentences, which it is your duty to improve. You may have to change the order of the clauses to make sense out of what he has written.

> **example:** Es geht mir besser.   Die Krankenschwestern sind sehr nett.
> **Es geht mir besser, weil die Krankenschwestern sehr nett sind.**

1. Ich sehe keine Berge aus dem Fenster. Es regnet im Moment.
2. Mein Zimmerkamerad schnarcht. Ich schlafe nicht gut.
3. Ich bin traurig. Ihr besucht mich nicht oft genug.
4. Das Essen schmeckt mir nicht. Ich esse wenig.
5. Das Essen schmeckt mir nicht. Es ist fast immer kalt.

6 While you are visiting Michael, you ask him questions about his activities in the hospital. To each question he reponds that he just did that yesterday.

> **example:**   Sprichst du mit dem Arzt?
> **Ja, ich habe gestern mit ihm gesprochen.**

1. Diskutierst du das Essen mit deinem Zimmerkamerad?
2. Protestierst du gegen das Essen?
3. Telefonierst du mit deiner Familie?
4. Probierst du es jeden Tag?

7 Add to each of Michael's responses his reason for his action. Then report that answer to a third party.
> **example:**   Sprichst du mit dem Arzt?
> a. **Ja, ich spreche mit dem Arzt, weil mir mein Fuß weh tut.**
> b. **Er spricht mit dem Arzt, weil ihm sein Fuß weh tut.**

1. Diskutierst du das Essen mit deinem Zimmerkamerad?
    a.
    b.

2. Protestierst du gegen das Essen?
    a.
    b.

3. Telefonierst du mit deiner Familie?
    a.
    b.

4. Probierst du es jeden Tag?
    a.
    b.

√ CHECK YOUR PROFICIENCY

CAN YOU:
__ make arrangements to stay in a youth hostel?
__ talk about excursions you have taken?
__ describe minor medical problems and give advice?
__ give reasons for your opinions?

DO YOU REMEMBER HOW TO:
__ specify locations?
__ use familiar forms of address for one or more people?
__ compare things of equal or unequal quality?
__ talk about things that happened in the past?

Mein »Ruf-doch-mal-an-Geschenk«

Damit wir öfter
miteinander
sprechen...

	DM	Pf	für Postscheckkonto Nr.
			99 66-500

Absender _____

Gebühren-frei

Für Vermerke des Absenders

Postscheckkonto Nr. des Absenders

PSchA | Postscheckkonto Nr. des Absenders | Postscheckteilnehmer

Postscheckkonto Nr. des Absenders

Empfängerabschnitt

DM   Pf

für Postscheckkonto Nr.
99 66-500

Absender und gegebenenfalls
eigene Fernmeldekontonummer

_____

_____

Verwendungszweck

Ruf-doch-mal-an-Geschenk

**Angaben über den Beschenkten
umseitig eintragen**

**Fernmelde-Kontokarte/
Postüberweisung**

DM   Pf

Die stark umrandeten Felder sind nur auszufüllen,
wenn ein Postscheckkontoinhaber das Formblatt als
Postüberweisung verwendet (Erläuterung siehe Rückseite)

(DM-Betrag in Buchstaben wiederholen)

für
Ruf-doch-mal-an-Geschenk
Sonderkonto der Deutschen Bundespost

in **5000 Köln 1**

Postscheckkonto Nr.
99 66-500
Postscheckamt
Köln

Ausstellungsdatum   Unterschrift

Einlieferungsschein/Lastschriftzettel

DM   Pf

für Postscheckkonto Nr.   Postscheckamt
99 66-500   **Kln**

Ruf-doch-mal-an-Geschenk
Sonderkonto der Deutschen Bundespost

in **5000 Köln 1**

Postvermerk

... damit wir öfter miteinander sprechen, habe ich heute _____ DM
auf Dein/Ihr Fernmeldekonto überwiesen. Das Geschenk wird der nächsten
oder übernächsten Fernmelderechnung gutgeschrieben
und vermindert entsprechend den Rechnungsbetrag.
Ruf doch mal an – ich freu' mich drauf!

_____

_____

_____

_____

_____

(Linien für persönliche Zeilen)

Chapter 14
MUSEUM

HÖREN

Stage 1

A1 Just listen several times to the dialogs for *Gespräche 1: Museum*. Talk along if you like.

A2 Practice saying the dialog lines. Use your "pause" button if you have one.

B1 Conversation 1
    1. What kind of museum is the person looking for?
    2. What do you think *hervorragend* means in this context?
    3. What do the two museums specialize in?

   Conversation 2
    1. How long will the two people have stayed in this city?
    2. Which museum do they decide to visit first? What is its specialty?
    3. What were their original plans for tomorrow?
    4. What is the second person's attitude toward the new plan?

   Conversation 3
    1. Why does the visitor ask about brochures and postcards?
    2. What happens to the visitor's package?
    3. How many adults and children want to see the museum?

Stage 2

B2 Conversation 1
    1. Was für ein Schild sehen die Museumsbesucher? Was bedeutet es?
    2. Wie lange wollen die Leute im Museum bleiben?
    3. Welche Jahreszeit ist es wahrscheinlich?
    4. Was wollen die Museumsbesucher wissen?

   Conversation 2
    1. Wo sind diese zwei Personen?
    2. Ist das Gebäude privat oder nicht? Wie wissen Sie das?
    3. Warum darf man seine eigenen Fotos nicht machen?

   Conversation 3
    1. Was für ein Museum ist dies?
    2. Was kann man hier sehen?
    3. Was ist ein "Kopfhörer"?
    4. Warum nimmt man einen Kopfhörer mit ins Museum?
    5. Sehen diese Leute das ganze Museum heute, oder nur ein bißchen?
    6. Was ist ein "Autoaufkleber"? Eine "Anstecknadel"?

C

2B:5.3.1 How many foreign tourists visited München in 1985? **a)** 2.7 million; **b)** 5.4 million; **c)** fewer than 1.35 million; **d)** as many as 1.5 million. What was the average daily attendance at the Oktoberfest? [7, 10]

2B:5.4.3 When might the Jewish Cultural Museum have to be closed? Why? When did it open? In what building is it located? How many visitors does it attract? [10]

SPRECHEN

Stage 1 1. You have just entered a museum lobby. Tell the clerk at the desk that you need to find the cloak room, the bathroom, and the entrance to the collection of 19th century art.

2.   The person at the desk reminds you that you should leave your belongings at the entrance to the museum. You apologize for having forgotten that you are carrying a large shopping bag that happens to be the size of the museum's prize exhibit.

3.   Your friend heard the person at the desk say something about that shopping bag, but didn't hear everything. Repeat what was said to you and what you replied.

4.   You have received permission to photograph some of the articles in the museum, but realize that you have left your tripod back at the hotel. Explain your situation to the clerk at the front counter and ask whether you might leave and reenter without having to pay again.

Stage 2   1.   Explain to the person at the hotel that you are interested primarily in seeing a museum that specializes in science and technology, but that you'd also like to find one in which you could learn about the plants and animals of the region.

2.   You'd like to purchase postcards that accurately represent the holdings of the museum you've just toured. Ask the appropriate questions at the front desk.

3.   The slides you are thinking of buying look as if they've been artificially colored to enhance the reds and greens in the paintings. Express your dismay to the clerk and ask whether the postcards and posters have been doctored in the same way.

4.   A small child, apparently not accompanied by anyone else in the museum, has been putting his fingers directly on some of the precious canvases. There is no guard in sight. Tell him what he needs to know.

LESEN

Stage 1   Consult **CT 336-37**, which describes six museums in Zürich. What are the different kinds of museums? Which ones appear to be connected with institutions of higher education? Which ones are not accessible to the handicapped? Of those the handicapped can visit, what provisions are made for wheelchair entrance and exit? Even if you didn't know anything about Zürich, which museum would appear to be the most centrally located? Why do you think that? Which museums have libraries? Which museum has the most generous visiting hours? The least generous?

Stage 2   1.   Are visitors permitted to take flash pictures in the Schweizerisches Landesmuseum? What is the price of admission? Of tours? How old is the museum? Is it public or private? What are the oldest collections in the museum? If you had just read *Wilhelm Tell* and are interested in crossbows, what word tells you whether you might be able to see one here? What words tell you that you can see jewelry, coins, furniture, flags, pewter, and sculpture here?

2.   What word tells you that the Suchard Museum is unique? Will you be able to take a streetcar directly to this museum from the Landesmuseum, or will you have to transfer?

3.   What are the oldest clocks in the clock museum? What kind of clock was carved? Neuenburg is the German name of the western Swiss city of Neuchâtel. What words indicate that French culture is represented in this collection? Are the clocks all from Switzerland?

4.   Now look at the description of the Deutsches Museum in München on pp. 28-29 of the **ST** *Drucksachen*. What three areas are the main emphases of its collection? If you were organizing a group tour of the museum, what would it cost? How many could participate? How long would it last? If you wanted to have a museum catalog sent to you by mail, what would the cost be? How many current journals does the museum have in its library? How often does the museum give tours of its library? What kinds of things does the museum have in its picture archive? What do you think the "Kerschensteiner Kolleg" is? Can a visiting scholar arrange for accommodations through the museum?

SCHREIBEN

Stage 1   You plan to meet a friend at the Schweizerisches Landesmuseum (**CT 337**) at 1:00 p.m. Write a short note to him, telling him when and where to meet you, and what streetcar lines he could take to get there. He might suspect that the museum isn't open during the noon hour, so you'll have to address that problem. Afterward you'll want to see the coffee museum. Tell your friend that it's not just a collection of coffee beans.

Lieber Karlheinz, . . .

Stage 2 After consulting pp. 28-29 of the **ST** *Drucksachen*, the description of the Deutsches Museum, write a note to two close friends, with whom you plan to spend a rainy day in the summer wandering about the 17 km of museum corridors. You realize that it is impossible to cover the entire museum in one day, so you will want to suggest things to see and do. Be sure to inform them about particulars of 1) buying a catalog to guide you through the museum, 2) eating lunch in a special place (since it will be raining too hard to eat in the city), 3) taking some pictures of the collections, and 4) buying souvenirs in the museum gift shop at the end of the day. In addition, tell them when to meet you and when you should plan to be finished with your visit.

Liebe Monika, lieber Erich, . . .

WANDERUNG

HÖREN

Stage 1

A1 Just listen several times to the dialogs for *Gespräche 2: Wanderung*. Talk along if you like.

A2 Practice saying the dialog lines. Use your "pause" button if you have one.

B1 Conversation 1
1. What do you conclude about the relationship between these two people?
2. What problem threatens to upset the relationship here? How is it resolved?
3. What time of year do you think it is?
4. From the context, what meanings do you attach to *um die Kinder besorgt sein, Wanderstiefel*, and *Schrank*?
5. What provision does each person want to make for eating on the hike?

Conversation 2
1. What words evoke the positive aspects of the hike?
2. What words evoke the negative aspects?
3. From the context, what do *Streichhölzer, braten, Riesenhunger*, and *Entfernungen* mean?
4. Check the arithmetic of the person totaling the distances.
5. What is the exact elevation distance covered on this hike?
6. What seems to have solved a physical problem on the hike?
7. What do you think the problem was?

Conversation 3
1. Are the people at the foot or the top of the mountain?
2. List the four different ways of descending the mountain. Give directions where appropriate.
3. What structures or buildings are mentioned? What is the function of the first one?
4. Are the people taking this hike for the first time?
5. Why does the Lärchenweg seem so attractive?
6. What activity will crown the day's achievement?

Stage 2

B2 Martin Jost, who is leading a weekend hike along the Hochwang in eastern Switzerland, is assigning tasks to various members of the party, which includes two members of his family as well as some newcomers to the region. German is their common language. Listen carefully, and then note down the tasks assigned, along with any reasons given for them. At the end write down any general instructions for all the hikers. Use the form below. Keep you notes: you will need them later.

Name	Aufgabe	Grund
1. Herr Segantini		
2. Markus		
3. Fräulein Wehling		
4 & 5. Herr & Frau Reinemann		
6. Katrin		
7. general instructions for all:		

c

1A:5.2.1-5 For each weather report take notes as follows: 1) for both Southern and Northern Bavaria — information about precipitation, temperatures, and wind direction; 2) extended forecast. <u>Segment 2</u>: Which mountain range is mentioned? <u>Segment 3</u>: Note the mistake the announcer makes and how he corrects himself. [9]

2A:1.2.5 How far did the boy fall? What was he trying to do? [11]

2B:4.1.1 After the introductory remarks and music the announcer gives an overview of the 6 reports that will be featured in the broadcast. For each one jot down one or two significant words, so that you could say very generally what each story might be about. Then concentrate on the separate items discussed under the title *"Wanderferien ohne Gepäck"*. Which is cheapest? demands the most hiking? lasts the longest? [2, 5, 9]

2B:4.2.3 What is the subject of the traveling exhibition? Which cultural periods are represented (one is mentioned in Chapter 10)? Which museums are sponsoring the show? [8]

SPRECHEN

Stage 1 1.   Your group of friends will be hiking all day long, with a break for lunch at the Königsee at the foot of the Watzmann, West Germany's second-highest mountain. Tell them:
  • What the day's plan is;
  • What to bring along for lunch;
  • What personal articles might be necessary for the hike. Think of the weather.

2.   Ask someone how far it is to the next spring or other source of water. Give reasons for your eagerness to drink something.

3.   You have just slipped and hit your knee against a rock. Tell a friend what happened and suggest what you would like to do now.

4.   You have returned to a favorite hiking area after four years' absence. Tell your companion what you did here before, and why this place is so special to you.

Stage 2 1.   You're preparing for a hike from St. Antönien (in the Prättigau of eastern Switzerland) up to the peaks that mark the Austrian border. The hike will include a night in the SAC (Schweizer Alpen Club) Carschinahütte (ca. 2200m) and a climb up the Sulzfluh (2817m) and the Drusenfluh (2830m), as well as a visit to the Lünersee (1970m) across the border in Austria.. Tell those with you:
  • What clothing items they will need to bring (don't forget the feet!);
  • What sorts of snack items they might like to bring;
  • What activities they can look forward to at the Lünersee;
  • How long you will be underway, and when you will return to your car in St. Antönien.

2.   You had an eventful hike. One of you forgot an important article of clothing, each thought the others were bringing an important part of the meals, you met some very interesting people at the Carschinahütte, and you saw some unusual animals near the peak of the Sulzfluh. Now that you are back at your base in Vaduz, the capital of Liechtenstein, tell your hosts what happened on the trip.

LESEN

Stage 1 1.   Look at *"Wanderungen am Schauinsland"* on **CT 146**. Would you be able to pause for a glass of refreshment during the hike described? If so, where? From what point on this map are you likely to have the best view of the surrounding area? What is the approximate elevation difference in feet between the bottom of the cable lift and the Schauinsland peak? Which place names mention a part of the body? (NOTE: In this part of the BRD the Standard German suffix <u>-lein</u> has the form <u>-le</u>.) Which names sound as if they have interesting histories?

2.   Do your best to guess from context the meaning of: *Aussichtsturm, rechnen, ca., abwärts, Zickzackweg, Freiterrasse.*

3.   From what point on this map are you likely to have the best view of the surrounding area?

4.   What is the approximate elevation difference in feet between the bottom of the cable lift and the Schauinsland peak?

Stage 2   As part of your university's overseas program in Graz, you are on a fall orientation hike around the Tannebenstock. (In which one of Austria's states is this mountain located?) In search of refreshment, you suddenly come upon the Gasthof Schinnerl, where you find out that there is a cave nearby. When you ask about it, someone hands you the brochure reproduced on p. 33 of the **ST** *Drucksachen*. How long would a guided tour of the cave last? Would you need a sweater? What if you visited in the winter? What part of the text tells you where to go to begin the tour? Is each visitor given a flashlight for the tour? What are the names of the main rooms in the cave? Which is the biggest? Do you climb up or down to get to the first one? Is the <u>Riesenglocke</u> above or below the <u>Großer Dom</u>? Which is higher, the <u>Riesenglocke</u> or the <u>Belvederegrotte</u>? What is the <u>Riesenglocke</u>, and where does it get its name? What is the <u>Riese</u>? Why is it called that?

SCHREIBEN

Stage 1   Refer again to the Schauinsland map on **CT 146**. You decided to take the hike from the Bergstation to Bärental, and now you're back at your room in Freiburg, where you want to describe the day's activities for your friend Nils, whom you met at a youth hostel in Wiesbaden and with whom you are corresponding regularly. You have only the one map of the Schauinsland area, and you intend to keep it because it has your notes from the hike on it. You can tell Nils what you did, though, and clearly enough that he gains a good impression of the landscape. Retrace your hike, being sure to tell him where the path went down (*hinunter*) and up (*hinauf*) to various points of interest, and tell him what you saw and whom you met along the way. He's an avid hiker and won't want to miss a bit of your excursion.

> Lieber Nils,
>
> Heute früh bin ich mit der Schauinslandbahn zur Bergstation hinaufgefahren. . . .

Stage 2   Now look again at your notes from the **B2** HÖREN exercise, in which Herr Jost was leading the small group of hikers along the Hochwang. They had a wonderful time, for the hike came off with very few mishaps. No one forgot any supplies, although there was some grousing about having to carry so much, and everyone enjoyed the night in a hay shed in the Fideriser Heuberge. Write an account of the trip through the eyes of Fräulein Wehling, being sure to tell what various people wanted to do and what had to be done for everything to come off smoothly (Don't forget to mention the mouse in the hay shed.).

STRUCTURAL EXERCISES

Note: Be sure you have reviewed your chapter grammar and read the relevant sections in the reference grammar.

1   Each of the following pairs of sentences describes two events. Use various subordinating conjunctions (*wenn, daß, weil, als, bevor, damit*) to combine the sentences in each pair. Be sure that the resulting sentence makes sense.

> **example:**   Wir waren lange im Museum.   Wir finden Museen interessant.
> **Wir waren lange im Museum, weil wir Museen interessant finden.**

>   1.   Ingrid hat das Deutsche Museum besucht. Sie war in München.
>   2.   Sie wollte vom Vater DM 4 haben. Sie hatte kein Geld für den Katalog.
>   3.   Sie hat das Geld gebracht. Sie konnte den Katalog kaufen.
>   4.   Ich war im Museum. Ich war schon drei Tage in München.
>   5.   Ingrid ist über Mittag im Museum. Sie kann dort essen.
>   6.   Ingrid ist um Mitternacht im Museum? Es ist möglich.

2   Write in either *wenn* or *als* according to the sense of each sentence.

>   1.   Das Wetter war herrlich, _____ wir in Nürnberg waren.
>   2.   Wir wollten immer am Wochenende wandern, _____ wir 1984 in Basel wohnten.

3. _____ du genug Geld hast, können wir Karten für die Schauinslandbahn kaufen.

4. _____ dein Vater kommt, wandere ich gern mit ihm.

5. Wir konnten zum Schauinslandgipfel hinaufsteigen, _____er letzten Winter hier war.

6. _____ ich jünger war, wollte ich immer Bergwanderungen machen.

3   Susanne Zeyse has kept an unusual diary, one which she writes <u>at the beginning of each day</u> rather than at the end. (She says she can be more optimistic that way.) Assuming that the day she describes below went as planned, peek into her diary and rewrite it from the more common perspective.

     example: Heute schreibe ich einen Brief an Eduard.
                      Heute habe ich einen Brief an Eduard geschrieben.

1. Heute fahre ich mit Vater in die Berge.

2. Wir machen eine lange Wanderung über den Ofenpaß.

3. Ich glaube, wir wandern etwa sieben Stunden.

4. Emil geht mit uns. Er ist immer so lustig.

5. Erich bleibt zu Hause. Er muß sein Zimmer aufräumen.

6. Annemarie ist heute auch mit uns. Sie will heute nicht arbeiten.

7. Wir steigen über den Paß, und dann essen wir.

8. Ich bringe Käsebrote mit.

9. Die Getränke kann Vater tragen. Er hat einen größeren Rucksack.

10. Wir kommen um 6 Uhr wieder nach Hause. Das Auto funktioniert natürlich wunderbar!

4   No matter how much good will Susanne brings to the venture, her father still has to do most of the work. But he wants to encourage Susanne and Annemarie to help him. On the last trip he was heard to issue the following orders to Susanne when she was the only one along. Since things rarely change, he'll be saying the same thing today — only to two people instead of one. Change each sentence accordingly:

1. Wach bitte auf, Susanne! Wir müssen gehen!

2. Iß den Toast, sonst hast du einen Riesenhunger unterwegs.

3. Hilf mir mal die Rucksäcke in den Wagen tun.

4. Bring diesmal die Wanderschuhe mit. Du hast sie letztes Mal vergessen.

5. Und vergiß den Regenschutz nicht.

6. Sei vorsichtig mit meinem Rucksack. Die Thermosflasche ist drin.

5   Susanne's little brother, Erich, has found her diary and cut it into bits with his new scissors. See if you can reconstruct her sentences before she comes home from the hike.

     example: ein Erich Dummkopf ist.   **Erich ist ein Dummkopf.**

1. regnet es heute wenn, eine finden Hütte dann trockene wir.

2. zwischen der der mir gut Wald der sehr Bergstation Talstation und gefällt.

3. der gehört Rucksack der Vater Flagge rote meinem große mit deutschen.

4. Mutter es leid mitkommt nicht mir daß tut.

5. Tagebuch tut weh mein Erich der wenn ihm nimmt Kopf.

√ CHECK YOUR PROFICIENCY

CAN YOU:
__ ask about what you will be seeing in museums?
__ talk at some length about preparations for a hike?
__ talk at some length about what you did in a museum or on a hike?

DO YOU REMEMBER HOW TO:
__ describe minor medical problems and give advice?
__ compare things of equal or unequal quality?
__ give reasons for your opinions?
__ ask for things for other people?

HÖREN

Stage 1

A1 Just listen several times to the dialogs for *Gespräche 1: Zimmervermittlung*. Talk along if you like.

A2 Practice saying the dialog lines. Use your "pause" button if you have one.

B1 Conversation 1
1. What clues tell you how many people are looking for a room?
2. Will they spend more than they planned for the room, or less?
3. What service will the *Zimmervermittlung* provide for them? What tells you?
4. In what part of the city is the hotel located? What is its name?

Conversation 2
1. What clue do you have to this person's profession?
2. What sort of room is he looking for?
3. Write the phrases that tell you a) in general and b) specifically where the hotel is.
4. How long will the person be staying at the hotel? What is the name of the hotel?

Conversation 3
1. What sort of hotel are the people looking for? Why do they need a hotel?
2. What difficulty do they encounter?
3. What suggestion are they given for overcoming that difficulty?
4. In what way will their accommodations not be terribly convenient?
5. What is the name of the town they want to see?

Stage 2

B2 Conversation 1
1. What is the name of the first person you hear?
2. What restrictions does the owner of the house seem to have on the room?
3. How was the owner informed about the people's visit? When?
4. What day is it? For how many days do the people want the room? Why?

Conversation 2
1. Why are these people in this city?
2. What speaks in favor of a room in the city center?
3. Do these people have a car? How do you know?
4. How many people will be getting together this evening? What if it were a year from now?

Conversation 3
1. Where does this conversation take place?
2. How long will the people stay here?
3. What difficulty has arisen?
4. What advice did the people receive in the *Zimmervermittlung*?
5. Where might the people well be spending their second night? Which place is closer to the center of town? What two clues tell you?

C

1B:7.1.1-2 Is the stock market up or down today? What is the value of the dollar? What is the change from yesterday? <u>Segment 2</u>: Observe the use of *steigen*. [P1, P2]

2A:2.1.3 What restriction does the announcer place on items offered through the radio "Fleamarket"? When can you start calling in to offer items? When does the program begin? [7, 12]

EVALUATE YOUR LISTENING COMPREHENSION

By now you should have listened — often several times — to almost all of the segments in the collection of broadcast materials. It's time to pause and see just how much progress you've made since your first listening exercise. If you were to return to the early chapters and do a few exercises in each (something we indeed recommend), you would doubtless find them much easier now. You might also notice an increase in your endurance — your ability to comprehend large amounts of lower-level material — and in your tolerance for language distinctly above your level. What then seemed like an endless babble may well appear now much shorter and filled with bits and pieces which you can understand individually, and which, when you put them together, show that you can understand what you need to understand even if you haven't gotten every word.

The following items offer a self-check of lower-level listening proficiency. If you are quite confident of your listening skills, skip the material in the rest of this section and wait for the check of higher-level competence in the next chapter.

1B:8.1.2   List the two sets of winning lottery numbers. Since the announcer repeats them, you should be able to get them all correctly without replaying the tape. What day does the announcer mention?

2B:5.2.2   Where does the news event occur? Which people will the new social workers help with what problems?

The first exercise checked your ability to manage simple information presented quickly. The targets of the second were large-scale comprehension and willingness to guess at meanings. As a further check and exercise, try skipping through **C** tape #1, listening to whatever comes up and taking notes accordingly. By now you should be able to recognize, for example, a weather report. If that is what you find yourself hearing, then take notes on temperature, precipitation, sky conditions, and wind direction. Your ability to recognize low-level factual information, like numbers, dates, colors, family terms, and common objects, should be solid. You should also be able to understand how things relate to each other in space (*in Berlin, nach Berlin, aus Berlin*) and time (*heute abend* vs. *morgen abend, will* vs. *wollte*).

SPRECHEN

Stage 1   You ask for accommodations for yourself and your companion in a quiet part of town.

1. The accommodations suggested are too expensive for you. Ask about alternatives in location and facilities.

2. The place sounds just fine. Ask the person at the desk to call the hotel for you and ask whether the room is still available.

3. Ask the desk clerk to see whether the people could hold the room for another few hours. You want to do some errands in the city before taking public transportation to the hotel.

4. You and your 22-year old friend are dead tired. All rooms in the city are booked already. Ask about directions to the cheapest type of accommodations you have encountered on your trip so far.

Stage 2   1. You are waiting for the bus and overhear another couple — obviously foreigners — talking about finding a room in the very same place recommended to you a few minutes ago in the *Zimmervermittlung*. Be friendly, especially when they ask you whether this is the right bus line to the hotel. (Don't worry: there's room for you all there!) In the course of some small talk, find out whether they might be a nice couple to explore the city with this evening.

2. The *Zimmervermittlung* in this city is not a staffed office, but an outdoor shelter with a series of pictures of hotels describing the facilities in each. The two telephones next to the display are busy, and there is a line of anxious tourists in back of each one. You enter a nearby place of business, explain your predicament, and try to convince the clerk that you should be allowed to use the phone. Be sure to use your new inventory of polite phrases, and to offer to pay for the call.

3. The *Zimmervermittlung* has given you the names of two very different hotels in town. One is near the city center, very swanky, with enticing facilities and services. The other is on the outskirts of the city, with what you are told is an outstanding kitchen specializing in local dishes. The second promises to be a good deal less luxurious than the first, with few of the amenities. Explain the situation to your companion and try to convince him/her that the choice you have made is the right one. Give good reasons for your decision.

4.   You are the companion. Try to convince your friend that he/she has made the wrong decision. Be sure to give solid reasons for your opinion.

LESEN

Stage 1   Consult p. 6 of the **ST** *Drucksachen*. Imagine that you are the clerk at the Trier *Zimmervermittlung*, with the job of communicating to people who know very little German the essential information about **a)** an inexpensive hotel and **b)** an expensive hotel. Now practice the same task, but this time with someone whose German is quite good — for example, that Japanese couple you've seen from time to time during your travels in the Federal Republic.

Stage 2   In Preliminary Chapter 2 you first looked at a list of facilities in a hotel. Now return to that document (**CT 321**) and look for some specific information. (You may find a dictionary helpful.) How many clues can you find that locate this city in a Warsaw Pact country? In what city does this hotel seem to be located? Consider the articles this hotel will lend (*ausleihen*) to its guests; do people seem to stay here mainly for business or for pleasure? What words tell you that this hotel will make dining reservations for you at various restaurants throughout the city? If you wanted to keep jewelry in a safe place, does this hotel provide the necessary security — or are you warned simply not to bring valuables with you? Could you cash a traveler's check here at 6 a.m.? If so (or if not), where would you go to do that? How long does it take the hotel laundry to wash things for the guests? What instructions are the guests given if they want to have something laundered? How does one get in touch with the hotel laundry? What is the hotel check-out time? Which of the requests and admonitions in the third column seem unusual to you? What are the words for: hair dryer, ironing, valuables, money exchange, (hotel) reception, (time) extension, day of departure, and events?

SCHREIBEN

Stage 1   Return to the Stage 2 SCHREIBEN exercise in Chapter 2 (*Im Hotel*), which uses the Trier map and the list of hotels and restaurants from that city. Now that you have chosen appropriate rooms for your relatives' visit to Trier, write a note to Mr. Erich Honecker, a resident of Trier who speaks a little English and has agreed to meet your family at the station, accompany them to their hotels, and give them a city tour the next day. Tell Mr. Honecker, who does not read English, which hotels you have selected for your family, and give him the reasons for your choice so that he can explain everything to your family. Be sure to ask him to tell your family that you will be meeting them in a couple of days when your living group's trip to Berlin is over.

Stage 2   Look again at the Trier hotel list on p. 6 of the **ST** *Drucksachen*. Write a note to the *Verkehrsverein der Stadt Trier*, the Trier Chamber of Commerce. Explain to them the plans your 30-member garden club has for a visit to their city, and ask whatever questions you think are relevant to the visit. Be sure to tell them how many people are involved, where they would like to stay, and why they would like to stay there. Assure them that your group is interested in many different summer activities. Begin your note *"Sehr geehrte Herren, . . . "*

WOHNUNG

HÖREN

Stage 1

A1   Just listen several times to the dialogs for *Gespräche 2: Wohnung*. Talk along if you like.

A2   Practice saying the dialog lines. Use your "pause" button if you have one.

B1   Listen several times to the description of a room in a house. Someone is telling where various articles of furniture have been put. Draw an outline of a rectangular room and write in the articles according to what you hear on the tape. Be sure to place the door and windows in their proper position. When your drawing is complete, be ready to describe the room fully to a classmate.

B2 In this conversation you hear Gerhard and Luise talking about various rooms in their apartments. Make a chart such as the following to take notes on the conversation. Fill in information about each room for each person. Be prepared to discuss the similarities and differences with a classmate.

ZIMMER	GERHARD	LUISE
Wohnzimmer		
Schlafzimmer		
Küche		

C

1B:6.3.1 What is the male speaker's occupation? What household appliance is discussed? Observe the use of *werden* in the phrase *"Da wird's dann teuer."* [5]

1B:6.3.2 What can you do with this appliance? **a)** cook; **b)** clean; **c)** refrigerate; **d)** get rid of garbage.

1B:6.3.4 What can you do with this product? **a)** cook; **b)** clean; **c)** refrigerate; **d)** get rid of garbage. [5]

1B:6.3.5 Fill in the blanks: *"Ich nehme nur Ajax ___ _____ _____, _____ _____ _____ glänzt, _____ _____ _____ ___ aus."* [5, 13]

1B:6.3.7 What product do the Ungeheuer people sell? How much does one of their special items cost? How long does the sale last?

1B:6.4.1 Observe the Chapter 16 expression *"Meine Güte"* at the start. How can you tell that the announcer is speaking to the men in the audience? [5, 9]

2B:5.2.3 What is the title of the pamphlet highlighted in the feature? How long is it? How much does it cost?

2B:5.3.2 The broadcast comes direct from the convention and exposition center in Koblenz, where a home products show is being held. What day(s) might it be? How large (in metrical units) is the exhibit space in the year the report was broadcast (1986)? How does that compare with the exhibit area in the first year the event was staged? Collect some figures about attendance.

SPRECHEN

Stage 1 1. You and your beloved have just been shopping for some clothing: a new jacket, socks, underwear, a skirt, a suit, a raincoat, running shoes, and a cap for the baby. Decide where you will keep each of the items in your new apartment. When you have decided, tell your beloved that you suddenly don't feel very well — but you do feel well enough to remind him/her where to put each of the things.

2. You have been preparing for your family's visit for days now. You've picked up in the apartment and scrubbed it from top to bottom, and you've spent money for fresh flowers for the kitchen table. But now your family has called and said they'll be coming next week instead of this afternoon. Tell a close friend what has happened and how you feel.

3. Your well-meaning friend has just put away everything you bought — but into the wrong places. Be polite, but firm, in correcting the errors.

Stage 2 1. Your family has just arrived for a visit while you're studying at the University of Graz. They have lots of luggage — more than you can accommodate in your student apartment. You advise them to leave some of their boxes in the luggage locker at the train station, to put their suitcases into your friend's car for the trip to the apartment, and to bring their hand luggage and shopping bags with them to the taxi.

2. Now you have arrived at your apartment. Decide with your friend where each of the suitcases and packages should go — in your apartment or his/hers, and where in each.

3. Among other things, your family has brought you some bad news from home regarding the health of a distant relative. Express your regrets, ask how the relative is doing now, and say how much you like that person. Also say a few words about what you did when you and the now ailing relative last saw each other.

4.   For some reason, your father is taking a lot of time arranging his affairs in the city. You had planned to have supper together and go to a concert, but that might not be possible now. Speculate about what you will do a) if he comes soon and b) if he doesn't show up for another hour. Then tell your two younger siblings to go looking for him.

LESEN

Stage 1   Look at the apartment advertisements on **CT 153**. For each one, decide whether the money you are paying for your room this year would be enough to finance the apartment abroad. Find the apartment that seems best to fit your style of living, your pocketbook, and your space needs. What if you were sharing the apartment? What would have to be different?

Stage 2   Compare carefully the English and German versions of text from an East German government brochure on **CT 155**. Underline parts of the German text that are not translated into English. Note where the sentence structure of the German text differs significantly from that of the English. Does the English sound "translated"? Why (not)? What conclusions do you reach about the challenges of translation in general?

SCHREIBEN

Stage 1   Look again at the apartment advertisements on **CT 153**. For each apartment, list in order the features you find most attractive. Now write a note to your friends in Konstanz, telling them about the two apartments that you think might best fit your needs. Be sure to tell them why you think so. Having compared the two, choose one. Be sure to invite your friends to come visit you once you have moved in and organized everything.

Stage 2   Look again at your **B2** HÖREN exercise, in which you heard about Gerhard's and Luise's apartments. Your friends in Konstanz know these two people, and they will be delighted to hear how they are doing. Write another note to Konstanz in which you tell about either Gerhard's place or Luise's. Then tell your friends why you think your new apartment is really superior to both.

STRUCTURAL EXERCISES

1   Be polite! Change the tone of the following snippets from the *Zimmervermittlung* to conform to your gentle and considerate nature.

       example: Stehen Sie auf!   **Würden Sie bitte aufstehen?**

    1.   Bitte, rufen Sie für uns das Hotel Seegarten an.
    2.   Kommen Sie sofort! Ich muß in die Stadt.
    3.   Gib mir mein Geld zurück.
    4.   Haben Sie immer noch ein Doppelzimmer frei?
    5.   Seien Sie in einer Stunde dort. Sonst verlieren Sie das Zimmer.
    6.   Zeigen Sie mir den Fahrplan!
    7.   Wie teuer ist das?

2   Your companion has ventured some opinions with which you agree. Support the statements you hear without sounding like an echo chamber.

       example: Das Hotel ist ruhiger.   **Richtig — das Hotel ist nicht so laut.**

    1.   Das Doppelzimmer kostet nicht sehr viel.
    2.   Mit der Tramlinie 5 ist es näher.
    3.   Es ist besser, wenn wir sofort fahren.
    4.   In der Pension sieht man weniger Touristen.
    5.   Das Hotel Lindauer Hof ist teurer als die Jugendherberge.
    6.   Das Hotel Möwe ist kleiner als das Hotel Seeblick.
    7.   Beim Imbiß muß man nicht so lange auf das Essen warten.

3 You have been very busy putting things where they belong, but all of a sudden you're not sure you've done a good job. First tell your friend where the things are, and then suggest where you two should move them.

> **example:** a. Ich habe den Fernseher in die Ecke gestellt.
> b. **Der Fernseher steht in der Ecke.**   **Stellen wir ihn ins Schlafzimmer.**

1. Ich habe den Stuhl neben den Tisch gestellt.
    a.
    b.

2. Ich habe den Schreibtisch ins Schlafzimmer getan.
    a.
    b.

3. Ich habe den Teppich auf den Küchenboden gelegt.
    a.
    b.

4. Den Schrank habe ich neben die Treppe gestellt.
    a.
    b.

5. Das kalte Bier habe ich auf den Herd gestellt.
    a.
    b.

6. Den Müll habe ich ins Badezimmer getragen.
    a.
    b.

7. Ich habe meine alten Schuhe unter das Bett geworfen.
    a.
    b.

4 A person in your living group is accusing you of doing things wrong. Set the record straight by saying that you have either not done those things or already done them — depending on what puts you in the better light.

> **example:** Du sollst die Wohnung saubermachen.
> **Aber ich habe sie schon saubergemacht!**

1. Du sollst mal im Wohnzimmer aufräumen. Es sieht wie ein Saustall aus.
2. Ruf Gabriele an. Sonst kommt sie heute abend nicht.
3. Du gibst für die Lebensmittel immer zu viel Geld aus. Sei doch sparsamer.
4. Vergiß nicht: du mußt den Schlüssel am Eingang abgeben.
5. Es ist schon neun Uhr. Du mußt deine Sachen auspacken.
6. Trag doch den Müll hinaus. Hier stinkt's.
7. Bleib nicht immer in deinem Zimmer. Du sollst mal ausgehen.

√ CHECK YOUR PROFICIENCY

CAN YOU:
__ use the subjunctive to express hesitation or politeness?
__ create the comparative form of adjectives and adverbs?
__ use common prepositions with appropriate cases to describe motion and location?
__ describe <u>past</u> activities when verbs like*anrufen* or *auspacken* are used?

DO YOU REMEMBER HOW TO:
__ express politeness with other means than the subjunctive?
__ use *nicht so* __ as an alternate to the comparative?
__ use *nach* and *zu* (with dative case!) to express motion?
__ use separable-prefix verbs in the <u>present</u> tense (*Sie sagt, daß der Zug bald <u>abfährt</u>*.)?

Chapter 16
STADTPLAN / FAHRPLAN

HÖREN

Stage 1

A1 Just listen several times to the dialogs for *Gespräche 1: Stadtplan / Fahrplan*. Talk along if you like.

A2 Practice saying the dialog lines. Use your "pause" button if you have one.

B1 Listen carefully to the conversation between two visitors to München. Each took different public transportation and saw different things. Write down what kind of transportation each used, what each one saw, and what was noteworthy about each place.

Stage 2

B2 Listen to the plans several visitors to München have for the day. Take notes on how Herr Albrecht, Frau Gunter, and Frau Helbling intend to reach their destinations, what they plan to do there, and why they have each chosen these activities.

C1
1A:4.2.3 List the number and location of the station you are listening to. What does the announcer think many of her listeners are doing? What time of the year might it be? Listening only <u>once</u>, list the basic information about the traffic problems she describes: highway stretch and, where she gives it, the road number and the length of the tie-up. [3]

C2
1B:6.2.6 Whatever the business is selling, where is it located in relation to Deckendorf? What customer convenience does it offer? Which season is mentioned? If you are trying to figure out what is being advertised, consider what kinds of things are suggested by the mention of a season and the provision of the location of one specific store (examples: diamonds, boats for water skiing), and also which things are unlikely under those circumstances (examples: toothpaste, records, brand-name appliances). Final hint until Chapter 18: The item is named repeatedly, and the word appears in a longer German word that many American hikers or lovers of oom-pah music would recognize.

1B:6.3.6 When is the Outdoor Exposition open (days of week, times of day)? What do the sponsors offer to encourage people to drive to it? [13]

1B:6.4.2 Observe the use of *sein* with *gefahren*. When did Frau Schmidt make her trip to the furniture store in Wolfratshausen? Did she buy anything? [5]

SPRECHEN

Stage 1
1. You are at a kiosk, where you want to find out what sorts of things will be happening in the city where you will be for the next three weeks. You also need to buy a map of the city.

2. The clerk at the kiosk offers you a choice of materials. Echo the choice, thus gaining time to make up your mind while people in back of you are growing impatient. Now choose the correct things.

3. You made a mistake in your choice, although it is possible the mistake was not your fault: You got the old edition of the schedule of events, and the map of the city seems to have been written for someone who speaks French, not German. Having taken the purchase back to the kiosk, make the best case you can for an exchange.

4. The city map you bought shows one-way streets and parking facilities, which are important for people with cars, but you've arrived by train and would rather have a map showing various kinds of public transportation. Do your best to convince the clerk at the Kiosk that you shouldn't have to pay extra for the correct map.

Stage 2
1. You don't care for the atmosphere in the Hofbräuhaus, where things have become a bit rowdy since you arrived two hours ago. Someone bumped your head with his elbow, and you don't care for all the noise and forced camaraderie. Explain in convincing detail to your German hosts why you'd rather try your luck elsewhere — at the Viktualienmarkt, for example.

2.   You are the host of the person above. Apologize for the psychic wounds and, using your map of München, tell the person how to find the Viktualienmarkt.

3.   You have the choice of taking the bus or the U-Bahn to your destination. Choose one, giving good reasons for your choice.

4.   You mistakenly took the U-Bahn in the wrong direction, which will cause you to be at least 45 minutes late to a supper engagement on the outskirts of the city. Call your host and be as contrite as you can, begging forgiveness for your silly mistake. Tell your host when you will be arriving.

5.   While waiting for the U-Bahn, you see a flower stand. You resolve to bring your host an even bigger bouquet than the one you have been carrying around for nearly an hour now. After entering the flower store, explain to the clerk what has happened and ask whether the flowers you brought with you can be incorporated into a larger and more impressive bouquet. Be sure to be polite, but direct: You don't want to miss the U-Bahn!

LESEN

Stage 1 In the lower right corner of the Mannheim city map on **CT 310** you will find the first part of the word *Planetarium*, a popular attraction described in the brochure on **CT 342**. What words or groups of words in the brochure would be especially important for you if you were the driver of a car? Become familiar with Mannheim by tracing the route to the planetarium from **a)** the Hauptbahnhof, **b)** the Nationaltheater, **c)** the Schloß.

Stage 2 Consult the Mannheim city map while you ponder where to eat after the last Thursday presentation in the planetarium. The restaurants in the city are listed in the *Gaststättenverzeichnis* on **CT 322**. Taking note of the column *Lage / Umgebung* in the list, find on the map where you would go for a Greek meal. (Are you sure the restaurant you chose is open?) Would the French restaurant be open? What choices would you have if you wanted to eat after the last planetarium show on a Saturday? Which of the restaurants you found is closest to the planetarium?

SCHREIBEN

Stage 1 Using the *Bildwörterbuch* nature display on **CT 300-01**, and remembering what you did after the visit to the planetarium, write a brief diary entry summarizing the day's activities. You should include high points of your visit to the planetarium as well as the memorable meal afterward and the eventful walk back to your hotel.

Stage 2 Some Austrian friends of yours were to meet you in front of the planetarium, but you had to hurry away to buy tickets for your train trip back to Bremen. You decide to leave them a note at the planetarium, telling them how to get to the Hauptbahnhof and where you can be found there. You would like them to see the historic Friedrichsplatz on their way. Give them appropriate directions, including a summary of what they will see between the planetarium and the station.

U-BAHN — S-BAHN

HÖREN

Stage 1

A1 Just listen several times to the dialogs for *Gespräche 2: U-Bahn — S-Bahn*. Talk along if you like.

A2 Practice saying the dialog lines. Use your "pause" button if you have one.

B1 While you look at your transit map of München on **CT 166**, listen to what a visitor to that city is saying about the public transportation network. Decide whether each of the three statements is true or false; if part of a statement is false, change it to make it correct.

C1
2A:1.1.2   How old was the counterfeiter the police caught in Nürnberg? Where did he manufacture the funny money? Just what was his scheme for passing it? What two smaller and very elementary words comprise the German word for 'counterfeiter'? [6]

2A:1.1.3   As the story is reported, how long have the rescuers been searching through the rubble of the hotel? How many victims are dead so far? How much hope is there for the rest? [2, 6]

C2
2B:5.4.2   A Catholic clergyman delivers a little talk about St. Joseph, whose name-day (*Namenstag*) is celebrated in heavily Catholic areas like Bavaria. Observe the use of the Chapter 16 connector *ob*, and indeed of other verb-last conjunctions, like *daß*. How many saints' days were once celebrated officially? [10]

EVALUATE YOUR LISTENING COMPREHENSION

Chapter 15 contained a self-evaluation of lower-level comprehension. Now try these more advanced tasks:

1A:5.2.1-5   Listening only <u>once</u> to these more difficult weather reports, can you note — all correctly — the temperatures, presence or absence of precipitation, wind direction, and period covered by the report? This exercise will test your stamina and speed in processing items that, taken individually, are not very difficult. [9, 14]

1B:6.2.5   Is the man going on a business or a pleasure trip? Is he going alone? Why does he want to be able to speak the local language? What is being advertised: **a**) a travelers' legal protection service; **b**) a language school; **c**) a self-taught language course; **d**) a company that offers jobs to multi-lingual applicants? The final question checks your ability to eliminate possibilities by noting the presence (or absence!) of key vocabulary.

2A:1.4.1   You will hear just the headline summary of a longer news broadcast. The first time you listen, figure out how many news events are being summarized. It's not cheating if you help yourself out by noting when the announcer wets his lips, rustles his paper, or changes tone of voice between stories. Note also which of the stories, if any, mentions your own country; more than a few travelers abroad, in times of fast-developing political crises, have found themselves straining to comprehend at least part of the news broadcast in another language. On second listening, try to list for each story one or two key words that are part of the *Wie, bitte?* vocabulary up to now or are very similar in English and German. The third story is the toughest one; listen for a long word containing *Arbeit*, and for a phrase that includes a number.

SPRECHEN

Stage 1   1.   You ask someone to show you how the automatic ticket machine works. Explain that you are a stranger to this city and have never seen a machine like that before.

2.   You are the person who has been asked about the ticket machine. Explain that you're also not from here and cannot help. Be polite.

3.   You'll be in München for several weeks and ask for advice about what kind of bus ticket to buy. Be sure to explain how often and where you will be riding. (The city map will help you out.)

Stage 2   Continuing to use the city map of München, as well as the transit map on **CT 166**, give advice about public transportation to someone wanting to travel between **a**) the <u>Deutsches Museum</u> and the university; **b**) Freising (north) and Wolfratshausen (south); **c**) the <u>Nationaltheater</u> and <u>Sendlinger Tor</u>.

LESEN

Stage 1   Note the advertisement for the Hotel drei Löwen in the "Erasmus" *Zugbegleiter* on **CT 319**. Why would you be unlikely to take public transportation to the Hauptbahnhof? Which buses could you catch near your hotel to go to Sendlinger Tor? Using the scale above the München map, estimate how long it would take you to walk that distance if you walked 7 km/hr.

Stage 2   Return to the Stage 2 LESEN exercise in the first half of this chapter. What bus lines traverse both of Mannheim's rivers? What buses would one have to take to reach the planetarium from **a)** the Hauptbahnhof, **b)** the Nationaltheater, **c)** the Schloß? Which bus line would take you directly from the planetarium to a restaurant (cf. *Gaststättenverzeichnis*, **CT 322**) where you can enjoy a meal outside on a warm summer evening?

SCHREIBEN

Stage 1   Copy down as carefully as you can the directions given in the second B1 HÖREN exercise, describing a trip from the Universität München to Dachau. Then give directions back to the university. Be sure to correct any mistakes you hear on the tape.

Stage 2   Using words such as *umsteigen*, *Verbindung*, *Fahrschein*, and *Zone*, write a note to that nice Japanese couple you've met repeatedly. They'll want to know how to get to the university in München, where you're studying, from the Starnberger See, where they've been sampling some of the local fish specialties.

STRUCTURAL EXERCISES

1.   Recount important events from your own life, telling just when they took place. The time indicated should be in relation to the present time: "a month ago", "three years ago", etc.

> **example**:   die Schweiz besuchen
> **Ich habe vor einem Jahr die Schweiz besucht.**

Handy phrases you may want to use are *zum ersten Mal* (for the first time) and *das letzte Mal* (the last time).

> **example**:   Ich habe die Schweiz zum ersten Mal vor fünf Jahren besucht.

2.   Now make sentences relating to your life (*Ich*) and that of your family (*Wir*). Be sure to use the appropriate helping verbs when talking about the past. Choose from the following and add others of your own:

> ein Museum besuchen / ein Haus bauen / ein Auto kaufen / in den Bergen wandern /
> mit dem Zug fahren / den Freund (die Freundin) kennenlernen / meinen Geburtstag
> feiern / klassische Musik hören / meine erste Semesterarbeit schreiben / aufstehen /
> fernsehen / tanzen / Deutsch anfangen / nach Hause fahren

3.   Prepare for class conversation with your regular partner by anticipating the questions:

> "Wann (an welchem Tag) war das genau?" and "Wo war das genau?"
> **example**:
> So, du hast die Schweiz zum ersten Mal vor 5 Jahren besucht. Wann war das genau?
> — Das war am 15. Mai 1984. Wir waren in einem alten Volkswagen . . . .

4.   Having talked so much in German class, you now have laryngitis. Using the phrases given in the first exercise (above), write out directions to a classmate who will be interviewing someone else. Above all, you want to find out not <u>when</u> the actions took place, but <u>whether</u> they have taken place at all.

> **example**:   ein Auto kaufen   **Frag ihn, ob er ein Auto gekauft hat.**

√ CHECK YOUR PROFICIENCY

CAN YOU:
__ obtain maps and timetables?
__ locate landmarks on a city map?
__ discuss parking facilities and options?
__ describe how to use mass transit?

DO YOU REMEMBER HOW TO:
__ describe the arrangement of an apartment?
__ talk about your experiences on an outing?
__ deal with minor medical problems?
__ express your plans for the immediate future?

HÖREN

Stage 1

A1 Just listen several times to the dialogs for *Gespräche 1: Mensa*. Talk along if you like.

A2 Practice saying the dialog lines. Use your "pause" button if you have one.

B1

1. How many students will there be all together when the couple returns from Berlin?
2. What are the two sets of plans regarding the Chiemsee?
3. Which plan is adopted? Why?
4. How many will be going to the Chiemsee? Why not all? When are they going?
5. What sorts of activities will take place after the visit to the Chiemsee?

Stage 2

B2

1. What do the initials WG seem to stand for?
2. Write down words and phrases that express the positive aspects of Sigrid's life.
3. What are *Nebenkosten*? Why are they so low?
4. How many people seem to be living where Sigrid lives?
5. What are some apparent disadvantages to dormitory life?
6. What German words seem to convey the English meanings "sit" and "natives"?

B3

1. What two main topics are discussed?
2. Name the countries that are mentioned in the dialog.
3. Where is the foreign student from? Does he have a scholarship?
4. What time of year does it seem to be? What are the clues?
5. How well does the German student know the geologist?
6. What German words seem to convey the English meanings "member", "earn, afford", "be enough", "reliable", and "subleaser"?

B4

1. After all is said and done, is the first person hungry or not?
2. Is the problem of a medical nature?
3. What German words seem to convey the English meanings "appeal to", "borrow", "either . . . or"?

C

2A:2.2.1

1. How long, according to the announcer, has Vico Toriani been in show-biz? Something the interviewer says in his first remarks will help you pin down the entertainer's age as well — he may not be 65 after all.

2. Ninety seconds into the interview, after he modestly discusses his charm, Toriani tells how he began to make it big right after World War II. Transcribe his remarks, beginning: *"Es ist halt so. Ich hatte doch sehr viel Glück* [good luck]. *Ich meine, der erste Glücksgedanke* [lucky thought] *war ja der, daß*

_____ _____ _____ _____, ____ _____ _____ _____ _____ ____,

_____ _____ ____ *gehen."*

3. Three minutes into the conversation, the interviewer asks Toriani whether his being Swiss has aided his career. What does Toriani value most about being Swiss? Note also as much as you can about his birth, youth, marriage, and current residence. [2, 9, 13]

SPRECHEN

Stage 1   1.   Introduce yourself and three friends without repeating the phrase in which you provide names.

       2.   A new acquaintance has assumed you are from New York.
   • You're not from New York. Explain why your acquaintance shouldn't have assumed you were.
   • You are from New York. Explain why your acquaintance should have assumed you were.

       3.   Think of three common ethnic food dishes. Tell why you do or don't like each item, or why you have no opinion.

Stage 2   1.   Recall the several kinds of sausages you have been exposed to thus far in *Wie, bitte?* Assume you have gained some personal familiarity with them. Express and justify your preferences. Try to say more than *gut* or *schlecht*.

       2.   How many ingredients of the following food items can you name in German? Taco; omelette; milkshake; pizza; chili; New England boiled dinner; sushi.

       3.   Explain the placement or final location of the various ingredients of: **a**) a hamburger; **b**) a banana split; **c**) a taco salad.

       4.   State and support your recommendation about food near your: **a**) college or university; **b**) home; **c**) workplace.

       5.   Describe how someone you know usually **a**) shops for groceries; **b**) takes care of his/her apartment.

LESEN

Stage 1   Consult your several menus and jot down food or drink items that contain national adjectives (English examples: "Irish Coffee", "Polish sausage").

Stage 2   1.   Consult your menus again and try to figure out why *russische Eier* have that name.

       2.   Both English and German can pose problems when it comes to talking about nationalities. (What are the citizens of Afghanistan called, and what is the adjectival form?). Read section 1 on **CT 172**, concentrating on the pattern: *X-isch* often = *aus, in, von X.* Imagine that you have communicated with people in or from these countries: Ireland, Iran, Belgium, Iceland, Poland, Mexico, Brazil, the Soviet Union, Japan, Australia, New Zealand, the Netherlands. Then experiment with the pattern

          Ich habe mit ein__ _____ Freund(in) _____ gesprochen.

Then check your dictionary to see how well you were able to guess the nationalities.

SCHREIBEN

Stage 1   You're in München and you're off to buy exotic foods and local ingredients for exotic dishes. Your destinations are the <u>Viktualienmarkt</u>, the open-air market just south of <u>Marienplatz</u>, and the nearby <u>Alois Dallmayr</u> store, a world-famous gourmet emporium. Make a shopping list of foreign foods you want to buy ready-made, or of local ingredients for exotic dishes you will concoct yourself. Use these patterns:

          indisches Bier   Hackfleisch für indisches Reisfleisch

Stage 2   You are working in a German-speaking country for a subsidiary of an American company. The company wants to celebrate the Fourth of July, but in a cosmopolitan manner, with plenty of international, ethnic, and American regional food. It's your job to sketch out the poster for the picnic. Besides providing the customary information about when and where, list some of the food and drink items. You might offer short explanations. The Mannheim restaurant list on **CT 322** and the ad for Sam's nightclub in **CT 197** can offer inspiration for juicy phrases.

        example: Dos Equis (mexikanisches Bier)

UNIVERSITÄT

HÖREN

Stage 1

A1   Just listen several times to the dialogs for *Gespräche 2: Universität*. Talk along if you like.

A2   Practice saying the dialog lines. Use your "pause" button if you have one.

B1
1. For what reasons is the first person not studying biology?
2. Why does the first person feel that biology is a restrictive major?
3. What are the second person's plans?
4. Why are these plans especially felicitous?
5. What German words in the *Gespräche* seem to be the equivalent of: minor, master's (degree), research year?

B2
1. The first person you hear is working his way through college. What are his jobs?
2. How far along in his studies is he?
3. What sort of a bibliography is he working on?
4. What German words in the *Gespräche* seem to be the equivalent of: put together, academic fields, hired, tutoring.

Stage 2

B3
1. Von welchen zwei Ländern hört man in diesem Gespräch?
2. Was studieren diese Studenten wohl <u>nicht</u>?
3. Von welchen traditionellen Hauptfächern spricht man?
4. Was lernt man in diesen Fächern besonders gut?
5. Warum scheint heute ein praktisches Wissen so wichtig zu sein?
6. Was soll man vor allem auf der Universität lernen?
7. Welche deutschen Wörter im Gespräch geben folgende englische Ausdrücke wieder: *revolves, in agreement, solve, don't get so excited.*

B4
1. Was sind die positiven Seiten vom Sport?
2. Was sind die negativen Seiten?
3. Warum hat die eine Person so wenig Zeit?
4. Was bedeutet für die andere Person "junge Leute"?
5. Welche deutschen Wörter im Gespräch geben folgende englische Ausdrücke wieder: *kinds of sports, moves around, required, exhausted.*

C

1A:2.2.2   When and on what station will the educational program (*Schulfunk*) be broadcast? When and in what languages, other than German, could you hear the news? What station are you listening to "now"? What topic will the psychologist discuss, and when? [8]

1B:8.2.2   See how many of the sports events you can identify; many have international names or are simply English words (for more vocabulary see the *Bildwörterbuch* display on **CT 304-05**). Note down at least a half-dozen words for foreign (=non-German!) nationalities, countries, or cities. Feel free to check the horserace report at the end to see whether you would have won if you had bet your age, the date, or the middle two digits in your Social Security number. [P2]

2A:1.1.1   Traffic in Würzburg is being rerouted around ceremonies marking the beginning of construction of a center for biosciences at the university. How many and which sciences are involved and when is the project to be completed? [4, 6]

2A:1.2.3   What is the title of the new stamp series? How many designs will be issued initially? Observe the word *Dauerserie*, meaning "regular" or "permanent" series. [10, 12]

2A:1.2.4.   Listen for words that have to do with buildings. Who has been attacking them, and when? [12]

2A:1.3.3   What nationality terms are used to describe a group that might have attacked the disco? Two people were killed; can you identify them by nationality, age and sex? [1, 13]

2A:1.3.4   Observe the use of the word *Mensch* in this and the preceding segment. How would you translate it if you were in charge of preparing the English-language version of the news?

SPRECHEN

Stage 1
1. Tell what's where at your school; mention at least 5 places.
2. What can a person do to make more friends at your college or university?
3. You just assumed that ⊗ was studying math. Explain why.
4. Why study German? Tell **a)** a friend; **b)** a German; **c)** your German teacher.
5. Describe your study habits — both the good ones and the bad ones.

Stage 2
1. Tell how you got lost on campus when you first arrived.
2. How can a student majoring in _____ keep from getting personally one-sided?
3. What should students majoring in _____ study so they can have an extra edge on the job market?
4. Explain in simple words what the following people study and do: foresters; neurophysiologists; entomologists; stock brokers; civil and mechanical engineers.
5. How did your parents' education resemble or differ from your own?; ("My dad keeps telling how he had to walk miles through the snow to school . . . ")
6. Tell what you recall of your first day at school.

LESEN

Stage 1
1.   Shop through your various printed materials and construct from them a specialized vocabulary suitable to your major or hobby. Aim at 20 words. Examples: Your major is history, so from **CT 344-45** you list items like *Krieg* and *Bundespräsident*; if it's geology, use the *Lurgrotte* brochure on p. 33 of the **ST** *Drucksachen* and list *unterirdisch* or *Schluchten*.

2.   Look at the museum overview on **CT 335**. Pick five employees of a range of establishments and write down the subjects they likely studied in college.

Stage 2   Look at the Trier information on pp. 18-19 of the **ST** *Drucksachen*. Pick a tour appropriate to your studies or other interests and plan questions to ask on it.

SCHREIBEN

Stage 1   Make up an outline transcript of 5 subjects you have studied, how long you studied them, and your grades. Here is the German grading scale:

    sehr gut   gut   genügend   mangelhaft   ungenügend

Stage 2   Write a short letter of inquiry about a study-abroad program that pertains to your major or other special interests. Tell enough about yourself that the people at the other end can advise you properly about coursework, finances, foreign language skills, etc. See the Afterword on **CT 270-73** for some ideas.

STRUCTURAL EXERCISES

1   Nationality adjectives. Convert between the forms *aus X* and *X-isch*.

> **example**: die Studenten aus Amerika = die amerikanischen Studenten

> 1.   Das sind französische Weine. = Das sind Weine _____
> 2.   Das ist eine Studentin aus Japan. = Das ist _____
> 3.   Wir kaufen Bier von Mexiko. = Wir kaufen _____
> 4.   Sie studiert an einer Universität in England. = Sie studiert _____
> 5.   Ich kenne einen indischen Physiker. = Ich kenne _____

2   You're collecting quite a set of souvenirs from all over Europe. List 5 of them; follow this pattern:
Das ist ein__ _____ aus ____ .   Ich habe ein__   _____sch__ _____ gekauft

3   Look at the concert schedule on **CT 8**. Many of the performers have foreign (= non-German) names. List some of them and guess their nationalities. Now do the same with the Freiburg doctors' list on **CT 5**.

> **example**: Janet Marsh. Ich glaube, sie ist Engländerin / aus England.

4   List the souvenirs you have bought for 5 people (family, friends, etc.). Tell whom they're for, using both of the patterns below.

> Das ist eine italienische Kassette <u>für</u> meinen Bruder.

> Ich habe <u>ihm</u> auch Weingläser aus Frankreich gekauft.

5   You and 3 friends decided to treat yourselves to some souvenirs. Tell what you bought; some of the gifts were exchanged within your group, and some of them were kept by the purchaser.

> **example**: I bought Larry a cassette, and he bought himself a poster.

6   Look at **CT 196-97** and pp. 24-25 of the **ST** *Drucksachen*, which are schedules of cultural events. Find events or kinds of events that are repeated, and make a chart telling when and how often they are repeated.

> **example**:   city tour   every day at 3

7   List 5 people, their majors, and why they are studying what they do.

√ CHECK YOUR PROFICIENCY

CAN YOU:
__ carry on a discussion in a student cafeteria?
__ talk about your living accommodations?
__ discuss your studies and your future plans?
__ identify the national origin of foreign students?

DO YOU REMEMBER HOW TO:
__ talk about getting around in a city?
__ find accommodations through a room-finding service?
__ deal with minor medical problems?
__ express your plans for the immediate future?

Ausgabe 1985

Mietvertrag

Herausgegeben vom Verein der Haus- und Grundeigentümer
Chur und Umgebung, **Surselva, Thusis** und **Domat/Ems**

Vermieter	_____
vertreten durch	_____
Mieter	_____
bisherige Adresse	_____

Liegenschaft	_____ Ort
Mietobjekt	_____ Stock
zur Benützung als	_____ für Personen
zur Mitbenützung	_____
	_____

Mietbeginn	_____ mittags 12 Uhr
Kündigung (Art. 1)	-monatlich zum voraus auf Ende März / Ende September
	_____
	Der Vertrag ist frühestens kündbar auf _____

Mietzins (Art. 2, 3 und 4)	Der Nettomietzins beträgt	Fr. _____
	Heizkosten akonto / pauschal	Fr. _____
	Warmwasserkosten akonto / pauschal	Fr. _____
	Treppenhausreinigung	Fr. _____
	TV-Anschluss	Fr. _____
		Fr. _____
	zahlbar monatlich*	Fr. _____

Viertel- / halbjährlich / jährlich* zum voraus.
(Nicht Passendes streichen)

HÖREN

Stage 1

A1   Just listen several times to the dialogs for *Gespräche 1: Kaufhaus*. Talk along if you like.

A2   Practice saying the dialog lines. Use your "pause" button if you have one.

B1   Conversation 1
1. What is the customer looking for?
2. Where is it to be found?
3. What else is located on that floor?
4. How will the customer probably get there?
5. Write down the name of the department where the customer is now.
6. How did the customer get to the store? How do you know?
7. What suggests that the customer might not be alone?

Conversation 2
1. What is the customer shopping for?
2. What time of year is it?
3. What is the customer's size?
4. Does the customer shop for this article often? Is he picky?
5. What seems to be the matter with the selection?

Conversation 3
1. What four gift suggestions does the sales clerk make?
2. Why does the customer reject the second and third suggestions?
3. Which is the least personal?
4. What pressure does the clerk try to apply to the customer?
5. What statement of the customer's would the recipient probably like to hear?
6. Are the customer and the recipient married?
7. What German words seem to convey the English meanings "these days", "sweets", and "suggest"?

Stage 2

B2   Conversation 1
1. In welchem Kaufhaus sind die zwei Personen jetzt?
2. Sind sie Gechwister? Mann und Frau? Ein Liebespaar?
3. Was möchte der Mann gerne kaufen?
4. Hat er diesen Artikel schon gesehen?
5. Was wissen Sie über die Preise im Fachgeschäft?

Conversation 2
1. Was sucht die Kundin?
2. Was sagt der Verkäufer Positives über den Artikel?
3. Welche Größe hat sie wohl anprobiert?
4. Was gefällt der Kundin nicht? Warum?
5. An welche Lösung denkt die Kundin?
6. Wie lange dauert es, bis man das Problem gelöst hat?
7. Das Geschäft befindet sich in einer Großstadt. Welche Großstadt könnte dies wohl sein?

Conversation 3

1. Was ist die Hauptgeschenkkategorie in diesem Gespräch? Welche Geschenkartikel gehören in diese Kategorie?
2. Was werden die Kunden wahrscheinlich kaufen?
3. Was sind die anderen Geschenkvorschläge? Warum kauft man diese Geschenke nicht?
4. Was ist das Verhältnis zwischen diesem Mann und der Frau, die das Geschenk bekommen soll? Zwischen den zwei Frauen?
5. Sieht dieses Paar die andere Frau sehr oft? Wie wissen Sie dies?
6. Was deutet auf das Alter dieses Paares hin?

C1

1B:6.1.3   How many countries — according to the ad, at least — does DHL serve in Europe? elsewhere? [P2]

1B:6.1.4   What quality of fish goes into the product, at least according to Capt. Igloo's claim? [P2, 2 13]

1B:6.2.2   The ad features items of clothing. For each, try to figure out what it is, how much it costs, and what type of person it is intended for. How old is the ad?

1B:6.2.4   In what year did the German national soccer team go to Mexico? [6, 10]

1B:6.2.5   Where is the couple planning to travel? [See the self-evaluation in Chapter 16.]

1B:6.2.6   Is the ad for a department store or a specialty store? What product are they advertising? [16]

1B:6.3.2   What feature of the product does the ad emphasize — a) innovative design; b) bargain price; c) snob appeal; d) traditional design? [15]

1B:6.3.3   Does the ad use *du*- or *Sie*-address? The product is a diet drink; see the *Bildwörterbuch*, **CT 308**, for words for 'thin' and 'fat'.

The ads in the preceding group make heavy use of vocabulary from recent chapters. Associate the words on the left with the companies, products, etc. on the right.

braten	DHL
frisch	fishsticks
Leder	Hertie clothing items
mitmachen	Fuji film
passen	insurance for vacation travel
Polizei	shop in Deckendorf
saftig	Bosch
unmöglich	diet drink

C2   1. The financial market report lists the stocks of two major department store chains, Karstadt and Kaufhof; note their current value and ± change.

1B:7.1.3

2. At the end of the financial report, note the currency exchange rates. If the task seems overwhelming, divide it into smaller ones. On first listening, list just the names of the currencies; on subsequent listening, fill in the numbers. [1, 6]

SPRECHEN

Stage 1   1. A clerk has asked you whether he can be of service. You're just looking, but you're grateful to him anyway.

2. It occurs to you that your spouse has a birthday coming up. You describe her interests and ask for advice about appropriate gifts.

3. Most of the suggestions made to you don't seem to be right, but one of them does. Ask more about that — size, color, price, etc.

4. You've decided to buy the article, and now you'd like to have it gift-wrapped and delivered as a surprise on your spouse's birthday.

Stage 2   Use the department store directory on **CT 180**.

1.   That Japanese couple keeps crossing your path throughout your European trip, and you encounter them in the department store restaurant. One of them is on crutches, the victim of a minor auto accident. First find out from them what has happened since you saw them last.

2.   Now find out why they are in this store. (They're buying a few things they need on their trip, as well as some souvenirs for their family at home.)

3.   React appropriately to their gift suggestions and tell them where each of the items is likely to be found.

4.   Bearing in mind the crutches, suggest how they might best get around in the store.

LESEN

Stage 1   Refer to the KaDeWe Etagenplan on **CT 180** and the *Bildwörterbuch* in the **Class Text**. Write out two lists of words — one of nouns, one of verbs — that are implied by the broad range of goods and services available on the fourth floor (3. OG.). Example from the 6th floor: *Betten (schlafen, machen, träumen, aufwachen . . . / das Kissen, das Federbett . . .).*

Stage 2   Now make categories of goods and services available at KaDeWe: things of interest to men, women, children, and animals; food; customer services; household; entertainment. To whom do most things seem to appeal? Why?

SCHREIBEN

Stage 1   1.   A friend of yours from Dayton, who speaks no German, wants to buy a few items in the department store in the city. Write out on a sheet of paper what he must say to the store clerk in each instance. Remember that he will not be able to understand a spoken or written reply to questions.

2.   Your "friend" has played a practical joke on you, which you don't appreciate after all the trouble you've taken to help him out. Now even the score by writing out a message to a store clerk that will probably be embarrassing to your friend.

Stage 2   Refer to the store directory and to your Bildwörterbuch. You are writing out instructions to two friends who will be shopping at KaDeWe and who are terrified by elevators and escalators. They are looking for stationery supplies, needlepoint patterns, a travel iron, some wax flowers, headphones for a portable radio, some lipstick, and lottery tickets. Tell them where to find what, bearing in mind that they want to be as efficient as possible about getting about the store, which they'll probably enter from Parkhaus I on the third floor (2. OG.)

FUNDBÜRO

HÖREN

Stage 1

A1   Just listen several times to the dialogs for *Gespräche 2: Fundbüro*. Talk along if you like.

A2   Practice saying the dialog lines. Use your "pause" button if you have one.

B1   Conversation 1
1. What is the word for the lost article?
2. List the steps used to describe the article.
3. What objects are used to define the article?
4. What two expressions are used to describe what the article is carried in?

Conversation 2
1. What is the lost article?
2. Where is it likely to be found?
3. Why is it not likely to be found in the other place?
4. Is the owner confident that it will be found?
5. What German words seem to convey the English meanings "fished around", "counter", and "nobody"?

Conversation 3
1. What article has been lost?
2. What words describe the size, color, and function of the article?
3. Where are the people talking?
4. Guess from context the meaning of *Blockschrift*.

Stage 2

B2   Conversation 1
1. Was sind die verlorenen Gegenstände?
2. Wohin geht der Besitzer zuerst?
3. Warum hat der Mann seine Sachen verloren?
4. Glauben Sie, daß er sie finden wird? Warum (nicht)?

Conversation 2
1. Was ist verlorengegangen? Beschreiben Sie es so gut wie möglich.
2. Hat man es gefunden?

Conversation 3
1. Was kann man nicht finden?
2. Wo hat man es verloren?
3. Ist es noch verloren?
4. Hat man es wirklich verloren? Oder hat jemand es gestohlen?
5. Wieso scheint es möglich zu sein, daß man es gestohlen hat?
6. Wer ist die dritte Person?
7. Welche Rolle hat diese Person in der Situation gespielt?

C1

2A:1.3.5   The news item tells of a fatal hit-and-run accident. The victims are described in great detail, because they cannot be identified. In Chapter 12 you listened for the basic information about the car and the victims. Now listen for information about the victims' clothing. One is male, one female. Listen first for items and maybe colors; on subsequent listening you might note qualifications like textile patterns or shades of color. For vocabulary help see the *Bildwörterbuch* displays on body parts and clothing, **CT 294-95,** and categories and qualities, **CT 308.** [12]

2A:2.1.3   List at least 2 of the 3 items that the announcer mentions as examples of things people might offer on the Fleamarket of the Air. List the 2 hobbies she mentions. Observe the Chapter 18 verb *sich melden*. [7, 12, 15]

C2

2B:5.2.2   Note the 2 words that begin with *Familie-*. How widespread will the new social service be in Bavaria? Does the report talk about male counselors, female counselors, or both? [See the special self-evaluation section in Chapter 15.]

2B:5.2.4   The speaker, a psychologist, summarizes the results of a call-in program about friendship. He lists 11 points. In which of them does he mention marriage? Challenge: Read again the section about "Words for 'thing'" on **CT 184** and then summarize the psychologist's sixth point. [12]

2B:5.3.2   How many times has the Household and Consumer Exposition in Koblenz been staged? How long has this year's exposition been going on? Observe the verbs *sich umschauen* and *mitspielen*. [15]

SPRECHEN

Stage 1   1.   Something of great sentimental value to you has disappeared. You are at the Fundbüro, where you describe it in as much detail as possible, telling just why it means so much to you.

2.   Speculate about where it could have disappeared — and why. You might find it helpful to use the Bildwörterbuch section on Categories/Kategorien (**CT 308-09**).

Stage 2   You think the article on the shelf behind the official is yours, but there is no ready means of identification on it. Do your best to convince her that you are indeed the owner. Perhaps someone who knows you well could vouch for your honesty.

LESEN

Stage 1   Read the descriptions of bicycle tours of München on **CT 186**. Make several lists from the information in the text: **a**) the street names (can you identify the street where the tour originates?); **b**) the museums; **c**) the political institutions; **d**) areas of natural beauty.

Stage 2   Guess from the context of the tour description on **CT 186** the meanings of the following words. Break down each word into its individual components and write down other words you know that are related to these components.

> **example**: Volkssänger: das Volk, der Sänger, singen)
>
> Gartenbaustil / Stadtummauerung / Außenfresko / Fassadenmalerei / Verkaufsstände / Ausgangspunkt.

SCHREIBEN

Stage 1   Refer to the second Versuchen Sie doch exercise on **CT 189**. You have indeed lost your umbrella and the bag of gifts, and the visit to the Fundbüro was fruitless. Now you're on the train to Bonn and don't know what you are going to say to your relatives. Put off that decision, therefore, by writing to the friends you just left in Hamburg, telling them the details of the loss and search. Don't forget to tell them what a wonderful time you had visiting them in spite of everything.

STRUCTURAL EXERCISES

Note: Be sure you have reviewed your chapter grammar and read the relevant sections in the reference grammar.

1   You are in a department store with your 8-year-old cousin from Konstanz. You have been asked by his parents to buy him some summer clothing. Ask the little fellow how he likes each article of clothing suggested by the salesclerk, and then give your opinion on the size, the color, and the price. Be sure to be polite to the clerk at the end of the excursion.

> **Example:**   Hose   "Gefällt dir diese Hose?"   "Ich glaube, die ist ihm zu groß."
>   "Rot gefällt mir gut."   "40 DM ist uns ein bißchen teuer."
>
> Hemd / Badeanzug / Sandalen / Shorts / Strümpfe / Windjacke

2   Your stepsister, who never did learn much about politeness and subtlety, is trying out her German in a department store. You've shopped here before, and know that the salesclerk she's speaking to can be rather curt, even snappy, if not addressed politely. Correct each of sis's statements, using a more polite verb form.

> **Example:**   Ist das viel besser?   Wäre das viel besser?
>
> Können Sie es mir zeigen?   Haben Sie es auch in blau?
> Darf ich es mal anprobieren?   Wissen Sie, wie ich es waschen soll?
> Muß ich es kalt oder warm waschen?   Was sagen Sie dazu?
> Das ist mir viel zu groß.

3 The little cousin in **1** (above) has all sorts of questions, which he is too bashful to ask the clerk. Relay them to the clerk with the introductory phrase *"Er möchte wissen, ..."* Be sure to represent your position (and his) accurately.

> **Example:** Wie spät ist es? Er möchte wissen, wie spät es ist.

> Wieviel kostet das kleine blaue Hemd?

> Warum heißt es hier "Taiwan"?

> Wo kann ich es anprobieren?

> Was bedeutet "bügelfrei"?

> Wer hat diese Schuhe gemacht?

> Wie kann ich mein Taschenmesser tragen, wenn die Badehose keine Taschen hat?

> Warum hat der Strumpf ein Loch drin?

> Wohin geht der Verkäufer, wenn er Kleider kauft?

√ CHECK YOUR PROFICIENCY

CAN YOU:
__ ask directions and make other inquiries in department stores?
__ negotiate purchases?
__ describe objects in some detail?
__ tell where, when, and under what circumstances something happened?
__ make spur-of-the-moment decisions or changes in plans?

DO YOU REMEMBER HOW TO:
__ conduct postal transactions?
__ deal with minor medical problems?
__ make plans for an excursion to a museum or to the countryside?
__ talk with a landlord about the specifics of room rental?
__ discuss — and justify — your study plans?

Kataloganforderung

Bitte senden Sie mir . . .
☐ schnellstens weitere umfangreiche Informationen (2– 80 Pf. – Briefmarken liegen bei) über:

Land/Ort

Termin:
☐ Ich habe Interesse an folgenden Fahrten, die nicht auf dieser Karte stehen:

Name
Vorname
Straße/Nr.
PLZ   Ort
Bitte helfen Sie uns und geben Sie uns an, wo Sie diese Karte entnommen haben.
Stadt/Land
genauer Ort (Uni, schwarzes Brett . . .)
Datum

So wird's gemacht:
Bitte dieses Blatt in frankiertem Briefumschlag (Absenderangabe und zwei 80-Pfennig-Briefmarken nicht vergessen!) senden an:

S & L –aktiv reisen–
Postfach 12 04 08
4000 Düsseldorf 12

Bitte schreiben Sie klar und deutlich, weil wir das Adressfeld für die Zusendung des Kataloges verwenden.
Anschriftenfeld für Katalogzustellung!

Anrede
Vorname, Name
Straße, No.
PLZ, Ort

Chapter 19

FREIZEIT: NATUR UND SPORT

HÖREN

Stage 1

A1 Just listen several times to the dialogs for *Gespräche 1: Freizeit: Natur und Sport*. Talk along if you like.

A2 Practice saying the dialog lines. Use your "pause" button if you have one.

B1   Conversation 1
1. Von welchen "Sportarten" handelt dieses Gespräch?
2. Was spricht gegen den zweiten Sport?
3. Was sagt das Schild genau?
4. In welchem Teil der BRD befinden sich diese Personen jetzt?

   Conversation 2
1. Welche Wörter haben mit Wasser zu tun?
2. Welche Ferienaktivitäten sind nicht mit dem Wasser verbunden?
3. Was passiert auf einer Sonnenaufgangswanderung?
4. Wörterbuch-Frage: Was braucht man, wenn man Federball spielen will?

   Conversation 3
1. Von wie vielen Generationen hört man im Gespräch?
2. Welche Freizeitaktivitäten werden hier genannt?
3. Wo findet jede der Aktivitäten statt?
4. Erraten Sie aus dem Kontext heraus (oder schlagen Sie im Wörterbuch nach): <u>Alm</u>, <u>Lech</u>, <u>Gipfelwanderung</u>.

Stage 2

B2   Segment 1
1. Wie viele Personen machen wahrscheinlich ihre Ferien zusammen?
2. Welche Wörter hängen thematisch mit <u>herumliegen</u> zusammen?
3. Welche Wörter bedeuten etwas Aktives?
4. Warum scheint frische Luft für die faule Person besonders wichtig zu sein?
5. Welche Wörter haben für Sie eine negative Bedeutung?
6. Welche Wörter drücken Ärger aus?

   Segment 2
1. Von welchen Sportarten hören wir in diesem Gespräch?
2. Was ist im Gespräch nicht ganz logisch?
3. Was bedeutet "FdH"?
4. Welche negativen Wörter hören Sie im Gespräch?
5. Welche positiven Wörter hören Sie?
6. In welchem Land ist man wahrscheinlich?
7. Welche Rolle spielt das Auto in diesem Sport?

   Segment 3
1. Was für eine Fahrt beschreibt man hier?
2. Wie lange dauert die Fahrt?
3. Mit welchem Verkehrsmittel macht man die Fahrt?
4. Wie viele Personen machen die Fahrt zusammen?
5. Wie kommt man nach der Fahrt wieder nach Hause?
6. Welche Fluß-, Stadt- und Ländernamen hören Sie?
7. Welche Adjektive beschreiben die Natur?
8. Welches Problem kann es unterwegs geben?
9. Erraten Sie aus dem Kontext heraus: <u>Ziel</u>, <u>Ausrüstung</u>, <u>versperren</u>, <u>Vorkenntnisse</u>, <u>windet</u>.

C1

1B:8.2.1

You will hear some soccer scores. Review the special vocabulary of soccer and the list of general sports vocabulary ('score,' 'goal,' etc.) in the *Bildwörterbuch*, **CT 304-05**. How many games are reported? Note their scores — you should be able to get all the numbers relatively easily, and in each case except the last you should be able to identify one of the teams by its home city. How long do the games seem to have been going on? In how many has the score not changed since the last report? Observe the use of *sich ändern*. [1, 8]

C2

2B:4.3.1

Identify both soccer teams by nationality. Where was the game played, and when? Write down a few phrases that show the first sportscaster's opinion of how well the German team played. Why did the other team not play as well as might have been expected?

After the game another sportscaster interviews two players as they head for the locker room. He criticizes the play toward the end of the game. Transcribe the reply, beginning *"Es kann auch nur passieren, er* ___ ____ _____ _____ _____." How long has it been since the Germans have beaten the other team? How many participles (*gedacht, gespielt*, etc.) can you hear? [8, 12]

2B:4.3.2

When and where will the dog show be held? How many such shows have there been? How many species are being shown? List the countries mentioned, and any breeds you can. What will be exhibited besides the pooches? [11]

C3

2A:3.1.2

What is the Wagner company advertising? What do they claim as their strongest selling point? (The key word is used in English and many other languages as well.) To get a better feeling for Bavarian accent and dialect, try to recognize in their Bavarian form these phrases as rendered into standard High German: *"wie ich dann gesehen habe," "gar nichts oder nur ein paar Mark," "da ist mir zum ersten Mal aufgegangen* [then I realized for the first time]." [5, 8]

SPRECHEN

Stage 1

1. You want to go either **a)** skiing or **b)** swimming. Find out how much longer the facilities will be open and make inquiries about appropriate equipment for both.

2. Tell your companion that it's too early/late in the day to indulge your interests in an outdoor sport. Ask what else your friend is interested in and suggest that the two of you do that.

3. Indicate your enthusiasm for the hike your friend wants to take. Say something about the details of the hike you will especially relish.

Stage 2

1. The bicycle rental office won't be open when you want to bring your bicycles back from the weekend trip. Make alternate arrangements with the clerk.

2. A good friend has suggested that you both learn to fly. Cite advantages and disadvantages of the plan.

3. You're at a mountain resort in Austria, with lots of tempting activities. You could go swimming and windsurfing, or you could head for the hills and either take some gentle hikes or do some serious rock climbing. Bicycle rental and a cable car to a nearby peak are both available. Plan a weekend's activities, assuming you might want to combine the various possibilities. Don't forget that a tasty meal or two would be a nice reward for some good hard play.

LESEN

Stage 1

Look at the Hotelverzeichnis on **CT 320**. Where would you go if you wanted to pick bouquets of wild rhododendron ("Alpine roses")? Do some lake fishing? Go horseback riding? Take a bike excursion? Do some target shooting? Practice your archery? Play water polo? Go wind surfing? Soothe your aching back?

Stage 2   Consult the Freizeit document on **CT 343**, one that should be familiar to you by now. In what country does the activity take place? What is the Indio? What are its main advantages? What equipment does one need in the Indio? What if it's rainy and cold? How much would this activity cost for five adults for one day? What if the weather were miserable? What does the price of the activity include? Assuming one would wear special clothing for a bad weather trip, what would one do with one's regular clothing? Would a family with 10-year-old twins be able to make this trip? How much would it cost? What is the last time one can make reservations for this activity? Where does one find out the telephone number to make reservations? Where does the activity begin? How does one get there from the capital of this country? If one leaves from the capital in the morning, must one return there in the evening?

SCHREIBEN

Stage 1   Pick one of the hotels listed in the Hotelverzeichnis on **CT 320** and write a letter of inquiry about your upcoming vacation. You want to indulge as many of your sporting interests as you can, but you also want to enjoy some good cooking and companionship with other vacationers. Be sure you tell the people what you're interested in, perhaps inquiring about sports and services not listed in the advertisement, and let them know what you're especially looking forward to and why. Begin your letter "*Sehr geehrte Familie X*".

FREIZEIT: HOBBYS UND MUSIK

HÖREN

Stage 1

A1   Just listen several times to the dialogs for *Gespräche 2: Freizeit: Hobbys und Musik*. Talk along if you like.

A2   Practice saying the dialog lines. Use your "pause" button if you have one.

B1   Conversation 1
          1. Von welchen Hobbys spricht man?
          2. Von welchen Verkehrsmöglichkeiten hören wir im Gespräch?

       Conversation 2
          1. Besitzt der Jazz-Sammler wahrscheinlich ein Instrument?
          2. Wann war er in New York?
          3. Wie alt ist seine Plattensammlung?
          4. Warum ist er ein so großer Jazzfreund?
          5. Was macht er auch gern abends?

       Conversation 3
          1. Was macht man?
          2. Schreiben Sie die Namen der Zutaten (*ingredients*) auf!
          3. Welche Zutaten findet man in einem Garten?
          4. Erraten Sie aus dem Kontext heraus: Fett, Fleischbrühe, Gewürz, Eßlöffel, Würfel, schälen
          5. Was ist süß in diesem Rezept? Was ist sauer?

Stage 2

B2   Conversation 1   (Zum Nachschlagen: Basteltisch, Seelenruhe, Kneipe)
          1. Welcher Sport wird erwähnt?
          2. Welche negativen Wörter hören Sie?
          3. Von welchen Zimmern hören wir? Was macht man in diesen Zimmern?
          4. Welche Wörter haben mit Musik zu tun?
          5. Welche Verben beschreiben etwas Ruhiges?
          6. Welche Verben beschreiben etwas Aktives?

Conversation 2
1. Welche Wörter haben mit Hitze zu tun?
2. Wo sind diese Personen?
3. Zeigt man oder erklärt man nur, was hier passiert?
4. Warum wird das Brot nicht schmutzig?
5. Was muß man zuerst machen, um Brot zu backen?

C1

2A:1.2.1 How precisely does the report give the size of the group of neo-Nazi juveniles? How do the gang members feel about being called neo-Nazis? Observe the verb *sich fühlen*, 'to feel.'

2A:1.2.5 The 14-year-old boy was trying to help his aunt, who had gotten caught in a safety net while skiing near a steep drop. What happened next? For vocabulary help, consult the *Bildwörterbuch* display on sports, **CT 305**. [11, 14]

C2

2B:4.2.1 What Mozart piece will be played at the open rehearsal? How much are tickets, and where and when can they be obtained? Would it be reasonable to try to be first in line for tickets and then use the money you save over ordinary ticket prices to have an unhurried lunch before the concert? [8]

2B:4.2.2 What station are you hearing, and what time of the day is it? What event does the broadcast commemorate? What is the full date (day, month, year) of "today" in the broadcast? [8]

2B:4.2.3 The sponsors of the traveling art exhibition are the Metropolitan in New York and the Germanisches Nationalmuseum in Nürnberg. What were the sources from which works for it were collected? Outline the schedule of the exhibition. [8, 14]

2B:5.2.3 The brochure *"Wohnen mit _____"* gives information about the quality and safety of various consumer items. List as many as you can; the list begins after the words *"und Sicherheit von."* To polish up your list, reread *Struktur* 2, section 2 on "Noun dative plurals" on **CT 198**. How much can you note about how to get a copy of the brochure? [15]

2B:5.4.3 How many private museums are there in Bavaria, <u>including</u> the Jewish Museum in Augsburg? How many museums of Jewish culture are there? How many members are there in the Jewish community in Augsburg? Why might the museum be closed? [10, 14]

SPRECHEN

Stage 1   1.   You'd like to get together with friends soon to play some music. Suggest a time and a place, remembering that your landlord is grumpy and that making music together always makes the three of you hungry.

2.   Seeing the stamps in the store window (*Hobbybedarf*) in Innsbruck has made you think about your own collection at home. Describe your collection to the shopkeeper and ask how she thinks you might best improve it.

Stage 2   1.   You have met some students from Africa in the Mensa and are exchanging information about your different cultures. Tell them what sorts of things you like to do in your spare time and tell them how your habits differ from those of many other Americans.

2.   Describe your favorite dessert recipe. Don't forget to make the necessary quantity and temperature conversions.

LESEN

Stage 1   Look at the "Erasmus-Zugbegleiter" on **CT 319**. What is being advertised? What people are addressed? What is a *Subskriptionspreis*? If you wanted to have a book about the "Krokodil" sent to you, how much would it cost? You could pay for it at your local post office; how? Are color pictures of the locomotives available? What does the name of the company seem to indicate? What do you think *Dampf- und E-Lokomotiven* are? Guess from context the meaning of *Sammlerobjekt, Nachdruck, Entwicklungen, Leckerbissen*.

Stage 2   Consult the *Hotelverzeichnis* on **CT 320**. Where would you stay if you wanted to see how farm families lived in the 19th century? If you wanted to buy some goods in another country and avoid paying customs duty? If you wanted to indulge your fascination for outdoor chess?

SCHREIBEN

Stage 1   You are taking part in the program offered by the <u>Hotel Zum Roten Bären</u> on **CT 340**. Send a note back home to your friends telling them what you have been up to and why.

Stage 2   Drawing on the information in the catalog of musical giants on **CT 195**, write a note to friends telling them what sort of concert you would like to attend on the evening of your birthday, and why. Be sure they know how much you have been looking forward to spending this evening with them.

STRUCTURAL EXERCISES

Note: Be sure you have reviewed your chapter grammar and read the relevant sections in the reference grammar.

1   You have been spending a week on a farm in the Austrian Voralpenland that offers the popular vacation *"Urlaub am Bauernhof"* (See **CT 192**). Write to your friends back in Hannover a list of the things that you enjoy.

>   **Example**:   Es macht mir viel Spaß, früh aufzustehen.
>   Es macht mir viel Spaß, mit der Bauernfamilie zu sprechen.

2   Add to your letter to Hannover observations about 1) the antiquated methods of doing some farm chores; and 2) the surprising presence of some modern conveniences.

>   Example: Hier melkt man die Kühe <u>noch</u> ohne Maschine.
>   Frau Loretz hat <u>schon</u> einen Computer in der Stube.

3   Use *nicht mehr* and *kein- . . . mehr* in a part of your letter to tell what things are no longer done on the farm.

>   **Example**:   Diese Familie backt <u>nicht mehr</u> das eigene Brot.
>   Sie kaufen immer bei der Bäckerei im Dorf ein.

4   Your letter might also include another kind of comment about activities. Say why you're looking forward to (or not looking forward to) certain things. Where appropriate, use sentence adverbs (*vielleicht, unbedingt, eigentlich, hauptsächlich, überhaupt nicht, vor allem*) to reinforce your comments.

>   **Example**:   Ich <u>interessiere mich</u> hauptsächlich <u>für</u> Schweine.
>   Ich <u>freue mich auf</u> die Fütterung jeden Morgen.

√ CHECK YOUR PROFICIENCY

CAN YOU:
__ talk in some detail about leisure activities?
__ describe how things are done?
__ recall some experiences you have had on weekends?
__ make plans for leisure activites?

DO YOU REMEMBER HOW TO:
__ express politeness in dealing with other people?
__ give instructions for arranging things in an apartment?
__ give directions for using mass transit facilities?
__ discuss your university studies and your plans after graduation?
__ describe lost items accurately enough to recover them?

HÖREN

Stage 1

A1 Just listen several times to the dialogs for *Gespräche 1: Konzert*. Talk along if you like.

A2 Practice saying the dialog lines. Use your "pause" button if you have one.

B1 Conversation 1

1. Was möchte Christel noch vor der Oper machen?
2. Warum scheint dies unmöglich zu sein?
3. Erraten Sie aus dem Kontext heraus: Ordentliches, längst, Gang, einverstanden.

Conversation 2

1. Wissen Sie, was für ein Konzert Herr Lehmann hören möchte?
2. Warum geht er heute doch nicht ins Konzert?
3. Welcher Tag ist "heute"?
4. Welchen Vorschlag macht die Person an der Theaterkasse?

Conversation 3

1. Wer scheint mehr von der Vorstellung zu verstehen, Eduard oder Ottilie?
2. Ist die Vorstellung ein Konzert oder eine Oper? Wie wissen Sie das?
3. Wie könnte man auch hier die Musik besser verstehen?
4. Wie traditionell ist diese Vorstellung?
5. Erraten Sie aus dem Kontext: Übertext, Handlung, projiziert

Stage 2

B2 Conversation 1

1. Warum sind die Karten dieses Jahr besser als die letztes Jahr im freien Verkauf?
2. Warum waren die Karten letztes Jahr schwer zu bekommen?
3. Was gibt es heute abend Besonderes im Programm?
4. Erraten Sie aus dem Kontext heraus: abonniert, Dirigent, einmalig.

Conversation 2

1. An welchem Abend kann man "Zar und Zimmermann" sehen?
2. Wer hat diese Operette geschrieben?
3. Was kann man im Musikinstrumentenmuseum hören? Wann?
4. Was wählt der Mann wahrscheinlich am 27.? Warum?

C1

1A:2.1.1 Note the program offerings for the 3 stations; how much time do you have before the sports report begins? [P1]

1A:2.1.2 What day is it? What station are you listening to? Which of the "Giants of German Music" listed on **CT 195** is featured in the musical offering? Could you be certain that you could still listen to his piece on the program? [9]

1A:2.1.3 The fellow whose family sends him greetings over the radio — how often is he on the road? to where? What does his family wish him? [4]

1A:2.2.1 Is the talk-show psychoanalyst male or female? What is the call-in phone number? Which of the "Giants of German Music" listed on **CT 195** is featured on another station, and which of his works would you hear? [8]

1A:2.2.2   Which of the "Giants of German Music" listed on **CT 195** is/are featured in the musical offering? when and on which station? what kind of compositions? On which station(s), and when, could you hear something other than classical music? What will you hear if you stay tuned to this station? [8, 17]

   C2

1A:2.3.1   What time of the day might it be? Does the announcer describe music just played or music about to be played? How many ways can you tell?

1A:2.3.2   Which of the "Giants of German Music" listed on **CT 195** is/are featured in the musical offering? What time is it "now"?

1A:3.1.2   Why does the announcer think the song is appropriate? How quickly can you say, in 25 words or less, why someone you know considers a certain song to be his or her song? [4, 11]

1A:3.2.2   What did the announcer receive in the mail? How precisely can you determine just who wants better weather? [4, 11]

SPRECHEN

Stage 1   1.   You're not sure whether tickets to the Czech Philharmonic are still available. Call the ticket office and identify yourself, explain how many tickets you want for this evening, and ask when the performance begins.

2.   When you find out that it will not be possible to have all the seats you want together, present some options to your friends: you could sit in different places (some couples would have to split up), go another evening, or perhaps some could go tonight and others two nights from now.

3.   Tell the person at the ticket office that you'll be right down to pick up the tickets. You've decided to take the seats and see if you can trade seats with some other concertgoers once you're inside the hall.

4.   You've just seen the ad (**CT 203**) for the <u>Zigeunerbaron</u>, one of your favorite operettas. Tell your friends all about it — location, time, special features — and then explain to them that you'll meet them for a snack in the city after you've seen this presentation and they've heard the Czech Philharmonic.

Stage 2   1.   There's a folk festival (music, handicrafts) in the small concert hall of the <u>Städtisches Kunsthaus</u> where you have been doing some term paper research. Tickets for the concert are sold out, but you know the management by now and think you can get seats for yourself and your two friends. Tell them your plan.

2.   You've arrived at the <u>Kunsthaus</u>, only to be greeted by a stranger at the door. Do your best to explain the situation to the new person, even though she steadfastly refuses to let you in without a ticket.

3.   Your friends are disgusted that you have let them down. Suggest an alternate plan — the Joe Cocker concert you read about on the university bulletin board yesterday morning. Be contrite.

LESEN

Stage 1   You have just read in the paper that the Litauisches Kammerorchester will be playing, among other things, Mozart's Klavierkonzert C-dur KV 415. Find out from your music library (or a musician friend) what the "KV 415" means.

Stage 2   1.   Brush up on your musical facts by reviewing the Chapter 8 (<u>Opernkasse</u>) reading exercise dealing with the burial sites of famous German-speaking composers. (You will find the composers listed alphabetically in the CT glossary.)

2.   Read the column "Live is Live" in the Berlin calendar of events on **CT 335**. Write down the English/American words that seem to have been borrowed into German. What do you suppose accounts for their number? Which musical offering does the author of the article think is the very best? How often can your hear live Latin American music? Where? Can you hear music more often in the "Quartier Latin", the "Quasimodo", or the "Metropol"? What does the very last sentence of the article appear to mean?

SCHREIBEN

Stage 1 Look at the "Platzl" ticket on **CT 200**. It is one of four you have bought for yourself, your companion, and another couple. Write a polite invitation to the other couple to join you for the evening, which will include a number of interesting activities. Because the other couple is unfamiliar with München's local traditions, be sure to suggest what they should wear and what they should expect. If you remember from Chapter 16 where "Platzl" is, tell them also how to get there from the private room they have rented for the month at the northern end of the Englischer Garten.

Stage 2 Unfortunately, the other couple overindulged at "Platzl", something your companion was afraid might happen if you didn't phrase your invitation correctly. There was a misunderstanding with another customer, and a bit of a ruckus as well, which led to an official invitation to your friends to spend the night in police custody. Now you must explain to their landlady why they will probably not be able to join her for lunch tomorrow. Just leave her a note, since it's very late now and you don't want to wake her.

WEINPROBE

HÖREN

Stage 1

A1 Just listen several times to the dialogs for *Gespräche 2: Weinprobe*. Talk along if you like.

A2 Practice saying the dialog lines. Use your "pause" button if you have one.

B1 Conversation 1
1. Wo befinden sich diese zwei Leute?
2. Welche Farben hören Sie? Was ist mit den Farben gemeint?
3. Wie können beide Seiten von einer Weinprobe profitieren?

Conversation 2
1. Welche Namen von Weinanbaugebieten hören Sie?
2. Wie heißt der trockenere Wein?
3. Woher kommt der süßere Wein?

Stage 2

B2 Conversation 1
1. Was trinkt Herr Wehner normalerweise am Abend? Warum?
2. Wann trinkt er Alkohol? Was für Alkohol?
3. Welche Weinsorten hören Sie? Sind sie rot oder weiß?

Conversation 2
1. Was ist mit dem Wort *Blume* gemeint?
2. Welche negativen vergleiche macht Franz?
3. Was für Pläne hat Franz? Wann?
4. Was sind Emmis Pläne?

C1

1B:6.1.3 Observe how the DHL World-Wide Express company uses the "Ride of the Valkyries" theme from Wagner's opera *Die Walküre* to suggest how fast they deliver the goods. [P2, 18]

1B:6.1.5 Note the subjects of 2 of the 4 stories featured in West Germany's most popular newspaper. Transcribe the slogan at the end of the commercial: "*Bild lesen* _____ _____ _____" [P2, 6]

1B:6.2.1 What part of tennis star Boris Becker's life does *Bild der Frau* claim to reveal? Observe the use of the adjectives *schön* and *toll* ; who was Linda Christian and what did she do that was so superlative? [5, 6]

1B:6.3.3   Observe and transcribe the repeated use of reflexive pronouns in the *du*-form: "*Mach* _____ _____, *halt* _____ _____." If you can't hear the difference between *dich* and "*damit der Durst* [thirst] *nicht dick macht*", you are in good company. [12, 18]

1B:6.3.6   How much more than camping does the exposition cover? How much is the parking fee? [13, 16]

C2

2A:2.1.4   What musical piece has the announcer just played? When is the next holiday? When will the famous enterainer Vico Toriani be interviewed? [7]

2A:2.2.1   About 90 seconds into the interview with Vico Toriani, the Swiss "All-around Entertainer" is asked about his early years in show business. List the media (radio, nightclubs, etc.) in which he has worked, and when. How many "platters" (*Tonträger*) did his biggest hit single sell? [2, 9, 13, 17]

2A:2.2.2   After Vico Toriani sings "*Tango der Nacht*", the announcer relays a song dedication from a wife to her husband on the occasion of their being married 6 months. He then tells a joke about a friend who had a quarrel with his wife. Can you get the punch line? "My wife crawled to me on her knees, and said: '_____.'" [13]

SPRECHEN

Stage 1   Look at the picture of the three people at a wine-tasting (**CT 206**). Taking each person in turn, practice saying what each one seems to be thinking about: the wine, the atmosphere, the other people, the plans for augmenting the wine cellar at home.

Stage 2   1.   One of the people at your table, an American, wants to try a bit more of the wine that was just served, but doesn't speak any German. He also wants to know whether that vintage is especially good, at what temperature the wine should be drunk, and when the grapes for this particular wine were harvested. Attract the host's attention and do your best to help the man out.

2.   Look at the wine nomenclature on **CT 206**. Now explain to a German-speaking Korean at the wine-tasting what the difference is between an *Auslese* and a *Spätlese*. Do so in simple terms: the person's German isn't as good as yours.

LESEN

Stage 1   Look at the Freiburg excursion list on **CT 339** for a wine-tasting excursion, and compare it with the tasting offered by the Hotel Markgräfler Hof (**CT 340**). Which one seems more complete?

Stage 2   Refer to the wine classifications on **CT 206**. Using a dictionary, see how many words you can find that are related to: *Beendigung, ausschließlich, krank, fehlerhaft, reif, naturgemäß, gekeltert, verwendet, ergibt, Gegensatz, konzentriert, wichtig,* and *ernten.* (Example: krank — Krankenkasse, Krankenschwester, Krankenwagen, Krankheit) What words in the text do you think are related to *Frost, wiegen,* and *sauer*?

SCHREIBEN

Stage 1   Look again at the description of the weekend "*Alles über badische Weine*" on **CT 340**. List the phrases which tell you that you will: a) learn about different kinds of grapes; b) learn about the geography of this part of Baden; c) have a meal you won't soon forget; d) see where wines are actually produced; e) learn about laws regarding wine production; f) enjoy a festive conclusion to the weekend.

Stage 2   Consult the Mannheim *Gaststättenverzeichnis* on **CT 322**. Two of the restaurants in Mannheim seem to offer not only a good selection of wines, but also special rooms where wine tastings could take place. With the information on this list in mind, write a formal letter to an acquaintance of yours, the head of the Remstalkellerei in Beutelsbach (just east of Stuttgart, zip code 7056). Your note should give the information necessary for his upcoming wine-tasting visit to Mannheim with eight of his employees — location of the restaurants in the city, their facilities, and perhaps your recommendation of one restaurant over the other based on your experience there.

STRUCTURAL EXERCISES

Note: Be sure you have reviewed your chapter grammar and read the relevant sections in the reference grammar.

1 On the ballet stage before you is a large empty box on a table. Dancers dressed as animals are performing various feats in and around this box. Describe for your blind companion what is happening on stage. Use as many prepositions as you can without being ridiculous.

       Example: Das Huhn fliegt <u>über den Karton</u>.   Das Huhn fliegt <u>darüber</u>.

2 Redo exercise 1, but recount the action for a friend who was unable to see the ballet with you.

       Example: Das Huhn <u>ist</u> über den Karton <u>geflogen</u>.   Das Huhn ist darüber geflogen.

3 One of the dancers at the ballet is not a human, but a chimpanzee named Fritz, which makes this ballet a perennial favorite for children. Fritz's trainer describes for a grade school class what the chimp does all day, from getting dressed to going to bed at night. Using different verbs, but especially the reflexive ones in your Reference Grammar (**Verbs §§ 41-46**), write the description of Fritz's activities — and those of the trainer. Feel free to use *gern* where appropriate.

       Example: Jeden Tag <u>freue ich mich auf</u> meine Arbeit.
                       Fritz steht früh auf und <u>zieht sich an</u>. Dann <u>holt er sich</u> gern eine Banane.
                       Dann . . .

√ CHECK YOUR PROFICIENCY

CAN YOU:
__ make arrangements to hear a concert?
__ talk about things to do inside a concert hall?
__ discuss the quality of a performance?
__ ask informed questions about the process of wine making?

DO YOU REMEMBER HOW TO:
__ describe leisure time activities?
__ talk about the recent past?
__ give directions for the use of mass transit facilities?
__ describe an illness or injury well enough to get help?

Ein-lieferungs-schein Bitte sorgfältig aufbewahren	Zum Aufkleben	des Nummernzettels	**Paketkarte**	Zum Aufkleben der Zettel für besondere Versendungsformen
		Absender		

Wert (in Ziffern) _____ DM   Entrichtete Gebühr _____ Pf

Gebühr (Pf)   Vermerke über besondere Versendungsformen und Vorausverfügungen (s. Rückseite)

Empfänger

Gewicht (kg)   Empfänger

(Straße und Hausnummer, „Paketausgabe" oder „Postlagernd")

Gewicht bei Paketen mit Wertangabe _____ kg _____ g

Postannahme

(Postleitzahl)   (Bestimmungsort)

Zum Aufkleben der Zettel für besondere Versendungsformen

Im Rokokotheater

Mittwoch, 2. und Freitag, 4. Mai, 20 Uhr

Deutsche Oper Berlin

Uraufführung

OPHELIA

Oper in fünf Szenen. Libretto (nach einer Idee des Komponisten) von Herbert Meier

Musik von Rudolf Kelterborn

Catherine Gayer, Patricia Johnson, Silvia McNair (Titelpartie), Yoko Nomura, Barbara Scherler, Barbara Vogel, Donald Grobe, Otto Heuer, Volker Horn, Rolf Kühne, David Knutson, Peter Maus, Miomir Nikolic, William Pell, Richard Salter und Paul Wolfrum

Musikalische Leitung: Arturo Tamayo
Inszenierung: Hans Hollmann
Bühnenbild: Hans Hoffer
Kostüme: Frieda Parmeggiani

Radio-Sinfonieorchester Stuttgart

Im Rokokotheater

Samstag, 5. Mai, 20 Uhr

PHILHARMONISCHE CELLISTEN KÖLN

Leitung: Werner Thomas

Werke von Georg Christoph Wagenseil, Bernhard Heinrich Romberg, Milij Balakirew, Heitor Villa-Lobos, Mario Castelnuovo-Tedesco, Jean Françaix, Reinhold Glière, Manuel de Falla, Alberto E. Ginastera, Werner Thomas-Mifune und Wilfried Hiller

Im Rokokotheater

Sonntag, 6. Mai, 20 Uhr

Deutsche Oper Berlin

OPHELIA

Oper in fünf Szenen. Libretto (nach einer Idee des Komponisten) von Herbert Meier

Musik von Rudolf Kelterborn

Catherine Gayer, Patricia Johnson, Silvia McNair (Titelpartie), Yoko Nomura, Barbara Scherler, Barbara Vogel, Donald Grobe, Otto Heuer, Volker Horn, Rolf Kühne, David Knutson, Peter Maus, Miomir Nikolic, William Pell, Richard Salter und Paul Wolfrum

Musikalische Leitung: Arturo Tamayo
Inszenierung: Hans Hollmann
Bühnenbild: Hans Hoffer
Kostüme: Frieda Parmeggiani

Radio-Sinfonieorchester Stuttgart

Jagdsaal linker Zirkel

Sonntag, 6. Mai, 20 Uhr

MUSIKVEREIN-QUARTETT WIEN

(Küchl-Quartett)

Rainer Küchl (Violine), Eckhard Seifert (Violine), Peter Götzel (Bratsche), Franz Bartolomey (Violoncello)

Werke von Wolfgang Amadeus Mozart, Leoš Janáček und Ludwig van Beethoven

---

Konzertsaal linker Zirkel

Dienstag, 8. Mai, 20 Uhr

PHILIP JONES BRASS ENSEMBLE

Werke von Gg. Fr. Händel, Musik der englischen Renaissance und Flämische Tanzmusik · Leitung: Philip Jones

Im Rokokotheater

Mittwoch, 9. Mai, 20 Uhr

INTERNATIONAL MENUHIN MUSIC ACADEMY

Werke von Antonio Vivaldi, Francesco Manfredini, Pietro Locatelli, Gioacchino Rossini, Giacomo Puccini und Niccolò Paganini

Solisten: Alberto Lysy und Matthias Enderle (Violine)
Leitung: Alberto Lysy

Konzertsaal linker Zirkel

Donnerstag, 10. Mai, 20 Uhr

I. SCHWETZINGER SERENADE

Das Südwestdeutsche Kammerorchester Pforzheim spielt Werke von Gg. Fr. Händel, Henryk Mikolaj Górecki, Benedetto Marcello, Robert Volkmann und W. A. Mozart

Solist: Klaus Becker (Oboe) · Leitung: Dirk Joeres

EINTRITTSPREISE
ENTRANCE FEES · PRIX DES CARTES D'ENTREE

Im Rokokotheater
ERÖFFNUNGSVORSTELLUNG »OPHELIA«
PREMIERE »LA CENERENTOLA«
25,-, 45,-, 65,-, 85,- DM

WIEDERHOLUNGEN »OPHELIA«
»LA CENERENTOLA«
25,-, 42,-, 58,-, 68,- DM

Im Rokokotheater
»DER ROSENKAVALIER«
15,-, 28,-, 40,-, 52,- DM

Im Rokokotheater
PHILHARMONISCHE CELLISTEN KÖLN
INTERNATIONAL MENUHIN MUSIC ACADEMY
NUOVA COMPAGNIA DI CANTO POPOLARE
STUTTGARTER KAMMERORCHESTER
SERENATA AMOROSA
GALA-ABEND FAYE ROBINSON
22,-, 30,-, 40,-, 52,- DM

Im linken Zirkel
SCHWETZINGER SERENADEN
MUSIKVEREIN-QUARTETT
PHILIP JONES BRASS ENSEMBLE
KLAVIERABEND CECILE LICAD
GITARRENABEND CARLOS BONELL
28,-, 36,- DM

Pfarrkirche St. Pankratius
KIRCHENKONZERT
12,-, 16,-, 22,- DM

Unsere Besucher weisen wir darauf hin, daß eine kurzfristige Rückgabe von Karten nicht bzw. nur in ganz bestimmten Ausnahmefällen möglich ist.

VORVERKAUFSKASSEN
BOOKING OFFICES · LOCATION

SCHWETZINGEN: Verkehrsverein Schwetzingen e.V.
Schloßplatz, Tel. 0 62 02/49 33

HEIDELBERG: Zigarrenhaus Grimm
Am Bismarckplatz
Telefon 0 62 21/2 09 09

MANNHEIM: Verkehrsverein Mannheim e.V.
Bahnhofplatz 1
Telefon 06 21/10 10 11

Prospekte bei folgenden Verkehrsämtern

Baden-Baden
Badenweiler
Bad Rappenau
Bad Schönborn
Basel/Schweiz
Berlin
Bonn
Bruchsal
Darmstadt
Eberbach/Neckar
Frankenthal/Pfalz
Frankfurt
(auch beim Deutschen
Reisebüro im Hauptbahnhof)
Freiburg/Breisgau
Freudenstadt
Hannover
Heilbronn
Karlsruhe
(auch Musikhaus Schlaile)
Kaiserslautern

Konstanz
Lahr
Landau/Pfalz
Ludwigshafen
Luzern/Schweiz
Mainz
Mosbach
München
Neustadt/Weinstraße
Offenburg
Pforzheim
Pirmasens
Reutlingen
Saarbrücken
Schwäbisch Hall
Speyer
Stuttgart
Tübingen
Ulm/Donau
Weinheim
Worms

AUSKÜNFTE · INFORMATIONEN · RENSEIGNEMENTS
durch die Geschäftsstelle der Festspiele
in Schwetzingen, Postfach 19 41, Telefon 0 62 02/49 33

FÜR DIE NACHSTEHEND GENANNTEN VERANSTALTUNGEN BESTELLE ICH KARTEN UND BITTE UM ÜBERSENDUNG PER NACHNAHME:

Sollten Plätze in der von mir gewünschten Preisgruppe nicht mehr verfügbar sein, dann bin ich mit der Übersendung von Karten der nächst höheren Preislage einverstanden.
JA/NEIN
(Zutreffendes bitte unterstreichen)

Datum	Veranstaltung	Anzahl	Preis	Summe

NAME:
WOHNORT UND STRASSE:

HÖREN

Stage 1

A1   Just listen several times to the dialogs for *Gespräche 1: Ausflüge*. Talk along if you like.

A2   Practice saying the dialog lines. Use your "pause" button if you have one.

B1   Conversation 1

    1. Wie viele Personen wollen den Ausflug machen?
    2. Wer hat den Auflug organisiert?
    3. Wie lange soll der Ausflug dauern?
    4. Welche Tageszeit ist es jetzt?
    5. Wo übernachtet man heute abend?
    6. Wie kommt man dorthin? Warum?

   Conversation 2

    1. Welche geographischen Namen hören Sie?
    2. Wie ist das heutige Wetter?
    3. In welchen deutschsprachigen Ländern ist man wahrscheinlich <u>nicht</u>? Warum?
    4. Wohin führen die beiden Wege von der Berghütte?
    5. Welche Wörter zeigen, daß die Kapelle schwer zu erreichen ist?

Stage 2

B2   Having just been on an excursion, two people have made a tape (*das Tonband*) to send to a friend back home. Listen to the tape and answer the following questions:

    1. Wie heißt der Freund? Wie heißen seine Bekannten in Österreich? Was ist seine Bekannte wohl von Beruf?
    2. Hören wir mehr vom Ausflug oder von der Fahrt zum Ausflugsort?
    3. An welchem Tag fährt man? An welchem Tag macht man das Tonband?
    4. Schreiben Sie die geographischen Namen auf, die Sie hören. Finden Sie auf einer Karte die Stadt, wo die Reise beginnt, und den Ort, wo der Aufstieg beginnt.
    5. Wie lange dauert die Hinfahrt nach Tirol? Warum?
    6. Schreiben Sie die Wörter auf, die die Verkehrslage beschreiben.
    7. Wie viele Personen fahren dorthin? Wie viele nehmen am Ausflug teil?
    8. Wo übernachtet man ? War man schon früher dort?
    9. Welchen Berg besteigt man? Welche Landesgrenze betritt man auf dem Gipfel?

C1
1A:5.2.1-5   Since you're going on an excursion, concentrate on the information about precipitation in general and mountain conditions in particular. Take the notes you think you need to take. Check your ears: Which verb tense did you hear at the end of Segment 5? — "*Vom Bayrischen Rundfunk <u>hören</u> or <u>hörten</u> Sie Nachrichten.*" [9, 14]

C2
2B:4.1.1   Early in the segment the announcer summarizes the upcoming reports about travel and vacation issues. Try to list the first three items. In the section later about hiking vacations, note words that describe staying or sleeping overnight. [2, 5, 9, 14]

2B:4.1.2   The report in the second half of the segment deals with customs regulations for tourists; what nationality of tourists visiting which countries? How much have import duties on goods brought back by such tourists changed, and over what period of time? What is the word for "duty-free"? [2, 12]

2A:1.1.4   How dangerous is the contaminated wine if you drink some of it? Describe the kind(s) of wine that should be safe to consume. [2]

SPRECHEN

Stage 1   1.   A pair of hikers has approached you and asked directions to a well-known landmark you just visited. Tell them how to get there, how long it will take, and what they will probably see underway.

2.   They recognize from your slight accent that you were not raised here, and they ask you how long you have been acquainted with the area. Recount one of your early adventures here with your parents when you were very young.

Stage 2   1.   You've lost your way in the mountains again, probably because you have ventured out without either a compass or a map. The trail signs you see point to towns and peaks whose names you don't recognize. Tell the person whom you encounter on the trail where you were trying to go, and find some believable excuse for being lost in spite of your general familiarity with the area.

2.   You're on the <u>Bodensee</u> for a long weekend — an ideal time to relax and get to know your friends from the youth hostel a bit better. There are many activities you could undertake, most involving some physical exertion: water sports, biking, hiking, a ferryboat ride across the lake to Romanshorn, perhaps even a ride on the gondola to the <u>Pfänder</u> at the east end of the lake. Make suggestions to your friends, outlining the advantages and disadvantages of each.

LESEN

Stage 1   Look at the advertisement for the <u>Palasthotel</u> on **CT 26**. If you were seriously contemplating a two-day stay here, what sort of person (age, interests, etc.) would you probably be? Write down a list of German adjectives describing what you might assume is a typical hotel guest, and then write a list of corresponding adjectives describing yourself. How do the two lists differ?

Stage 2   1.   The <u>Palasthotel</u> just didn't fill the bill for you, but the advertisement on **CT 56** looks attractive. List the words and phrases that seem especially enticing. Can you describe a typical guest of this place?

2.   You might try to relieve your stress another way. Consult the weather information on **CT 94** to see if a hike might be in order. Then make a list of clothing and equipment appropriate to the hike.

SCHREIBEN

Stage 1   Combine the materials on **CT 116** to describe an excursion you would like to take. Use the possibilities for expressing simultaneity on **CT 212** to tell what you would like to do on the excursion.

Stage 2   1.   Look carefully at the picture on **CT 130**, which shows four young travelers. Note what city they are in, find that city on a map, and then pick any one person and write what that person might say in a letter home about the others in the group (their appearance, personality, nationality, and interests) and what they did on a day's excursion in that area.

2.   Consult the map of Oberbayern on **CT 158**. Starting from one of the towns, plan a two-day bike trip, describing the geographical features and man-made landmarks you see underway. Your description can take the form of a suggestion to two of your friends from that nice youth hostel in Hannover (*"Liebe Freunde, . . ."*).

REISEBÜRO

HÖREN

Stage 1

A1   Just listen several times to the dialogs for *Gespräche 2: Reisebüro*. Talk along if you like.

A2   Practice saying the dialog lines. Use your "pause" button if you have one.

B1   Conversation 1

1. Schreiben Sie die geographischen Namen auf, die Sie hören, wobei Sie jeden Namen dem entsprechenden Land zuteilen.
2. In welcher Stadt befinden sich diese Gesprächspartner?
3. Wo finden die Ferien wahrscheinlich statt? Warum?
4. Warum kennt die Reisebüroangestelle das Gebiet so gut?
5. Wie kommt man zu diesem Ferienort? Wie lange dauert es? Wie oft muß man umsteigen?
6. Erraten Sie aus dem Kontext heraus: <u>Bademöglichkeit</u>, <u>auffrischen</u>, <u>Gastfreundschaft</u>, <u>Verbindung</u>.

Conversation 2

1. Welche Worte zeigen, daß man "mehr als Tourist" sein möchte?
2. Welches Image hat man vom Schwarzwald, d.h. wie stellt man sich das Leben dort vor?
3. Wie weiß die Angestellte über den Schwarzwald Bescheid?
4. Erraten Sie aus dem Kontext heraus: <u>Inhaberin</u>, <u>sich auskennen</u>, <u>abgelegen</u>, <u>entsprechend</u>, <u>Vollverpflegung</u>.

Stage 2

B2

1. Was wäre der Vorteil von einer Reise in die USA?
2. Welche Länder schlägt man als Reiseziel vor?
3. Schreiben Sie die "Nachteile" von jedem Land auf.
4. Was spricht dafür, daß diese Leute "Geld wie Heu" haben?
5. Aus welchem Teil der BRD stammen diese Leute wohl? Wo leben sie jetzt?
6. Was wären die Vorteile vom Urlaub am Bauernhof?
7. Warum entscheiden sich die Leute wahrscheinlich für den Bauernhof-Urlaub?

C1
1B:6.1.1
What prize(s) does the noodle company offer, and how many of them? What special ingredient is in the noodles? Consult the *Bildwörterbuch* display on **CT 301** to learn the names of the animals you heard. [P1, P2, 12]

1B:6.1.2
What sauces can you get with Chicken McNuggets Shanghai? To sound "Chinese" the actor in the ad makes a mistake in German word order; correct his German: "*Sie müssen* ___ _____ _____." Your ears and grammar are really good if you can hear later mistakes in the dative plural article. [P2, 2, 12]

2A:2.1.1
What day and time of day is it likely "now"? How many ways can you support you opinion about what day it is (or is not)? The announcer mentions television; how can you be sure that you are <u>not</u> hearing a TV broadcast without the picture? Is the announcer happy because he's had a good time on vacation, or because he expects to have a good time? [1, 9]

C2
2B:5.2.2
Is the family-counselor program a private or governmental project? What is its status? **a)** It's been stopped. **b)** It's been started. **c)** It's definitely going to be started. **d)** Its sponsors hope to start it. [15, 18]

2B:5.3.1
Does the news story report <u>past</u> tourism statistics, assess <u>current</u> tourism, or predict <u>future</u> tourism? Assuming the statistics are typical for other years, how important are foreign visitors to München's tourist industry? [7, 10, 14]

SPRECHEN

Stage 1   You are interested in spending some time in the Austrian Alps. It's late spring, and the possibilities extend from high-country skiing (the snow is best in the early morning) to hiking in the lower valleys, where the first wildflowers are blooming. Because of the precarious status of the U.S. dollar, your funds are limited, but you want to make the most of your time. Ask the travel agent about possible package tours, and solicit recommendations for the best places to go.

Stage 2 You've never been to the Westerwald, between Bonn and Marburg. You have a week, and you want to use the time to get to know one small area well. Find out what sorts of activites are available, and ask about the price and nature of accommodations. When the travel agent tries to convince you to spend most of your time in the urban areas to either side of the Westerwald, tell him why you prefer to concentrate on small-town life and the stress-reducing solitude of the forest.

LESEN

Stage 1 Look at the ad for the Condor travel agency on **CT 217**. Which cities would you not include on a tour? Why? Which would you substitute? Why? Be prepared to give your reasons in German to the class.

Stage 2 Read the advertisement and train schedule on **CT 212**. You and three friends, tired of the incessant rain in the north, will be taking the IC train from Hamburg as far south as you can. What is the southernmost city you can reach on this train? The westernmost? How much will tickets cost for each of you to each of these places? If you needed sleeping accommodations on the train, how much would they cost? (Will you need them?) Look at a map of Switzerland, and then consult the last half of the train schedule. Where does it appear that the train divides its cars according to their final destination? Does the train go to Lausanne via Spiez and Brig? How do you know? What phrases in the advertisement suggest that **a**) the price of sleeping accommodations depends in part on how and how far you travel? **b**) sleeping on the train is a good way to make use of those lost nights during your vacation? **c**) there are special arrangements for people who travel frequently?

SCHREIBEN

Stage 1 Note the location of the travel agency on the plan of the <u>Hauptbahnhof</u> in München (**CT 31**), where you intend to meet friends to plan a trip to the Frisian Islands. They will be arriving on the S-Bahn, Linie 15. Leave them a note telling them how to find you when they get there. Now rephrase the note, assuming they're arriving on the bus from their culinary excursion to the Starnberger See.

Stage 2 1. Find Marburg and its river, <u>die Lahn,</u> on your map of West Germany, and then look at the map of Marburg on **CT 132**. Now find the travel agency and practice giving directions to it from the castle and from the swimming pool.

2. Return to the exercise in Stage 1 (above). Write a friendly letter to the travel agency, in which you outline your reasons for a change of itinerary. Begin your letter: *"Sehr geehrte Herrschaften, . . ."*

STRUCTURAL EXERCISES

Note: Be sure you have reviewed your chapter grammar and read the relevant sections in the reference grammar before doing these exercises.

1 You are talking with a friend who is a bit hard of hearing and who keeps saying *"<u>Wie, bitte</u>?"* Combine the ideas expressed in the pairs of phrases in three different ways so the friend is sure to understand what you say about your excursion. Either causation or simultaneity may be involved.

Example: **Armbanduhr kaputt / Zug verpassen**
Meine Armbanduhr war kaputt. Ich habe den Zug verpaßt.
Weil meine Armbanduhr kaputt war, habe ich den Zug verpaßt.
Meine Armbanduhr war kaputt, also habe ich den Zug verpaßt.

1. Magenschmerzen / wandern können
2. Gutes Wetter / Aufstieg genießen
3. Regnen / zu Hause bleiben
4. Auf der Paßhöhe stehen / nach Italien sehen
5. Eine schnelle Fähre haben / viele Nordseeinseln sehen
6. Im Schlafwagen reisen / sich ausruhen
7. Einen Bären sehen / spät im Dorf ankommen
8. Den Reiseführer mißverstehen / den Weg verfehlen

9. Zum Paß hinaufsteigen / viele Pflanzen finden

10. Wildspezialitäten servieren / Hunger haben

2 In order to find out what sort of vacation to recommend, the clerk in the travel agency asks you what things you have already seen and done. As it turns out, you haven't yet seen or done anything she suggests — but you'd like to. Using the cues, write both her question and your answer.

> **Example:** **über die Grenze fahren?**
> Sind Sie schon mal über die Grenze gefahren?
> Nein, ich bin noch nicht über die Grenze gefahren.
> Aber wenn ich meinen Paß bekomme, möchte ich das machen.

1. ein Fahrrad mieten?
2. den Loftleidir-Flug nach Island buchen?
3. Alpenpflanzen sehen?
4. um den Comer See wandern?
5. eine Fähre nach den friesischen Inseln nehmen?
6. das Matterhorn besteigen?
7. den Stefansdom in Wien besichtigen?
8. eine Stadtrundfahrt von Ost-Berlin machen?
9. das Geburtshaus von Mozart besuchen?
10. an einer Abendfahrt auf dem Rhein teilnehmen?

3 You have been doing various things for some time now, and you tell an inquisitive person how long that has been. From the information given, formulate both the question and the response.

> **Example:** nach Sylt kommen **(2 Jahre)**
> Wie lange kommen Sie schon nach Sylt?
> Wir kommen seit zwei Jahren nach Sylt.

1. hier in Innsbruck sein **(1 Monat)**
2. Zeitungsartikel schreiben **(10 Jahre)**
3. diesen Wein trinken **(25 Jahre)**
4. Ihre Wanderschuhe tragen **(2 Wochen)**
5. in Leipzig studieren **(10 Monate)**
6. unabhängig sein **(3 Jahre)**
7. an diesem Volksfest teilnehmen **(1 Woche)**
8. mit Ihrem Bruder telefonieren **(15 Minuten)**
9. Briefmarken sammeln **(30 Jahre)**
10. schilaufen **(1 Tag)**

4 Return to the activities in #3, which you intend to continue doing. Add to your comments an appropriate period of time and reason for the continued activity.

> **Example:** nach Sylt kommen **(2 Jahre)**
> Ich komme noch ein Jahr nach Sylt. Dann habe ich kein Geld mehr.

√ CHECK YOUR PROFICIENCY

CAN YOU:
__ plan an excursion, giving reasons for your suggestions?
__ talk about your activities in various cities?
__ arrange for travel to East bloc countries?
__ ask for and give directions to places in cities and in the out-of-doors?

DO YOU REMEMBER HOW TO
__ deal wih minor medical problems?
__ arrange for private accommodations for an extended period of time?
__ ask questions and talk about mass transit facilities?
__ discuss your university studies in detail?

Ein Angebot der **DB touristik**

Ost-Expreß '82
Januar – Dezember 1982

Sonderfahrten

UdSSR China

DB
Reisedienst der
Bundesbahndirektion Hannover

_____
(Tagestempel für die Annahmestelle)

Zur Weiterleitung an die **Fka Hannover Hbf**

ANMELDUNG (bitte in Druckschrift ausfüllen)

Für Reise Nr. _____ vom _____ bis _____

nach _____

melde(n) ich (wir) _____ Personen an _____

_____ Damen _____ Herren _____ Ehepaare

Ich (wir) wünsche(n) folgende Unterkünfte:
                                    Unterbringung im Zug
_____ Einzelzimmer   2-Bett-Abteil _____

_____ Doppelzimmer   3-Bett-Abteil _____

Einsteigebahnhof: _____

Die Sonderfahrkarten möchte(n) ich (wir) bei der Fahrkarten-
ausgabe / dem DER-Reisebüro / der Verkaufsagentur der DB in

_____ in Empfang nehmen.

Mit der Anmeldung werden die im Programm angegebenen
Reisebedingungen anerkannt.

Anschrift des Bestellers:
_____

_____

Tel.: _____

_____   _____
(Datum)   (Unterschrift des Bestellers)

– Bitte Rückseite ebenfalls ausfüllen! –

FRAGEBOGEN FÜR VISAERTEILUNG
(Reisepaß und 6 Paßbilder beifügen)

1. FAMILIENNAME | | | | | | | | |

   Namensänderung
   Mädchenname

2. Vornamen | | | | | | | | |

3. Geburtsdatum u. Ort

Tag	Monat	Jahr	Ort		Land

4. Staatsangehörigkeit | | | |

5. Ständige Anschrift

Ort	Straße	Hausnummer

6. Berufliche Stellung, Arbeitsstätte u. Anschrift

7. Wann waren Sie das letzte Mal in Polen:
                         in der UdSSR:

8. Wurde Ihnen bereits ein polnisches / sowjetisches Visum
   verweigert?   Wann und wo?

9. Bei verheirateten Damen Name und Vorname des Mannes:

10. Ihre Verwandten in Polen / in der UdSSR:

   (Name, Geburtsdatum, Anschrift)

   _____

   _____

   _____

   _____

   _____

   _____

   _____

   _____

   _____
                                    (Unterschrift)

HÖREN

A1   Just listen several times to the dialogs for *Gespräche 1: Berlin — die geteilte Stadt*. Talk along if you like.

A2   Practice saying the dialog lines. Use your "pause" button if you have one.

B1   Conversation 1
1. Wo findet dieses Gespräch statt?
2. Ist die Grenzkontrolle immer noch sehr streng?
3. Schauen Sie sich Seite 348 im Haupttext an. Was ist <u>Neues Deutschland</u>? Wie würden Sie auf diesen Vorschlag reagieren, wenn Sie die andere Person wären?
4. Wie ernst ist der Vorschlag gemeint?
5. Hat man Zigaretten und Alkohol dabei?
6. Erraten Sie aus dem Kontext heraus: <u>verhaften</u>, <u>Gefängnis</u>.

Conversation 2
1. Was wäre der Vorteil von einer Übernachtung in Ostberlin?
2. Was wäre der Nachteil?
3. Wo übernachtet man wahrscheinlich? Warum?
4. Wie könnte man am besten über das Ostberliner Leben Bescheid bekommen? Gibt es diese Möglichkeit?
5. Erraten Sie aus dem Kontext heraus: <u>wahnsinnig</u>, <u>erleben</u>, <u>Kittchen</u>.

B2   Conversation 1
1. Warum hat man früher an der Grenze so streng kontrolliert?
2. Ist die Kontrolle immer noch so streng?
3. Warum durften die Grenztruppen Einreisende stoppen und untersuchen?
4. Erraten Sie aus dem Kontext heraus: <u>herrschen</u>, <u>Einfahrt</u>, <u>hindern</u>, <u>Zugang</u>, <u>erschweren</u>, <u>Viermächteabkommen</u>, <u>unterbrochen</u> (*from* unterbrechen), <u>Hoheitsgebiet</u>.

Conversation 2
1. Wie vergleicht man hier Berlin mit Bonn?
2. Wer sind die vier Alliierten?
3. Was wären die Vorteile von einem wiedervereinigten Berlin?
4. Was wären die Nachteile?
5. Wie denken die anderen europäischen Länder darüber?

C1

1A:4.2.2   Which word does the announcer mispronounce and then correct? There is a traffic tie-up in Augsburg. Until when? Does the announcer give a reason for it? How long is the delay at the border? [4]

1A:4.2.3   What, according to the woman announcer near the start, is the reason for the heavy traffic? What season is it? Can you guess more precisely than just the season? As you did in Chapter 16, listen to her report of traffic jams, noting highway number, stretches between major cities, and length of tie-up; but this time listen also for which side of the *Autobahn* is blocked. What is the cause of the traffic problem in Nürnberg? At the end (male announcer), note the delays for at least two of the border crossing points. [3, 16]

C2

2B:4.2.3   In which region of Germany was the art featured in the traveling exhibition created? How will it be transported to New York? [8, 14, 19]

2B:4.3.2   What day(s) could "today" be? How many exhibitors will be at the dog show? [11, 19]

SPRECHEN

Stage 1   Look at the picture on **CT 221**. There have been some difficulties at the border. Describe what has happened and how the problems will be resolved.

Stage 2   1.   Describe the picture of the Berlin Wall on **CT 220**.

2.   You have been in Berlin long enough to see the major attractions in both parts of the city. In your hotel is someone who is in the city on business but has one day to devote to a major museum visit. The big question: Is it going to be the group of museums on the Museumsinsel in East Berlin, or the world-famous paintings and Egyptian collection in the West Berlin suburb of Dahlem? Considering transportation, costs, and your acquaintance's interests, give some advice.

LESEN

Stage 1   Look at the picture in the lower left on **CT 220**. In what country do you think this picture was taken? Prepare to describe in German what an eternal flame is supposed to mean.

Stage 2   1.   Read the article *"Ein Besuch in Ostberlin"* on **CT 329**. What reference do you find to Berlin as a "divided city"? What subtle criticism of the west do you find? What evidence do you find that much of East Berlin has been rebuilt, renamed, or converted? To what extent does this article assert that much of western culture is rooted in East Berlin — or at least celebrated there?

2.   Part of the East Berlin information on **CT 329** deals with money exchange and other regulations concerning finances. Assemble all the information you can find and see if you can give reasons for the regulations.

3.   Which entry into East Berlin may be used by both West Germans and visitors from other countries? In what sense is the information about this entry not consistent in the article? Could a visitor from Canada gain entry into East Berlin after midnight? If you wanted to take a bus tour of East Berlin leaving from West Berlin, would you likely pay the tour company in *Mark* or *Deutsche Mark*? What document(s) would you have to bring with you?

SCHREIBEN

Stage 1   Choose one of the bus tour companies listed on **CT 329** and write a letter of inquiry about tours to East Berlin. Be sure to tell them the sorts of things you will want to see, and ask if there will be time to visit various attractions at different times of the day.

Stage 2   Read the city tour information about East Berlin on pp. 20-21 of the **ST** *Drucksachen*. Now write a short note back to your German teacher in Rochester, comparing the Berliner Dom with cathedrals you already know in Köln, Trier, and Freiburg. Because your teacher is interested in religion, add whatever you can find about other religious structures.

BERLIN — "HAUPTSTADT DER DDR"

HÖREN

Stage 1

A1   Just listen several times to the dialogs for *Gespräche 2: Berlin — "Hauptstadt der DDR"*. Talk along if you like.

A2   Practice saying the dialog lines. Use your "pause" button if you have one.

B1   Conversation 1
1. Spricht man hier mit einem Ostberliner oder einem Westberliner?
2. Wie gut kennen sich diese Gesprächspartner?
3. Welchen Grund für den Mauerbau gibt die DDR an?
4. Welcher Grund scheint glaubhafter zu sein?
5. Erraten Sie aus dem Kontext heraus: <u>Auswanderung</u>, <u>verhindern</u>, <u>abgegeben</u>, <u>Einmarsch</u>, <u>Regierung</u>.

Conversation 2
1. Was versteht der Ostberliner unter dem Wort "Freiheit"?
2. Meinen Sie, daß er nach dem Westen reisen möchte? Warum (nicht)?
3. Warum würde es zuviel kosten, nach dem Westen zu reisen?
4. Erraten Sie aus dem Kontext heraus: <u>Einkommen</u>, <u>kostenlos</u>, <u>Bewegungsfreiheit</u>.

Stage 2

B2   You are taking notes for your study abroad group's trip to East Berlin. Listen to the tour guide's descriptions of various monuments and public buildings, and note the main attractions of each. Make a special effort to write down words and phrases that strike you as being propaganda.

C1   Observe how the stock reports use two ways to indicate possession: *von* + dative case (see **CT 98**), and
1B:7.1.1,2   the genitive case, which is described in the *Struktur 1* section of this chapter (see **CT 222**). Can you note the many instances of the past tense form discussed most recently in Chapter 21 (see **CT 218**)? [P1, P2, 15]

C2   The on-the-scene radio announcer interviews the organizer of the consumer-products exposition.
2B:5.3.2   Compare the expositions of 1980 and 1986 in terms of exhibit area and number of exhibitors. How much larger in exhibit size will the exposition grow, according to the organizer? What conveniences are offered now to attract more visitors? How much do they cost? [15, 18]

2B:5.3.3   Why, in general, are the three women going to prison? Try to note more exactly at least one of the three counts of the guilty verdict returned against them. [3]

SPRECHEN

Stage 1   Assemble ten questions you would like to ask someone from East Berlin about life in a socialist country. The questions should deal with all aspects of life: work, leisure time, travel, study, and so on.

Stage 2   From what you know about life behind the Iron Curtain, give answers to your ten questions that reflect the thoughts of someone born and raised in East Berlin.

LESEN

Stage 1   Use the map on **CT 227** to locate where the photographs on the page were taken. Then identify the landmarks in the picture on the top right.

Stage 2   Follow the war years (1939-45) in the East Berlin city history on p. 36 of the **ST** *Drucksachen*. Underline those parts of the history that seem less than objective in their treatment of the Soviet role in the war.

SCHREIBEN

Stage 1   Look back at the German text on **CT 155**. List ten words and phrases that would likely be the core of a message from someone wanting to underscore East German progress in the last forty years.

Stage 2   1.   Consult the notes you took for the **B2** listening exercise for this part of Chapter 22, the monologue by the East German tour guide. Write down the things you think your group would like to see, and give reasons for your choices.

2.   Look at p. 36 of the **ST** *Drucksachen*, part of a city history of East Berlin. Write succinct newspaper headlines that capture the substance and tone of each of the first five entries for the year 1933. (What does *KPD* mean?)

STRUCTURAL EXERCISES

Note: Be sure you have reviewed your chapter grammar and read the relevant sections in the reference grammar.

1   As a European history major, you have been asked to interpret for a group of Austrians who are planning to tour East Berlin. You would like the experience (and the pay), but there are commitments to your study abroad group that must be met before you can undertake anything new. Explain **a)** to your study abroad group leader what the Austrians would like you to do, and then **b)** to the Austrians what your other commitments are. Use *sollen*, and then the *wollen, daß . . .* construction.

> **Example:**   **Zeigen Sie uns den Berliner Dom.**
> Ich soll ihnen den Berliner Dom zeigen.
> Sie wollen, daß ich ihnen den Berliner Dom zeige.

Austrian wishes:

1. Erklären Sie uns, wie wir zur "ewigen Flamme" kommen.
2. Finden Sie bitte die Milch-Mokka-Bar "Tutti-Frutti!"
3. Zeigen Sie uns, wo sich Hitler erschossen hat.
4. Erklären Sie uns die amerikanische Rolle im zweiten Weltkrieg.
5. Geben Sie uns ein paar Tips zum Ostberliner Nachtleben.

Group commitments:

6. Hol den Gruppenleiter um 18 Uhr am Bahnhof ab.
7. Schau unten am Eingang, ob die Post schon gekommen ist.
8. Hilf dem armen Brian mit der Verlängerung seines Visums.
9. Schreib endlich deinen Beitrag zur Gruppenarbeit über das Leben in der DDR.
10. Bring die Susanne schnell zum Krankenhaus!

2   You have been asked to say what activities various national groups like to engage in: sports, cooking, hiking, and so on. Pick ten nations and describe what the males, females, or both groups like to do.

> **Examples**:   Der Kanadier spielt gern Eishockey.   Die Amerikanerinnen studieren gern.

3   Look at the drawing of the extended family on **CT 296**. Write ten sentences using both the genitive case and *von* with the dative to describe the people.

> **Example:**   Der Großvater des Kindes/vom Kind mit dem Teddybären
> hat einen Schnurrbart.

√ CHECK YOUR PROFICIENCY

CAN YOU:
__ say something about various historical sights in West and East Berlin?
__ arrange for an extended stay in East Berlin?
__ anticipate East German opinions about social and political matters?
__ offer reasonable rebuttals to propaganda from both East and West?

DO YOU REMEMBER HOW TO:
__ arrange for accommodations in a private room or dormitory?
__ compare North American and European educational systems?
__ ask about finding lost items and describe them in detail?
__ ask important questions about trying on and buying clothing?

HÖREN

A1   Just listen several times to the dialogs for *Gespräche 1: Gedenkstätten*. Talk along if you like.

A2   Practice saying the dialog lines. Use your "pause" button if you have one.

B1   Conversation 1

1. Wie wissen wir, daß wenigstens eine Person im Gespräch ziemlich alt ist?
2. Warum hat man im Krieg nichts von den KZs gehört?
3. War die alte Person im Krieg ein Parteimitglied? Warum (nicht)?
4. Wie viele haben der Partei angehört?
5. Erraten Sie aus dem Kontext heraus: <u>besorgt</u>, <u>im Gegenteil</u>, <u>Parteiangehöriger</u>, <u>Wahl</u>.

        Conversation 2

1. Wie viele Personen im Gespräch sind aus Berlin?
2. Was haben die Grenztruppen gemacht?
3. Welches Bild bekommen Sie von der Mauer durch das Gespräch?
4. Erraten Sie aus dem Kontext heraus: <u>Grenzwächter</u>, <u>Kreuze</u>, <u>Kränze</u>, <u>Mitmenschen</u>, <u>Friedensmauer</u>, <u>durchstrichen</u>, <u>Leidensmauer</u>.

B2
1. Wie viele dieser Studenten sind aus der DDR?
2. Welche Worte zeigen die Unabhängigkeit der DDR von der Sowjetunion?
3. Welche Worte zeigen, daß die Sowjetunion in der DDR nicht immer etwas Positives ist?

B3   Listen to the account of a family's fortunes during and after the War, and take careful notes on the activities of each person. The people are: Onkel Gustav, Friedrich, Dorothea, Opa, Oma, and Heinz.

C1   <u>Note:</u> Many of the segments in this chapter illustrate use of the passive (see **CT 228** and **232**). Listen carefully for the various forms of the key verb *werden*.

1B:8.1.1,2   Observe the use of the past-tense passive: numbers <u>were drawn</u> (*wurden gezogen*). How big is one of the lottery prizes? What day or part of the week is it? [P1, 15]

C2

2A:1.2.1   What do the "Green Jacket" gang members call the people they beat up, and what do other people call the gang members now? [10, 19]

2A:1.2.4   What were the targets of the bomb attacks, and how were the explosives delivered? Observe the use of *wurden* in the passive structures (see **CT 232**). How many attacks have there been, and in what period of time? [12, 17]

2A:1.2.5   Which relative was the boy trying to help? Did he lose his ski pole before, while, or after he tried to help her? [11, 14]

2A:1.3.3   What caused the disaster in the disco? When did it occur? At least one American died — what was he doing in Germany? [1, 13, 17]

2A:1.3.4   How did the 4 people die? [1, 11, 17]

SPRECHEN

Stage 1 You've now seen lots of memorials in Europe, and it strikes you that you have seen many fewer in the United States. When you are asked about this, explain the difference. Take this opportunity to characterize the wars that have taken place on American soil.

Stage 2 You're speaking with a student at the Humboldt-Universität in East Berlin. Ask about the role played by the Soviet Union in the final attack on Berlin during World War II. Keeping in mind the fact that there are now Soviet soldiers stationed on East German soil, ask about the relationship between the two countries.

LESEN

Stage 1 1.   What do the commemorative tablets on **CT 230** and **CT 232** tell you about Switzerland? What does the sign on **CT 231** mean? What country do you think it is in?

2.   Compare WW2 casualties for the United States, the Soviet Union, and Germany both in sheer numbers and in percentage of population. Compare the Jewish casualties in all countries.

Stage 2 Tombstones tell us a good deal about history and about personal circumstances within larger historical contexts. On **CT 240** you will find a picture of a tombstone found in the Jewish cemetery in Freiburg. Who is buried here? What was the maiden name of the wife? What is Nissan, if not the name of a Japanese automobile company? Why do you suppose the memorial shows two different ways of showing dates? What do *geb.* and *gest.* stand for? Find out what you can about Theresienstadt.

SCHREIBEN

Stage 1 Look at the map on **CT 235**. How many East bloc countries are mentioned? In what context? List country names, adjectives of nationality, and the names of citizens (example: die Schweiz/Schweizer, schweizerisch/der Schweizer, die Schweizerin).

Stage 2 1.   Look again at the Schnurmann tombstone on **CT 240**. Write a brief historical account of the lives of these people, including the reasons for what happened. Are you <u>sure</u> they are buried here?

2.   Read the sign from a church wall in Bern on **CT 242**. What does it commemorate? Look up any names with which you are unfamiliar and prepare a written outline for a brief oral report.

RENTNER

HÖREN

Stage 1

A1   Just listen several times to the dialogs for *Gespräche 2: Rentner*. Talk along if you like.

A2   Practice saying the dialog lines. Use your "pause" button if you have one.

B1   Conversation 1
1. Warum mußten die Frauen am Kriegsende so schwer arbeiten?
2. Was für Arbeit haben die Frauen geleistet?
3. Was ist der "Trümmerberg" in Stuttgart?
4. Erraten Sie aus dem Kontext heraus: <u>Wiederaufbau</u>, <u>zustandegebracht</u>, <u>eingesetzt</u>, <u>beseitigt</u>.

Conversation 2
1. Warum ist Elsa nicht mehr mit Harald verheiratet?
2. Warum wohnt sie nicht beim Sohn?
3. Wo wohnt sie jetzt?
4. Was findet man Positives am Altersheim?

     5. Hat Elsa bei <u>einer</u> Person gelebt oder <u>zwei</u>, bevor sie ins Altersheim gekommen ist?

     6. Warum ist Elsa heute nicht mehr so gesund?

     7. Sind diese Gesprächspartner gut befreundet oder nicht?

Stage 2

B2   Conversation 1

     1. Ist Frau Kunert älter oder jünger als die anderen?

     2. Welchen Krieg hat das Ehepaar durchgemacht?

     3. Welche Wörter zeigen, daß sie ihr heutiges Leben als etwas Positives anschauen?

     4. Hat das Ehepaar Kinder?

     5. Ist das Ehepaar gesund?

     6. Denkt das Ehepaar gern an den Krieg? Wie wissen Sie das?

     Conversation 2

     1. In welchen Städten hat die alte Frau gelebt?

     2. Warum ist sie von der Stadt D- weggezogen?

     3. Hat man in Ostpreußen in der Stadt oder auf dem Land gelebt?

     4. Lebt der alte Mann noch? Was ist ihm im Krieg passiert?

     5. Hatte das Ehepaar Kinder?

C1

2A:1.3.1   Whose well-being is being discussed? Read section 2 of **CT 238** and then tell what the problem is. [1, 11]

C2   Talk for 30 seconds about the speaker's view of what friendship means — even if all you do is just to

2B:5.2.4   construct a list that begins, *"Naja. Er spricht von . . . "* More ambitious would be to try to represent his opinions: *"Er sagt, daß . . . "* Still more challenging would be a presentation of your own views in response to those of the speaker: *"Er sagt, es ist sehr schwer, einen Freund zu finden, aber . . . "* [12, 18]

SPRECHEN

Stage 1   Look at the picture of the Swiss farmers on **CT 236**. What do you think they're talking about? With a classmate, practice a typical discussion — but not necessarily in Swiss German.

Stage 2   Describe to your old high-school German class what conditions in Berlin were like just before the Nazis assumed power. Then compare life before the war with life just after Berlin was liberated in 1945, and with present-day life in Berlin some two generations later. Do your best to account for the differences.

LESEN

Stage 1   Look at the text *"Wohnen im Alter"* on **CT 236**. Guess from the entire context of the advertisement the meaning of the words *umsorgt, bevormundet, pflegebedürftig, teilhaben,* and *gesellschaftlich.*

Stage 2   Return to the city tour information about East Berlin on pp. 20-21 of the **ST** *Drucksachen*. The retirees in the city have seen many changes during their lives. Which of the buildings were constructed after the Second World War? Which important building would a person in his late 90's have seen built when he was a child? When he was in his early 30's, he may have taken part in the centennial celebration of a structure designed by Karl Friedrich Schinkel. About how old was he when the structure received its current name? (How do you know this was not the structure's original name?)

SCHREIBEN

Stage 1 Look at the picture of the man with the boy on **CT 196**. Write down some of his thoughts. Then write what he would say about how his life has changed **a)**in the last 20 years and **b)**in the last 10 years.

Stage 2 Return one more time to the city tour information about East Berlin on pp. 20-21 of the **ST** *Drucksachen*. The retiree in his late 90's has put down on paper a few words about the Schinkel structure, but wants you to flesh out the history for him. Do your best, incorporating the following words: *gebaut, Architekt, Unter den Linden, Statuen, 100-Jahr-Feier, neuer Name.*

STRUCTURAL EXERCISES

Note: Be sure you have reviewed your chapter grammar and read the relevant sections in the reference grammar.

1 Each of the following sentences deals with a family's experiences during and after the Second World War. Rephrase them to place the people and things that were the objects of each activity more squarely in the center of the action.

> **Example:** **Man brachte uns Kinder zuerst in die Stadt zu den Großeltern.**
> Wir Kinder wurden zuerst in die Stadt zu den Großeltern gebracht.

1. Die Nazis holten Onkel Fritz.
2. Wir haben ihn nie wieder gesehen.
3. Man rief Tante Emma als Krankenschwester in die Armee.
4. Wir haben sie wieder 1944 in Osnabrück gefunden.
5. Meine Familie schickte mich in Nürnberg in die Schule.
6. Wir verkauften den alten Opel vor dem Krieg.
7. Unsere Verwandten aus der Stadt besuchten uns immer, weil wir einen Garten hatten.
8. Die Bomben zerstörten die Kirche in unserer Nachbarschaft.
9. Nach dem Krieg haben wir die Kirche wieder aufgebaut.
10. Unsere Häuser öffneten wir den Flüchtlingen aus dem Osten.

2 Rephrase each of the following sentences using both the dative and the genitive to express "one of".

> **Example:** **Ein Freund von mir lebte nach dem Krieg in München.**
> Einer von meinen Freunden lebte . . .   Einer meiner Freunde lebte . . .

1. Eine Kusine von mir hat im Krieg einen Lastwagen gefahren.
2. Ein Kind von ihr hat einen amerikanischen Soldaten geheiratet.
3. Ein amerikanischer Soldat in Kaiserslautern hat mir geschrieben.
4. Ich habe ihm das Foto von einer Freundin zugeschickt.
5. Und er hatte mir ein Foto von einem Freund zugeschickt!
6. Wir haben uns dann in einem Cafe in Mainz kennengelernt.
7. Er hat mir einen Ring von seiner Mutter gegeben.
8. Ich habe ihm eine Kirschtorte von meiner Schwester gebracht.

3 If we'd had any money during the war, some good things might have happened. Hypothesize about the past according to the example.

> **Example:** **Wir hatten kein Geld. Sonst . . . ein größeres Haus kaufen.**
> Sonst hätten wir ein größeres Haus gekauft.

1. Sonst . . . meine Studien beginnen.
2. Sonst . . . die alte Kuh nicht für das Fleisch töten.
3. Sonst . . . nicht immer zu Hause sitzen.
4. Sonst . . . nicht mit dem Hunger kämpfen.
5. Sonst . . . den Freund von der Schwester wiedersehen.
6. Sonst . . . einen höheren Lebensstandard haben.

7. Sonst . . . ein Auto kaufen.

8. Sonst . . . das Haus renovieren.

9. Sonst . . . ein kleines Geschäft aufmachen.

10. Sonst . . . die dänische Grenze vor dem Krieg erreichen.

4 Accusations are flying about your family's involvement in the war. Pass them along to your parents, and then provide your own denial.

Example: Man sagt, . . . (**wir**) Steak essen.
Man sagt, wir hätten Steak gegessen. Aber wir haben kein Steak gegessen!

1. (**wir**) immer Ausflüge machen

2. (**ich**) immer nur Radio hören

3. (**ihr**) zuviel Benzin brauchen

4. (**wir**) Schnaps trinken

5. (**ihr**) den Nazis helfen

6. (**Rosa**) Liebesbriefe an Hitler schreiben

7. (**wir**) ein Landhaus in Bayern mieten

8. (**ihr**) Offiziere der Luftwaffe einladen

9. (**ihr**) eine Bombe an Herrn Churchill schicken

10. (Rosa) zu Hause eine Naziuniform anziehen

√ CHECK YOUR PROFICIENCY

CAN YOU:

__ describe important historical events?

__ hypothesize about the past?

__ report what someone else has said about the past?

__ change the perspective of a sentence by using the passive voice?

DO YOU REMEMBER HOW TO:

__ talk about leisure time activities?

__ describe in detail how things are done?

__ ask important questions about mass transit facilities?

__ handle minor medical emergencies?

DEUTSCHE BUNDESPOST

Telegramm

Verzögerungsvermerke

Empfangen von

Empfangen

Datum   Uhrzeit

Platz   Namenszeichen

Datum   Uhrzeit

Gesendet

Platz   Namenszeichen

Leitvermerk

Via/Leitweg

Uhrzeit

Aufgabetag

Wortzahl

Bezeichnung der Aufgabe-TSt

Aufgabe-Nr.

aus 7800 Freiburg im Breisgau/1

Gebührenpflichtige Dienstvermerke

=

=

Name des Empfängers, Straße, Hausnummer usw.

Bestimmungsort – Bestimmungs-TSt

Bitte Rückseite beachten.

Die stark umrahmten Teile sind vom Absender auszufüllen.

Feste Gebühr
(Nur bei Auslandstel)   DM _____ Pf

Wortgebühren   DM _____ Pf

Sonstige Gebühren   DM _____ Pf

Zusammen   DM _____ Pf

Angenommen

Wörter geändert

Wörter gestrichen

Wörter hinzugesetzt

**Auf ungenügende Anschrift/
Besonderheiten/
Dienstzeit hingewiesen**

Absender (Name und Anschrift, ggf. Ortsnetzkennzahl und
Telefonnummer, **diese Angaben werden nicht mittelegrafiert**)

A5, Kl. 38fc

fp   1ds ·10.84 / 8 7 6 5 4 3

937 200 099-5
TO Anl. 1

HÖREN

Stage 1

A1 Just listen several times to the dialogs for *Gespräche 1: Die alte Heimat — damals*. Talk along if you like.

A2 Practice saying the dialog lines. Use your "pause" button if you have one.

B1 Conversation 1
1. Wann und von wo ist diese Familie ausgewandert?
2. Wie viele Generationen sind schon in Amerika geboren?
3. Was ist in Michigan passiert?
4. Wie viele Familienmitglieder sind nach Amerika ausgewandert?
5. Erraten Sie aus dem Kontext heraus: <u>Schar</u>, <u>getauft</u>, <u>Nachtwächter</u>, <u>Einbrecher</u>.

      Conversation 2
1. Schreiben Sie die Namen der Verkehrsmittel (z.B. Auto, Flugzeug) auf, die Sie hören.
2. Welche Städtenamen hören Sie?
3. Wie viele Familienmitglieder sind ausgewandert?
4. Wohin sind sie gefahren?
5. Warum wollten sie nach New York?
6. Warum hat es in Hermann so viele Familien von "zu Hause" gegeben?
7. Erraten Sie aus dem Kontext heraus: <u>umständlicher</u>, <u>Vorfahren</u>, <u>komischerweise</u>, <u>sich ansiedeln</u>, <u>Molkerei</u>, <u>sich ausbreiten</u>.

Stage 2

B2 A person is speculating about the reasons his ancestors left Europe. Listen carefully, and list in your own words as many reasons as you can. Then tell in your own words what many modern Swiss families are doing and why.

C1

1A:1.2.1 Was the news report broadcast just before the segment, or is it going to be heard afterward? [P2, 2, 3]

1A:1.3.4 Was the news report broadcast just before the segment, or is it going to be heard afterward? [P2, 3, 7]

1A:2.3.2 The announcer mentions Bach, Beethoven, and the news. According to what can be heard in the segment, which statement is true at the time she speaks?
    a) So far this evening she has played Beethoven's Second and Bach's Twentieth.
    b) This evening she has already played Beethoven's Second; the news is at 8, followed by a Bach piece.
    c) So far this evening she has played Beethoven's Second and something by Bach.
    d) She's going to play Beethoven's Third and then, after the news, something by Bach. [20]

1A:3.2.1 Because of the Easter holiday, the poor announcer is overworked. How many requests for birthday and anniversary greetings has she received, and how many will she try to pass on now?

The greetings for the couples celebrating forty-fifth wedding anniversaries — they were married sometime around 1941 — are interesting. The congratulations for the first couple come from the "Bund der Kriegsblinden" — the Federation of Blind War Victims. Read the statistics about civilian and military casualties on **CT 235** to understand why one can't be certain who was blinded during the Second World War — the husband, the wife, or both. The couple may have been quite old, even in 1986, since by 1945 the German military was drafting some of the very same men who had been excused from military service in the First World War because — twenty-seven years earlier — they had been too old.

The other couple celebrating their forty-fifth wedding anniversary offers a more cheerful picture. How many grandkids and great-grandchildren do they have?

About 4 minutes into the segment the announcer reads the greetings to those celebrating their ninetieth birthdays. One of them shares a name with a famous German composer (see **CT 195**). Who is it? [3, 11]

C2

2B:5.4.1

Concentrate on verb tenses, time phrases, the word *rot*, and passive constructions to select the statement which best fits the announcer's statements:

a) St. Joseph's Day used to be an official holiday, and it is still celebrated unofficially.

b) St. Joseph's Day is still an official holiday.

c) St. Joseph's Day used to be an official holiday, but now it's just a day like any other.

d) People shoot off fireworks on St. Joseph's Day.

Concentrate on a relative pronoun construction and verb tenses to determine whether the name "Joseph" is more or less common now than it was in earlier times. [3, 10]

2B:5.4.2

The Catholic clergyman who is speaking about St. Joseph's Day says that the life of that saint has a message for people today. Which group does he have in mind? **a)** practicing Catholics; **b)** Catholics, whether or not they attend church; **c)** young people; **d)** everyone.

How many saints' days are formally celebrated each year now in Catholic areas? **a)** more than 50; **b)** 50; **c)** fewer than 50.

How does the speaker seek to demonstrate that saints' days had a progressive influence on the social policies of earlier times?

a) The many saints' days effectively reduced the earlier six-day work week to five days.

b) St. Joseph, who was a carpenter, illustrated the dignity of manual labor.

c) The many saints' days gave people more time to build cathedrals.

d) The many saints' day reminded the rulers of society of their responsibilities to the working classes. [10, 16]

SPRECHEN

Stage 1

On **CT 240** there is a picture of a person taking a picture of an old house. Shortly after this picture was taken, the person spoke some German words into a tape recorder to document this visit to the old family homestead. What were the words?

Stage 2

1. Tell as much as you know about how **a)** your parents and **b)** your grandparents met.

2. Speculate about what course your life would have taken if you had not been born **a)** when or **b)** where you were.

LESEN

Stage 1

Read the documents found on **CT 241**. Whose documents were they? Where are they from? Why are they written in German?

Stage 2

On **CT 246** you will find a page from an East German government publication. Remembering the average East German income shown on **CT 154**, compare those things for which prices are given on this page with equivalent services in the United States. Write down words and phrases that account for the differences.

SCHREIBEN

Stage 1

Look at the picture of the römisch-germanisches Museum in Köln on **CT 96**. Write a short description of the differences between the buildings you see.

Stage 2

1. **CT 210** shows two pictures that contrast old and new ways of life. Write a short description of what life used to be like and what it is like now. Write why you think the change was or was not necessary.

2.   Look again at the church documents on **CT 241**. Write a note to distant relatives in Karl-Marx-Stadt, telling them about these documents you've just found in an old trunk in the attic. Surely you remember this person, someone you knew well when you were younger. Write about his relationship to you, and then write a brief history of his life, including his parents' emigration from present-day East Germany.

DIE ALTE HEIMAT — JETZT

HÖREN

Stage 1

A1   Just listen several times to the dialogs for *Gespräche 2: Die alte Heimat — jetzt*. Talk along if you like.

A2   Practice saying the dialog lines. Use your "pause" button if you have one.

B1   Conversation 1

1. Warum sind diese Wohnhäuser in der BRD so modern?
2. Warum ist das amerikanische Haus nicht so modern eingerichtet?
3. Sind die Deutschen kritisch?
4. Vergleichen Sie das deutsche Haus mit dem amerikanischen Haus.
5. Sagen Sie etwas zur Ehe bei den Amerikanern (gesund/nicht gesund — typisch/nicht typisch?)
6. Erraten Sie aus dem Kontext heraus: <u>Überraschung</u>, <u>gestehen</u>, <u>übel nehmen</u>, <u>Ausnahme</u>, <u>Großteil</u>.

Conversation 2

1. Ist das Bild von den USA in diesem Gespräch positiv oder negativ?
2. Welche Ausdrücke zeigen, daß die BRD heutzutage ein sehr modernes Land ist?
3. Welche Ausdrücke sind für Sie eher negativ als positiv?
4. Wieso kann es einem Land "zu gut" gehen?
5. Erraten Sie aus dem Kontext heraus: <u>Wohlstand</u>, <u>dem Boden gleich</u>, <u>auf die Beine bringen</u>, <u>Wirtschaftswunder</u>.

Stage 2

B2
1. Aus welchen Ländern kommen die Gesprächspartner?
2. Von welchen Ländern oder kulturellen Gruppen hören Sie im Gespräch?
3. Um welche kulturelle Gruppe geht es hauptsächlich im Gespräch?
4. Schreiben Sie die Ausdrücke auf, die mit dem Hauptproblem zu tun haben.
5. Was scheint das größte Problem zu sein?
6. Welche Probleme sind mit den Kindern verbunden?
7. Welche Länder haben die gleichen Probleme?
8. Welche Rolle spielt Geld im ganzen Problemkreis?
9. Erraten Sie aus dem Kontext heraus: <u>herholen</u>, <u>Gastgewerbe</u>, <u>Mischehen</u>, <u>berücksichtigen</u>, <u>formulieren</u>, <u>Mehrzahl</u>, <u>anbeten</u>, <u>Einwandererstrom</u>, <u>Arbeitslosigkeit</u>, <u>Arbeitslosenunterstützung</u>, <u>Kulturraum</u>, <u>Zusammenleben</u>.

C1

1B:7.1.2   Is the market generally higher or generally lower today? List today's and yesterday's share prices for Volkswagen.

Listen for the word *Rentenmarkt*. It is related to *Rentner*. The later is a person who draws a pension. *Die Rente* is income from investments, and can refer more specifically to the yield from pension funds or annuities. How much is the annuity market down today?

What is the exchange rate for dollars today, and how has it changed from yesterday?

How many different ways does the announcer have of expressing a rise or improvement in values? [P2, 15, 22]

C2
2A:1.1.3
How many hundred people are searching for how many hundred victims? Observe the relative pronoun construction, *"Menschen, die . . . unter . . . Hotel . . . sind."* Of the 11 victims found so far, how many are seriously injured? [2, 6, 16]

2A:1.3.2
Did the mother die before or after the sextuplets were delivered? How many of them are girls? Did all 6 survive birth? [1, 11, 13]

2A:1.3.5
Were the two accident victims in a car, on bicycles, or on foot when they were killed? When was the accident? Who are the police looking for now, besides the hit-and-run driver? Listen for the many passive constructions in the segment, particularly at the start, since the focus is on the victims and since the person who killed them, having committed hit-and-run, cannot be named. Verbs to observe are *anfahren, verletzen, identifizieren, vermissen.* [12, 18]

2A:3.1.1
What is the speaker's feeling about how long the special Salvator beer will be available? How closely can you determine the range of dates possible for "today"? [1, 5, 8]

2A:3.1.3
Concentrate on a relative pronoun to determine whom the speaker is greeting. He mentions earlier times — how much earlier? [5]

SPRECHEN

Stage 1
Find an old family picture and identify the people as closely as you can. Begin with description of them as they appear in the picture, and compare them with the people they later became. Be sure to define relationships carefully. (You will find that relative clauses come in handy here.)

Stage 2
Now find a more recent picture of your family. First describe their physical features, and then talk about their personalities — including any little quirks that characterize your family and no other.

LESEN

Stage 1
1.   Read *"Der Arbeiter"*, a short description of a slide show at the BMW museum in München on p. 39 of the **ST** *Drucksachen*. How have robots changed the lives of workers in a modern factory? What about workers' jobs in such a modern automated factory? (Look up the verb *warten* in your dictionary to find its unusual meaning here.)

2.   Now read *"Jugend und Ausbildung"* on the same page. What do the newer, more complicated machines imply for the training of young factory workers? What interest does the company have in spending a good deal of time and money in training programs? What has changed the entire face of the business or commercial aspect of the modern corporation?

Stage 2
The paragraph *"Frauen in der Industrie"* in the BMW museum materials (p. 39 of the **ST** *Drucksachen*) lists two main difficulties faced by women in the search for equality in the workplace. What are they? What is a *Doppelbelastung*? What appears to be a possible solution to the problems?

SCHREIBEN

Stage 1
The paragraph *"Soziale Einrichtungen"* in the BMW museum materials (p. 39 of the **ST** *Drucksachen*) tells what social services are available to BMW employees. For each of the long compound nouns expressing an answer to the needs of individual workers, write a sentence or two of explanation for someone who might not understand the word. Example: *Kinderferienlager — In den Schulferien können Kinder dorthin gehen, meist an einen Ort im Wald oder in den Bergen. Sie lernen neue Spiele und Lieder und schlafen in Schlafsäcken in Hütten.*

Stage 2
Read the paragraph *"Technik"* in the BMW museum materials. Beginning with what you already know about the time before the Industrial Revolution in the 19th century, write a paragraph describing differences in the workplace that have been brought about by the introduction of new technologies in this century. Have all the changes been for the better?

Chapter 24: STRUCTURAL EXERCISES

STRUCTURAL EXERCISES

Note: Be sure you have reviewed your chapter grammar and read the relevant sections in the reference grammar.

1   The following tape-recorded account of the beginning of the1932 emigration of a family from Europe needs to be edited and prepared for dissemination in a newsletter for an upcoming family reunion. Recast this conversational-past narration in the more formal past tense, omitting the narrative crutches such as "You know?" and "Right?". Remember that as the narrator intrudes into the story, you should refer to him not as *ich*, but as one of the group (*er*). Make other changes of perspective as necessary.

> **Example:** **Und endlich sind wir von Le Havre losgefahren.**
> Und endlich fuhren sie von Le Havre los.

> Ich habe meine Sachen schon eine Woche vorher eingepackt. Wir Kinder sind einfach sehr neugierig gewesen — und etwas ängstlich, natürlich. Nun, der große Tag war da. Onkel Martin hat uns mit seinem Auto abgeholt und zum Bahnhof gebracht. Aber, weißt du, wir haben schon dort große Probleme gehabt. Vater hat unser ganzes Geld vergessen und er mußte wieder nach Hause. Onkel Martin hat ihn also dorthin und zurück gefahren. Dann ist der Zug nicht gekommen, weil am Fuhrwerk etwas kaputt war. Endlich haben wir die Lokomotive aus der Ferne gesehen und haben so gewußt, daß unsere Träume wahr werden. Im Zug ist nicht viel passiert, nur sind alle etwas nervös gewesen. Und an der Grenze haben wir unsere Pässe vorgezeigt. Der Beamte hat uns gefragt, ob wir auswandern, weil wir soviel Gepäck mitgetragen haben. Mutter hat "Ja" gesagt und dazu ein bißchen geweint — weißt du? Die Mutter hat mir so leid getan, weil sie ihre ganze Familie wahrscheinlich nicht mehr sehen würde. Aber in Le Havre — im Hafen also — ist alles viel besser gegangen. Mutter hat versprochen, nicht mehr zu weinen. Und wir Kinder haben zum ersten Mal in einem richtigen Hotel geschlafen und gegessen! Am Morgen der Abreise haben wir dann das Schiff gesehen und große Augen gemacht . . . .

2   The narrator of the above account, Anton, also showed some pictures to the interviewer and explained who the various people were. The pictures will be printed in the newsletter. Recast the narrator's statements in more formal German by using relative pronouns as well as the narrative past tense.

> **Example:** **Der erste ist mein Bruder. Der ist schon 1936 gestorben.**
> Der erste ist sein Bruder, der schon 1936 starb.

1. Dann kommt Gudrun. Die war bei der Abreise die Jüngste.
2. Neben Gudrun steht Katrin. Mit der hat Gudrun später einen Laden aufgemacht.
3. Der Nächste ist Christian. Seine Tochter hat einen Mann aus Ohio geheiratet.
4. Neben Christian sitzt Jakob. Mit ihm habe ich lange einen Briefwechsel geführt.
5. Hinten steht der Vater. Ich habe ihn nach diesem Tag dann nicht mehr gesehen.
6. Am Ende siehst du Emilie. Die hat mit ihrem zweiten Mann sieben Kinder gehabt.
7. Links von Emilie steht Onkel Gustav. Der ist mit seiner Familie 1934 ausgewandert.
8. Onkel Gustav hatte drei Jungen. Ich habe immer mit denen gespielt.
9. Das ist Tante Grete. Die war die Frau von Onkel Gustav. Ich habe sie sehr geliebt.
10. Das sind dann die Zwillinge. Ihren Geburtstag haben wir immer gern gefeiert.

3   The narrator sighs a bit, recalling the old days, and wonders what might have happened if things had been different. Complete his speculations both creatively and correctly.

> **Example:** Wenn wir nicht ausgewandert wären, . . .
> . . . hätten wir dieses schöne Land nie gesehen.

1. Wenn der Krieg nicht begonnen hätte, . . .
2. Wenn Vater nicht schon 1935 gestorben wäre, . . .
3. Wenn Gudrun und Katrin keinen Laden aufgemacht hätten, . . .
4. Wenn Chrsitians Tochter den Mann aus Ohio nicht geheiratet hätte, . . .
5. Wenn Emilie nach dem Tod ihres ersten Mannes Witwe geblieben wäre, . . .
6. Wenn Onkel Gustav in Gaishausen geblieben wäre, . . .

7. Wenn Tante Grete länger gelebt hätte, . . .
8. Wenn die Flugkarten nach Frankfurt nicht so viel gekostet hätten, . . .
9. Wenn wir in den ersten Jahren ein Telefon gehabt hätten, . . .
10. Wenn ich nicht später nach Seattle weitergereist wäre, . . .

√ CHECK YOUR PROFICIENCY

CAN YOU:
__ talk about your family relationships?
__ tell your personal history in some detail?
__ give opinions about both past and present events?
__ speculate about what might have happened if things had been different?

DO YOU REMEMBER HOW TO:
__ make arrangements to hear a concert?
__ discuss the quality of a rock or classical concert?
__ ask questions about the process of making something?
__ discuss the possibilities of excursions to various places?

Deutsche Demokratische Republik

Ministerium für Auswärtige Angelegenheiten

Transitvisum

zur einmaligen Reise durch das Hoheitsgebiet
der Deutschen Demokratischen Republik
über die für den Transitverkehr
zugelassenen Grenzübergangsstellen
auf den vorgeschriebenen Verkehrswegen
und der kürzesten Fahrtstrecke

i. A.

Während des Transits ist ein Wechsel des Transportmittels nur mit Zustimmung der zuständigen Organe der DDR gestattet. In der Binnenschiffahrt berechtigt das Transitvisum zum Landgang an den dafür zugelassenen Orten.

A 19/3

GM 6942947

Dieses Transitvisum berechtigt

Name

Vorname

Geburtsdatum

Reisedokument-Nr. I-5/6,5/3.5   BRD/WB

mit _____ Kind/ern

zur Fahrt in dem für die unverzügliche Durchreise benötigten Zeitraum
durch die Deutsche Demokratische Republik
nach BRD/Westberlin

Einreise   Ausreise

21.07.18
Schwanheide

HÖREN

Stage 1

A1   Just listen several times to the dialogs for *Gespräche 1: Wäscherei*. Talk along if you like.

A2   Practice saying the dialog lines. Use your "pause" button if you have one.

B1   Conversation 1
1. Wie heißt der Kunde?
2. Werden die Hemden gewaschen oder gereinigt?
3. Wann sind die Hemden dann fertig? Warum erst dann?
4. Wollte der Kunde seine Hemden selbst waschen?

        Conversation 2
1. Welche Probleme hat der Kunde?
2. Wann soll das Waschmittel zugegeben werden?
3. Wie viele Maschinen müssen benutzt werden?
4. Warum sagt der Kunde, daß die Wäsche immer teurer wird?

Stage 2

B2
1. Wie ist die Jacke schmutzig geworden?
2. Soll sie gereinigt oder gewaschen werden? Wozu entscheidet sich die Kundin?
3. Wie können die Blusen und Hemden am saubersten werden?
4. Kommt die Kundin oft hierher? Warum (nicht)? Macht sie die Wäsche gern?
5. Wo ist ihr Mann? Warum hilft er nicht?
6. Welches Mißverständnis hören Sie?

C

2B:4.1.2   The second half of the segment deals first with customs regulations governing tourists entering West Germany from other Common Market countries (=*EG-Länder*). How much wine, how much hard liquor, and how many cigarettes can be brought duty-free into the Federal Republic under the present regulations, and how do those quantities differ from those specified in earlier regulations? Observe the passive construction "*dürfen ... eingeführt werden.*" Note the same information for West Germany's neutral neighbors by transcribing the final sentence: "*Aus Österreich* _____ _____ _____ _____ _____ _____ _____ __ _____ _____, *sowie* _____ _____ *Schnaps,* _____ _____ _____ _____ _____ _____ _____." [2, 12, 21]

2B:4.2.3   Observe the passive with modal verb construction in the very first sentence: "*kann ... bewundert werden*" (*bewundern* = to admire). Listen for a second passive construction, beginning with wurden, to learn what security measures were taken to protect the art works on their trip to New York. [8, 14, 19, 22]

2B:5.4.3   Note how many times you hear the verb *schließen*, and how often the passive is used, in this report about the possible closing of the Museum of Jewish Culture in Augsburg. Transcribe the end of the very first sentence: "*Nach der Meldung einer Nachrichtenagentur [According to a news-service report],* _____ _____ _____ _____ _____ _____ _____ *Geldmangel möglicherweise* _____ _____ _____ _____ _____ _____." [10, 14, 19]

Observe later the phrase used to describe a specialist at the museum: "*ein wissenschaftlicher Mitarbeiter*".

EVALUATE YOUR LISTENING COMPREHENSION

The following items request comprehension of simple facts and construction of elementary inferences. Chapter 26 offers a check of higher-level comprehension.

1A:1.4.1-4   Can you understand the time and the station identification upon one listening only? Does the announcer tell what time it was, what time it is, or what time it will be? In segment 4, is the program "Bayern-Magazin" over or not yet begun? [7, 10, 13]

1A:2.1.2   What is the latest time it can be "now"? What is the minimum length of the classic music broadcast on stations 2 and 4? What special group of listeners does the announcer address? [9, 20]

1A:5.2.5   What time is it? Has it been raining in Southern Bavaria? How low in the mountains will snow fall? Did the new report precede the weather, or is it to follow? [9, 14, 21]

1B:6.1.8   What two reason does the coffee manufacturer give for buying EduScho? [P2, 5, 9]

1B:6.3.6   Transcribe the exact name of the event. For what 4 activities does it offer information and materials? [13, 16, 20]

1B:6.4.3   What special group of people is the target of the ad for brain tonic, and how does it claim to help them? [5, 13]

SPRECHEN

Stage 1   You have a deep stain on your shirt and need it taken care of right away. When the employee at the cleaner's expresses doubt about cleaning the shirt, you become upset. But you must catch public transportation within two hours and absolutely must have the shirt done by then — it's the only good one you have. In your desperation, you offer to pay double.

Stage 2   You are the employee in the situation above. You don't understand why the person is so upset — after all, the stain didn't happen in your establishment! There are other regular customers in line with their orders, and you feel put upon. But agree to discuss the matter with the boss anyway.

LESEN

Stage 1   Look at the control panels of the washing machines shown on **CT 250**. Do the pointers move clockwise or counterclockwise during the entire wash-rinse cycle? How do you know?

Stage 2   1.   Look at the long text on **CT 250**, the one that describes the washing procedure. How does the door of the machine open? What part of these instructions can be taken care of at home before going to the laundromat? How do these instructions differ from those in American laundromats?
2.   Look at the SENSO ad on **CT 255**. Where is this product made? How many ounces of detergent does this box contain? How are imperatives expressed on the SENSO box? Which words and phrases describe gentle treatment of clothing? Why should some woolens be washed separately from others?

SCHREIBEN

Stage 1   Read "*Willkommen . . .*" on **CT 192**. In as much detail as you think pertinent, tell how various articles of clothing got dirty and give instructions for washing each.

Stage 2   The instructions you gave in the exercise above were misunderstood. The good shirts are now a different color, there is dark lint on the light pants, and the jeans are still filthy. Write another note, expressing your disgust and frustration, and say what must be done now.

FOTOENTWICKLUNG

HÖREN

Stage 1

A1   Just listen several times to the dialogs for *Gespräche 2: Fotoentwicklung*. Talk along if you like.

A2   Practice saying the dialog lines. Use your "pause" button if you have one.

B1   Conversation 1
              1. Welche Frage hat der Kunde?
              2. Wie sagt die Angestellte, daß alles im Labor automatisch vor sich geht?
              3. Wie weiß man im Labor, welcher Film wem gehört?
              4. Aus dem Kontext heraus erraten: behilflich, Umschlag, Kennzeichen, geklebt.

              Conversation 2
              1. Welche Fragen hat der Kunde?
              2. Scheint dies ein gewöhnlicher Kunde zu sein?
              3. Aus dem Kontext erraten: Keine Ursache, Linse, Wunsch, Chemikalien, Führungen.

Stage 2

B2   1. Wie viele Filme insgesamt möchte der Kunde zur Entwicklung abgeben?
              2. Wann wird die Entwicklung bezahlt?
              3. Welche Wünsche hat der Kunde noch dazu?
              4. Welches englische Wort hören Sie im Gespräch?
              5. Wann sind die Bilder fertig? Wann sind die Vergrößerungen fertig?
              6. Aus dem Kontext heraus erraten: Großlabor, mitbezahlt, geraten.

C1

1B:6.1.9 When do you get the full nectar-like effect of Langnese honey? What does that experience do for your attitude toward the rest of the world? Copy down a sentence that tells how selective the Langnese folks are about the honey they produce. [P2, 5, 9]

1B:6.2.4 How is Fuji promoting its film? List up to 3 ways. [6, 10, 18]

1B:6.2.6 What kind of leather fashions does the store have? *"Ledermode, ____ es _____ ____ _____ gibt."* [16, 18]

1B:6.3.1 What machine is being repaired? What damaged it? Observe the past subjunctive: *"Mit Kalgon wäre das nicht passiert."* Can you jot down the slogan sung at the end? [5, 15]

1B:6.3.2 Note the relative pronoun at the start: *"Das ist wichtig für alle, _____ sich schon lange ein Mikrowellengerät kaufen wollten."* Where can you put the compact Bosch microwave? Where should you go for more information? [15, 18]

1B:6.3.7 Why is Ungeheuer BMW having the sale? [15]

C2

2A:1.1.1 What is the title of the politician who is laying the cornerstone for the new building at the university? What other dignitary is mentioned? Read section 3 about word formation on the **Class Text** *Struktur 1* page (**CT 258**), and then listen for phrases containing verbs that mean "unite" and "simplify". [4, 6, 17]

2A:1.4.1 How many of the news summaries deal with labor and industry? What is the Bavarian Social Democratic Party planning to do? [See the special self-evaluation section in Chapter 16.]

2A:1.4.2 How many of the news stories mention government officials or institutions? How does the medical school professor think doctor training programs can be improved? [13]

SPRECHEN

Stage 1 1. Look at the beach picture on **CT 190**. Describe five photos taken by a person involved in this activity, and then give special developing and mounting instructions for each.
           2. Repeat the exercise for the rock-climbing picture.

Stage 2 You are thinking of leaving some film for developing and name various sizes as gifts for various family and friends. When the clerk suggests a special offer, including free film, you decide you can't pass it up. Be sure to find out when your pictures will be ready.

LESEN

Stage 1 Look at the signs on **CT 258**. Where would each sign be found?

Stage 2 Look at the picture of the camera store to the left on **CT 256**. In what city is the store located? How do you know? Using a transit map familiar to you by now, which public transportation would you take to Herne's? Bearing in mind the cost of photo printing, do you think the store window shown on page 255 (left) is located in the same country? Why (not)? What special advantages might Herne's offer over other stores? Does it cost more to make a picture from a negative or a slide? Is the *"Bild vom Bild"* text from Herne's? How do you know? Why was the customer who received the note from the photo lab (page 256) probably disappointed?

SCHREIBEN

Stage 1 Write the two present passive sentences you see in the sign *"Unsere Leistungen. . ."* on **CT 252**. How else can they be expressed? Which sentences in the active voice could be expressed in the passive?

Stage 2 The door shown on **CT 257** tells where various articles are to be found in a store. What German store name might be found over the door? List as many verbs as you can that are suggested by the nouns in the listing. (Example: *Glückwunschkarten — schreiben, heiraten*)

STRUCTURAL EXERCISES

1 You are passing along instructions in a laundromat / camera store, where the boss is a bit too overbearing for your taste. Convert the boss's instructions from imperatives to sentences with *man* and then to passive constructions. NOTE: *nicht müssen ≠ nicht dürfen*!

Example: Kochen Sie das nicht!
Das darf/soll man nicht kochen.   Das darf/soll nicht gekocht werden.

1. Trennen Sie die Kochwäsche von der Feinwäsche!
2. Machen Sie das nicht alles in einer Maschine!
3. Bringen Sie den Sommeranzug zur chemischen Reinigung!
4. Lesen Sie zuerst die Gebrauchsanweisungen!
5. Tun Sie nicht so viel Waschpulver hinein!
6. Waschen Sie die rosa Unterwäsche nicht mit den Jeans zusammen!
7. Bringen Sie diese Filme um drei Uhr ins Zentrallabor!
8. Verkaufen Sie nicht so viel Fugi-Film!
9. Entwickeln Sie den Film kostenlos! Das ist mein Freund.
10. Bestellen Sie die Dias zum Sonderpreis! Das ist meine Frau.

2 Back in the youth hostel, you are telling some of your Swedish friends about life in rural Austria. You can do this by using *man* as the all-purpose agent, or you can use a passive construction. Do the latter.

Example: Man kehrt die Straßen jeden Tag.
Die Straßen werden jeden Tag gekehrt.

1. Man öffnet die Geschäfte täglich um 7.30 Uhr.
2. Man hängt die Federdecken jeden Morgen zum Fenster hinaus.
3. Man macht jeden Tag von Mittag bis 14 Uhr eine Arbeitspause.
4. Man wählt nur die besten Politiker.
5. Man besucht die Kirche jeden Sonntag.
6. Abends trinkt man beim Kartenspiel manchmal ein wenig Schnaps.
7. Morgens früh füttert man das Vieh.
8. Man renoviert die alten Kapellen an den Wanderwegen.
9. Man schließt die Fensterläden, wenn das Wetter stürmisch wird.
10. Man unternimmt gern lange Bergwanderungen in den Schulferien.

√ CHECK YOUR PROFICIENCY

CAN YOU:
__ explain the separation of articles of clothing for washing?
__ give instructions for operating a washing machine?
__ arrange to have your film processed in a camera store?
__ explain special film processing requests?

DO YOU REMEMBER HOW TO:
__ arrange for travel to East bloc countries?
__ make arrangements for an extended stay in an East bloc city?
__ deal with political and social opinions that differ from your own?
__ talk about human misfortunes and discuss important historical events?

Chapter 26
UNHÖFLICHKEIT — HÖFLICHKEIT

HÖREN

A1   Just listen several times to the dialogs for *Gespräche 1: Unhöflichkeit — Höflichkeit*. Talk along if you like.

A2   Practice saying the dialog lines. Use your "pause" button if you have one.

B1   Conversation 1
  1. Warum kann niemand dieses Argument gewinnen?
  2. Warum hält der Deutsche nicht viel von den USA?
  3. Kritisiert er eher die Innenpolitik oder die Außenpolitik der Amerikaner?
  4. Erraten Sie aus dem Kontext heraus: <u>notwendig</u>, <u>den Rücken kehren</u>, <u>engagiert</u>, <u>Rohstoffe</u>, <u>unbeliebt</u>.

        Conversation 2
  1. Wie gut kennen sich diese Gesprächspartner?
  2. Wie viele Personen treffen sich am Samstag Abend?
  3. Was wissen Sie über Kiesemans?
  4. Erraten Sie aus dem Kontext heraus: <u>bezogen</u>, <u>Firma</u>, <u>gemütlich</u>.

B2
  1. Wissen Sie, was verkauft werden soll? Was kann es <u>nicht</u> sein?
  2. Beschreiben Sie, wie die Hausfrau auf den Hausierer reagiert.
  3. Wie alt ist die Firma des Hausierers?
  4. Warum möchte die Hausfrau lieber im Dorf einkaufen?
  5. Welche positiven Argumente wendet der Hausierer an?
  6. Erraten Sie aus dem Kontext heraus: <u>Versuch</u>, <u>überzeugt</u>, <u>woanders</u>, <u>Ladenpreis</u>, <u>augenblicklich</u>, <u>sich hineinzwängen</u>

C   EVALUATE YOUR LISTENING COMPREHENSION

2A:1.1.2   Aside from the small cost of manufacturing the coins, how much did the counterfeiter make each time he passed one of his phony coins? Write down a word that shows that he has been caught. [6, 16]

2A:1.2.3   Who will be on the stamps, and how many will there be? [10, 12, 17]

2A:2.1.2   How many people, and from where, wrote to request the song? Have they tried before? [1, 12]

2A:2.1.3   What items will the fleamarket accept, under what conditions can they be offered, and how does one get them mentioned on the air? If you want to try this as a speaking exercise, picture yourself offering advice to a friend; use the verbs *können*, *müssen* and *dürfen*. [7, 12, 15, 18]

2B:4.1.1   If you go on any of these tours, what happens to your baggage? [2, 5, 9, 14, 21]

2B:5.2.3   What is the title of the publication, how long is it, how much does it cost, and where can you obtain it? What does it offer advice about? [15, 19]

SPRECHEN

   Find three pictures of people doing impolite things. Describe the pictures, then say what each person should be doing instead.

   Look at the picture on **CT 200**. A member of the audience suddenly stands up and says something to the conductor. Practice the ensuing dialog.

LESEN

Stage 1 Look at the three lines at the bottom of **CT 54**, beginning with "LINKS GEHEN . . . " and ending with " . . . *bevor der Zug hält.*" In each case, create a sentence telling someone face-to-face but politely to obey the impersonal command expressed by the sign.

Stage 2 You have observed someone violating the regulations or ignoring the directions expressed in the signs you read in Stage 1. What's past is past, but you can still comment about it. By all means try to use the past subjunctive ("You should have . . . "), but don't forget how bitingly effective you can be with just a "tsk-tsk" observation ("Too bad you didn't . . . ").

SCHREIBEN

Stage 1 Your student-housing roommate in the Goethe Institut German for Business program is a slob who knows everything about macro-economics and nothing about home economics. Pick three of the worst offenses and describe them in writing. Try the following formats: 1) notes for a heart-to-heart talk where you don't want to lose your temper or forget your German; 2) a pithy note to the roommate who's never around when you want to talk, with back-up threats in case there is not a change for the better; 3) notes for a talk with the director of the Goethe Institut — you want a new roommate.

Stage 2 Refer to the Stage 2 speaking exercise above. As a music critic, you have been taking notes for your article in the next day's edition of the local paper. You realize that there's material here that would interest more than just music lovers, and you plan a front-page story — assuming you can keep up with the rapid-fire conversation and activity within the concert hall after the house manager has called the police. Write your account of the happenings.

WILLKOMMEN UND ABSCHIED

HÖREN

Stage 1

A1 Just listen several times to the dialogs for *Gespräche 2: Willkommen und Abschied*. Talk along if you like.

A2 Practice saying the dialog lines. Use your "pause" button if you have one.

B1
1. Wie wissen Sie, daß Herr Dr. Hentschel schon mal hier war?
2. Ist dies eher das Geographische Institut der Universität oder die Hauptarbeitsstelle des ADAC (Allgemeiner Deutscher Automobil-Club)? Warum meinen Sie das?
3. In welchem deutschprechenden Land findet das Gespräch wohl nicht statt?
4. Ist Herr Dr. Hentschel wahrscheinlich allein oder mit seiner Familie in dieser Stadt?
5. Erraten Sie aus dem Kontext heraus: <u>stellen . . . zur Verfügung</u>, <u>Flügel</u>, <u>umbauen</u>, <u>erweitern</u>, <u>verlegt</u>.

Stage 2

B2
1. Wann findet das Gespräch statt — morgens oder nachmittags?
2. Was sind Steve und Cathy von Beruf?
3. Sind Steve und Cathy mit "Mama" verwandt?
4. Wie fahren Steve und Cathy nach Hause?
5. Erraten Sie aus dem Kontext heraus: <u>Gewöhnliches</u>, <u>es geht . . . um den Kaffee</u>, <u>ungern</u>, <u>Stipendium</u>, <u>bestehen</u>, <u>anderthalb</u>, <u>Forschung</u>, <u>sich bewerben</u>, <u>klappen</u>.

C1

2A:1.1.5 What dignitary eulogized Mr. Nixdorf? What achievements did he praise — can you list two? How big was the Nixdorf company when Heinz Nixdorf became its head? Estimate how many employees the company probably has now in West Germany. [7, 13]

2A:1.2.2   About how many foreign companies were represented at the fifty-third Week of Fashion Exhibition in München? What dignitary was there to open the exposition? [10]

2A:1.3.3   Have the police arrested suspects in the bombing? One of the fatalities was an American soldier; do you find it odd that the news media care whether or not he was "colored" (*farbig*)? The other fatality was a young woman. Observe the passive with past tense modal: "*konnte . . . identifiziert werden.*" What more is now known about her? About how many Americans were among the 30 persons who were severely injured? [1, 13, 17, 23]

C2
2B:5.3.2   The name of the event is the "_____- *und Verbraucher* _____." What was the attendance the previous year, and was the organizer happy with that figure? What attendance does the organizer hope for this year? What does he think of the relatively poor attendance on opening day? When was opening day? What day is "today"? What expression does the announcer use to bid the organizer farewell at the end of the chat? [15, 18, 22]

2A:2.1.4   What is the upcoming broadcast schedule for this station? [7, 20]

2A:2.2.3   The verb *sich verabschieden* ("to take one's leave") is a fancy way of saying good-bye. Like the announcer in the segment, with this "Mumbo-Jumbo" we will now take our leave. Your *Wie, bitte?* listening exercises are finished. You might want to pause a moment to think about all you have listened to, and about how much you know now that you didn't know before. *Auf Wiederhören!* [13]

SPRECHEN

Stage 1   You are going over to your host family's house for the last visit before you head back home. It has been an exciting year, with lots of ups and downs, and you feel that you've grown immeasurably. Practice saying what you have been planning for a while now — different things to your host parents and your siblings, who you hope will all come see you in Houston someday.

Stage 2   As part of your last week abroad, you have just taken part in one of the activities illustrated or implied in the collection of pictures and other realia on the front and back covers of the **CT**. Describe the activity, telling in detail what made it so special at this time.

LESEN

Stage 1   Look at the menu from the Wall Cafe on pp. 10-13 of the **ST** *Drucksachen*. List how many activities are available for an unforgettable farewell party.

Stage 2   Look at the list of East Berlin hotel facilities on **CT 321**. You have used one of the services or pieces of equipment offered in the lists headed "*Wir vermitteln* [We arrange]" or "*Wir leihen aus* [We lend out]". Can you formulate a sentence or two in which you express your thanks for the service rendered and describe a little more how it helped you? Example: "Thanks for helping me order the flowers. My friends really liked them." If you are looking for a challenge, imagine how you might convey that same warmly human information while offering as well a tip in much-coveted Western currency to someone who is by no means a "servant" but who will indeed appreciate — and perhaps even expect — a "gift."

SCHREIBEN

Stage 1   Look at the picture on **CT 156**. The student in the picture is about to return to the United States, and is thinking about some missed opportunities while in Europe. List ten thoughts beginning with the important word "*Wenn . . .*"

Stage 2   Write a note to a few of your friends inviting them to that farewell party at the Wall Cafe. Be sure to list the activities you will be involved in to give an idea of what sort of party it will be. Don't forget to tell them when the party will start and what they should wear.

STRUCTURAL EXERCISES

Note: Be sure you have reviewed your chapter grammar and read the relevant sections in the reference grammar.

1   Look back at the third structural exercise at the end of Chapter 24. Change your answers to include a modal verb in the past subjunctive.

   Example: Wenn wir nicht ausgewandert wären, . . .

   . . . <u>hätten wir dieses schöne Land nie sehen können</u>.

   1.   Wenn der Krieg nicht begonnen hätte, . . .
   2.   Wenn Vater nicht schon 1935 gestorben wäre, . . .
   3.   Wenn Gudrun und Katrin keinen Laden aufgemacht hätten, . . .
   4.   Wenn Christians Tochter den Mann aus Ohio nicht geheiratet hätte, . . .
   5.   Wenn Emilie nach dem Tod ihres ersten Mannes Witwe geblieben wäre, . . .
   6.   Wenn Onkel Gustav in Gaishausen geblieben wäre, . . .
   7.   Wenn Tante Grete länger gelebt hätte, . . .
   8.   Wenn die Flugkarten nach Frankfurt nicht so viel gekostet hätten, . . .
   9.   Wenn wir in den ersten Jahren ein Telefon gehabt hätten, . . .
   10. Wenn ich nicht später nach Seattle weitergereist wäre, . . .

2   During a stay with distant relatives in southern Austria, you have discovered your great-grandmother's letters back home to her family at the turn of the century. Unfortunately, someone has cut apart one of the letters, the one that tells her initial impressions of life in the new world. Reconstruct the original order of the sentences and find the secret message in the initial small letters.

   1.   Die Bauernhöfe liegen weit auseinander.
   2.   So starke Winde hatte ich noch nie erlebt.
   3.   Thomas hat sofort eine Bauernfamilie aus der Heimat kennengelernt.
   4.   Trotzdem ist das Gemeinschaftsleben hier wirklich sehr zufriedenstellend.
   5.   Das heißt: wenn man Zeit hätte, mit ihnen zu sprechen!
   6.   Ich glaube, ich bin sehr froh, wenn der Frühling kommt und wir auf die Felder können.
   7.   Ich weiß also nicht, wie man den Kontakt zu den Nachbarn aufrechterhalten soll.
   8.   Die sind uns dann auch am Anfang mit Rat und Tat zur Seite gestanden.
   9.   Ihr würdet lachen, wenn Ihr uns alle bei diesen Zusammenkünften sehen könntet.
   10. Nun, meine Lieben, ich muß den Kleinen helfen und das Abendessen noch vorbereiten.
   11. Meine Lieben, ich weiß nicht, was ich über dieses Land sagen soll.
   12. Alles ist hier so furchtbar wild.
   13. Ich hoffe recht bald von Euch zu hören, denn ich vermisse Euch alle sehr.
   14. Zu Hause habe ich nie getanzt — aber hier in Amerika fühlt man sich einfach irgendwie freier.
   15. Sie hat mir gesagt, es gibt einem hier vor allem das Wetter sehr zu schaffen.
   16. Ich glaube wohl, daß Ihr uns auch vermißt. Behüte Euch Gott in weiter Ferne.
   17. Mit vielen lieben Grüßen — Eure Anna
   18. Und man sagt, daß es im Hochwinter viel Schnee gibt.
   19. Mit der Frau komme ich besonders gut aus, die ist aus Kärnten.
   20. Dafür bin ich natürlich sehr dankbar, weil ich sonst nicht durchgekommen wäre.
   21. Jeden Freitag Abend trifft sich die ganze Nachbarschaft im Dorf zu einem Tanz.

√ CHECK YOUR PROFICIENCY

CAN YOU:
__ handle yourself with dignity in the face of unreasonable arguments?
__ talk your way out of awkward situations?
__ ask for favors?
__ bid farewell in a natural and graceful manner?

DO YOU REMEMBER HOW TO:
__ talk about kinship and narrate personal history?
__ compare cultures?
__ advance opinions and speculate about things?
__ describe how certain machines work?

Dialog Translations

Preliminary Unit 1
I Beg Your Pardon? Who? What?

Not understanding

You folks talk American?	I beg your pardon?
In my opinion this statement needs no explanation.	I beg your pardon?

Greetings

Good morning.	Good morning.
Hello.	Hello.
Good evening.	Good evening.

Names

What is your name, please?	Schmidt. Anna Schmidt.
Good morning, Mr. ___	Good morning, Mrs. ___
Good-bye.	Good-bye, Miss ___

What is your last name, please?	My name is ___
Thank you. And your first name?	_____

Who is that?	That's ___

What's your name, please?	Schmidt. My name is Benno Schmidt.

Country & Nationality

Are you an American?	Yes.
Are you an American?	No, a Canadian.
Well, well — from Canada.	Yes, from Toronto.

More personal information

And how old are you?	I'm 22.
What are you studying?	Math.

Preliminary Unit 2
Where? When? How Much?

Excuse me!

Oh, excuse me!	That's all right.
Excuse me . . .	Yes?

Where is . . .? (in the train)

Is that Wiesbaden?	No, that's not Wiesbaden. That's Mainz.

Where is . . .? (reading a map)

Where is Aachen?	Aachen? There.
Where?	That's Cologne, and here's Aachen.

Is Freiburg in Switzerland?	No, in the FRG.
What did you say?	In the Federal Republic of Germany.

Where is Frankfurt?	Frankfurt an der Oder is in the GDR.
	Frankfurt am Main is in the FRG.
And Graz?	That's in Austria.

Time and Day

What time is it?	I don't know. Sorry.
Excuse me. What's the time?	It's 10 o'clock.
What's today?	Monday.
Tomorrow's Wednesday, right?	No, not Wednesday. Tuesday.
Is today Friday?	No, Thursday. Yesterday was Wednesday.

How much does that cost?

How much?	5 marks.
How much does that cost?	That costs 16 marks.

Chapter 1 — Conversations 1
Tickets and Passports, Please

1

CONDUCTOR	Tickets, please.
JOHN	Huh?
WILL	I beg your pardon?
CONDUCTOR	Your ticket, please.
JOHN	OK. Here. Uh, here.
WILL	There you are.
CONDUCTOR	All right. Thank you.
JOHN	Thanks.
WILL	Thanks.
CONDUCTOR	You're welcome.
JOHN	Well, I guess it's German from here on.
WILL	I beg your pardon?

2

CONDUCTOR	Hello. Tickets, please.
ANDREAS	Tickets. Here you go.
CONDUCTOR	OK, thanks. Good-bye.
ANDREAS	Thank you. 'Bye.

3

PASSPORT OFFICIAL	Good morning. Passports.
COLIN	What did you say?
PASSPORT OFFICIAL	Passports. Your passports, please.
COLIN	Oh. Yeah . . .Yes. My passport. There you are.
PASSPORT OFFICIAL	All right. Thank you.

4

PASSPORT OFFICIAL	Hello. Passports, please.
LOREN	There you go. Uh, when will we be in Aachen?
PASSPORT OFFICIAL	I don't know. Is this your luggage?
LOREN	That? No, that's not my luggage.
PASSPORT OFFICIAL	Not your luggage. All right. Thank you.
LOREN	Don't mention it. Good-bye.

5

CONDUCTOR	Good evening. Your ticket, please.
TED	My ticket? Here it is.
CONDUCTOR	Thanks a lot. That's fine.
TED	Thank you. When do we get to Cologne?
CONDUCTOR	In 2 hours. At 8 p.m.
TED	I beg your pardon?
CONDUCTOR	Oh, you're an American. This evening at 8 o'clock.
TED	Thanks very much. Good-bye.
CONDUCTOR	Good-bye. . . . Tickets, please . . . .

Chapter 1 — Conversations 2
Snack Bar

1

OWNER	What'll it be?
MR. FREI	A glass of beer, please.
OWNER	One beer. . . . there you go.
MR. FREI	Thank you. How much is that?
OWNER	2 marks, please.

2

WAITRESS	OK, bratwurst, potato salad, and a beer. 7 marks 20.
MR. GLATTHARD	Here are 10 marks 20.
WAITRESS	And 3 marks change. Thank you.
MR. GLATTHARD	Thank you. Good-bye.
WAITRESS	Good-bye.

3

MRS. SUTTER	Good evening.
OWNER	Good evening. What would you like?
MRS. SUTTER	I'd like a currywurst with French fries.
OWNER	And anything to drink?
MRS. SUTTER	How much is a bottle of mineral water?

OWNER	2 marks 10. Would you like that?
MRS. SUTTER	Yes, please.

4

MISS HEBBEL	Do you have tea?
OWNER	No, we don't have tea. Would you like coffee?
MISS HEBBEL	Yes, please. Black.
OWNER	And anything to eat?
MISS HEBBEL	Nothing, thanks.
OWNER	All right — 2 marks 50.

5

OWNER	OK, 3 marks 10.
MRS. SCHILLING	There you are. 100 marks.
OWNER	Oh, 100 marks? I don't know, . . .
MRS. SCHILLING	Wait — I have 10 pfennig.
OWNER	Thanks a lot. OK, 3 marks. . . . And 20, 30, 40, 45, 50, 55, 70, . . ., no, 60, 65, 70, 75, 80, 85, 90, 92, 94, 96, 97 marks change.

Chapter 2 — Conversations 1
In the Hotel

1

MR. AMRHEIN	Good evening. Can I help you?
MR. JÖRY	I'd like a double room, please.
MR. AMRHEIN	All right. And how long will you be staying?
MR. JÖRY	Just one night.

2

MR. BECK	Good evening. We need two adjacent singles, please.
MRS. RANCKE	Fine. With a bath?
MR. BECK	With a shower — do you have one with shower and one without?
MRS. RANCKE	Of course. All together that'll be 145 marks a night.

3

MR. GELLERT	Evening.
MISS ZIPPERT	Hello. Do you have a room for one night?
MR. GELLERT	Yes, we do. Would you like a single or a double?
MISS ZIPPERT	Um . . . How much is a double with bath?
MR. GELLERT	Let's see — a double with bath costs 100 marks.
MISS ZIPPERT	I think that's a little too much. And without a bath?
MR. GELLERT	80 marks.
MISS ZIPPERT	OK, the double without bath, please.

4

MRS. LANDOLF	And you'd like it for two nights, right?
MRS. QUIESE	That's right, for tonight and tomorrow. How much is that?
MRS. LANDOLF	For two nights? That'll be 90 marks all together — with breakfast, of course.
MRS. QUIESE	Fine.
MRS. LANDOLF	All right, that's room number 7. Here's the key. . . . And is that your luggage there?
MRS. QUIESE	No, my luggage is still in the taxi.

Chapter 2 — Conversations 2
Hotel Restaurant

1

WAITER	Enjoy your drinks, folks.
MR. & MRS. BÜHLER	Thanks very much.

2

WAITER	Here you are. Two pork chop dinners, and two glasses of red wine. Enjoy your meal.
MR. & MRS. MÄHDER	Thank you.

3

MR. BLATTER	I'd like number 1, please.
WAITER	And for the lady?
MR. BLATTER	Uh . . .
MRS. BLATTER	Number 4, please.

4

TIM GRADY	Oh, waiter?!
WAITER	Yes? Can I help you?
TIM GRADY	"Seelachsfilet." Can you tell me what that is, please?
WAITER	Oh, that's fish. And today it's very good.

5 MISS MEISTER   We'd both like the pork chop with potatoes and bean salad, please.
WAITRESS   OK, the special. And what would you like to drink?
MISS MEISTER   Bring us two glasses of red wine, please.

6 MRS. WITTKOWSKI   This restaurant is really great, isn't it?
MRS. ENGEL   It sure is, and the pork chop tastes wonderful.
MRS. WITTKOWSKI   The wine, too. Should we have another glass?
MRS. ENGEL   Why not? Oh, waiter?! Two more glasses, please.
WAITER   I beg your pardon?
MRS. ENGEL   Please bring us two more glasses of white wine.
WAITER   OK, I'd be happy to.

7 BILL   Drat! I dropped my knife and I don't know the word to use to get another one.
JACK   Let me try something. Oh, waiter?!
WAITER   Yes? Do you need something?
JACK   Yes. For the pork chop. He needs . . .
WAITER   Salt?
JACK   No, we have that already.
BILL   I need a . . . for my chop I need a . . . .
WAITER   Oh, a knife! You don't have a knife!
BILL   Right. A knife. I need a knife.
WAITER   I'll bring it right away.

8 MRS. CAMENISCH   Miss?! The check, please.
WAITRESS   All right, that was two orders of sausage salad and two beers, wasn't it?
MRS. CAMENISCH   And the two rolls, too.
WAITRESS   OK, two rolls. That'll be 13 marks all together, please.

9 MR. FRISCH   Waiter, we'd like the check, please.
WAITER   Is that all together?

Chapter 3 — Conversations 1
Ticket Window

1 MRS. HOFFMANN   When is the next train to Cologne, please?
OFFICIAL   1:17.

2 MR. SAXEN   How much is a ticket to Cologne, please?
OFFICIAL   9 marks 70. 19.40 for the round-trip.
MR. SAXEN   I beg your pardon?
OFFICIAL   Aachen to Cologne, 9.70. From Aachen to Cologne and back to Aachen, 19.40.

3 DR. VAZER   Good morning. A ticket to Cologne, please.
OFFICIAL   One to Cologne. One-way or round-trip?
DR. VAZER   One-way, please.
OFFICIAL   OK, 8 marks 10, please. Track 7 at 11:25.
DR. VAZER   Track 7. Where is that?
OFFICIAL   Take a left here, and then go 50 meters.

4 MR. STEIGER   Two to Düsseldorf, please, round-trip.
OFFICIAL   We're closed. Go to window 4, please.
MR. STEIGER   Oh, sorry. Thanks.

5 MISS FELDER   Excuse me. Where's the women's rest room?
MRS. UHLIG   I don't know. Ask that lady over there.

6 MISS FELDER   Excuse me. Is there a women's rest room around here?
MRS. SZADROWSKY   You'll find the rest rooms to the right, around the corner.
MISS FELDER   What was that?
MRS. SZADROWSKY   To the right, around the corner there. Do you understand?
MISS FELDER   Oh, OK — to the right. Fine. Thanks a lot.

Chapter 3 — Conversations 2
Travel Provisions

1

MR. WIESER	Hello. Two oranges and a chocolate bar, please.
MRS. REINIG	OK — anything else?
MR. WIESER	No, thanks. That's all.
MRS. REINIG	4 marks 30, please.
MR. WIESER	4 marks . . . and . . . 10, 20, 30 pfennig.
MRS. REINIG	Thank you. 'Bye. Wait — don't forget your ticket!
MR. WIESER	Thanks very much. Good-bye.

2

MR. CASPAR	. . . and two rolls and some Swiss cheese.
MRS. STOPS	This piece of Emmenthaler is 180 grams. Is that enough?
MR. CASPAR	No, not for two people. A little bit more, please. Let's say 250 or 300 grams.
MRS. STOPS	OK, this piece here, then. 280 grams. And anything else?

3

MISS HEUSS	All right. That comes to 3.90.
MR. BITZBERGER	Here are 100 marks.
MISS HEUSS	Oh, 100 marks! Don't you have anything smaller?
MR. BITZBERGER	Just a second . . . Yes, I think so. 1 mark, 2, 2.50, 3, 3.50, 60, 70, 80, 90.
MISS HEUSS	Thanks very much.

4

MRS. KITZHABER	And we'll take a package of nuts, too.
MISS BERNHARD	The nuts, too? Isn't that too much?
MRS. KITZHABER	No, I love nuts. I think I'll eat them right here.
MISS BERNHARD	But we'll eat the chocolate later on the train, won't we?

Chapter 4 — Conversations 1
On the Train

1

MRS. PRINZ	Hello. Is someone sitting here?
MRS. WAGNER	No, that seat's taken. I'm sorry.
MRS. PRINZ	Oh. Thanks. 'Bye.

2

MR. FILZER	What time is it, please?
MR. WETTSTEIN	Umm, I think it's quarter to 10. Just a second . . . Yes, it's 9:46.

3

MR. HAMBURGER	Are you going to Basel, too?
DOCTOR SCHLUMPF	No, just to Cologne.
MR. HAMBURGER	Cologne? Terrific city. So much to see. Of course, the cathedral is fantastic, but you already know that, don't you? And the zoo for the kids! And . . .

4

MR. BLOCH	Hi. Are these seats already taken?
MR. TRÄGER	No, there's room here. Have a seat.
MR. BLOCH	Thanks. I'll get my family and be right back.
MR. BLOCH	Well, I'm back. This is my family — my wife, my son, and my two daughters.

5

MRS. BRÜCKNER	So are you an American?
MARK FRY	I am, yes, but he's Canadian. I work for a bank in Cologne, and he'll be studying in Munich until July.
MRS. BRÜCKNER	Oh, Cologne is really interesting. The cathedral, the museum, the zoo and so on . . . Mmm . . . Tell me, does he always sleep so much?
MARK FRY	No, but you know, he works so hard these days. He's a physics major.
MRS. BRÜCKNER	Oh — but that's too bad. Now he's not seeing anything, and the trip to Cologne is so beautiful — but even more beautiful in the summer.

Chapter 4 — Conversations 2
Where is the Street?

1

MRS. BENJAMIN	'Scuse me. Where's the Hotel Krone?
MR. WEISHAUPT	Hotel Krone. Sorry. I don't know. The tourist office is around the corner. Ask there.

2

MR. REICH	Excuse me. Do you know where the Thielen Hotel is?
MR. BEERLI	Take the number 10 bus to the train station. You'll be there in 10 minutes.

3   Miss Schaller   The youth hostel? That's not far from here. Go up here a few more blocks. You'll see a bakery. Then go left 200 meters.
         Jack Alin   Just a second. That's two more blocks . . .

4   Mrs. Fischer   . . . You'll find it with no problem.
         Mrs. Mohr   Thanks. And where can I find a cab here?
         Mrs. Fischer   That costs too much. It's better to walk.
         Mrs. Mohr   But I have too much luggage. I think I'll take a cab.

5   Mrs. Stolzboden   So keep driving through town. Just go straight. You'll see the Hessen Hotel on the left, . . . a bank, . . . the post office, . . . and then the train station.
         Miss Metzger   OK, fine. A hotel on the left, the post office, then a bank . . .
         Mrs. Stolzboden   No. The hotel, then the bank — that's the Deutsche Bank — and now the post office.
         Miss Metzger   And then I'll find the station.
         Mrs. Stolzboden   Right. And then you'll find the station. But keep going straight.

6   Gianni Strumolo   Excuse me. We're looking for the city museum. Here's the address.
         Mr. Christoph   That's not far from here. But today is Monday. I think it's closed today.

Chapter 5 — Conversations 1
Transit Stop

1   Mr. Kündig   When does the next bus to Brühl get here?
         Mr. Muhmenthaler   At 10:23 and then at 10:43 — every 20 minutes.

2   Mrs. Zippert   Excuse me, please. Does this bus go to the train station?
         Mrs. Mütterl   No, but the number 12 S-Bahn takes you right there.

3   Miss Weideli   . . . No, number 13 doesn't go right to Offenbachplatz. You have to change buses.
         Mr. Ambach   Change? Where?
         Miss Weideli   OK — take number 13 to Bachstraße. You have to get out there. And then take number 9.

4   Mr. Rohr   Do I have to change buses?
         Mrs. Ranke   Yes, at the market place. You'll see the stop to the left as you get off.
         Mr. Rohr   And how long do I have to wait there?
         Mrs. Ranke   Not very long. The buses run every 30 minutes.
         Mr. Rohr   Every 30 minutes? But it's so cold.

5   Miss Bürger   Excuse me. I'm looking for the hospital. Is it far from here?
         Miss Leuthold   No, that's not very far. But it's really raining. You'll be better off taking a cab.

Chapter 5 — Conversations 2
Hotel — Bath or Shower

1   Mrs. Mixnitz   Hello. May I help you?
         Mr. Strebel   A single with a shower, please.
         Mrs. Mixnitz   Certainly. And for how long?
         Mr. Strebel   For two nights, please.

2   Mrs. Penne   Good evening, folks.
         Mrs. Albrecht   Hello. We need a double, please.
         Mrs. Penne   All right. And with a bath or shower?
         Mrs. Albrecht   A shower, please.
                      . . .
         Mrs. Penne   Fine. There we are. That'll be 64 marks . . . And here's your key.

3   Mrs. Gratwohl   Now, you'll find the bath on the 3rd floor, to the right. That's 5 francs extra.
         Mr. Daetwyler   OK. And where is our room?
         Mrs. Gratwohl   On the second floor, to the left. . . . Wait — you don't have a room key yet.
         Mr. Daetwyler   And for the bath? Do we need a key?
         Mrs. Gratwohl   Yes. I'll give you the key right away. You can get soap and towels down here.

4   Angela Sproul   And where can I take a shower?
         Miss Reiser   The shower is on the same floor, around the corner to the left. Do you know how it works?
         Angela Sproul   What do you mean, exactly? Hot and cold and so on? "Hot" is "H" and "Cold" is "K", isn't it?

	Miss Reiser	No. Not all our guests understand German as well as you do. It's very simple. Hot is on the left and red, and cold is on the right and blue. Don't forget: red is hot, and blue is cold.
	Angela Sproul	OK: red — hot . . . blue — cold. Thanks a lot.

5
	Mrs. Girsberger	So go up one flight, and then left.
	Mrs. Tiemens	That's number 28?
	Mrs. Girsberger	Yes, 28. And towels you'll find up in the room.
	Mrs. Tiemens	And soap, too?
	Mrs. Girsberger	Yes, soap also.
		. . .
	Mrs. Tiemens	(on room phone) Yes, this is room 28. I don't have any towels, and I'd really like to take a bath.
	Mrs. Girsberger	Oh, I'm so sorry. I'll bring them up to you right away. Do you need soap, too?
	Mrs. Tiemens	Maybe. . . . No, we already have soap . . . . Wait. My husband says we also need toilet paper.

Chapter 6 — Conversations 1
Currency Exchange

1
	Mr. Schorer	Change money? Yes, window 1, please.
	Tom Green	Thank you. Do I need my passport?
	Mr. Schorer	Well, maybe. You have it with you, don't you?
	Tom Green	I'm afraid not. It's in the hotel.

2
| | Allen Krill | 1.78. Is that the exchange rate for traveler's checks? |
| | Miss Hostetler | No, for cash. |

3
	Vince Jacobs	$350 in marks, please.
	Mr. Jacobi	$350. Just a second. That makes 722.85. Would you like a 500-mark bill, or do you need small bills?
	Vince Jacobs	Give me five 100-mark bills, please, and then four 50s.
	Mr. Jacobi	All right. 1, 2, 3, 4, 500 marks, 550, 600, 650, 700 marks . . . 10, 20, 285. And there's your receipt.

4
	Mrs. Brauner	All right, five traveler's checks for 100 Canadian dollars, that makes 182 marks. I need your signature, too, down to the left, and today's date up to the right.
	Bill Bradley	Do you need my passport, too? It's in the hotel.
	Mrs. Brauner	No, I don't need it. Your signature is enough. But don't forget the date.
	Bill Bradley	OK. My signature down to the left, and the date goes up to the right.

5
	Miss Drechsler	20 marks in small bills, please.
	Mr. Kaiser	Of course. Would you like a 10 and two 5-mark pieces?
	Miss Drechsler	No, let me have four 5-mark pieces, if you would. They're for the ticket machine.
	Mr. Kaiser	OK. Here you are: 5, 10, 15, 20.

Chapter 6 — Conversations 2
Convenience Store

1
	Mr. Eisler	A chocolate bar, please, and a package of raisins, and . . .
	Mrs. Gottwald	Just a second. Here are the raisins. Then the chocolate — was that with nuts?
	Mr. Eisler	Yes, please. Also, do you have the *International Herald Tribune* ?
	Mrs. Gottwald	No, we don't have any more from today. Or would you like yesterday's?

2
	Marianne Wolz	Yes, I need a ticket for the streetcar. The machine next door isn't working.
	Mr. Sartorius	Yep, it's always broken — or so it seems. So — a streetcar ticket — or do you want a 24-hour ticket?
	Marianne Wolz	Is that a lot more expensive?
	Mr. Sartorius	A ticket costs you 1.50, and the 24-hour ticket is 12 marks. It's cheaper if you do a lot of riding.

3
	Mr. Schürer	Anything else for the trip?
	Professor Locher	Yes, maybe some fruit. Right — apples.
	Mr. Schürer	Fine. How many would you like?
	Professor Locher	Two, please, and an orange. And I see you have no bananas, right?
	Mr. Schürer	Yes, we have no bananas. That is, we have no bananas today. We did yesterday, but not today. Sorry.

4   TED ADORNO   Excuse me. Do you have *Time* magazine from the U.S.?
        MRS. KNÜSEL   Newspapers and journals from the States are left over there. Do you not see them?
         TED ADORNO   Yes, I do. We can speak German. I understand you just fine. But *Time* isn't there.
        MRS. KNÜSEL   Sorry. You do speak good German. So there aren't any more *Times*. We still have *Newsweek* .
         TED ADORNO   OK, I'll take that. And also a *Kölner Zeitung*.

Chapter 7 — Conversations 1
City Tour

1   MR. DIMITZ   Good morning. Can you tell me when the next sightseeing tour leaves?
          MISS NEFF   The next one starts at 2:30 p.m. — in an hour. But for how many people? We don't have much
                       more room.
          MR. DIMITZ   Do you still have four seats? We want to be sure to do it today. Tomorrow we have to leave
                       already.
          MISS NEFF   Just a second, I'll look. Our computer knows everything. . . . Yes, we still have four seats. May I
                       have the names, please?

2   MRS. STROBEL   . . . No. All seats are booked for the first tour tomorrow. But there's a second tour at 3 o'clock.
                       Would you like that?
        PROFESSOR RAU   Well, maybe. First I have to ask my husband. He's still in the hotel, and I don't want to call him.
                       The children are still asleep.
        MRS. STROBEL   Tell you what: Ask your husband, and then give us a call tomorrow morning at 9.
        PROFESSOR RAU   Maybe I can come back this afternoon.

3   DOCTOR PFANNER   . . . Of course. We'll stay in the cathedral for an hour. There's a lot to see there.
          MR. RIEMER   Can we take pictures inside?
        DOCTOR PFANNER   By all means. Just not with a flash. That will disturb the service. The next one begins at 11 o'clock.
          MR. RIEMER   Then I'll have to get my tripod. Do I have enough time?
        DOCTOR PFANNER   Yes, our bus isn't leaving until 9:15.
          MR. RIEMER   Great. I'll meet you downstairs in 5 minutes.

4   MRS. ISSLER   All right, everybody — an hour in the museum. The entrance you'll see over here to your left.
          MISS KAUL   And where do we meet after that?
        DOCTOR ZÄHNER   And when's lunch?
          MRS. ISSLER   Meet me in front of the restaurant on the cathedral square — around 12:15. I'll get us a table.
          MISS KAUL   What are we doing after lunch?
        DOCTOR ZÄHNER   Can we go shopping? I'd like to get a few postcards of the river.
          MRS. ISSLER   Our bus is picking us up at 1:45. If you eat fast, ...

Chapter 7 — Conversations 2
Pastry Shop

1   MRS. MAHLER   Is there a table up front by the window? Then we can see when our bus is coming.
       MRS. HAUPTMANN   There are too many people there. Let's look for something in the back. Or don't you want to sit
                       next to the rest rooms?

2   MR. SCHERER   I'd like a piece of nut cake, please, and mineral water.
          MISS GALLER   All right. And for you, ma'am?
          MR. SCHERER   She'd like nut cake, too, please.
          MRS. SCHERER   But with coffee.
          MISS GALLER   All right — two nut cakes, mineral water, coffee. Shall I bring a cup or a pot?

3   MS. CONNORS   I'd like raspberry ice cream, please.
           MR. LUTZ   And for you, sir?
         MR. CONNORS   (no answer)
         MS. CONNORS   Sorry. He doesn't speak German. Please bring him some chocolate ice cream.
           MR. LUTZ   Do you want a dish or a cone?

4   MR. SCHULZ   You're leaving the day after tomorrow already?
        MR. GRAUNING   Yes. What else should we do?
          MR. SCHULZ   Let's see — you've been in the cathedral, of course, and to the Rhine park.
        MR. GRAUNING   And to the museum next to the cathedral, and to the synagogue on Rathenau Square.
          MR. SCHULZ   Hm . . . What else is there to see?
        MR. GRAUNING   Something for the children, maybe? The circus, or . . .

MR. SCHULZ	Oh, the zoo! You just have to see the zoo. And tonight you can take a cruise on the Rhine.
MR. GRAUNING	Great, if we find a babysitter.

5

MR. FREUDENBERG	Boy. Two concerts, three museums, and five churches in 2 days — that's a lot.
MISS DANZER	That's too much for me. And then we sit in a pastry shop in the afternoon and stuff ourselves.
MR. FREUDENBERG	Maybe we ought to go dancing or hiking.
MISS DANZER	Or swimming — if not in the river, then in a pool.

Chapter 8 — Conversations 1
Opera Ticket Office

1

MRS. ALTORF	Do you still have tickets for *Der Freischütz* ?
MISS DORPEN	For this evening? I'll check. . . Yes, I still have four orchestra seats.
MRS. ALTORF	Are they all together in one row?
MISS DORPEN	No, two are in the third row, and two right behind them in the fourth row.

2

MR. DIENER	Do you still have anything for tonight?
MRS. WEISS	No, I'm sorry. For tonight I don't have anything left.
MR. DIENER	Oh, too bad. But how about tomorrow?
MRS. WEISS	Yes, that'll work. How many tickets would you like?

3

DOCTOR HUMBERT	Hello. I'd like two tickets for tonight, if you still have anything.
MR. DEUTSCH	Oh, I'm sorry, but we're all sold out for tonight.
DOCTOR HUMBERT	On, no! But we just have to see *Der Freischütz* !
MR. DEUTSCH	We still have tickets for the twelfth.
DOCTOR HUMBERT	Not until the twelfth? But we have to leave on the eleventh.

4

MRS. DR. KOPP	Hello. Do you still have tickets for *Aïda* on the 5th of October?
MISS GRÄDEL	No, I'm sorry, but we don't have any more tickets for the 5th. Or for the 7th.
MRS. DR. KOPP	Oh, that's such a shame. When <u>do</u> you have any for?
MISS GRÄDEL	For the 6th, but that isn't *Aïda* . On the 8th there's no performance. And for the 9th all we have left are standing-room tickets.
MRS. DR. KOPP	And for next week? Maybe we can stay a few more days.
MISS GRÄDEL	We still have lots of good seats for next Monday and Wednesday. What's better for you? Monday is the 10th, and Wednesday the 12th.
MRS. DR. KOPP	I think we want to come sooner — so let's say the 10th.

Chapter 8 — Conversations 2
Old Town

1

MR. BIRKEL	Boy, that was really great — the cathedral, the parks, the museum . . .
MRS. BIRKEL	And there are always new things and old things together here in Cologne — it's a modern city and a medieval city at the same time.
MR. BIRKEL	Right, and there aren't all that many cars in the old part of town. It's easy to be a pedestrian around here.
MRS. BIRKEL	I'll say — the pedestrian mall on Hohe Straße is really pretty. And the Rhine promenade must be several kilometers long.
MR. BIRKEL	Well, now — how about tonight? Shall we get tickets for the evening cruise on the Rhine? The city was so beautiful last night — I'd like to see it from the river.

2

MRS. KURSTEINER	Let's go up there to the city hall.
KARL KURSTEINER	No, I'm too tired. I don't want to see anything else. How far is the hotel from here?
MRS. KURSTEINER	Only a 15-minute walk. And we'll see the city hall anyway if we want to go right to the hotel.
KARL KURSTEINER	Well, I'm staying in the room this afternoon.

3

MISS KLEE	It's 12:15 already. Shall we walk through the old part of town first and then eat later?
MR. KANDINSKY	Fine. I'm not hungry yet, but I'd like to eat something around one.
MISS KLEE	Great — but that meal last night was horrible. We're not going to eat in the hotel again today, are we? Maybe on the Cathedral Square . . .
MR. KANDINSKY	Good idea. But now where shall we go first?
MISS KLEE	Well, I'd like to see the Sankt-Aposteln Church. I think it's on the Neumarkt, not far from the opera. And after an hour we'll find something to eat. How's that sound?
MR. KANDINSKY	Sounds fine to me. I think this stairway takes us down to Mittelstraße. We can probably see the church easily from there.

4   MISS HAMELN   So this is the Sankt-Aposteln Church. How old is it? I don't see a sign.
         MR. MEINRAD   Let's take a look at the guide . . . . "Neumarkt — 11th century; church — Romanesque."
         MISS HAMELN   So it's not Gothic like the cathedral, and not Roman like the wall near the city museum.
         MR. MEINRAD   No, this church is from the 12th century. "Heavily damaged in World War II."
         MISS HAMELN   Probably before 1945.
         MR. MEINRAD   "Altar — 1975."
         MISS HAMELN   That's not all that old. After all, I was born in 1970.

Chapter 9 — Conversations 1
Breakfast

1   MR. BOSSART   Zo, good morning. You sleep very late, yes. I was think we have to knock up your room. Do you become coffee or tea?
         MR. SPALDING   Feel free to speak German if you want.

2   MRS. LEUTENEGGER   OK, folks. Two breakfasts. Anything else?
         MR. HOLLINGER   I'd like tea instead of coffee.
         MRS. LEUTENEGGER   Black tea. Coming right up.
         MRS. HOLLINGER   And I'd like a 4-minute egg, please.
         MRS. LEUTENEGGER   OK, one tea and a soft-boiled egg. Fine.
         MR. HOLLINGER   Hm. . . I don't have a knife. Would you please bring me a knife?
         MRS. LEUTENEGGER   Of course. And I'll bring you a spoon for the soft-boiled egg. You already have forks. Do you need anything else?
         MRS. HOLLINGER   Our daughter would like a small cup of hot chocolate.

3   MR. ROTH   Good morning. Is there room for me here?
         MR. RICHIGER   Well, good morning, Mr. Roth. Please sit down.
         MR. ROTH   Thanks. . . . Enjoy your meal.
         MR. RICHIGER   Thanks. Same to you.
         MR. ROTH   Nice day, if it stays this way.
         MR. RICHIGER   That was wonderful last night, wasn't it?
         MR. ROTH   A marvelous evening. I think Cologne is really very interesting.
         MRS. RICHIGER   Is there anything like that where you live?
         MR. ROTH   In the U.S.? Well, ...

4   MISS KUPPER   Would you please pass the rolls?
         MRS. LEHMANN   Sure. Would you like the marmalade, too?
         MISS KUPPER   No, thanks. I already have enough. By the way, were you at the opera last night, too, at *Der Freischütz* ?
         MRS. LEHMANN   I'm afraid not. We wanted to buy tickets, but they didn't have any more for last night.
         MISS KUPPER   Oh, too bad. Were you able to get something for tonight?
         MRS. LEHMANN   Yes, but the seats were very expensive. We had to pay 60 marks a ticket.

Chapter 9 — Conversations 2
What Do You Recommend?

1   MR. SLOANE   We don't know the city very well yet. What do you recommend, Mr. Pfenninger?
         MR. PFENNINGER   Well, you really have to go to the zoo.
         MR. SLOANE   Fine, but please tell us how to get there.
         MR. PFENNINGER   OK. You go to the cathedral. From there you take the streetcar, number 11 or 16. It doesn't matter which one: both take you right there.
         MR. SLOANE   And 11 or 16 back again?
         MR. PFENNINGER   That's right. . . . Have a nice day.

2   MISS BACH   Well, nice weather today, folks. Back to the cathedral?
         DOCTOR GROB   No, we might do that Sunday, if it's raining.
         MISS BACH   Sunday? Then you can hear an organ concert there at 2:30.
         DOCTOR GROB   Great. But today we want to take the ferry to the Rhine park. And we also wanted to buy tickets for the evening cruise on the Rhine.
         MISS BACH   Do you know where the ticket office is?
         DOCTOR GROB   Right on the Rhine, isn't it, not far from the cathedral?
         MISS BACH   Right — or you can also buy tickets in the tourist office. That's right near here.

3   MR. WIESEL   The America House? Let me see your city guide. OK. Look here. You already know where the opera house is, right?

SUSAN PETERS   Right. We've been there twice already. OK, so we go to the opera house. Then what?

MR. WIESEL   From there you have to go farther to the Sankt-Aposteln Church — that's four or five blocks — about 250 meters.

SUSAN PETERS   And how do we get there?

MR. WIESEL   Your best way is through the Neumarkt. Then you'll see the church on your right.

SUSAN PETERS   So the church is on the right.

MR. WIESEL   Then a little farther on the left is the America House on Hahnenstraße.

SUSAN PETERS   And that's the way we get to the America House?

MR. WIESEL   Yep. Just keep your eyes open, and you're sure to find it.

4   MR. GRETHEN   Good morning, ladies. Well, how did it go yesterday?

MRS. OERTIG   Very nice tour.

MR. GRETHEN   And the climb up the tower, too?

MRS. OERTIG   No, I'm afraid not. We couldn't climb the tower. The weather was too bad. Too much fog.

MR. GRETHEN   Oh, that's a shame. And you had your heart set on that, too. But today the weather is sure to be better.

MRS. OERTIG   Tell me — does it always rain so much here?

Chapter 10 — Conversations 1
Cathedral

1   MR. ENGELS   What horrible weather! I'm sorry, everyone, but we're not allowed to climb the tower. It's too dangerous in this weather, especially for children.

MRS. VON SCHOLZ   Aw — and I really wanted to take a picture of the city from up there.

MR. ENGELS   Of course you did. But that'll work much better on a sunny day. Then the streets aren't so wet.

MRS. VON SCHOLZ   Well, all right. Maybe I could come back tomorrow, or the day after.

2   MR. BRIEST   And on the left you see the Sankt-Ursula Church, folks, and over to the right . . .

MRS. GÜRLÜK   Excuse me. How old is this church? A thousand years?

MR. BRIEST   Almost a thousand years old. It was built in the 12th century. And from the east side we have a beautiful view of the Hohenzollern Bridge . . .

MRS. GÜRLÜK   Man! Is it ever long!

MR. BRIEST   Ahem! . . . This bridge was built in 1907 and is more than 500 meters long.

3   MRS. WERDENBERG   Now, that was really terrific. And now I'd like to buy some postcards.

MISS SACHSEN   All right. You'll find them at the entrance in front.

MR. WERDENBERG   And color slides of the cathedral, too?

MISS SACHSEN   Probably. But if you don't find any, you can get souvenir items in all the shops.

MRS. WERDENBERG   And stamps? Can I get them here at the entrance, too?

MISS SACHSEN   Yes, I think so. But there's a kiosk right next to the cafe. You're sure to find your stamps there.

MR. WERDENBERG   And I can get polaroid film there too?

MISS SACHSEN   Hm. I'm afraid not. For that you have to go to a camera store. But that's right near here, too, down by the station.

4   MRS. VON HAAG   I'd like two rolls of slide film, please, DIN 21.

MISS BETTNER   All right. What kind would you like, and how many exposures?

MRS. VON HAAG   Agfa, please. 24 exposures, if you have it.

MISS BETTNER   I'm sure we do. . . . Right, here they are. And did you want something else?

MRS. VON HAAG   Yes, I'd like to get some postcards of the city, but I don't see them here.

MISS BETTNER   Oh, yes, we have a big selection. Look up there by the door, on the big board.

MRS. VON HAAG   Oh, I'm sorry. And you have stamps, too, don't you?

MISS BETTNER   Of course. We have them, too. Are you sending them to another country?

Chapter 10 — Conversations 2
Presents

1   MRS. KNECHT   All right. Next?

BOB KAUFMANN   I'd like a T-shirt with a picture of Cologne.

MRS. KNECHT   We have lots with pictures. Did you want one with the cathedral?

BOB KAUFMANN   Maybe, but I was thinking of something else. Something with the Rhine, or . . .

MRS. KNECHT   Here's a T-shirt with a Rhine steamer. Nice, isn't it?

BOB KAUFMANN	Oh, that is nice. Do you have it in my size?	
MRS. KNECHT	I think so. What size do you wear?	

2

MISS MEYER	Hello. Are you next?
MRS. KÜTTEL	Yes. I'm looking for a present for my son. He's 10.
MISS MEYER	Fine. Does he like to read? We have good children's books.
MRS. KÜTTEL	No, not really.
MISS MEYER	What are his hobbies? Sports, maybe? We also have everything for kids who like sports.
MRS. KÜTTEL	It doesn't really matter. Just not any video games. He shouldn't watch so much TV.

3

MR. ZELLJADT	Excuse me. How do I get to the toy department?
MRS. BEHLER	Toys are on the fifth floor. One flight up.
MR. ZELLJADT	Thanks a lot. And the men's department?
MRS. BEHLER	That's downstairs, on the second floor.
MR. ZELLJADT	I'm sorry — which floor did you say?
MRS. BEHLER	The second floor. From the escalator you go around the corner to the left.

4

MRS. BÜHLMANN	OK, 11 marks 20 is your change. There's your receipt, and here are the four wine glasses.
TOM TANKERSLEY	Thanks a lot. They're presents for my parents in the U.S. Can you please wrap them up well?
MRS. BÜHLMANN	Be glad to. Do you need a plastic sack, too?
TOM TANKERSLEY	Yes, thanks. And one more question: where do I find casettes with folk music from Cologne?
MRS. BÜHLMANN	Cassettes and records you'll find in the basement. There are also picture books, posters, and postcards there if you want some other presents for your family.

Chapter 11 — Conversations 1
Zoo

1

MISS HUBER	. . . All right, two adults and two children — 17 marks, and 3 marks is your change. And would you like to rent an umbrella? It's quite wet.
MRS. VON SALIS	And pretty cold, too. Are all the animals outside?
MISS HUBER	No, not all of them. . . . May I suggest something? We have a famous primate house, and it's also warmer inside than outside.
MRS. VON SALIS	Oh, that sounds good.

2

MR. FRANZEN	Well, shall we see the bears first? The polar bears are right over there.
MISS GLATT	No, I'd rather visit the fish and then the birds. They're more interesting.
MR. FRANZEN	Oh, no. I think big animals are better. Maybe I'll go see the elephants and then the rhino. And you go see the ducks.
MISS GLATT	OK, fine. Do you see the snack bar over there? I'll see you there in an hour.

3

KÖBI FÄSSLER	Lookit! A seal. Or is it a sea lion?
MRS. FÄSSLER	That must be a seal. Sea lions are bigger and have longer teeth.
KÖBI	He looks like Uncle Max. Give him something to eat. What does he like to eat?
MRS. FÄSSLER	Don't you see the sign? "Next feeding 3:00." Let's wait for 15 minutes. I'll buy a few fish and you can throw them to the seal.
KÖBI	And he'll always catch them, won't he? And he doesn't have any hands!

4

ANGELIKA STOCK	Look, Mommy. A crocodile. He looks dead.
MRS. STOCK	The crocodile's asleep right now. First he eats a lot, and then he sleeps for a long time.
ANGELIKA	Hey, crocodile! Don't be so lazy! Get up!
MRS. STOCK	Not so loud! Read the sign: "Crocodiles jump and bite. . ." You know, crocodiles eat people every day in Africa. You'd better take my hand now.
ANGELIKA	Mommy, I want to see the snakes, too!

Chapter 11 — Conversations 2
Evening Cruise on the Rhine

1

MRS. DACHSEN	Hurry up. Our boat leaves in 20 minutes.
MR. DACHSEN	I thought it wasn't leaving until 7:30.
MRS. DACHSEN	No, read the schedule: "Special Trip 'Rhine in Flames.' Departure from the Rhine bridge at 7:00 p.m."
MR. DACHSEN	OK, I'm coming. Give me the room key. And this time don't forget your jacket.
MRS. DACHSEN	I've already got it — and my hat. Are you taking your sweater along, too?
MR. DACHSEN	I sure am. It's pretty cool already — not more than 60°.

2   MR. MARTENS   Hello. Is there room here?
    MR. SIEBERT   Sure, there's room. Be my guest.
    MR. MARTENS   Oh, thanks. By the way, my name's Martens.
    MR. SIEBERT   Mine's Siebert. Nice to meet you. My wife . . .
    MR. MARTENS   Good evening, Ms. Siebert. And this is Ms. Behrens.

3   MRS. MAREK   Nice weather for an evening cruise, isn't it?
    MRS. BAUER   Marvelous — and much cooler and fresher in the evening than during the day. Is this your first evening cruise, too?
    MRS. MAREK   Oh, this is the first time we've been on the Rhine at all. By the way, do you know the name of that castle over there?
    MRS. BAUER   Just a second. I'll check in our guidebook . . . Köln, Königswinter, Rolandseck. . . . That has to be the Drachenfels.

4   KARL BRUGGMANN   Gabi, we've known each other for a week already. We've got to celebrate. Shall we order another bottle of wine or champagne?
    GABRIELE FLICK   Yes, and the Loreley is coming up soon. This is all so romantic, especially when the ship's band is playing. And I so love to dance with you.
    KARL BRUGGMANN   Waiter, what would you recommend, the Steinberger Auslese or the Fuchsmantel Wackenheimer Riesling Kabinett?
    MR. STALDER   That all depends. They're both excellent. The Steinberger Auslese is a little sweeter, and the Fuchsmantel a bit dryer. I prefer the Fuchsmantel myself — the '81 is especially good.

Chapter 12 — Conversations 1
Post Office

1   CATHY KERNER   I'd like to send these two letters and the postcards air mail to the United States, please.
    MRS. WENNE   All right. This one costs 1.10, and the other letter is heavier — it'll cost 1.70. And ten postcards are 7 marks. That makes 9.80 all together.
    CATHY KERNER   What was that? I didn't understand you.
    MRS. WENNE   9 marks and 80 pfennig.
    CATHY KERNER   Thank you. And how much is a postcard to Canada?
    MRS. WENNE   That's 70 pfennig, too. All together that would be 10 marks 50.

2   PROFESSOR NEU   I'd like ten 70s, please.
    MR. STALDER   I don't have any more 70s right now. Can I give you 50s and 20s?
    PROFESSOR NEU   They're for postcards, but I think it'll be all right.
    MR. STALDER   And do you need anything else?
    PROFESSOR NEU   Yes, please — some air mail stickers.

3   RICHARD LYMAN   I'd like a postal parcel, size 3, please.
    MRS. STEINER   All right. And you'll have to fill out these forms if you're sending it abroad.
    RICHARD LYMAN   Is there a special book rate?
    MRS. STEINER   Yes, if the package doesn't weigh more than 5 kilos.
    RICHARD LYMAN   I have another question. I bought presents for my family — wine glasses and so on.
    MRS. STEINER   Then it's better to buy a box with styrofoam.

4   HOWARD LEICHTER   I'd like to call my family in the U.S., please. Could you explain how to do that?
    MR. THIELE   Go into booth number 2. The country code for the U.S. is 0 01. So you dial the entire number. And come back here when you're finished.
    HOWARD LEICHTER   Thanks very much. And how much will that cost?
    MR. THIELE   A long-distance call to the U.S. costs 4 francs 80 for each time unit. A unit is one minute.
    HOWARD LEICHTER   I might not have enough money on me.
    MR. THIELE   That's all right. Your family can pay for the call.

5   BARRY GOODMAN   How much is the small package?
    MR. BOENINGER   I don't know yet. Just a second.
    BARRY GOODMAN   Wait — could you please give me back the first letter and the big package? I have to write down the ZIP codes.
    MR. BOENINGER   OK, that's that. The two letters are 4 marks 60, and the two packages are 26 marks 90. That's 31 marks 50 together, please.

Chapter 12 — Conversations 2
In the Train Compartment

1 MR. WIDNER Hello. Are there two more empty seats here?
DOCTOR VON SPOHR I think so, if they're not reserved. Take a look at the sign outside.
MR. WIDNER There's nothing on it. I'll go get my luggage and be right back.
DOCTOR VON SPOHR OK, but be careful. The train's going to leave right away.

2 BEATE Well, Cologne was really great! And we saw so much.
KONRAD . . . And ate and drank and sang . . .
BEATE But didn't sleep much.

3 SVEN Excuse me, sir, this is a non–smoker.
MR. BLATTER This is a non–smoker? Sorry, I didn't see the sign.

4 MRS. BECK Why aren't we leaving?
MR. BECK I heard that the train from Bremen has been delayed.

5 KÄTHE <u>There</u> you are again. Did you find the dining car?
SUSANNE No. The conductor told me there isn't one.
KÄTHE But surely there's a snack cart.

6 MR. BURCKHARDT Did you say you're from Canada? I didn't know that. I thought you were an American.
MS. THOMPSON What did you say? I didn't understand you. There's so much noise.

Chapter 13 — Conversations 1
Youth Hostel

1 MRS. HENTSCHEL Do you two have sleeping bags or your own sheets with you, or do you want to rent them?
HANS KRÖGER We'd like to have blankets, if that's OK — and pillows, too. We already have sheets.
MRS. HENTSCHEL All right. Now — just two more things: From 10:00 on we have to have it quiet in the sleeping rooms, and don't be up and about tomorrow morning before 7:00.
HANS KRÖGER Fine with me — those are the normal quiet hours. I'm dead tired anyway. We were on the road for a long time today.

2 MR. HENTSCHEL And do you have your I.D. with you?
ERNA GÄBLER I think so, yes. Right — there it is. Here.
MR. HENTSCHEL And you'll find the house rules on the board there, to the left.
ERNA GÄBLER Um — I have one more question. My friend and I wanted to go to the concert in the city park tonight, and —
MR. HENTSCHEL — and you want to stay out late, right? OK, but please don't stay out past 10:00. We lock up at 10 on the dot. And please don't leave things like money or cameras in the room when you go out.

3 BRIGITTE LOOS And what all did you see there?
ERIKA WOLFEN Oh, man, it was great. There were a few guys from the Munich Touring Club. We took a terrific bike trip through upper Bavaria with them.
BRIGITTE LOOS Fantastic. I love the Alpine foothills. Last year I went on a hike with my class from Oberammergau to Innsbruck.
ERIKA WOLFEN Oh, neat. But I like to bike better — and always to go from hostel to hostel because it's so cheap. And I meet so many new people.
BRIGITTE LOOS And the youth hostels are always clean. I don't much like helping out in the kitchen, though.
ERIKA WOLFEN But it's really fun if everyone cooks or cleans up together after the meal.

4 ANGELA PASSAU No, I'm not allowed to smoke in the lounge. The youth hostel parents told me that last night.
CHRISTIANE JUNG Well, I think they're right. You can smoke if you get a hotel room somewhere in town. But not here.
ANGELA PASSAU And of course you can't drink, either — not to mention drugs!
CHRISTIANE JUNG I think that's a really good thing about youth hostels. The hostel mother & father are there and act almost like parents — only not our <u>own</u> parents.
ANGELA PASSAU Exactly. I can really talk to them if something's bothering me. This morning I had a problem, and we talked about it while we were doing the dishes.

Chapter 13 — Conversations 2
Illness

1

HARALD	I think I have a cold.
UTE	What? Again?
HARALD	Yes, since Tuesday. The youth hostel was terribly cold.
UTE	Hm. For 3 days already. Maybe we'd better stay home today.

2

LISELOTTE	Well, how are you doing?
CHRISTIANE	I have a headache, even when I'm lying down.
LISELOTTE	Maybe because you drank too much last night.
CHRISTIANE	Well, . . . but the stomach ache . . . and I've had a little fever since yesterday morning .
LISELOTTE	Too bad you bent the ol' elbow so much.
CHRISTIANE	Oh, leave me alone! Don't we have any aspirin or anything?
LISELOTTE	Yes, I have some pills with me, but maybe you should go to a doctor if it's really serious.
CHRISTIANE	No, I think a few hours' rest are the best doctor.
LISELOTTE	Yeah, I think so too. Tomorrow you'll be fine again.

3

MR. HIRT	Now, please tell me where it hurts . . . Here?
MR. RUDOLF	No, a little higher, around the knee. And my hip really hurts now, too. Man, is that ever painful!
MR. HIRT	And it'll get worse if you keep walking on it. Just stay put. I'll call a doctor.
MR. RUDOLF	OK. I think I'll lie down a little in the meantime. Ow!
MR. HIRT	You've got to see a doctor right away. I'll call the hospital. It's better for you to go in an ambulance than in my car.

4

MS. BETHKE	Now, I'm telling you, that's bad, Ms. Vogt. You really ought to go to a specialist, to the eye doctor.
MS. VOGT	But you know, Ms. Bethke, I've never been sick before in my whole life, and now all of a sudden . . .
MS. BETHKE	Then you've really got to be careful. If you don't go to the doctor right away, that can get a lot worse.
MS. VOGT	I know, I know. That's what my husband says, too. But you know, I get a little afraid when I hear the word "hospital."
MS. BETHKE	Oh, pooh — why? You can't be afraid. After all, you were born in a hospital!

Chapter 14 — Conversations 1
Museum

1

MR. ZELIKOWITSCH	Excuse me. What kinds of museums are there here in Freiburg?
MRS. WALTHER	Oh, every kind, really — we have eight museums here. I'll give you a guidebook and a few pamphlets. Do you already know what you'd like to see?
MR. ZELIKOWITSCH	Well, we just came from Cologne. We saw the art museum and the Roman-Germanic museum when we were there.
MRS. WALTHER	Then I'd suggest that you visit our Museum of Freiburg City History. And if you stay here longer, you should also see the Museum of Modern Art.

2

BOB ROSENKRANTZ	Two adults and two children, please. Is there a discount for foreign students?
MISS STOFFEL	Of course. All students pay half price. And admission is free for children.
BOB ROSENKRANTZ	Fine. Would you like to see our student I.D.s?
MISS STOFFEL	No, that won't be necessary. OK — 2 times 2.50, please. And you'll have to leave your bags and coats in the check room before you enter. You can leave your baby carriage there, too, if you like.
BOB ROSENKRANTZ	Thank you. May I take my camera along with me?

3

MRS. ZANGERL	Pardon me. That camera there — is it yours?
MRS. KIESEMANN	Oh, yes, that's mine. I almost forgot it.
MRS. ZANGERL	Unfortunately, you can't take flash pictures here, because that disturbs the other visitors.
MRS. KIESEMANN	Oh, excuse me. I didn't know that. And I really wanted to take a picture of the Grünewald altar.
MRS. ZANGERL	Too bad you didn't bring a tripod. But you can buy postcards and posters at the front desk.

4

MR. LAUTENBACH	Yes, we were told that you sell pictures of the Grünewald altar here. We couldn't take a picture of it because I had only a flash and no tripod.
MISS FEHR	That's too bad. But we have lots of pictures of that altar because it's so famous. Did you want postcards, posters, or color slides?

MR. LAUTENBACH Probably postcards, but I like that poster there a lot. Do you have it a little smaller? We're traveling.

MISS FEHR I'm sorry, but we don't have it any smaller. But you can buy it in a mailing tube. The poster comes already packed for mailing, so you can send it overseas.

Chapter 14 — Conversations 2
Hike

1

JENS Say, Hans-Dietrich! Have you ever been up on that mountain there?

HANS-DIETRICH Oh, sure — that's called Schauinsland. From up there you can see for miles. That's where they get the name: "Look into the country."

JENS And how high is the top of the gondola?

HANS-DIETRICH 1220 meters — and the peak is even higher: 1284 meters. But with the gondola you get up there in just a few minutes.

JENS But can't you fall?

HANS-DIETRICH No, Jens, the gondola isn't at all dangerous.

2

MRS. DÄNIKEN Christa, if you want to go along, you'll have to put on your sweater. That blouse just isn't warm enough.

CHRISTA But I'd rather stay down here and play with Katrin.

MRS. DÄNIKEN But we're going to have a picnic. We're going to take our packs and hike until we're tired, and then we'll eat somewhere in the sun —

CHRISTA And can we take the gondola back down?

MRS. DÄNIKEN Of course, Christa. But first we'll hike on farther before we come back.

3

ERIKA Sit down, Emil. Did you forget something?

EMIL Erika, you're not going to believe this. But the basket with the food is still at home on the kitchen table.

ERIKA Oh, no! And I'm so hungry, too. Well, OK — let's go back down. Then we can grab the food and come right back. I've always told you —

EMIL You're not mad at me, are you?

ERIKA What do you mean, "mad," Emil? Of course not. I have to get a jacket anyway — it's pretty cool up here with that wind.

EMIL Sure is. I didn't see the clouds this morning. I hope it doesn't rain.

4

MR. SCHILLER Look, you two. Do you see the trees to the left of the path?

ANNAGRET Do you mean the fir trees, Mr. Schiller?

MR. SCHILLER Right. When I was young, we kids played cowboys and Indians and Robinson Crusoe there. We built a little cabin, too.

ANNAGRET Is your cabin still there?

MR. SCHILLER No, I don't think so. But run on down there and take a look.

5

MRS. DR. ZAHND Did you climb up here, Professor, or did you take the gondola?

PROF. LENZEN We took the gondola — my foot still hurts.

MRS. DR. ZAHND Your foot? What happened?

PROF. LENZEN Well, it was on a short hike down from Schauinsland — through the forest, you know. I hit my foot against a rock, and it's been hurting for 3 weeks now.

Chapter 15 — Conversations 1
Room-Finding Service

1

MR. LAUCH For two nights, right? And how much were you thinking of spending?

MR. GROSS Not more than 60 marks, if it's without a bath.

MR. LAUCH Just a second. I have two possibilities. The "Krone" — that's right near here — and the "Lamm" — but that's farther from the center of town.

MRS. GROSS Well, it would be better closer in. But is the "Krone" quiet? We couldn't sleep at all well yesterday in the "Bahnhofshotel."

MR. LAUCH Well, the "Krone" is on Königstraße, and of course there's lots of traffic there. The "Lamm" is a lot quieter and costs less.

MRS. GROSS Well, dear, shall we try the "Lamm"?

MR. GROSS Yes, I think so. Would you please give them a call for us?

2 MISS AMBRUGG   Too bad the hotels are all full. A private room would be a possibility. Do you want to try private?

    MR. MARTIN   Well, yes, if all the hotels around the station are full. Would you have anything for 50 or 60 francs?

    MISS AMBRUGG   On Heidengasse, in the south part of town, there are a couple of possibilities in that price range — and maybe even cheaper. You take the #5 streetcar.

    MR. MARTIN   And about how expensive are they?

    MISS AMBRUGG   Both of them are quite reasonable: 25 francs a night per person, including breakfast.

    MR. MARTIN   So that would be 50 francs for two people for one night, including breakfast. Fine.

    MISS AMBRUGG   Shall I go ahead and call the people? You're going on out there right away, aren't you?

3 MRS. LATTIG   But if you want to have the room, then you'll have to come right away. I have to go into town.

    MR. HANSEN   We'll come right away, if you can wait another 20 minutes.

    MRS. LATTIG   Certainly, Mr. Hansen. Take the S-Bahn, number 10, to the third stop, which is Mozartstraße. The house is right across the street. The S-Bahn runs every 5 minutes.

    MR. HANSEN   OK. Number 10 to the third stop. Thanks very much, Mrs. Lattig. Good-bye.

    MRS. LATTIG   Good-bye. I'll see you soon.

4 MISS PFAFF   OK, a double in the Europa Hotel.

    DOCTOR FORSTER   Just where is that?

    MISS PFAFF   I'll show it to you on the map. We're here on Ringstraße. The hotel's not even 200 meters from here, on Kantstraße, on the right-hand side.

    DOCTOR FORSTER   How long will they hold the room? Our luggage is still at the station in the locker.

    MISS PFAFF   You have an hour to get there. So I'm going to give you this piece of paper. You pay 5 marks here, and you get it back later on your hotel bill.

Chapter 15 — Conversations 2
Apartment

1 MR. BÜRGEN   OK. I imagine there's enough room for your things in the cabinet. You can put your suitcase up on top of the cabinet after you've unpacked everything.

    MR. SOHLICH   And the backpack? It's pretty big.

    MR. BÜRGEN   You can put it on the floor of the cabinet.

    MR. SOHLICH   And the toilet is down the hall?

    MR. BÜRGEN   Yes, down the hall. You'll find the shower in the basement. But you said you wanted to go to town right away?

    MR. SOHLICH   Yes. Our other suitcase is still in the locker. And we wanted to get some things at the grocery store.

2 MRS. JANKUHN   Then you'll find the kitchen nook over there next to the living room. You have a cabinet between the stove and the couch. That way you don't see right into the kitchen.

    MISS KÖHLER   And the refrigerator — where . . .?

    MRS. JANKUHN   In the corner. Look — right there to the left of the sink.

    MISS KÖHLER   Great — a very practical setup. And cleaning — do you have a vacuum cleaner in the house?

    MRS. JANKUHN   Yes, you'll find the vacuum downstairs next to the back door.

    MISS KÖHLER   That's by the door to the garage. Fine.

    MRS. JANKUHN   Everyone cleans his own room and carries out his trash. And every 4 weeks you'll have to scrub the stairs, so they stay clean.

    MISS KÖHLER   And when is it my turn?

    MRS. JANKUHN   In 2 weeks — on the 15th. And the rent is always due on the first.

3 MR. KRAUS   So, you're back again. Everything OK?

    MS. SEITZ   Just fine. I unpacked my suitcase, and then we called our friends.

    MR. KRAUS   You can take a shower now if you want. I cleaned up a little bit in the bathroom.

    MS. SEITZ   Thanks. That was nice of you.

    MR. KRAUS   But might I ask you not to take terribly long showers? Electricity is more expensive here than in the U.S.

    MS. SEITZ   Of course. By the way, it looks as if the lamp next to my bed isn't working.

    MR. KRAUS   Aha — it appears that no light appears.

    MS. SEITZ   Funny, eh? Do you suppose you have a new bulb?

4 MRS. BURGER   When you go out, just leave the key in the restaurant or at the hotel desk. That's a little different here from the way you do it in America.

    MR. DRABKIN   Of course. We learned that in Aachen — or, rather, on the train to Cologne, when I found the hotel key in my pocket.

Chapter 16 — Conversations 1
City Map — Timetable

1

MR. BLOCH — Would you like the large street map, or did you want the monthly program guide with the small city map?

GRETE ERNST — Look, Thomas, we already have the Michelin guide. It has street maps for every big city.

THOMAS BENEDIKT — Yes, I know. But there's no program guide in it. And we do want to do things, don't we?

GRETE ERNST — Sure. But today is already the 29th. We should ask if he has the latest monthly guide.

2

MRS. LAMPRECHT — Bavarian National Museum. Let's have a look — M 29. That's in the northeast part of town. Looks like it's pretty far from the station.

MR. LAMPRECHT — Well, we could take the number 55 bus right on out there.

MRS. LAMPRECHT — I'd just as soon not take the bus. How much would a taxi be?

MR. LAMPRECHT — Let's do this: first we'll take the S-Bahn to Marienplatz. That's in the center of town.

MRS. LAMPRECHT — Fine. We can visit the town hall and the toy museum before lunch.

MR. LAMPRECHT — And after lunch we could take a walk through the Hofgarten.

MRS. LAMPRECHT — But we have to be at my cousin's at 4 o'clock.

3

MS. OTT — But don't you think the parking garage is much too expensive?

MR. THALMANN — Yep, especially if we want to stay more than a couple of hours.

MS. OTT — OK, then I have a suggestion. Michael, Georg, and Konrad visited Munich last year, and they just parked their car on the street at the end of a bus line.

MR. THALMANN — And then they took the bus back into town. Very clever. Let's do that.

4

HARALD WEINRICH — So there you are! What happened, anyway?

MONIKA LERNER — We ate in town and then we went to the National Museum.

MARTIN LERNER — Then we wanted to take the streetcar to your place — you said number 55.

MONIKA LERNER — We misread the sign . . .

MARTIN LERNER — You misread the sign. And then we got onto number 53 and rode all the way to Josephsplatz.

HARALD WEINRICH — OK, so you got off there, and . . .

MONIKA LERNER — We had to wait for the next U-Bahn, and it didn't come until 5:33 . . .

HARALD WEINRICH — Well, that's OK. But why didn't you call me?

Chapter 16 — Conversations 2
Subway — Streetcar

1

WILLIAM LEWIS — Excuse me. Do you know if I can buy a ticket for the S-Bahn here?

MS. ACKERMANN — You get that from the machine over there. Do you know how it works?

WILLIAM LEWIS — No, I don't. Could you please show me?

MS. ACKERMANN — Sure. Look here: in the yellow zone — that's this part of town here — it costs 1 mark 20. In the blue zone it's more expensive — 2 marks.

WILLIAM LEWIS — I have to go to Leopoldplatz.

MS. ACKERMANN — That's in the blue zone. So you have to press the blue button and put your coin in here. Then you get your ticket.

2

MS. FELLMANN — Hello. Can I buy an S-Bahn ticket here?

MS. EISENHAUER — Sure. What kind of ticket do you want — for a week, a month, . . .

MS. FELLMANN — I'm staying here a few weeks and riding 3 or 4 times a day.

MS. EISENHAUER — Well, then a monthly ticket would be best. 65 marks, please.

MS. FELLMANN — How long is it valid? 30 days, or just until the end of the month?

3

MR. JAEGER — Excuse me, young man. Would you please get up? This lady would like to sit down.

MR. POST — What did you say? Oh, of course. Please have a seat. Can I help you with your packages?

MS. KNIEBEL — Thank you. That's very nice of you.

MR. POST — Glad to help. . . . By the way, I have to go to Heidestraße. Do you know if I have to change streetcars?

MS. KNIEBEL — Heidestraße? Oh, that's not far from the art museum, behind the botanical garden. I don't think you have to transfer.

4

MR. HOFER — May I please see your ticket?

MS. KELLER — My ticket? Oh, yes, of course. There you are.

MR. HOFER — Hmm. But this ticket isn't valid in this part of town.

MS. KELLER — But I just bought it 10 minutes ago.

Mr. Hofer	But you got on at Bärenplatz. The ticket isn't valid on this side of the river. You need another ticket for the blue zone.
Ms. Keller	Oh, good grief. What am I going to do now?
Mr. Hofer	Well, normally you'd have to pay a fine — and buy the right ticket.
Ms. Keller	I didn't know that was another zone. I'm not from here.
Mr. Hofer	That's OK. But now you know. Well, I hope you enjoy your stay with us.

Chapter 17 — Conversations 1
Student Union

1

Erich Kopp	Enjoy your meal. . . . Is there room for one more?
Georg Franzen	Sure, have a seat.
Erich Kopp	My name's Erich Kopp, from Friesland.
Georg Franzen	Nice to meet you, Erich. I'm Georg Franzen.
Gisela Mautner	Then I need to introduce myself, too: I'm Gisela Mautner.
Erich Kopp	Hi, Gisela. Are you from here?
Gisela Mautner	No, from Baden-Baden.

2

Thomas Richter	Now, <u>that</u> I wouldn't eat if I were you. It looks so — what's the word I want? — unnatural. No one can eat that.
Gisela Brusecki	Maybe you're right: a little more color in the vegetables would be good.
Thomas Richter	"Roast Chicken with Spätzle" — that sounds much better. And I'm going to have a green salad, too.
Gisela Brusecki	Are the sausages boiled or grilled? I'd really like to get a juicy bratwurst with bean salad.
Thomas Richter	Take a look: "Today's Special: two wieners with a roll and potato salad — 4 marks 70." Not bad. That's much cheaper than bratwurst, and it tastes much better, too.
Gisela Brusecki	Well, maybe. . . . Are you going to have grape juice, too?

3

Hanni Klinger	"Indisches Reisfleisch" — what's that, anyway?
Ute Nelz	Oh, that's hamburger with rice, raisins, green peppers, curry —
Hanni Klinger	Well, we'll see. Something Mexican would be good, too.
Ute Nelz	Not for me. That'd be too spicy. Besides, I could go for a good American hamburger.
Hanni Klinger	My, my — a middle-class meal for the American Studies major. But I'd like something exotic.
Ute Nelz	Oh, great. Something exotic in the dining hall — and we'll get Greek oysters at McDonald's, right?

4

Franz Moser	Well, what do you guys think? "Wanted: tenant for the month of August. Sublet nice furnished two-room apartment on the 8th floor" — That'd be OK, wouldn't it?
Benedikt Gerber	We'll see. That's in the student apartment complex, and we'd probably have married couples with kids in the building —
Benedikt Gerber	If you don't see anything else, we ought to take a look at the place. We wouldn't be home much anyway.
Franz Moser	Right. And if the apartment's nicely furnished —
Heinz Konrad	Or do we want to try a co-op? Maybe an older house, someone from school —

Chapter 17 — Conversations 2
University

1

David Hensley	No, it's not an exchange program. Our college sends 15 students to Munich every year.
Anni Reichardt	And they're allowed to study anything here?
David Hensley	Yes, but the first term we have special courses.
Anni Reichardt	But then you take regular courses in the second semester, don't you?
David Hensley	Yes, most of us. But those are usually lectures and seminars on history, art, literature — you know, the humanities.
Anni Reichardt	And science courses, too?
David Hensley	No, those we can take at home. This is our best chance to get to know European culture.

2

Peter Peiser	Linguistics? Really? Why?
Ralph Biermann	Well, I'm just interested in languages. After all, I was born overseas. Every day we had other languages in our house: Italian, French, even Swedish.
Peter Peiser	So you want to be an interpreter or something like that?

RALPH BIERMANN   No, not necessarily. I'm interested in the scientific side of linguistics: language history, structure, the process of learning a language — things like that.

PETER PEISER   So not really <u>what</u> people say, but <u>how</u> they say it. Personally, I think the What is more interesting than the How. But to each his own.

3   SANDY PALMER   So you start school when you're 5, too?

ALEX SCHIWOW   Yes, but usually not until we're 6. And then our school lasts a year longer than yours does.

SANDY PALMER   You aren't out of school until you're 19? And then you start college?

ALEX SCHIWOW   Not necessarily. After our Abitur the guys have to go into the army or do alternative service.

4   KAREN STEEN   And when do you have to choose a major? Also before your third year?

BERT BRANDT   No, right away. But when you've done the Abitur, you generally know what you want to study.

KAREN STEEN   So is it impossible to change majors? We do that a lot.

BERT BRANDT   Yes, I think that's a good feature of your system. But it's possible here, too. You just can't be a student forever!

KAREN STEEN   That's what my parents keep saying.

BERT BRANDT   And here it's the state that says you can't be a student forever. That's because the state pays for the education.

KAREN STEEN   For everyone?

BERT BRANDT   Yes, but not as many people study here as in your country.

Chapter 18 — Conversations 1
Department Store

1   MR. RUNKEL   Hello. What can I help you with?

MR. ZDANEK   Hi. Just browsing, thanks.

2   MR. HOHLER   Hello. Maybe you can help me. I'm looking for some shirts for my son — he's 8 — but I don't see anything here for him yet.

MS. NIEHOFF   Oh, not here, no. The sizes for his age are over there by the wall.

MR. HOHLER   Oh, fine. I didn't see them.

3   MS. ZSCHAMMER   Boy, I really like that a lot, I must say.

MS. KOHL   Isn't it nice, though? I think it's really cute, too.

MS. ZSCHAMMER   Would you have it in pink? That's my favorite color.

MS. KOHL   Well, this year we didn't have much in pink at all. I'm afraid there's nothing left in pink.

MS. ZSCHAMMER   Oh, what a shame I didn't come sooner. But we were on vacation. Do you suppose you'd know where else I could look in town?

MS. KOHL   Well, you might try at Aschinger or the new Mode-Hof on Severinstraße.

MS. ZSCHAMMER   Of, of course. Aschinger. Thanks very much for your help.

MS. KOHL   Sure. Any time.

4   MS. ROHR   What do you think? Is this all right, or is it too small for me?

MS. WINKLER   Well, I really think you could go ahead and wear a size larger.

MS. ROHR   Me, too — and that would be a lot more comfortable, wouldn't it?

5   MS. WIRTZ   No, unfortunately the new summer suits are already sold out. I'm sorry.

MR. HOELSCHER   Oh, rats —

MS. WIRTZ   But we still have a fine selection of beautiful suits. Look over here on the left — these can be worn in the fall and the spring, too.

MR. HOELSCHER   Hm, I'd have to think about that. You see, I already have two fall suits — and I really don't care for these colors all that much.

MS. WIRTZ   I see what you mean — a lighter color would certainly be better, but it would also be nice if you could wear the suit more than just in the summer.

MR. HOELSCHER   Yes, you're quite right. Still, I think I'd rather wait. But thanks a lot for your help.

Chapter 18 — Conversations 2
Lost and Found

1   MR. LECHNER   And you really don't remember any more?

DR. STIERLE   No, and I just don't understand it. How is it possible to lose two such big suitcases in the train station?

MR. LECHNER   Think about it again, maybe you'll remember after all. You still had the suitcases at the ticket window.

	Dr. Stierle	Yes, I still had them there. And then we walked over to the snack bar, and I put them in a corner there.
	Mr. Lechner	Right. Aren't they there in the corner?
	Dr. Stierle	No, I already looked.
	Mr. Lechner	Then we'd better check the lost and found. Maybe they'll know what we can do.
2	Dr. Stierle	So — let's sit down a little bit. They've got their hands full here.
	Mr. Lechner	Well, all right. But we really do have to hurry. The train's leaving in 25 minutes.
	Dr. Stierle	Right, but if I don't find my suitcases I can't go along. Hah — now it's our turn.
	Ms. Meinert	May I help you?
	Dr. Stierle	Hello, yes. I've lost two big suitcases, dark green ones. Have you seen them?
	Ms. Meinert	Do you mean those there? They were on a luggage cart at the snack bar, and the redcap brought them here.
3	Ms. Dr. Beck	Can you help me? I've lost my purse.
	Mr. Steirer	We'll see. What does your purse look like?
	Ms. Dr. Beck	It's a light brown suede purse.
	Mr. Steirer	And the contents?
	Ms. Dr. Beck	My wallet, sunglasses, keys, make-up, and so on — and my I.D.
	Mr. Steirer	Hm. Without identification you can't identify yourself. We do have a purse like that, but I can't give it to you if I don't know just who you are.
	Ms. Dr. Beck	Well, why don't you just take a look at the picture on the I.D.?
	Mr. Steiner	Hm. Sure — why not? Let's do that.
4	Ms. Glatthard	Hello. I can't find my son. Can you please help me?
	Mr. Koch	Hm — you ought to check with the police. We just get luggage and things like that here, not people.
	Ms. Glatthard	Fine. And where do I find the police?
	Mr. Koch	You'll find the station between the ticket window and the Kühne Travel Agency. That's up on the second floor.
	Ms. Glatthard	Oh, thank you so much.
	Mr. Koch	Not at all — just don't worry. You'll find him.
	Ms. Glatthard	Yes, and when I do . . .

Chapter 19 — Conversations 1
Leisure Time — Outdoors and Sports

1	Mr. Roffler	You can find swimsuits in the Roffler sports store on Bahnhofstraße. Or they're less expensive in the department store next door. But the best selection is in the sports store.
	Ms. Hardt	So Roffler then. And could you also tell me how to get to the outdoor pool?
	Mr. Roffler	Oh, you want to go to the pool? From Roffler you go up Bahnhofstraße about 200 meters.
	Ms. Hardt	And do you know how late they're open today?
	Mr. Roffler	They close in less than an hour.
	Ms. Hardt	Thanks very much for the information, Mr. . . . . uh . . .
	Mr. Roffler	Roffler. Please say hello to my brother.
2	Ms. Schwerin	I wanted to go skiing today. Are all the lifts operating?
	Ms. Buchholz	Yes, but not the Rothorn lift. It won't be operating again until Tuesday.
	Ms. Schwerin	Fine. And one more question: I have cross-country skis . . .
	Ms. Buchholz	Oh, that's fine, you can use those, too. You take the trail back to the Schwarzsee, then to the east toward Reute —
	Ms. Schwerin	Wait, just a second. That sounds a little complicated. Would you by any chance have a map of the area?
3	Stefan Marx	Shall we meet here again next week?
	Trina Seiler	Great, Stefan. And I'll bring along something to eat.
	Stefan Marx	Fine — but maybe you ought to discuss that with the other members. Next weekend is the big climb up the Schwarzhorn.
	Trina Seiler	Oh, neat. My parents wrote me that I should join in the climb.
	Stefan Marx	Too bad they emigrated. Otherwise they could go along.
	Trina Seiler	Right. The plans with the hiking club are just great. I really do want to spend the day with all of you.
	Stefan Marx	More than just the day, Trina. We start the climb at 10 at night. Then we see the sunrise before we come back down.
	Trina Seiler	Terrific! I'm already looking forward to it.

4

MR. SPENGLER	. . . and that would be for the whole weekend, right?
ARTUR ZSCHOKKE	Right, until Sunday evening, around 5 or 6.
MR. SPENGLER	Well, we close right at 6. You'll have to be here at 5:45 at the latest.
EMMA ZSCHOKKE	Oh, we can certainly make that.
MR. SPENGLER	Fine. That'll be 20 marks per day, and a 50 mark deposit. Do you have any other questions?
ARTUR ZSCHOKKE	Yes, it looks like this tire could use some air.

Chapter 19 — Conversations 2
Leisure Time — Hobbies and Music

1

PROFESSOR ZEHNDER	Oh, do you collect coins, too?
MR. PETERS	Yes, I've been collecting for 11 years.
PROFESSOR ZEHNDER	Really? You must have a marvelous collection.
MR. PETERS	Yes, it is rather large, but I'm not all that interested in quantity. Quality is much more important to me.
PROFESSOR ZEHNDER	My sentiments exactly. The best coins are beautiful and also rare.
MR. PETERS	Yes, but it's too bad that the value has more to do with rarity than with beauty.

2

MRS. MAURER	So what kind of hobbies does your son have?
MR. FRINGS	Well, he likes to make things — planes and such.
MRS. MAURER	And did you have an idea of how much you wanted to spend?
MR. FRINGS	Well, it shouldn't be more than 50 marks.
MRS. MAURER	I'll show you a few things. Then you can decide just what you want. And be sure to tell me when you've found something.

3

GABI VON WEBERN	Did you bring your instrument with you?
WALTRAUT SABIN	Yes. I'll be staying here for 6 months, and I didn't want to leave it at home. I practice every day — for years now.
GABI VON WEBERN	Well, what are your plans for Thursday evening? I play in a little group. We meet at my place at 8. You could sit in if you want.
WALTRAUT SABIN	Sure. What kind of music do you play? I'm really most interested in classical, but I've also played jazz in clubs.
GABI VON WEBERN	We play all sorts of things: classical, jazz, some musicals . . . it's mainly a group of music lovers. You're certainly welcome aboard.

4

MS. ASCHINGER	OK, now the headphones fit you perfectly. Did you want to take them like this, or should I put them back in the box?
MS. TRÜB	You can just leave them attached to the recorder. I'd like to listen to some music on the train.
MS. ASCHINGER	Didn't you say you're traveling to East Berlin?
MS. TRÜB	Yes, We want to see for ourselves what life is like there.
MS. ASCHINGER	Well, then you ought to go to the Deutsche Oper. It's supposed to be really beautiful after the renovation. And in East Berlin you can buy good records cheaply, too.
MS. TRÜB	Oh — one more thing: are there problems at the border if you have a machine like this?
MS. ASCHINGER	Don't worry. They're not all that strict anymore.

Chapter 20 — Conversations 1
Concert

1

MR. WEGMANN	It says in the paper that there are still some tickets for the Bach B-Minor Mass. How about it?
MS. WEGMANN	That depends. Do we have to go into the city just to get the tickets? If we do, I'm not interested.
MR. WEGMANN	I think we can order them by phone. But it doesn't say anything about that here. Shall I call?
MS. WEGMANN	OK by me. But if there are just standing-room tickets, we'll have to decide if it's worth it.

2

MS. STRAUSS	All right, here you are. Two orchestra seats together, third row on the left. The cloak room is downstairs.
LISA VOGEL	All right, thanks. Do I have time for a cigarette?
MS. STRAUSS	Hm — the performance begins in just a few minutes.
LISA VOGEL	Well, I can wait an hour for a smoke.
MS. STRAUSS	Actually, it's an hour and a half until the first intermission. You know that the *Meistersinger* is a very long opera. The performance lasts four and a half hours.
LISA VOGEL	Can I get something to eat during the intermission? Otherwise, that's too much Wagner on an empty stomach.

3 MR. KARSTEN   I have a request. Could I change places with you? Then I can sit next to my wife.

MR. BOENISCH   Why, of course. I thought about that myself before the intermission. You're taller than I am, and I couldn't see the entire stage.

MR. KARSTEN   Thanks very much. That's very nice of you.

MR. BOENISCH   I assume you're an American. How do you like our production of *Porgy and Bess*?

MR. KARSTEN   Excellent. I didn't know that people here were so interested in American composers.

4 MR. NILITSCHKA   To Baslerstraße? That'll take a while because of the opera traffic. Did you like it?

PROF. FLEISCHMANN   Yes. *Aïda* is always wonderful, even if I didn't understand much.

MR. NILITSCHKA   Yes, Italian operas are very often sung in German translation here. The music is much more important than the words. Often even I don't understand the German myself.

PROF. FLEISCHMANN   We saw *Aïda* in Rome, too, with the elephants on stage in the open-air theater.

MR. NILITSCHKA   Hm. You can't really compare the two productions. Putting elephants on stage — only in Rome! Those are productions for tourists, not opera lovers.

Chapter 20 — Conversations 2
Wine-Tasting

1 MS. LAßWITZ   May I offer you some of the '83 now? That was an excellent year — maybe the best in the last 10 years, and also the most expensive.

MS. WIESINGER   Can the '83 be compared to the '81?

MS. LAßWITZ   The '81 is too sweet for me. I prefer a dry wine.

MS. WIESINGER   A sweeter wine tastes better to me. And with a little cheese and fruit.

MS. LAßWITZ   Yes, you seem to be interested in our wines. May I invite you to our next tasting?

MS. WIESINGER   Oh, gladly. When would that be?

MS. LAßWITZ   It's going to be on October 4th, at 2 p.m.

2 MR. NIKOLAUS   Do we still have time to try the *Spätlese*? Our bus is leaving in a few minutes.

MS. MÖHN   By all means — you should try it before you leave. Then you can decide whether you like the *Spätlese* or the *Auslese* better . May I pour you some?

MR. NIKOLAUS   Of course. Should this wine be served chilled?

MS. MÖHN   Usually Mosel wines are served between 60° and 64°. They shouldn't be too cold.

MR. NIKOLAUS   I really like the taste of this wine. Like roses in springtime.

MS. MÖHN   It is, isn't it? Would you like to take a few bottles along?

3 MS. DÖRFLER   When are the grapes actually harvested in the fall?

MS. MEISTER   It all depends. The grapes for a *Kabinett* wine are harvested earlier than for a *Spätlese*, and the *Auslese* harvest comes even later, when the grapes are completely ripe.

MS. DÖRFLER   And how long does the wine stay in the barrels before it's bottled?

MS. MEISTER   That varies quite a bit. Sometimes just a few months, but the Rhine wines almost never more than 3 years.

4 CHARLES PORTER   We were here last week and thought the Johannisberger *Kabinett* was very good.

MR. SCHMÜCKING   So you took part in the wine festival?

CHARLES PORTER   Yes, we did. And we have a question: How difficult is it to send wine to the United States?

MR. SCHMÜCKING   It's really not worthwhile for just a few bottles. You can take them through customs yourself.

CHARLES PORTER   But we wanted a whole case. That's too heavy.

MR. SCHMÜCKING   We can take care of all that for you. You just need to fill out a few forms.

Chapter 21 — Conversations 1
Excursions

1 MR. FREUDENBERG   Hello. Nice view, isn't it? Do you mind if we sit down with you?

MS. FREUDENBERG   We want to rest a bit, too. This mountain gets higher every year.

TOM DOOLEY   Of course, please have a seat.

MR. FREUDENBERG   Thanks. First I have to shed this pack.

KWANG KIM   May I help you with it? It looks heavy.

. . .

MS. FREUDENBERG   Yes, we've been taking this hike for 40 years now, every year on our anniversary.

MR. FREUDENBERG   Everything has changed over the years. 40 years ago there wasn't any freeway through the valley.

MS. FREUDENBERG   Well, dear, it's getting late. Time for us to go.

MR. FREUDENBERG   It was nice talking with you. Have a good day. Good-bye.

2

MR. SAWYER	May I sit here with you?
MR. BEHRENS	Sure. In this restaurant it's always hard to find an empty table.
MR. SAWYER	I just arrived today. Maybe you could recommend some game dish.
MR. BEHRENS	The elk steak is fantastic. Here it's served with a wonderful berry sauce.
MR. SAWYER	*Bear sauce* ? We saw bears in the zoo, but . . .
MR. BEHRENS	No, no. You misunderstood me. Berries — plants, not animals.
MR. SAWYER	Aha: elk steak with berry sauce. Thanks, Mr. . . .
MR. BEHRENS	Behrens. My name is Behrens. Really. Funny, huh?

3

MS. MARTI	Excuse me. I think we're lost. We wanted to see the Hohenfels Castle.
MS. SCHREIBER	Oh, you've taken the wrong trail.
MS. MARTI	Oh, no! How is that possible?
MS. SCHREIBER	Well, because of the steep climb you didn't notice that you kept going farther south.
MS. MARTI	Oh, well — do you know if we can reach the castle on this trail?
MS. SCHREIBER	OK, this trail leads on through the woods and then up to the pass. Then you can't miss the trail down to the castle from there.

4

MR. ZAUCHER	But if you climb up, it will take you at least two and a half hours. The climb will make you tired, and you won't enjoy the descent.
MS. KARLEN	Mr. Zaucher's right, dear. We'd just be thinking about the next stretch of trail ahead. If we start at the pass, we'll enjoy it more.

Chapter 21 — Conversations 2
Travel Agency

1

MR. JUNG	Good morning. I was just at the Chamber of Commerce. They said you have information about package trips from Munich to Austria.
MS. EIGER	Yes — what did you have in mind? Day trips to Innsbruck or Salzburg?
MR. JUNG	First I was thinking of a weekend trip to Vienna, and maybe later a longer trip to Czechoslovakia.
MS. EIGER	Then we have lots to offer you. Are you interested in group tours?
MR. JUNG	Group tours? Well, only if they're less expensive and if you have enough time for yourself. I like to be independent.
MS. EIGER	I'll give you a few brochures first. You can look at them, and then we can talk more about what you want to do.

2

MS. MÖNCH	I'm very interested in the two-day trip to Lindau. Could you give me some details about it?
MS. GLADBACH	Glad to. "Round trip by train to Lindau, second class. Two nights in the Europahof, including breakfast, 200 marks. Leaves every Friday at 2:30 p.m. from May 24th to October 25th."
MS. MÖNCH	I'll be traveling alone. Is that the price for a single?
MS. GLADBACH	No, that's the price per person in a double. For a single there's a 20 mark surcharge.
MS. MÖNCH	Well, that sounds very nice, but I thought I might like to take a day out for a trip into Switzerland.
MS. GLADBACH	You can do that, too. Let me suggest this: If you rent a bicycle in Lindau, you can ride it to Friedrichshafen. Then you take the ferry from Friedrichshafen to Romanshorn in Switzerland. There you ride along the shore of Lake Constance.
MS. MÖNCH	And maybe stay for a day in Stein am Rhein, right, and take the ferry back to Meersburg?
MS. GLADBACH	Exactly. That way you'd see a lot and enjoy the fresh air. That's really worth doing.

3

MS. KEULER	To Leipzig? You'd have to book your trip 6 weeks in advance because of the visa.
DR. BOND	But we'll be in Europe for just 2 more weeks.
MS. KEULER	There's another possibility. You can get day visas for East Berlin right at the border crossings in the city. You just travel to West Berlin, by train or plane. You have to get hotel reservations in advance.
DR. BOND	Do I have to cross the border every day if I want to stay longer?
MS. KEULER	No. You get your extension automatically at your hotel. So you can take care of that there.

Chapter 22 — Conversations 1
Berlin — the Divided City

1

MR. TÜTSCH	Too bad we had to wait so long at the border. He wanted us to open every suitcase!
MS. TÜTSCH	But long waits have been fairly rare since 1972 — that's what the guidebook says. And the other official was quite nice.
MR. TÜTSCH	Yes, he was most interested in your new chess computer.

2 MS. WALTHERS — So that's the wall. And on the other side East Berlin and the Brandenburg Gate.

MS. FRICK — Then the big building on this side must be the Reichstag. What does the guidebook say about it?

MS. WALTHERS — "Destroyed by fire in 1933. Bombed in 1945. Rebuilt after the war. Chief symbol of the empire and the Nazi period. . . ."

MS. FRICK — So — it wasn't far from here that Hitler shot himself — that was on April 30, 1945.

MS. WALTHERS — ". . . Now a museum with the exhibition 'Questions asked of German History.' Closed Saturdays."

3 MS. HÄNDEL — What are those children doing with the flowers?

MR. HAHN — That's the eternal flame for the victims of fascism and militarism.

MS. HÄNDEL — Those are big words. What do children know about them?

MR. HAHN — Actually, they learn a lot about them in school — and in the Pioneers and the Free German Youth.

MS. HÄNDEL — Well, it's time to go outside. I think I hear a march.

MR. HAHN — Yes, the soldiers are coming now. The ones from East Germany are marching, and the ones from the United States are taking pictures.

4 MS. SCHUCHARDT — Yes, this is the Hotel Metropol. Please speak louder, we have a bad connection.

MR. ROSENGRANT — I'd like information about staying with you. That would be in mid-April. And I also wanted to ask if I can pay with my VISA card.

MS. SCHUCHARDT — Of course. Credit cards are welcome — with payment in international currencies.

MR. ROSENGRANT — And where is the best place to cross the border?

MS. SCHUCHARDT — For Americans there are various possibilities — first of all Checkpoint Charlie for cars and pedestrians, and then Friedrichstraße if you take the U-Bahn. That's a little closer, but it's open only during the day.

MR. ROSENGRANT — Do I have to apply for a visa in advance?

MS. SCHUCHARDT — No, you can get a day visa at the border crossing, and we'll renew it for you here in the hotel.

Chapter 22 — Conversations 2
Berlin — "Capital of the GDR"

1 MS. SCHREIBER — The wall was built in 1961. Before that everyone could travel freely to the west.

ANDREW TALMAN — And afterwards?

MS. SCHREIBER — After the wall we all knew that our home was here. And today our standard of living is the highest among the socialist countries.

ANDREW TALMAN — What would you say to the people who fled before 1961 if you could speak with them?

MS. SCHREIBER — I'd tell them, "Too bad you left. Just look what we've accomplished."

2 MR. SONNEMANN — All right, this is Bebel Square, formerly Opera Square. Here in 1933 the fascists burned books by Jewish as well as all liberal authors.

CAROL BARNES — Books by whom, for example?

MR. SONNEMANN — Naturally those by Marx and Lenin. The Americans in the group would probably be interested to know that even books by Jack London were banned during the Nazi period.

3 MISS LEOPOLD — But what does freedom mean when you have to live on the street, as you do in New York?

ANGELA SACCO — Too bad you aren't allowed to travel to the United States. There aren't all that many poor people.

MISS LEOPOLD — But they're there, and in our socialist country you don't see any poor people.

ANGELA SACCO — Nor any rich people, either!

MISS LEOPOLD — Yes, that's just what I mean — here everyone is equal, and the government guarantees us training and a job.

ANGELA SACCO — Really? Does the factory worker earn just as much as the Secretary General of the party?

4 MR. SCHWEITZER — That means that the average annual income in East Germany is 12,000 marks.

ADRIANUS KEIJ — How much does a new car cost?

MR. SCHWEITZER — 17,000 marks. But you have to wait a few years. I could sell my old Wartburg tomorrow for 35,000 marks.

ADRIANUS KEIJ — Now hold on! A new car costs 17,000 marks, and a used one 35,000?

MR. SCHWEITZER — Right, twice as much, because there's no waiting period.

5 MR. LIEBKNECHT — Who paid for the renovation of the church, if I might ask? It wasn't the state, was it?

MS. GUSTAV — The government paid a part of the cost, and West German Christians helped with the restoration of the paintings.

Chapter 23 — Conversations 1
Memorials

1   MR. DR. SCHULZE   Dachau, where we're driving today, was one of the first concentration camps.

ANDREW GOODMAN   And lots of Jews were sent there already in 1933, weren't they?

MR. DR. SCHULZE   Well, actually not right at the beginning. Most of the prisoners were political opponents of Hitler's — communists, Social Democrats, journalists and so on.

MS. DR. SCHULZE   And all you knew was that this person or that was arrested because he was an "enemy of the state."

ANDREW GOODMAN   Unbelievable. And yet a few people still believe to this day that there was no Holocaust!

2   MS. DR. SCHULZE   That's right — 6 million human beings died in the concentration camps. And we didn't know anything about all of that until the war was over.

ANDREW GOODMAN   Well, anyway, my grandmother told me I shouldn't travel to Germany. My grandfather and both my aunts were killed there.

MR. DR. SCHULZE   But maybe a look into the past could help you understand it all.

3   MONIKA WALTHERS   Say, I don't really understand this. In the city guide to East Berlin it says, "The city was destroyed by English and American airplanes."

EBERHART HAYM   So? That's right. Didn't you read about the air raids yourself?

MONIKA WALTHERS   Sure, but now listen to this: "The city was liberated by the Soviet heroes," and I happen to know that the Russians had 7,500 planes in the attack on Berlin.

EBERHART HAYM   So you think they're saying that none of these planes killed any people or destroyed parts of the city, right?

MONIKA WALTHERS   Exactly. How can they say stuff like that?

EBERHART HAYM   Today the Russians have to be heroes, because East Germany is one of the East Bloc countries.

4   HERB BAUSCHINGER   Unbelievable. So many dead, and so many families destroyed.

MS. BAUSCHINGER   Right. But also think of the 12 million refugees from the eastern territories who had to flee to the west.

HERB BAUSCHINGER   Were they really Germans?

MS. BAUSCHINGER   Yes, most of them. And that's really ironic, because one of Hitler's pet words was "room for living."

HERB BAUSCHINGER   . . . that is to say, more room for his German people.

MS. BAUSCHINGER   But the great emigration didn't begin until after the war was over. That's why the Wall was built in 1961 — to put an end to the emigration.

Chapter 23 — Conversations 2
Retired People

1   MS. SENSENBRENNER   Yes, my husband was drafted into the army already in 1939. He didn't come back from Russia until 1951.

WILLIAM LINGLE   Not until 1951? But how is that possible? The war was over back in 1945.

MS. SENSENBRENNER   I know, but many didn't come home until much later.

WILLIAM LINGLE   And during that time you never saw him, either?

MS. SENSENBRENNER   No, I did once — when he was in the hospital. But the children were already big by the time they saw their father again.

2   MS. EBERHARD   Well, we just couldn't take it any more at home. I had to put my mother in a retirement home.

MS. STAMMLER   Oh, was that because of your work, or because of the care?

MS. EBERHARD   Both, really.

MS. STAMMLER   But you said that the retirement home is really good.

MS. EBERHARD   Yes, I'm very satisfied with it.

MS. STAMMLER   And you probably wouldn't have lasted much longer — taking care of her, I mean.

3   MS. STEIERT   You know, lots of people say that we didn't fight against Hitler and are therefore also responsible for the whole Nazi catastrophe.

MR. STEIERT   But it wasn't that simple. They made us lots of promises, and those were hard times after the First World War.

EMILY SANDERSON   Yes, I know — poverty, inflation, unemployment.

MS. STEIERT   But we're doing quite well now. We have our apartment and our government pension.

MR. STEIERT   And our little garden provides a lot — not just vegetables, but also peace and quiet.

EMILY SANDERSON   I'm really happy you're both doing well.

4

MR. TSCHARNER	The war years were tough on us Swiss, too. People think we just sat at home.
RETO CATHOMAS	Well, I don't. After all, I understand you and my grandfather were in the border guard.
MR. TSCHARNER	That's right. We were supposed to make sure nothing happened.
RETO CATHOMAS	But how did that work with being neutral? No one was allowed to attack Switzerland, right?
MR. TSCHARNER	My dear Reto, what do you mean, "allowed?" Hitler was just afraid that he'd lose too many soldiers here. Otherwise he'd have attacked us, too.
RETO CATHOMAS	No, I mean — Switzerland was neutral, wasn't it?
MR. TSCHARNER	Well, "neutral" — sure, but let's say neutral on the side of the Allies.

Chapter 24 — Conversations 1
The Old Family Home — Back Then

1

CHRISTIANE PRIER	The Archive closes in half an hour. I was just tidying up before we close.
KEVIN SMITH	I'm looking for documents about my relatives. My family name is Smith, but it was different earlier. My great-grandfather's name was Friedrich Wilhelm Schmidt.
CHRISTIANE PRIER	And when did he emigrate to America?
KEVIN SMITH	In 1885 — that's what it says in the big German Bible at home. We have a few letters, too.
CHRISTIANE PRIER	It would be better if you could come by again tomorrow morning.
KEVIN SMITH	Are there documents like that in the church, too?
CHRISTIANE PRIER	Yes, especially birth dates. That's important, because the Town Hall was destroyed in the war.

2

MAGDA SEIFERT	We're pretty closely related.
SUSAN WERNER	Yes, we are. Do I have this right, now? You're my great-grandfather's oldest sister's granddaughter.
MAGDA SEIFERT	Right — exactly. Let me show you another picture.
SUSAN WERNER	The young man wearing the uniform — is that my great-grandfather, too?
MAGDA SEIFERT	No, that's his younger brother, just before he died. He was killed in France in 1916.
SUSAN WERNER	And the woman holding the two children in her arms?

3

SHAWN HINES	And what became of the other children?
INGEBORG SAILER	Gerhardt — that's your grandmother's second-oldest cousin — studied law at the University of Leipzig. That's what Karl Marx University was called then. He became a lawyer and married a girl from . . .

4

ELIZABETH BÜTOW	Tell me how your grandparents met. Was that after the war?
ELISABETH BUETOW	No, before. My grandfather had a stationery store downtown. One day my grandmother came into the store and . . .

5

ADAM SNYDER	My father had to do a lot of traveling back then.
JOHANNA SCHNEIDER	And that was the reason for the divorce?
ADAM SNYDER	Maybe. But it would have happened even if he had been home more.
JOHANNA SCHNEIDER	Well, let's change the subject. So you went to school in South Carolina?
ADAM SNYDER	When I was four, we moved to Winnebago County. I went to grade school there, from 1973 to 1979. Then 3 years of junior high and 3 years of high school. I studied at the University of Michigan from 1985 to 1987. I've been in the army since August of '87.

Chapter 24 — Conversations 2
The Old Family Home — Now

1

HEINZ STRAUCH	It would have been better, if you had taken the "Wetterstein." It goes right to Murnau.
BARBARA FIELD	Yes I knew that. But I wanted to see Nuremberg.

2

CHAD SKAGGS	What's the difference between Bavaria and Prussia?
HERTA FRANKE	Kind of like Texas and New York. As you know, Bavaria is in the south, and is the largest state in the Federal Republic. Prussia is — or was — in the north. As a state Prussia doesn't exist any more.
CHAD SKAGGS	Are the people different?
HERTA FRANKE	The dialects are very different — and the cultural differences are pretty great, too.

3

KARL JÄGER	Your Aunt Rosie is a Pink Lady? What's that?
CARLA YEAGER	A woman who works in the hospital, and . . .
KARL JÄGER	That's what we call a nurse.
CARLA YEAGER	No. She helps only because she wants to — as a volunteer.

4	GEORG WEIGAND	So you pay 60 pfennigs for a liter of gas, but we pay twice as much.
	RICK PETERSON	But there are big geographical differences. For example, you live in Bonn, and your father lives in Augsburg.
	GEORG WEIGAND	Right. That's 529 kilometers — 5 hours by train.
	RICK PETERSON	My mother-in-law lives in New Jersey. We live in Sacramento. That's almost 3000 miles, let's say 4800 kilometers.
	GEORG WEIGAND	And your parents— where do they live?
	RICK PETERSON	Not far from us — in Anaheim. That's just 350 miles — about 500 or 600 kilometers.
	GEORG WEIGAND	And you don't think that's far?
5	KATE MUELLER	Right, and that costs a bundle — $400 a month.
	TRINA MÜLLER	$400!! So she shells out a third of her entire income — before taxes — for child care.
	KATE MUELLER	But both parents want a career. My sister had to go right back to work.
	TRINA MÜLLER	Then there's a big difference between our systems. In the GDR, mothers get 6 months off with pay. Child care is free.
	KATE MUELLER	Right, but you can't make a direct comparison.
6	HOWE BAKER	And if Grandfather hadn't emigrated to America, what then?
	ERNA SCHNEIDER	He would probably have kept on being a baker.
	HOWE BAKER	And then he wouldn't have gotten to know my grandmother.
	ERNA SCHNEIDER	Yes, everything would have been different. You wouldn't even be here!

Chapter 25 — Conversations 1
Laundry

1	MR. LANDAU	My. You have quite a load there. Let's see how much that weighs . . . O.K., 7 kilos. We can do that in one machine.
	MR. NIKOLAISEN	Great. When can I pick up the laundry?
	MR. LANDAU	Today, if you come by before 6 p.m.
	MR. NIKOLAISEN	Fine. May I leave the suitcase here?
	MR. LANDAU	Of course. We'll pack everything up for you.
	MR. NIKOLAISEN	Oh, one more thing: please don't boil the laundry.
2	MS. KRÜGER	I don't know if we can wash all that in one machine or not.
	MS. BALZ	Maybe it should be done in two machines. With the shirts in with the delicates.
	MS. KRÜGER	Right, they certainly can't be boiled.
	MS. BALZ	It would also be better if you didn't boil the new jeans. Otherwise they'll fade too much.
	MS. KRÜGER	Whatever you think. Then we'll need two machines.
	MS. BALZ	Or maybe I should wash the jeans myself.
	MS. KRÜGER	As you wish — but we don't have any self-service here.
3	CLAUDIA MARGNELLI	Do you know how to operate this machine?
	RALPH BAKER	Sure — the directions aren't so easy for foreigners to understand. Have you already separated the regular wash from the delicates?
	CLAUDIA MARGNELLI	Yes — most of the things shouldn't be boiled.
	RALPH BAKER	Then you set both machines for color wash. That way nothing gets boiled.
	CLAUDIA MARGNELLI	But will the jeans get clean, too?
	RALPH BAKER	Certainly. German technology.
4	CHRISTINE H.	Would you like me to do that for you?
	MR. HAWTHORNE	Oh, no, thanks — if you'd just show me how this works, then I can do it myself.
	CHRISTINE H.	I'd be glad to. But what kind of laundry do you have?
	MR. HAWTHORNE	Well, I don't know the German terms very well. Shirts and socks, jeans and underwear.
	CHRISTINE H.	O.K. — shirts are delicate, so you should wash them in one machine. And the jeans and socks are color wash, so that would be another machine.
	MR. HAWTHORNE	And the other things are whites, right? So I need three machines.
	CHRISTINE H.	Right. And you'll see the operating instructions up here on the board. Is everything O.K.?

Chapter 25 — Conversations 2
Photo Developing

1	MS. SCHRANZ	Interesting. Where did you take this picture, if you don't mind my asking?
	MR. BEINECKE	In East Berlin. We were there for 7 days.

2
MR. HUMMEL — I'd like an enlargement of this color picture.
MS. SCHMITTEN — Oh, that's very nice. Is that East Berlin?
MR. HUMMEL — No, Dresden. That's our student group. The enlargement is a present for my girlfriend.

3
MS. FONTANE — Hello. I'd like to leave these films for developing.
MS. BRUNN — Fine. Normal size, right? And did you want matte or glossy?
MS. FONTANE — Matte. You said "normal size." What is the normal size?
MS. BRUNN — 9 x 13 cm is normal. The next size would be 13 x 18.
MS. FONTANE — Hm. What's the difference in price?
MS. BRUNN — Not much, really. We're having a special this week on the 13 x 18. Let's see: 24 exposures . . . that would be 31 marks instead of 39, and you get a free roll of film.
MS. FONTANE — Fine. And when can I pick up my pictures?
MS. BRUNN — Tomorrow at this time. We develop everything ourselves here.

4
MR. FLYNN — How long will that take? We're leaving tomorrow.
MR. NÄFF — Let's see. 100 ASA — that's American film.
MR. FLYNN — Right — I brought it to Austria with me.
MR. NÄFF — No problem. That's 21 DIN. We can do it just fine — no special treatment will be necessary.
MR. FLYNN — Do you develop the pictures here?
MR. NÄFF — No, in our main lab.
MR. FLYNN — But that takes a lot of time, doesn't it?
MR. NÄFF — Actually not. It's just 2:00 now. You can leave your films here. They'll be picked up today and then brought back in 24 hours.

5
MR. JÜRGENS — I'd like prints made from these slides.
MS. KLETT — Well, that'll take a few days. Are you in a hurry?
MR. JÜRGENS — No. I'll be here for another 2 weeks. But is it expensive?
MS. KLETT — No. In fact, we're having a special for all sizes: 10 x 15, 15 x 25, 20 x 30.
MR. JÜRGENS — I'd like these three in 20 x 30, but are the slides sharp enough?
MS. KLETT — Let's take a look . . . The two slides from the hike, yes. We can't make the other one that big, though. You didn't have enough light.

Chapter 26 — Conversations 1
Impoliteness — Politeness

1
A) Stop!
B) Leave me alone! If you don't stop, I'll call for help!
C) If you don't stop that right away, I'll call the conductor.
D) Or else I'm gonna give you a knuckle sandwich!
E) Oh, that was rude, crude, vulgar and socially unacceptable!

2
A) Quiet, please!
B) May I ask you to be quiet?
C) Could I ask you to be quiet, please?
D) I'm asking you for the last time to be quiet. Otherwise I'll go to the hostel parents.
E) Shut up!

3
MR. HENNING — The Americans want more and more nuclear weapons in Europe. Why do you keep electing presidents like that?
LINDA MARKS — A) Maybe you're right. I don't know.
B) Oh, well — I don't think politics is all that interesting.
C) Well, it's not as simple as you think.
D) OK, first of all: I'm not the President. And second: He doesn't speak for all Americans.
E) Do you think all Germans think that way?
F) But the Russians also seem to want to have more and more arms in Europe.
G) And what if there aren't any more nuclear weapons and American soldiers in West Germany?
H) And have you always elected the very best politicians here?

4
ERNST BOHRER — Why did you say that? Surely you don't mean that!
HUGO FRIEDRICH — A) I think you misunderstood me.
B) I didn't really mean that.
C) I'm sorry you took it that way.

5 KLAUS WENDT   You just shouldn't have done that!
       ANNA KOHL   A) Yeah, that's right. That was really stupid of me.
                   B) I don't think it was all that bad.

6 MR. BRACHER   Could you come to our place on Saturday evening?
       MS. KÖNIG   A) Sorry, but I can't. That's really nice of you, but I have a previous engagement.
                   B) Thanks for the invitation. But I'm afraid we can't. We've already made plans.
                   C) Love to. That would be great. When should we be there?

7 MS. TIEMENS   Excuse me. Can you do me a favor?
       MS. BERGMANN   Sure, of course. How can I help you?

Chapter 26 — Conversations 2
Welcome and Farewell

1 JOHN ALLEN   I got a Fulbright Fellowship to study political science here.

2 MR. STROBEL   OK, I'd like to introduce someone. This is Mr. Anderson from Chicago. He's doing some on-the-job training with us in international economics. That's Ms. Mager there on the left, from the international division.
       ROY ANDERSON   Pleased to meet you, Ms. Mager.
       MR. STROBEL   And next to her is Ms. Alpers from the sales division.
       ROY ANDERSON   Hello, Ms. Alpers.

3 BENNO KEHL   I'm delighted that you're staying with us. Make yourself comfortable.
       JUDY ATTERHOLT   Thanks very much. I already feel right at home.

4 JIM STEPHENS   Hello, I'd like some flowers for one of my co-workers who has invited me to supper.
       MS. BREMER   Fine. Were you thinking of a certain kind?
       JIM STEPHENS   Do you have red roses?
       MS. BREMER   Yes, but in Germany red roses signify love.
       JIM STEPHENS   I didn't know that. Hm — I don't know the different kinds of flowers. Could you recommend something?
       MS. BREMER   You probably want a colorful bouquet. Of course, I'll have to know how much you want to spend.
       JIM STEPHENS   Oh, somewhere between 20 and 30 marks.
       MS. BREMER   For that you'll get a beautiful bouquet. If you can't decide, you can also pick out something in our display window.

5 ANN BLACKLER   We're very grateful to you for showing us your town. We hope you can visit us sometime.
       MR. LUDWIG   I hope you enjoyed your trip. I know you had your hands full with your business obligations.
       PETE HEROLD   Well, we had enough time to take a short trip to Berlin. I wish we'd been able to visit Dresden, too.
       MR. LUDWIG   Yes, and you should have gone to Leipzig, too. But maybe next time.

6 TOM JEFFERS   High time for us to go. Thanks so much for everything!
       MS. BACHMANN   We enjoyed it too. Well, bon voyage! And say hello to your family! Have a safe trip home!

Chapter Glossaries

NOUN PLURALS are indicated unless the noun follows one of two regular patterns:

If the word ends in -e, add -n	der **Name**, plural **Namen**
If the word does not end in -e, add -e	das **Gespräch**, plural **Gespräche**

Preliminary 1

NOUNS

der

Amerikaner, - American (male); The adjective is **amerikanisch**
Familienname last name, family name
Herr, -en Mr.; gentleman
Main no pl the Main River
Morgen, - morning
Name (last) name
Vorname first name, given name

die

Amerikanerin, -nen American (female)
Frau, -en Mrs., Ms.

Kanadier, - (male) Canadian; **Kanadierin** (female)
Mathematik no pl mathematics

das

Fräulein, - Miss, Ms.; waitress!
Gespräch conversation, talk
Kanada no pl Canada

OTHER

also so, therefore, well, oh, OK
alt old
Auf Wiedersehen! Good-bye!
aus dat from, out of
bitte please; here you go; you're welcome
danke thanks

das that; the
Guten Abend hello; Good Evening
Guten Morgen hello; Good Morning
Guten Tag Hello (late a.m. to early p.m.)
ich I
ist is
ja yes; of course, after all
nein no
Sie you (formal)
studieren study; major in
und and
was what
wer who
wie how
Wie heißen Sie? What is your name?
Wie ist der Name? What is your name?

Preliminary 2

NOUNS

der

Abend evening (including "night" before sleeping time)
Dienstag Tuesday
Donnerstag Thursday
Freitag Friday
Mittwoch Wednesday
Montag Monday
Samstag Saturday
Sonntag Sunday

die

Bundesrepublik Deutschland (BRD) no pl the Federal Republic of Germany (FRG); West Germany

Deutsche Demokratische Republik (DDR) no pl German Democratic Republic (GDR); East Germany
Entschuldigung, -en Excuse me! pardon
Mark, - BRD & DDR currency unit
Schweiz no pl Switzerland
Uhr, -en o'clock

das

Deutschland no pl Germany
Österreich Austria

OTHER

da there, here
gestern yesterday

heißen be named, be called **ich heiße** my name is
heute today
hier here
Ich weiß nicht I don't know
in in
kosten cost
morgen tomorrow
nicht not
sind are
spät late
tut mir leid I'm sorry
war was
weiß (I) know, (he/she) knows
wieviel how much
Wieviel Uhr ist es? What time is it?
wo where

Chapter 1

NOUNS

plural only

Pommes frites French fries

der

Ausweis ID card
Franken, - Swiss Franc
Groschen, - Austrian coin

Imbiß, Imbisse fast food place, snack bar
Kaffee no pl coffee; 2 coffees, please **2(mal) Kaffee, bitte**
Kartoffelsalat potato salad
Kontext context
Moment moment; Wait a moment!
Paß, Pässe passport
Paßbeamte passport official (male); **Paßbeamtin** (female)

Pfennig, - or **-e** 1/100th of a mark
Rappen, - Swiss coin (1/100 of a Franken)
Salat salad
Schaffner, - conductor
Schilling, - or **-e** Austrian monetary unit
Tee tea

die

Bratwurst, ̈e type of (grilled) sausage
Currywurst, ̈e curried sausage; 2 orders of currywurst **zwei Stück, zweimal Currywurst**
Fahrkarte ticket (train, etc.)
Flasche bottle
Funktion, -en function
Kellnerin, -nen waitress (waiter = **der Ober, Kellner**)
Kontrolle control (post); check, inspection
Ordnung *no pl* order; routine »**in Ordnung**
Paßkontrolle passport check
Situation, -en situation
Sprache language; speech
Strategie strategy
Struktur, -en structure

Stunde hour; time; lesson
Wurst, ̈e sausage »**Bratwurst**

das

Bier, - or **-e** beer (note: **2 Bier** 2 beers; **Biere** kinds of beer)
Brötchen, - breakfast roll
Gepäck *no pl* baggage, luggage
Glas, - or **̈er** glass (note: **zwei Glas Wein** 2 glasses of wine)
Mineralwasser *no pl* mineral water
Ticket, -s ticket (transportation)
Visum, Visen visa

OTHER

ach! oh!
bitte schön / sehr you're welcome; there you go; yes? can I help you?
danke schön / sehr thanks a lot

essen eat
gut good; well
haben have
heute abend this evening
in Ordnung OK, all right
ist gut OK, all right, sure
mit with
möchten would like (to)
nichts nothing
schwarz black
so OK, now then, that's it, well then
trinken drink
um __ Uhr at __ o'clock
versuchen try, attempt
wann when (in questions)
wir we
zu to, at; too **zuviel** too much
zurück back, change (money)

Chapter 2

NOUNS

plural only

Herrschaften ladies and gentlemen; gentlemen; everyone

der

Appetit *no pl* appetite »**Guten Appetit**
Bohnensalat bean salad
Fisch fish
Ober, - waiter; (direct address) **Herr Ober!**
Rotwein red wine
Schlüssel, - key
Wein wine
Weißwein white wine
Wurstsalat sausage salad

die

Dame lady, woman
Dusche shower (bath)
Nacht, ̈e night
Nummer, -n number, size (of clothing, shoes, etc.)
Salzkartoffel, -n boiled (salted) potatoes
Tagesspezialität, -en today's special

das

Bad, ̈er bath(-tub, -room)
Doppelzimmer, - double room in hotel

Einzelzimmer, - single room in hotel
Frühstück breakfast
Hotel, -s hotel
Kotelett, -s (meat) chop, cutlet
Messer, - knife
Restaurant, -s restaurant
Salz *no pl* salt
Seelachsfilet, -s salmon filet
Taxi, -s taxi
Zimmer, - room

OTHER

auch also, too, even
beide both
bißchen (a) little (of something) »**ein bißchen**
bleiben stay (remain)
brauchen need, require
bringen bring, fetch
doch sure(ly), indeed, by all means; but, however, nevertheless
ein bißchen a little
etwas something
fantastisch fantastic, great
für for
gern(e) gladly, with pleasure; Sure! Glad to!
glauben believe, think
Guten Appetit! Enjoy your meal!
Herr Ober! waiter!
im in the

ist recht OK, all right, fine
kein no, none, not any
lang(e) long; for a long time »**wie lange**
machen do, make; **das macht X** that totals X; **das macht nichts** that's OK
natürlich sure, of course, certainly
noch still, yet
nur only
oder or
ohne without
pro per
schmecken taste
schön fine, great, beautiful
schon already; really
sehr very
sofort right away, at once, immediately
teuer expensive
uns us
warum why
wie lange how long
wohl well, good; probably, likely
wunderbar great, fine, wonderful
zahlen pay
Zum Wohl! cheers! here's mud in your eye!
zum to; to (the)
zusammen together
zweimal two (of something), twice, two orders of _

Chapter 3

NOUNS

der

Dank *no pl* thanks »**vielen Dank**
Fahrkartenschalter, - ticket counter, window
Käse cheese
Proviant *no pl* provisions, supplies (of food)
Reiseproviant *no pl* travel food, snacks
Schalter, - counter, ticket window
Schweizerkäse *no pl* Swiss cheese
Zug, ¨e train

die

Damentoilette women's restroom
Ecke corner
Frau, -en woman
Karte ticket; map; card; menu
Nuß, Nüsse nut
Orange orange
Person, -en person, human being
Schokolade *no pl* chocolate(s)
Tafel, -n bar (of chocolate, soap)
Toilette restroom, toilet, bathroom

das

Abteil (train) compartment
Gleis track (railroad)
Gramm, - gram (1 lb. = approx. 500g)
Meter, - meter (= 1.1 yard)
Päckchen, - pack, packet; parcel, small package
Stück, - or **¨e** piece, unit (**2 Stück** _ 2 pieces of _)

OTHER

aber but, however
alles everything
danke vielmals thanks a lot
dann then
einfach one-way
einmal one (order of) __
es gibt there is, there are
finden find
fragen ask, inquire
gehen go; walk
genug enough
geschlossen closed, shut

hin there, toward there; **hin und zurück** there and back, round trip
lieben love; like (something) a lot
links to the left
mal once, just; **Xmal** Xtime(s): **viermal** four times
mehr more
nach to, toward, after
nächst next
nehmen take
noch etwas something else/more
rechts to the right, on the right-hand side
sagen say, tell
sie she; they; her; them
sonst nichts nothing else
sonst noch (et)was anything else
um around
vergessen forget
verstehen understand
viel many
vielen Dank thanks a lot, many thanks
vielmals a lot, often
weiter furthermore; farther
wohin where to
zuviel too much

Chapter 4

NOUNS

der

Bahnhof, ¨e train station
Bruder, ¨ brother
Doktor, -en doctor (title of address — includes Ph.D., etc.)
Dom cathedral
Freund friend (male), boyfriend
Frühling spring (season)
Hauptbahnhof, ¨e central RR station
Herbst fall (autumn)
Platz, ¨e seat; (market) square; place
Sohn, ¨e son
Sommer, - summer
Vater, ¨ father
Winter, - winter
Zoo, -s zoo

die

Adresse address (street)
Auskunft, ¨e information; details
Bank, -en bank (financial)
Familie family (singular!)
Frau, -en wife
Jugendherberge youth hostel
Konditorei, -en pastry shop
Linie line; bus or streetcar line
Minute minute

Mutter, ¨ mother
Physik *no pl* physics
Post *no pl* post office; mail; postal system
Reise trip, journey
Schwester, -n sister
Stadt, ¨e city
Straße street; block
Tochter, ¨ daughter

das

Kind, -er child
Museum, Museen museum
Stadtmuseum, -museen city museum
Verkehrsbüro, -s chamber of commerce; tourist information office
Viertel, - quarter; (one) fourth; **Viertel vor drei** 2:45

OTHER

arbeiten work
besetzt occupied, busy
besser better
bis until, up to, by; **bis zu** up to, as far as, until the
deutsch German
dies this
dort (over) there
durch through

ein paar a couple (of), a few (not necessarily a pair)
fahren travel, drive
frei free
geradeaus straight ahead
gleich (time) right away, directly
holen get, fetch
immer always, ever
interessant interesting
jetzt (right) now
kommen come
leicht easy, easily; light
mir (to) me
nehmen Sie Platz take a seat
paar »**ein paar** a few, a couple, some
reisen travel
richtig right, correct
schade too bad, a shame
schlafen sleep
sehen see; understand
suchen look for, seek
und so weiter (usw.) and so forth (etc.)
viel much
von from, of, belonging to
vor before, in front of
weit far
wieder again; back
wissen know (facts)
zu Fuß on foot

Chapter 5

NOUNS

der

Bus, -se bus
Gast, ⸚e guest, customer
Mann, ⸚er man (male person); husband
Marktplatz, ⸚e market place
Stock, ⸚e story, floor

die

Haltestelle stop (transit)
S-Bahn, -en suburban/urban train, streetcar
Seife soap
Treppe stairs, stairway

das

Deutsch *no pl* German (language) **auf deutsch** in German
Handtuch, ⸚er towel
Krankenhaus, ⸚er hospital
Telefon telephone
Toilettenpapier *no pl* toilet paper

OTHER

all all, every **alle X Minuten** every X minutes
am at the, by the, on the
aus•steigen get out (of bus, etc.)
baden bathe, swim
bekommen get, receive
blau blue (color, not emotion)
braun brown
dahin to there, that way
direkt direct(ly)
duschen (take a) shower
einfach easy, easily, simple, simply
erst first
extra extra, additional(ly)
funktionieren work, function, operate, run
ganz quite, complete(ly)
geben give
gelb yellow
genau exact(ly)
grau gray
grün green
heiß hot
hoch up, high, upstairs; **eine Treppe hoch** one flight up
kalt cold (temperature)
kann can (I/he/she/it)
meinen mean (intend, imply)
müssen must, have to
noch kein still no
oben up there, upstairs, above
regnen rain
rosa pink
rot red
sein his, its
so . . . wie as . . . as
sollen be supposed to, should really
stark strong(ly); severe(ly); heavy, heavily
um•steigen transfer (transit)
unten down below, downstairs
warten wait
weiß white
wenn if; when, whenever
zweit- second

Chapter 6

NOUNS

der

Apfel, ⸚ apple
Automat, -en vending machine
Fahrkartenautomat, -en ticket vending machine
Fünfziger, - fifty (banknote or stamp)
Geldwechsel *no pl* currency exchange
Kiosk kiosk, newsstand
Kurs exchange rate
Professor, -en professor
Reisescheck, -s traveler's check
Schein bill (money), banknote, certificate

die

Banane banana
D-Mark, - West German mark

Quittung, -en receipt
Rosine raisin
Straßenbahn, -en streetcar
Stundenkarte transit ticket valid for one hour
Unterschrift, -en signature
Zeitschrift, -en magazine, journal
Zeitung, -en newspaper

das

Datum, Daten (calendar) date
Geld *no pl* money, currency
Obst, -sorten fruit

OTHER

bar (in) cash
billig cheap
das heißt that is, means

denn then, anyway, indeed (expresses interest or impatience)
kanadisch Canadian
kaputt broken, out of order
klein small, little
können can, be able to
leider unfortunately
mit along (with)
na well . . .
naja well now . . .
nebenan right nearby; next door; in the next room
scheinen seem; shine
schreiben write
sprechen speak, talk
unterschreiben sign
vielleicht maybe, perhaps
wechseln (ex)change
wollen want (to)

Chapter 7

NOUNS

plural only

Leute people

der

Babysitter, - baby sitter
Becher, - cup (for ice cream)

Blitz flash (photo, lightning)
Computer, - computer
Domplatz, ⸚e cathedral square
Eingang, ⸚e (building) entrance
Fluß, Flüsse river
Gottesdienst religious service
Nachmittag afternoon; **heute nachmittag** this afternoon

Rhein *no pl* the River Rhine
Rheinpark, -s park on the Rhine
Stadtplan, ⸚e city map
Tisch table
Verkehr *no pl* traffic; trade, business; dealings
Zirkus, -se circus

die

Ansichtskarte (picture) postcard
Fahrt, -en trip (vehicular)
Kirche church
Nußtorte nut cake
Rundfahrt, -en tour, excursion
Stadtmitte city center
Stadtrundfahrt, -en round-trip city tour
Synagoge synagogue
Tasse cup
Tüte cone (ice cream); small sack, paper bag
Zeit, -en time

das

Eis, -sorten ice cream, ice
Essen, - food, meal
Fenster, - window
Himbeereis, - raspberry ice cream
Kännchen, - small pot (of coffee, etc.)
Konzert concert; concerto

Mittagessen, - lunch
Schokoladeneis, - chocolate ice cream
Schwimmbad, ⸚er swimming pool
Stativ tripod

OTHER

ab away, down, off
ab•fahren leave, depart
ab•holen pick up, fetch
an at, on
an•fangen begin
an•rufen call up (telephone)
auf *dat* on
beginnen begin, start
bestimmt certain(ly), particular(ly), definite(ly)
dürfen may, be allowed/permitted
ein•kaufen shop, make purchases
fotografieren photograph, take pictures
früh early
gibt es Is there . . . ? *acc*
hinten behind, to the rear

man one, a person, people, they
mich me *acc, dir obj*
nach•sehen look, check
neben *dat* next to
Pardon Excuse me
reservieren reserve, book
reserviert reserved, booked
schnell quick(ly)
schwimmen swim
sitzen sit
stören disturb, annoy, bother
tanzen dance
treffen meet (by arrangement); **wir treffen uns später** we'll meet later
übermorgen day after tomorrow
vom (=von dem) of the; from the
vorn(e) in front
wandern hike, walk
weg away, off, gone
weg•fahren leave, go away (vehicular)
wie viele how many
zuerst first *adv*; first of all; at first

Chapter 8

NOUNS

der

Altar, Altäre altar
April *no pl* April
August *no pl* August
Dezember *no pl* December
Februar *no pl* February
Fußgänger, - pedestrian
Januar *no pl* January
Juli *no pl* July
Juni *no pl* June
Krieg war
Mai *no pl* May
März *no pl* March
November *no pl* November
Oktober *no pl* October
Park, -s park
September *no pl* September
Stadtführer, - city guide (book)
Stehplatz, ⸚e standing room (tickets)
Tag day
Weltkrieg World War

die

Abendfahrt, -en evening trip
Altstadt, ⸚e Old Town
Fußgängerzone pedestrian zone
Garderobe hat & coat check at restaurants, etc.; tall, free-standing wardrobe closet
Idee idea, thought

Kasse cashier's station; ticket office
Mauer, -n wall (external)
Nähe *no pl* neighborhood, vicinity; nearness **in der Nähe** near
Oper, -n opera
Opernkasse opera ticket office
Promenade promenade
Reihe row (seats)
Vorstellung, -en performance
Woche week
Zone zone

das

Abendessen, - dinner, supper
Auto, -s automobile, car
Hotelzimmer, - hotel room
Jahrhundert century
Kino, -s movie theater
Rathaus, ⸚er city hall
Schild, -er sign(post); nameplate, number plate
Theater, - theater

OTHER

aus•sehen look (appear, seem)
ausverkauft sold out
besichtigen see, view
bummeln stroll, wander
dritt third
führen lead
furchtbar horrible
geboren born

gotisch Gothic (art & architecture style)
hinauf up(ward)
hinter behind, in back of
hinunter down
hoh- high; without endings: **hoch**; **höher** higher
hungrig hungry
kaufen buy
keine mehr no (not any) more
kilometerlang kilometers long
lesen read
Mittel- middle __, central __ ; **das Mittelalter** Middle Ages
modern modern
müde tired
neu new
noch nicht not yet
nun now, now then, well
nur noch ju__ __ (left, remaining)
primal great!
romanisch Romanesque (art & architecture style)
römisch Roman
Sankt Saint
sowieso anyway, anyhow
stimmen be right, make sense
wahrscheinlich probably
wirklich really
zerstört destroyed
zur (=zu der) to the

Chapter 9

NOUNS

der

Löffel, - spoon
Nebel, - fog, mist
Schwarztee *no pl* straight tea
Turm, ̈e tower
Wunsch, ̈e wish, desire

die

Fähre ferryboat
Gabel, -n fork
Marmelade *no pl* jam, marmalade
Turmbesteigung, -en tower climb, ascent

das

Amerikahaus, ̈er U.S. cultural facility
Ei, -er egg
Orgelkonzert organ concert

Verkehrsamt, ̈er tourist (information) office
Vierminutenei, -er softboiled egg, 4-minute egg
Wetter *no pl* weather

OTHER

auf•passen watch out, pay attention, look sharp
aus•geben spend money, pay
bei at, by, near, with; **beim (=bei dem)**
besteigen climb, ascend
dahin•kommen get to there
egal all the same; **das ist mir egal** I don't care
empfehlen recommend
etwa about, approximately, roughly
gar quite; **gar nicht** not at all
gleichfalls The same to you!
halb half; **halb drei** 2:30, half past two

hätte would have; **hätte gern** would like to have
hatte had
herrlich wonderful, glorious
hören hear, listen
kennen know, be acquainted with
konnte was able to, could
reichen pass (food, etc.), hand
ruhig calm(ly) **können + ruhig + verb = go ahead and + verb**
schlecht bad, poor
selbstverständlich obviously, of course, certainly
statt instead of
übrigens by the way, incidentally
unbedingt certainly, without fail; absolutely
weichgekocht softboiled
zu Hause at home (location)

Chapter 10

NOUNS

plural only

Eltern parents

der

Artikel, - article, item
Bekannte acquaintance (male)
Diafilm slide film
Film film (camera or movie)
Sport *no pl* sports, physical training
Sportler, - athlete
Touristenartikel, - tourist item; souvenir

die

Abteilung -en department
Aufnahme photo, exposure
Aussicht, -en view, prospect
Auswahl *no pl* selection, range, choice
Bekannte acquaintance (female)
Briefmarke postage stamp
Brücke bridge
Frage question
Größe size (of clothes, etc.)
Herrenabteilung, -en men's department
Kassette (audio) cassette
Marke brand, make (of product)
Ostseite East side
Plastiktasche plastic carrying bag
Platte record (music); from **die Schallplatte**
Rolltreppe escalator
Seite page, side

Spielwarenabteilung, -en toy department
Tafel, -n board, display, sign; plaque
Tasche satchel, purse, pocket
Volksmusik *no pl* folk music

das

Ausland *no pl* abroad; foreign countries
Bild, -er picture
Bilderbuch, ̈er picturebook
Buch, ̈er book
Café, -s cafe
Dia(positiv), *pl* **Dias** *or* **Diapositive** slide (film)
DIN (Deutsche Industrie Norm) *no pl* set of German industrial standards
Farbdia, -s color slide
Foto, -s photograph
Fotogeschäft camera store
Geschäft shop, store; business
Geschenk gift, present
Hobby, -s hobby
Jahr year; **im Jahre 1989** in 1989
Kinderbuch, ̈er children's book
Plakat poster; placard
Plastik *no pl* plastic
Rheinschiff Rhine excursion boat
Schiff ship, boat
Spiel game
T-shirt, -s T-shirt
Untergeschoß, -geschosse basement, cellar
Videospiel video game
Weinglas, ̈er wine glass

OTHER

als than
anderes else, different »**etwas anderes**
atheistisch atheist(ic)
besonders especially
einmalig unique
ein•packen pack (up), wrap (up)
entschuldigen excuse (oneself)
etwas anderes something else/different »**anderes**
evangelisch Protestant *adj*
fast almost
fern far, distant; tele__
fern•sehen watch TV
gefährlich dangerous
groß big, large; tall
höher higher (from **hoch**)
hübsch pretty; handsome
jüdisch Jewish
jung young
katholisch Catholic
Kölner from Köln
könnte could, might be able to
konservativ conservative
liberal liberal
Mensch! Man! Wow!
naß wet
schauen look
sicher certain(ly), sure(ly)
sonnig sunny
stammen (aus) date from
streng strict, severe
überall everywhere, all over
welch which

Chapter 11

NOUNS

der

Affe ape, primate
Bär, -en bear
Eisbär, -en Polar bear
Elefant, -en elephant
Erwachsene adult male
Fahrplan, ⁻e schedule (transportation)
Grad, - degree (temperature)
Hut, ⁻e hat
Kabinett *no pl* Kabinett (wine quality designation)
Mensch, -en human being, person
Onkel, - uncle
Pulli (Pullover), Pullis (Pullover) sweater, pullover
Regenschirm umbrella
Reiseführer, - travel guide
Riesling *no pl* Riesling (grape or wine)
Seehund seal
Seelöwe sea lion
Sekt German sparkling wine; champagne
Vogel, ⁻ bird
Zahn, ⁻e tooth
Zimmerschlüssel, - room key

die

Abfahrt, -en departure
Auslese select vintage
Ente duck
Erwachsene adult female
Flamme flame
Fütterung, -en feeding (animals)
Hand, ⁻e hand
Jacke jacket, coat
Kapelle band (music)

Loreley *no pl* famous Rhine rock
Mutti, -s Mom(my)
Rheinbrücke Rhine bridge
Rheinfahrt, -en Rhine river boat excursion
Schiffskapelle ship's orchestra
Schlange snake; waiting line
See sea, ocean
Sonderfahrt, -en special excursion
Viertelstunde quarter-hour

das

Affenhaus, ⁻er monkey house
Krokodil crocodile
Mal time (occurrence, occasion)
Nashorn, ⁻er rhinoceros
Schloß, Schlösser castle
Tier animal

OTHER

auf•stehen get up, stand up, rise, arise
ausgezeichnet excellent
bald soon
beißen bite
berühmt famous, well-known
bestellen order, reserve
besuchen visit, attend, go to
darauf on that, to that
darauf (ankommen) depend (up)on; **es kommt darauf an** it all depends
denken think
diesmal this time
draußen outside
drinnen inside
drüben over there
Es freut mich (sehr) (Very) glad/pleased to meet you »**freuen**
Es kommt darauf an it all depends

etwas somewhat
fangen catch
faul lazy
feiern celebrate
fressen eat (animal activity)
freuen please, make happy »**es freut mich sehr**
frisch fresh (foods)
gerade just now, recently
größer bigger, larger
gucken look (casual or child talk)
jed- each, every
klingen sound
kühl cool
laut loud(ly)
lieber rather (used with verb); prefer, like __ -ing more
Mach schnell! Hurry up!
mieten rent
mit•nehmen take along, with
nach•schauen check, look up, take a look, have a look
nicht (wahr)? *invites agreement* right? Doesn't it? etc.
romantisch romantic
schnell•machen hurry up
selber *intensifier* (by) myself, yourself, etc.
spielen play
springen jump
süß sweet
tot dead
trocken dry
überhaupt at all
vor•stellen introduce
wahr true »**nicht wahr?**
werfen throw
ziemlich rather, quite

Chapter 12

NOUNS

der

Anruf telephone call
Brief letter (mail)
Lärm *no pl* noise
Luftpostaufkleber, - airmail sticker
Nichtraucher, - non-smoker
Plastikschaum *no pl* styrofoam
Siebziger, - 70 (postage stamp, etc.)
Speisewagen, - dining car
Wagen, - car (auto or train)
Zwanziger, - 20 (banknote or stamp)

die

Einheit, -en unit (of measure)
Ermäßigung, -en reduction, discount

Kabine booth
Luftpost *no pl* airmail
Postkarte post card
Postleitzahl, -en ZIP code
Speise food, fare
Übersee *no pl* overseas
Verspätung, -en delay
Vorwahl, -en area code

das

Büfett buffet, snack counter
Ferngespräch long-distance call
Formular form, blank
Kilo, -s kilogram (2.2 lb)
Kilogramm, - kilogram (35 oz)
Nichtraucherabteil non-smoking compartment
Paket package, carton

Postpaket mailing carton

OTHER

ander- other, different *adj*
an•schauen look at
aus•füllen fill out
beschreiben describe
bezahlen pay (needs a direct object)
daß *conj* that
einige some, a few
erklären explain
fertig finished, ready
gegessen eaten (from **essen**)
per Luftpost via air mail
schicken send
schwer heavy; hard, difficult
singen sing

stehen stand
toll fantastic, great, "crazy"
Verzeihung! pardon me!

wählen dial
wär- would be (from **sein**)
wieder•geben give back, return

wiegen weigh
zurück•kommen return, come back

Chapter 13

NOUNS

plural only

Ferien vacation (general)
Herbergseltern youth hostel supervisors
Kopfschmerzen headache
Magenschmerzen stomach ache

der

Arm arm
Arzt, ⁼e doctor (male)
Aufenthaltsraum, ⁼e lounge, waiting room
Augenarzt, ⁼e eye doctor
Club, -s club; also spelled **Klub**
Junge boy, fellow
Krankenwagen, - ambulance
Schlaf no pl sleep
Schlafraum, ⁼e (dormitory-style) sleeping area
Schlafsack, ⁼e sleeping bag
Schmerz, -en pain, ache
Spaß no pl fun **es macht Spaß** it's fun
Spezialist, -en specialist
Stadtpark, -s city park
Touring-Club, -s travel club

die

Angst, ⁼e worry, anxiety, fear **Angst haben (vor** dat) be afraid (of)
Ärztin, -nen doctor (female)
Bettwäsche no pl bed linens
Decke blanket, comforter
Droge drug
Hausordnung, -en house rules
Hüfte hip
Kamera, -s camera
Klasse class
Klinik, -en private hospital; clinic
Krankheit, -en illness, ailment
Küche kitchen
Radtour, -en bicycle trip

Ruhe no pl rest; (peace &) quiet, peacefulness
Ruhestunde quiet hour(s)
Sache thing, item
Schulklasse school class, grade
Tablette pill, tablet
Wanderung, -en hike, walk

das

Bayern no pl Bavaria
Bett, -en bed
Fieber no pl fever (98.6°F = 37,1°C)
Geschirr no pl utensils, knives & forks; "dishes"
Geschirrspülen no pl dish-washing
Herz, -en heart
Kissen, - pillow
Knie, - knee
Leben, - life
Oberbayern no pl upper Bavaria (between München and the Alps)
Problem problem
Voralpenland no pl Alpine foothills
Wort word (in context); plural ⁼er with individual unrelated words

OTHER

ab dat & sep pref after, from (a certain time) on
ab•schließen close, lock up
ängstlich worried
Au(a)! ouch!
auch wenn even if, even though
auf einmal suddenly; all at once
aus•bleiben stay out
aus•gehen go out
best best adj **am besten** best (of all) adv
dabei along, there; meanwhile, while (doing something)
diskutieren discuss
eigen own adj
eigentlich actually, really
erkältet sein have a cold

ernst serious(ly)
gewöhnlich usual(ly)
helfen dat help **hilf mir!** help me!
ins (=in das) into the
inzwischen in the meantime, meanwhile
irgendwo somewhere
kennen•lernen meet, get acquainted
kochen cook, boil
krank sick
lassen let, leave, allow
laufen run, walk
letzt last
liegen lie (be prone), be situated
los loose; wrong; free; away
los•gehen get going, start up
Münchner from München
nie never
pünktlich on time, punctual
rad•fahren ride a bicycle
rauchen smoke
recht haben be right (persons); **du hast recht** you're right
reden talk, speak
rufen call (out); shout
ruhig calm(ly), peaceful(ly)
sauber clean
schließen close, shut »**geschlossen**
schlimm bad, serious; unfortunate
schmerzen hurt, ache
seit dat since, for (time span)
Spaß machen be fun, enjoyable **es macht mir Spaß** I enjoy it; **es macht Spaß** It's fun
spülen wash, rinse
tief deep
totmüde dead tired
unterwegs on the way, on the road, en route
weh tun dat ache, hurt
weil because, since
wenig little; few pl; **ein wenig** a little
werden become
wunderschön beautiful

Chapter 14

NOUNS

der

Baum, ⁼e tree
Berg mountain
Eintritt entry, admission (price)
Fuß, ⁼e foot
Gipfel, - peak, summit (mountain)

Hunger no pl hunger; **Hunger haben** be hungry
Indianer, - Indian (North American)
Kinderwagen, - stroller
Küchentisch kitchen table
Mantel, ⁼ coat; cloak
Museumsbesucher, - museum visitor
Nord(en) no pl (the) north
Ost(en) no pl (the) east

Photoapparat camera (not movie)
Prospekt brochure, pamphlet, leaflet; catalog
Rucksack, ⁼e knapsack, backpack
Stein rock, stone
Student, -en male student
Studentenausweis student ID
Süd(en) no pl (the) south
Wald, ⁼er forest, woods

Wanderweg (hiking) path
West(en) *no pl* (the) west
Wind wind (weather)

die

Bahn, -en railway, cableway
Bergstation, -en station at top end of cable railway; **Station** station, stop
Bluse blouse
Hälfte half (of something)
Hütte (mountain) cabin, hut
Kunst, ¨e art
Menge bunch, a lot; amount, quantity; crowd
Postverpackung, -en postal packing
Seilbahn, -en gondola, overhead cableway
Sonne sun
Stadtgeschichte city history
Studentin, -nen female student
Tanne fir tree
Tragetasche tote bag, carrying bag
Wolke cloud

das

Kunstmuseum, -museen art museum

Land ¨er country, land, nation; province; countryside
Picknick, -s picnic
Preußen *no pl* Prussia

OTHER

ab•geben check, deposit, turn in
als when
an•ziehen put on (clothes)
ausländisch foreign
bauen build
bevor before *conj*
böse angry; **mir böse** angry with me
daher thus, from that, hence
damit so that *conj*
gefallen *dat* please; **das gefällt mir** I like that
gegen *acc* against
gehören *dat* belong (to X) **es gehört mir** it belongs to me
germanisch Germanic
hinein•gehen enter, go in
hin•setzen set down; **setz dich hin, setzen sie sich hin** sit down
hinunter•fallen fall down

hoffen hope
kilometerweit kilometers away
kurz short, for a short time
mit•kommen come along, with
nieder down; (in place names) Lower
nördlich northern, (to the) north
Ober- upper, chief (as part of noun compounds)
östlich (to the) east
passieren happen, occur
schlagen hit, strike
setzen set, put, place; **setz dich, setzen Sie sich** sit down
soviel so much
steigen climb
unwichtig unimportant
verkaufen sell
verpacken pack, wrap up
vor•schlagen suggest, propose
warm warm
was für what kind of
westlich west(ern)
wieso why, how come
zurück•fahren return, go back

Chapter 15

NOUNS

der

Ausgang, ¨e exit
Flur entrance hall, hallway
Herd stove, range
Hotelschlüssel, - hotel key
Keller, - cellar, basement
Koffer, - suitcase
Kühlschrank, ¨e refrigerator
Müll *no pl* garbage, refuse, trash
Schatz *no pl* sweetheart, darling
Schrank, ¨e cabinet, closet, cupboard
Stadtteil part, district of a city
Staubsauger, - vacuum cleaner
Strom *no pl* electricity; current (river or electrical)
Supermarkt, ¨e supermarket
Zettel, - slip of paper; note

die

Bahnhofsnähe *no pl* vicinity of the railway station
Birne pear; lightbulb (**Glühbirne**)
Garage garage
Heizung, -en heating (system)
Hintertür, -en back door
Hotelrechnung, -en hotel bill
Kochnische kitchenette
Lampe lamp
Miete rent (payment)

Möglichkeit, -en possibility; chance; opportunity
Preislage price range
Rechnung, -en bill, check
Ringstraße beltway, circumferential street
Station, -en station; stop
Stube small comfortable room
Theke counter, bar
Wohnung, -en apartment, home, dwelling
Zimmervermittlung, -en room-finding service

das

Badezimmer, - bathroom
Becken, - basin, bowl, sink
Europa *no pl* Europe
Haus, ¨er house
Hotelrestaurant, -s hotel restaurant
Quadratmeter, - square meter
Saubermachen *no pl* cleaning (up)
Schließfach, ¨er baggage locker
Sofa, -s sofa, couch

OTHER

anders different *adv*
Auf Wiederhören! Good-bye! (on the phone), Talk to you later!
auf•räumen clean up, pick up, tidy up
aus•packen unpack
belegt occupied, taken

bitten ask, request (inquire = **fragen**)
fällig due
frei•halten hold, keep open, keep clear
gegenüber opposite, across the way *adv*
hinaus out (inside to outside)
hinaus•tragen carry out
hin•fahren go, travel (away)
inklusive including, included
komisch funny (odd)
legen lay, set, put
lernen learn
näher closer, nearer
nett nice, neat; friendly
praktisch practical(ly); almost
preiswert reasonable (price)
privat private(ly)
probieren try, have a look at; taste
putzen clean, polish
recht- right (hand)
südlich southern, southerly
unter *acc/dat* under; (in place names) Lower
vermieten rent (out)
voll full
weniger less, fewer
Wiederhören short form of **Auf Wiederhören**
würde would (conditional)
zeigen show, indicate
zwischen *acc/dat* between

Chapter 16

NOUNS

der

Aufenthalt stay, visit, stopover
Fahrschein transit ticket
Führer, - guidebook, guide, leader
Garten, ¨ garden
Gott, ¨er God
Hof, ¨e yard, courtyard; farm; royal court; hotel, inn
Hofgarten, ¨ courtyard garden
Knopf, ¨e button
Monat month
Ort place, location; town
Spaziergang, ¨e stroll, walk
Straßenplan, ¨e street map
Vorschlag, ¨e suggestion, proposal

die

Buslinie bus line
Endstation, -en end of the line, terminus
Geldstrafe fine, penalty
Güte no pl goodness, kindness; **Meine Güte!** My goodness!
Kusine cousin (female); **der Vetter** male cousin

Monatskarte monthly pass (for public transit, etc.)
Münze coin
Strecke stretch, section, leg (of a trip)
Wochenkarte weekly ticket (bus, etc.)

das

Dorf, ¨er village
Kunsthaus, ¨er art museum
Monatsende end of the month
Monatsprogramm program for the month (concerts, etc.)
Nationalmuseum, -museen National Museum
Parkhaus, ¨er parking structure
Programm TV channel; radio station; schedule
Spielzeugmuseum, -museen toy museum

OTHER

am besten best of all
an•kommen arrive
behindert handicapped
Bescheid wissen know how, be informed
botanisch botanical

drin (=darin) inside, in it, in that
drücken press
ein•steigen get on, board (bus, etc.)
ein•werfen insert (money into slot)
endlich finally
falsch wrong, incorrect (of things) **Sie haben unrecht** you're wrong
fremd strange, foreign **fremd sein** be a stranger
Grüß Gott Hi! Howdy!
gültig valid
nordöstlich northeast(ern), (to the) northeast
normalerweise normally, ordinarily
Not- emergency (as part of compound)
ob whether, if
parken park
schlau clever, sneaky, wily
schwarz•fahren ride without a valid ticket
sich oneself (reflexive)
täglich daily
un- un-, in-
ungültig invalid, no good
unternehmen undertake, do
viermal four times
wünschen wish

Chapter 17

NOUNS

plural only

Spätzle type of southern German noodle

der

Curry no pl curry (powder)
Deutsche German (male)
Dolmetscher, - interpreter, translator
Hamburger, - hamburger; citizen of Hamburg
Kurs university course
Paprika no pl paprika; pepper (vegetable)
Reis no pl rice
Schüler, - student (male); **Schülerin** (female)
Sonderkurs special class
Staat, -en government; state, nation
Traubensaft no pl grape juice
Untermieter, - subletter, subleaser
Wiener, - wiener (hot dog)
Zivildienst no pl alternate service

die

Amerikanistin, -nen (female) specialist in American studies

Armee army
Auster, -n oyster
Deutsche German (female)
Farbe color
Geisteswissenschaft, -en humanities (academic subjects)
Geschichte history
Hochschule college, university
Kultur, -en culture; civilization
Linguistik no pl linguistics
Literatur, -en literature
Lust, ¨e pleasure, joy; desire; **Lust haben** like, be interested in __-ing, want to __
Mensa, Mensen university cafeteria
Mittelklassenmahlzeit -en middle-class meal
Naturwissenschaft, -en science
Schule school
Schulzeit, -en time in school
Sprachgeschichte linguistic history
Sprachwissenschaft, -en linguistics
Staatsuniversität, -en state university
Tageskarte menu of the day
Uni, -s university, college
Universität, -en university
Vorlesung, -en lecture; course
Wissenschaft, -en academics, science (not just physical sciences)

Wohngemeinschaft, -en apartment collective, commune

das

Abitur no pl high-school exit/univ. entrance exam
Austauschprogramm exchange program
Brathuhn, ¨er roast(ing) chicken
Ehepaar (married) couple
Fleisch meat, flesh
Friesland no pl Frisia (northwest German coastal regions & islands)
Gemüse vegetable(s)
Gymnasium, Gymnasien high school (college prep track) **Oberschule** American high school
Hackfleisch no pl ground meat (usually beef)
Hauptfach, ¨er major (academic)
Hochhaus, ¨er high-rise building
Mexiko no pl Mexico
Semester, - semester, term (quarter = **das Quartal)**
Seminar seminar
Studentendorf, ¨er student residence area
Studentenheim dormitory

Studium, Studien study/studies,
   program of study
Tierchen, - little animal

OTHER

alle *pron* everyone
amerikanisch American *adj* (the noun
   is **Amerikaner/in**)
ändern (sich) change
außerdem besides, in addition (to
   that)
braten roast; bake; fry, grill
dauern last, take (time)
eingerichtet furnished, arranged
englisch English
europäisch European *adj*
exotisch exotic
fein fine
finanzieren finance

französisch French *adj* **der Franzose**
   Frenchman; **die Französin**
   Frenchwoman
gebraten roasted; baked; fried, grilled
gekocht boiled; cooked
gesucht wanted (newspaper ad)
griechisch Greek
indisch Indian
interessieren interest; **sich**
   interessieren für/*acc* be interested in
italienisch Italian
jemand someone
Mahlzeit! mealtime greeting
meistens mostly
mit•machen participate, take part; go
   along, have to do with, be associated
   with
möbliert furnished
möglich possible

nämlich of course, as you know; you
   see
niemand no one
oft often; **öfter** more often
saftig juicy
scharf sharp, spicy
schwedisch Swedish
sondern but rather
über *acc*/*dat* over, above, beyond;
   about, concerning
unmöglich impossible
unnatürlich unnatural
usw. (und so weiter) etc. (and so forth)
vor•stellen (sich) *acc* introduce
   (oneself)
wissenschaftlich scholarly, scientific,
   academic

Chapter 18

NOUNS

der

Anzug, ⸚e suit
Geburtstag birthday
Geldbeutel, - wallet, pocketbook
Gepäckkarren, - baggage cart
Inhalt content(s), ingredients
Karren, - cart
Personalausweis ID card
Sommeranzug, ⸚e summer suit
Träger, - baggage carrier
Urlaub vacation (from work), holiday

die

Breite width, breadth
Hilfe *no pl* help, assistance, aid
Höhe height, elevation
Kosmetik *no pl* cosmetic(s)
Länge length
Lieblingsfarbe favorite color
Mode fashion(s)
Polizei *no pl* police (force)
Sonnenbrille sunglasses
Wand, ⸚e wall (interior)

das

Alter *no pl* age; old age
Büro, -s office

Ding thing (usually concrete)
Fundbüro, -s lost and found office
Hemd, -en shirt
Kaufhaus, ⸚er department store
Leder *no pl* leather
Pech *no pl* bad luck; **so ein Pech!**
   What lousy luck!
Reisebüro, -s travel bureau, agency
Wildleder *no pl* deerhide, suede »**Leder**
Zeug *no pl* stuff, gear, things

OTHER

an•probieren try on (clothing)
aus•weisen (sich) identify (__self)
beeilen (sich) hurry
bequem comfortable; **es sich** *dat*
   bequem machen make oneself
   comfortable
breit wide, broad
bunt colorful, many-colored
dankbar grateful, thankful
dienen *dat* serve
dunkel dark; **dunkelgrün** dark green
einmal once
erinnern remind **sich erinnern an** *acc*
   remember
gern geschehen glad to do it; my
   pleasure »**geschehen**
geschehen happen

hell light, clear, bright; **hellbraun** light
   brown
hierher over here (motion)
irgendetwas something (or other)
lila purple
marschieren march, trot
melden report officially; declare
mit•fahren go along (by vehicle), travel
   along (with)
nichts +*adj*-**es** nothing that is +*adj*:
   nichts Gutes, etc.
passen *dat* fit; suit; be proper
recht very, pretty, quite
schmal narrow
solch such, like that/these etc.
stellen put, place, position; **eine Frage**
   stellen ask a question
Tja Oh well, Gee, Hmm
tragen wear; carry, bear
überlegen (sich) consider, reflect (on);
   das muß ich mir überlegen I'll have
   to think about that
um•schauen (sich) look around,
   browse
unverständlich incomprehensible
verlieren lose
verloren lost
womit with what
z.B. (=zum Beispiel) for example

Chapter 19

NOUNS

der

Abstieg descent, way down
Apparat apparatus, appliance
Aufstieg climb, ascent

Badeanzug, ⸚e swimsuit
Gruß, ⸚e greeting
Jazz *no pl* jazz
Kassettenrekorder, - cassette recorder
Klub, -s club (organization)
Kopfhörer, - headphones
Laden, ⸚ shop, store

Langlaufschi, -er cross-country ski
Liebhaber, - enthusiast, fan, amateur,
   lover (of __)
Lift (ski) lift; elevator
Münzensammler, - coin collector,
   numismatist
Reifen, - tire (car, bicycle)

Sammler, - collector
Sammlerwert value to a collector
Sonnenaufgang, ¨-e sunrise, sunup
Wander-Klub, -s hiking club
Wert worth, value

die

Freizeit *no pl* free time, leisure time
Gegend, -en area, vicinity;
   neighborhood; region
Grenze border, boundary; limit
Gruppe group; combo
Information, -en information
Kneipe pub, bar, saloon, dive
Luft, ¨-e air, atmosphere
Musik *no pl* music
Natur *no pl* nature
Qualität, -en quality
Quantität, -en quantity, amount
Renovierung, -en renovation,
   restoration
Richtung, -en direction (north, etc.)
Sammlung, -en collection
Schallplatte phonograph record
Schönheit *no pl* beauty, loveliness
Schwierigkeit, -en difficulty, trouble
Seltenheit, -en rarity, rareness
Tour, -en tour, trip, outing

das

Fachgeschäft specialty shop
Flugzeug airplane
Freibad, ¨-er open-air swimming pool
Instrument instrument; tool, implement
Mitglied, -er member (of a group)
Musical, -s musical show
Pfand, ¨-er deposit
Sportgeschäft sporting goods store
Wochenende weekend

OTHER

an•hören listen (to) **sich** *dat* **etwas
   anhören** listen to something
aus•wandern emigrate
basteln tinker, build, put together (as a
   kit)
Bescheid sagen *dat* inform, let
   someone know
Betrieb »**in Betrieb**
freuen auf (sich) *acc* look forward to
geöffnet open(ed)
großartig wonderful, superb, splendid
hauptsächlich primarily, mainly,
   mostly
herzlich heartily, cordially

in Betrieb working, in working order
klasse! great, terrific!
klassisch classic(al)
knapp scarce, in short supply; barely
   (almost not)
kompliziert complicated
leben live, be alive
mit•bringen bring, take along
nachts at night
öffnen open, unlock
perfekt perfect
sammeln collect, gather
schaffen manage; do
schi•laufen ski, go skiing
selten seldom, rarely
spätestens at the latest, no later than
teil•nehmen participate, take part; +
   an/*dat* take part in
üben practice, exercise
verbringen spend (time)
vor allem above all
vor•haben plan (to do something)
wichtig important
willkommen welcome
zirka circa, about
zu•machen shut (door, etc.)

Chapter 20

NOUNS

der

Jahrgang, ¨-e vintage year
Komponist, -en composer
Magen, - stomach (internal organ)
Moselwein Moselle wine
Opernkenner, - opera fan
Rheinwein Rhine wine
Schlager, - hit (song)
Text text; lyrics
Tourist, -en tourist
Zoll, ¨-e customs, duty

die

Aufführung, -en performance, staging
Bühne stage; platform
Ernte harvest
Kiste box, case, crate, chest
Messe mass (religious service, musical
   piece)
Pause intermission, break; rest
Rose rose
Spätlese *no pl* late vintage (wine
   quality designation)

Traube grape
Übersetzung, -en translation
Weinprobe wine-tasting
Zigarette cigarette

das

Faß, Fässer barrel, vat
Freilichttheater, - open-air theater
Parkett *no pl* theater stalls, parquet
Weinfest wine festival

OTHER

an•bieten offer
an•nehmen assume, presume, accept
aus•ziehen (sich) take off (one's
   clothes), undress
dafür for that, in favor of that
dagegen against, opposed to that
daran about that, at that, on that
darüber about that, over that
ein•laden invite
ein•schenken pour (wine, etc. into a
   glass)
entscheiden (sich) decide
erledigen accomplish, do, finish up

ernten harvest
leer empty
lohnen (sich) es lohnt sich it's worth
   it (the effort, doing)
manchmal often
meinetwegen OK with me
mindestens at (the) least, no less than
miteinander together, with each other
moll minor (musical key)
nebeneinander next to each other
reif ripe; mature
servieren serve (dining)
statt•finden take place
tauschen exchange, swap
telefonisch by telephone
um . . . zu in order to . . .
um•ziehen (sich) change (one's
   clothes)
vergleichen compare
verschieden varied, various; different
vollreif fully ripe; mature
während while, during
wegen because of, due to

Chapter 21

NOUNS

der

Ausflug, ⁻e excursion, outing, sidetrip
Bodensee *no pl* Lake Constance
Grenzübergang, ⁻e border crossing point
Hirsch deer, stag
Hochzeitstag wedding day
Preis price; prize
Tagesausflug, ⁻e day trip, excursion
Weg way; path
Zuschlag, ⁻e surcharge, extra charge

die

Autobahn, -en freeway, expressway
Beere berry, grape
Beerensoße berry sauce
Burg, -en castle
Gruppenreise group excursion
Paßhöhe elevation of a pass
Pauschalreise package tour
Pflanze plant

Soße sauce
Übernachtung, -en overnight stay
Verlängerung, -en extension; renewal
Wildspezialität, -en wild game special dish
Wochenendreise weekend trip
Zugreise train trip

das

Fahrrad, ⁻er bicycle
Gasthaus, ⁻er inn, restaurant
Hirschfilet, -s venison filet
Ostberlin *no pl* East Berlin
Tagesvisum, -visen 24-hour visa
Tal, ⁻er valley

OTHER

ab•legen take off, remove (coat, etc.)
allein alone; only
aus•ruhen (sich) rest (up)
automatisch automatic
bemerken remark, observe, comment
buchen book, reserve

damit with that/those
entlang along
erhalten get, receive
erreichen reach, get to, attain
folgend following, subsequent
freitags on Fridays
genießen enjoy
hinauf•steigen climb (up)
höchst highest; **höchste Zeit** (it's) high time, about time
lustig jolly, merry; fun
mißverstehen misunderstand
steil steep
tatsächlich really, actually; indeed
unabhängig independent
unrecht haben (of people) be (in the) wrong
verfehlen miss (destination)
verlaufen (sich) lose one's way (walking)
vieles much
voraus ahead; **im voraus** in advance
weiter- __ further, continue to __

Chapter 22

NOUNS

der

Angriff attack, raid
Arbeiter, - worker, laborer
Arme (the) poor (one, person)
Autor, -en author; **Autorin** (female)
Bombenangriff bombing raid
Brand, ⁻e fire, blaze
Christ, -en Christian (person)
Fabrikarbeiter, - factory worker (male)
Faschismus *no pl* fascism
Faschist, -en fascist
Flüchtling refugee
Generalsekretär General Secretary
Kleine the little one (child)
Lebensstandard, -s standard of living
Militarismus *no pl* militarism
Pionier pioneer
Reiche rich person (male)
Reichstag *no pl* upper house of German parliament (1871-1945)
Sekretär secretary (male); **Sekretärin** (female)
Soldat, -en soldier
Teil part, section; share
Wartburg *no pl* kind of automobile

die

Ausbildung *no pl* training, instruction, practical education
Ausstellung, -en exhibit(ion), show

Blume flower
Bombe bomb
Fabrik, -en factory
Freiheit, -en freedom
Hauptstadt, ⁻e capital city
Heimat, -en homeland, native land
Jugend *no pl* youth (time of life)
Kreditkarte credit card
Marschmusik *no pl* march music
Mitte center, middle; **Mitte April** in the middle of April
Nazizeit *no pl* the Nazi era
Partei, -en political party
Restaurierung, -en restoration, renovation
Stelle job; place, spot, location
Verbindung, -en connection
Währung, -en national currency
Wartezeit, -en wait, waiting period
Weltstadt, ⁻e cosmopolitan city
Zahlung, -en payment

das

Beispiel example, instance; **zum Beispiel (z.B.)** for example
Einkommen, - income
Gebäude, - building
Gemälde, - painting
Hauptsymbol primary symbol
Kaiserreich empire
Opfer, - victim
Reich empire
Schach *no pl* chess

Symbol symbol
Tor gate, gateway; archway

OTHER

arm poor; **der/die Arme** poor person
auf•machen open (up)
bedeuten mean, signify
davon about that, of that, from that
doppelt double, twice (as much)
durchschnittlich (on the) average
eben exact(ly), precisely
erschießen shoot (dead); **sich erschießen** shoot oneself
ewig eternal(ly), forever
garantieren guarantee
gebraucht used, second-hand; **Gebraucht__** used __
genausoviel just as much
geteilt divided, split
international international
jährlich yearly, annual(ly)
leisten do, accomplish, achieve; *refl* afford
nachher afterwards
reich rich
relativ relative(ly)
renovieren renovate, restore
samstags on Saturdays
sozialistisch socialist
verboten prohibited
verbrannt burnt (up) »**verbrennen**
verbrennen burn (up)

verdienen earn (money), deserve
verlängern lengthen, extend; renew
vorher before, previously

weg•gehen go away (on foot)
wem *dat* (to, for) whom
wen *acc* whom

Chapter 23

NOUNS

plural only

Alliierten the WWII Allies (US, USSR, Great Britain, France)

der

Anfang, ⁼e beginning, start
Blick glance, look; view
Bundeskanzler, - Federal Chancellor (equivalent of President or Prime Minister)
Gegner, - opponent
Großvater, ⁼ grandfather
Held, -en hero
Journalist, -en journalist
Jude Jewish person (male); **Jüdin** (female)
Kommunist, -en communist
Lebensraum *no pl* room to live (for a population)
Luftangriff air-raid
Opa, -s grandpa
Ostblockstaat, -en eastern bloc nation
Raum, ⁼e room; space
Rentner, - pensioner, retiree; **Rentnerin** (female)
Russe Russian (male); **Russin** (female)
Schweizer, - Swiss (male); **Schweizerin** (female)
Sowjet -s Soviet (citizen)
Sozialdemokrat, -en Social Democrat (SPD party member)
Staatsfeind enemy of the state
Tote dead person (male); **die Tote** (female)
Zivilist, -en civilian

die

Arbeit, -en work, labor, task; job, position
Arbeitslosigkeit *no pl* unemployment
Armut *no pl* poverty
Auswanderung, -en emigration
Bevölkerung, -en population, populace
Emigration, -en emigration, exile
Entspannung, -en relaxation
Gedenkstätte memorial, monument
Grenzwache border guard
Großmutter, ⁼ grandmother
Inflation *no pl* inflation ($)
Kriegszeit, -en wartime
Massenvernichtung, -en mass extermination
Nazikatastrophe the Nazi catastrophe
Neutralität *no pl* neutrality
Pflege *no pl* care; nursing; attention; maintenance
Rente pension (retirement)
Tante aunt
Vergangenheit *no pl* the past
Wehrmacht *no pl* German imperial army

das

Altersheim retirement home
Ende end, outcome; **zu Ende** finished, over
Gebiet region, area
Konzentrationslager (KZ), - concentration camp
KZ (=Konzentrationslager), -s concentration camp
Lieblingswort, ⁼er favorite phrase
Ostgebiet eastern region(s)
Rußland *no pl* Russia

Spital, ⁼er hospital
Volk, ⁼er people; nation

OTHER

an•greifen attack
aus•halten bear, endure, stand
beenden finish, complete, end
befreien liberate, (set) free, release
behaupten claim, assert, maintain
beides both (things)
deswegen therefore, thus, consequently
fliehen flee, escape
hin•kommen get there, arrive
ironisch ironic
kämpfen fight
meist most
nach Hause home(ward)
nachdem *conj* after
neutral neutral
politisch political(ly)
schuld guilty; **schuld sein an**/*dat* be guilty of
sorgen take care (**für** of); **sich sorgen um** *acc* worry about
soweit so far; as far as
sowjetisch Soviet
sterben die
töten kill
unglaublich unbelievable, incredible
unvorstellbar inconceivable
verhaften (put under) arrest; **verhaftet** under arrest
versprechen promise
vorbei past, gone
wieder•sehen see again
wurde *past tense* of **werden**
zufrieden contented, satisfied
zu•hören listen to

Chapter 24

NOUNS

der

Anwalt, ⁼e lawyer (male); **Anwältin** (female)
Bäcker, - baker
Beruf profession
Dialekt dialect
Enkel, - grandson
Kindergarten, ⁼ kindergarten
Tod *no pl* death
Unterschied difference
Urgroßvater, ⁼ great-grandfather

Verwandte relative (male)
Vetter, - cousin (male); **die Kusine** female cousin

die

Bibel, -n Bible
Enkelin, -nen granddaughter
Grundschule elementary school
Jura *no pl* law (academic subject); **das Gesetz** law, ordinance
Krankenschwester, -n nurse; **Krankenpfleger** male nurse
Meile mile

Mittelschule junior high school
Oberschule high school
Scheidung, -en divorce
Schwiegermutter, ⁼ mother-in-law
Steuer, -n tax
Uniform, -en uniform
die Verwandte relative (female)

das

Archiv record office; archives
Benzin *no pl* gasoline
Dokument document
Drittel, - third (the ordinal is **dritt-**)

Geburtsdatum, -daten birthdate
Gehalt, ̈er salary
Mädchen, - girl
Schreibwarengeschäft stationery store
System system

OTHER

einander each other
eng tight(ly), close(ly)
existieren exist
fallen fall; die in battle
geographisch geographical(ly)
gewesen been (*past participle* of **sein**)

halten hold; stop (transit)
heiraten marry, get married; **verheiratet** married
kulturell cultural
verwandt related
vorbei•kommen come by (visit)
wohnen live (reside)
zerstören destroy

Chapter 25

NOUNS

der

Ausländer, - foreigner
Glanz *no pl* glossy finish; gleam, shine
Lehrling apprentice
Meister, - master; expert
Preisunterschied difference in price
Sonderpreis special price

die

Anweisung, -en instructions
Buntwäsche *no pl* colored wash
Entwicklung, -en development
Feinwäsche *no pl* delicate laundry
Fotoentwicklung, -en film developing
Freundin, -nen friend (female), girlfriend
Gebrauchsanweisung, -en operating instructions, manual
Kochwäsche *no pl* hot-water laundry
Maschine machine; engine

Pflegewäsche *no pl* delicates, special-attention laundry
Selbstbedienung *no pl* self-service
Socke sock (usually man's)
Sonderentwicklung, -en special processing (film)
Studentengruppe student organization
Technik *no pl* technology; engineering
Unterwäsche *no pl* underwear
Vergrößerung, -en enlargement (photographic)
Wäsche *no pl* laundry
Wäscherei, -en laundry (establishment)
Weißwäsche *no pl* light or white laundry

das

Entwickeln *no pl* developing
Farbfoto, -s color photo
Labor, -s laboratory, lab

Licht, -er light
Sonderangebot special offer
Zentrallabor, -s central laboratory

OTHER

allerdings of course, however
bedienen operate
eilig in a hurry, hurriedly; **ich habe es eilig** I'm in a hurry
ein•gehen shrink
ein•stellen set
entwickeln develop
kostenlos free
matt matte finish (photo)
minimal minimal(ly)
normal normal
trennen separate, divide
tun do, make
waschen wash
zurück•bringen bring back, return

Chapter 26

NOUNS

der

Abschied *no pl* farewell, leave-taking; **Abschied nehmen** take one's leave
Gefallen, - favor
Präsident, -en president
Strauß, ̈e bouquet, bunch of flowers

die

Atomwaffe atomic weapon
Auslandsabteilung, -en foreign department, export-import department
Blumenart, -en kind of flower
Einladung, -en invitation
Fresse trap, mug, kisser
Geschäftssache business matter

Höflichkeit, -en politeness, courtesy
Kollegin, -nen colleague, co-worker (female); **Kollege** (male)
Liebe love
Politik, *no pl* politics
Unhöflichkeit, -en impoliteness, rudeness
Verkaufsabteilung, -en sales department
Waffe weapon
Wirtschaft, *no pl* economics; business

das

Maul, ̈er (animal) mouth, trap; **halt's Maul!** shut up!
Praktikum, Praktika practical training, internship
Stipendium, Stipendien scholarship

OTHER

auf•hören quit, stop doing
aus•suchen pick out, look for
danken *dat* thank
dumm dumb, stupid
entschuldigen (sich) take a raincheck
erstens first of all, in the first place
gewiß certain, specific
hauen punch, hit, sock
hoffentlich (subject) hopes that; hopefully
sonst or else, otherwise
unverschämt rude, crude, vulgar, socially unacceptable
zweitens secondly, in the second place

Reference Grammar
TOPIC SUMMARY

NOUNS

1 Function of nouns
2 Noun spelling
3 Gender of nouns
4 Guessing noun gender
5 Plurals
6 Plural formation patterns
7 Dictionary symbols
8 Gender in the plural
9 Number and case (see **Adjectives §§3-7**)
10 Possession in nouns: *von*; the genitive
11 Compound nouns
12 Irregular nouns
13 Adjectival nouns
14 Dative plurals in *-n*
15 Accusative of definite time
16 Infinitives as nouns

PRONOUNS

1 Definition and function of pronouns
2 Pronouns replace noun phrases
3 Kinds of pronouns
4 Demonstrative pronouns
5 Personal pronouns
6 Perspective in personal pronouns
7 Accusative personal pronouns
8 Dative personal pronouns
9 Possessive pronouns
10 Endings of possessive pronouns
11 *du, dich, dir, dein*
12 *ihr, euch, euer*
13 Personal pronoun summary
14 Pronouns combined with prepositions; *da-*
15 Relative pronouns
16 Definite and indefinite pronouns
17 *man*
18 *jemand, niemand*
19 *nichts, etwas, alles*
20 Interrogative pronouns
21 *wem, wen*
22 Reflexive pronouns

ADJECTIVES AND ADVERBS

1 Adjectives and adverbs defined
2 *der/die/das* as gender markers
3 Subjects; *d-* in the nominative case
4 Direct objects; *d-* in the accusative case
5 Indirect objects; *d-* in the dative case
6 Possession; *d-* in the genitive case
7 Summary of the definite article
8 Summary of the indefinite article; *kein*
9 *ein-, kein-* as pronouns
10 Endings of unpreceded adjectives

11 Adjective endings after *ein*: masculine and neuter nominative and accusative
12 Adjective endings after *ein*: feminine nominative and accusative
13 Adjective endings after *ein*: dative
14 Adjective endings after *ein*: genitive
15 Summary of adjective endings after *ein*
16 Adjective endings after *d-*: nominative and accusative
17 Adjective endings after *d-*: genitive and dative
18 *welch-, dies-, jed-, solch-*
19 Endings of adjectives in series
20 Adjectival nouns
21 Adjectival nouns of national identity
22 Comparison: positive, comparative, superlative
23 Positive forms
24 Comparative forms
25 Comparative forms with umlauted stem vowel
26 Comparative forms with endings
27 *so . . . wie*
28 *-er als*
29 Comparison strategy
30 Use of adverb + comparative form for greater precision
31 Superlative forms
32 Umlauted and irregular superlatives
33 Definition of adverbs
34 Adverb phrases
35 Superlative adverbs ending in *am -sten*
36 Word order of adverbs
37 Combining adverbs for greater precision
38 *noch, nicht mehr, kein- . . . mehr*
39 *schon, erst, noch nicht, noch kein-*
40 *gern, lieber, am liebsten*
41 *hin*
42 *her*
43 *-lang* for adverbs of time and distance

VERBS

1 Verb stem and ending
2 Tense: past, present, future
3 Tense signals
4 Present tense: stem vowel remains
5 Subjects match endings
6 Person and number
7 Pronouns and endings
8 *du* + *-st*
9 *ihr* + *-t*
10 Present tense + adverb = future tense
11 Present tense + *seit*
12 Stem-changing verbs
13 Stem changes with *du*
14 The verb *sein*
15 *du bist, ihr seid*
16 *er, sie, es hat*
17 *du hast*

How — and why — to use the Reference Grammar

PURPOSE — The **Reference Grammar** on the following pages serves a variety of purposes. Above all, it supplements the *Struktur* pages in the **Class Text**, which are short treatments of German structure that promote lively class sessions applying new linguistic features to real-life contexts. The **Reference Grammar**, which is intended for study outside class, gives more complete explanations and examples of spoken and written German.

ORGANIZATION — As a whole, the **Reference Grammar** is organized according to the relative importance of linguistic features at this level, from nouns to word order. Each section — nouns, pronouns, and so on — begins with basic structures and proceeds to more complex ones. In this way you can always review a topic or read ahead in it, according to your needs or curiosity. Most paragraphs in the **Reference Grammar** are cross-referenced to chapters in the **Class Text**. You will see, for example, that §20 of *Adjectives and Adverbs* in the **Reference Grammar** refers you back to chapters 17 and 22 in the **Class Text**, where that structural feature is introduced and practiced. Likewise, in the *Struktur* sections of **Class Text** chapters 17 and 22 you will find marginal references to **A.A. §20**. The paragraphs that do not have **Class Text** cross-references are intended to supplement each of the **Reference Grammar** sections and to give you information that will be useful when you encounter structural questions in the extensive authentic reading materials.

USE — When you are working on the structural exercises at the end of each **Class Text** chapter, be sure to read the appropriate **Class Text** *Struktur* section first, and then the keyed **Reference Grammar** paragraph(s). If the presentation still seems unclear, use the review feature of the Reference Grammar to go over preceding paragraphs and refresh your memory.

Some students may find that the **Class Text** structural presentations are complete enough that they can get along without reading the **Reference Grammar**. One of your considerations, therefore, will be how much to use it — if at all. We caution you, however, that your proficiency in German derives both from your daily practice in the language and from your ability to apply knowledge of its structures. Solid grammar is the keystone of any standard language, and knowledge of vocabulary and structure is what underlies the notion of "fluency". You will be furthering your progress in German when you can actively monitor the things you say and write, just as your use of English is fostered by careful conscious attention to the forms of your language.

SOME TECHNICAL TERMS — The <u>parts of speech</u> referred to in the **Reference Grammar** are defined in their individual sections, but here are some quick definitions for ready reference.

- **Nouns** name persons, places, things, qualities, or states, and are often the subjects of sentences: <u>Mr. Holmes</u>, <u>Arkansas</u>, <u>cave</u>, <u>darkness</u>, <u>panic</u>.
- **Pronouns** replace or substitute for nouns: <u>she</u> (Mrs. Holmes), <u>they</u> (the journalists), <u>we</u> (<u>you</u> and <u>I</u>).
- **Adjectives** describe nouns: <u>dark</u>, <u>forthright</u>, <u>ambivalent</u>, <u>hairy</u>.
- **Adverbs** tell more about verbs, adjectives, and even other adverbs: She sings <u>well</u>, he is <u>extremely</u> worried, they ran <u>too</u> fast.
- **Verbs** show action, state, or relation. They also indicate time: She <u>falls/fell</u>, he <u>is/was</u> afraid, it <u>becomes/became</u> chilly.
- **Prepositions** define relationships and precede nouns and adjectives: <u>in</u> her heart, <u>between</u> the two friends, <u>with</u> anxiety.

SCOPE — We do not intend this **Reference Grammar** to be an exhaustive grammar of German. However, it does contain all the structural information required for solid performance at a fairly advanced level. You will probably want to keep the **Reference Grammar** for use in your subsequent study of German.

CURIOUS? — If you want to learn more about the structures of German, there are a number of linguistic discussions available in English. Herbert Lederer's *Reference Grammar of the German Language* (New York: Charles Scribner's Sons, 1969) is the most complete. John Waterman's *History of the German Language* (Seattle: Univ. of Washington Press, 1976) is a good introduction to the origins of modern German. Linguistic matters of all sorts are dealt with imaginatively by Victoria Fromkin and Robert Rodman in *An Introduction to Language* (New York: Holt, Rinehart and Winston, 1988). Students and teachers alike are certain to profit from William G. Moulton's classic *A Linguistic Guide to Language Learning* (New York: Modern Language Association, 1966). If you are curious about your progress in German, and about the process of learning a second language in general, read the Afterword on pp. 270ff. of the Class Text and ask your teacher to show you the *ACTFL/ETS Proficiency Guidelines*, which both inspired and informed the writing of *Wie, bitte?*. They are summarized in the **Class Text** *Afterword* on **CT 270-271**.

Reference Grammar

NOUNS

§1 **Nouns** identify. They may identify something animate (a <u>person</u>, a <u>tree</u>) or inanimate (a (1) <u>rock</u>, a <u>city</u>), including abstract concepts such as <u>difficulty</u> or <u>justice</u>. A noun may stand by itself:

> <u>power</u> corrupts

or it may be part of an entire **noun phrase**:

> the tall woman with the Great Dane

§2 Nouns in written German can be identified readily; they all begin with **capital letters**: (1)

> der Amerikaner die Österreicherin
> der Paß die Fahrkarte   das Gepäck

A spelling note: When a word ends in -*ss* or -*sst*, the -*ss* is written *ß*: *Paß, heißt*. *ss* is also written *ß* after long vowels and double vowels (diphthongs): *stoßen, heißen*.

§3 All German nouns are classified by **gender**. You will note that each noun in the chapter (1)

Gender of nouns vocabulary lists appears with *der, die,* or *das*:

> der Paß **die** Fahrkarte   **das** Gepäck

In form and function, *der, die,* and *das* all correspond to English 'the'. In German, however, the differences among the three forms *der, die, das* play an important grammatical role. They indicate whether a noun is "masculine", "feminine", or "neuter".

> <u>**Der**</u> represents **masculine** nouns such as <u>Paß</u>.
> <u>**Die**</u> signifies **feminine** nouns such as <u>Fahrkarte</u>.
> <u>**Das**</u> represents **neuter** nouns such as <u>Gepäck</u>.

The correct forms of the nouns are <u>*der* *Paß*</u>, <u>*die* *Fahrkarte*</u>, and <u>*das* *Gepäck*</u>. **<u>Die</u> Paß*, **<u>das</u> Fahrkarte*, and **<u>der</u> Gepäck* are impossible combinations for a native speaker of German. Obviously, there is nothing especially masculine about a passport, or feminine about a ticket. These words have what is called <u>grammatical gender</u>. But nouns referring to humans generally show <u>natural gender</u>, such as <u>*der Kanadier*</u> or <u>*die Frau*</u>.

No doubt you can confidently predict natural gender. After more exposure to German you may begin to predict grammatical gender. For now, though, **you must memorize the gender of each noun.** If you do not know the gender, you will be unable to use the noun correctly, and you may confuse your listeners.

Nouns in the dictionary of this text are grouped by *der, die,* or *das* in order to encourage their identification with one of these three gender signs.

§4 In some instances it is possible to make an intelligent guess about the gender of a noun. Especially important may be the **ending** of the noun. Here are some principles:

a) <u>Characteristic endings</u>: Nouns that end in -*er* and denote nationality are **masculine**: *der Amerikaner* 'American (man)', *der Kanadier* 'Canadian (man)'.

Also **masculine** are nouns that end in -*er* and denote professions: *der Lehrer* 'teacher', *der Schaffner* 'conductor'.

Corresponding **feminine** nouns are derived from these masculine forms. They end in -*in*: *die Amerikanerin, die Kanadierin, die Lehrerin, die Schaffnerin*.

Most nouns ending in -*e* are **feminine**: *die Fahrkarte* 'ticket', *die Straße* 'street'. These include nouns formed from adjectives such as *die Länge* 'length' and *die Breite* 'width'.

b) <u>Characteristic suffixes</u>: Nouns ending in the suffixes *-heit*, *-keit*, *-schaft*, and *-ung* are always **feminine**: *die Schönheit* 'beauty' (from *schön* 'beautiful'), *die Wichtigkeit* 'importance' (from *wichtig* 'important'), *die Freundschaft* 'friendship', *die Hoffnung* 'hope' (from the verb *hoffen* 'hope').

All nouns ending in the suffixes *-chen* and *-lein* are **neuter**; the two suffixes suggest smallness: *das Häuschen* 'small house', *das Kindlein* 'little child'.

§5
Plurals

Just as in English, German nouns generally have both **singular** and **plural** forms. English (1) noun plurals usually end in '-s':

| tables | parties | cats | houses |

(Note that the sound represented by the written 's' may vary, and that spelling changes can be complicated!)

But there are also many nouns whose plurals do not end in '-s':

| mice | women | oxen | children | feet |

Some nouns do not even show distinctive plural forms:

| sheep | fish | moose | a <u>ten-foot</u> pole |

And some nouns have no plural forms at all:

| evidence | milk | inflation | darkness |

Long ago German nouns could be identified by groups, and plural forms were reasonably predictable. Today, however, it is very difficult to guess what a noun's plural form might be.

SINGULAR	PLURAL
Mann	Männer
Flasche	Flaschen
Wurst	Würste
Engländer	Engländer
Ticket	Tickets
Kanadierin	Kanadierinnen

Because of the variety of plural forms, the plural of each noun **must** be learned along with the singular.

§6 There are several common patterns of plural formation in German. (1)

- Feminine nouns ending in *-e* add *-n*: *die Fahrkarte, die Fahrkarten; die Schule, die Schulen* 'school, schools'.

- *-er* nouns of nationality or profession have no additional ending: *der Engländer, die Engländer* 'Englishman, Englishmen', *der Bäcker, die Bäcker* 'baker, bakers'.

- The feminine *-in* nouns of nationality or profession add *-nen*: *die Amerikanerin, die Amerikanerinnen, die Autorin, die Autorinnen.*

- Nouns with the feminine suffixes *-heit*, *-keit*, and *-ung* add *-en*: *die Schönheiten* 'beauties', *die Möglichkeiten* 'possibilities', *die Hoffnungen* 'hopes'.

- Some German noun plurals end in *-s*. They are usually words borrowed from other languages, such as English or French:

  | die Hobbys | die Hotels | die Autos |

- <u>Masculine</u> and <u>neuter</u> nouns that end in *-el, -en, -er, -chen,* and *-lein* have no additional plural ending:

der/die Schlüssel	key/keys
der/die Wagen	car/cars
der/die Arbeiter	worker/workers
das/die Hündchen	puppy/puppies
das/die Häuslein	cottage/cottages

You can remember this rule by recalling *Elener Chen–lein*, the girl who sat in front of you in the fourth grade.

NOTE: In the dative plural all nouns (other than those whose plurals end in *-s*) end in *-n*.

NOMINATIVE PLURAL: die Tage   DATIVE PLURAL: nach zehn Tage<u>n</u>

§7 Many dictionaries show noun plurals by using a kind of shorthand: (1)

der Mann, ⸚er

This entry means that the word *Mann* is masculine (<u>*der*</u> *Mann*), that the plural adds an *-er* to the stem, and that the stem vowel (*M**a**nn*) is umlauted (*M**ä**nner*). (Note the similarity to English 'man—men'.) Dictionary entries for the other words listed above are

die Flasche, -n	die Wurst, ⸚e	der Engländer, -
das Ticket, -s	die Kanadierin, -nen	

§8 Gender is irrelevant in the plural. That is, regardless of gender, the dictionary forms of   (1) all plural nouns are identified by *die*: *die Männer, die Tickets, die Kanadierinnen.* This does not mean that all nouns somehow "become" feminine in the plural!

§9 In addition to **gender** (masculine, feminine, neuter) and **number** (singular, plural), all   (5) German nouns appear in one of four different **cases** according to their function within a sentence. For a discussion of the case system, see **Adjectives §§3-7.** Be sure to read that section before proceeding with this discussion of nouns.

§10 Nouns can show **possession** in a number of ways: (22)

a) **Personal names** add an *-s*, just as English names do. This is true of both masculine and feminine names: <u>*Karls*</u> *Freundin,* <u>*Martinas*</u> *Mutter.*

b) Phrases such as 'my father's friend' are expressed in the form

the friend   of   my father

One common equivalent uses the dative preposition *von*:

der Freund   **von**   { mein<u>em</u> Vater
                              mein<u>er</u> Schwester
                              mein<u>en</u> Eltern

c) Written German often uses the <u>genitive case</u> (without *von*!) to express possession. The genitive case is sometimes encountered in spoken German as well:

der Freund   { mein<u>es</u> Vaters
                  mein<u>er</u> Schwester
                  mein<u>er</u> Eltern

- In the genitive case, most singular **masculine and neuter nouns** end with an *-s*. An *-e-* is often inserted before the *-s* after nouns of one syllable. The article or other limiting word also ends in *-es*:

NOMINATIVE	GENITIVE
der Vater	Vorname d<u>es</u> Vater<u>s</u>
der Großvater	Freunde mein<u>es</u> Großvater<u>s</u>
das Jahr	Ende d<u>es</u> Jahre<u>s</u>

- **Feminine nouns** have no characteristic genitive ending. The article or other limiting word, if there is one, ends in *-er*:

die Kinder mein<u>er</u> Tante der Preis d<u>er</u> Fahrkarte

- **Plural nouns** have no characteristic genitive ending. The article or other limiting word, if there is one, ends in *-er*:

die Eltern mein<u>er</u> Freunde

- **Spoken German** tends to avoid genitive constructions. Speakers most often paraphrase by using the preposition *von* with the dative. See **Nouns §10b** above.

NOTE: The genitive is commonly used to express <u>indefinite past and future time</u>, time about which the speaker is not certain. The most common such expression is *eines Tages* 'one day', a staple of storytelling or planning:

> Eines Tages wurde der König aber krank und ließ seine drei Söhne zu sich kommen.
> *But one day the king became sick and bade his three sons come to him.*

> Wir müssen unbedingt eines Tages zusammen Kafee trinken!
> *We'll just have to get together for coffee sometime!*

§11
Compound nouns
Compound nouns are formed from two or more nouns, or from nouns and other parts (2) of speech such as adjectives or verbs. The last element of a compound noun is always a (10) noun, and this noun always determines the gender of the compound:

noun + noun:	der Sport	+ <u>das</u> Fest	⇒	<u>das</u> Sportfest
	die Kartoffel	+ <u>der</u> Salat	⇒	<u>der</u> Kartoffelsalat
verb + noun:	fahren	+ <u>die</u> Karte	⇒	<u>die</u> Fahrkarte
	sprechen	+ <u>die</u> Stunde	⇒	<u>die</u> Sprechstunde (office hours)
adjective + noun:	weiß	+ <u>der</u> Wein	⇒	<u>der</u> Weißwein
	groß	+ <u>die</u> Mutter	⇒	<u>die</u> Großmutter
verb + 2 nouns:	braten + die Wurst	+ <u>der</u> Stand	⇒	<u>der</u> Bratwurststand

§12
Irregular nouns
A very few singular nouns add an *-n* or *-en* in the accusative, dative, and genitive cases:

NOMINATIVE	but	ACCUSATIVE, DATIVE, GENITIVE
Herr		Herrn
Student		Studenten
Soldat		Soldaten
Junge		Jungen
Mensch		Menschen

§13
Adjectival nouns
(See **Adjectives §16**) One of the nouns in §12, *der Junge* 'boy', is really a noun formed (10) from an adjective (*jung* 'young', hence 'the young one'). This is a very common principle (22) of word formation in German, and extends to neuter nouns as well as masculines and feminines:

der Deutsche	*the German (man)*	der Alte	*the old man*
die Deutsche	*the German (woman)*	die Alte	*the old woman*
die Deutschen	*the Germans*	das Alte	*that which is old; old stuff*

Because these words are nouns, they are all capitalized, and because they are also adjectives, they have the appropriate endings:

ein Bekannter von mir	*an acquaintance of mine* (masculine nominative singular)
Ich habe einen Bekannten in . . .	*I have an acquaintance in . . .* (masculine accusative singular)
Das sind unsere Verwandten.	*Those are our relatives.* (nominative plural)

§14
With few exceptions, all nouns in the **dative plural** end in *-n*. If no *-n* is present in the (19) normal plural form, one must be added. The addition of the *-n* causes no changes in the rest of the noun. Looking at the group of six nouns in §5, we see that *Flaschen* and *Kanadierinnen* already end in *-n*. Therefore, no additional *-n* is necessary in the dative plural. But the other four nouns do not end in *-n*. Three of the plurals seen in context are

die Männer	mit den Männer<u>n</u>
die Würste	mit den Würste<u>n</u>
die Engländer	mit den Engländer<u>n</u>

Das Ticket / die Tickets presents a special case. Those nouns that have plurals ending in *-s* do not add an *-n* in the dative plural. Typically, these words are of foreign origin, usually English or French. The most common ones are

das Taxi	das Restaurant
das Radio	das Baby
das Hotel	die Kamera

In the dative plural: *mit den Taxis / Hotels / Babys*, etc.

§15 The **accusative case** is used to express **definite time**. Common expressions of definite (17)
time — time about which the speaker is certain — are found in (21)

Es hat einen Tag / zwei lange Tage gedauert.
Wir spielen den ganzen Tag.
Wir bleiben eine Woche in Berlin.
Das dauert wenigstens eine Stunde.

§16 **Infinitives** (See **Verbs §1**) may function as nouns. When they do, they are always <u>neuter</u> (13)
Infinitives nouns and are capitalized. They have the meaning 'the act of ___-ing'. (21)

Das Schwimmen macht mir immer Spaß.
I always like swimming.

The word for 'food', *das Essen*, is formed in this way, and no longer means just 'the act of eating'.

Infinitival nouns are often used as the object of the preposition *bei* in a phrase meaning '<u>in the</u> act of __-ing'. *Bei* then combines with *dem*, the neuter dative definite article, as *beim*:

Beim Bergsteigen kann er nicht so gut atmen.
He can't breathe very well when he's mountain climbing.
Beim Aufwachen ist sie immer müde.
She's always tired when she wakes up.

Colloquial German even makes prepositional phrases into nouns:

Ins Bett gehen > das Insbettgehen
Vor dem Insbettgehen trinkt er eine Tasse Tee.
He drinks a cup of tea before going to bed.

PRONOUNS

§1 Pronouns refer to something or someone that has already been mentioned.   (1)

> Where's Margaret?   Margaret's in town.
> What's Margaret doing there?   Margaret's buying Margaret some clothes.
> Well, Margaret's mother is looking for Margaret.

Obviously, this conversation sounds more natural if pronouns such as <u>she</u>, <u>herself</u>, and <u>her</u> substitute for the name <u>Margaret</u>. Similarly, the statement 'She's in town' makes no sense unless the listener knows who 'she' is.

§2 Pronouns can replace entire noun phrases: (3)

> What ever happened to
> that nice young **man** who used to come over to mow your lawn?
> I_____ I
>   ↑
>   **He** moved to Tennessee.

§3 There are several kinds of pronouns:

Kinds of pronouns

DEMONSTRATIVE pronouns	§4
PERSONAL pronouns	§5
POSSESSIVE pronouns	§9
RELATIVE pronouns	§15
INDEFINITE pronouns	§16
INTERROGATIVE pronouns	§20
REFLEXIVE pronouns	§22

§4 **Demonstrative** pronouns have the same forms as the definite article (*der, die, das*) in all   (1)

Demonstrative cases except the genitive singular and the dative plural, where they are identical to the   (6) **relative** pronouns (See **Pronouns §15**). **Demonstrative** pronouns point to things or people, demonstrating (often visually) what or whom the speaker is referring to.

The "all-purpose" demonstrative pronoun *das* can be used to point to tangible objects or to something abstract:

> **Das** ist mein Vater.   **Das** ist eine gute Idee.

The object of reference can be either singular (as in these two examples) or plural:

SINGULAR	PLURAL
Das <u>ist</u> Luise.	**Das** <u>sind</u> Ueli und Luise.
Das <u>ist</u> Rotwein.	**Das** <u>sind</u> gute Menschen.

When demonstrative pronouns refer to <u>people</u>, the context is usually quite casual:

> Franz kommt morgen.   Franz? Ach, gut — **der** ist wirklich nett.
>   . . . He's a great guy.

When a difference must be made between something near and something far, a contrast between *dies* 'this' and *das* 'that' is common:

> <u>Dies</u> ist meine Wurst, und <u>das</u> ist Ihre Wurst.

§5 **Personal pronouns** are found in first, second, and third person, both singular and plural: (3)

Personal

	SINGULAR	PLURAL
FIRST PERSON	ich	wir
SECOND PERSON	Sie	Sie
THIRD PERSON	er / sie / es	sie

Personal pronouns are used to refer to nouns when no special emphasis is called for:

> Wann beginnt denn die Oper? **Sie** beginnt schon um 7.
> Ich glaube, Manfred studiert Philosophie.   Ja, ich weiß. **Er** ist sehr klug.

§6 Be sure to consider **perspective** when you use personal pronouns. That is, consider who **(3)**
is speaking or being spoken about:

> **Ich** glaube, **ich** gehe nach Hause. **ich** bin furchtbar müde.
> > Wie, bitte? **Sie** gehen schon? Aber es ist noch früh!

> Arthur und ich fahren nach Rom. **Wir** bleiben eine Woche dort.
> > So? Sie und Arthur? und was machen **Sie** denn in Rom?

> Ich habe eine gute Idee: Sie kommen um 5 und bleiben bis 6.
> Ich komme um 6, und dann gehen **wir** zusammen ins Kino.
> > Gut. Also ich komme um 5 und bleibe bis 6.
> Sie kommen um 6 — das ist eine gute Idee — und dann gehen **wir**. Prima!

§7 Many **accusative** forms of the personal pronouns are identical to the nominative forms: **(8)**

Accusative

	SINGULAR	PLURAL
FIRST PERSON	mich	uns
SECOND PERSON	Sie	Sie
THIRD PERSON	ihn / sie / es	sie

§8 **Dative** personal pronouns: **(9)**

Dative

	SINGULAR	PLURAL
FIRST PERSON	mir	uns
SECOND PERSON	Ihnen	Ihnen
THIRD PERSON	ihm / ihr / ihm	ihnen

§9 **Possessive pronouns** exist in first, second, and third person forms in the singular and **(1)**
Possessive the plural. They establish the relationship between someone and something "possessed" **(5)**
or "owned" by that person: **(6)**

EXAMPLE	"OWNER"	THING "OWNED"
my cows	*I*	*cows*
your father	*you*	*father*
her dark eyes	*she*	*eyes*
their semester grades	*they*	*grades*

Here the relationships are between

> *I* and *my*   *you* and *your*   *she* and *her*   *they* and *their*.

In German the relationships are

	SINGULAR		PLURAL	
	pronoun	*possessive*	*pronoun*	*possessive*
FIRST PERSON	ich	mein	wir	unser
SECOND PERSON	Sie	Ihr	Sie	Ihr
THIRD PERSON	er / sie / es	sein / ihr / sein	sie	ihr

§10 The possessive pronouns, which derive from pronoun forms, are often called possessive **(1)**
adjectives. This is so because they are base forms, to which **endings** may be added to **(5)**
indicate the gender, number, and case of the following noun:

MASCULINE	FEMININE	NEUTER	PLURAL
Ihr Paß	mein**e** Fahrkarte	Ihr Gepäck	Ihr**e** Tickets

The endings for all possessive adjectives are the same as those for *ein-* and *kein-*, and for this reason many German grammars refer to this entire group of words as the *ein-words*.

| | EIN / KEIN | | | | POSS. ADJS. (EX.: IHR='HER') | | | |
	Masc.	Fem.	Neut.	Pl.	Masc.	Fem.	Neut.	Pl.
NOMINATIVE	ein	eine	ein	keine	ihr	ihre	ihr	ihre
GENITIVE	eines	einer	eines	keiner	ihres	ihrer	ihres	ihrer
DATIVE	einem	einer	einem	keinen	ihrem	ihrer	ihrem	ihren
ACCUSATIVE	einen	eine	ein	keine	ihren	ihre	ihr	ihre

§11 **The forms of *du*, the second person familiar pronoun, are similar to those of *ich*.**   (11)

NOMINATIVE	ich	du
DATIVE	mir	dir
ACCUSATIVE	mich	dich
POSSESSIVE PRONOUN	mein-	dein-

§12 The plural of *du* is *ihr*, 'my (two or more) good friends'. *ihr*, like the other personal   (13)
pronouns, appears in various forms according to its function in the sentence: (19)

NOMINATIVE	ihr
DATIVE	euch
ACCUSATIVE	euch
POSSESSIVE PRONOUN	euer-

NOTE: When endings are added to *euer-*, the stem reduces to *eur-*:

Das ist **euer_** Zimmer   BUT: mit **eurem** Vater   für **eure** Freunde

§13 **SUMMARY: paradigms of personal pronouns, singular & plural**

Summary

FIRST PERSON

	SINGULAR	PLURAL
NOMINATIVE	ich	wir
GENITIVE	mein-	unser-
DATIVE	mir	uns
ACCUSATIVE	mich	uns

SECOND PERSON

| | familiar | | polite | |
	SINGULAR	PLURAL	SINGULAR	PLURAL
NOMINATIVE	du	ihr	Sie	Sie
GENITIVE	dein-	eur-	Ihr-	Ihr-
DATIVE	dir	euch	Ihnen	Ihnen
ACCUSATIVE	dich	euch	Sie	Sie

THIRD PERSON

| singular | | | | plurals |
	MASCULINE	FEMININE	NEUTER	(ALL)
NOMINATIVE	er	sie	es	sie
GENITIVE	sein-	ihr-	sein-	ihr-
DATIVE	ihm	ihr	ihm	ihnen
ACCUSATIVE	ihn	sie	es	sie

§14 Like nouns, pronouns can be combined with prepositions, and personal pronouns are no   (20)
exception. Typical short phrases using dative and accusative prepositions are

DATIVE	ACCUSATIVE
mit uns	für mich
bei ihr	ohne ihn
von ihm	gegen uns
zu ihnen	durch sie

Combinations of this sort are common <u>when the pronouns refer to people</u>.

<u>When the pronouns refer to objects</u>, they occur as the form *da-* in combination with the preposition, with *da-* being the equivalent of English 'it' or 'that'.

damit	*with it*	dafür	*for it, for that*
dabei	*along with that*	dadurch	*through that, thereby*
danach	*after that*	dagegen	*against that*
davon	*from that*		

All prepositions are combined with *da-* without showing case.

If the preposition begins with a vowel, the first part of the *da-* construction becomes *dar-*:

daraus   darum   darin   daran   darüber

§15
Relative

Relative pronouns are pronouns that refer to a person or thing already mentioned. Their equivalents in English are 'who', 'whom', 'that', and 'which'. As in English, they come after the words they refer to (their <u>antecedents</u>) and stand at the beginning of a <u>relative clause</u>.   (24)

ANTECEDENT ↓   ↓ RELATIVE PRONOUN
*The fellow **who** wore the hat is my brother.*
↑ RELATIVE CLAUSE

<u>FORM</u>: Relative pronouns have the same forms as the <u>demonstrative pronoun</u>:

	MASCULINE	FEMININE	NEUTER	PLURAL
NOMINATIVE	der	die	das	die
GENITIVE	dessen	deren	dessen	deren
DATIVE	dem	der	dem	denen
ACCUSATIVE	den	die	das	die

<u>USAGE</u>: Relative pronouns establish a direct link between their antecedents and the additional information supplied in their clause, and must occur in the same number and gender as their antecedents. The <u>case</u> in which relative pronouns occur is determined by their usage within the relative clause. The case of the antecedent is irrelevant to the case of the relative pronoun. Because relative clauses are also subordinate clauses, the finite verb is placed at the <u>end</u> of the clause.

nominative   Das war der Junge, <u>der</u> immer so schön <u>singt</u>.

The relative pronoun is masculine and singular because *Junge* is masculine and singular; it is nominative because it is the subject of *singt*, the verb in its own clause.

genitive   Die Frau, <u>deren</u> Hand meine Katze gebissen <u>hat</u>, heißt Marx.

The pronoun is feminine and singular because *Frau* is feminine and singular; it is genitive because of possessive relationship between *Frau* and *Hand*.

dative   Wo ist denn das Kind, <u>dem</u> ich die DM 20 gegeben habe?

The pronoun is neuter and singular because *Kind* is neuter and singular; it is dative because it is the indirect object in its own clause: I gave the money <u>to the child</u>.

accusative   Der Berg, <u>den</u> du siehst, heißt die Zugspitze.

The pronoun is masculine and singular because *Berg* is masculine and singular; it is accusative because it is the direct object of *du siehst*.

NOTE: English often omits relative pronouns:

The man () I saw   The child () I gave the money to

but relative pronouns <u>must</u> be used in all relative clauses in German.

§16
Indefinite

All the pronouns you have seen so far are **definite** ones. They refer to real people or things. There are a number of **indefinite pronouns** that do not refer to anyone or anything specific: *man, jemand, niemand, nichts, etwas,* and *alles.*   (8)
(14)
(17)

§17 The most important of these pronouns is *man*, the equivalent of 'one, people, they, you' (14)
in English. If speakers of North American English used the word 'one' as a pronoun very
often, the correspondence would be clear. But we have a variety of colorful ways of
avoiding 'one' on this side of the Atlantic Ocean.

> *People* aren't as nice as they used to be.
> *They* say it's going to rain tomorrow.
> *You* just can't get a good cigar anymore.

All of these homespun expressions have equivalents using *man* in German. But this
pronoun is by no means confined to casual conversation down at the courthouse square.
Man, which is derived from *der Mann*, refers to any person of either sex, and is always
accompanied by a third person singular verb:

> Man muß nicht lange auf die Straßenbahn warten.

Man is used in generalizations and never refers to someone specific. Often a sentence
with *man* replaces one in which the passive voice or an infinitive phrase is used:

> Das <u>wird</u> leicht <u>gemacht</u>.   That'<u>s</u> easily <u>done</u>.
> Das <u>ist</u> leicht <u>zu machen</u>.   That'<u>s</u> easy <u>to do</u>.
> Das kann <u>man</u> leicht machen.   <u>You</u> can do that easily.
> Das macht <u>man</u> leicht.   <u>You</u> do that easily.

Man is often used prescriptively:

> So etwas tut man einfach nicht!   *You just don't do something like that!*
> Man nimmt die Gabel in die linke Hand.   *You take your fork in your left Hand.*

§18 *Jemand* and *niemand* contain the word *man*, and both also refer to people. *Jemand* is (17)
simply 'someone or other' — the identification of a single human being, rather than
'they, people', as the source of the action. Both pronouns, like *man*, are used with third
person singular verb forms.

> Jemand hat das Fenster aufgemacht.   <u>Someone</u> opened the window.
>   (It wasn't the wind.)

Niemand is the opposite of *jemand*, 'nobody, no one in particular':

> <u>Niemand</u> hat das Fenster aufgemacht. Das war der Wind.

§19 *Nichts*, *etwas*, and *alles* all refer to things: '<u>Nothing</u>', '<u>some</u>thing', and '<u>every</u>thing'. (8)
Again, the accompanying verb is in the third person singular.

> <u>Nichts</u> ist so gut wie italienisches Eis.
> Möchten Sie <u>etwas</u> essen?   Nein, danke. Ich habe Eis gegessen.
> Wo ist denn das italienische Eis?   Rainer hat <u>alles</u> gegessen!

When used as a pronoun, *etwas* can be defined by a following neuter adjectival noun,
whose case is determined by the usage of the phrase within the entire sentence. Most
frequently that adjectival noun has the nominative or accusative ending *-es*:

> Was möchtest du trinken? Kaffee?   Nein. Etwas Kaltes, bitte.
>
> Mutti! Der Hansjürgen hat etwas Dummes gesagt!

Etwas is also an adverb meaning 'somewhat'.

> Heute ist es <u>etwas</u> kalt, nicht?   Ja, <u>etwas</u> kälter als gestern.

Like *etwas*, *nichts* is often followed by an adjectival noun:

> Was hat denn der Arzt gesagt?   <u>Nichts Gutes</u>. Tut mir leid.

Alles is often found in the phrase *Alles Gute!* — 'Best wishes', literally 'I wish you
everything that is good'.

§20
Interrogative
Interrogative pronouns, as their name suggests, are used to ask questions. They may (22)
refer to people ('Who?' 'Whom?' 'Whose?') or to things ('What?'). The interrogative
pronouns do not show gender, and are both singular and plural.

	PEOPLE	THINGS
NOMINATIVE	wer	was
GENITIVE	wessen	see **Pronouns §21**
DATIVE	wem	see **Pronouns §21**
ACCUSATIVE	wen	was

All these forms are used in either <u>direct or indirect questions</u>. A direct question ends
with a question mark; an indirect question is concealed within a statement or another
question.

DIRECT: *Who are you?*   INDIRECT: *I don't know <u>who you are</u>.*
                                          Do you know <u>who that is</u>?

Wer, the nominative form, is used when the interrogative is the subject of a question:

<u>Wer</u> ist das?   <u>Wer</u> sind denn diese Leute?

Wessen, the genitive form, is the equivalent of English 'Whose?'.

<u>Wessen</u> Mantel ist das?   Ist das Heidis Mantel?

Wem shows that the identity of the recipient of an action is unknown:

↓ SUBJECT (nominative)
<u>Wem</u> hat er denn das Geld gegeben?
↑ RECIPIENT (dative)

Wen asks a question in which the direct object of the verb is an unknown person:

<u>Wen</u> hast du am Bahnhof gesehen?   War das Hildegard?

§21
Both *wem* and *wen*, which are the equivalents of English 'whom', can be the objects of (22)
prepositions, just as English 'whom' can:

<u>Mit wem</u> bist du eigentlich zum Zoo gegangen?
<u>Für wen</u> haben Sie denn in Köln gearbeitet?

Colloquial English places the prepositions at the end of such questions:

Who(m) did you work for?

But standard German does not permit this. If there is a connection between preposition
and interrogative pronoun, as there is in this English question, the two words must
appear together. The English written standard requires the same form as the German:

For whom did you work?

Was, the neuter interrogative pronoun, does not have dative or genitive forms.
Colloquial German allows speakers to say *Von was?* and *Mit was?*, using the accusative
form as a dative. The standard language requires that the *was* be couched in a *wo-*
construction, in which the *wo-* does <u>not</u> mean 'where':

<u>Womit</u> spielst du denn?   *What are you playing with?*
Weißt du, <u>wovon</u> er erzählte?   *Do you know what he was talking about?*

If the preposition begins with a vowel, the *wo-* becomes *wor-*: *woraus, woran.*

Older forms of English used the equivalent of *wo-* constructions in '<u>where</u>-', still present
in the word 'whereby' ('by what') and 'wherein' ('in what').

§22
Reflexive
Reflexive pronouns refer back, or reflect back, on the subject of a sentence. By definition (17-
they cannot appear in either the nominative or the genitive case. The subject may be 20)
doing something on her own behalf, in which instance the reflexive pronoun appears in (25)
the <u>dative</u> case. If the subject does something to himself directly ('He bit himself'.), the
reflexive pronoun appears in the <u>accusative</u> case. (See the discussion of verbs used with
reflexive pronouns in **Verbs §41ff**.)

Forms: The reflexive pronouns are identical in form to the personal pronouns with the exception of the second person polite (*Sie*) and the third person singular (*er, sie, es*) and plural (*sie*), where the pronoun is *sich* 'yourself/yourselves, him-/her-/itself, themselves'.

Usage: The action in the sentence reflects back on the subject. Subject and object must be the same person.

reflexive:	Der Wolf beißt <u>sich</u> (himself) in den Fuß.
not reflexive:	Der Wolf beißt <u>ihn/sie</u> (someone else) in den Fuß.
reflexive:	Ich kaufe <u>mir</u> später einen neuen Pullover.
not reflexive:	Ich kaufe <u>ihm/ihr</u> später einen neuen Pullover.

NOTE: Many verbs have special meanings when they are used with reflexive pronouns. See **Verbs §41ff**.

Caution: *Selber* also means 'self'. It is not a reflexive pronoun, however, but rather an intensifier. It puts greater emphasis on a person already referred to:

↓ DIRECT OBJECT

Gib mir den Hammer. Ich mache <u>das</u> <u>selber</u>.

↑ INTENSIFIER

ADJECTIVES & ADVERBS

§1   **Adjectives** and **adverbs** are descriptive words. **Adjectives** tell us more about nouns: **(5)**
how <u>big</u> they are, how <u>colorful</u>, <u>important</u>, <u>tasty</u>, <u>obtuse</u>, and so on. **Adverbs** give more   **(13)**
information about verbs (how <u>well</u> someone sings, how <u>high</u> she flies, <u>when</u> they will
arrive, <u>where</u> the party will be), about adjectives (they're <u>unusually</u> calm, <u>incredibly</u>
rich), and even about other adverbs (he ran <u>extremely</u> fast).

§2   In **Nouns §3** you read about *der*, *die*, and *das* as gender markers of nouns: *der*-nouns are   **(5)**
Definite articles   masculine, *die*-nouns are feminine, and *das*-nouns are neuter. *Der*, *die*, and *das* are three
of the forms of the definite article, the most important and useful adjective in German.
'Definite' means 'known, obvious, old information', '<u>the</u> one we all know about'. There
is an indefinite article in German as well, expressing 'new or unspecified information'.
(See **Adjectives §8**). The German definite article *d-*, with all its forms, is an essential tool
in the manipulation of the language. If the forms of *d-* are not handled with precision,
then communication will be severely inhibited and some grave misunderstandings can
occur. **LEARN THESE FORMS!**

§3   *Der*, *die*, and *das* identify masculine, feminine, and neuter nouns when used as the   **(5)**
Nominative   subject of a sentence:

> <u>Der</u> Kartoffelsalat kostet DM 2,20.
> <u>Die</u> Fahrkarte ist nicht zu teuer.
> <u>Das</u> Zimmer hat keine Dusche.

When a noun is the **subject** of a sentence, it appears in what is called the **nominative
case**. *Der Kartoffelsalat*, *die Fahrkarte*, and *das Zimmer* are all nominative forms. The subject
directs the action of a sentence and fits the verb ending (See **Verbs §7**). Nouns that are
not the subject of a sentence, but are identical with the subject, also appear in the
nominative case:

>   ↓SUBJECT NOUN   ↓PREDICATE NOUN
> Ihre <u>Mutter</u>   ist   <u>Universitätsprofessorin</u>.

When the definite article is used in the plural, all nouns — <u>regardless of gender</u> — that
appear in the nominative case are identified by the article *die*:

> <u>der</u> Paß: Bitte, wo sind <u>die</u> Pässe?
> <u>die</u> Fahrkarte: <u>Die</u> Fahrkarten kosten DM 36,—.
> <u>das</u> Hotel: <u>Die</u> Hotels in Frankfurt sind sehr elegant.

SUMMARY: definite articles in the <u>nominative</u> case

MASCULINE	FEMININE	NEUTER	PLURAL
der	die	das	die

§4   German nouns may appear in four different grammatical cases, according to their   **(6)**
Accusative   sentence usage. For example, subject nouns or pronouns can act with the verb to have a
direct effect on objects in the rest of the sentence, the predicate. These nouns in the
predicate are **direct objects**, and almost without exception they appear in the **accusative
case**.

>   ↓ SUBJECT   ↓ DIRECT OBJECT
> Meine <u>Mutter</u> kauft immer <u>Schokolade</u> mit Nüssen.

When a noun has a nonsubject function in a sentence, the form of its definite article may
change. Before feminine and neuter nouns in the **accusative** (direct object) case, the
definite articles *die* and *das* do not change. Before masculine nouns, however, the definite
article appears as *den* in the accusative.

> Haben Sie <u>den</u> Kartoffelsalat?
> Morgen kaufe ich **die** Fahrkarte nach Berlin.
> Wir möchten **das** Zimmer für heute und morgen.

When the definite article is used in the accusative **plural**, it appears for all genders in the form *die*:

<u>der</u> Paß:	Haben wir <u>die</u> Pässe?
<u>die</u> Fahrkarte:	Heute kaufe ich <u>die</u> Fahrkarten.
<u>das</u> Hotel:	Ich finde <u>die</u> Hotels in Salzburg sehr komfortabel.

SUMMARY: definite articles in the <u>accusative</u> case

MASCULINE	FEMININE	NEUTER	PLURAL
den	die	das	die

NOTE: The accusative is used to express definite time. See **Nouns §15.**

§5
Dative
Sometimes a noun or pronoun is neither the subject of a verb nor its object, but rather a (7) beneficiary, or recipient, of the action in a sentence.

In the sentence

> *He bought the old horse some medicine.*

the subject is 'He', the direct object is 'medicine', and the animal for which it was bought, 'the old horse', is different from the subject. 'The old horse' is the one for which the action is performed, and appears in the **indirect object** case, called the **dative.** By no means does this example mean that 'horse' is always in the dative case, or that 'medicine' must always be an accusative. This action took place at the veterinarian's office. If 'some medicine' is stricken from the sentence, the meaning changes entirely:

> *He bought the old horse.*

Now 'He', the subject, acted directly on 'the old horse', the accusative object of the verb 'bought'. This action took place at the sale barn.

A person hearing or reading a noun that appears in the dative case can tell immediately what its function is by the form of the preceding article:

der Mann:	Ich gebe **dem** Mann einen Reiseführer.
die Frau:	Wir kaufen **der** Frau zwei Pfund Äpfel.
das Kind:	Schenken wir **dem** Kind eine Modellbahn?

When the definite article precedes nouns in the dative plural, it has the form **den,** regardless of the gender of the noun:

> Bringen Sie <u>den</u> Männern eine Flasche Wein, <u>den</u> Frauen je ein
> Liter Pils und <u>den</u> Kindern Kola oder Orangensaft.

The dative is not used just as an indirect object case. Many prepositions govern the dative case as well. (See **Prepositions §4ff.** and **§20ff.**)

> Gehen Sie mit <u>der</u> Frau da.
> — Mit <u>ihr</u>?
> Ja, mit <u>ihr</u>. Nicht mit <u>dem</u> Mann. Er ist ein Idiot.
> — Gut, also mit <u>ihr</u>, nicht mit <u>ihm</u>.

SUMMARY: definite articles in the <u>dative</u> case

MASCULINE	FEMININE	NEUTER	PLURAL
dem	der	dem	den

§6
Genitive
Another set of forms of the definite article shows that a noun is in possession of (22) something. That possession may be tangible, as in

> the <u>doctor's</u> children

or it may be intangible, as in

> the end <u>of the day</u>.

In these examples, the nouns that show possession — the doctor and the day — appear in the **genitive case**, also called the **possessive case** in English grammar. The definite articles that precede genitive nouns have characteristic forms:

der Arzt:	Der Sohn **des** Arztes wohnt in Salzburg.
die Tante:	Die Kinder **der** Tante heißen Vetter.
das Hotel:	Die Zimmer **des** Hotels sind wunderschön.

For an explanation of the *-(e)s* ending on genitive nouns, see **Nouns §10**.

When the definite article appears in the genitive plural, all genders have the form *der*:

der Computer:	Der Preis **der** Computer ist zu hoch.
die Maus:	Es ist unmöglich, eine **der** Mäuse zu fangen.
das Problem:	Das war nur der Anfang **der** Probleme.

SUMMARY: definite articles in the <u>genitive</u> case

MASCULINE	FEMININE	NEUTER	PLURAL
des	der	des	der

NOTE: The genitive is used to express indefinite time. See **Nouns §10**.

§7   Definite articles in all cases, singular and plural

	MASCULINE	FEMININE	NEUTER	PLURAL
NOMINATIVE	der	die	das	die
GENITIVE	des	der	des	der
DATIVE	dem	der	dem	den
ACCUSATIVE	den	die	das	die

§8   Indefinite articles, forms of *ein-*, precede nouns that introduce new information or (2)
describe any member of a category. They correspond to English 'a' or 'an', as opposed to (5)
the definite article 'the'. The paradigm of the indefinite article bears a strong (6)
resemblance to that of the definite article (§7):

	MASCULINE	FEMININE	NEUTER
NOMINATIVE	ein	eine	ein
GENITIVE	eines	einer	eines
DATIVE	einem	einer	einem
ACCUSATIVE	einen	eine	ein

Note that *ein-* has no ending in the masculine and neuter nominative or in the neuter accusative. Note also that, by definition, *ein* has no plural forms. Moreover, the absence of an article in the plural signals an indefinite plural. Plural endings do exist, however, for *kein*, the negative of *ein*:

	PLURAL
NOMINATIVE	keine
GENITIVE	keiner
DATIVE	keinen
ACCUSATIVE	keine

Kein has singular forms also, since it negates singular nouns as well as plural ones. These endings are the same as those for **ein**. As the negative of **ein**, **kein** has the meaning 'none, not any, -n't . . . any'.

§9 Sometimes *ein* and *kein* follow nouns that have been used in a previous clause. Here (23)
they are similar to 'one' and 'none' in English, and take on the function of pronouns.

Where did my pet turtles go?	Here's <u>one</u>!
Do you have some money?	No, I don't have <u>any</u>.

In these situations *ein* and *kein* add the endings that would be present if the nouns in question were there:

Wo sind meine Schildkröten?	Hier ist ein**e** (Schildkröte)!
Haben Sie einen 10-Mark-Schein?	Nein, ich habe kein**en** (Schein).

This principle applies even in those cases where *ein* and *kein* do not have endings themselves, in the masculine nominative and the neuter nominative and accusative. Here *ein* and *kein* borrow endings from the definite article, with *eines* shortened to *eins*:

↓ <u>der</u> Bleistift

MASCULINE NOMINATIVE: Wo ist ein Bleistift?   Hier ist ein<u>er</u>.

↓ <u>das</u> Auto

NEUTER ACCUSATIVE: Wer hat ein neues Auto?   Ich habe ein<u>s</u>.

Ein can also anticipate an understood noun in the German equivalent of 'one of . . '. Here, too, *ein* borrows endings from the definite article if they are not already part of the *ein* declension. The 'of' phrase is rendered either by *von* and the dative or by the genitive:

↓ anticipates <u>der</u> Freund

Wer ist das?   Das ist ein<u>er</u> von meinen Freunden.
              Das ist ein<u>er</u> mein<u>er</u> Freunde.
                                  ↑ genitive plural

↓ anticipates <u>die</u> Freundin
Das ist ein<u>e</u> von meinen Freundinnen.
Das ist ein<u>e</u> mein<u>er</u> Freundinnen.
              ↑ genitive plural

§10   Definite and indefinite articles always come before the nouns they modify. Other (9) adjectives, however, may either precede or complement the nouns they modify — just as in English.

preceding: *the <u>old</u> <u>gray</u> mare*
complementary: *the mare is <u>old</u> and <u>gray</u>*

When adjectives <u>follow</u> the nouns they modify, their form stays the same in German:

kalt: Das Wetter ist <u>kalt</u>.
schön: Die Autos waren sehr <u>schön</u>.

But when adjectives <u>precede</u> the nouns they modify, they carry endings according to the function of the nouns in the sentence. When the adjectives stand <u>alone</u> in front of nouns, these endings correspond closely to the endings of the definite article. The examples show nominative forms:

MASCULINE: d<u>er</u> Wein   kühl<u>er</u> Wein
FEMININE: d<u>ie</u> Milch   frisch<u>e</u> Milch
NEUTER: d<u>as</u> Obst   gut<u>es</u> Obst
PLURAL: d<u>ie</u> Kinder   lieb<u>e</u> Kinder

§11   One of the adjectives preceding a noun must indicate the function of that noun in the (9) sentence. When the adjective is a form of the <u>definite</u> article *d-*, that task has been performed. (*Der* before *Mann* shows, for example, that the following noun is masculine and nominative and singular.) When the adjective is a form of the <u>indefinite</u> article *ein-*, however, it fails in three instances to indicate the function of the following noun:

	MASCULINE	NEUTER
NOMINATIVE	ein	ein
ACCUSATIVE		ein

In these situations the adjective following *ein* takes over and says something about the noun that follows according to the principle outlined in §10:

	MASCULINE	NEUTER
NOMINATIVE	ein alter Mann	ein altes Haus
ACCUSATIVE		ein altes Haus

§12   In the feminine the adjective following *eine* also carries the *-e* ending: (9)

NOMINATIVE	eine alte Frau
ACCUSATIVE	eine alte Frau

§13 In all other situations the adjectives following variations of *ein-* and the other *ein-* words (10)
(*kein* and the possessive pronouns) have the ending *-en*. The full paradigm of endings for (16)
the **nominative, dative, and accusative** is

	MASCULINE	FEMININE	NEUTER	PLURAL
NOM	ein_ alter Mann	eine alte Frau	ein_ liebes Kind	meine lieben Kinder
DAT	einem alten Mann	einer alten Frau	einem lieben Kind	meinen lieben Kindern
ACC	einen alten Mann	eine alte Frau	ein_ liebes Kind	meine lieben Kinder

§14 In the **genitive** case the endings on adjectives following *ein-* words are all *-en*:

eines alten Mannes   einer alten Frau eines lieben Kindes   meiner lieben Kinder

§15 **SUMMARY: ENDINGS ON ADJECTIVES FOLLOWING *EIN-* WORDS**

	MASCULINE	FEMININE	NEUTER	PLURAL
NOMINATIVE	-er	-e	-es	-en
GENITIVE	-en	-en	-en	-en
DATIVE	-en	-en	-en	-en
ACCUSATIVE	-en	-e	-es	-en

§16 **Adjectives that follow the definite article** take endings that are either *-e* or *-en* in the (8)
nominative and accusative: (10)
(12)

	MASCULINE	FEMININE	NEUTER	PLURAL
NOM.	der alte Mann	die alte Frau	das alte Auto	die alten Autos
ACC.	den alten Mann	die alte Frau	das alte Auto	die alten Autos

NOMINATIVE: -e   Sind Sie der Nächste? Sind Sie die Nächste?
                      Montag ist der zehnte, Mittwoch der zwölfte.
                      Der andere Brief ist schwerer.
                      Die große Postkarte nach Kanada . . .

ACCUSATIVE: -en   Für den zwölften haben wir noch Karten.
                      Geben Sie mir den ersten Brief.

PLURAL: -en   Die beiden Briefe sind DM 4,60.
                      Für die beiden Pakete . . .

§17 **Genitive and Dative adjectives after the definite article** have an *-en* ending: (18)
(16)

	MASCULINE	FEMININE	NEUTER	PLURAL
GEN.	des alten Mannes	der alten Frau	des alten Autos	der alten Autos
DAT.	dem alten Mann	der alten Frau	dem alten Auto	den alten Autos

Wir müssen schon am elften wegfahren.
. . . in der dritten Reihe
Die Fußgängerzone in der Hohen Straße . . .

§18 The adjectives *welch-* 'which' and *dies-* 'this' take endings that are identical to those of the (10)
definite article. The adjectives that follow them are declined according to the paradigms
illustrated in §16 and §17.

        Welcher Student war denn das?
               — Ach, das war dieser junge Student aus den USA.
        Wirklich? Was machen wir denn mit diesen amerikanischen Studenten?
               — Welche meinen Sie denn? Die sind nicht alle so schlimm.

The same endings are used with *jed-* 'every' and *solch-* 'such'.

§19 Once an adjective ending pattern has been established in a phrase, the endings on all
adjectives are the same:

        ein böser alter Mann   eine nette alte Frau   ein liebes kleines Kind
        mit einem großen, schweren, schwarzen Hammer

§20 An adjective may refer to a person without a following noun. In this case the adjective (17)
itself becomes a noun, and is capitalized. Except in the plural, the form of the definite (22)
article leaves no doubt about the gender of the person. The adjective maintains its
proper ending.

> der alte Mann ⇒ <u>der Alte</u>　　die alte Frau ⇒ <u>die Alte</u>　　die alten Leute ⇒ <u>die Alten</u>
>
> mit dem Alten 'with the old man'
> mit der Alten 'with the old woman'

This is the origin of the word for 'boy', *der Junge*, literally 'the young male'.

Note the similarity to English adjectival nouns: the old, the just, and so on.

> *The rain it raineth on the just*
> *And also on the unjust fella.*
> *But mostly on the just because*
> *The unjust steals the just's umbrella.*

Reflecting on this crime, we also find neuter nouns made from adjectives:

> <u>das Böse</u> = *evil, that which is evil, the evil thing, etc.*
> <u>das Gute</u> = *the good, that which is good, the good thing, etc.*

Other common parallels are *das Positive, das Negative, das Interessante.*

§21 Adjectival nouns showing national identity follow the principle established in §20. (17)
Although there are abundant examples of nouns of national origin such as *der
Amerikaner, die Amerikanerin*, many such nouns are really formed from adjectives and
thus must have adjective endings to reflect their gender and function within a sentence.

Identical to the pattern of *der Junge*, therefore, are *der Deutsche* and *die Deutsche*, with
datives

> mit dem Deutschen (masc.)　　　mit der Deutschen (fem.),

accusatives

> für den Deutschen (masc.)　　　für die Deutsche (fem.),

and plurals

> die Deutschen　　　　mit den Deutschen　　　　für die Deutschen.

§22 Adjectives are frequently used to compare one thing to another, or to establish a
hierarchy including "standard" quality, the **positive** form, "better" quality, the
comparative form, and "best" quality, the **superlative** form.

§23
Positive The **positive** form of an adjective is the form in which it appears in glossaries: *gut, alt,* (4)
neurotisch, weitsichtig, and so on.

NOTE: When endings are added to *hoch*, the stem becomes *hoh-*.

§24
Comparative The **comparative** form of an adjective compares one thing to another, the equivalent of (4)
English adjectival forms ending in '-er' ('higher') or preceded by 'more' ('more
interesting'). Of these two forms, German uses only the first: All adjectives form their
comparative by adding *-er*.

POSITIVE	COMPARATIVE
schön	schöner
weit	weiter
interessant	interessanter

NOTE: Although many speakers of English use the superlative (best, highest, etc.) to
compare two things, German <u>must</u> use the comparative.

§25 An important variation in the comparative form is the umlauting of a stem vowel, especially in one-syllable adjectives:

POSITIVE	COMPARATIVE
alt	älter (note English *old—elder*)
warm	wärmer
kurz	kürzer

Hoch has a special comparative form: *höher.*

There are a few "irregular" comparative forms, the most notable of which is *besser,* from the positive *gut.* (Note English 'good-better'.)

§26 The comparative forms of adjectives are still adjectives, which may come after a noun:

> Ich glaube, das Kotelett ist heute besser.

— or before it, in which case they must have appropriate adjective endings according to §§10-19:

> Ich finde, der längere Mantel ist schöner.

These endings provide essential signals and are never abbreviated, even where redundancy seems likely with adjectives ending in *-er*:

> ↓ comparative suffix
> ein tapfererer Soldat   *a braver soldier*
> ↑ adjective ending

§27 Comparison can be carried out without the *-er* ending. If object A is <u>better than</u> object B, **(11)** then object B is <u>not as good as</u> object A. The formula used to compare two things from the <u>perspective of the lesser</u> of the two is *so . . . wie*, the equivalent of English 'as . . . as':

> Die Berge sind schön, aber das Meer ist schöner.
> — Ja, ich finde die Berge auch nicht <u>so schön wie</u> das Meer.

§28 Another way of stating the comparison in §26 would be from the <u>perspective of the</u> **(11)** <u>greater</u> of the two. Here the word *als* is used after the word describing the greater:

> Das Meer ist <u>schöner als</u> die Berge.
> — Ja, ich finde das Meer auch schöner.

§29 **Comparison strategy:** If for some reason you do not know a specific word you want to **(15)** use in a comparison, think of an antonym and use another kind of comparative construction:

> Die Berge in Wyoming sind . . . sind . . . (*"Hmm . . . 'higher than'? How do you say 'higher', anyway?. . . aha —"*) Die Berge in Vermont sind nicht <u>so hoch wie</u> die Berge in Wyoming.
> — So, in Wyoming sind die Berge also <u>höher</u> — sehr interessant.

§30 Not all things that are compared differ to an equal degree. One thing may be marginally **(11)** better than another, or better by far. The hierarchy of adverbs used to lend greater precision to the comparison is

<u>etwas</u> besser	<u>ein bißchen</u> besser
	<u>noch</u> besser
<u>viel</u> besser	<u>weit</u> besser

§31
Superlative The **superlative** form of an adjective, ending in *-st* in German as it does in English, **(20)** compares the accompanying noun to others and finds it superior to all the rest. The superlative is used when <u>three or more</u> unequal things are being compared.

Adjectives with stems ending in a *t-* or *s-* sound normally add an *-e-* before the <u>*-st*</u> ending: *interessantest-.* A conspicuous exception is the superlative of *groß: größt-.*

There are two environments for superlative forms: one <u>before</u> nouns and one <u>after</u> nouns. When a superlative adjective comes **after** the noun it modifies ("Alpine milk is the richest") it is couched in the formula *am . . . -sten*:

> Geranien sind schön, und Tulpen sind auch schön.
>   — Ja, aber Rosen sind <u>am schönsten</u>.
> Konrad hat viel Geld, und Jürgens Vater ist Millionär. . .
>   — aber Elisabeth ist <u>am reichsten</u>.

When the superlative adjective comes **before** the noun it modifies, it must have the appropriate adjective ending:

> <u>kleinst</u>- Christina ist die kleinst<u>e</u> Tänzerin in der Gruppe.
> <u>teuerst</u>- Die teuerst<u>en</u> Diamanten finde ich nicht schön.

This rule also applies when there is no <u>apparent</u> following noun, but one is strongly implied:

> Die teuersten Diamanten sind auch <u>die schönsten</u> (Diamanten).
> Ja, Hunde sind gute Haustiere. Aber <u>die besten</u> (Haustiere) sind Fische.
>   — Wie, bitte? Die besten Hunde sind Fische??
>   — Nein, nein. Die besten Haustiere sind Fische.

§32   Adjectives that umlaut their stem vowels in the comparative do so as well in the (20) superlative. Note the following common irregular comparative and superlative forms:

POSITIVE	COMPARATIVE	SUPERLATIVE
gut	besser	best-
viel	mehr	meist-
nahe	näher	nä<u>chst</u>-
hoch, hoh-	hö<u>her</u>	höchst-
groß	größer	größt-

NOTES: 1. *Mehr* does not take adjective endings; *viel* takes endings only in the plural. 2. *Nahe*: Compare archaic English 'nigh', 'nearer', 'next'. The 'next' place is literally the 'nearest' one.

§33

Adverbs   It was stated in §1 that adverbs modify adjectives, verbs, and other adverbs. Adverbs generally do not have forms that are different from the forms of adjectives. In English, most adverbs have a characteristic suffix '-<u>ly</u>'. Whereas German does have an equivalent suffix *-lich*, it is used for both adjectives and adverbs (*möglich* 'possible', 'possibly'). English speakers sometimes have difficulty coming to terms with adverbs such as *gut*, whose equivalent, 'good', we learn as an adjective only: Her voice is <u>good</u> (adjective), but she sings <u>well</u> (adverb).

Adverbs answer the questions 'When?', 'Where?', 'How?', 'How far?', 'To what extent?', etc. That is, they tell <u>time</u>, <u>location</u>, <u>direction</u>, <u>manner</u>, <u>extent</u>, cause, and purpose. They may be one-word adverbs, such as *doch, immer, auch, heute*, or adverb phrases which combine adverbs with each other or with prepositional phrases.

CATEGORY	QUESTION WORD	ADVERB	PREPOSITIONAL PHRASE
TIME	wann	heute	vor der Klasse
LOCATION	wo	hier	vor dem Haus
DIRECTION	wohin	dorthin	in die Stadt
	woher	hierher	aus der Stadt
MANNER	wie	schnell	mit dem Auto
EXTENT	wie	sehr	durch die ganze Welt
CAUSE	womit	damit	mit einem Hammer
PURPOSE	warum	deshalb	wegen dem Wetter
or REASON	wozu		
	wieso		

§34 Even if adverbs are several words long, their function in a sentence does not change. In this first sentence, both adverbs modify the verb *spielt*:

↓ adverb tells when

Der Cellist spielt <u>am 29. März</u> <u>im Auditorium Maximum</u>.

↑ adverb tells where

<u>In der Stadthalle am linken Ufer des Rheins</u> gibt es am Freitag ein tolles Konzert.

↑ adverb tells where

§35 Although there are no differences in form between the positive and comparative forms of adjectives and adverbs, the superlative form of adverbs exists only in the *am . . . -sten* framework described in **§31**.

Von allen Sängerinnen singt Barbara weitaus <u>am schönsten</u>.

§36 **Word order.** Adverbs of time are often placed first in a sentence.   (4)

Word order

<u>Morgens</u> ißt er ganz wenig.
In the mornings he eats very little.

Other kinds of adverbs show emphasis in first position — in English as in German.

<u>Mit meinem Hund</u> gehe ich im Stadtpark spazieren.
With my dog I go walking in the city park.

Often there is more than one adverb in a sentence, in which case the more or most important one comes first, with the verb following. Of course, the importance of an adverb is determined by the speaker, not by some abstract set of rules.

The rule of thumb "time—manner—place" is often cited for the order of adverbs in a German sentence.

↓ how

<u>Am Donnerstag</u> gehe ich <u>mit meinem Hund</u> <u>im Stadtpark</u> spazieren.

↑ when   ↑ where

But this assumes that no single adverbial element is emphasized over any other. All things being equal, this is an appropriate order, but in the real world of daily communication the "rule" is probably broken more often than it is obeyed. The principle of "most important first" is the one to remember.

§37 Adverbs can be doubled, as in English, to lend greater precision to a statement. (13) Obviously, 'tonight' does not say as much as 'tonight at 8'. Generally the more general statement is made first, then the more specific:

↓ general

Wir kommen <u>morgen Abend</u> <u>um sieben Uhr</u>.

↑ specific

↓ general   ↓ general

Er findet uns <u>im Park</u> <u>neben dem Rathaus</u>.   Ihr Koffer ist <u>oben</u> <u>im zweiten Stock</u>.

↑ specific   ↑ specific

§38 The adverb *noch* has to do with time that has begun in the past and has continued into (8) the present. It is an adverb that looks back, saying that a prior condition <u>still</u> exists. (19)

Sind Sie <u>noch</u> hier? Ich dachte, Sie sind schon lange weg.
Are you still here? I thought you'd left long ago.

The combination of *noch* with *immer* as *noch immer* or *immer noch* provides special emphasis:

Ist er denn <u>immer noch</u> in Bonn? Don't tell me he's still in Bonn!

One **negative** of *noch* is **nicht mehr**, used to negate <u>an entire idea</u>. The condition that began in the past <u>no longer</u> exists.

Ja, also, er <u>war</u> heute hier — jetzt aber <u>nicht mehr</u>. Ich weiß nicht, wo er ist.
(IDEA: Ist er noch hier?)

Another negative of *noch* is *kein-* ... *mehr*. This phrase is used to negate <u>nouns</u>:

Entschuldigung. Haben Sie heute <u>noch Zeit</u>? Es tut mir leid, daß ich so spät komme.
— Nein, jetzt habe ich <u>keine Zeit mehr</u>. Warum waren Sie nicht früher hier?

§39 In a sense the adverb *schon* is the opposite of *noch*, because *schon* often has to do with (19)
time that is beginning in the present and extending into the future. A question using (21)
schon asks whether an expected (future) condition already exists. Elaboration often
contains the adverb *erst* 'just, not until'.

Sind Sie <u>schon</u> hier? Ich dachte, Sie kommen <u>erst</u> um 8 Uhr.
— Ja, ich weiß. Es ist jetzt <u>erst</u> 7 Uhr 30. Hoffentlich ist das nicht zu früh.

NOTE: In combination with other adverbs of time, *schon* points not forward, but back in
time. The continuity with present time is still firmly established.

Sie wohnt schon lange (zwei Jahre, zehn Monate) in Köln.
She's been living in Cologne for a long time (two years, ten months) now.

The **negative** forms of *schon* parallel those of *noch* (§37). *Noch nicht* 'not yet' negates an
entire idea:

Ist sie <u>schon</u> hier? Ach, ich hoffe es!
— Nein, sie ist <u>noch nicht</u> hier. Ich sage es Ihnen, wenn sie kommt.
(IDEA: Ist sie hier?)

NOTE: *Noch nicht* is <u>not</u> the negative of *noch*!

Noch <u>kein</u>- negates nouns:

Haben Sie Ihren Brief schon?
— Nein, ich habe <u>noch keine Post</u> bekommen.   (noun: Post)
Aber warum nicht?
— Nun, ich war <u>noch nicht</u> bei der Post.   (idea: bei der Post sein)

§40 The adverb *gern* shows that the action of a verb is gladly or willingly undertaken. By (10)
extension, it is used in sentences that tell what someone's interests or hobbies are. *Gern*
also reinforces *möchte*.

Möchten Sie mit mir einkaufen gehen?   — Ja, <u>gern</u>. Ich komme <u>gern</u> mit.

Ja, mein Franz spielt so <u>gern</u> mit seiner Modelleisenbahn. Schade!
— Warum schade? Es ist schön, daß Ihr Enkel <u>gern</u> spielt.
Aber Franz ist mein Mann! Er ist doch 87 Jahre alt!
— Nun, seien Sie nicht so. Ich möchte auch <u>gern</u> so lange leben.

Lieber, the comparative of *gern*, is used to show preference for one thing over another.

Tennis ist ein schöner Sport. Aber ich schwimme <u>lieber</u>.

Was möchten Sie <u>lieber</u> machen? Reiten oder im Gummiboot paddeln?
Ich glaube, ich möchte <u>lieber</u> paddeln. Es ist doch so furchtbar heiß.

Am liebsten is the superlative of *gern*, showing a preference for one thing over several
others.

Ja, Hummel und Scarlatti höre ich sehr gern. Aber <u>am liebsten</u> höre ich Schostakowitsch.

So. Jetzt haben wir ein ganzes Wochenende. Was möchten Sie <u>am liebsten</u> machen?

§41 The adverb *hin* shows motion <u>away from the speaker</u>. It often reinforces another (8)
directional adverb in the sentence, and is frequently a part of a separable verb prefix.
Combining with *wo* it means 'Where to?'.

Die ganze Familie ist 1880 <u>nach Amerika</u> <u>hin</u>gezogen.
Zuerst wollten sie nach New York <u>hin</u>, aber dann kamen sie nach New Orleans.

<u>Wo</u> gehen Sie <u>hin</u>, bitte?   or   <u>Wohin</u> gehen Sie, bitte?
↑_____↑ *Where are you going?*   ↑

Hin can combine with prepositions to indicate a more precise direction:

Steigen Sie nur <u>hinauf</u>.   *Go ahead and climb on up.*
Ach, mein Hut ist von der Turmspitze <u>hinunter</u>gefallen!
                                    ↑ *down away (from me)*

§42 The adverb *her* is used to indicate motion <u>toward the speaker</u>. Combining with *wo* it **(8)**
means 'Where from?'.

Kommen Sie bitte <u>her</u>!
<u>Wo</u> kommen Sie <u>her</u>, bitte?   or   <u>Woher</u> kommen Sie, bitte?
↑_____↑ *Where do you come from?*   ↑

In this function it is often combined with prepositions to indicate more precisely the
direction taken.

<u>Herein</u>, bitte!   Kommen Sie bitte <u>herunter</u>.
Please come in. Please come down here (toward me).

In spoken German, the difference between *hin* and *her* is frequently obscured, with a
variant of *her* being used more often and simply with the meaning 'with motion'.

Und plötzlich ist der Bergsteiger in die Gletscherspalte heruntergefallen.
And suddenly the mountain climber fell down into the crevasse.
(The speaker would have to be down in the glacier for the strict <u>her</u> rule to apply.)

'Raus!   *Get out of here!*

Understandably, the phrase *hin und her* means 'back and forth'.

§43 The adverbial suffix *-lang* attaches to <u>noun plurals</u> in order to indicate distance or
duration of time.

der Tag, -e	tagelang
die Woche, -en	wochenlang
der Monat, -e	monatelang
das Jahr, -e	jahrelang
das Meter, -	meterlang
die Meile, -n	meilenlang

VERBS

§1 **Verbs** appear in the glossary of this text in their **infinitive** forms, and consist of a verb (1) stem plus an ending. The ending of the infinitive is either -*en* or -*n*:

STEM	ENDING	INFINITIVE
komm-	+	-en	⇒	kommen
wander-		-n		wandern

§2 Verbs identify the **time** of the action in a sentence relative to the speaker's own time. (1) This time can be in the past, the present, or the future. The **present** is the fine line between the **past** (extending from a second ago back into prehistory) and the **future** (extending from now into all time to come).

§3 Verbs indicate time by signals in their structure. **Present** time is signaled by the stem (1) vowels and their specific variants. **Past** time is revealed by special changes or additions to the verb stem. **Future** time is most often expressed by the present tense in German.

§4 Most verbs show **present** time through their stems, with the stem vowel unchanged: (1)

kommen: ich komme

§5 Verbs also identify the **subject** of a sentence, or its **actor**. They do so by means of (1) **endings** that conform to the subject. These endings match only the subject of the verb, never other elements in the sentence.

§6 **Subjects** are identified by **person**. The person may be **first person**, or "I". (Remember (1) this by considering that many people always think of themselves <u>first</u>.) If "I" is the first person, then "you" is the **second person**. "I" could be called the speaker and "you" the listener, the one whom "I" addresses directly. Everyone and everything else — that is, "he", "she", and "it" — is considered **third person**. If "I" is the speaker and "you" the listener, then the others are the ones talked about: those "over there", not included in our little circle.

Subjects are also identified by **number**. "I" is **singular** in number, since there"s only one of me. If another individual is included, then the "I" becomes **plural**: "we".

In English the second person "you" can be either singular or plural, according to the number of people meant: "you, my friend" or "you, my friends". (The phrase "you all [y'all]" is a handy way of illustrating a second person plural form.)

The third person pronouns all have "they" as their plural form.

SINGULAR	PLURAL
he	
she	they
it	

§7 This is the pattern of German pronouns used in Chapters 1-10, and of the **present tense** (1)
Present tense verb endings that show agreement with the subject: (2)

	SINGULAR	PLURAL
FIRST PERSON	ich komm-e	wir komm-en
SECOND PERSON	Sie komm-en	Sie komm-en
THIRD PERSON	er komm-t / sie komm-t / es komm-t	sie komm-en

You must learn that the pronoun *ich* matches the verb ending -*e*, the pronoun *er* matches the verb ending -*t*, and so on. There is no such thing as *<u>er kommen</u> or *<u>ich kommt</u>; these are impossible forms.

Of course, these correspondences hold true for nouns as well: *Er kommt* could be *Karl kommt*, and *wir kommen* could be *Erika und ich kommen* (See **Pronouns** §6).

Verbs with stems ending in *-t, -d*, or certain groups of consonants add an *-e-* before the third person singular ending *-t*:

      es findet   sie arbeitet   er öffnet

§8 The second person singular familiar pronoun *du* is always paired with the verb ending (11) *-st*: *du kommst, du studierst, du bringst*. Just as *du* has a close relative in archaic English 'thou', the *-st* ending is historically the same as in older English forms 'thou hast', 'thou preparest', 'thou anointest'.

§9 The second person plural pronoun *ihr* is always paired with the verb ending *-t*: *ihr geht,* (13) *ihr kommt, ihr fahrt ab*.

§10 The verb conjugation illustrated in §7 is the standard pattern for most present-tense (4) verbs. The **present tense** is used to describe actions or situations in <u>present time</u>. It is also used to refer to <u>time in the near future</u>, especially when the sentence includes a future time expression:

      Ich <u>treffe</u> Sie <u>um 4 Uhr</u> am Rathausplatz.
      Wir <u>fahren</u> <u>morgen abend</u> mit dem Rheindampfer.

These two German sentences could be translated with the English present tense:

      I'm meeting you at 4. . . .Tomorrow evening we're taking. . . .

But we also commonly use the helping verbs 'will' and 'going to' to show future time:

      I'll meet you . . . / I'm going to meet you . . .
      We'll leave . . . / We're going to leave. . .

§11 The patterns described in **§10** are easily understood by speakers of English. But the (13) German present tense can also refer to actions that began in the past and are continuing (21) in the present. The preposition *seit* (with the dative case) is used to tell how long the action has been taking place:

      Er wohnt seit März in Innsbruck.
            He's been living / has lived in Innsbruck <u>since</u> March.
      Ich spiele Poker schon seit 20 Jahren.
            I've been playing / have played poker <u>for</u> 20 years.

This structure is used <u>only</u> if the action is continuing in the present. If it is not, then it belongs to the past, and a past tense must be used.

§12 A number of verbs change their stem vowels in the <u>third person singular</u> (*er/sie/es* form). (4) Most of these verbs have the stem vowel *-e-*:

INFINITIVE	3RD PERSON SINGULAR
essen	er ißt
vergessen	er vergißt
sprechen	sie spricht
treffen	er trifft
nehmen	sie nimmt (irregular)
geben	es gibt
sehen	sie sieht (note: ie, not i)

A very few of these stem-changing verbs have the stem vowel *-a-*:

fahren	sie fährt
tragen	er trägt
schlafen	sie schläft

German is not alone in changing the pronunciation of stem vowels in the third person singular. Note that the vowels in the English infinitives 'say' and 'do' differ from those in the third person forms 'he says' ('sez') and 'she does' ('duz').

§13 Those verbs that change their stem vowel in the third person singular make the same **(11)** change for the second person familiar (*du*) form as well. Because *du* is used, the verb ending is *-st*:

du ißt   du sprichst   du nimmst   du fährst

Note that *ß* + *s* ⇒ *ß* in the *du* form of *essen*.

§14 The verb *sein* 'to be' has forms unlike those in the standard pattern seen in §7. Its present **(1)** tense paradigm is

	SINGULAR	PLURAL
FIRST PERSON	ich bin	wir sind
SECOND PERSON	Sie sind	Sie sind
THIRD PERSON	er/sie/es ist	sie sind

The function of *sein* is to join other sentence elements. This coupling, or linking function is like the equal sign in mathematics. Two things are seen to be related, or placed in the same light. This is also true of *werden* 'become' and *heißen* 'be called'.

Das ist mein Vater.   Es ist Annemarie Wir sind Studenten.

If two things are to be seen as the same, then they also appear in the same grammatical case. Because *Das*, *Es*, and *Wir* are all the subjects in the examples above, and therefore appear in the nominative case, then *Vater*, *Annemarie*, and *Studenten* are also nominative. The phrase *mein Vater* shows clearly that *Vater* is a nominative form (See **Pronouns §10**).

§15 Two other forms of *sein* are not included in the chart above. They are the second person **(12)** familiar forms, matching the pronouns *du* and *ihr*: **(13)**

SINGULAR	PLURAL
du bist	Ihr seid
Du bist nicht mehr so jung.	Seid Ihr schon wieder hungrig?

§16 *Haben*, another high-frequency verb, also has irregular forms in the singular. The third person singular of haben is *hat*, not *habt*.

Sie möchte kommen, aber sie hat keine Fahrkarte.

§17 Matching the third person form *hat* is the *du* form *hast*: **(12)**

Wieviel Geld hast du denn heute? Genug für das Kino?

§18 There are other important verbs whose present tense is "irregular", that is, whose **(5)** conjugation does not fit the pattern in §7. These include *möchten*, the other modal verbs, and *wissen*. *Möchten* is used here to establish the pattern for these essential verbs:

	SINGULAR	PLURAL
FIRST PERSON	ich möchte	wir möchten
SECOND PERSON	Sie möchten	Sie möchten
THIRD PERSON	er/sie/es möchte	sie möchten

Note that the third person singular form does not have the familiar *-t* ending. In this group of verbs, the *ich* form and the *er/sie/es* form are identical.

§19
Modals
The **modal verbs** are normally used in combination with the infinitive forms of other **(5)** verbs. They impart a special tone to a statement or question, establishing a "mood" in which the action of the main verb is carried out.

Used by itself, **möchten** is the German equivalent of 'would like' in English:

Ich möchte eine Weißwurst, bitte.

But when *möchte* is combined with another verb, it means 'would like to':

Wir möchten in die Schweiz fahren.

Here *möchten*, the modal verb, agrees with the subject of the sentence, *wir*, but it is clear that the main action of the sentence has to do with traveling to Switzerland. *Möchten* imparts a special mood or tone to what is said.

§20 The other modal verbs and their special meanings are   (5)

KÖNNEN	*can, may, be able to*	(action is <u>possible</u>)
MÜSSEN	*must, have to, gotta*	(action is <u>physically necessary</u>)
SOLLEN	*supposed to*	(action is <u>morally necessary</u>)
WOLLEN	*want to*	(action is <u>very desirable</u>)
DÜRFEN	*may, be allowed to*	(action is <u>permissible</u>)

§21 Two major patterns apply to the use of the modal verbs: (5)
                                                                                                  (7)

1.   Modals are followed by infinitives, and these infinitives appear at the end of the clause in which the modal appears. (This means that the infinitive normally comes at the end of a sentence.) Be careful not to conjugate the infinitive to agree with the subject of the sentence! Once you have conjugated one main verb (here the modal) to agree with the subject, further conjugation is downright wrong.

2.   The infinitive appears by itself at the end of the sentence without any other word that might be thought to equal English 'to'. Note the difference between the two languages:

Wir **wollen** im Herbst nach Österreich <u>fahren</u>.
We **want to** <u>go</u> to Austria in the fall.

In addition to the verbs listed in §20, the common verbs *sehen*, *hören*, and *lassen* may function as modals, with complementary infinitives.

Endlich <u>sehe</u> ich ihn <u>kommen</u>.	*I finally see him coming.*
<u>Hörst</u> du sie <u>singen</u>?	*Do you hear her singing?*
<u>Lassen</u> Sie mich doch <u>gehen</u>!	*Let me go!*

§22 *Können*: Action is possible. Someone 'is <u>able</u> to' do something.   (5)

	SINGULAR	PLURAL
1	Ich <u>kann</u> kein Spanisch verstehen	Wir <u>können</u> Sie um 11 sehen.
2	Sie <u>können</u> mich später finden.	<u>Können</u> Sie es morgen kaufen?
3	Er/Sie <u>kann</u> es nicht sagen.	Sie <u>können</u> es schon vergessen.

§23 *Müssen*: Action is physically necessary. Someone '<u>has</u> to' do something.   (5)

	SINGULAR	PLURAL
1	Ich <u>muß</u> einfach mehr schlafen.	<u>Müssen</u> wir schon gehen?
2	Sie <u>müssen</u> hier bleiben!	<u>Müssen</u> Sie das wissen?
3	Er/Sie <u>muß</u> weiter arbeiten.	Sie <u>müssen</u> um 10 Uhr fliegen.

NOTE: The negative of *müssen* does not mean 'must not', but rather 'do(es) not have to'. (See **Verbs §26**)

Das müssen Sie nicht essen.
   You don't have to eat that if you don't want).
   (<u>not</u> *You mustn't eat that.*)

§24 *Sollen*: Action is morally necessary. One 'is <u>obligated</u> to' do something.   (5)

	SINGULAR	PLURAL
1	Ich <u>soll</u> zu Hause bleiben.	Wir <u>sollen</u> immer nett sein.
2	Sie <u>sollen</u> keine Angst haben.	Sie <u>sollen</u> Ihre Eltern fragen.
3	Er/Sie <u>soll</u> das wissen.	<u>Sollen</u> sie immer ruhig bleiben?

Sollen is also used in the sense 'is said to be':

Innsbruck <u>soll</u> sehr schön <u>sein</u>.
   Innsbruck <u>is said to be</u> very beautiful.
   <u>People say that</u> Innsbruck <u>is</u> very beautiful.

§25 *Wollen*: Action is desirable. Someone 'wants to' do something.   **(6)**

	SINGULAR	PLURAL
1	Ich will keinen Fisch essen!	Wir wollen immer studieren.
2	Wollen Sie mehr Wein?	Sie wollen ein Pils, ja?
3	Er/Sie will eine Wurst haben.	Wollen sie einen Zwanziger?

NOTE: *Wollen* does <u>not</u> mean 'will'. The two words have the same origin, but vastly different meanings today. Remember that 'I will go tomorrow' is simply *Ich gehe morgen*.

§26 *Dürfen*: Action is permissible. Someone 'is <u>allowed</u> to' do something.   **(7)**

	SINGULAR	PLURAL
1	Darf ich hier Platz nehmen?	Wir dürfen nicht mitkommen. Schade.
2	Ja, das dürfen Sie machen.	Natürlich dürfen Sie ein Taxi nehmen.
3	Er/Sie darf nicht gehen	Dürfen sie alle zum Zoo kommen?

NOTE: In the word 'dare', English retains the old meaning commonly expressed by its close relative *dürfen*:

> <u>Dare</u> I mention the credit card bill?
> We <u>dare</u> not say anything to Mother.

NOTE: The negative of *dürfen* means 'must not':

> Das dürfen Sie nicht essen!   You mustn't eat that!

§27 The last of these unusual, but very common, verbs is *wissen*:   **(4)**

	SINGULAR	PLURAL
1	Das weiß ich nicht mehr	Danke, wir wissen es schon.
2	Wissen Sie die Adresse?	Sie wissen seinen Namen, ja?
3	Er/Sie weiß , wo ich wohne	Wissen sie, wieviel das kostet?

Wissen is used to indicate knowledge of something as a fact. It is not used in the sense of 'know a person'. The verb *kennen* is used for that:

> Ich weiß seinen Namen.   I know that fact.
> Aber ich kenne ihn nicht gut.   I don't know him well.

§28 The second person singular familiar (*du*) forms of the modals and *wissen* add an -*st* to the   **(11)**
singular stem:

INFINITIVE	SINGULAR STEM	*DU* FORM	
möchten	möchte	möchtest	
können	kann	kannst	
müssen	muß	mußt	(note spelling)
sollen	soll	sollst	
wollen	will	willst	
dürfen	darf	darfst	
wissen	weiß	weißt	(note spelling)

§29 The second person plural familiar (*ihr*) forms of these verbs add -(e)*t* to the plural stem: **(13)**

INFINITIVE	PLURAL STEM	*IHR* FORM
möchten	möcht-	möchtet
können	könn-	könnt
müssen	müss-	müßt
sollen	soll-	sollt
wollen	woll-	wollt
dürfen	dürf-	dürft
wissen	wiss-	wißt

§30
Prefixes
Many verbs change their meaning by adding prefixes to the infinitive. These changes can   **(7)**
be very subtle, and they can also be quite dramatic.   **(11)**

> She looked over the contract.
> She overlooked the fine print.

Some of the prefixes are found connected to the verbs in their infinitive forms, but unconnected to the verbs when they are used in the normal process of description in present tense. These prefixes are called **separable prefixes**.

Other prefixes remain attached to the verbs in all forms. These are called **inseparable prefixes**.

English has a number of verb prefixes as well. Notice how the meaning of the verb 'pass' changes when the preposition 'by-' is added as a prefix, or how 'construct' is changed by the prefix 're-'. In these examples, 'by' is something like a separable prefix in that it is often used in its own right; some other English examples are 'out-', 'with-', 'over-', and 'under-'. On the other hand, 're-' acts as an inseparable prefix because it cannot stand alone as an independent word. Other prefixes of this sort in English are 'inter-', 'de-', 'dis-', 'ab-', and 'pre-'.

§31
Separable
Most **separable prefixes** are taken from the inventory of prepositions found in Prepositions §4, §13, and §20. Sometimes they change the meaning of verbs in very predictable ways, as in the case of *ausgehen, durchgehen,* and *untergehen*:   (7) (11)

aus	*out*	+ gehen *go*	⇒ ausgehen	*go out, exit*
durch	*through*	+ gehen	⇒ durchgehen	*go through*
unter	*under*	+ gehen	⇒ untergehen	*go down* (the sun), *decline* (the Roman Empire)

In other instances the meaning of the separable prefix verb cannot necessarily be guessed by knowing the meaning of the individual elements, for many words have figurative as well as literal meanings. For example, the combination of *an* 'on, at' and *nehmen* 'take' produces *annehmen* 'take on, accept, assume' — but from the literal meaning of a 'taking on', as in

He <u>assumed</u> his new duties as division chief.

we also derive a figurative meaning:

He <u>assumed</u> his new duties would be easy.

And in the case of some separable prefix verbs, all we can do is scratch our heads and wonder how they came to have their current meanings — although there are usually perfectly good historical reasons. A case in point is the combination of the prefix *auf* 'up, on' with the verb *hören* 'hear, listen': *Aufhören* means 'stop'. Clearly you must learn the special meaning of each new prefixed verb, for the whole is sometimes quite different from its parts.

Word order: In normal use in the present tense, the separable prefix appears not in combination with the verb, but at the <u>very end of the clause</u>. If the infinitive is called for — at the end of a clause after a modal verb, for example — the prefix attaches to it. Separated or attached, the prefix is thus in final position. Example — *einkaufen* 'go shopping':

> ↓ end of clause
> Kaufen Sie später <u>ein</u>, oder kommen Sie jetzt mit?
> Ich kaufe heute Nachmittag <u>ein</u>.
> Ich möchte später <u>einkaufen</u>.

For an account of separable prefix verbs in infinitive phrases, see **Verbs §39**.

§32
Inseparable
Inseparable verb prefixes are just that: They never separate from their verbs. Also, only rarely can a meaning be associated with an inseparable prefix. This means that the inseparable verbs created by the addition of the prefix must simply be memorized as individual vocabulary items without regard to the larger word family to which they belong historically. Examples of this sort of unpredictability are   (22)

kommen	*come*	bekommen	*get, receive*	entkommen	*escape*
hören	*hear*	gehören	*belong*	verhören	*interrogate*

In at least one common pair the inseparable verb means the opposite of its base form:

kaufen   *buy*   verkaufen   *sell*

Again, the inseparable prefix remains with the verb at all times:

	SINGULAR	PLURAL
1	Ich verkaufe	wir verkaufen
2	Sie verkaufen	Sie verkaufen
3	er/sie verkauft	sie verkaufen

§33   One relatively small group of prefixed verbs contains verbs with prefixes that look separable (i.e., are identical to a few prepositions), but may or may not be, according to the meaning of the verb. Understandably, these verbs can be confusing, since their written form gives no hint about the nature of their prefixes.

For example, *über<u>setz</u>en* and *<u>über</u>setzen* are two verbs with the same written form, but different meanings. The first, which the underlining shows to be accented on the verb stem, is the more common of the two and means 'translate'. It is an inseparable verb.

Sie <u>übersetzt</u> nicht gern. Sie liest einfach lieber.

The second, which is accented on the prefix, is separable. It means 'set over'.

Sie <u>setzt</u> ihren Koffer auf den Gepäckkarren <u>über</u>.

In verb pairs of this sort, the pronunciation of the verbs gives the clue to their meaning and usage. If the prefix is stressed, then the verb has the more literal or physical meaning (here literally 'set across' or 'transfer') and is separable. If the verb stem is stressed, then the verb has a figurative or nonphysical meaning (here 'set across from one language into another') and is inseparable. Dictionaries use conventional means of differentiating the two kinds of verbs, usually with a mark before the stressed syllable: *über'setzen* 'translate' vs. *'übersetzen* 'set across'.

§34   **Verb complements** are words or phrases that complete an idea begun by a verb. In their (12)
Complements   simplest form, they are single words: (13)

Jetzt ist Hannelore wieder <u>gesund</u>.

Here the meaning of the sentence is unclear until the last word. The sense of the statement could be changed completely with the substitution of *krank, hier,* or *müde*. The single word could also be changed to *in Stuttgart, auf einer Reise,* or *böse auf ihren Mann,* and in each instance the impact of the sentence hinges on the last phrase.

Note that the verb complement appears at the end of the sentence. In <u>subordinate clauses</u> (after subordinating conjunctions such as *wenn*) the verb complement appears <u>near</u> the end, just before the verb:

Es macht ihm immer eine große Freude, wenn er <u>im Café</u> sitzt.

§35   In many instances the **verb complement** is a **prepositional phrase**, introduced by a (13)
preposition that combines with the verb to create a special meaning. Using the English (20)
verb <u>work</u>, we can construct sentences of very different meanings using the different phrases <u>work with</u>, <u>work at</u>, <u>work under</u>. In addition, we can work <u>under pressure</u> and work <u>under a supervisor</u>, and even work <u>under cover</u> or <u>under an assumed name</u> or <u>under a tent</u> — all with different meanings that cannot be anticipated or perceived when we hear merely the word <u>work</u>.

These combinations of verbs and prepositions contribute much to our flexibility as speakers and writers of English. We wait <u>for</u> things, speak <u>about</u> them, and are interested <u>in</u> them. In German, as in English, the preposition that combines with the verb is important in determining the meaning of the whole sentence. However, because German prepositions are used with specific cases (See **Prepositions §4, §13, §20**), these cases must be kept in mind in constructing the prepositional phrase that completes the idea begun by the verb. Of course, those prepositions that are always used with specific cases continue to govern those cases only.

von   **dative**   Sie spricht immer _von_ ihrer Reise nach Österreich.
für   **accusative**   Ich interessiere mich _für_ die Buchdruckkunst.

However, the prepositions used with either the dative or the accusative (**Prepositions §20**) provide some difficulties. When these prepositions are used as verb complements to give special meaning to verbs, the "motion toward" vs. "location or motion within" distinction no longer applies. Now the verb and preposition combination must be learned with a specific case to be associated with a special meaning. For example, the preposition _auf_ means 'on, onto'. When combined with the verb _warten_ and used with the accusative case, it means 'for':

Er _wartet_ am Bahnhof _auf_ seinen Bruder.
He's waiting for his brother at the station.

Thus we must learn _warten auf_ with accusative as the equivalent of 'wait for'. If this seems inconvenient, it is also absolutely necessary. For if _warten auf_ is used not with the accusative, but with the dative, _auf_ maintains its literal meaning of 'on'.

Er _wartet_ am Bahnhof _auf_ seinem Bruder.
He's waiting on top of his brother at the station.

Understandably, serious miscommunication can arise if the cases governed by verbal complements are not scrupulously learned. To facilitate your learning, dictionaries indicate these cases either by giving clear examples (_Er wartet auf den Zug_, in which _den_ is clearly an accusative form) or by supplying the case: _warten auf_/acc. or _warten auf_ w/acc.

§36   Sometimes the verb complement is a **verb** itself. As in English 'go', the German verb _gehen_ can be supplemented by an infinitive of another verb to indicate an activity about to take place. As with the other complements, the infinitive that completes the idea comes at the end of the clause: (12) (13)

Heute morgen _gehe_ ich mit meiner Mutter _einkaufen_.

After a modal verb, the complement can no longer come at the very end of the clause, because another infinitive is there:

Ich _möchte_ mit dir einmal einkaufen _gehen_.

Other verbal complements include stehenbleiben and kennenlernen.

Bitte, _bleiben_ Sie noch einen Moment _stehen_.
Ich _lernte_ ihn in einer Jugendherberge _kennen_.

§37
Dative   A number of verbs govern not the accusative case, but the dative. Generally, the verb phrases are ones in which a condition or an action on behalf of someone is either explicit or implied. Two clear examples are the verbs _helfen_ 'help' and _dienen_ 'serve':   (14) (18)

Bitte, helfen Sie mir!	_Please help me!_ (Give aid to me)
Womit kann ich Ihnen _dienen_?	_What can I help you with?_
	(help = give service to)

The group of verbs that govern the dative case includes _gehören_ 'belong to'. Since something must belong to someone, it seems natural that that person should appear in the dative case:

Mir? Nein, das gehört _mir_ nicht. Vielleicht gehört es _meiner_ Mutter.

Gefallen is the verb most commonly used to indicate liking. Because it is used so often, its special meaning must be understood: it does not mean 'like', but rather 'be pleasing to'. When we use _gefallen_, we must rethink our English inclination to say 'I like it' and say instead 'It is pleasing to me'. This may sound stiff in English, but

Es **gefällt** mir

is perfectly normal to a German speaker. Other examples:

Gefällt Ihnen das?	_Do you like that?_
Der Film hat uns wirklich sehr gut _gefallen_.	_We really liked the movie._

Note that what appears as the object in the English 'I like it' is really the subject when the action of liking is seen from the German perspective, and that the English subject 'I' turns into the German dative object *mir*.

Similarly, one expression with the verb *gehen* and two with the verb *tun* are used to indicate physical well-being:

Wie geht es Ihnen/dir heute?	How "does it go with you" today? (How are you?)
Danke, es geht mir gut.	I'm fine, thanks.

NOTE: Never respond to *Wie geht's?* with *Ich bin gut*, which is an assertion of superiority.

Ach, das tut mir/uns furchtbar leid.	Oh, I'm/we're terribly sorry. (literally: That does sorrow to me/us.)
Mein Fuß tut mir weh.	My foot hurts. ('does woe' to me.)

Other verbs using the dative case include *antworten* 'answer' and *schmecken* 'taste (good)'.

Antworte mir!	Answer me! (Give an answer to me.)
Das schmeckt mir nicht.	That doesn't taste good (to me).

§38   We make a distinction in English between the verb forms 'he eats', 'he is eating', and 'he does eat':

> He eats bread (habitually)
> He is eating bread (at this very moment)
> He does eat bread (but he'd rather not)

Standard German does not have equivalent verbal forms, but deals with these matters by other means. (The verbal forms are present in colloquial German, however.) This feature of English, and its absence in the German standard, suggests why German speakers learning English make characteristic mistakes such as

> I eat my toast now.
> Go we now home, yes?

English also sets traps for English speakers learning German. Beginning students often make the mistake of translating word for word such phrases as

I am eating	≠	Ich bin essen
I don't drink milk	≠	Ich tue nicht trinken Milch.

English speakers must recognize that an entire verb form in English is rendered by an entire verb form in German. Here 'am eating' is the equivalent of German *esse*, and 'do drink' is *trinke* in German. Whatever you want to say, be careful not to formulate your thoughts in English and then transfer them bit by bit into German.

§39
Infinitive phrases   You have seen that infinitives do not show tense: They are "infinite" in their meanings in the same way that "finite" forms such as *gehst* and *trägt* signify a specific person, number, and tense. Infinitives are used not just in dictionary glossaries, and not just as complements to modal verbs, but also as the focus of action in **infinitive phrases**. **(19) (20)**

> Es macht immer Spaß, bei Hans und Irma zu übernachten.

Here the infinitive *übernachten* combines with *zu* to describe an activity that is not restricted to any specific tense or person. An individual could say this sentence with reference to himself, or the action of spending the night could be described by an entire swarm of Hans and Irma's relatives. Also, the person saying the sentence could indicate that it <u>was</u> always fun or <u>will</u> always <u>be</u> fun to spend the night at that house. The tense of the entire sentence is determined by the tense of the verb in the main clause (here *macht*), and the infinitive never needs to change its form.

The structure of an infinitive phrase is illustrated by the sentence above: an introductory comma separates the phrase from the rest of the sentence, and the infinitive preceded by

zu comes at the very end of the phrase. If the infinitive has a separable prefix (See **Verbs §31**), the *zu* is enclosed between the infinitive and the prefix:

> Es ist immer schön, unsere Eltern anzurufen.

§40 An infinitive phrase that is introduced by the particle *um* expresses purpose. That is, **(20)** something is done for a specific reason. The equivalent in English is 'in order to', with the 'to' showing that we also have the infinitive phrase in English:

> Sie geht in die Stadt, um ihren Bruder bei der Polizei abzuholen.

The infinitive phrase introduced by *um* answers the question *Warum?*

The preposition *ohne* may also begin an infinitive phrase, the resulting construction showing how something is done: namely, without some specific other activity:

> Jörg ging einkaufen, ohne sein ganzes Geld auszugeben.
> *Jörg went shopping without spending all his money.*

The equivalent construction in English is 'without -ing'.

§41
Reflexives
Reflexive constructions involve actions that are directed back upon the subject of the **(17)** verb: He bit himself, they threw themselves at her feet. In English reflexive constructions **(20)** involve a pronoun ending in -self/-selves. In German the pronoun is identical to the personal pronoun except for the second person polite (*Sie*) and the third person singular (*er, sie, es*) and plural (*sie*), where it is *sich*.

In their simplest form, reflexive actions involve doing something for oneself: buying oneself a cold drink or a new hat, doing oneself a favor, finding oneself a seat on a bus. Here the reflexive pronoun is in the dative case, since the action is performed for oneself, in one's own interest:

> Ich kaufe mir morgen einen neuen Mercedes.

There is nothing inherently reflexive about these constructions. They could be used in the same way without specifying the person for whom an action is taken. (*Ich kaufe morgen einen neuen Mercedes.*) But the situation itself is reflexive: The subject is the beneficiary of the action.

§42 Reflexive constructions often have direct equivalents in English. We are often called **(18)** upon to introduce or identify ourselves: **(20)**

> Darf ich mich vorstellen?   *May I introduce myself?*
> Sie kann sich nicht ausweisen.   *She can't identify herself.*

These constructions both include a verb and a reflexive pronoun in the accusative case, because the verb is understood to be acting directly back upon the subject.

§43 Most reflexive constructions, however, do not have direct equivalents in English and **(18)** must therefore be learned as specific vocabulary items including verb and reflexive **(20)** pronoun. In the glossary to this text, verbs that are used with a reflexive pronoun are identified by a *sich* accompanying their infinitives. Common verb-pronoun combinations include

sich (hin)setzen	*sit down*	Bitte, setzen Sie sich (hin).
sich beeilen	*hurry*	Warum mußt du dich so beeilen?
sich waschen	*wash*	Er kann sich noch nicht gut waschen.
sich erinnern	*remember*	Wie heißt er? Ich erinnere mich nicht.
sich umschauen	*look around*	Wir schauen uns nur um, danke.
sich anziehen	*get dressed*	Zieh dich doch schnell an!
sich fühlen	*feel*	Wie fühlst du dich heute? Besser?
sich erkälten	*catch cold*	Ich habe mich wieder erkältet.
sich entscheiden	*decide*	Hm — ich kann mich nicht entscheiden.
sich lohnen	*be worth it*	DM 20? Das lohnt sich gar nicht.
sich freuen	*be happy*	Heute ist schön. Ich freue mich sehr.

§44 A number of reflexive verb/pronoun combinations are used with specific **prepositions**, **(19)**
Prepositions just as in English. Remember that the case governed by the preposition must be learned **(20)**
so that you can use the expression effectively. Among the most common combinations
are

sich freuen auf (acc.)	*look forward to*
	Ich freue mich immer auf Weihnachten.
sich freuen über (acc.)	*be happy about*
	Er freut sich über sein neues Baby.
sich erinnern an (acc.)	*remember*
	Erinnerst du dich an deinen alten Freund Max?
sich interessieren für (acc.)	*be interested in*
	Interessieren Sie sich für Jazz?
sich beschäftigen mit (dat.)	*be busy with*
	Sie hat keine Zeit. Sie beschäftigt sich mit ihren Steuern.
sich wundern über (acc.)	*be amazed about*
	Wir wundern uns über dein Glück.
sich gewöhnen an (acc.)	*get used to*
	Man gewöhnt sich eigentlich an alles.

§45 In some reflexive constructions the subject is not the direct goal of the verb's action, but **(19)**
the indirect goal. In these situations there is an accusative object of the verb, but the **(20)**
subject is still involved as a point of reference. One example of this sort of construction
has already been cited in **§41**.

Ich kaufe mir morgen einen neuen Mercedes.

Here *Mercedes* is the direct object of the verb, and *mir* tells for whom the action is being
undertaken. The car could just as well be bought for someone else.

Some common verbs are used with dative reflexive objects. Here the reflexive is dative,
and the other object is accusative.

sich etwas überlegen	*consider something*
sich etwas anschauen	*take a look at something*
sich etwas vorstellen	*imagine something*
sich etwas anhören	*(take a) listen to something*

In each of these, the *etwas* reflects an accusative object of the verb, and the *sich* reflects a
dative object referring back to the subject of the sentence.

Ich möchte es mir anschauen

thus means 'I'd like to look at it (*es*) for myself (*mir*)'. The verb cannot be used with
another dative object: I cannot look at something with someone else's eyes. Similarly, I
cannot take note of something or listen to music or consider something for anyone other
than myself. Others will have to do their own taking note, listening, and considering.
Other sentences with these verbs:

Nun, überlegen Sie es sich mal.	*Well, think about it a bit.*
Schau es dir doch an.	*Take a look at it.*
Ich möchte mir deine neue Kassette anhören.	*I'd like to listen to your new tape.*
Das kann ich mir gut vorstellen.	*I can well imagine that.*

§46 An important group of reflexive constructions deals with parts of the body: washing **(20)**
hands, brushing teeth, and so on. When the specific parts of the body are mentioned, one
does not simply perform these acts — one does them on one's behalf, thus calling for a
dative reflexive pronoun. The functions include, but are not limited to

sich die Hände/das Gesicht/die Füße (etc.) waschen
sich die Haare kämmen / trocknen
sich die Zähne putzen

This formula extends to clothing as well:

> sich das Hemd (etc.) anziehen / umziehen / ausziehen

Obviously, it is possible to use the verbs *waschen, kämmen, trocknen, putzen,* and *anziehen* as simple active verbs taking an object other than oneself, especially when parents are performing these duties for young children:

> Diese Eltern waschen ihre Kinder nicht oft genug.
> Ich muß meinen Sohn wieder anziehen.

But when reference is made to specific parts of the body or items of clothing, then a dative noun or pronoun must be used to show whose body or clothing is involved. Note the difference between a nonreflexive function and a reflexive one:

> NONREFLEXIVE: Mutter trocknet ihr (*the daughter*) die Haare zu lange.
> REFLEXIVE: Mutter trocknet sich (*herself*) die Haare zu lange.
>
> NONREFLEXIVE: Ich putze meinem Sohn die Zähne.
> REFLEXIVE: Ich putze mir die Zähne.

§47   All the verb forms discussed so far have been in what is called the **indicative mood**. (2)
Imperative   Mood has to do with the attitude of the speaker toward what he is saying. Statements in (3) the indicative mood are made in a straightforward and nonrestrictive fashion in a variety of tenses. The **imperative mood**, on the other hand, is used to **give commands**. Imperative forms do not indicate time — we cannot command others to 'have done' or to 'will do' something, but just to 'do' it in present time.

> yes: *Please buy me a Toblerone*   (present)
> no: *Please bought me a Toblerone.*   (past)
> no: *Please will buy me a Toblerone.*   (future)

When individuals are being addressed, both English and German place the verb in first position to give commands.

§48   Signs in public places usually warn or inform by simply using an infinitive at the end of (2) the imperative statement: (3)

> **Bitte nicht mit dem Wagenführer <u>sprechen</u>.**
>   *Please do not speak to the driver.*
> **Bitte nicht <u>hinauslehnen</u>.**
>   *Do not lean out of the window.*
> **Nicht <u>öffnen</u>, bevor der Zug hält!**
>   *Do not open until the train stops!*
> **Nicht <u>rauchen</u>.**
>   *No smoking.*

§49   When commands are directed at people known to the speaker as *Sie,* German uses the (2) *Sie* form of the verb: (3)

> **Bringen Sie** uns bitte zwei Glas Rotwein.   *(Please)* **bring** us . . . .
> **Bleiben Sie** bitte zwei Nächte!   *(Please)* **stay** . . . .

The verb *sein* is an exception to this pattern, but the difference between the infinitive and the *Sie* imperative form is insignificant in the spoken language:

> **Se<u>i</u>en Sie** bitte vorsichtig! *Please **be** careful!*

The prefix of a **separable verb** appears at the end of the command:

> Bitte, **rufen Sie** mich später am Nachmittag **an**.
>   *Please call me later this afternoon.*

§50   Understandably, there are also special imperative forms that apply to individuals well (11) known to the speaker as *du*. Almost all verbs use just the verb stem for this purpose. Note that the pronoun *du* itself does not appear:

> **Komm** schnell!   **Schlaf** nicht ein!   **Sei** bitte ruhig!

Verb stems ending in -d or -t and stems of -n infinitives (*wandern, handeln*) add an -e in the *du* imperative:

> **Finde** deinen Bruder und bring ihn hierher.
> **Arbeite** mit beiden Händen.
> **Wandre** nicht so weit!

Some other verbs, those with stems ending in -*ieren* or in certain groups of consonants, also frequently add an -e in the *du* imperative:

> **Studiere** Philosophie, das ist interessanter.   **Öffne** das Fenster, bitte.

Verbs with stems in -e- that normally change in the *du* and *er/sie/es* forms make the change in the *du* imperative as well:

> **Nimm** die Linie 7 zum Stadion.
> **Gib** der Oma diese Plätzchen, und **sprich** nicht mit dem bösen Wolf!

Other stem-changing verbs, those with stems in -a-, do not make the vowel change in the *du* imperative:

> **Lauf** schneller, sonst verpassen wir die Tram!   **Schlaf** gut, meine Liebe.

§51   The *ihr* imperative simply uses the *ihr* form of the verb. As in the *du* form, the pronoun   (14)
does not appear in the imperative:

> **Wartet** doch, ich komme schon!
> **Nehmt** mir diesen Brief bitte mit zur Post.
> **Seid** lieb zueinander, Kinder!

§52   When we give orders to <u>ourselves</u>, we speak as if we were speaking to a second person.   (8)

> *Come on, bear down, fella!*
> *Stop that twitching and play it right for once!*

But sometimes our commands include another person as well as ourselves, so that the people involved are *wir*, not just *ich*. In English these commands take the form of suggestions, couched in tones that may range from gentle to severe:

> *Let's go have some ice cream.*
> *Let's pay attention to what we're doing for once!*

In German these suggestions use the first person plural form of the verb and add the personal pronoun *wir*:

> <u>Fahren wir</u> doch in die Stadt zum Zirkus.
> <u>Bleiben wir</u> heute zu Hause.

The verb *sein*, as in the formal imperative, has a distinctive *wir* imperative form:

> **Seien wir** jetzt freundlicher zueinander, ja?

§53   In addition to the indicative and the imperative, German has a third mood, the   (15)
Subjunctive   **subjunctive**. The subjunctive is commonly used to express **politeness** or **tentativeness**,   (16)
especially in a few very high-frequency verbs such as *sein, haben, werden, wissen*, and the   (18)
modals. This is the subjunctive function that beginners are most likely to encounter first. English equivalents of polite expressions are "Would you have . . . ?" or "Do you suppose you could . . .?" The body language that accompanies this kind of language is often cautious and tentative rather than forthright or aggressive.

The subjunctive is also used to express **hypotheses** — to guess what would be true if certain other things were to be one way or another. The sentence "If it rained right now, we'd be drenched" contains two verbs in the subjunctive mood. It is a hypothesis: 'In fact, it is not raining right now, and we are not being drenched'. Since the adverb 'right now' implies that we are dealing with present time, the use of the verb forms 'rained' and '(woul)d be drenched' instead of the present tense 'is raining' and 'are being drenched' tells us that the speaker is supposing what might be the result of some hypothetical action.

§54 **Subjunctive forms.** We have seen that English resorts to the use of past tense forms (15)
('rained') to talk about a contrary-to-fact situation in present time. German does the very (16)
same thing — to no one's surprise, perhaps, since the two languages are closely related. (18)
In fact, English also uses apparently past forms in order to express politeness or
tentativeness: "Could you perhaps . . .?"

In dealing first with the most common German subjunctive forms, it will be helpful to
list the past tense forms from which they are derived:

INFINITIVE	PAST STEM	PRESENT SUBJUNCTIVE
sein	war-	wär-
haben	hatt-	hätt-
werden	wurd-	würd-
wissen	wußt-	wüßt-
können	konnt-	könnt-
müssen	mußt-	müßt-
dürfen	durft-	dürft-
sollen	sollt-	sollt-
wollen	wollt-	wollt-

The characteristic difference between the past stem and the present subjunctive is the
umlauted stem vowel, which immediately says to the listener 'hypothesis! politeness!
tentativeness!' (*Sollen* and *wollen* are obvious exceptions to the pattern, but because of
other clues built into an entire subjunctive sentence, their non-umlauted stem vowels
still do not hinder the transmission of the important subjunctive message.) To these
present subjunctive stems are then added endings that match the subject. Example: *hätt-*

	SINGULAR	PLURAL
FIRST PERSON	ich hätte	wir hätten
SECOND PERSON	du hättest	ihr hättet
	Sie hätten	Sie hätten
THIRD PERSON	er/sie/es hätte	sie hätten

Just as in the simple past tense, the third person singular has no *-t* ending.

§55 Although it is the "polite" subjunctive that one encounters, recognizes, and uses first, it (18)
is the subjunctive of **hypothesis** that is more widespread and that gives greater
flexibility to both the written and spoken language. The forms listed above are used to
hypothesize as well as to express politeness or tentativeness, and other verbs (virtually
all can be used to hypothesize) also have subjunctive forms that are derived from their
past stems. Although functions may differ, the forms are the same.

In its capacity to express hypotheses, the subjunctive exists in two **tenses**, the **present**
and the **past**. The <u>present subjunctive</u> is used to describe those things that might be, but
are not:

        PRESENT   *If he <u>saw</u> a bear now, he'd <u>run</u>.*

The sentence is contrary to fact: He doesn't see a bear now, and he's not running now.
The statement is pure hypothesis. The <u>past subjunctive</u> describes things that might have
been, but were not:

        PAST   *If he <u>had seen</u> a bear then, he <u>would have run</u>.*

This is also contrary to fact: He didn't see a bear then, and he didn't run. Note that each
of these sentences consists of a clause beginning with <u>If. . .</u> and a clause stating a result.
Appropriately, these are called the "if clause" and the "result clause". Subjunctive forms
are used in each one, because contrary-to-fact situations are stated in each. The verb is
placed at the end of its clause because *wenn*, a subordinating conjunction, is used in
German <u>if</u> clauses.

§56 The **present subjunctive**, in English as well as German, is formed from the simple past **(18)**
Present stem, as seen in the examples <u>rained</u> and <u>saw</u> above. In the case of the **regular verbs**,
subjunctive those that form their past stems by adding *-te* to the present stem, the past is identical to
the present subjunctive. Exceptions are, as ever, the high-frequency verbs listed in §54.
Note the close correspondence to English forms.

PAST INDICATIVE	PRESENT SUBJUNCTIVE
Ich <u>kaufte</u> ein Geschenk.	Wenn ich ein Geschenk <u>kaufte</u>, . . .
I <u>bought</u> a present.	*If I <u>bought</u> a present, . . .*
Er <u>holte</u> mir ein Bier.	Wenn er mir ein Bier <u>holte</u>, . . .
He <u>fetched</u> me a beer.	*If he <u>fetched</u> me a beer, . . .*
Ich <u>hatte</u> einen Porsche.	Wenn ich einen Porsche <u>hätte</u>, . . .
I <u>had</u> a Porsche.	*If I <u>had</u> a Porsche, . . .*
Das <u>wußte</u> sie schon.	Wenn sie das schon <u>wüßte</u>, . . .
She <u>knew</u> that already.	*If she <u>knew</u> that already, . . .*

In order to establish a realistic context for the subjunctive, however, there must be some
clear factual situation to which the subjunctive provides an alternative. The second
column above is more properly compared to some real situation in the present tense:

Ich kaufe kein Geschenk. Aber wenn ich ein Geschenk <u>kaufte</u>, . . .
I'm not buying a present. But if I <u>bought</u> (<u>were buying</u>) one, . . .

Er holt mir kein Bier. Aber wenn er mir ein Bier <u>holte</u>, . . .
He's not fetching me a beer. But if he <u>fetched</u> (<u>were fetching</u>) me one, . .

Note that there are various possibilities for the English subjunctive here: 'If I <u>bought</u>', 'if I
<u>were buying</u>', 'if I <u>were to buy</u>', 'if I <u>happened to buy</u>', 'if I <u>should buy</u>' — all expressing
a hypothesis. In German the single form *kaufte* functions for all these English
equivalents.

For **irregular verbs**, those that do not form their past stem with *-t*, the same principle of
usage applies. As opposed to the regular verbs, however, these normally umlaut the
vowel of the past stem before adding the characteristic subjunctive endings. Of course,
only *a*, *o*, and *u* can be umlauted.

INFINITIVE	PAST STEM	PRESENT SUBJUNCTIVE
sein	war	wär-
werden	wurde	würd-
heißen	hieß	hieß-
kommen	kam	käm-
gehen	ging	ging-
laufen	lief	lief-

§57 'If' clauses can be used alone to express wishes ('If my prince would come . . .'). **(18)**
However, they are usually not left unfinished, as they are in §56 above, but are
completed by a result clause. When the 'if' clause is the first syntactical element, the verb
in the main clause must come next as the second element in the entire sentence:

       1   **2**
<u>Wenn ich ein Geschenk kaufte</u>, <u>hätte</u> ich kein Geld mehr.
If I bought a present, I wouldn't have any more money.

This sentence can be rearranged — in German as in English — by placing the result
clause first:

  1 **2**
Ich <u>hätte</u> kein Geld mehr, wenn ich ein Geschenk kaufte.
I wouldn't have any more money if I bought a present.

§58 *Würde*: **the all-purpose subjunctive form.** *Würde*, the present subjunctive of *werden*, is   **(18)**
würde used widely for all functions of the subjunctive — polite, tentative, and hypothetical.

POLITE:	Würden Sie mir bitte das Salz reichen?
TENTATIVE:	Würden Sie vielleicht eine Nummer größer vorziehen?
HYPOTHETICAL:	Würden Sie es kaufen, wenn Sie das Geld hätten?

The combination of *würde* and an infinitive produces the same result as the present
subjunctive form of that infinitive. That is,

würde + haben	=	hätte
würde + sein	=	wäre
würde + gehen	=	ginge
würde + kaufen	=	kaufte

Ich <u>würde</u> ins Theater <u>gehen</u>, wenn ich as Geld hätte.
Ich <u>ginge</u> ins Theater, wenn ich das Geld hätte.

Style and level of diction are important factors in the use of the subjunctive in modern
German. In colloquial speech, the use of *würde* with an infinitive to form the present
subjunctive is widespread in both if clauses and result clauses.

COLLOQUIAL: Wenn ich den Bären <u>sehen würde</u>, <u>würde</u> ich <u>weglaufen</u>.

In less colloquial speech *würde* is not used in if-clauses, but frequently occurs in result
clauses:

FORMAL:	Wenn ich den Bären sähe, <u>würde</u> ich <u>weglaufen</u>.
MORE FORMAL:	Wenn ich den Bären sähe, liefe ich weg.

Even allowing for differences in level of speech, most German speakers today do not
choose to combine *würde* with *sein, haben*, or the modal verbs.

§59 **The past subjunctive,** as stated above, is used to describe those actions that might have   **(23)**
Past subjunctive taken place, but did not: **(24)**

PAST: *If he <u>had seen</u> a bear, he <u>would have run</u>.*

In English the past subjunctive is formed by combining the past participle of the main
verb with the present subjunctive form of its helping verb. In this sentence the verbs in
question are *sehen*, which takes the helping verb *haben*; and *laufen*, which takes the
helping verb *sein*. Again, because *wenn* is used, the finite verb — here the helping verb
that agrees with the subject — comes at the very end of the clause:

Wenn er einen Bären <u>gesehen hätte</u>, <u>wäre</u> er <u>gelaufen</u>.

Just as with the present subjunctive, the order of clauses can be reversed without
changing the meaning. As ever, the main verb is in second position:

Er <u>wäre gelaufen</u>, wenn er einen Bären <u>gesehen hätte</u>.

The past subjunctive with modals combines *hätte* with a double infinitive.

Wenn ich es hätte sehen können, hätte ich keine Angst gehabt.
If I'd been able to see it, I wouldn't have been afraid.

Note that, although *wenn* normally places the auxiliary in final position, a double
infinitive is always the very last element in a sentence. (See **Verbs §75**)

§60 The subjunctive mood is used to report what someone else has said. Typically, such   **(23)**
indirect discourse is introduced by a phrase such as *sie sagte* or *sie meinte*, in order to
make it clear that the statement is someone else's opinion. When the original statement is
in the <u>present tense</u>, the <u>present subjunctive</u> is used to relate it:

original statement by Marta:	"Hans <u>ist</u> eigentlich ganz nett."
related by another person:	Marta sagte, Hans <u>wäre</u> eigentlich ganz nett.
or:	Marta sagte, daß Hans eigentlich ganz nett <u>wäre</u>.

When the original statement is in past time, then it is related by the <u>past subjunctive</u>:

> original: "Der Winter <u>war</u> doch furchtbar kalt."
> retold: Er sagte, der Winter <u>wäre</u> furchtbar kalt <u>gewesen</u>.
> **or:** Er sagte, daß der Winter furchtbar kalt <u>gewesen wäre</u>.

> original: "Jemand <u>hat</u> unseren Wagen <u>gestohlen</u>."
> retold: Sie sagten, jemand <u>hätte</u> ihren Wagen <u>gestohlen</u>.
> **or:** Sie sagten, daß jemand ihren Wagen <u>gestohlen hätte</u>.

§61
Future tense

German normally uses the present tense with an adverb of time to indicate future action. A formal **future tense** does exist, however, occurring frequently in writing and occasionally in speaking. It is formed with the verb *werden* as a helping verb, followed at the end of the clause by an infinitive — similar in construction to modal clauses.

> Morgen <u>werden</u> wir alle mit dem Postbus nach Trimmis <u>fahren</u>.

Werden is the finite verb, agreeing with the subject and holding second place in the sentence unless used in a subordinate clause:

> Er sagte, <u>daß</u> wir alle morgen mit dem Postbus fahren <u>werden</u>.

NOTE: In the future tense a modal verb occurs in final position, after its dependent infinitive.

> Morgen wirst du es besser verstehen <u>können</u>.

§62
Past tense

The **past tense**, sometimes called the **narrative past**, is used to describe events — usually a series of events — that occurred in past time. By its very nature, the past tense is heavily used in newspapers and other sources that report and analyze past occurrences. With the exception of the common verbs *sein, haben, wissen, denken, werden*, and the modals, the past tense is not frequently used in normal conversation.   **(9) (21) (24)**

§63

These high-frequency past tense forms are some of the most important ones commonly used in both writing and speaking: **(9) (21) (24)**

INFINITIVE	PAST STEM
sein	war
haben	hatte
wissen	wußte
können	konnte
müssen	mußte
dürfen	durfte
sollen	sollte
wollen	wollte

§64

The **formation of the past tense** depends on the kind of verb involved — regular or irregular. The **regular verbs** form the past stem by the addition of a *-te* to the present stem: **(9) (21) (24)**

INFINITIVE	PRESENT STEM	PAST STEM
kaufen	kauf-	kaufte-
studieren	studier-	studierte-
kosten	kost-	kost<u>ete</u>-

The conjugation of the past tense is similar to that of the present tense, with the exception of the third person singular forms, which are identical to those of the first person:

	SINGULAR	PLURAL
FIRST PERSON	ich kauf te	wir kauf te **n**
SECOND PERSON	du kauf te **st**	ihr kauf te **t**
	Sie kauf te **n**	Sie kauf te **n**
THIRD PERSON	er/sie kauf te	sie kauf te **n**

§65
Irregular verbs The **irregular verbs** do not have past stems with *-te*. Instead, their past is formed by (21) vowel change, and sometimes with a slight difference in consonant structure as well. (24) There are good historical reasons for each of these past forms, and with more exposure to German you will develop a "feel" for what the past tense of an irregular verb might be. The only way to learn these forms at the beginning is to memorize them along with their infinitives. The infinitive is called the <u>first principal part</u> of a verb, and the past stem is called the <u>second principal part</u>.

<u>INFINITIVE</u>	<u>PAST STEM</u>
sein	war
heißen	hieß
essen	aß
trinken	trank
bleiben	blieb
gehen	ging

Additional examples of irregular verbs with all their principal parts are listed on the back flyleaves of the Class Text.

The conjugation of the irregular verbs in the past is identical to that of the regular verbs:

	SINGULAR	PLURAL
FIRST PERSON	ich blieb	wir blieb **en**
SECOND PERSON	du blieb **st**	ihr blieb **t**
	Sie blieb **en**	Sie blieb **en**
THIRD PERSON	er/sie/es blieb	sie blieb **en**

§66 In addition to the regular and irregular verbs, there are a few that seem to be (21) combinations of the two kinds. Again, there are good historical reasons for their forms, (24) but from a modern viewpoint they appear to be anomalies. These verbs combine the *-te* suffix of the regular verbs with the vowel change of the irregular ones:

<u>INFINITIVE</u>		<u>PAST STEM</u>
bringen	*bring*	brachte
denken	*think*	dachte
kennen	*know*	kannte
nennen	*call*	nannte
rennen	*run*	rannte
wissen	*know*	wußte

§67 As you have already seen in the discussion of the present perfect, English and German (21) verbs, especially the most common ones, tend to be remarkably similar in form. Regular (24) verbs in English have past stems ending in <u>-d</u> (such as <u>said</u> from <u>say</u>), a sound that is a close relative of German *-t*. Irregular verbs in English generally show the vowel change characteristic of their German cognates (words with which they share a common origin):

tragen — trug   draw — drew

Some useful examples:

<u>IRREGULAR (vowel change)</u>		<u>REGULAR (-**d** (Eng.) / -**t** (Ger.))</u>	
drink — drank	trinken — trank	*have — had*	haben — hatte
eat — ate	essen — aß	*dare — dared*	dürfen — durfte
forget — forgot	vergessen — vergaß	*make — made*	machen — machte
find — found	finden — fand	*love — loved*	lieben — liebte
come — came	kommen — kam	*say — said*	sagen — sagte
sleep — slept	schlafen — schlief	*hear — heard*	hören — hörte
see — saw	sehen — sah	*play — played*	spielen — spielte

§68
Present perfect

The **present perfect tense**, sometimes called the **conversational past**, is used in everyday (12) speaking about events in past time. <u>It does not describe a time different from that described by the past tense</u>. Both tenses can talk about the same time, illustrating that "tense" and "time" are not one and the same. When the telling involves a single event in past time, then the present perfect is usually the tense chosen for the job. When a chain of events is discussed, then the past tense is frequently used. The term "conversational past" says a good deal about the usage of this new tense: It is used in speaking — but is also very common in writing. Very often the small group of high-frequency words listed above — *sein*, *haben*, *wissen*, and the modals — are used in the past tense while the other verbs in a discussion appear in the present perfect.

§69
The **formation of the present perfect** requires the use of the <u>past participle</u> of a verb in (12) combination with either *haben* or *sein* as a helping verb. The past participle is the name (13) for the third principal part of a verb. If 'drink' and 'drank' are the first and second (15) principal parts of 'drink', then 'drunk' is the third. It is used in combination with a form (22) of the helping verb 'have', which is the only helping verb in modern English:

> They <u>have drunk</u> all the tea! What do we do now?

Past participles of **regular verbs** are formed by combining the present stem (the infinitive minus the *-n* or *-en* ending) with 1) the prefix *ge-* and 2) the suffix *-t*.

> holen: **ge + hol + t**

The principal parts of *holen* are thus

FIRST	SECOND	THIRD
holen	holte	geholt

The only additional information needed to use the verb *holen* in all its tense forms is the helping verb, which — as for virtually all regular verbs — is *haben*. Traditionally, the helping verb is learned in its third person singular form along with each verb's past participle:

> holen — holte — hat geholt

For both regular and irregular verbs, the past participle comes at the very end of the clause.

> Wir <u>haben</u> heute keine Bananen <u>gekauft</u>.
> Sie <u>hat</u> in der Stadtmitte nur Rockmusik <u>gehört</u>.

NOTE: The past participles of **separable verbs** include the *ge-* prefix between the prefix and the stem:

> Sie hat das Brot schon <u>eingepackt</u>.

The past participles of **inseparable verbs** do not add the *ge-* prefix:

> Müllers haben ihr Haus schon <u>verkauft</u>.

NOTE: The past participles of verbs ending in *-ieren* do not add the prefix *ge-*. All *-ieren* past participles end in *-t*.

> Sie hat <u>studiert</u>. Wir haben schon <u>telefoniert</u>.   Haben Sie es <u>reserviert</u>?

§70
Irregular verbs

Irregular verbs form their past participle by adding to the verb stem the *ge-* prefix and (12) the suffix *-en*. Usually the vowel of the verb stem is changed as well.

> singen: **ge + sung + en**

Most verbs use *haben* as a helping verb.

> Herr Fischer-Dieskau <u>hat</u> wunderschöne Lieder <u>gesungen</u>.
> Endlich <u>haben</u> sie oben auf dem Berg <u>gestanden</u>.

§71
There are a number of irregular verbs that use *sein* as a helping verb, just as an older (14) form of English once used the verb 'be':

> Lo! An angel <u>is</u> come . . . .

These verbs in German are intransitive — they do not take objects. They also show a change of location or condition. A change of location includes verbs such as *laufen*, *kommen*, *gehen*, *fahren*, and *steigen*. A change of condition includes not only *sterben* 'die' (some would say this implies a change of location!), but the common *einschlafen* 'go to sleep', *werden* 'become', and *aufwachen* 'wake up', which is a regular verb.

> Er ist früh am Abend eingeschlafen und erst spät am Morgen aufgewacht.

Two common verbs that do not fit this pattern, but that are used with sein, are *sein* itself and *bleiben*:

> Wir sind nur kurz im Westerwald gewesen.
> Wie lange sind Sie eigentlich in der Steiermark geblieben?

§72   The past participles of a few unusual verbs are noteworthy. They seem to be regular in having a *-t* suffix, yet their stems show a vowel change:

INFINITIVE		PAST PARTICIPLE
bringen	*bring*	hat gebracht
denken	*think*	hat gedacht
kennen	*know*	hat gekannt
nennen	*call*	hat genannt
senden	*send*	hat gesandt
wissen	*know*	hat gewußt

§73   It is impossible to tell from the infinitive form of a verb whether it is regular or irregular, a feature shared by English. (This is a dilemma that inspired the poet E. Scumas Rory to pen the verse at the end of this paragraph.) *Fragen* 'ask' and *sagen* 'say', for example, are both regular verbs, with the past participles *gefragt* and *gesagt*. But *tragen* 'carry' is irregular, with the past participle *getragen*. Should you have to guess what a verb's past participle might be, then use English as your guide. Remember: English and German are closely related, and the most common verbs tend to be old and therefore similar in both languages. Note the similarity between the first two verbs in the list above, *bringen* and *denken*, and their English counterparts, 'bring/brought', 'think/thought'.

> The peeping Tom designed to peep
> On Miss Godiva when she's sleep,
> Wherefore on hands and knees he crept
> And underneath her curtain pept.
>
> Behind him, though, a watchman crope,
> Pursuing peepers while she slope
> And pounced on Tom because he pope. (Thunks, 7)

§74
Past perfect   The **past perfect tense** is used to refer to events that took place before another past tense already referred to in a discussion. The past perfect can exist only with reference to this other tense, and cannot stand alone. The statement "She hadn't seen him for years" makes no sense unless we know that she was just visiting him or was looking for him. The statement "She hasn't seen him for years" does make sense, since it is firmly established in present time. Normally our frame of reference is

> present time — time before present time.

If we establish our frame of reference in the past instead of the present, then this scheme is shifted to become

> past time — time before past time.

The English past perfect tense refers to time before past time by using the past tense of the helping verb 'have', just as it was seen above to use the present tense of 'have' for the present perfect tense:

> PRESENT PERFECT: We *have met* the enemy, and he is ours.
> PAST PERFECT: We *had met* the enemy, and he was ours.

German operates the way English does, using the <u>past</u> tense forms of the helping verb *haben* and *sein*, as appropriate to the individual verb. This means that in the German past perfect tense, *war* and *hatte* are the helping verbs instead of *ist* and *hat*.

> Als ich ihn sah, <u>hatte</u> er das Geschenk schon <u>bekommen</u>.
> TIME: 1. *He received the present.*   2. *I saw him.*
> Als ich in Dübendorf ankam, <u>war</u> die Familie schon <u>abgefahren</u>.
> TIME: 1. *The family departed.*   2. *I arrived in Dübendorf.*

Because the past perfect tense has to exist within a past context, German sentences using the past perfect often contain the word *nachdem*, a subordinating conjunction meaning 'after' and establishing the time relationships:

> <u>Nachdem</u> er den Fisch <u>gekauft hatte</u>, fuhr er schnell nach Hause.
> Sie stieg in den Sportwagen, <u>nachdem</u> sie Max <u>geküßt hatte</u>.

§75
Double infinitive

When modal verbs are used in the present perfect tense, they appear in their infinitive form at the end of the clause in combination with the infinitive form of the verb that is used to complete their meaning. This construction is called a **double infinitive**. The same construction is used in the future tense. Note the differences in the four tenses:

PRESENT	Sie <u>will</u> nicht zum Zirkus <u>mitgehen</u>.
PAST	Sie <u>wollte</u> nicht zum Zirkus <u>mitgehen</u>.
PRESENT PERFECT	Sie <u>hat</u> nicht zum Zirkus <u>mitgehen wollen</u>.
FUTURE	Sie <u>wird</u> nicht zum Zirkus <u>mitgehen wollen</u>.

NOTE: *Sehen*, *hören*, and *lassen*, which can function as modals (See **Verbs §21**), use the double infinitive construction in the perfect.

> Endlich habe ich ihn <u>kommen sehen</u>.   *I finally saw him coming.*
> Hast du sie <u>singen hören</u>?   *Did you hear her sing/ing?*
> Er hat mich nach einer Stunde <u>gehen lassen</u>.   *He let me go after an hour.*

§76
Voice

The verbs discussed up to this point have all been in one of three **moods**: the indicative, the imperative, and the subjunctive. They have also occurred in a variety of **tenses** that described time relationships. Verbs also have **voices**, the active voice and the passive voice. Paragraphs §§1-75 have treated verbs in the <u>active voice</u>, in which the subject of each sentence was performing an action. In the <u>passive voice</u> the subject of a sentence is acted upon by someone or something else in the sentence. Note the difference:

(22)
(23)

> ACTIVE: *They took him to the station in a Volkswagen.*
> PASSIVE: *He was taken to the station in a Volkswagen.*

The first sentence is in the active voice: 'They' is the subject, and 'him' is the object of the verb <u>took</u>. The second sentence is in the passive voice: the subject does not act, but is acted upon.

§77
Passive voice

The **passive voice** combines a form of the verb *werden*, acting as a helping verb, with a past participle. In the English passive illustration in §76, 'was' is the helping verb and 'taken' is the past participle. In German the passive sentence would be

(22)
(23)
(24)
(25)

> Er <u>wurde</u> in einem Volkswagen zum Bahnhof <u>gebracht</u>.
> He <u>was (being) taken</u> to the station in a Volkswagen.

Wurde, of course, is a past tense form of the verb *werden*, and the sentence says that an action took place in the <u>past</u>. If the helping verb were *wird*, in the present tense, the action would be taking place in the <u>present</u>:

> Er <u>wird</u> in einem Volkswagen zum Bahnhof <u>gebracht</u>.
> He<u>'s being taken</u> to the station in a Volkswagen.

In this sentence the true actors are missing: we do not know who is taking him to the station. If the agents were to be added to the sentence, they would be in a dative phrase with the preposition *von*:

> Er wird <u>von drei Männern</u> in Schwarz zum Bahnhof gebracht.
> He's being taken to the station <u>by three men</u> in black.

§78 Other passive tenses are encountered less frequently in spoken German. They are the
<u>present perfect</u>, the <u>past perfect</u>, and the <u>future</u>.

In the **present perfect** the verb *werden* still functions as a sign of the passive, but must
have the helping verb *sein. Werden* appears in the form *worden* after the past participle:

> Er <u>ist</u> schon zum Bahnhof <u>gebracht worden</u>.
> > He<u>'s</u> already <u>been taken</u> to the station.

In the **past perfect** the helping verb changes from the present to the past tense, according
to the principle established in §74:

> Er <u>war</u> schon zum Bahnhof <u>gebracht worden</u>, als ich ihn sah.
> > He <u>had</u> already <u>been brought</u> to the station when I saw him.

The **future** tense of the passive voice causes casual observers to throw up their hands in
dismay because the sign of the future tense and the sign of the passive voice are one and
the same verb, *werden*. Bear in mind, however, that the future is simply a form of *werden*
plus an infinitive at the end of the clause.

> ↓ future sign   ↓ passive sign
> Er <u>wird</u> zum Bahnhof gebracht <u>werden</u>.

Here the infinitive in the sentence is not an <u>active infinitive</u>, *bringen* 'bring', but rather a
<u>passive infinitive</u>, *gebracht werden* 'be brought'.

§79 When the passive voice is used with **modals**, the construction is parallel to that of the   **(25)**
future passive (§78). The modal verb is used in combination with a passive infinitive,
and the construction parallels exactly that in English. As in all modal constructions, the
infinitive comes at the end of the sentence:

> ↓ modal   ↓past part. ↓passive sign
> Das <u>kann</u> schnell <u>gemacht</u> <u>werden</u>.

> ↓ passive sign
> That <u>can</u> <u>be</u> <u>done</u> quickly.
> ↑modal   ↑past part.

§80 English speakers tend to avoid heavy use of the passive voice, and German speakers
often seek substitutes for the passive as well. One mechanism for replacing the passive
voice, of course, is a switch to the active. Where no agent is present in the passive
version (as in many of the sentences in §78), **man** is added to provide an active subject.
Remember that *man* does not specify an individual, but simply 'they, someone'.

> PASSIVE: Er <u>wurde</u> zum Bahnhof <u>gebracht</u>.
> ACTIVE: <u>Man brachte</u> ihn zum Bahnhof.

A different substitute for the passive is the use of an infinitive phrase, the combination of
zu and an infinitive:

> PASSIVE: Er wird nur schwer verstanden.
> > He can be understood only with difficulty.
> ACTIVE: Er ist schwer zu verstehen.
> > He's hard to understand.

§81 After an action has been performed, it can be described as a completed action. A door   **(22)**
that <u>has been closed</u> (passive construction) is a <u>closed</u> door (adjectival description). A
piece of cheese that <u>has been melted</u> (passive construction) is properly described as
<u>melted</u> cheese (adjectival description). On the one hand we have a true passive voice,
and on the other we have what is often called the **false passive**, or **statal passive**. The
<u>false passive</u> is really just the use of an adjective, which may come before or after a noun:

> That door is now <u>closed</u>.
> We discuss those things behind <u>closed</u> doors.

Grammatically, all participles are adjectives, and here they can be seen clearly in that function. Because they are adjectives, they must agree with the nouns they precede:

Das ist eine geschlossene Tür.

Note the different ways of describing the same object:

PASSIVE:	Die Tür ist geschlossen worden.
PASSIVE SUBSTITUTE:	Man hat die Tür geschlossen.
FALSE PASSIVE:	Die Tür ist geschlossen.
ADJECTIVE:	Das ist eine geschlossene Tür.

Note also the fundamental difference between a door that is just swinging shut at the moment

Die Tür wird geschlossen

and one that is already closed:

Die Tür ist geschlossen.

Confusion can arise from the English equivalent, since the English verb 'be' is both a sign of the passive and a simple descriptor:

The door is closed every day at four. (It swings shut then.)
The door is closed every day at four. (When we come at four, it is shut tight.)

PREPOSITIONS

§1   Prepositions are words that provide information about how something or someone —   (7) the **object** of the preposition — is related to the fundamental action of a statement or question. The groups of words in which prepositions appear — the **prepositional phrases** — tell <u>how</u>, <u>where</u>, <u>when</u>, <u>in what direction</u>, or even <u>why</u> something happens.

> *He went shopping <u>with his brother</u>.*   (how)
> *They bought clothes <u>at Clyde's</u>.*   (where)
> *That was <u>in the afternoon</u>.*   (when)
> *Then they went <u>into the city</u>.*   (in what direction)
> *They walked <u>because of the weather</u>.*   (why)

§2   Prepositions always have **objects**, words that follow them. That object is always either a   (7) noun or a pronoun. Other words, most often adjectives, may provide more information about the object.

PREPOSITION	OBJECT OF PREPOSITION
with	*(his) brother*
at	*Clyde's*
in	*(the) afternoon*
into	*(the) city*
because of	*(the) weather*

§3   Prepositions cause their objects to appear in specific grammatical **cases**. (For an   (7) explanation of cases, see **Adjectives §§3-7**.) Some prepositions are always followed by the **dative** case, some are always used with the **accusative** case, and some can govern either of the two cases depending on the nature of the action in the sentence. In these instances, the use of the dative or the accusative has nothing to do with the other function of these cases as indirect or direct object cases. The object of a preposition is never an indirect object or a direct object.

§4   Common prepositions <u>always</u> used with the <u>dative</u> case are   (7)

Dative   **aus**   **bei**   **mit**   **nach**   **seit**   **von**   **zu.**

They govern the dative case whether their meaning is literal or figurative:

> . . . aus dem Haus   *out of the house*
> . . . aus dem Jahre 1907   *dating from the year 1907*
> . . . aus den Vereinigten Staaten   *from the U.S.A.*

§5   As the examples above show, *aus* has a broad range of meaning within the framework of   (3) 'out of'. Perhaps the most common use is in combination with the name of a city or   (7) country, indicating "point of origin". If someone is *aus Berlin*, then that person is taken to   (10) be a native of Berlin.

The point of origin can also be <u>in time</u>, mainly in discussing historical origins:

> Der Dom stammt <u>aus dem 14. Jahrhundert</u>.   *dates from the 14th century*
> Diese Kirche ist <u>aus dem Jahre 1766</u>.

Aus can also indicate a source, or original material.

> Hatte George Washington wirklich Zähne aus Holz?
>   *Did George Washington really have wooden teeth?*

§6   *Bei* often indicates spatial proximity — nearness, or presence.   (10)   (21)

A town can be located <u>near</u> another (usually larger) one:

> Beutelsbach <u>bei</u> Stuttgart.

If someone lives <u>next to</u> (or <u>by</u>) a church, then

> Er wohnt <u>bei</u> der Kirche.

When I am <u>at</u> the barber shop, then
> Ich bin <u>bei</u>m (=bei dem) Friseur.

If I live <u>with</u> my parents in their house, then
> Ich wohne <u>bei</u> meinen Eltern.

If I have no money <u>with</u> (or <u>on</u>) me, then
> Ich habe kein Geld <u>bei</u> mir.

Bei can also indicate <u>occasion</u>, <u>circumstance</u>, or <u>condition</u>, as in

<u>bei diesem Wetter</u>	*in this weather*	<u>bei 40 Grad Kälte</u>	*at -40°*
<u>Berlin bei Nacht</u>	*Berlin at night*	<u>beim Fußballspiel</u>	*at the soccer game*

Bei often appears with a verbal noun to show simultaneous action:
> <u>Beim Singen</u> macht er oft die Augen zu.
>> *While/When he sings, he often closes his eyes.*

Verbal idiom: *helfen bei* 'help with':
> <u>Hilf</u> ihr <u>bei</u> der Arbeit.   *Help her with her work.*

§7 *Mit* implies <u>accompaniment</u> or <u>instrument</u>.   **(7)**
> Bitte, kommen Sie <u>mit</u> mir nach Hause.   **(9)**
> Das ist der Mann <u>mit</u> dem roten Bart.
> Schlagen wir es <u>mit</u> einem Hammer.

§8 *Nach* means 'to, toward' when used with the names of cities or countries: **(3)**
> Annegret fährt morgen <u>nach</u> Hannover.   **(7)**
> Wann kommen Sie denn <u>nach</u> Amerika?

It also means 'after' in either a spatial sense:
> Das Mädchen springt <u>nach</u> dem Fußball. (where to?)

or a temporal sense:
> <u>Nach</u> dem Konzert gehen wir essen.   (when?)
> Es ist schon 10 Minuten <u>nach</u> zwei.

Nach is also part of the common idioms:

<u>nach</u> Hause	*(in the direction of) home*
Meiner Meinung <u>nach</u>	*in my opinion*
fragen <u>nach</u>	*inquire/ask about/after*
Er fragte <u>nach</u> ihrer Mutter.	*He asked about her mother.*

§9 *Seit* has exclusively temporal meaning — 'since'.
> <u>Seit</u> dem Krieg wohnt sie allein.

In this sense it figures prominently in combination with present tense verbs to indicate activity that began in the past and is still continuing (See **Verbs §11**):
> Wir studieren schon <u>seit</u> sieben Jahren.
>> *We've been studying <u>for</u> seven years now.*

§10 *Von* implies <u>separation</u> of something from something else.   **(7)**
> Wir fliegen <u>von</u> Amsterdam nach Vancouver.   **(9)**
> Das ist ein Brief <u>von</u> meiner Schwester.

Von also is used with nouns and pronouns as a substitute for the genitive (possessive) case ('of'):
> Ist das nicht die Mutter <u>von</u> Ihrem Mann?
> Das war ein Teil <u>von</u> der Altstadt.
> Die Bedeutung <u>von</u> diesem Artikel verstehe ich einfach nicht.
> Er ist ein guter Freund <u>von</u> mir.

NOTE: You can avoid misunderstandings in the use of the words *Freund* and *Freundin* (either 'male/female friend' or 'boy/girlfriend') by contrasting

> Das ist mein Freund / meine Freundin   *That's my boyfriend / girlfriend*

with

> Das ist ein Freund / eine Freundin von mir . . . *a friend of mine*

Von contracts with *dem* to produce **vom**.

> Hedwig kommt gerade <u>vom</u> Büro.

§11 *Zu* shows <u>direction toward</u> someone or something that is not a city or country: (7)

> Komm <u>zu</u> mir, Hänschen!   (9)
> Gehen wir <u>zur</u> Post.
> Ich möchte <u>zum</u> Zirkus.

Zu is frequently used to mean 'to the house of':

> Kommen Sie um acht Uhr <u>zu</u> mir, heute Abend gibt's eine kleine Fete.

Zu contracts with following *dem* and *der* to produce *zum* and *zur*.

> Gehen wir <u>zum</u> Rathaus, ja?   Nein, ich gehe lieber <u>zur</u> Paulskirche.

Note the following special uses of *zu*:

> Was möchtest du <u>zum Frühstück</u>?   *for breakfast*
> Den möchte ich gern <u>zum Freund</u> haben.   *as a friend*
> Mit der Zeit <u>wurde</u> sie <u>zu einer guten Schriftstellerin</u>.   *became a good writer*
> Egon <u>gehört zu den besten Pianisten</u>.   *is one of the best pianists*

§12 The prepositions *bei*, *von*, and *zu* appear with definite articles in the following   (7)
contractions: (9)

bei	+ dem	⇒ **beim**		
von	+ dem	⇒ **vom**		
zu	+ dem	⇒ **zum**	zu + der	⇒ **zur**

The contraction is normally made unless the definite article is emphasized for a good reason:

> Bei <u>dem</u> Wetter gehe ich nicht.   *I'm not going in <u>this</u> weather.*

§13 Another group of prepositions is used only with the **accusative** case: (8)

Accusative   **bis**   **durch**   **für**   **gegen**   **ohne**   **um**

§14 *Bis* 'until, up to' occurs in many time expressions without a following article:

> bis Dienstag   bis nächste Woche   bis 1990

When a following article is present, *bis* is most often supplemented with *zu* in the expressions *bis zum* . . . and *bis zur* . . . :

> <u>Bis zum</u> Krieg wohnten wir in Danzig.
> Die Straßenbahn Linie 12 fährt <u>bis zur</u> Kasernenstraße.

§15 *Durch* closely parallels the English word 'through' in both literal and figurative senses: (8)

> Fahren Sie ganz <u>durch</u> die Stadt, und fragen Sie noch einmal dort.
> <u>Durch</u> die Zimmervermittlung finden wir immer gute Hotelzimmer.

§16 *Für* is most often the equivalent of English 'for'.   (8)

> Hier ist ein Geschenk <u>für</u> dich.   —<u>Für</u> mich? Ach, wie schön.

Be careful in time expressions, however, where English 'for' is usually <u>not</u> the equivalent of *für*:

> Wir waren <u>drei Wochen</u> in Wien.
> *We were in Vienna <u>for three weeks</u>.*

> Er studierte <u>ein ganzes Jahr</u> in Bonn.
> *He studied in Bonn <u>for a whole year</u>.*

When used with time expressions, *für* has the meaning 'with the intention of staying for ___'.

> Sie fliegen <u>für ein Semester</u> nach München.
> *They're flying to München, where they'll be staying for a term.*

> Wir sind <u>für 14 Monate</u> nach Chur gezogen.
> *We moved to Chur, where we spent 14 months.*

§17 *Gegen* means 'against' in both physical and nonphysical senses:

> Das Auto ist <u>gegen</u> den Baum gefahren und ist jetzt wertlos.
> Nein, ich bin <u>gegen</u> Ihren Plan. Tut mir leid.

§18 *Ohne* is the equivalent of English 'without'.   (8)

> Ich, glaube, wir machen es <u>ohne</u> Ihre Hilfe.
> Gehen Sie wirklich <u>ohne</u> uns? Ach, schade.

§19 *Um* means 'around, about' in a physical sense:

> Die Kinder laufen <u>um</u> das Haus und suchen Ostereier.
> *. . . around the house* (either inside or outside)

When used with clock time, *um* means 'at':

> Wir treffen uns <u>um</u> drei Uhr vor dem Glockenturm.
> Ihr Zug fährt <u>um</u> 17 Uhr 40.
> <u>Um</u> Viertel vor acht sehe ich Sie im Cafe Wollmer.

Note the use of *um* in the verbal idiom *bitten um* 'ask for'.

> Peter hat seine Mutter <u>um</u> hundert Schilling gebeten.
> *Peter asked his mother for 100 ÖS.*

§20
Dat. — Acc.
A special group of prepositions is used with either the dative or the accusative, (7)
depending on the action expressed in the sentence: (15)

an	**auf**	**hinter**	**in**	**neben**
über	**unter**	**vor**	**zwischen**	

When the prepositional phrase answers the question *Wo?* 'Where?', these prepositions are used with the <u>dative</u> case. If the prepositional phrase answers the question *Wohin?* 'Where to?', then they are used with the <u>accusative</u>.

wo = dative   **wohin = accusative**

The crucial distinction between accusative and dative is not one of motion versus no motion, but of motion <u>toward</u> something (<u>accusative</u>) versus either location or motion <u>within</u> something (<u>dative</u>). It is possible for lots of movement to be taking place within a confined area — a child chasing a cat around in a room, for example. Because this is within a confined area, the preposition *in* would be used with the dative.

§21 *An* expresses physical location on or movement onto a **vertical** surface. It contracts with (7)
dem to yield *am*:

> In der Mensa hängen die Annoncen immer <u>am</u> Schwarzen Brett.   **dat.**
> Wollen wir den Zettel <u>an das</u> Schwarze Brett hängen?   **acc.**

An is also used to indicate location next to or movement toward something, usually a vertical surface:

> Wer steht <u>an</u> mein<u>er</u> Tür?   **dat.**   . . . <u>at</u> my door
> Gehen Sie bitte <u>an das</u> Fenster.   **acc.**   . . . <u>to</u> the window

But note this exception, decidedly a horizontal surface:

> Wir fahren morgen <u>ans</u> Meer.   **acc.**   . . . <u>to</u> the ocean

An is an important part of verbal idioms. Note case usage:

> teilnehmen <u>an</u>   **dat.**   *take part <u>in</u>*   denken <u>an</u>   **acc.**   *think <u>of</u>*
> arbeiten <u>an</u>   **dat.**   *work <u>on</u>, <u>at</u>*   glauben <u>an</u>   **acc.**   *believe <u>in</u>*

Am introduces dates and days, telling when things are happening:

> Erich kommt <u>am</u> 22. Juli wieder nach Hause.
> Ach, schön, das ist <u>am</u> Dienstag, nicht?

§22 *Auf* expresses physical location on or movement onto a **horizontal** surface.   **(7)**

> Ich glaube, ich schlafe heute Nachmittag <u>auf dem</u> Sofa.   **dat.**   **(15)**
> Bitte, legen Sie Ihre Sachen einfach <u>auf den</u> Stuhl.   **acc.**

Auf is also often used to indicate location at or motion toward a place, usually a building in a town.

> Mein Vater arbeitet immer noch <u>auf der</u> Post.   **dat.**
> Brigitte muß schnell auf <u>die Post</u>.   **acc.**

Note the use of *auf* (acc.) in *warten auf*:

> Wartet <u>auf</u> mich!   *Wait <u>for</u> me!*

§23 *Hinter* indicates location or movement **behind** something: **(15)**

> Die Arbeiter bauen etwas <u>hinter dem</u> Bahnhof.   **dat.**
> Gehen Sie <u>hinter den</u> Bahnhof. Da finden Sie den Kiosk.   **acc.**

§24 *In* shows location **within** or movement **into** something: **(7)**

> Arbeiten Sie gern <u>in der</u> Stadt?   **dat.**   **(15)**
> Ich muß schnell <u>in die</u> Stadt fahren.   **acc.**

NOTE: As a separable verb prefix, *in* assumes the form *ein*:

> <u>ein'treten</u>   *step in, enter*

§25 *Neben* expresses location or movement **next to** something: **(15)**

> Mein Büro steht <u>neben der</u> neuen Aula der Universität.   **dat.**
> Ach, stellen Sie die Lampe bitte <u>neben die</u> Couch.   **acc.**

§26 *Über* indicates location or movement **over** something: **(15)**

> Der weiße Mond hängt <u>über dem</u> Garten.   **dat.**
> Der flinke braune Fuchs springt <u>über den</u> faulen Hund.   **acc.**

When the meaning is 'about', *über* is always used with the accusative:

> Das ist eine Geschichte <u>über</u> eine schöne Prinzessin.

§27 *Unter* shows location or movement **under** something: **(15)**

> Die Maus hat <u>unter dem</u> Schreibtisch geschlafen.   **dat.**
> Die Katze ist <u>unter den</u> Schreibtisch gesprungen.   **acc.**

§28 *Vor* expresses location or movement **in front of** something: **(7)**

> Zwei große Polizisten stehen <u>vor der</u> Tür.   **dat.**   **(15)**
> Der Schauspieler tritt <u>vor das</u> Publikum.   **acc.**   **(16)**

Vor is also used in time phrases to mean 'ago'. It <u>precedes</u> its object:

> **V<u>or</u>** 5 Minuten / 2 Wochen / ein<u>em</u> Tag / ein<u>er</u> Stunde **war er hier.**
> *He was here 5 minutes / 2 weeks / a day / an hour / **ago**.*

Note the important verbal idioms dealing with fear: *angst haben vor* and *sich fürchten vor* (dat.).

> Wer <u>hat angst vor</u> dem großen bösen Wolf?
>> *Who's afraid of the big bad wolf?*

> Rotkäppchen <u>fürchtet sich</u> nicht <u>vor</u> ihm.
>> *Little Red Riding Hood's not afraid of him.*

§29   *Zwischen* shows location or movement **between** two things: (15)

> Der Junge schläft gern <u>zwischen seinen</u> Eltern.   **dat.**
> Der Hund lief <u>zwischen meine</u> Beine und aus dem Haus.   **acc.**

§30   **IMPORTANT**: Remember that the **location/movement toward** distinction between   (15) dative and accusative applies **only** to the group of prepositions discussed in §§20-29. Do not apply this rule to the prepositions that take only the dative or only the accusative. Many beginning students believe, for example, that the prepositional phrase in "All our canaries flew <u>out the window</u>" should use the accusative case because of the obvious motion implied. But no matter how much motion is involved, *aus* still takes the dative case: *<u>aus dem</u> Fenster*.

WORD ORDER

§1 Human language is <u>sequential</u>. Sounds (or their written versions) precede and follow (1) each other. All languages have principles of word order. Such principles describe how speech elements can be combined. Some principles of word order tell what must be done, others what can but need not be done, and still others what is downright impossible in a language.

Many speakers of a language do not have a conscious, analytic knowledge of its principles of word order, but all normal human beings acquire a detailed working knowledge of the structural patterns of their native language. Typically we absorb notions of word order unconsciously, by trial, error, and example, before we learn conscious rules. Certain patterns just "sound right".

Learners of foreign languages acquire their knowledge in many different ways, in accord with their personalities and with the method of instruction or exposure. Students with informal exposure to a language, perhaps through family background or travel abroad, may approach word order "by ear". Some language classes emphasize that attitude. Other students may prefer to work with carefully formulated "textbook" rules of word order.

Both approaches have their benefits, and we hope that in your study of German the notion of what "feels right" will go hand in hand with a clear knowledge of what "is right". The important thing to remember is that principles of word order are not abstract, pointless formulas to be memorized and parroted back, but rather descriptions of how genuine human speech works. Thus it is important that you consider not only what the language looks like on the printed page, but also what it sounds like when it is spoken and heard. <u>Rhythm, pitch, intonation, and pace are all vital factors in the understanding of word order</u>. When you study, be sure to pay attention to SOUND as well as sight.

§2 The basic principle of <u>English</u> word order is that in statements (or "declarative (1) sentences") <u>the subject immediately precedes the verb</u> (<u>and objects follow the verb</u>).

SUBJECT	VERB	OBJECT
The <u>dog</u>	<u>bit</u>	the <u>man</u>.
<u>They</u>	<u>threw</u>	a <u>party</u> for the emperor.
His <u>son</u>	<u>loved</u>	a famous <u>economist</u>.

From these sentences it would be impossible to understand that the man was doing the biting, or to be sure that the famous economist returned the son's love. In the second sentence, the form <u>they</u> confirms for speakers of English that the <u>party</u> cannot be the subject of the sentence.

Sometimes the subject is the second element of an English sentence:

Generally <u>it</u> rains on our picnic.
With a heavy heart, <u>I</u>'ve decided to resign.

Note that **subject — verb — object** is a <u>basic principle</u> of English word order, and only that. There are sentences with object — subject — verb order, such as "<u>Him</u> I like, but <u>her</u> I don't", but it is hard to imagine an English sentence with object — verb — subject order: "The <u>ball</u> kicked <u>she</u> in front of the bus". In English, it is the **sequence** of forms that gives meaning to a sentence. If that were not true, then "The dog bit the man" could be understood in two ways.

§3 The most important feature of declarative sentences in German is that **the verb comes** (1)
second.   (6)
                                                                                           (10)

FIRST	SECOND	REST OF STATEMENT
Ich	habe	keine Pommes frites.
Heute	fahren	wir nach Freiburg.
Mein Gepäck	ist	das nicht.
Morgen um 14 Uhr 52	sind	wir in Köln.

In German the subject often precedes the verb, but that is not by any means a hard and
fast rule. The first element may be the subject, or it may be an object of some kind, or
even a long phrase telling when, where, or how the action of the sentence will take place.
In the last example above, the verb is the sixth <u>word</u> in the sentence, but it is the <u>second</u>
element. The first five words are a long adverb phrase telling 'when'.

Placement in first position lends emphasis to a word or phrase that would not
command such attention if it were placed in the middle or at the end of a sentence. <u>If this</u>
<u>first element is not the subject of the sentence, then the subject must follow the verb</u>
<u>immediately</u>.

§4 Word order in German **questions** is very similar to that in English ones. In each (1)
Questions language, a form of the verb must come first in a question — unless there is an
introductory question word, or <u>interrogative</u>, present.

(INTERROGATIVE)	VERB	SUBJECT	REST OF SENTENCE
	Fahren	Sie	heute nach Stuttgart?
	Are	you	traveling to Stuttgart today?
Warum	fahren	Sie	heute nach Stuttgart?
Why	are	you	traveling to Stuttgart today?

§5 In German, as in English, it is often true that "the tone makes the music". That is, it is
possible to say a sentence with normal declarative word order (See **Word Order §2**), but
with intonation that says "This is a question" to the listener. Listen carefully to the
intonation patterns in the sentences

She <u>likes</u> him. (He's nice.)She likes <u>him</u>? (Yuk!)
<u>She</u> likes <u>him</u>? (What a mismatch!)

Das ist mein Gepäck. (Yep, that's mine, all right.)
<u>Das</u> ist <u>mein</u> Gepäck? (Yeek! It didn't look like that before!)

§6 There can be more than one verb in a German sentence, but in each independent clause (5)
— in each clause that can stand alone in the sentence — only one of those verbs is the (7)
<u>finite</u> verb, one that agrees in number with the subject. In the case of the **modal** verbs, (10)
those that are used with a following infinitive, the modal itself comes in second position,
thus obeying this firm word order rule (See **Verbs §21**).

↓ modal   ↓ infinitive
Ich <u>kann</u> ihn nicht so gut <u>verstehen</u>.
2   **end**

The finite verb in second position may be an auxiliary (*sein* or *haben*); see **Verbs §69**.

§7 **Conjunctions** are used to tie — or <u>conjoin</u> — two sentence elements. (2)
Conjunctions Möchten Sie Bier **oder** Apfelsaft? (4)
Ich nehme ein Zimmer mit Dusche **und** eins ohne Dusche.

Sometimes the second element is an entire sentence, and the result is a <u>compound</u>
<u>sentence</u>:

Wir fahren am Dienstag.		Sie fahren am Donnerstag.
Wir fahren am Dienstag	**und**	sie fahren am Donnerstag.

The word order of the second sentence is unchanged if one of the following common **coordinating** conjunctions is used:

und	*and*	**denn**	*because*
aber	*but*	**sondern**	*but (rather)*
oder	*or*		

§8 The coordinating conjunction *sondern* deserves special mention. Like *aber*, it has the (17) English equivalent 'but', and it does appear when two sentence elements are being compared. However, *sondern* is used when the two elements are mutually exclusive.

> Ich finde ihn ganz nett, <u>aber</u> er ist doch sehr krank, nicht wahr?
> Gut, ich komme mit, <u>aber</u> es wird schon spät.

In these examples, it is certainly possible for someone to be sick and nice at the same time; it is also possible for someone to come along even if it is getting late. In neither of these cases are the possibilities <u>mutually exclusive</u>. The use of *sondern* rejects any compatibility between two choices, and is therefore often reinforced by *nicht* or *kein*:

> Nein, sie liebt nicht Helmut, <u>sondern</u> Jürgen.
> Im deutschen Süden ist das Klima nicht hart, <u>sondern</u> mild.
> Es ist nicht wichtig, was man sagt, <u>sondern</u> was man macht.

§9 There is a group of conjunctions that change the word order of the clauses in which they (12)
Subordinating appear. Unlike the coordinating conjunctions (§§6-7), the **subordinating conjunctions** (14) place the main verb at the very end of the clause. A common example of these (21) conjunctions is *wenn* 'if, whenever'.

> **2**
> Ich bleibe noch eine Weile, <u>wenn</u> Sie schnell <u>kommen</u>.

Note that *kommen*, the verb that matches the subject (the finite verb), appears at the end of the clause. The use of the subordinating conjunctions might seem to violate that supreme principle of German word order explained in §3, but it does not. The <u>main</u> verb in this sentence is *bleibe*. It appears in the main clause, which can stand alone as an independent unit:

> Ich bleibe noch eine Weile.

The *wenn* clause, on the other hand, cannot stand alone. For good reason, it is called a <u>dependent</u> (or <u>subordinate</u>) <u>clause</u> because it needs another clause, an <u>independent</u> (or <u>main</u>) <u>clause</u>, for support.

The *wenn* function can be managed <u>without</u> *wenn*:

> Hast du Geld? Ja? Dann gehen wir einkaufen.

but *wenn* expresses conditions more clearly and efficiently:

> Wir gehen einkaufen, <u>wenn</u> du Geld hast.

§10 Another high-frequency subordinating conjunction is *daß* 'that'. Again, *daß* cannot stand (12) alone. The clause

> *that she's staying all day*

requires introduction by 'She said', 'I hear', or another similar phrase.

> Sie **bleibt** den ganzen Tag.
> Wir wissen, <u>daß</u> sie den ganzen Tag **bleibt**.

The *daß* function can be managed <u>without</u> *daß*:

> Vater kommt am Mittwoch wieder. Wir wissen das.

but *daß* relates one action to another more clearly and efficiently:

> Wir wissen, <u>daß</u> Vater am Mittwoch wieder kommt.

§11   The subordinating conjunction *als* 'when' is used to relate two events in past time. It,   (14)
      too, places the finite verb at the very end of its clause.

      Es regnete immer, <u>als</u> wir im Nordwesten <u>lebten</u>.

      Note that there are two subordinating conjunctions with the apparent meaning 'when'.
      However, there is a fundamental difference between *wenn* and *als*. *Wenn* is used in the
      sense of 'whenever' — that is, in describing a repeated action in past, present, or future.
      Als, on the other hand, occurs only in sentences dealing with <u>past time</u>, and specifically a
      <u>single event</u> in past time. If the context of the above sentence were such that the speaker
      lived in the Northwest on several different occasions, then <u>als</u> would be incorrect; <u>wenn</u>
      would be the proper word, indicating repeated action in past time.

      The *als* function can be managed <u>without</u> *als*:

      Wir waren 2 Jahre in der Schweiz. Das Wetter war immer schön.

      but *als* better expresses that two things happen at the same time:

      Das Wetter war immer schön, <u>als</u> wir in der Schweiz waren.

§12   Another subordinating conjunction, *ob*, is frequently confused with *wenn*, and again   (16)
      English is the source of the confusion — for 'if' is the meaning most commonly assigned
      to both. Whereas *wenn* means 'if' in hypothetical situations, however, — 'If I only had
      some worms, I'd go fishing'. — *ob* means 'if' in the sense of 'whether', a word used much
      less frequently today than 'if'. The simple test is thus: in cases where 'whether' can be
      substituted for 'if', use *ob*. *Ob* is often used in subordinate clauses following main clauses
      containing the verb *wissen*.

      Daniela? Moment, bitte — ich weiß nicht, <u>ob</u> sie zu Hause ist.
      Wissen Sie, <u>ob</u> es heute regnen soll?

      The *ob* function can be managed <u>without</u> *ob*:

      Arbeite ich heute abend? Ich weiß nicht.

      but *ob* eliminates the need to formulate artificial questions:

      Ich weiß nicht, <u>ob</u> ich heute abend arbeite.

§13   There are many other subordinating conjunctions, but the ones given in the above   (13)
      paragraphs are the most important. Some others: (14)
                                                                                          (21)

      | **obwohl** | *although* | **weil** | *because* |
      | **nachdem** | *after* (See **Verbs §74**) | **bevor** | *before* |
      | **seitdem** | *since* (involving time) | **damit** | *so that* |
      | **bis** | *until* | **während** | *while* |

§14   A number of the conjunctions above have English equivalents that are identical in form
      to the corresponding English prepositions. Be sure to make the distinction between the
      two parts of speech. **Prepositions** take a noun or pronoun object, and **conjunctions**
      introduce an entire clause.

      | PREPOSITION: | Nach dem Krieg . . . | *after the war* |
      | CONJUNCTION: | Nachdem der Krieg vorbei war, | *after the war was over,* |
      | PREPOSITION: | Seit dem Jahre 1949 | *since the year 1949* |
      | CONJUNCTION: | Seitdem wir hier wohnen . . . | *since we've been living here* |
      | PREPOSITION: | Bis nächste Woche | *until next week* |
      | CONJUNCTION: | Bis du wiederkommst, . . . | *until you come back again* |
      | PREPOSITION: | Vor dem Konzert | *before the concert* |
      | CONJUNCTION: | Bevor wir ins Konzert gehen, . . . | *before we go to the concert* |

§15 **Interrogative words** can also function as subordinating conjunctions. That is, they can **(18)** introduce clauses that give more information about something in the main clause; and they can place the verb at the end of the subordinate clause.

> Weißt du, <u>wann</u> er von den Wanderferien <u>zurückkommt</u>?
> Können Sie mir bitte sagen, <u>wieviel</u> das alles <u>kostet</u>?
> Wissen Sie, <u>wo</u> ich die Meierstraße finden <u>kann</u>?

§16 When the compound tenses — that is, those tenses that consist of more than one verbal **(13)** element — are used in subordinate clauses, it is the <u>finite verb</u> that is placed at the <u>very end</u> of the clause. This takes precedence over the rule that places past participles and dependent infinitives at the very end.

>   ↓ auxiliary   ↓ verb   verb   auxiliary
> Wann <u>hast</u> du sie eigentlich das letzte Mal <u>gesehen</u>?   ↓   ↓
>   —Ich weiß nur, <u>daß</u> ich sie seit Jahren nicht mehr <u>gesehen</u> <u>habe</u>.

>   ↓ auxiliary   ↓ verb
> <u>Kann</u> er das wirklich <u>tun</u>?   verb ↓   ↓ auxiliary
>   — Ich weiß nicht, <u>ob</u> er das wirklich <u>tun</u> <u>kann</u>.   Mal sehen!

§17 Subordinate clauses occur not only as a second element of a longer sentence, as in the **(14)** examples above, but can be in first position as well. When they do appear in first position, remember that <u>the finite verb in the main clause must be in second position</u>.

>   1   2
> <u>Als wir in der Schweiz waren</u>, <u>war</u> das Wetter immer schön.
>   ↑ finite verb

>   1   2
> <u>Wenn Sie schnell kommen</u>, <u>bleibe</u> ich noch eine Weile.
>   ↑ finite verb

>   1   1   1
> <u>Als ich mit meinen Freunden nach Hause kam und sah, daß mein kleiner Sohn</u>
>   1   1   2
> <u>mit seinem Hamster in der Ecke hinter dem Buchregal schlief</u>, <u>war</u> ich böse.
>   ↑ finite verb

§18 When **two nouns** occur together, the one that is <u>definite</u> comes first. **(12)**

>   1   2
> Zu Weihnachten gebe ich <u>meinem Bruder</u> <u>einen Pullover</u>.
>   ↑ definite ↓   ↑ indefinite ↓
> Zu weihnachten gebe ich <u>meinen Pullover</u> <u>einem Freund</u>.

§19 When **a noun and a pronoun** occur together, it is the pronoun that has word order **(12)** priority and comes closer to the verb. When there are two pronouns, it is the <u>accusative</u> pronoun that comes first.

>   1   2
> Was mache ich mit dem Pullover? Ich gebe <u>ihn</u> <u>meinem Bruder</u>.
>   pronoun ↑   ↑ noun

> Bitte, bringen Sie <u>es</u> <u>mir</u> später.
>   direct object ↑ ↑ indirect object

§20 **Word order of *nicht*.** *Nicht* generally follows both noun and pronoun objects, and **(6)**
adverbs of time. When it negates a whole clause, it comes at the end of the clause. **(18)**

↓ object
Nein, er hat <u>es</u> <u>meinem Vater</u> <u>nicht</u> gesagt.
↑ object

Es ist heute <u>nicht</u> so schön.
↑ adverb of time

Wir sehen ihn heute abend <u>nicht</u>.

Nicht precedes other sentence elements, including predicate nouns, adjectives, adverbs,
and verb complements.

noun:	Das ist <u>nicht</u> mein Gepäck.
adjective:	Es wird heute <u>nicht</u> so regerisch.
adverb:	Fahr <u>nicht</u> so schnell.
verb complement:	Wir haben <u>nicht</u> Fußball gespielt.

Nicht also negates what it immediately precedes. (See **Word Order §8**)

Ich kaufe heute <u>nicht</u> Käse, sondern Joghurt.

Nicht may also appear at the very end of a sentence in order to invite confirmation of
something that has been said. It has a wide variety of English equivalents, all of which
are simply *nicht (wahr)?* in German.

Hm. Sie sind Kanadierin, nicht wahr?	*. . .aren't you?*
Er kommt aus Wien, nicht?	*. . .isn't he?*
Sie wohnen alle in Madrid, nicht?	*. . .don't they?*

Reference Grammar
CHECKLIST OF COMMON ERRORS

- **confusion of sounds or spelling; capitalization**

  ~~Ik~~ ich ~~siet~~ Zeit ~~Amerikanish~~ amerikanisch ~~vas~~ was ~~nür~~ nur

- **wrong vocabulary choice**

  1. A word may have several distinct equivalents in another language.

     right: [thing is] correct = *richtig*   not left = *rechts*;

                   [person] is right = *recht haben*   right, privilege = *das Recht*

  2. Words that look or sound alike may not mean the same thing at all.

                stay ≠ *stehen*   *vor* ≠ for

  Remedies: Look up the word in an English-German dictionary, and then look it up in the German-English part of the dictionary. If you don't have time for that, use simpler words or constructions that you are sure of.

- **failure to consider gender of nouns**

  1. Use of "duh" for all articles — ~~duh~~ die Frau, ~~duh~~ der Mann, ~~duh~~ das Kind

  2. German article, but wrong gender — ~~der~~ die Fahrkarte, ~~die~~ der Paß

  Remedies: In speaking you may just have to guess, since you can't take time to check a dictionary. Otherwise, failure to check gender is inexcusable. Learn major patterns of noun formation.

- **failure to conjugate verbs according to both subject and tense**

         ~~Ich gehen gestern nach Hause.~~   Ich bin gestern nach Hause gegangen.

  The error is especially likely when the subject and verb are separated from each other in a manner not encountered in English.

         ~~Ich rufe Sie gestern nicht an, weil ich arbeiten müssen.~~

         Ich habe Sie gestern nicht angerufen, weil ich arbeiten mußte.

- **incorrect verb placement**

  1. The main conjugated verb must appear in second position in all statements.

     ~~Heute ich gehe zum Bahnhof.~~   Heute gehe ich zum Bahnhof.

     The error is most likely when the statement begins with a time or location phrase.

  2. Verb complements appear at the end of main clauses.

     ~~Ich muß gehen nach Hause um zwei Uhr.~~

     Ich muß um zwei Uhr nach Hause gehen.

  3. The verb appears last in subordinate and relative clauses.

     ~~Ich glaube, daß wir gehen ins Restaurant.~~

     Ich glaube, daß wir ins Restaurant gehen.

- **imitation of the English progressive form of verbs (to be + (verb)-ing)**

  ~~Wir sind zum Bahnhof gehen.~~   Wir gehen zum Bahnhof.

            We're going to the station.

- **Incorrect formation of the past tense**

  ~~Ich habe geschriebt.~~   ~~Sie hat nichts gesagen.~~

  Ich habe geschrieben.   Sie hat nichts gesagt.

  Remedies: Note which verbs are regular, and memorize irregular verbs. Trust English; related verbs often follow the same patterns: *leben, lebte, habe gelebt* / live, lived, have lived; *trinken, trank, getrunken* / drink, drank, drunk.

- **wrong verb tense**

    1. Action that continues from the past into the present must be expressed in the present tense; _seit_ introduces the related time phrase.
        ~~Ich habe hier für zwei Monate gewohnt.~~
        Ich wohne seit zwei Monaten hier.
        I've lived (been living) here for two months.

    2. Overuse of the one-word past tense in imitation of English, especially in ordinary conversation.
        ~~Heute morgen aßen wir im Hotel.~~
        Heute morgen haben wir im Hotel gegessen.
        This morning we ate in the hotel.

- **use of _haben_ where _sein_ is required in the present perfect**
    ~~Ich habe nach Hause gegangen.~~   Ich bin nach Hause gegangen.

- **neglect of differences among grammatical cases**

    1. use of the nominative as the universal case
        Ich nehme ~~der~~ den Bus zu ~~der~~ dem Bahnhof.

    2. confusion of pronouns (especially _Sie_ 'you' / _sie_ 'she' / _sie_ 'they')
        Ist sie hier? Ja, ~~ich bin~~ sie ist hier.

    3. confusion of accusative and dative objects
        Ich kaufe ~~meinen~~ meinem Bruder ein T-Shirt.

    4. use of the accusative case after _sein_
        Das ist ~~einen~~ ein Fahrplan.

- **confusion of _du_ and _Sie_**
    Bitte, sagen Sie mir ~~deine~~ Ihre Telefonnummer.
    (or: Bitte, sag mir deine Telefonnummer.)

- **confusion of pronouns, especially _Sie/sie_**
    sie= she, her (accusative); they, them (accusative)
    ihr = her (dative, genitive); you (familiar plural, nominative only)

- **Incorrect negation (_nicht_/_kein_- /_nichts_; placement of _nicht_)**

    1. use of _nicht_ as a universal negation, with no provision for _kein_
        Wir haben ~~nicht~~ keine Bananen.

    2. confusion of _nicht_ and _nichts_
        Ich wußte nicht**s**.   _I didn't know anything._
        Ich wußte nicht.   _I didn't know._

    3. incorrect placement of _nicht_
        negation of <u>entire</u> action:
            Wir sind gestern <u>nicht</u> nach Hamburg gefahren.
            We didn't go to Hamburg at all, anytime.
        negation of <u>part of</u> the action:
            Wir sind <u>nicht</u> gestern nach Hamburg gefahren.
            Whether or not we went to Hamburg, we didn't go yesterday.

- **Incorrect choice of _wann_, _wenn_, _als_, _ob_**
    ~~Wann~~ <u>Wenn</u> es 6 Uhr ist, können wir essen.
    ~~Wann~~ <u>Als</u> ich 12 Jahre alt war, . . .
    Können Sie mir sagen, ~~wenn~~ <u>ob</u> Sie Wienerschnitzel haben?

Drucksachen

Karte Map

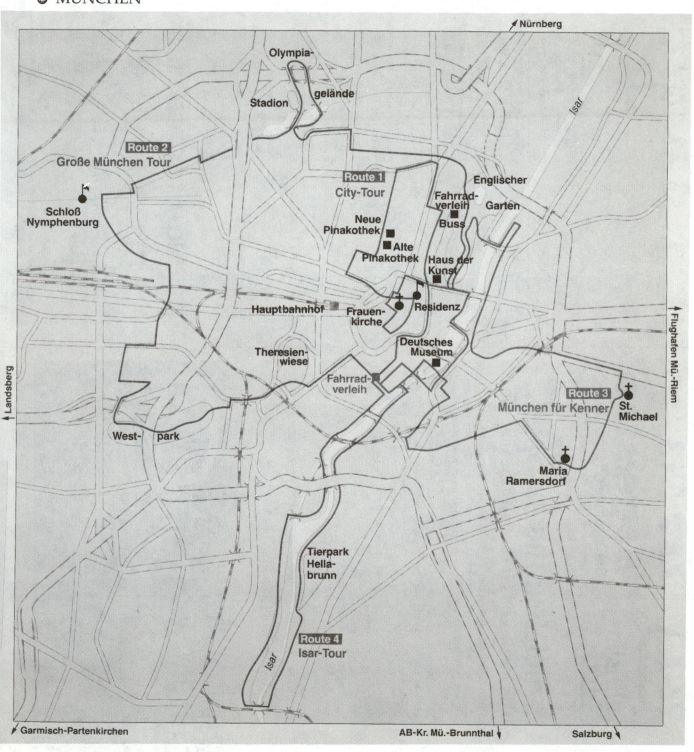

Zugbegleiter   Train Pamphlet

März 1986

IC 513 Wetterstein
Braunschweig/Hannover – Köln – München – Mittenwald

IHR ZUG-BEGLEITER

Ankunft	km	Abfahrt		Anschlüsse	
10.38 ↰ **Düsseldorf** Hbf 🛄		**10.40**		**Intercity hotel ibis Düsseldorf** Tel. (02 11) 1 67 20	
	↓		D 10.46	Düsseldorf-Benrath 10.53 Leverkusen-Mitte 11.04	(300)
				Köln-Deutz 11.13	(450)
	40		E 10.56	Düsseldorf-Bilk 10.59 Neuss 11.08, weiter als Nahverkehrszug in Richtung Mönchengladbach Hbf	(300)
			11.05	in Richtung Köln Hbf (hält nicht in Leverkusen-Wiesdorf)	
			S	S-Bahnanschlüsse bestehen in Richtung:	
				Düsseldorf-Garath – Langenfeld (Rhl)	(396)
				Düsseldorf Flughafen	(397)
				Hilden – Solingen-Ohligs	(397)

🛄 = Gepäckträgerservice Ruf-Nr. (02 11) 3 68 04 40

Ankunft	km	Abfahrt		Anschlüsse	
11.03 Köln Hbf 🛄		**11.06**		**Intercity hotel ibis Köln** Tel. (02 21) 13 20 51	
	↓	4 X	E 11.12	Porz (Rhein) 11.22 Troisdorf 11.29	(420)
	33			Siegburg 11.35 Hennef (Sieg) 11.40	
				Eitorf 11.49 Herchen 11.54	
				Schladern (Sieg) 12.01 Au (Sieg) 12.07	
				Wissen (Sieg) 12.14 Betzdorf (Sieg) 12.23	
				Niederscheiden 12.34 Siegen 12.39	
				Haiger 13.02 Dillenburg 13.07	
				Herborn (Dillkreis) 13.12 Wetzlar 13.27	
				Gießen 13.38	
			D 11.15	Düren 11.36 Aachen Hbf 11.58 Verviers-C 12.23	(440)
				Liège G 12.42 Brussel/Bruxelles N 13.44	
				Brussel/Bruxelles C 13.49	
				Brussel M/Bruxelles 2 13.53 Gent-St-Pieters 14.27	
				Brugge 14.51 Oostende 15.08	
			11.16	Opladen 11.33	(400)
			D 11.20	Brühl 11.32	(600)
			E 11.21	Horrem 11.34 Langerwehe 11.53	(440)
				Eschweiler Hbf 12.00 Stolberg (Rhl) Hbf 12.04	
				Aachen Rothe Erde 12.10	
			S 11.22	Bergisch Gladbach 11.41	(491)
			D 11.24	Köln Süd 11.30 Liblar 11.44 Wellerswist 11.51	(430)
				Euskirchen 12.00 Mechernich 12.15 Kall 12.24	
				Blankenheim (Wald) 12.40 Dahlem (Eifel) 12.50	
				Jünkerath 12.55 Gerolstein 13.10	
				Kyllburg 13.33 Bitburg-Erdorf 13.39 Speicher 13.51	
				Kordel 14.05 Ehrang 14.11	
			E 11.24	Dormagen 11.38	(470)
			11.24	Overath 11.55 Dieringhausen 12.24	(415)
				Gummersbach 12.32	
		4 X	11.27	in Richtung Bonn-Beuel – Linz (Rhein) – Neuwied	(610)
			11.30	in Richtung Düren – Aachen Hbf	(440)
			S 11.42	Köln-Chorweiler Nord 11.57	(491)

🛄 = Gepäckträgerservice Ruf-Nr. (0221) 14 13 4 60
4 = nicht 29. V.

Fortsetzung ▶

Bielefeld macht Spaß.
Das ideale Ziel für Ihren Wochenend-Trip.

Mitten im Teutoburger Wald die grüne Großstadt Bielefeld. Mit einem Angebot für Individualisten.

Stadturlaub in Bielefeld – das ist mehr als chic einkaufen, stadt-bummeln, Sehenswürdigkeiten- und Museen-Besuch – das ist Oper, Operette und Schauspiel im Stadt-theater und im Theater am Alten Markt – das ist Kino, Bowling und Kegeln – das sind Dichterlesungen, Jazz und Kabarett im Bunker Ulmenwall – das ist die Oetkerhalle mit einem Musikprogramm von ernst bis heiter und das sind nicht zuletzt die Diskotheken und Studentenkneipen von „progressiv" bis „gemütlich".

Stadturlaub in Bielefeld – das ist Abwechslung und Anregung zu-gleich. In einer Stadtlandschaft mit 4.800 ha Wald, 400 Bauernhöfen und 521 km Wanderwegen. Bei Ihrem Besuch der freundlichen Stadt am Teutoburger Wald können Sie sich von all dem selbst über-zeugen und Ihr Herz für Bielefeld entdecken.

Verkehrsverein Bielefeld
Tourist-Information im Leinenmeisterhaus
Am Bahnhof 6
4800 Bielefeld 1
Tel. (05 21) 17 88 44

Tourist-Information
im Rathaus
Niederwall 25
4800 Bielefeld 1
Tel. (05 21) 17 88 99

13.27 Mannheim Hbf — 13.32

Ankunft	km	Abfahrt	Anschlüsse	
→		IC 13.31	"Tiziano" **Karlsruhe Hbf 14.00 Offenburg 14.33 Freiburg (Brsg) Hbf 15.02 Basel Bad Bf 15.39 Basel SBB 15.46 Olten 16.29 Luzern 17.07 Bellinzona 19.23 Lugano 19.51 Chiasso 20.16 Como SG 20.47 Milano C 21.25**	(700)
	17			
Ⓐ ✗		13.37	Ludwigshafen (Rhein) Hbf 13.41	(660)
✗		13.38	Bad Dürkheim 14.39	(668)
△ ✗		13.40	Schwetzingen 13.58 Graben-Neudorf 14.23, weiter in Richtung Karlsruhe Hbf (hält nicht in Altrip und Karlsruhe-Hagsfeld)	(701)
△		13.40	Viernheim 14.09 Weinheim 14.23	(568)
		D 13.41	Ludwigshafen (Rhein) Hbf 13.45 Schifferstadt 13.53 Haßloch (Pfalz) 13.59 Neustadt (Weinstr) Hbf 14.05 Kaiserslautern Hbf 14.29 Landstuhl 14.39 Homburg (Saar) Hbf 14.50 St Ingbert 15.03 Saarbrücken Hbf 15.14	(670)
E ✗		13.41	Mannheim-Friedrichsfeld 13.48 Ladenburg 13.53 in Richtung Heidelberg Hbf	(550)
E ✗		13.44	Böhl-Iggelheim 14.25 Lambrecht (Pfalz) 14.42 Einsiedlerhof 15.09 Kindsbach 15.12	(702)
		E 14.06	Hauptstuhl 15.21 Bruchmühlbach-Miesau 15.25 Limbach (bei Homburg/Saar) 15.36 Rohrbach (Saar) 15.42 Saarbrücken Ost 15.56	(670)

🔟 = nicht 29. V.

11.24 Bonn Hbf — 11.26

Ankunft	km	Abfahrt	Anschlüsse	
→		11.38	Remagen 11.56, weiter in Richtung Koblenz Hbf	(600)
	59	D 11.44	Bad Breisig 12.08 Andernach 12.16	(600)
		4 ✗ 11.46	in Richtung Euskirchen	(433)

🛒 = Gepäckträgerservice Ruf-Nr. (0228) 715366
4 = nicht 29. V.

11.57 Koblenz Hbf — 11.59

Ankunft	km	Abfahrt	Anschlüsse	
→		IC 12.06	Boppard 12.21 Bad Salzig 12.25 St Goar 12.34 Bingerbrück 12.57, weiter als Eilzug Bingen (Rhein) 13.01 Gau Algesheim 13.07 Ingelheim 13.11	(600)
	92	D 12.13	Cochem (Mosel) 12.46 Bullay (DB) 12.55 Wengerohr 13.08 Trier Hbf 13.32 Wasserbillig 13.49 Luxembourg 14.17 u in Trier Hbf E 13.38 Saarbrücken Hbf 15.00	(620)
7 Ⓐ		E 12.13	Niederlahnstein 12.19 Bad Ems West 12.29 Bad Ems 12.33 Nassau (Lahn) 12.41 Diez 13.02 Limburg (Lahn) 13.06, weiter als Nahverkehrszug Weilburg 13.50 Stockhausen (Lahn) 13.59 Wetzlar 14.15 Gießen 14.28	(540)
8 †		12.13	Niederlahnstein 12.19 Bad Ems 12.35 Limburg (Lahn) 13.14 Weilburg 13.50 Gießen 14.28	(540)
8 †		E 12.15	Neuwied 12.27	(610)
		E 12.17	Niederlahnstein 12.22 Braubach 12.29 St Goarshausen 12.45 Aßmannshausen 13.02 Rüdesheim (Rhein) 13.06 Eltville 13.18 in Richtung Rüdesheim (Rhein) – Wiesbaden Hbf	(610)
11		12.20	Kobern-Gondorf 12.38	(610)
8 ⓒ		12.23	Mayen Ost 13.37	(620)
		D 12.30	Bingerbrück 13.09	(603)
		12.33	Bad Kreuznach 13.38 Bad Münster am Stein 13.43 Alsenz 13.54 Rockenhausen 14.05 Winnweiler 14.15 Enkenbach 14.25 Hochspeyer 14.32 Kaiserslautern Hbf 14.40 Pirmasens Hbf 15.24	(600)
7 ✗		12.41	in Richtung Kobern-Gondorf – Cochem (Mosel) – Trier Hbf	(620)

🛒 = Gepäckträgerservice Ruf-Nr. (0261) 12282
7 = nicht 29. V.
8 = auch 29. V.
10 = ab Bingerbrück ✗, nicht 29. V.
11 = ✗ außer ⑥ an Schultagen

12.47 Mainz Hbf — 12.49

Ankunft	km	Abfahrt	Anschlüsse	
→	70	S 12.53	Wiesbaden Hbf 13.04	(594)
7 Ⓐ		S 12.54	Armsheim 13.31 Alzey 13.42 (hält nicht zwischen Mainz Hbf und Klein-Winternheim-Ober Olm)	(655)
7 Ⓐ		12.55	Bodenheim 13.06, weiter in Richtung Worms Hbf – Ludwigshafen (Rhein) Hbf	(660)
		S 13.06	Frankfurt (Main) Flughafen 13.32 Frankfurt (Main) Hbf 13.48	(594)
7 Ⓐ		13.21	Groß Gerau 13.44 Darmstadt Hbf 13.58	(552)
7 ✗		13.28	Bodenheim 13.39 Worms Hbf 14.19	(660)

7 = nicht 29. V.

Upper table

Ankunft	km	Abfahrt	Anschlüsse

hotel ibis Ulm — Tel. (07 31) 61 90 01

15.52 Ulm Hbf   **15.54**

→   85

E 15.58 Neu-Ulm 16.01 Leipheim 16.12 (900)
Günzburg 16.16 Offingen 16.22
Burgau (Schwab) 16.28 Jettingen 16.31
Dinkelscherben 16.41 Gessertshausen 16.48
Diedorf (Schwab) 16.52 Westheim (Schwab) 16.56
Neusäß 16.59

12 Ⓒ 15.58 in Richtung Augsburg Hbf (900)
12 Ⓐ 16.03 Ehingen (Donau) 16.43 (755)
12 Ⓐ 16.09 Giengen (Brenz) 16.58 Heidenheim 17.12. (788)
weiter in Richtung Aalen

E 16.10 Neu-Ulm 16.12 Senden 16.21 Vöhringen 16.27 (975)
Bellenberg 16.29 Illertissen 16.34
Altenstadt (Iller) 16.39 Kellmünz 16.44
Memmingen 16.54 Grönenbach 17.05
Dietmannsried 17.13 Kempten (Allg) Ost 17.20
Kempten (Allg) Hbf 17.23

D 16.12 Laupheim West 16.27 Biberach (Riß) 16.37 (750)
Bad Schussenried 16.52 Aulendorf 16.56
Mochenwangen 12 17.05 Ravensburg 17.11
Meckenbeuren 17.20 Friedrichshafen Stadt 17.28
Friedrichshafen Hafen 17.33

12 †   16.15 Ehingen (Donau) 17.04 (755)
12 Ⓐ 16.20 in Richtung Augsburg Hbf (900)
12 Ⓐ 16.26 in Richtung Memmingen (975)
Ⓐ E 16.38 Ulm-Donautal 16.42 Erbach (Württ) 16.48 (750)
Schemmerberg 17.02

Ⓒ = auch 29. V.
Ⓐ = nicht 29. V.
† = hält nur ⑥ und †.
auch 29. V.

Meldung aus dem Schwarzwald:

Alle Welt berichtet vom „Waldsterben" und dabei am liebsten (oder auch bequemsten!?) am Beispiel des weltbekannten und prominenten Schwarzwaldes.

Was erfährt aber zur gleichen Zeit der Gast im Schwarzwald? Einen nach wie vor ungebrochenen Erholungswert der Landschaft. Darauf kann man sich verlassen. 97 Prozent der Befragten bestätigen dies.

Deshalb:

Wer den Schwarzwald liebt, besucht ihn und überzeugt sich selbst.

Lower table

Ankunft	km	Abfahrt	Anschlüsse

13.42 Heidelberg Hbf   **13.44**

→ 12 112

13.48 Meckesheim 14.14 Sinsheim (Elsenz) 14.28 (561)
Steinsfurt 14.34 Bad Rappenau 14.54
Bad Wimpfen 15.01 Bad Friedrichshall-Jagstfeld 15.04,
weiter in Richtung Heilbronn Hbf

D 14.00 Eberbach 14.25 Neckarelz 14.40 (560)
Heilbronn Hbf 15.04 Bietigheim-Bissingen 15.25

12 = ✗, nicht 29. V.,
ab Sinsheim (Elsenz) ✗ außer ⑥

14.51 Stuttgart Hbf   **14.57**

→ 94

E 15.11 Stuttgart-Bad Cannstatt 15.16 (760)
Esslingen (Neckar) 15.22 Plochingen 15.30
Wendlingen (Neckar) 15.39 Nürtingen 15.44
Metzingen 15.55 Reutlingen Hbf 16.01
Tübingen Hbf 16.11

E 15.13 Stuttgart-Bad Cannstatt 15.17 Waiblingen 15.25 (787)
Schorndorf 15.36 Lorch (Württ) 15.46
Schwäbisch Gmünd 15.51 Böbingen (Rems) 16.00
Aalen 16.13 Wasseralfingen 16.19 Goldshöfe 16.23
Bopfingen 16.38 Nördlingen 16.47

E 15.21 Winnenden 15.41 Backnang 15.48 (785)
Sulzbach (Murr) 15.59 Murrhardt 16.05
Gaildorf West 16.16
Schwäbisch Hall-Hessenthal 16.25
Crailsheim 16.44

D 15.25 Böblingen 15.46 Horb 16.12 Rottweil 16.47 (740)
Tuttlingen 17.06 Singen (Hohentwiel) 17.33
Schaffhausen 17.57 Zürich HB 18.44
Zug 19.29 Arth-Goldau 19.45
🚐 Konstanz 18.00

D 15.27 Ellwangen 16.32 Crailsheim 16.47 (785)
Dombühl 17.03

S S-Bahnanschlüsse bestehen in Richtung:
Stuttgart-Vaihingen – Böblingen
Esslingen (Neckar) – Plochingen (791)
Waiblingen – Schorndorf/Backnang (791)
Ludwigsburg – (793)
Marbach (Neckar)/Bietigheim-Bissingen (795)
Leonberg – Weil der Stadt (796)

Ankunft	km		Abfahrt	Anschlüsse	
17.08 München Hbf			**17.18**		
↓ 54			E 17.54	Petershausen (Oberbay) 18.18 Reichertshausen (Ilm) 18.25 Pfaffenhofen (Ilm) 18.31 Wolnzach Bf 18.39	(920)
		Ⓢ		S-Bahnanschlüsse bestehen in Richtung:	
				Ostbahnhof – Neubiberg – Hohenbrunn – Höhenkirchen-Siegertsbrunn – Kreuzstraße	(991)
				Moosach – Oberschleißheim – Freising	(991)
				Deisenhofen – Holzkirchen	(992)
				Dachau Bf – Petershausen	(992)
				Johanneskirchen – Ismaning	(993)
				Pasing – Olching – Maisach	(993)
				Trudering – Haar – Grafing Bf – Ebersberg (Oberbay)	(994)
				Grafrath – Geltendorf	(994)
				Unterpfaffenhofen-Germering – Herrsching	(995)
				Markt Schwaben – Erding	(996)
				Gauting – Starnberg – Tutzing	(996)
				Baierbrunn – Wolfratshausen	(997)

▲ = ab Holzkirchener Bahnhof
△ = ab Starnberger Bahnhof
[5] = am 1. III., ⑤ und ⑥ vom 7. bis 15. III., täglich vom 21. III. bis 5. IV., ⑤ und ⑥ ab 11. IV., auch 18. V.
[15] = nicht 29. V.
[16] = auch 29. V.

Ankunft	km		Abfahrt	Anschlüsse	
17.53 Weilheim (Oberbay)			**17.55**		
↓ 21		⑥ 🚌	17.58	Peißenberg 18.10 Schongau 18.43	(902)
18.09 Murnau			**18.11**		
↓ 26			18.19	Bad Kohlgrub 18.40 Oberammergau 19.00	(963)
18.32 Garmisch-Partenkirchen			**18.47**		
↓ 11			18.45	Griesen (Oberbay) 19.02 Ehrwald Zugspitzbahn 19.18 Reutte in Tirol 19.47	(973)
19.00 Klais			**19.01**		
↓ 6					
19.07 Mittenwald					
			20.12	Scharnitz 20.21 Seefeld in Tirol 20.35, weiter in Richtung Innsbruck Hbf	(960)

Ankunft	km		Abfahrt	Anschlüsse	
16.35 Augsburg Hbf			**16.37**		
↓ 62		[15] Ⓐ	16.40	Kaufering 17.21 Landsberg (Lech) 17.35	(982)
		[15] Ⓐ	16.41	Mering 16.55 Geltendorf 17.25, weiter in Richtung Weilheim (Oberbay) (hält nicht in Kaltenberg und Greifenberg [Oberbay])	(960)
		[16] Ⓒ	16.48	Aichach 17.16	(911)
		[15] Ⓐ	E 16.51	Augsburg-Oberhausen 16.54 Langweid (Lech) 17.01 Herbertshofen 17.05 Meitingen 17.08 Nordendorf 17.12 Mertingen Bf 17.21 Donauwörth 17.27	(910)
		[15] Ⓐ	16.58	Bobingen 17.11 Schwabmünchen 17.19 Buchloe 17.31	(970)
		[16] Ⓒ	17.03	Mering 17.16 Geltendorf 17.42, weiter in Richtung Weilheim (Oberbay) (hält nicht in Kaltenberg, St Ottilien, Greifenberg [Oberbay] und Raisting)	(960)
		[15] Ⓐ	E 17.11	Gablingen 17.20 Bäumenheim 17.44	(910)
			E 17.20	Bobingen 17.31 Schwabmünchen 17.38 Buchloe 17.52 Kaufbeuren 18.13 Biessenhofen 18.20 Günzach 18.35, weiter in Richtung Kempten (Allg) Hbf	(970)

[15] = nicht 29. V.
[16] = auch 29. V.

17.08 München Hbf 17.18

Ankunft	km		Abfahrt	Anschlüsse	
↓ 54		[5] IC	17.15	„Erasmus" **Rosenheim 17.54 Kufstein 18.18 Wörgl 18.41 Jenbach 18.58 Innsbruck Hbf 19.22**	(950)
		△	E 17.27	Freising 17.51 Landshut (Bay) Hbf 18.13 Neufahrn (Niederbay) 18.31 Eggmühl 18.43 Hagelstadt 18.49 Köfering 18.53 Obertraubling 18.58 Regensburg Hbf 19.04	(930)
		▲ [15] Ⓐ	E 17.31	München Ost 17.42 Mühldorf (Oberbay) 18.31 Töging (Inn) 18.42 Neuötting 18.47 Perach 18.51 Marktl 18.57 Buch (Inn) 19.01 Julbach 19.04 Simbach (Inn) 19.10	(940)
		▲ [16] Ⓒ	E 17.31	München Ost 17.41 Markt Schwaben 17.56 Dorfen Bf 18.14 Ampfing 18.25 Mühldorf (Oberbay) 18.31, weiter als Nahverkehrszug Tüßling 18.41 Heiligenstadt (Oberbay) 18.44 Altötting 18.50 Kastl (Oberbay) 18.56 Gendorf 18.58 Burgkirchen 19.01 Pirach 19.05 Burghausen (Oberbay) 19.14	(940)
		△	E 17.32	München Harras 17.40 Holzkirchen 18.00 Warngau 18.07 Schaftlach 18.12 Reichersbeuern 18.19 Bad Tölz 18.26 Gaißach 18.29 Obergries 18.34 Lenggries 18.38 🚌 Tegernsee 18.39	(955)
		[15] Ⓐ	E 17.38	München Ost 17.47 Grafing 18.05 Rosenheim 18.22 Raubling 18.30 Brannenburg 18.35 Flintsbach 18.39 Oberaudorf 18.46 Kiefersfelden 18.50 Kufstein 18.54	(950)
		△ [15] Ⓐ	E 17.43	Moosburg 18.21 Ergoldsbach 18.50 Niederlindhart 19.11 Mallersdorf 19.14 Laberweinting 19.19 Sallach 19.23 Geiselhöring 19.28 Radldorf (Niederbay) 19.36 Straubing 19.44	(930)
			D 17.45	Oberstaufen 19.52 Röthenbach (Allg) 20.05 Lindau Hbf 20.34 Bregenz 20.51 St Margrethen 21.07 Rorschach 21.24 St Gallen 21.39 Winterthur 22.33 Zürich Flughafen 22.38 Zürich HB 22.50	(970)
		△ Ⓑ	E 17.50	Darching 18.23 Miesbach 18.33 Agatharied 18.36 Hausham 18.40 Schliersee 18.43 Fischhausen-Neuhaus 18.55 Fischbachau 19.04 Geitau 19.09 Osterhofen (Oberbay) 19.13 Bayrischzell 19.16	(955)

Fortsetzung ▶

Hotelverzeichnis   Hotel Listing

TRIER

Zeichenerklärung:
Fw fl. warm. Wasser · Z Zentralheizung · T Zimmertelefon · L Lift · G Garage · eigener Parkplatz · D Diät/Diätkost · K Konferenzraum · R Restaurant · TV Television

Zimmerpreis für Übernachtung mit Frühstück (einschl. Bedienung u. MwSt.) in DM

(Rubrik: Deutsch — HOTEL-RESTAURANTS)

Telefon-Vorwahl: 06 51

Name, Straße, Telefon, Telex	Stadtplanquadrat	Zahl der Betten	Bad/Dusche + WC 1-Bett-Z von–bis	Bad/Dusche + WC 2-Bett-Z von–bis	Bad/Dusche 1-Bett-Z von–bis	Bad/Dusche 2-Bett-Z von–bis	fl. Warmwasser 1-Bett-Z von–bis	fl. Warmwasser 2-Bett-Z von–bis	Zuschlag Halbpension	Zuschlag Vollpension	Kinderrabatte	Ausstattung
Holiday Inn, Zurmaiener Straße 164, Telefon 2 30 91, Telex 4-72 808	A 3	335	109,— 119,—	139,— 179,—					18,—	36,—		FwZTLGPDRK 10 – 300 Hallenbad, Sauna, Solarium
Hotel Deutscher Hof, Südallee 25, Telefon 4 60 21, Telex 4-72799	D 3	180	55,— 60,—	93,— 95,—			35,— 38,—	70,— 75,—	15,—	30,—		FwZTLGPDRK 10 – 150 Kegelbahnen
Dorint-Hotel Porta Nigra, Porta-Nigra-Platz 1, Telefon 2 70 10, Telex 4-72 895	B 3	176	106,— 116,—	162,— 250,—					27,—	48,—		FwZTLGPDRK 10 – 400
Europa Parkhotel Mövenpick, Kaiserstraße 29, Telefon 71 95 - 0, Telex 4-72 858	C 3	170	119,50	169,—					22,—	44,—		FwZTLGPDRK 8 – 1200 Tanzkeller
Hotel Eurener Hof, Eurener Straße 171, Telefon 8 80 77, Telex 4-72 555	E 5	130	75,— 79,—	115,— 130,—	51,—		39,—	76,—	19,50	39,—		FwZTLGPRK 100, Sauna, Hallenbad, Liegewiese
Hotel Biesiusgarten, Olewiger Straße 135, Telefon 3 10 77	über C 1	115	60,— 70,—	95,— 115,—			45,—	65,—	17,—	28,—		FwZTLGPRK 20 – 110 Liegewiese
Faßbenders Central-Hotel, Sichelstraße 32, Telefon 7 40 77	B 2	60	40,— 50,—	70,— 80,—	40,—	70,—			10,—	20,—		FwZPDRK 20 – 40 Liegewiese
Hotel Zum Christophel, Simeonstraße 1, Telefon 7 40 41/4 42 44	B 3	24	40,— 60,—	90,— 95,—			32,— 35,—	65,—	13,—	25,—		FwZTGRTVRK 20 – 40
Hotel Feilen-Wolff, Kölner Straße 22, Telefon 8 67 63	B 5	50	50,—	75,— 85,—					n. V.	n. V.		FwZTGPRK 50
Hotel Zur Post, Ruwerer Straße 18, Telefon 51 00	links v. A 2	45	35,— 38,—	68,— 75,—			25,— 28,—	35,— 45,—	12,—	24,—		FwZPRK 50 Kegelbahn
Hotel Constantin an der Römerbrücke, St.-Barbara-Ufer 1 – 2, Telefon 7 53 85	D 4	40	48,— 100,—	72,— 148,—					15,—	30,—		FwZTGPDR
Hotel Haus Schneider, Eurener Straße 190, Telefon 8 87 74	E 5	38	40,—	66,—			34,—	60,—	15,—	25,—		FwZPRK 50
Hotel Estricher Hof, Straße Trier – Konz, Telefon 3 30 44/45	E 2	36	48,— 50,—	90,— 95,—					15,—	26,—		FwZTGPRDLK 50 Liegewiese
Hotel Pieper, Thebäerstraße 39, Telefon 2 30 08	B 2	35	43,—	76,—					11,—	n. V.		FwZTPDRK 40
Hotel Minnebeck, Eurener Straße 68, Telefon 8 88 05	E 5	33			32,—	58,—			n. V.	22,—		FwZTPKR
Hotel Breit, Paulinstraße 13, Telefon 2 57 74	B 3	29			35,—	60,—						FwZPK 40
Hotel Klosterklause, Balthasar-Neumann-Straße 1, Telefon 2 56 13	B 2	28					35,—	60,—	12,—	17,—		FwZPRGZK 40
Hotel Haus am Berg, Drosselweg 23, Telefon 6 98 43, Teletex 6 51 935 setrie	links v. A 4	27	32,— 36,—	58,— 62,—			28,— 32,—	50,— 54,—	Restaurant nur für Hausgäste			FwZGPTR Liegewiese
Altstadtstube Zum Frankenturm, Dietrichstraße 3, Telefon 4 82 25	C 3	26							10,—	n. V.		FwZRK
Hotel Zender, Ehranger Straße 207, Telefon 6 61 11	links v. A 2	26	32,— 38,—	55,— 60,—			35,—	70,—	n. V.	23,—		FwZGPRK 50 2 Kegelbahnen
Hotel Handelshof, Lorenz-Kellner-Straße 1, Telefon 7 39 33	D 4	25					28,—	56,—				FwZGP
Hotel Maximin, Ruwerer Straße 12, Telefon 5 25 77	links v. A 2	25					25,—	40,— 44,—	12,—			FwZGPKR
Hotel Am Ufer, Zurmaiener Straße 81 – 83, Telefon 4 54 04/7 64 87	B 4	24	50,— 60,—	85,— 95,—								FwZGPTRK 20 Tanz-Treff
Pension-Weinhaus Becker, Olewiger Straße 206, Telefon 3 37 81	über D 1	24	40,— 45,—	70,— 75,—								FwZPRK 120, Weinproben, Weinverkauf
Hotel Kugel, Kirchenstraße 17, Telefon 8 62 37	rechts v. E 4	23			30,— 35,—	50,— 60,—		40,— 50,—				FwZPRK 40
Hotel Reichert, Koblenzer Straße 1, Telefon 6 61 04	links v. A 4	23	48,—		22,—	44,—	20,— 22,—	40,— 44,—				FwZGPK 40 Kegelbahn

München: Wichtige Informationen   Munich: Basic Information

Wichtige Telefonnummern und Auskunftsstellen

Wichtige Telefonnummern

Funkstreife/Polizei	**Tel.: 110**
Feuerwehr	**Tel.: 112**

In mit einem roten Streifen am Dach gekennzeichneten Telefonzellen können obige Nummern kostenlos angerufen werden.

Rettungsdienst　　**Tel.: 22 26 66**

ADAC Südbayern
Ridlerstr. 35
Tel.: 51 95-0

ADAC-Pannendienst
Tel.: 76 76 76

ACE-Pannendienst
Tel.: 53 65 02

DTC–Deutscher Touring Automobil-Club
Amalienburgstraße 23
Tel.: 8 11 10 48

Alpine Auskunftsstelle
(Deutscher Alpenverein)
Praterinsel 5
Tel.: 29 49 40

Auskunftsstellen der Bundesbahn
Fahrplan Reisezüge und Bahnbus
Tel.: 59 29 91, 59 33 21
Fahrpreisauskunft
Tel.: 55 41 41
Reservierung von Sitz-, Liege- und Bettplätzen
Tel.: 128-59 94, 128-59 95
Auto im Reisezug
Tel.: 128-8 44 05, 128-8 44 25
Sonderzüge, -fahrten
Tel.: 128-58 46
S-Bahn-Fahrplan, im Hauptbahnhof
Tel.: 55 75 75

Flugauskunft
Tel.: 92 11 21 27

Jugend-Informations-Zentrum
Paul-Heyse-Straße 22
Tel.: 53 16 55
Mo–Fr 11–19 Uhr
Sa 11–17 Uhr
So und Fei geschlossen

> Weitere wichtige Rufnummern können Sie dem Monatsprogramm des Fremdenverkehrsamtes entnehmen.

Wichtige Postämter

Postamt 1
Residenzstraße 2
Tel.: 21 77-0

Öffnungszeiten:
Mo mit Fr 8–18 Uhr
Frühschalter 7–8 Uhr
Spätschalter 18–18.30 Uhr
Sa 8–12 Uhr
Frühschalter 7–8 Uhr
Spätschalter 12–13 Uhr
So und Fei geschlossen.

Postamt 32
Bahnhofplatz 1
Tel.: 55 98/4 01

Öffnungszeiten:
Täglich 0–24 Uhr
Öffentliche Telexstelle täglich
6.30–23 Uhr

Alle unter „hauptpostlagernd" eingehenden Sendungen werden beim Postamt 32 zur Abholung bereitgehalten. Postsparkassendienst, Auszahlung von Schecks und Geldwechsel auch nachts.

Postamt 87
Flughafen München-Riem
(Abflughalle)
Tel.: 41 41-1

Öffnungszeiten:
Mo mit Fr 8–18 Uhr
Sa 8–13 Uhr
So und Fei 10–11 Uhr
Spätschalter Mo mit Fr 18–21 Uhr
Sa 13–20 Uhr
Sonn- und Feiertage:
11–13, 14–19.30 Uhr.

> Internationale Telefonate können von allen Postämtern und von den Telefonhäuschen aus, die mit einem grünen Hinweisschild gekennzeichnet sind, geführt werden.

Fremdsprachige Apotheken

Bahnhof-Apotheke
Bahnhofplatz 2
Tel.: 59 41 19, 59 81 19

City-Apotheke
Schillerstraße 9
Tel.: 55 55 21/22

Europa-Apotheke
Schützenstraße 12
Tel.: 59 54 23

Internationale Inter-Apotheke
Ecke Luisen-/Elisenstraße 5
Hauptbahnhof Nordausgang
Tel.: 59 54 44/59 54 45

Internationale Ludwigs-Apotheke
Neuhauser Straße 8,
(Fußgängerzone)
Tel.: 2 60 30 21

Lerchen-Apotheke
Schleißheimer Straße 201
Tel.: 3 08 67 31

Schützen-Apotheke
Schützenstraße 5, Bayerstraße 4
Tel.: 55 76 61–63

Schwanthaler-Apotheke
Schwanthalerstraße 2
Tel.: 59 36 51/59 82 63

> Unter der Tel.-Nr. 59 44 75 erreichen Sie die Bandansage (in Deutsch) der dienstbereiten Apotheken.

Öffnungszeiten

Banken allgemein
Mo–Fr vorm. 8.30–12.30 Uhr,
nachm. 13.45–15.30 Uhr
Do nachm. 13.45–17.30 Uhr

Deutsche Verkehrs-Kredit-Bank AG
Wechselstuben:
Hauptbahnhof
Tel.: 55 70 35
Täglich 6–23.30 Uhr
Flughafen, Abflughalle
Tel.: 90 70 10
Täglich 7–20.30 Uhr
Flughafen, Ankunfthalle
Tel.: 90 84 33
Täglich 7–22 Uhr

Einzelhandelsgeschäfte allgemein
in der Innenstadt
Mo–Fr 9–18 Uhr
Sa 9–12/14 Uhr
langer Sa (1. Sa i. Monat) 9–18 Uhr

Kaufhäuser allgemein
Mo–Fr 8.30–18.30 Uhr
Sa 8.30–14 Uhr
langer Sa (1. Sa i. Monat) 8.30–18 Uhr

> Sowohl bei Banken als auch bei allen Geschäften können die angegebenen Öffnungszeiten im einzelnen etwas variieren.

Gaststättenverzeichnis   Restaurant List

FREIBURG

Cafés

Name	Straße	Tel.	Plq.	Sitzplätze	Ruhetag
Kornhaus	Münsterplatz 11	3 25 65	D4	140 +140 Garten	Dienstag
Lienhart	Salzstr. 11	2 48 78	D4	48	Sonntag
Mall-Café	Schiffstr. 5	3 72 82	D4	80	keinen
Milano	Schusterstr. 7	3 37 35	D4	120	keinen
Mozart	Habsburgerstr. 127	2 32 00	C4	60 +40 Terr.	Sonntag
Münstercafé	Münsterplatz 15	3 53 63	D4	90 +130 Garten	Winter/ Mittwoch
Panoramahotel	Wintererstr. 89	55 10 11	C5	60	keinen
Park-Café	Am Karlsplatz	5 50 55	D4	70	keinen
Pavillon-Café	Bei den Unikliniken	5 50 55	C3	70	keinen
Reiß	Schusterstr. 34	3 90 28	D4	35	Sonntag
Reiß	Kaiser-Joseph-Str. 221	28 03 93	D4	30	Sonntag
Rheingold	Eisenbahnstr. 47	3 60 66	D4	65	keinen
Schettler	Guntramstr. 57	27 25 63	C3	45	Donnerstag
Schmidt	Am Bischofskreuz 13	8 34 42	C2	39 +39 Garten	Montag
Schöpflin	Markgrafenstr. 6	49 40 77	D2	25	Montag
Schwarzes Kloster	Rathausgasse 48	2 69 41	D4	100	Sonntag
Sonnec	Schlierbergstr. 139	40 31 73	E3	40	Donnerstag
Steinmetz	Kaiser-Joseph-Str. 193	3 66 66	D4	130	Sonntag
Sternwaldstüble	Gerwigplatz 5	7 18 23	E4	35	Samstag Sonntag
Tessiner Stuben	Bertoldstr. 17	3 27 70	D4	75/120	Sonntag Feiertag
Unterlinden	Unterlinden 12	3 41 78	D4	16	Sonntag Sa. Mittag
Welle	Richard-Wagner-Str. 33	55 21 50	C4	40	Montag Samstag
Windlicht-Bistro	Fischerau 6	3 04 13	D4	35	Sonntag

Bierstuben

Name	Straße	Tel.	Plq.	Sitzplätze	Ruhetag
Alter Simon	Konviktstr. 43	2 51 73	D4	40	ab 12 Uhr keinen
Badischer Hof	Lehenerstr. 27	27 21 74	D3	30	Mittwoch
Binding-Brezel	Herrenstr. 40	2 40 97	D4	60	keinen
Dampfross	Löwenstr. 7	3 54 06	D4	45	keinen
Deutsches Haus	Schusterstr. 40	2 45 00	D4	70	Sonntag
Einbecker	Littenweilerstr. 13	6 39 33	E6	51	Mittwoch
Eschholz-Billard	Wannerstr. 21	27 33 12	E4	–	keinen
Keller-Klause	Günterstalstr. 53	7 48 21	E4	30	keinen
Klarastüble	Klarastr. 7	27 64 37	E4	35	Sonntag
Klosterbräustüble	Zähringerstr. 1a	5 42 16	B4	40	keinen
Krümmel-Gay	Salzstr. 13	3 39 30	D4	21	keinen
Mühlhauserstüble	Mühlhauserstr. 6	8 31 35	B2	35	Sonntag
Mühlenklause	Gilgenmatten 2	4 16 37	D2	50	Montag
Ole's Tenne	Kaiser-Joseph-Str. 264a	3 53 05	D4	90	keinen
Pfeife, Zur	Konviktstr. 41	2 63 23	D4	42	keinen

Bierstuben

Name	Straße	Tel.	Plq.	Sitzplätze	Ruhetag
Pit's Pilsstube	Gundelfingerstr. 25	5 64 38	A4	35	Sonntag
Roxy Bierbar	Bertoldstr. 56	3 50 85	D3	51	keinen
Schubertstüble	Heinrich-v.-Stephanstr. 12	7 32 92	E3	35	Sonntag
Stiefel	Schusterstr. 42	2 60 41	D4	30	keinen
Töff-Töff	Lehenerstr. 49	28 02 89	D3	20	keinen
Tulla-Eck	Tullastr. 13	5 35 15	B4	45	Samstag So. bis 18 Uhr
Vögele	Reutebachgasse 12a	5 36 15	B4	20	Sonntag
Zapfhahn, Zum	Moltkestr. 16	2 47 74	D3	25	Sonntag

Weinstuben

Name	Straße	Tel.	Plq.	Sitzplätze	Ruhetag
Alter Simpel	Insel 4	3 56 97	D4	60+60 Garten	keinen
Batzenbergstüble	Adelhauserstr. 7c	3 50 45	D4	45	Sonntag
Busse's Waldschänke	Waldseestr. 77	7 48 47	E5	120	Sonntag
Colombi	Rotteckring 16	3 14 15	D4	85	keinen
Einbecker	Littenweilerstr. 13	6 39 33	E6	51	Mittwoch
Engler's Weinkrügle	Konviktstr. 12	3 15 57	D4	60	Mittwoch
Enoteca	Schwabentorplatz 6	3 07 51	D4	24	Sonntag
Greiffenegg-Schlößle	Schloßbergring 3	3 27 28	D4	200 +80 Terr.	Montag
Gutenbergstüble	Habsburgerstr. 106	3 24 62	C4	20	Sonntag Feiertag
Henry, Bei	Talstr. 56	7 34 39	E4	70	Sonntag Montag
Karcher's Weinstube	Eisenbahnstr. 43	2 27 73	D3	80 +120 Terr.	keinen
Keller-Klause	Günterstalstr. 53	7 48 21	E4	30	keinen
Klosterbräustüble	Zähringerstr. 1a	5 42 16	B4	40	keinen
Markgräfler Hof	Gerberau 22	3 25 40	D4	40+20	Sonntag Mo. Mittag
Mühlhauserstüble	Mühlhauserstr. 6	8 31 35	B2	35	Sonntag
Oberkirch's Weinstuben	Münsterplatz 22	3 10 11	D4	140	Sonntag
Rappen	Münsterplatz 13	3 13 53	D4	120	keinen
Schubertstüble	Heinrich-v.-Stephanstr. 12	7 32 92	E3	35	Sonntag
Schwarzwälder Hof	Herrenstr. 43	3 23 86	D4	100	Mittwoch
Sichelschmiede	Insel 1	3 50 37	D4	80	keinen
Sonnec	Schlierbergstr. 139	40 31 73	E3	40	Donnerstag
Stiefel	Schusterstr. 42	2 60 41	D4	30	keinen
Tessiner Stuben	Bertoldstr. 17	3 27 70	D4	75 +120 Garten	Sonntag Feiertag
Töff-Töff	Lehenerstr. 49	28 02 89	D3	20	keinen
Trotte, Zur	Fischerau 28	3 07 77	D4	55	keinen
Vögele	Reutebachgasse 12a	5 36 15	B4	20	Sonntag
Webers Weinstube	Hildastr. 35	70 07 43	E4	66	Freitag
Zwiebel, Die	Münsterplatz 11	3 36 05	D4	75	keinen
Zwigard's Weinstuben	Mathildenstr. 14	27 51 35	C3	65	Sonntag

Speisekarte: Imbiß
Menu: Fast Food

mini bar
DSG

Unser mini bar-Verkäufer serviert Ihnen Warmes oder Kaltes zum Essen und zum Trinken direkt ins Abteil.

„Das Frühstück"

Fix und fertig servieren wir Ihnen Ihr Frühstück in der praktischen Einwegverpackung. Kännchen, Tasse, Teller, Besteck, Serviette und Erfrischungstuch – an alles ist gedacht. Im Nu bereiten wir Ihnen ein Kännchen Kaffee mit löslichem Bohnenkaffee und dazu gibt's Kaffeesahne und Zucker. Verschiedene Brotsorten sind eine gute Unterlage für Butter, Konfitüre, Streichwurst und Schmelzkäse. Und als kleine Süßigkeit: 1 Erfrischungsbonbon.

„Die Kalte Mahlzeit"

Ein reichhaltiges Menü erwartet Sie in der praktischen Einwegverpackung. Besteck, Teller, Serviette und Erfrischungstuch – alles ist dabei. Als Vorspeise gibt es Räucherlachs-Pastete und zum flämischen Kartoffelsalat geräucherten Hinterschinken mit Senf. Die vier halben Scheiben Brot können Sie belegen mit Butter und Schmelzkäse. Zwei süße Dessertriegel und ein Erfrischungsbonbon runden Ihr Menü ab.

Je nach Vorrat Art.-Nr.	D in Deutschland DM*	B in Belgien FB	F in Frankreich FF	A in Österreich ÖS**	NL in den Niederld. hfl	CH in der Schweiz Sfrs.
Speisen						
406 Frühstück (Inhalt: siehe oben)	7,80	130,–	18,60	57,–	8,70	7,20
381 Kalte Mahlzeit (Inhalt: siehe oben)	15,–	250,–	35,70	107,–	16,70	13,80
Imbiß						
587 1 Bockwurst, 1 Scheibe Brot, Senf	3,–	50,–	7,10	21,–	3,30	2,80
416 3 Döschen Streichwurst, 2 Scheiben Brot, 1 Portion Butter	5,–	83,–	11,90	36,–	5,50	4,60
414 1 Portion Käse 50 g, 3 Scheiben Brot, 1 Portion Butter	5,–	83,–	11,90	36,–	5,50	4,60
308 1 Stück Cabanossi 100 g	3,30	55,–	7,90	24,–	3,70	3,–
287, 288, 289 } 1 Portionspackung Brot	–,40	7,–	1,–	3,–	–,50	–,40
Warme Getränke						
359 1 Kännchen Kaffee	3,40	57,–	8,10	24,–	3,80	3,10
358 1 Känn. Tee (1 Doppelteebeutel)	3,40	57,–	8,10	24,–	3,80	3,10
Verschiedenes						
440 1 Päckch. Marmorschnitten Stck.	2,10	35,–	5,–	15,–	2,30	1,90
986 1 Tafel Schokolade 100 g	1,70	28,–	4,–	12,–	1,90	1,60
987 Leibniz-Keks 100 g	1,70	28,–	4,–	12,–	1,90	1,60
431 1 Becher Eiskrem (vom 1. April bis 30. September)	2,10	35,–	5,–	15,–	2,30	1,90
831 Zigaretten (Automat.-Packg.)***	3,45	–	–	–	–	–
Kalte Getränke						
877 1 Dose Exportbier } einschl. 0,33 l	2,50	42,–	6,–	18,–	2,80	2,30
878 1 Dose Pils } Trinkb. 0,33 l	2,50	42,–	6,–	18,–	2,80	2,30
880 1 Fl. Apollinaris Mineralwasser 0,33 l	2,40	40,–	5,70	17,–	2,70	2,20
892 1 Dose Pepsi-Cola 0,33 l	2,50	42,–	6,–	18,–	2,80	2,30
895 1 Dose Fanta 0,33 l	2,50	42,–	6,–	18,–	2,80	2,30
894 1 Dose Florida Boy Orange (ohne Kohlensäure) 0,33 l	2,50	42,–	6,–	18,–	2,80	2,30
903 1 Dose Apfelsaft 0,33 l	2,50	42,–	6,–	18,–	2,80	2,30
Spirituosen						
801 Jägermeister 2 cl	3,10	–	–	–	–	–
802 Doornkaat 2 cl	2,80	–	–	–	–	–
800 Weinbr. Dujardin „Imperial" 2 cl	2,90	–	–	–	–	–

* In diesen Preisen sind Bedienungsgeld und Mehrwertsteuer enthalten.
** Einschließlich Mehrwertsteuer (8% für Speisen, 18% für Getränke).
*** Kein Verkauf auf Strecken der Deutschen Reichsbahn.

DSG
Deutsche Schlafwagen- und Speisewagen-Gesellschaft m.b.H.
Guiollettstraße 18-22
6000 Frankfurt am Main 1

MILCH   (0,2 l)

Nußmilch	2,30
Moccamilch	2,30
Kirschmilch	2,30
Zitronenmilch	2,30
Bananenmilch	2,30
Maracuja-Orangenmilch	2,30
Nußmilch mit Sahne	2,60
Moccamilch mit Sahne	2,60
Milch naturell	2,00
"Eimer Milch" 0,4 l	3,00

Zigaretten, Tabak mit Blättchen und Streichhölzer
erhalten Sie in unserem Automaten am Treppenauf-
gang. Unser Streichholzheft hat das dekorative Wall-
cafe-Design.

Das gibt's, . . .

daß man einigen Freunden Dias zeigen will; gemeinsame Aktionen gegen Ungerechtigkeiten plant; wichtige Ereignisse diskutieren muß; der gesamte Spiel-
kreis plötzlich ungeheuren Appetit auf Eis bekommt . .

und es passiert, . . .

daß man nirgendwo einen Raum dafür findet.
Wir haben einen Gruppenraum.
Reservieren kann man mündl. oder telef. (32 46 86),
für regelmäßige oder einmalige Treffen, kurz- oder
langfristig, für 4 bis maximal 20 Personen.

FRÜHSTÜCK BIS 23.00 UHR

Kleines Frühstück: Tasse Kaffee, Ei, Butter, Konfitüre, Roggenbrötchen, Brot	5,00
Frühstück: Kännchen Kaffee, Tee oder Kakao, Ei, Butter, Käse, Salami, Konfitüre, Roggen- brötchen, Toast, Brot	8,00
Knäcke-Frühstück: Tasse Kaffee, 2 Sorten Käse, Ei, Butter, Konfitüre, 3 Scheiben Knäckebrot	6,00
Müsli-Frühstück: Schale Müsli, Kännchen Milch, Schälchen Nüsse u. Rosinen, Marmelade	5,00
mit Orangensaft statt Milch	6,00
Amerikanisches Frühstück: 2 Eier mit Schinken, Toast, Ananas, Orangensaft und 1 Tasse Kaffee	9,00
Sekt-Frühstück für zwei Personen: Sekt Kännchen Kaffee, Tee oder Kakao, 2 Eier, 2 Sorten Käse, Salami, Konfitüre, Honig, Butter, 2 Roggenbrötchen, 4 Sorten Brot	24,00
Sekt-Frühstück für 1 Person: Sekt, Kännchen Kaffee, Tee oder Kakao, Ei, 2 Sorten Käse, Salami, Konfitüre, Honig, Butter, Roggenbrötchen, Brot	13,00

Selbstverständlich können Sie statt einer Tasse auch
ein Kännchen bekommen, der Differenzbetrag wird
verrechnet.

WEITERES ZU DEN GEDECKEN:

Portion Butter	0,90
gekochtes Ei	0,90
Roggenbrötchen	0,50
Scheibe Toast oder Brot	0,40
1 Scheibe Käse	1,00
2 Scheiben Knäckebrot	0,60
Portion Honig	0,70
Portion Konfitüre	0,60
Portion Käse Tartare	0,90
Portion Salami	1,00
Portion Schinken	1,30
Portion Camembert	1,70

KUCHEN

Apfelstrudel mit Sahne	3,50
Apfelstrudel mit heißer Vanillesoße	3,50

oder:
— Unseren Apfelstrudel — mit Äpfeln frisch vom Markt,
  geschnitten, mit selbstzubereitetem Strudelteil umhüllt —
  verkaufen wir auch

AUSSER HAUS!

Buchweizenkuchen	3,50

— mit Schokolade oder Preiselbeeren,
  jenachdem, was gerade frisch gebacken wurde

Schneemustorte	3,50
Obstkuchen nach Jahreszeit	3,00
Marmorkuchen	2,50
Nußkuchen	2,50
(mit Sahne + DM 0,50)	

Häufig backen wir auch Kuchen außerhalb der Reihe.
Fragen kostet nichts!

KALTE ERFRISCHUNGEN MIT EISKREM

Wiener Eiskaffee	(Vanilleeis, Kaffee, Schlagsahne)	3,60
Wallcafé-Shake	(Vanilleeis, Kakao, Rum, Schlagsahne	4,50
Sorbet	Tiroler Landwein, Zitroneneis)	4,50
Barbarossa	(prickelnder Rotwein, Erdbeereis)	4,50

EISKREM

Hawaiibecher	(Vanille-, Erdbeereis, Ananas, Sahne, Waffel)	5,50
Schwarzwaldbecher	(Kirchstrudeleis, Schwarzw. Kirschwasser, Kirschen, Sahne, Waffel)	5,80
Noisettebecher	(Vanille-, Nußeis, Eierlikör, Sahne, Krokant, Waffel)	5,80
Mohrenbecher	(Schokoladeneis, Rum, Sahne, Waffel)	5,80
Spezialbecher	(Vanilleeis, Früchte, Cointreau, Sahne, Waffel)	5,80
Kinderbecher "Tutti-Frutti"	(Vanille-Erdbeereis, Früchte, Sahne, Waffel	4,00

Nicht für große Kinder!

Portion Eis	3,70
Kleine Portion Eis	3,20
Portion Eis mit Sahne	4,40
Portion Eis mit Früchten	4,40
Portion Eis mit Früchten und Sahne	4,70
Kleine Portion Eis mit Sahne	3,90
Kleine Portion Eis mit Früchten	3,90
Kleine Portion Eis mit Früchten und Sahne	4,20

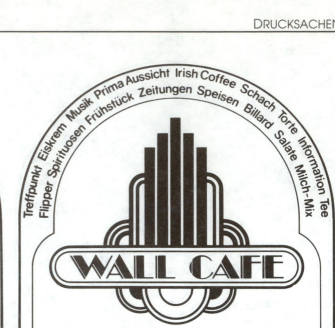

HEISSE KÖSTLICHKEITEN

Irish Coffee	(Kaffee mit 2 cl Tullamore, Dew Whiskey, Zucker, Schlagsahne)	5,80
Kaffee Orange	(Kaffee mit 2 cl Cointreau, Zucker, Mandarinen, Schlagsahne)	5,80
Kaffee Royal	(Kaffee mit 2 cl Asbach Uralt, Zucker, Schlagsahne)	5,80
Pharisäer	(Kaffee mit 2 cl Rum, Zucker, Schlagsahne)	5,80
Schoko Caprice	(Kakao mit 2 cl Cointreau, Zucker, Schlagsahne)	5,80
Schoko Tia Maria	(Kakao mit 2 cl Rum, Zucker, Schlagsahne)	5,80
Russ. Schokolade	(Kakao mit 2 cl Wodka, Zucker, Schlagsahne)	5,50
Grog mit 4 cl Rum		5,00
Glühwein		4,50

Der Kaffee ist das Unwesentlichste von allen Dingen, die zu einem richtigen Kaffeehaus gehören. Man kann getrost behaupten, daß unter hundert Besuchern dieser Bildungsanstalten kaum zehn sind, die von dem Drange nach dem unentbehrlichen Schälchen hingeführt werden. Die übrigen Neunzig gehen hinein, weil — weil — ja,
warum denn?
Warum?!
Nun, wohin soll man denn sonst geh'n! Wo soll man sein ''Lesebedürfnis'' befriedigen? Wo soll man die ''wichtigsten'' Neuigkeiten erfahren? Wo soll man seine Bekannten treffen? Wo soll man Schach oder Tarock spielen? Wo soll man seine Zeit todtschlagen? Und schlägt man sie nicht todt, ja, um Himmelswillen, was soll man mit diesem lästigen Überfluß an Zeit denn anfangen?

Edmund Wengraf, 1891

KAFFEE

Kaffee	Kännchen	3,60
	Tasse	1,80
Café Crême (Kaffee mit Schlagsahne)	Tasse	2,10
Italienischer Espresso		2,20
Italienischer Capuccino		2,40
Kakao mit Schlagsahne	Kännchen	4,00
	Tasse	2,10

TEE   (Kännchen)

Traditionell im Kännchen gebrüht, keine Teebeutel!

Bitte beachten Sie, daß Tee ein Naturprodukt ist und sein volles Aroma erst nach 3 — 5 Minuten entfaltet.

Himalaya Hochgewächs, Darjeeling	4,20
Jasmin mit Honig	4,20
Earl Grey, engl. Mischung	4,20
Russische Mischung	4,00
Russische Mischung mit Maraschinokirsche	4,20
Ceylon Mischung	4,00
Ostfriesische Mischung	4,00
Ostfriesische Mischung mit Schlagsahne	4,20
Sweet Orange	4,50
Bourbon Vanille	4,50
Granny's Apfeltee	4,50

Mancher strebsame junge Mann hierzulande, der für die Bildung seines Genius etwas tun wollte, hat seine Laufbahn damit begonnen, daß er sich zunächst das geeignete Kaffeehaus aussuchte.

J. A. Lux. 1922

SPIRITUOSEN

Rum	2 cl 40 %	2,50
	4 cl	3,80
Bacardi	2 cl 38 %	3,30
	4 cl	5,00
Calvados	2 cl 40 %	3,30
	4 cl	5,00
Pernod	2 cl 43 %	3,30
	4 cl	5,00
Korn	2 cl 32 %	1,50
	4 cl	2,50
Gin, deutscher	2 cl 40 %	2,50
	4 cl	3,80
Gin, Gordon's	2 cl 40 %	3,30
	4 cl	5,00
Wodka, deutscher	2 cl 40 %	2,50
	4 cl	3,80
Wodka, Moskowskaya	2 cl 40 %	3,30
	4 cl	5,00
Fernet Branca	2 cl 42 %	3,00
	4 cl	4,80
Underberg	2 cl 49 %	3,00
Ouzo	2 cl 40 %	3,00
	4 cl	4,80
Malteserkreuz	2 cl 43 %	3,00
Tequila	2 cl 40 %	3,30
	4 cl	5,00
Grappa	2 cl 43 %	3,50
	4 cl	5,50
Campari	2 cl 25 %	3,00
	4 cl	4,80

WEINE

Weißweine:

Rheinhessen	Bechtheimer Pilgerpfad		
	– süffig, blumig –	0,2 l	3,80
Mosel	Ürziger Schwarzley, Riesling		
	– lieblich, würzig,schöner Riesling		
		0,2 l	4,00
Baden	Sasbacher Vulkanfelsen, Müller-Thurgau		
	– fruchtig, feines Bukett –		
		0,2 l	4,50
Rheinpfalz	Leinsweiler Herrlich, Huxel Spätlese		
	– duftig, mild –	0,2 l	5,00
Elsaß	Edelzwicker	0,2 l	4,40

Roséweine:

Rheinpfalz	Ungsteiner Kobnert, Portugieser Weißherbst		
	– fruchtig, frisch, saftig –		
		0,2 l	4,40

Rotweine:

Frankreich	Château Flaugerges		
	– frisch, viel Körper, vollmundig –		
		0,2 l	3,50
Frankreich	Beaujolais Villages	0,2 l	5,00

Sekt:

MM – Extra	1/4 Fl.	7,50
Henkell Trocken	1/1 Fl.	30,00
Fürst v. Metternich	1/1 Fl.	39,00

Bowle nach Saison

Speisekarte: Restaurant   Menu: Restaurant

JACOBI immer in Mode...mitten in Köln

Restaurant
Café

Zum Frühstück (bis 11 Uhr)

Tasse Kaffee, Tee oder Schokolade 2 Brötchen, Butter und Konfitüre, 1 gek. Ei	3,40
Kännchen Kaffee, Tee oder Schokolade 2/2 belegte Brötchen nach Wahl	5,—
1 gekochtes Ei	—,55
Portion Butter	—,65

Warme Getränke

Tasse Bohnenkaffee mit Milch und Zucker	1,60
Kännchen Bohnenkaffee	3,20
Tasse Kaffee Hag	1,60
Tasse Schokolade mit Zwieback und Sahne	1,80
Glas Tee mit Zitrone oder Sahne	1,60
Kännchen Tee mit Zitrone oder Sahne	2,80
Grog von Rum 4 cl. Portions-Fläschchen	2,60
Irish Coffee	5,50

Eierspeisen

3 Stck. Spiegeleier oder Rührei mit Salat und Pommes frites	7,50
3 Stck. Spiegeleier oder Rührei mit Schinken, Salat und Pommes frites	8,—
Rührei mit Spargel, Toast und Salat	7,—
Omelette mit Spargel, Toast und Salat	9,—
Omelette mit Champignons	9,—
Omelette mit Schinken, Pommes frites und Salat	9,—
Omelette mit Spargel, Pommes frites	9,—

Warme Speisen (bis 17.30 Uhr. Zubereitungsdauer ca. 15 Min.)

Feines Ragout im Näpfchen mit Toast	5,80
Blätterteig-Pastetchen mit feinem Ragout	7,—
Ungarischer Gulasch, Pommes frites oder Salzkartoffeln, Salat *) **)	9,90
Schweinekotelett mit gem. Salat u. Pommes frites	10,20
Jägerschnitzel mit gem. Salat u. Pommes frites	11,—
Wiener Schnitzel mit gem. Salat und Pommes frites	14,60
Rumpsteak mit Meerrettich o. Champignons grosser Salat-Teller und Pommes frites *)	15,—
1/2 Masthähnchen mit Salat und Pommes frites	8,—
Schweinekotelett „Ungarisch" mit Buttererbsen und Pommes frites	10,60
Nordsee-Scholle ohne Gräten gebraten mit gemischtem Salat, Pommes frites	9,90

Unsere Tagesspezialitäten

Montag

Rheinischer Sauerbraten mit Rosinensauce, 2 Stck. Kartoffel-Klößen und Apfelmus-Ananas	10,30

Dienstag

mild geräuchtes Kasseler-Rippenspeer auf Sauerkraut und Kartoffel-Püree	10,30

Mittwoch

Eisbein mit Sauerkraut und Kartoffel-Püree	10,30

Donnerstag

Ungarischer Saftgoulasch mit 2 Kartoffel-Klößen und gemischtem Salat	10,30

Freitag

Rotbarsch-Filet gebacken, Remouladen-Sauce, Pommes frites und Salat	10,30

Warme Küche bis eine Stunde,
Kalte Küche bis eine halbe Stunde vor Geschäftsschluß.
Wir bitten um Ihr Verständnis.

*) Sorbinsäure   **) Ameisensäure

Beilagen

Salzkartoffeln	1,40
Pommes frites	1,60
Kartoffelsalat	1,60
Salat oder Gemüse	2,20
Apfelmus mit Ananas	1,60

Suppen

Ochsenschwanzsuppe mit Brötchen	2,50
Hühnerbrühe mit Einlage und Brötchen	2,50
Hühnerbrühe mit Einlage, Ei und Brötchen	3,—
Serbische Bohnensuppe	3,—

Kalte Speisen

'ne halven Hahn (Käse, Röggelchen, Butter)	2,30
1 Stck. Leberwurst, Kartoffelsalat	3,70
Wurst- oder Käseschnittchen	3,75
Schnittchen gekochter Schinken oder Braten, garniert	6,50
Strammer Max mit Mayonnaisensalat	7,—
3/2 russische Eier garniert	4,80
Fleischsalat oder Heringssalat mit Brötchen	3,20
Sülze mit Sauce Remoulade und Pommes frites	6,10
Kasseler Rippchen mit Kartoffelsalat	6,90
Schweinekotelett mit Mayonnaisensalat	6,70
Zartes Roastbeef rosa gebraten mit Remouladen-Sauce, Röstkartoffel oder Mayonnaisensalat	8,70
Eiersalat, Champignons, Spargel, Toast und Butter	6,80
Salatplatte mit Spiegelei	7,—
Riesenbockwurst mit Brötchen	3,70
Riesenbockwurst mit Kartoffelsalat	4,30
Riesenbockwurst mit großer Portion Pommes frites	5,—
JACOBI-Spezialplatte	8,—
Heringsstip im Steintopf, „Hausfrauen-Art", Kartoffeln oder Pommes frites, oder Brot	7,50
„KÖLNER-DOM"-Teller gekocht. Schinken, Stangenspargel, Geflügelsalat-Eiersalat, Weißbrot	9,50
1/2 Belegtes Brötchen	1,60

Unsere Hauskonditorei empfiehlt

Rodonkuchen	1,70
Dresdner Käse-Apfel-Torte	2,10
Sahne-Torten ab	2,60
Obst-Torten ab	2,10
Obst-Torten mit Sahne ab	2,60
Buttercreme-Torten ab	2,60
Portion Schlagsahne	1,40

Reiche Auswahl an Kuchen und Torten in erstklassiger Qualität (auch zum Mitnehmen) finden Sie täglich frisch an unserem Büfett. Beachten Sie bitte unsere Tages-Kuchenkarte!

Eiscreme-Spezialitäten

Gemischtes Eis, Vanille, Schokolade, Erdbeer	2,50
Gemischtes Eis mit Sahne	3,—
Eiskaffee mit Sahne	2,60
Eis-Schokolade mit Sahne	2,60
Ananas-Melba	3,60
Pfirsich-Melba	4,50

RHEINGOLD-EISBECHER
Vanille-Eis, Früchte, Nüsse, Himbeersaft, Sahne — 4,60

SCHWARZWÄLDER EISBECHER
Vanille-Eis, Erdbeer-Eis, Früchte, Kirschwasser, Sahne — 5,50

JACOBI-EISBECHER
Vanille-Eis, Erdbeer-Eis, Früchte, Mandeln, Johannisbeer-Gelee, Sahne, Orig. Chartreuse — 5,80

KINDER-EISBECHER mit Früchten und Sahne — 3,70

Kalte Getränke

Flasche DOM-Kölsch	0,33 l	2,10
Flasche STERN-Pils	0,33 l	2,10
Flasche STERN-Urkraft (Malz)	0,33 l	2,10
Flasche KÖNIG-Pils	0,33 l	2,50
Glas COCA-COLA		1,80
Glas FANTA		1,80
Flasche Looza-Tomatensaft	0,2 l	2,—
Flasche Mineralwasser Apollinaris	0,25 l	1,80
Schorle, weiß oder rot	0,2 l	2,40
Apfelsaft-Schorle	0,2 l	2,—
Apfelsaft	0,2 l	2,10
Orangensaft aus Konzentrat		2,—
Traubensaft	0,2 l	2,50
Schwarzer Johannisbeersaft	0,2 l	2,50

Spirituosen

Doppelkorn	2 cl	1,60
Doppelwacholder	2 cl	1,60
Doornkaat	2 cl	1,90
Steinhäger Schlichte	2 cl	1,90
Schwarzwälder Kirschwasser	2 cl	2,50
Asbach Uralt	2 cl	2,40
Underberg, Orig.-Flasche	2 cl	2,—

Weine

Pokal Rhein-, Mosel- oder Rotwein	0,1 l	2,40
Karaffe Rhein-, Mosel- oder Rotwein	¼ l	4,60
CINZANO, rot, weiß oder dry	5 cl	2,70

Sekt

Glas Sekt mit Orangensaft	3,80
Glas Campari / Soda mit Eis	3,80
Glas Campari / Orange mit Eis	5,50
Piccolo Matheus Müller einschl. Sektsteuer	5,50

Alle Preise einschl. Bedienungsgeld und Mehrwertsteuer
Für Ihre Garderobe können wir leider nicht haften.

SCHUMA-KAFFEE KÖLN

Für den verwöhnten Gaumen:

Hawai-Toast mit Salat	7,—
Geflügelsalat „Miami" mit Toast und Butter	8,50
Spezialtoast mit Ragout fin, Spargel, Champignons, Sc. Hollandaise, mit verschied. Salaten umlegt	7,—

Parkscheine können wir hier nicht einlösen. Dagegen vergüten wir Ihnen beim Einkauf ab DM 5,— am Lösungstage in allen Abteilungen unseres Hauses ab DM 1,— Parkgebühr sämtlicher der Parkgemeinschaft Köln e. V. angeschlossenen Parkhäuser und des Parkhauses Gürzenich.

A-Z für Touristen   A to Z for the Tourist

Wien · Vienna · Vienne · Viena · ウィーン

Informationen

Autofahren und Verkehrsvorschriften

Die allgemeinen Verkehrsvor-
schriften unterscheiden sich im
allgemeinen nicht wesentlich von
denen anderer Länder (Rechts-
fahrordnung). Es wurden aber
aus Gründen der Verkehrssicher-
heit, der besseren Ausnützung des
Parkraumes und der Erhaltung
des Verkehrsflusses einige Son-
derregelungen getroffen, die Sie
kennen und beachten
müssen.
Die Höchstgeschwindigkeit im
Ortsgebiet beträgt 50 km/h. Hup-
verbot besteht generell in ganz
Wien. Es wird empfohlen, für
Fahrten innerhalb Wiens öffentliche Verkehrsmittel zu benützen.
In Straßen mit Parkverbot dürfen
Sie höchstens 10 Minuten halten.
In Kurzparkzonen ist das Parken
an Werktagen zwischen 8 und 18
Uhr (Samstag 8–12 Uhr) nur mit
Parkscheinen für die Dauer von
maximal 1½ Stunden gestattet.
Achtung: Die Tafeln „Parkverbot" mit dem Zusatz „Kurzpark-
zone" sind nur am Beginn
und am Ende der Zonen
aufgestellt.
Parkscheine gibt es bei den Vorverkaufsstellen der Wiener Verkehrsbetriebe, bei vielen Tank-
stellen, in Tabak-Trafiken sowie
in den Filialen einiger Geldinsti-
tute. Die Entwertung geschieht
durch Anzeichnen von Jahr, Monat, Tag und Uhrzeit.

Banken und Wechselstuben

Die Öffnungszeiten bei den
Wiener Banken und Sparkassen-
zentralen sind Montag, Dienstag,
Mittwoch, Freitag, 8–15 Uhr,
Donnerstag 8–17.30 Uhr (Filialen
von 12.30–13.30 Uhr geschlossen). Von Montag bis Samstag
können Sie auch in vielen Reisebüros, täglich in den Wechselstuben im Westbahnhof
(7–22 Uhr), im Südbahnhof

(6.30 bis 22 Uhr), im Bahnhof
Wien Mitte (Montag bis Freitag
7.30–19 Uhr, Samstag, Sonn- und
Feiertag 7.30–13 Uhr), im City
Air Terminal (8–12.30 Uhr und
14–18 Uhr), am Flughafen
(6.30–23 Uhr) und in der Tourist-
Information Opernpassage
(9–19 Uhr) Geld wechseln.

Donau-Rundfahrten in Wien

Von April bis Oktober täglich
um 13 Uhr.
Von Mai bis September täglich
um 13 und 16.30 Uhr.
Von Mai bis Oktober jeden Donnerstag, Freitag und Samstag um
20.30 Uhr.
Abfahrt bei der DDSG-Station
Schwedenbrücke-Donaukanal.
Informationen: DDSG-Reise-
dienst. A-1021 Wien. Handels-
kai 265. Tel. 26 65 36.

Fiaker

Standplätze auf dem Stephansplatz, Heldenplatz, Josefsplatz
und in der Augustinerstraße
(gegenüber der Albertina).

Flughafen

Internationaler Flughafen Wien-
Schwechat, 19 km von der Innenstadt entfernt.
Flughafen-Transfers:
Autobus: Regelmäßige Busverbindung zwischen dem Flug-
hafen und der Innenstadt (City
Air Terminal, Wien 3, beim
Hotel Hilton). Von 6–8 Uhr alle
30 Minuten, von 8–19.20 Uhr alle
20 Minuten. Bei Ankunft von
Kursmaschinen stehen auch
nach 19.20 Uhr Transferbusse zur
Verfügung. Außerdem zwischen
dem Flughafen und West- und
Südbahnhof. Von 6 bis 19 Uhr
alle 30 Minuten ab Westbahnhof
(15 Minuten später vom
Südbahnhof) und von 7 bis
19 Uhr alle 30 Minuten ab
Flughafen.
Eisenbahn: Bahnverbindung
zwischen Flughafen und Wien-
Mitte (City Air Terminal) und
Wien-Nord (Praterstern)

zwischen 7.30–20.30 Uhr ca. jede
Stunde.
Shuttle Service: Kleinbusverbin-
dung zwischen dem Flughafen
und Ihrem Hotel. Bestellung
direkt am Flughafen, im Hotel
oder bei Ihrer Fluglinie.

Geld

Die Währungseinheit ist der
Schilling zu 100 Groschen. Es
gibt Münzen zu 5, 10, 50
Groschen und Münzen zu 1, 5,
10, 20, 25, 50, 100, 500, 1000
Schilling, außerdem Banknoten
zu 20, 50, 100, 500 und 1000
Schilling.

Gottesdienste

Katholische Gottesdienste ab
6 Uhr. Auskünfte Tel. 53 25 61.
Evangelische Gottesdienste:
Auskünfte Tel. 52 83 92; Israeliti-
scher Gottesdienst im Tempel,
1010 Wien, Seitenstettengasse 4,
Tel. 63 45 16; Altkatholische
Kirche, 1010 Wien, Wipplinger-
straße 6, Tel. 63 71 33; Wiener
Islamisches Zentrum, 1210 Wien,
Am Hubertusdamm 17–19,
Tel. 30 13 89; Islamischer Gebets-
raum, 1090 Wien, Türken-
straße 3, Tel. 34 46 25; Anglikani-
scher Gottesdienst, 1030 Wien,
Jaurèsgasse 17–19, Auskünfte:
Tel. 73 15 75; Mormonen: Auskünfte Tel. 37 32 57; Methodi-
sten: Auskünfte Tel. 43 72 45.

Informationsstellen und Zimmer-vermittlung

Für Autoreisende:
Offizielle Tourist-Information
an der Autobahn A1 (Westauto-
bahn) Autobahnstation Wien-
Auhof. ganzjährig. April bis Oktober 8–22 Uhr. November bis
März 10–18 Uhr. Offizielle Tourist-Information an der Autobahn
A2 (Südautobahn) Abfahrt Zentrum. April bis Juni und Oktober
bis März täglich 10–18 Uhr. Juli
bis September täglich 8–22 Uhr.
Für Flugreisende:
Offizielle Tourist-Information in
der Ankunftshalle des
Flughafens, täglich 9–22 Uhr.
Juni–September täglich bis
23 Uhr.

Für Schiffsreisende:
In der Schiffsstation Wien-
Reichsbrücke befindet sich ein
Auskunftsschalter der DDSG
mit Zimmervermittlung
(7.30–20 Uhr).
Während Ihres Wien-Aufenthaltes:
Offizielle Tourist-Information.
Opernpassage, Telefon 43 16 08,
täglich 9–19 Uhr.
Österreich-Information
1040 Wien. Margaretenstr. 1
(Ecke Wiedner Hauptstraße)
Telefon 57 57 14. Montag bis
Freitag 9–17 Uhr.
Bahnreisende finden in bzw. bei
Westbahn- und Südbahnhof Rei-
sebüros. die eine beschränkte Aus-
wahl von Hotels vermitteln.

Klima

Wien liegt 171 m über dem
Meeresspiegel. Das Klima ist
teils atlantisch, teils kontinental
beeinflußt.
In den trockenen, sonnigen
Sommermonaten steigt die
Temperatur bis etwa 30°C. Im
Winter fällt das Thermometer bis
knapp unter 0°C. Die schönsten
Jahreszeiten mit ihren milden
und sonnigen Tagen sind der
Frühling und der Herbst in
Wien.

Kurzentrum Wien-Oberlaa

Eine der wärmsten Schwefel-
thermalquellen Österreichs,
diverse therapeutische Einrich-
tungen, Thermalbad, Tennis,
Kurpark, ca. 15 Minuten vom
Stadtzentrum entfernt.
Auskünfte: Heilquelle Oberlaa,
Kurbetriebsgesellschaft m.b.H.,
1100 Wien, Kurbadstraße 10,
Tel. 68 16 11.

Notfälle

Bei Notfällen können Sie in
Wien über die Telefonnummern
122   die Feuerwehr
133   die Polizei
144   die Rettung
herbeirufen.

Post- und Telegrafenämter

Adressen siehe Telefonbuch
unter „Post". Im allgemeinen
sind die Postämter von Montag

bis Freitag von 8–18 Uhr geöffnet. Das **Hauptpostamt** (Wien 1., Fleischmarkt 19) und alle Bahnhofspostämter haben auch Nacht- und Sonntagsdienst. Telegrafenzentrale: 1., Börseplatz 1. Postdienstliche Auskünfte: Telefon 83 21 01. Briefmarken sind in allen Postämtern und Tabak-Trafiken erhältlich. Briefmarken-Automaten vor den meisten Postämtern.

Shopping

Hauptgeschäftsstraßen sind in der Inneren Stadt (1. Bezirk): die Kärntner Straße (zwischen Opernkreuzung und Stock-im-Eisen-Platz) mit den kleinen Seitengassen, der Graben (zwischen Stock-im-Eisen-Platz und Kohlmarkt), der Kohlmarkt (zwischen Graben und Michaelerplatz), die Rotenturmstraße (zwischen Stephansplatz und Kai); ferner die Mariahilfer Straße (zwischen Messepalast und Westbahnhof), die Favoritenstraße (zwischen Südtiroler Platz und Reumannplatz) und die Landstraßer Hauptstraße.
Geschäftszeiten:
Die Geschäfte sind im allgemeinen von Montag bis Freitag von 9–18 Uhr, Samstag von 9–12 Uhr geöffnet. Lebensmittelgeschäfte öffnen schon vor 8 Uhr, halten aber oft Mittagspause von 12.30 bis 15 Uhr. Die Geschäfte im West- und Südbahnhof sind täglich von 7–23 Uhr geöffnet (Lebensmittel, Tabakwaren, Schreibartikel, Bücher, Blumen). In diesen Bahnhöfen befinden sich auch Friseur, Bäder und Fotoautomaten.
Einkaufstips:
Das Wiener Kunsthandwerk bietet Erzeugnisse an, die nach alter handwerklicher Tradition hergestellt werden und ihrer Schönheit, Güte und Preiswürdigkeit wegen in aller Welt geschätzt sind. Besonders beliebte Artikel sind Petit-Point-Arbeiten, Gebrauchs- und Ziergegenstände aus handbemaltem Wiener Augarten-Porzellan, Goldschmiede-Erzeugnisse, handgefertigte Puppen, Kunstkeramik, Emailarbeiten, Schmiedeeisen-Erzeugnisse, Lederwaren aller Art und anderes mehr.
Für Sammler und Kunstfreunde werden die Wiener Antiquitätenläden eine unerschöpfliche Fundgrube sein. In Antiquariaten, Buch- und Kunsthandlungen und zahlreichen Gemäldegalerien kann man wertvolle alte Bücher, Bildbände, Stiche, Radie-

rungen, Aquarelle oder Ölbilder erwerben.
Kunstauktionen veranstalten das staatliche „Dorotheum", 1. Bezirk, Dorotheergasse 19, große Privatgalerien und Antiquitätenhandlungen. Die zur Versteigerung gelangenden Gegenstände können vorher besichtigt werden. Ausrufungspreis und Versteigerungstermine sind angeschrieben.
Flohmarkt, Wien 6, Naschmarkt bei der U-Bahnstation Kettenbrückengasse. Jeden Samstag 8–18 Uhr (nicht an Feiertagen).

Spanische Reitschule

1010 Wien, Hofburg. Vorführungen der Spanischen Reitschule finden Sonntag vormittag (10.45) und Mittwoch abend (19 Uhr) statt, ausgenommen in den Monaten Jänner, Februar, Juli, August und Dezember. Die genauen Termine entnehmen Sie bitte dem Detailprogramm des Wiener Fremdenverkehrsverbandes. Kartenbestellungen sind unbedingt erforderlich und sollten so früh als möglich für die Sonntagsvorführungen an die Spanische Reitschule, für die Mittwoch- und die Kurzvorführungen nur an Wiener Theaterkarten- und Reisebüros gerichtet werden.
Das Training (Morgenarbeit) kann täglich außer Sonntag und Montag von 10 bis 12 Uhr besichtigt werden.

Stadtrundfahrt

Die beiden Wiener Rundfahrtengesellschaften **Cityrama Sightseeing Tours** und **Vienna Sightseeing Tours** bieten ein reichhaltiges Angebot an Besichtigungs- und Ausflugsfahrten.
Auskünfte und Buchungen bei allen Reisebüros und in den Hotels.

Taxi

Funktaxiruf: 31 30, 43 69, 62 82, 91 90
Der Fahrpreis wird durch amtlich geichte Taxameteruhren angezeigt. Gepäckzuschlag bei Gepäck über 20 kg S 10,–. Preis für Fahrten außerhalb des Stadtgebietes nach freier Vereinbarung. Standplätze gekennzeichnet.

Verkehrsmittel

Speziell für Wien-Besucher: **72-Stunden-Netzkarte.** Gültig für U-Bahn. Schnellbahn. Stadtbahn. Straßenbahn und Autobus. Preis 92 öS. Erhältlich bei: Tourist-Informationsstellen. Tabak-Trafiken. Reisebüros im Westbahnhof und Südbahnhof. Informationsstellen der Wiener Verkehrsbetriebe in den U-Bahn-Stationen Karlsplatz. Stephansplatz. Praterstern sowie bei allen Vorverkaufsstellen der Wiener Verkehrsbetriebe.
Für Straßenbahn, Autobus, Stadtbahn, U-Bahn und Schnellbahn gibt es innerhalb der Stadtgrenzen einen einheitlichen Tarif, mit dem Umland einen Verkehrsverbund. Fahrscheine können Sie im Vorverkauf in den Vorverkaufsstellen und in Tabaktrafiken (in Blöcken zu 5 Stück) verbilligt oder im Wagen beim Automaten zum vollen Fahrpreis besorgen. Fahrscheine werden nur bei Fahrtantritt markiert. In schaffnerlosen Wagen Entwerter, bei U-Bahn und Stadtbahn Entwerter bei den Bahnsteigsperren. Markierte Fahrkarten gelten inklusive Umsteigen bis zum Fahrziel. Kurzstreckenkarten und Streifenkarten für den Verkehrsverbund gibt es nur im Vorverkauf.

Aus dem Veranstaltungskalender

Aus der Fülle von Veranstaltungen in Wien finden Sie hier jene, die jährlich etwa zum gleichen Termin abgehalten werden. Das Detailprogramm für Ihren Wien-Besuch erscheint jeweils Mitte des Vormonats und wird auf Anforderung gerne zugesandt.

Frühling

Haydn-Tage (März)
Wiener Frühlings-Marathon (März)
Viennale Film-Festival (März)
Wiener Messen (März)
Spanische Reitschule, Vorführungen (März bis Juni)
Walzer- und Operettenkonzerte (April bis Oktober)
Rundfahrten mit der Donau-Dampfschiffahrts-Gesellschaft (April bis Oktober)
Wiener Festwochen (Mai, Juni)
Frühlingsfest im Prater (Mai)

Sommer

Blumenkorso im Prater (Juni)
Spectacvlvm (Juli)
Wiener Musik-Sommer (Juli, August)

Wiener Sängerknaben

In der Burgkapelle der Wiener Hofburg finden von Jänner bis Juni und von Mitte September bis Dezember an allen Sonntagen und röm. kath. Feiertagen um 9.15 Uhr Messen statt, zu denen die sogenannte Hofmusikkapelle – bestehend aus einem Chor der Wiener Sängerknaben sowie Mitgliedern des Staatsopernchores und -orchesters – Werke alter und neuer Meister aufführt. Schriftliche Bestellungen von Sitzplätzen sollen mindestens acht Wochen im voraus an die Hofmusikkapelle, Hofburg, A-1010 Wien, gerichtet werden (Stehplätze sind frei).
Ein separates Kartenkontingent wird an der Tageskasse in der Burgkapelle jeweils am Freitag ab 17 Uhr verkauft. Rechtzeitiges Anstellen (etwa ab 16.30 Uhr) ist zweckmäßig. Pro Person werden an der Tageskasse maximal zwei Karten abgegeben.

Zeitunterschied

In Österreich gilt die mitteleuropäische Zeit (MEZ). Zwischen Ende März und Ende September werden die Uhren um 1 Stunde vorgestellt.

Operettenvorstellungen (Juli, August)

Herbst

Messen mit den Wiener Sängerknaben (September bis Dezember)
Spanische Reitschule, Vorführungen (September bis Dezember)
Wiener Messen (September)
Schuberttage (November)
Antiquitätenmesse (November)
Antiquitätenschau im Kursalon (November)

Winter

Advent in Wien, Christkindlmarkt (Dezember)
Kaiserball in der Hofburg (31. Dezember)
Neujahrskonzert der Wiener Philharmoniker (1. Jänner)
Wiener Fasching: Philharmonikerball, Opernball und hunderte andere Bälle (Jänner bis März)
Operettenwoche, Maskenball am kaiserlichen Hof zu Wien (Februar)

Sehenswürdigkeiten   Sights to See

TRIER

ÖFFNUNGSZEITEN UND EINTRITTSPREISE DER SEHENSWÜRDIGKEITEN UND MUSEEN

Porta Nigra, Amphitheater, Barbara-* und Kaiserthermen

können besichtigt werden in der Zeit:

1. 1.–31. 3. täglich (außer montags) 9 – 13 und 14 – 17 Uhr
1. 4.–30. 9. täglich 9 – 13 und 14 – 18 Uhr
1. 10.–31. 10. täglich 9 – 13 und 14 – 17 Uhr
1. 11.–30. 11. täglich (außer montags) 9 – 13 und 14 – 17 Uhr

Im Monat Dezember sind alle Bauwerke geschlossen.

* Die Barbarathermen sind montags geschlossen.
Letzter Einlaß ist jeweils eine halbe Stunde vor Schließung des Bauwerks.

Eintrittspreise

	Einmaliger Besuch eines Bauwerks	Besuch aller Bauwerke
a) Erwachsene	2,– DM	6,– DM
b) Erwachsene in Gruppen ab 20 Personen	1,50 DM	4,50 DM
c) Jugendliche bis einschl. 18 J.	1,– DM	3,– DM
d) Jugendliche in Gruppen ab 20 Personen	0,70 DM	2,– DM
e) Rentner, Studenten, Schwerbeschädigte	1,– DM	3,– DM
f) Kinder unter 6 Jahren	freier Eintritt	
g) Familien (2 Erw. u. 3 Kinder)	5,– DM	15,– DM

Römische Palastaula (Basilika) ev. Kirche

Telefon (06 51) 7 24 68

Ostersamstag bis 31. Okt.: werktags 9 – 13 Uhr und 14 – 18 Uhr sonn- und feiertags 11 – 13 Uhr und 14 – 18 Uhr

1. November bis Karfreitag: werktags 11 – 12 Uhr und 15 – 16 Uhr sonntags 11 – 12 Uhr montags geschlossen.

Dom und Liebfrauenkirche

1. November bis 31. März: täglich 6 – 12 Uhr und 14 – 17.30 Uhr
1. April bis 31. Oktober: täglich 6 – 18 Uhr

Führungen im Dom und in der Liebfrauenkirche.
Preis: 1,– DM/Person.
Anfragen direkt an Dombüro, Telefon (06 51) 7 58 01.

Domschatzkammer:

1. November bis 31. März: werktags 10 – 12 und 14 – 17 Uhr sonntags 14 – 16 Uhr
1. April bis 31. Oktober: werktags 10 – 12 und 14 – 17 Uhr sonntags 14 – 17 Uhr

Eintritt: 1,– DM.

St.-Matthias-Abteikirche (Trier-Süd)

Täglich 7 – 12 Uhr und 14 – 18 Uhr.

Besichtigung der frühchristlichen Grabanlagen unter dem Friedhof von St. Matthias für kleinere Gruppen nach Anmeldung beim Pfarramt, Telefon (06 51) 3 26 34.

Kath. St.-Michael-Kirche, Am Mariahof 37

Telefon (06 51) 3 22 42

Modernes Gotteshaus mit Kunstwerken von Otto Herbert Hajek und Jakob Schwarzkopf (Glasfenster).

Geöffnet: täglich 11 – 12 Uhr und 15 – 17 Uhr.

St.-Paulin-Kirche (Trier Nord)

Telefon (06 51) 2 76 34

Täglich 8 – 12 Uhr und 14 – 18 Uhr. Donnerstags vormittags geschlossen.

Rheinisches Landesmuseum, Ostallee 44

Telefon (06 51) 4 83 68

Archäologische Funde von der Altsteinzeit bis zur Neuzeit, insbesondere römerzeitliche Mosaiken, Grabinventare, Grabdenkmäler mit Reliefdarstellungen aus Alltag und Berufsleben, Keramik, Glas, Münzen und Kleinkunst sowie frühchristliche Zeugnisse.

Geöffnet: montags bis freitags   9.30 – 16 Uhr
samstags   9.30 – 14 Uhr
sonntags   9.00 – 13 Uhr

Geschlossen am 1. Januar, 1. Mai, 24., 25., 26. und 31. Dezember.

Eintritt frei.

Städt. Museum Simeonstift (An der Porta Nigra)

Telefon (06 51) 7 18-24 49

Dokumente der Stadtgeschichte, Kunstwerke vom Mittelalter bis zum 19. Jahrh. aus Trier, spätantike Kunst, Wechselausstellungen zeitgenössischer Kunst.

Geöffnet täglich von 9 bis 17 Uhr; von November bis Februar montags geschlossen. Eintritt: Erwachsene 2,– DM; Schüler, Lehrlinge, Studenten, Soldaten und Rentner 1,– DM; Schüler bis 14 Jahre freier Eintritt.

Unterricht im Museum: nach Anmeldung jederzeit durch den Fachlehrer möglich.

Bischöfliches Museum, Banthusstraße 6

Telefon (06 51) 71 05-255

Kirchliche Kunst der Trierer Diözese, Funde aus frühchristlicher Zeit. Konstantinische Deckenmalereien.

Geöffnet: montags bis freitags   10 – 12 und 14 – 17 Uhr
samstags, sonn- und feiertags   10 – 13 Uhr

Eintritt: 1,– DM.
Schüler, Studenten, Gruppen: 0,50 DM.
Geschlossen vom 23. Dezember bis 2. Januar.

Schatzkammer und Ausstellung der Stadtbibliothek, Weberbach 25

Telefon (06 51) 7 18 – 24 30

Kostbare Handschriften, Gutenberg-Bibel und illustrierte Bücher, Urkunden und Dokumente aus Mittelalter und Neuzeit; Barock-Globen, Karten, Wechselausstellungen.

Geöffnet: bis 24. 3. und ab 2. 11. 1986, samstags 10 – 13 Uhr; 25. 3. bis 1. 11. 1986 montags bis freitags 14 – 17 Uhr, samstags 10 – 13 Uhr.

Eintritt: Erwachsene 2,– DM, Schüler, Studenten 1,– DM.
Führungen (1 Std.) Deutsch, Fremdspr. 30,– DM.
Gruppen nach Vereinbarung.
Katalog: 5,– DM.

Kulturzentrum – Tuchfabrik, Weberbach/Wechselstraße

Telefon (06 51) 7 18-20 44

Ausstellung: „2000 Jahre Stadtentwicklung Trier." Gezeigt wird Werden, Wachsen und Wandel des Stadtgrundrisses und der Stadtgestalt vor dem jeweiligen historischen Hintergrund. Es finden regelmäßig Konzerte und Theatervorstellungen statt. Genaueres siehe Tagespresse und „Fröhlicher Steuermann".

Geöffnet: dienstags bis samstags 10 – 17 Uhr, sonntags 12 – 17 Uhr.

Eintritt: Erwachsene 3,– DM, Schüler und Studenten 1,50 DM.
Katalog: 20,– DM.

Führungen nach Anfrage bei Herrn Strobel, Stadtplanungsamt, Telefon (06 51) 7 18-20 44.

Karl-Marx-Haus, Museum, Brückenstraße 10

Telefon (06 51) 4 30 11

Ausstellung: „Karl Marx (1818 – 1883). Leben – Werk – Zeit", Originaldokumente; Sonderausstellung; Videofilm: „Ein Gang durch das Geburtshaus von Karl Marx"; deutsch, englisch, französisch.

Geöffnet: November bis März: April bis Oktober:
dienstags bis sonntags: 10 – 13 und 15 – 18 Uhr   10 – 18 Uhr
montags nur: 15 – 18 Uhr   13 – 18 Uhr

Eintrittspreise:
Erwachsene 2,– DM, Gruppen, Schüler und Studenten 1,– DM, Schulklassen 0,50 DM (pro Person).
Führungen (45 Minuten):
Deutsch: 35,– DM
Fremdsprachen: 45,– DM
Geschlossen vom 24. Dezember bis Anfang Januar.

Studienzentrum Karl-Marx-Haus, Johannisstraße 28

Telefon (06 51) 4 30 11

Bibliothek, Forschung, Kommunikation, Sonderausstellungen.

Geöffnet: montags bis freitags: 10 – 13 Uhr und 14 – 17 Uhr.
Freier Eintritt.

Kunsthandwerkerhof, Simeonstiftplatz 2

Informationen über Kunsthandwerk, Beratung, praktische Vorführung und Verkauf.

Geöffnet: montags bis freitags   9 – 18.30 Uhr
samstags   9 – 14 Uhr

Glasbläser   Telefon (06 51) 4 16 61
Glasdekor   Telefon (06 51) 4 29 91
Goldschmiede   Telefon (06 51) 4 33 98
Batikbilder, Radierungen   Telefon (06 51) 4 58 28

Unverbindliche Besichtigung. Führungen sind nach Voranmeldung möglich.

Edelsteinausstellung „Hanspeter-Schleife", Fleischstraße 34 – 36

Werktäglich zu den üblichen Geschäftszeiten, Telefon (06 51) 7 64 49.

KABINENBAHN TRIER, ZURLAUBENER UFER

Telefon (06 51) 4 52 99, verkehrt täglich ab Ostern bis Mitte November ab 9 Uhr nach Bedarf.

Erwachsene, Gruppen ab 12 Personen:
einfache Fahrt 3,– DM
Hin- und Rückfahrt 4,– DM
Kinder: 4 – 14 Jahre, Gruppen ab 12 Personen:
einfache Fahrt 2,– DM
Hin- und Rückfahrt 3,– DM
Bei Gruppen haben Begleitpersonen freie Fahrt. Parkmöglichkeiten für Busse sind vorhanden.
Einzelpreis Erwachsene: einfache Fahrt 4,– DM
Hin- und Rückfahrt 5,– DM
Einzelpreis Kinder 4 – 14 Jahre: einfache Fahrt 3,– DM
Hin- und Rückfahrt 4,– DM

SCHIFFSFAHRTEN AUF DER MOSEL

Motorboot „Zurlauben" der Fahrgastschiffahrt Kolb

Ausflugsfahrt nach TRIER-PFALZEL (6 Stromkilometer)
Von Anfang Mai bis Mitte Oktober ab 11.00 Uhr mehrmals Fahrten ab Stadthafen Trier-Zurlauben. Nähere Auskünfte: Telefon (0 26 73) 15 15.

Fahrgast-Schiffahrt Kolb
Moselfahrten von Trier nach Bernkastel-Kues

Täglich von Anfang Mai bis Mitte Oktober 9.15 Uhr ab Stadthafen Trier-Zurlauben.
Auskunft: Telefon (0 26 73) 15 15.

Linienverkehr der „Navigation Touristique de l'Entente de la Moselle Luxembourgeoise" mit der „Princesse Marie-Astrid"

Von April bis September:
Sonntags: 10.30 Uhr ab Trier bis Schengen (Lux.)
Von Juni bis September:
Mittwochs: 14.15 Uhr ab Trier bis Mehring
Mittwochs: 18.00 Uhr ab Trier bis Grevenmacher (Lux.)
Von Juli bis September:
Samstags: 9.00 Uhr ab Trier bis Bernkastel-Kues

BESUCHSPROGRAMM IN TRIER

Ein Tag in Trier

Vormittags
Stadtrundgang[1] oder Stadtrundfahrt[2] von der Porta Nigra bis zum Amphitheater[3];
nachmittags
Fahrt mit der Kabinenbahn[3] von der Talstation Zurlauben zur Weißhausterrasse, Café-Restaurant (Aussicht auf Trier, Rosengarten, Fachhochschule, Wildfreigehege, Waldlehrpfad) und Waldspaziergang zum Kockelsberg[4], Café-Restaurant, zurück mit dem Stadtbus; oder Fahrt mit dem Motorboot[5] ab Stadthafen Zurlauben nach Pfalzel und zurück – mit ein- bis zweistündigem Aufenthalt in der ehemaligen Sommerresidenz der Trierer Kurfürsten;

abends
Besuch einer Weinstube, des Stadttheaters, eines Konzerts oder einer anderen Veranstaltung[6].

Zwei Tage in Trier

Erster Tag: siehe oben.
Zweiter Tag:
vormittags
Besuch der Museen und/oder der Kirchen St. Matthias[7] und St. Paulin[7], Rundgang durch die Hauptgeschäftsstraße in der ab 11 Uhr verkehrsfreien Innenstadt;
nachmittags
Bahnfahrt nach Saarburg oder Luxemburg; für Besucher mit eigenem Wagen Ausflugsfahrten nach den Vorschlägen der Tourist-Information.

Sechs Tage in Trier

Erster bis zweiter Tag: wie vor.
Dritter bis sechster Tag:
Vertiefung des Stadtrundganges und der Museenbesuche. Besuch der städtischen Parkanlagen (Palastgarten, Nells Park, Mattheiser Weiher) oder der Bäder (Städt. Hallenbad; Nordbad, Südbad: beheizte Freibäder).
Fahrt mit dem Stadtbus (siehe auch: Busfahrkarten für Trier-Besucher) in die neuen Stadtteile (Neuheiligkreuz, Mariahof, Auf der Hill, Irscher Berg, Tarforster Flur u. a.), Bus-Ausflugsfahrt Eifel – Mosel.
Fahrt mit der Bundesbahn oder dem Bus in den Hunsrück, Bustfahrt Stadt und Land Luxemburg[8].
Nachmittagsfahrt mit der Bahn oder dem Bus in das Ruwertal mit den Weindörfern Mertesdorf (Freibad), Kasel und Waldrach (Riveristalsperre) oder in das Kylltal mit Burg Ramstein, Kordel, Daufenbach.
Spaziergänge: Weinlehrpfad, Waldlehrpfad.

Anmerkungen zu den Programmvorschlägen:

[1] Wir empfehlen wegen der kurzen Entfernungen den Weg von der Porta Nigra zum Amphitheater zu Fuß zurückzulegen und für die Rückfahrt die Linie 6/16 oder 26 (Haltestelle Charlottenstraße) zu benutzen.
[2] Siehe dazu den Abschnitt „Führungen".
[3] Außerhalb der Verkehrszeit der Kabinenbahn (April – Oktober, siehe dazu auch den Veranstaltungskalender) 10- bis 15minütiger Fußweg ab Kaiser-Wilhelm-Brücke (Haltestellen der Buslinien 2 und 8) oder Fahrt mit dem eigenen Wagen.
[4] Mittwochs, samstags und sonntags ab Kockelsberg mit Linie 9.
[5] Motorbootverkehr zwischen Trier und Trier-Pfalzel von Mai bis Oktober (siehe dazu auch den Veranstaltungskalender), Bahn- und Busverbindung während des ganzen Jahres.
[6] Siehe dazu auch den Veranstaltungskalender.
[7] Bus 3 und 4.
[8] Siehe dazu auch den Veranstaltungskalender; außerhalb der Hauptreisezeit Fahrt mit fahrplanmäßigen Zügen oder dem Europa-Bus oder mit dem eigenen Wagen.

Jugendherbergen im Trierer Land

Bernkastel, Bollendorf, Brodenbach, Cochem, Daun, Dreisbach, Gerolstein, Hermeskeil, Idar-Oberstein, Manderscheid, Mayen, Morbach, Prüm, Saarburg, Tholey, Traben-Trarbach, Weiskirchen.

Alle Jugendherbergen sind geeignet für: Einzelgäste, Familien (zum Teil Familienzimmer), Schulklassen, Gruppen, Lehrgänge, Tagungen, Erholungsmaßnahmen.

Golf-Sport

Golf-Club Trier-Mosel e. V., 5559 Ensch-Birkenheck, Telefon (0 65 07) 43 74, oder 5500 Trier, Postfach 19 05.
Platz: 9 Loch mit Erweiterungsgelände auf 18 Loch, Par 72, 6 000 m – insgesamt 60 ha Wiesen, Wald und Weinberge, ganzjährig bespielbar.

WEINLEHRPFAD, KELLERBESICHTIGUNG, WEINPROBE

Der 2 km lange „Trierer Weinlehrpfad" rund um den Petrisberg beginnt oberhalb des Amphitheaters. Seine 39 Stationen zeigen „Sehenswertes und Merkwürdiges vom Anbau und Leben des Weinstocks". Der Weinlehrpfad endet im Winzerstadtteil Olewig; dort täglich zwischen 10 und 18 Uhr Gelegenheit zur Weinkellerbesichtigung mit Weinproben. – Spezialführer mit Karte und Weinproben-Wochenplan durch die TOURIST-INFORMATION TRIER oder an den Prospektautomaten am Beginn des Weinlehrpfades. Proben ab 4,– DM.
Vom 1. Mai bis 30. September täglich ab Anfang des Weinlehrpfades kostenlose ca. einstündige Führungen. Anschließend Gelegenheit zum Essen beim Winzer und Besichtigung des Betriebes. Die TOURIST-INFORMATION TRIER vermittelt auf Anfrage auch englischsprachige Führungen.
Weitere Weinlehrpfade finden Sie in Saarburg (ca. 3 km), Schweich (ca. 2 km) und Wiltingen (1,8 km).

WEININFORMATION MOSEL-SAAR-RUWER

Konstantinplatz 11, 5500 Trier, Telefon (06 51) 7 36 90
Die Weinstube an der Römischen Palastaula lädt ein zum Verkosten von Mosel-Saar-Ruwer-Weinen verschiedenster Jahrgänge, die sämtlich aus dem Bereich des Landkreises Trier-Saarburg und der Stadt Trier stammen – ein Wegweiser zum Weineinkauf ohne Risiko.

WALDLEHRPFAD

Der ca. 3 600 m lange Waldlehrpfad beim Wildfreigehege zeigt und erläutert heimische Gehölzarten.
Anfang und Ende: Parkplatz Drachenhaus.

STADTBAD, Südallee, gegenüber Kaiserthermen

Das ganzjährig geöffnete Hallenbad bietet in verschiedenen Becken 830 qm Wasserfläche. Dazu entsprechenden Freizeitraum und Einrichtungen wie Sauna, Solarium, Spielraum, Whirlpool, „Badehosen"-Cafeteria und ein Restaurant.

Stadtrundgang City Tour

BERLIN Vom Alexanderplatz zum Marx-Engles-Platz und züruck

Ministerium für Auswärtige Angelegenheiten

Schinkelbau aus den Jahren 1824/1828, der Bärenbrunnen von Hugo Lederer. Der achtgeschossige Gebäudekomplex des Ministeriums für Auswärtige Angelegenheiten der DDR am Ufer des Spreekanals begrenzt die Westseite des Platzes. Er wurde von 1964 bis 1967 nach Plänen des Architektenkollektivs Josef Kaiser, Herbert Aust, Gerhard Lehmann und Lothar Kwasnitza errichtet. Auch das Ministerium für Hoch- und Fachschulwesen der DDR hat hier seinen Sitz.

Ministerium für Hoch- und Fachschulwesen

Palast der Republik

Mit dem Palast der Republik hat der Marx-Engels-Platz seine architektonische und städtebauliche Vollendung erfahren. Das repräsentative Gebäude ist von 1973 bis 1976 von Bauschaffenden aus allen Bezirken der DDR nach Plänen der Architekten Heinz Graffunder (Chefarchitekt), Wolf Rüdiger Eisentraut, Christian Schulz, Karl-Ernst Swora, Manfred Prasser, Herbert Aust und Klaus Weber errichtet worden. Der Palast der Republik, in dessen

Volkskammer der DDR

Flügel zur Lustgartenseite die Volkskammer der DDR ihren Sitz hat, ist mit seinen vielfältigen Einrichtungen ein wahres Haus des Volkes, eine Stätte wichtiger Kongresse und internationaler Begegnungen wie auch eine Heimstatt sozialistischer Kultur, des Frohsinns und der Geselligkeit. 1976 und 1981 fanden im Großen Saal der IX. bzw. X. Parteitag der Sozialistischen Einheitspartei Deutschlands statt, die richtungweisende Beschlüsse zur Fortführung des erfolgreichen Kurses der Hauptaufgabe in ihrer Einheit von Wirtschafts- und Sozialpolitik zum Wohle des Volkes und zur Sicherung des Friedens faßten.

Theater im Palast

Neben dem Besuch eines der vielen Restaurants ist besonders empfehlenswert ein Abend im Theater im Palast (TiP), das sich speziell der szenischen Gestaltung literarisch-dramatischer Programme widmet. Der Palast der Republik ist einschließlich der Galerie im 2. und 3. Geschoß für alle Besucher täglich von 10 bis 24 Uhr geöffnet.

Berliner Dom

Der Berliner Dom steht in Nachbarschaft zu den neuen Bauten am Marx-Engels-Platz und wirkt als Bindeglied zu den historischen Bauten an der

32

Straße Unter den Linden und auf der Museumsinsel. Er wurde nach dem Abriß des alten Berliner Domes, der um die Mitte des 18. Jahrhunderts nach Plänen Johann Boumanns d. Ä. erbaut und in den Jahren 1816 bis 1822 von Karl Friedrich Schinkel umgestaltet worden war, an der Spree errichtet. Der heutige Dom ist in den Jahren 1894 bis 1905 nach Plänen des Architekten Julius Karl Raschdorff erbaut worden und gilt als ein Beispiel des Historismus und Eklektizismus; hier wurden viele über Jahrhunderte gültige traditionelle Strukturformen und Baustile mit- und nebeneinander verwandt. Die umfangreichen Arbeiten bei der Rekonstruktion des im zweiten Weltkrieg durch anglo-amerikanische Bomben erheblich beschädigten Gebäudes, für die allein 3500 Tonnen Sandstein benötigt wurden, zeugen von dem großen handwerklichen Können der Steinmetze, Maurer, Zimmerer aus zahlreichen Betrieben der DDR und sind eine bedeutende denkmalpflegerische Leistung.

Lustgarten

Gedenkstein zu Ehren der Widerstandsgruppe Herbert Baum

Unmittelbar vor dem Dom steht auf dem Lustgarten ein Gedenkstein zu Ehren der Widerstandsgruppe Herbert Baum, die am 18. Mai 1942 an dieser Stelle eine faschistische Hetzausstellung über die Sowjetunion in Brand setzte. Herbert Baum wurde am 11. Juni 1942 von den Faschisten ermordet.

Interhotel "Palasthotel"

Vom Marx-Engels-Platz zurück in Richtung Alexanderplatz führt die Karl-Liebknecht-Straße vorbei am Marx-Engels-Forum und am Palasthotel, das von 1977 bis 1979 errichtet worden ist. Das Hotel verfügt über 600 Gästezimmer, über Konferenzräume mit 650 Plätzen und über vielfältige gastronomische Einrichtungen, die insgesamt 1200 Gästen Platz bieten.

Heilig-Geist-Kapelle

Die Heilig-Geist-Kapelle, unmittelbar neben dem Palasthotel in der Spandauer Straße gelegen, entstand gegen Ende des 13. Jahrhunderts als Teil einer Hospitalanlage. Hauptschmuck der Kapelle ist der Giebel an der Spandauer Straße. Der Innenraum ist mit einem gut erhaltenen Sterngewölbe überdeckt, das vermutlich im 15. Jahrhundert entstanden ist. Die Kapelle wird von der Sektion Wirt-

33

schaftswissenschaften der Humboldt-Universität genutzt. In der Spandauer Straße laden die Milch-Mokka-Bar „Tutti-Frutti" und das Fischspezialitätenrestaurant „Gastmahl des Meeres" zur Einkehr ein. Hier ist auch die Buchhandlung „Das internationale Buch".

„Tutti-Frutti" „Gastmahl des Meeres"

In Richtung Alexanderplatz befinden sich in der Karl-Liebknecht-Straße das Haus der Ungarischen Kultur und das Polnische Kultur- und Informationszentrum. Beide Einrichtungen vermitteln durch Ausstellungen und Veranstaltungen viel Wissenswertes über ihre Länder; ihnen sind Verkaufssalons für Volkskunsterzeugnisse, Bücher und Schallplatten angeschlossen.

Haus der Ungarischen Kultur

Polnisches Kultur- und Informationszentrum

Zwischen der S-Bahn und der neuen Markthalle, in der es auf 6500 Quadratmetern Verkaufsfläche zahlreiche Geschäfte mit Basarcharakter gibt, lädt ein Altberliner Markt mit rustikalen Imbißständen zum Verweilen ein. Sehenswert ist hier der Marktbrunnen von Gerhard Thieme, der Berliner Originale wie den Wurstmaxen, die Blumenfrau und den Stoffhändler darstellt.

Markthalle

Altberliner Markt

Marktbrunnen

Auf der anderen Straßenseite (zu erreichen durch einen Fußgängertunnel) steht die Marienkirche. Die am Ende des 13. Jahrhunderts errichtete Kirche wurde bei einem Brand am 11. August 1380 beschädigt und erhielt im ausgehenden 14. Jahrhundert ihre jetzige Gestalt. Bemerkenswert ist ihre Ausstattung, besonders ein spätgotisches Wandgemälde in der Turmvorhalle: ein Totentanz. Das bronzene Taufbecken im Chor der Kirche stammt nach der Inschrift unter dem Figurenfries aus dem Jahre 1437. Die Marmorkanzel am nordöstlichen Langhauspfeiler ist eines der wenigen vollständig erhaltenen Werke des Baumeisters und Bildhauers Andreas Schlüter und stammt aus dem Jahre 1703.

Marienkirche

34

Die Straße Unter den Linden

Marx-Engels-Brücke

Eine der schönsten Brücken Berlins ist die Marx-Engels-Brücke, die vom Marx-Engels-Platz zur Straße Unter den Linden führt. Sie wurde 1822 bis 1824 nach einem Entwurf Karl Friedrich Schinkels errichtet. Auch die acht Statuen nach Motiven aus der griechischen Mythologie, die nach Restauration auf den Postamenten der Brücke wieder ihren Platz erhalten haben, gehen auf Anregungen Schinkels zurück. Die Ausführung der Schinkelschen Skizzen übernahmen acht Künstler, die zumeist Schüler so bedeutender klassizistischer Bildhauer wie Johann Gottfried Schadow und Christian Daniel Rauch waren: Gustav Bläser, Friedrich Drake, Karl-Heinz Möller, Hermann Schievelbein, Ludwig Wichmann, Albert Wolff, Emil Wolff und August Wredow. Die Brüstungsfelder der Geländer enthalten Darstellungen von arabeskenartig verschlungenen Seepferden, Tritonen und Delphinen, ebenfalls nach Entwürfen von Schinkel.

Unter den Linden

Die 1390 Meter lange und 60 Meter breite Straße Unter den Linden erstreckt sich vom Marx-Engels-Platz bis zum Brandenburger Tor. Bedeutende Baudenkmäler aus dem 18. und 19. Jahrhundert machen sie zu einer Sehenswürdigkeit ersten Ranges. Als Vorläufer der Straße Unter den Linden führte seit 1573 ein Reitweg vom kurfürstlichen Hohenzollern-Schloß zum Tiergarten. Kurfürst Friedrich Wilhelm ließ 1647 die erste Lindenallee anlegen. Anfang des 18. Jahrhunderts begann unter dem preußischen König Friedrich I. die Errichtung prunkvoller Bauten an der Straße Unter den Linden.

Museum für Deutsche Geschichte

Auftakt für die repräsentative Bebauung der Straße war der Bau des Zeughauses, in dem heute das Museum für Deutsche Geschichte untergebracht ist. Es ist das älteste erhaltene Gebäude der Straße und eines der schönsten historischen Bauwerke der Hauptstadt. Im Jahre 1695 war die Grundsteinlegung für den zweigeschossigen, um einen Innenhof gruppierten barocken Vierflügelbau, der als Waffenkammer für die brandenburgisch-preußische Armee dienen sollte. Während der bürgerlich-demokratischen Revolution von 1848 stürmten

35

WOCHENSPIELPLAN DER

Staatsoper

I, Opernring

Tageskasse: Hanuschgasse 3 / Goethegasse 1 —
53 24—26 55 — Abendkasse: 53 24—24 18

Tonbandauskunft über Programm und Besetzungen:
53 24—23 45

 (2 Rollstühle zugelassen)

Volksoper

IX, Währinger Straße 78

Tageskassen: Hanuschgasse 3 / Goethegasse 1 —
53 24—26 57 — Währinger Straße 78: 53 53 24—33 18
Abendkasse: 53 24/33 18 und 33 19

 (2 Rollstühle zugelassen)

Do 1. April

Bei aufgehobenem Abonnement — Preise D

BALLETT-TAGE

Schwanensee

Ballett in vier Akten von V. B. Begitschew und Wasily Geltser
Musik von Peter Iljitsch Tschaikowski

Dirigent: Stefan Soltesz
Choreographie von Rudolf Nurejew — Frei nach Petipa - Iwanow
Bühnenbild und Kostüme: Nicholas Georgiadis

Jacob-Scheuermann
Birkmeyer, L. M. Musil

Anfang **18.30** Uhr   Ende nach 22 Uhr

Bei aufgehobenem Abonnement — Beschränkter Kartenverkauf
Preise E

Kiss me Kate

von Cole Porter

Dirigent: Franz Bauer-Theussl
Regie: Heinz Marecek
Musikalische Szene u. Choreographie: Michael Maurer
Bühnenbild und Kostüme: Rolf Langenfass
Choreinstudierung: Karl-Heinz Dold

Koller, Holliday, Gordon
Minich, Grau, Liewehr, Kraemmer, Wasserlof,
Gerhard, Kandutsch, Randers, Dauscha, Jeschek,
Drahosch, Schellenberg

Anfang **19** Uhr   Ende etwa 22 Uhr

Fr 2. April

Bei aufgehobenem Abonnement — Preise D

BALLETT-TAGE

Dornröschen

Ballett in einem Prolog und drei Akten
Libretto: Iwan Wsewoloschski

Musik: Peter I. Tschaikowski

Choreographie: Rudolf Nurejew nach Marius Petipa
Bühnenbilder und Kostüme: Nicholas Georgiadis
Dirigent: Ernst Märzendorfer

Cech, Kirnbauer, Gaugusch
Nurejew, Molnar

Anfang 19 Uhr   Ende etwa 22.15 Uhr

Beschränkter Kartenverkauf — Preise D

Die ungarische Hochzeit

von Nico Dostal

Dirigent: Rudolf Bibl
Inszenierung: Robert Herzl
Bühnenbild: Pantelis Dessyllas
Kostüme: Leo Bei

Irosch, Kales, Tobisch, Mottl
Aichhorn, Huemer, Kolmann, Wasserlof, Randers,
Jeschek, Katzböck, Worisch

Anfang **19** Uhr   Ende etwa 21.30 Uhr

Sa 3. April

Preise D

BALLETT-TAGE

Dornröschen

Ballett in einem Prolog und drei Akten
Libretto: Iwan Wsewoloschski

Musik: Peter I. Tschaikowski

Choreographie: Rudolf Nurejew nach Marius Petipa
Bühnenbilder und Kostüme: Nicholas Georgiadis
Dirigent: Ernst Märzendorfer

Cech, Kirnbauer, Gaugusch
Nurejew, Molnar

Anfang 19 Uhr   Ende etwa 22.15 Uhr

Preise D

Zum 200. Male!

Wiener Blut

von Johann Strauß
Dirigent: Rudolf Bibl
Inszenierung: Otto Schenk
Bühnenbilder: Walter Hoesslin
Kostüme: Ronny Reiter

Holzmayer, Haas, Papouschek, Ch. Klein, Falzari,
Hofman, Kindler, Schalk
Minich, Dönch, Kuchar, Wasserlof, Gerhard, Kolmann,
Randers, Laurer, Jenewein

Anfang **19** Uhr   Ende 22 Uhr

MONTAG, 5. APRIL

Letzte Vorstellung im Abonnement 13. Gruppe
Beschränkter Kartenverkauf — Preise D

19 Uhr **Arabella**

Bei aufgehobenem Abonnement — Preise E

19 Uhr **Kiss me Kate**

DIENSTAG, 6. APRIL

Letzte Vorstellung im Abonnement 1. Gruppe
Beschränkter Kartenverkauf — Preise D

18.30 Uhr **La Bohème**

Im Abonnement 3. Gruppe und allg. Kartenverkauf — Preise D

19 Uhr **Pariser Leben**

WIENER THEATER

KAMMERSPIELE

I., Rotenturmstraße 20 — Telefon 63 28 33   Straßenbahn: 1, 2 — U-Bahn: Schwedenplatz

Täglich 20—22 Uhr (außer Montag)

Samstag, 27., und Sonntag, 28. März, auch 16—18 Uhr
Geschlossene Vorstellungen: 27. nachm. und 30. März
Beschränkter Kartenverkauf: 1. April

Der doppelte Moritz

von Toni Impekoven und Carl Mathern

Inszenierung: Peter Loos — Bühnenbild: Wolfgang Müller-Karbach — Kostüme: Ariane Maino

Marianne Chappuis, Gretl Elb, Monika Salcak-Prinz, Marianne Schönauer, Monika Strauch
Max Böhm, Kurt Jaggberg, Erich Padalewski, Helmut Schleser, Siegfried Walther

Theater in der Josefstadt in den Kammerspielen

„AUS DER REIHE"

Montag, 29. März, 19.30 Uhr — Allgemeiner Kartenverkauf
SONNTAG, 4. APRIL, 15 UHR — Allgemeiner Kartenverkauf

URAUFFÜHRUNG

KYBERNETISCHE HOCHZEIT

Musikalisches Zauberspiel von Lotte Ingrisch
Inszenierung und Ausstattung: Eva Kerbler
Musik: Spontan Music Trio — Choreographie: Sam Cayne

Marianne Chappuis, Cornelia Köndgen, Erni Mangold, Brigitte Neumeister, Elfriede Ramhapp, Michaela Rosen
Matthias Croy, Friedrich Fleischhacker, Karl Krittl, Herwig Seeböck, Siegfried Walther

Der Kartenvorverkauf findet an der Tageskasse der Kammerspiele (Telefon 63 28 33) täglich von 9 Uhr an ununterbrochen bis 18.30 Uhr, an der Tageskasse des Theaters in der Josefstadt täglich von 9 Uhr an ununterbrochen bis 18 Uhr und in den Kartenbüros statt.

Ensemble Theater Treffpunkt Petersplatz

Kartenreservierungen: 66 32 00

Täglich 19.45 Uhr (außer Sonntag und Montag)

Weill-Brecht

Die Dreigroschenoper

Regie: Dieter Haspel
Raum: Christian Feichtinger
Kostüm: Evelyn Luef
Musikalische Leitung: Ernst Istler

28. März 1982, Beginn 11 Uhr
AUFRISSE
(Texte von Wladimir Majakowski)
Sonntags-Matinee mit Maria Böhmberger und Walter Benn

Büro: 1010 Wien, Marc-Aurel-Straße 3/6, Telefon 66 32 00

FREIE BÜHNE WIEDEN

Leitung: Topsy Küppers
1040 Wien, Wiedner Hauptstraße 60 b — Telefon 56 21 22

Samstag, 27. März: 50. Vorstellung!

Österreichische Erstaufführung

TOPSY KÜPPERS in

Ich steige aus!

(I'm getting my act together and taking it on the road)
Musical von Gretchen Cryer und Nancy Ford

mit

Karin Friedl, Lorain Jones, Regina Riedl
und
FRED SCHAFFER

Regie: Conny Hannes Meyer
Musikalische Leitung: Prof. Heinz Hruza

Dienstag bis Samstag, jeweils 20 Uhr
Sonntag um 16 Uhr
Seniorenvorstellung zu halben Preisen

Theaterkassa: Montag bis Samstag 16—20 Uhr, Sonntag 14—16 Uhr
Telefonische Bestellung Tag und Nacht unter 56 21 22

Veranstaltungskalender Schedule of Events   MANNHEIM

Tageskalender
Mehrtägige Veranstaltungen
Ausstellungen
Juli

27.07. - 07.09. Ägidius Geisselmann – Gemälde
Kunstausstellung, Eröffnung 27.7., 11 Uhr, Öffnungszeiten Di - So 9.30 - 17 Uhr, donnerstags bis 21 Uhr, Eintritt frei
Ludwigshafen, Wilhelm-Hack-Museum, Berliner Straße 23

30.07. - 31.08. Schloßspiele Heidelberg
zur Aufführung kommen „Hans Sachs", heitere Volksoper von Albert Lortzing, „The Student Prince", musikalische Romanze von Sigmund Romberg in englischer Sprache, „Der geduldige Sokrates", Komische Oper von Georg Ph. Telemann sowie diverse Konzerte, Programme und Informationen beim Verkehrsverein Heidelberg, Tel. (0 62 21) 1 08 21, Vorverkauf Konzertkasse Heidelberg, Tel. (0 62 21) 2 10 76;
Städtische Bühne Heidelberg
Heidelberg, Schloß, Schloßhof und Englischer Bau

31.07. - 17.08. Zauber, Zauber – 12 Großmeister der Magie
präsentiert von Peter von Zahn, Vorstellungen Mo - So 20.30 Uhr, Sa, So und Mi zusätzlich 16 Uhr, Fr zusätzlich 24 Uhr, Eintritt 18, 24, 28, 34 und 38 DM, Vorverkauf Mannheimer Kartenhaus, Tel. 10 40 40;
Hoffmann Konzerte Mannheim
Mannheim, Rosengarten, Mozartsaal

Tageskalender
Einzelveranstaltungen

Einzelveranstaltungen
Juli

01. Di 09.30 Schiffsausflug nach Neckarsteinach
Ankunft in Neckarsteinach 13.15 Uhr, Rückfahrt ab Neckarsteinach 15.30 Uhr, Ankunft in Mannheim ca. 19 Uhr, Preis mit Rückfahrt 20 DM (Kinder 12 DM), einfache Fahrt 12 DM (Kinder 9 DM), Vorverkauf Verkehrsverein Mannheim, Tel. 10 10 11;
Rhein-Neckar-Fahrgastschiffahrt Heidelberg
Abfahrt Mannheim, Kurpfalzbrücke, Neckar

01. Di 10.00 Stadtrundfahrt Mannheim
mit Besichtigung des Kurfürstlichen Schlosses, Abstecher nach Ludwigshafen und Auffahrt zum Fernmeldeturm, Dauer ca. 2 Stunden, Preis 12 DM, Schüler und Rentner 9 DM, Kartenverkauf im Bus; Verkehrsverein Mannheim
Abfahrt Mannheim, Wasserturm

01. Di 11.00 Hauptversammlung der Fuchs Petroclub AG
Öl + Chemie Mannheim
Mannheim, Rosengarten, Stamitzsaal

01. Di 18.00 A Night in Casablanca
20.00
Amerikanischer Film von Archie Mayo mit Groucho, Chico und Harpo Marx, Eintritt 4 DM
Heidelberg, Deutsch-Amerikanisches Institut, Sofienstraße 12

01. Di 19.00 Gitarre, Laute, Mandoline – Konzert
mit Werken von J. S. Bach, Vivaldi, Vallet, Dowland u.a., Ausführende Gitarrenorchester und Schüler der Städtischen Musikschule Mannheim, Solist Takashi Tsunoda (Renaissance- und Barock-Laute), Leitung Takashi Ochi, Eintritt frei
Mannheim, Kammermusiksaal, E 4, 14

01. Di 20.30 Orchester der Stadt Heidelberg/Heidelberger Bachchor – IV. Chorkonzert
mit dem Werk „Alexanderfest" von Georg Friedrich Händel, Solisten Barbara Schlick (Sopran), Lutz-Michael Haderer (Tenor) und Roland Hermann (Baß), Leitung Rudolf Kelber, Eintritt 8,50 DM, Ermäßigung 4,25 DM, Vorverkauf Konzertkasse Heidelberg, Tel. (0 62 21) 2 10 76;
Bachverein Heidelberg
Heidelberg, Schloß, Schloßhof. Bei ungünstiger Witterung findet die Veranstaltung im Königssaal statt.

Tageskalender
Einzelveranstaltungen
Juli

01. Di 20.00 Zum Problem des vorgriechischen Ursprungs griechischer Heiligtümer: Olympia und Delphi
Vortrag von Professor Dr. Hans-Volkmar Herrmann, Universität Köln, Eintritt frei;
Studium Generale
Mannheim, Universität, Schloß, Hörsaal O 163

02. Mi 10.00 Stadtrundfahrt Mannheim
weitere Angaben s. 1. 7.

02. Mi 11.30 Schiffsausflug nach Worms
Ankunft in Worms 12.30 Uhr, Rückfahrt ab Worms 15.30 Uhr, Ankunft in Mannheim ca. 16.45 Uhr, Preis mit Rückfahrt 12 DM, (Kinder 8 DM), einfache Fahrt 8 DM (Kinder 6 DM), Vorverkauf Verkehrsverein Mannheim, Tel. 10 10 11;
Rhein-Neckar-Fahrgastschiffahrt Heidelberg
Abfahrt Mannheim, Kurpfalzbrücke, Neckar

02. Mi 15.30 Schmunzeln und Freude mit und über Elsbeth Janda
an der Orgel Georg Faßmann, Veranstaltung kostenlos, jedoch Parkeintritt;
Stadtpark Mannheim GmbH
Mannheim, Luisenpark, Seebühne

02. Mi 19.00 Spanische Klaviermusik – Konzert
mit Werken von Don Luis Milan, Antonio Soler und Isaak Albeniz, Ausführende Schüler der Klavierklasse Oda Retzlaff an der Städtischen Musikschule Mannheim, Eintritt frei
Mannheim, Kammermusiksaal, E 4, 14

03. Do 08.00 Sonderpostamt mit Sonderstempel anläßlich des Jubiläums „100 Jahre Automobil"
Schalter geöffnet bis 18 Uhr;
Verkehrsverein Mannheim und Deutsche Bundespost
Mannheim, Verkehrsverein, Bahnhofplatz 1, Verkehrspavillon

03. Do 09.30 Historische Erinnerungsfahrt an die 1. Fahrt des Motorwagens von Carl Benz am 3.7.1886
Auf dem Weg zu einem Empfang im Kurfürstlichen Schloß werden die Fahrzeuge folgende Route benutzen: Start am Benz-Denkmal (Augusta-anlage) - Planken - Paradeplatz - Kurpfalzstraße - Schloß. Aufstellung im Ehrenhof, wo sie bis ca. 14 Uhr besichtigt werden können. Es handelt sich um 15 Fahrzeuge, das älteste Automobil stammt aus dem Jahr 1886, das neueste Modell von 1953; Daimler-Benz AG, Stuttgart-Untertürkheim
Mannheim

Tageskalender
Einzelveranstaltungen

Juli

03. Do 10.00 Hafenrundfahrt Mannheim
14.30 mit Besichtigung der Stromhäfen und Hafenbecken an Rhein und Neckar, Dauer ca. 2 Stunden, Preis 9 DM (Kinder 6,50 DM), Kartenverkauf auf dem Schiff und beim Verkehrsverein Mannheim, Tel. 10 10 11;
Rhein-Neckar-Fahrgastschiffahrt Heidelberg
Abfahrt Mannheim, Kurpfalzbrücke, Neckar

03. Do 10.00 Stadtrundfahrt Mannheim
weitere Angaben s. 1.7.

03. Do 10.00 Jahreshauptversammlung der Bilfinger + Berger Bau AG
Mannheim, Rosengarten, Stamitzsaal

03. Do 15.00 Einweihung der Carl-Benz-Sporthalle anläßlich des Jubiläums „100 Jahre Automobil"
(nur für geladene Gäste)
Mannheim-Waldhof, Alsenweg

03. Do 16.00 Hallenfußballturnier anläßlich der Einweihung der Carl-Benz-Sporthalle
Namen der teilnehmenden Mannschaften werden in der Tagespresse veröffentlicht, Eintritt frei
Mannheim-Waldhof, Carl-Benz-Sporthalle, Alsenweg

04. Fr 09.00 Internationales Verkehrsforum des ADAC Nordbaden zum Thema „Jugendliche Fahranfänger"
Mannheim, Rosengarten, Musensaal

04. Fr 10.00 Stadtrundfahrt Mannheim
weitere Angaben s. 1.7.

04. Fr 19.00 Tauschabend für Ansichtskarten
Eintritt frei
Mannheim, Hauptbahnhof, Kaschemme, Lindenhofunterführung

04. Fr 20.00 Eli Freud – Orgelkonzert
mit Werken israelischer Komponisten, Eintritt 10 DM, Ermäßigung 5 DM, Karten nur an der Abendkasse
Mannheim-Lindenhof, Johanniskirche, Windeckstraße 1

05. Sa 10.00 Kinder kennen keine Grenzen – Kinderfest
mit dem Kinderzirkus Aladin und anderen Attraktionen, Ende ca. 16 Uhr;
Terres des Hommes Mannheim/Ludwigshafen
Mannheim, Paradeplatz

05. Sa 10.00 Stadtrundfahrt Mannheim
weitere Angaben s. 1.7.

Tageskalender
Nationaltheater Mannheim

Juli

Nationaltheater Mannheim

Ständiges Ensemble mit Oper, Operette, Musical, Ballett, Schauspiel, Kinder- und Jugendtheater; Großes Haus (1155 Plätze), Kleines Haus (635 Plätze) und Werkhaus-Studio (140 Plätze).

Kassenstunden und Kartenvorverkauf
Vorverkauf/Collinistraße 26; Öffnungszeiten Mo, Sa, So 11 - 13 Uhr, Di - Fr zusätzlich 14 - 18 Uhr – Telefondienst (06 21) 2 48 44/45/46/47 Mo und Sa 9 - 13 Uhr, Di - Fr 9 - 17 Uhr, So 11 - 13 Uhr.
Abendkasse/Goetheplatz, 1 Stunde vor Beginn der Vorstellung Tel. 16 80 - 252 und 257.

Preise

Großes Haus Platzgattung	Preisgruppen			
	I	II	III	IV
A Parkett 1. - 5. R. Orchesterreihen Logen I-IV	44,–	35,–	26,–	18,–
B Parkett 6. - 11. R. Logen V-VIII	37,–	31,–	22,–	16,–
C Parkett 12. - 17. R. Logen IX u. X Balkon 1. u. 2. R.	29,–	27,–	17,–	14,–
D Parkett 18. - 22. R. Logen XI u. XII Balkon 3. Reihe	22,–	20,–	12,–	12,–
E Parkett 23. Reihe Balkon 4. Reihe	13,–	12,–	8,–	8,–

Kleines Haus Platzgattung	Preisgruppen			
	I	II	III	IV
A Reihe 1 - 7	44,–	35,–	26,–	18,–
B Reihe 8 - 14	37,–	31,–	22,–	16,–
C * Reihe 15 - 18	29,–	27,–	17,–	14,–
D Reihe 19 - 21	22,–	20,–	12,–	12,–
E Reihe 22	13,–	12,–	8,–	8,–

Für musikalische Werke gelten die Preisgruppen I und II, für gesprochene Werke Preisgruppe III, für Märchenvorstellungen Preisgruppe IV.

Für alle Vorstellungen in Miete auch freier Verkauf; bei Theatergemeinde beschränkte Verkauf.

Tageskalender
Nationaltheater Mannheim

Juli

nationaltheater Mannheim

Spielplan Juli

01. Di 19.30 G **Don Pasquale** – Komische Oper von Gaetano Donizetti, letztes Mal, Miete J, PG II
19.30 K **Sommergäste** – Schauspiel von Maksim Gorkij, Miete A, PG III

02. Mi G **Geschlossen**
20.00 K **Zur schönen Aussicht** – Schauspiel von Ödön von Horvath, Miete M rot I, PG III

03. Do 20.00 G **Romeo und Julia** – Ballettabend, Musik von Peter Tschaikowsky, letztes Mal, Miete J, PG II
K **Geschlossen**
20.30 S **Wiener Gala** – Geschichten, Typen und ihre Lieder aus Wien, Casino, DM 12

04. Fr 19.30 G **Norma** – Oper von Vincenzo Bellini in italienischer Sprache, Miete F grün, PG II
K **Geschlossen**
20.30 S **Erstens will ich fröhlich sein, zweitens mich vergnügen** – Literarisches Kabarett, Casino, DM 6

05. Sa 19.30 G **Lady Macbeth von Mzensk** – Oper von Dmitrij Schostakowitsch, Erstaufführung, Miete S, PG I
K **Geschlossen**
20.00 S **Der Kontrabaß** – Stück von Patrick Süskind, DM 12

06. So 18.30 G **Rienzi** – Oper von Richard Wagner, Miete C, PG I
19.30 K **Reporter** – Schauspiel von Ben Hecht, Erstaufführung, Schauspielmiete, PG III

07. Mo 20.00 G **Der Opernball** – Operette von Richard Heuberger, Miete B, PG II
19.30 K **Sommergäste** – Miete K, PG III

08. Di 19.30 G **Lady Macbeth von Mzensk** – Miete O, PG II
20.00 K **Reporter** – Miete G, PG III

09. Mi 19.30 G **Die Macht des Schicksals** – Oper von Giuseppe Verdi in italienischer Sprache, Miete M blau, PG II
20.00 K **Zur schönen Aussicht** – Miete M rot II, PG III

Spielplanänderungen – auch Änderungen der Anfangszeiten – vorbehalten. Verbindlich sind die wöchentlich erscheinenden Spielplanplakate.
G = Großes Haus, K = Kleines Haus, S = Studio im Werkhaus, * = Theatergemeinde, PG = Preisgruppe

Museen　Museums

Museen und Sammlungen

Deutsches Museum
auf der Isarinsel (Ludwigsbrücke)
Tel. 217 91

Zählt zu den bedeutendsten technisch-naturwissenschaftlichen Museen der Welt, mit einer Führungslinie von ca. 17 km Länge. Anhand von 16000 Originalgeräten, Modellen und Nachbildungen demonstriert es auf 45000 m² Ausstellungsfläche die Geschichte der Naturwissenschaften und Technik auch auf den meisten Gebieten der neuesten Forschung.
1983: 1,2 Mio Besucher.

Öffnungszeiten:
Täglich von 9–17 Uhr, außer Neujahrstag, Karfreitag, Ostersonntag, 1. Mai, Pfingstsonntag, Fronleichnam, 17. Juni, 1. November, 24., 25. und 31. Dezember. Faschingssonntag und Faschingsdienstag nur von 9–13 Uhr, geöffnet.

Eintrittspreise:
Erwachsene DM 4,00, Kinder und Studenten DM 1,50, Planetarium DM 0,50. Ermäßigungen: Gruppen ab 10 Personen DM 1,50. Bibliothek Eintritt frei.

Residenz-Museum
Eingang Max-Joseph-Platz 3
Tel. 22 46 41

Öffnungszeiten:
Di mit Sa 10–16.30 Uhr, So und Fei 10–13 Uhr.

Eintrittspreise:
Erwachsene DM 2,50. Studenten und Gruppen Ermäßigung, Jugendliche in Begleitung Erwachsener frei.

Die 1385 begonnene Haupt-Stadt-Residenz der Wittelsbacher-Dynastie ist durch ihre Größe und Vielfalt ein begeisterndes Erlebnis. In den nachstehenden Rundgängen ist die Schatzkammer mit ihren reichhaltigen Sammlungen nicht enthalten.

Vormittags-Rundgang:
Ahnengalerie, Antiquarium, Schwarzer Saal, Schlachtensäle, Porzellan 19. Jh., ostasiatisches Porzellan, Kurfürstenzimmer,

Charlottenzimmer, Trierzimmer, Reiche Zimmer, Grüne Galerie, Päpstliche Zimmer, Nibelungen-Säle.

Nachmittagsrundgang
ab 12.30 Uhr:
Ahnengalerie, europäisches Porzellan 18. Jh., Hofkapelle, Reliquienkammer, Reiche Kapelle, Reiche Zimmer, Grüne Galerie, Päpstliche Zimmer, Silberkammer, Steinzimmer, Königszimmer, Nibelungensäle.

Altes Residenztheater
(Cuvilliés-Theater)
Eingang Residenzstraße 1
Tel. 22 46 41

Öffnungszeiten:
Mo mit Sa 14–17 Uhr, So und Fei 10–17 Uhr.

Eintrittspreise:
Erwachsene DM 1,50, Studenten und Gruppen erhalten Ermäßigung, Jugendliche unter 15 J. in Begleitung Erwachsener Eintritt frei.

Bezauberndes Rokokotheater, benannt nach seinem Erbauer François Cuvilliés.

Schatzkammer der Residenz
Max-Joseph-Platz 3
Tel.: 22 46 41

Kronen und Kleinodien; Goldschmiedewerke und Juwelen aus zehn Jahrhunderten.

Öffnungszeiten:
Di mit Sa 10–16.30 Uhr, So und Fei 10–13.00 Uhr.

Eintrittspreise:
DM 2,50.
Ermäßigung für Studenten und Gruppen.

Glyptothek
Königsplatz 3
Tel. 28 61 00

Sammlung griechischer und römischer Skulpturen.

Öffnungszeiten:
Di, Mi, Fr mit So 10–16.30 Uhr, Do 12–20.30 Uhr.

Eintrittspreise:
DM 3,00 für Glyptothek und Staatliche Antikensammlungen einzeln. DM 5,00 für beide Museen zusammen, Ermäßigungen an der Kasse erfragen.

Staatliche Antikensammlungen
Königsplatz 1
Tel. 59 83 59

Sammlung griechischer Vasen, griechische, etruskische und römische Kleinplastik, Goldschmuck, Glas.

Öffnungszeiten:
Di, Do mit So 10–16.30 Uhr, Mi 12–20.30 Uhr.

Eintrittspreise:
DM 3,00 für Staatliche Antikensammlungen und Glyptothek einzeln. DM 5,00 für beide Museen zusammen, Ermäßigungen an der Kasse erfragen.

Staatliche Sammlung Ägyptischer Kunst
Residenz, Eingang Hofgartenstr.
Tel. 29 85 46

Öffnungszeiten:
Täglich (außer Mo) 9.30–16 Uhr, Abendöffnung Di 19–21 Uhr.

Eintrittspreise:
Erwachsene DM 2,50; Kinder, Schüler, Studenten und Künstler Ermäßigung. So und Fei frei.

Bayerisches Nationalmuseum
Prinzregentenstraße 3
Tel. 21 68 1

Kunst, Kunsthandwerk und Volkskunde Europas, vom Mittelalter bis zum 19. Jh.

Öffnungszeiten:
April mit September:
Di–Fr 9.30–16.30 Uhr, Sa, So und Fei 10.00–16.30 Uhr.

Oktober mit März:
Di–Fr 9.00–16.00 Uhr, Sa, So, Fei 9.30–16.00 Uhr.

Eintrittspreise:
DM 3,00, So und Fei frei.

Achtung: Wegen Umbau sind die Fachsammlungen unregelmäßig geöffnet.
Genaue Auskunft unter der o. g. Telefonnummer.

Museen und Sammlungen

Prähistorische Staatssammlung
Lerchenfeldstraße 2
Tel.: 29 39 11

Sammlungsschwerpunkte „Vorge-
schichte in Bayern", „Römische
Kaiserzeit" und „Frühes Mittelalter".
Jährlich mehrere Sonderausstellungen (Termine s. Offizielles Monatsprogramm).

Öffnungszeiten:
Di bis So 9.30–16.00 Uhr
Do 9.30–20.00 Uhr.

Eintrittspreise:
DM 2,00.
So und Fei frei.

Zweigmuseum Burg Grünwald
Zeillerstraße 3, 8022 Grünwald
Tel. 6 41 32 18

Sammlungsschwerpunkte: „Vor-
und Frühgeschichte Münchens und
seines näheren Umlandes",
„Römische Steindenkmäler",
„Geschichte der Burg Grünwald".
Möglichkeit zur Turmbesteigung.
Jährlich wechselnde Sonder-
ausstellungen.

Öffnungszeiten:
Anfang März–Ende November:
Mittwoch mit Sonntag 10–16 Uhr.
Dezember–Februar geschlossen.

Eintrittspreise:
DM 2,00, DM 1,50 ermäßigt,
DM 0,50 für Kinder.

Münchner Stadtmuseum
St.-Jakobs-Platz 1
Tel. 233/23 70

Ständige Ausstellung „Münchner
Wohnkultur von 1700 bis 1900",
Raum mit den Moriskentänzern von
Erasmus Grasser.

Sonderausstellungen:
Puppentheatermuseum
Fotomuseum, Filmmuseum
Musikinstrumentenmuseum

Öffnungszeiten:
Täglich (außer Mo) 9–16.30 Uhr.
So und Fei 10–18 Uhr.

Eintrittspreise:
DM 3,00, Ermäßigungen,
So und Fei frei.

Staatliches Museum für Völkerkunde
Maximilianstraße 42
Tel. 22 48 44

Kunst und Kultur außereuro-
päischer Völker.

Öffnungszeiten:
Täglich (außer Mo) 9.30–16.30 Uhr.

Eintrittspreise:
Erwachsene DM 2,50 (Sonder-
ausstellungen mit gesonderten
Preisen), Kinder, Studenten und
Gruppen Ermäßigungen.
So und Fei frei.

Staatliche Münzsammlung
Residenz, Eingang Residenzstr. 1
Tel. 22 72 21

Münzen, Medaillen, Plaketten,
Geldzeichen, Gemmen und
Kameen.

Öffnungszeiten:
Täglich (außer Mo) 10–17 Uhr.

Eintrittspreise:
Erwachsene DM 2,00, Kinder
DM 0,20, Gruppen Ermäßigungen.
So und Fei frei.

Deutsches Jagd- und Fischereimuseum
Neuhauser Straße 53
Tel. 22 05 22

Öffnungszeiten:
1. April–31. Oktober:
täglich 9.30–17.00 Uhr
1. Nov.–31. März: täglich
9.30–16.00 Uhr. Abendöffnung:
Jeden Montag 19.00–22.00 Uhr.
Winterhalbjahr: Montags geschlossen.

Eintrittspreise:
Erwachsene DM 3,00, Kinder und
Studenten Ermäßigung.

Deutsches Theatermuseum
Galeriestraße 4 a
(Hofgartenarkaden)
Tel. 22 24 49

Öffnungszeiten:
Bibliothek Di–Do 9–12 Uhr
und 13–16.30 Uhr.
Fr 9–12 Uhr und 13–15.30 Uhr.
Sa, So und Mo geschlossen.
Sonderausstellungen täglich
10–16 Uhr, Mo geschlossen.

Eintrittspreise:
Erwachsene DM 1,00; Kinder,
Schüler, Studenten DM 0,50.

BMW-Museum
Petuelring 130 (gegenüber dem
Olympiagelände)
Tel.: 38 95/33 07

Die Ausstellung ZEITMOTOR zeigt
Vergangenheit, Gegenwart und
gibt Ausblick bis ins Jahr 2030.
100 Exponate, Videofilme, Diashows
und ein 70-mm-Film sind die Bau-
steine dieser Ausstellung.

Siemens Museum
Prannerstraße 10
Tel. 2 34/26 60

Wir zeigen in unseren Schau-
räumen den Weg der Elektrotechnik
und Elektronik anhand der
Geschichte des Hauses Siemens in
Modellen, Bildern und Demonstra-
tionsgeräten bis heute. Ergänzend
dazu stellen wir in den Studien-
räumen die Entwicklung einzelner
Produktgruppen vor. Führungen für
Gruppen nach Vereinbarung.

Öffnungszeiten:
Mo mit Fr 9–16 Uhr, Sa und So
10–14 Uhr, feiertags geschlossen.

Eintritt frei

Das Münchner Bildungswerk
führt folgende regelmäßige
Führungen für Gruppen durch:

Rundgang durch die Münchner
Altstadt
Alte Pinakothek
Neue Pinakothek
Bayerisches Nationalmuseum
Lenbachvilla
Prähistorische Staatssammlung
Residenz
Stadtmuseum
Kirchen in der Innenstadt

Nähere Auskünfte bzw.
jederzeitige Vereinbarungen
beim

Münchner Bildungswerk
Adolf-Kolping-Straße 1
8000 München 2
Dr. Jutta Thinesse-Demel
Tel.: 21 37-240

Informationen für Ihren Besuch im Deutschen Museum

Das Deutsche Museum hat die Aufgabe, die historische Entwicklung der Naturwissenschaft, der Technik und der Industrie zu erforschen, die wesentlichen Epochen durch belehrende und systematische Darstellungen zu veranschaulichen und durch hervorragende und typische Meisterwerke zu dokumentieren.

In den Ausstellungsabteilungen befinden sich etwa 16000 Objekte; die Ausstellungsfläche beträgt ca. 45000 m².

Die Studiensammlung enthält weitere 50000 Objekte, ist aber nur Fachleuten nach Anmeldung zugänglich.

Das Museum ist groß; bei Zeitmangel ist eine Vorauswahl ratsam, dabei hilft der »Wegweiser durch die Sammlungen« (ca. 170 Seiten, auch in Englisch, Französisch, Italienisch) mit Lageplänen, Abbildungen und erklärenden Texten. Preis DM 4,–, bei Versand zuzüglich DM 2,50, erhältlich im Museumsladen und in der Eingangshalle.

Klassenbesuche: Vorbereitungsmaterial »Sehen und Begreifen« für Schüler und Lehrer ist zu beziehen über das »Führungswesen«, Tel. (089) 2179252.

Führungen vermittelt das »Führungswesen«, Tel. (089) 2179252. Sonderführungen sind mindestens eine Woche vorher schriftlich anzumelden. Führungsdauer: ca. 2 Stunden; maximale Teilnehmerzahl: 25 Personen. Gebühren für Führungen: DM 60,–, in Fremdsprachen DM 80,–. Die Gebühren sind direkt an die Führungskraft zu richten.

Photographieren (auch mit Blitz) für private Zwecke ist erlaubt. Gewerbliche Photo-, Film-, Ton- und Fernsehaufnahmen sind nach Absprache mit der Pressestelle gegen Gebühr gestattet.

Behinderte Besucher gelangen über Rampen und Aufzüge in die Ausstellungen (mit Ausnahme der Abteilungen Planetarium, Bergwerk und Teile des Hüttenwesens). Eine Behindertentoilette befindet sich im 1. Obergeschoß (Abteilung Musikinstrumente). Zugang zum Restaurant von der Abteilung »Technische Chemie« (1. Obergeschoß); wenden Sie sich bitte an das Aufsichtspersonal (siehe auch »Zusatzinformationen für behinderte Besucher«).

Restaurant und Imbißraum befinden sich im Ausstellungsbereich; Speisewagen in den Sommermonaten auf dem Freigelände, Tel. (089) 22713 3.

Der Museumsladen führt populäre Literatur zu Technik und Naturwissenschaft, Kataloge, Plakate, Ansichtskarten, Dias sowie technisches Spielzeug und Geschenkartikel, Tel. (089) 299931. Ein Gesamtverzeichnis der »Lieferbaren Veröffentlichungen des Deutschen Museums« ist bei der Publikationsstelle, Tel. (089) 2179247, erhältlich.

Die Bibliothek bietet 700000 Bände und 4900 Zeitschriften (1700 laufende Zeitschriften in den Lesesälen).

Bibliotheksführungen finden jeden 2. Sonntag im Monat, 11 Uhr, statt. Zu sehen sind u. a. Lesesäle, Magazine, seltene Bücher.

Die Sondersammlungen der Bibliothek verfügen über eine umfangreiche Plansammlung, Firmenschriften, Denkmünzen, Porträts, Wasserzeichen, Nachlässe bedeutender Wissenschaftler und ein Luftbildarchiv.

In der Bildstelle im Bibliotheksbau befinden sich ca. 400000 Negative aus der Geschichte der Naturwissenschaft und der Technik, Tel. (089) 2179231. Schwerpunkt liegt auf Themen der Sammlungen und der Bibliothek des Deutschen Museums.

Das Kerschensteiner Kolleg ist eine Fortbildungsinstitution für Studenten, betriebliche Ausbilder, Lehrer und Wissenschaftler. (Einzelanmeldung nur bei Ausbilderkursen.)

Das Forschungsinstitut dient der Erforschung der Geschichte der Natur- und Ingenieurwissenschaften.

Im Kongreßzentrum (Kongreßsaal mit 2400 Plätzen, mehrere Sitzungsräume) werden Tagungen und Veranstaltungen abgehalten, Tel. (089) 2179241.

Sonderveranstaltungen, Matineen, Vorträge (siehe gesondertes Veranstaltungsprogramm, welches wie auch dieses Informationsblatt bei der Pressestelle, Tel. (089) 2179246, erhältlich ist).

Übernachtungen kann das Deutsche Museum nicht vermitteln. Anfragen sind zu richten an das Fremdenverkehrsamt München, Rindermarkt 5, 8000 München 2, Tel. 23911.

Deutsches Museum
VON MEISTERWERKEN DER NATURWISSENSCHAFT UND TECHNIK

Deutsches Museum

Postfach 260102 · 8000 München 26 · Telefon (089) 21791

Öffnungszeiten:
Museum und Bibliothek sind täglich von 9 bis 17 Uhr geöffnet.
Am Neujahrstag, Karfreitag, Ostersonntag, 1. Mai, Pfingstsonntag, Fronleichnam, 17. Juni, 1. November, 24., 25. und 31. Dezember sind Museum und Bibliothek geschlossen.
Am Faschingssonntag und -dienstag nur von 9 bis 13 Uhr, am 1. Mittwoch im Dezember von 9 bis 14 Uhr geöffnet.

Eintrittspreise:
Erwachsene DM 5,– Schüler, Studenten mit Ausweis DM 2,– Gruppen ab 20 Personen DM 2,– pro Person.
Wochenkarten für Schüler und Ausbildungsgruppen DM 6,–
Planetarium zusätzlich DM 1,– pro Person.
(Eintrittskarten im Erdgeschoß an der Information.)
Bibliothek und Sondersammlungen: freier Eintritt.

Öffentliche Verkehrsmittel:
Mit allen S-Bahnlinien (Haltestelle Isartor).
U-Bahnlinien 1 und 8 (Haltestelle Fraunhoferstraße).
Straßenbahnlinie 18 (Haltestelle Deutsches Museum).
Straßenbahnlinie 20 (Haltestelle Isartor).

Parkmöglichkeiten sind begrenzt;
Anfahrt mit dem Pkw ist nicht zu empfehlen.

Mitgliedschaft:
Als Mitglied (DM 48,– jährlich) können auch Sie das Deutsche Museum aktiv unterstützen. Sie erhalten u. a. unsere Zeitschrift »Kultur & Technik« und freien Eintritt in das Museum.
Jungmitglieder (Schüler, Studenten) erhalten für DM 6,– Jahresbeitrag freien Eintritt in das Museum.

Stand: 6.85

Vorführungen in den Ausstellungsabteilungen (Änderungen vorbehalten)

Uhrzeit	Erdgeschoß	1. Obergeschoß	2. Obergeschoß	3. Obergeschoß	6. Obergeschoß
9.45	Bergbau				
10.00	Modelleisenbahn	Luftfahrt	Automatische Ziegelfertigung (außer Mittwoch)		Planetarium
10.30	Lokomotiven / Formen und Gießen von Metallen / Luftfahrt		Handschöpfen von Papier		
11.00	Hochspannungsanlage / Modelleisenbahn	Experimente in der Chemie (Mo–Fr)	Raumfahrt		
11.30	Lokomotiven	Kunststoffverarbeitung / Technische Chemie		Landwirtschaftstechnik	
12.00	Modelleisenbahn				
13.00	Modelleisenbahn				Planetarium
13.30	Lokomotiven		Geschichte der Photographie		
13.45	Bergbau				
14.00	Modelleisenbahn / Hochspannungsanlage	Luftfahrt	Automatische Ziegelfertigung (außer Mittwoch)	Landwirtschaftstechnik	Planetarium
14.30	Formen und Gießen von Metallen / Luftfahrt				
15.00	Modelleisenbahn		Textiltechnik / Langsiebpapiermaschine (Mi–Fr) / Raumfahrt		Planetarium weitere Vorführungen (nach Möglichkeit u. Bedarf) 13.00; 15.00 (englisch)
15.30	Lokomotiven	Kunststoffverarbeitung / Technische Chemie			
16.00	Hochspannungsanlage / Modelleisenbahn				
Ganztägig		Musikinstrumente	Glasblasen / Keramikherstellung		

Dauer der Vorführungen: Bergbau und Automatische Ziegelfertigung 60 Minuten, alle übrigen 15 bis 20 Minuten

Filme in den Ausstellungsabteilungen (Änderungen vorbehalten)

10.00	Erdöl und Erdgas
14.00	
10.45	Bergbau
14.45	
11.30	Hüttenwesen
15.30	

Dauer ca. 30 Minuten

Dem Besucher stehen zahlreiche Filme zur Verfügung. Die Filmprogramme können zum Teil vom Besucher gewählt werden.

Ausflüge Excursions

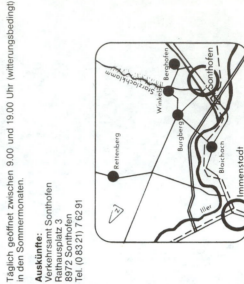

- – Mini-Autoscooter
- – Original-Düsenjäger FG 91 als Klettergerät
- – ferngesteuerte Pistenraupe und Miniautos
- – 3 Tennisplätze
- – Bonanza-Pferde-Reitbahn
- – Western-Eisenbahn
- – Oldtimer-Autobahn
- – Elektro-Miniboote im Silbersee-Jachthafen
- – Parkseilbahn
- – etc.

Auskünfte:
Freizeitpark »Illerparadies«
Fam. Stefan Mäusle
8961 Heising-Hinwang/Allgäu
Tel. (08374) 74 77

Vorschlag 2)

Starzlachklamm bei Sonthofen

Täglich geöffnet zwischen 9.00 und 19.00 Uhr (witterungsbedingt) in den Sommermonaten.

Auskünfte:
Verkehrsamt Sonthofen
Rathausplatz 3
8972 Sonthofen
Tel. (08321) 7 62 91

Kempten, im Herzen des Allgäus gelegen, bietet dem Besucher eine Vielzahl von Unterhaltungsmöglichkeiten in kultureller, geselliger und auch in sportlicher Hinsicht. Doch auch die gesamte Region hält für den Gast eine Fülle von Sehenswürdigkeiten bereit.

Wenn Sie während Ihres Kempten-Aufenthaltes die schönsten »Winkel« unseres Gebietes kennenlernen möchten, so geben wir Ihnen auf den folgenden Seiten einige Anregungen und Tips. Ob Sie nach Osten oder Westen, ob Sie nach Süden oder Norden fahren, Sehenswertes und Interessantes werden Sie überall finden.

Falls Sie zu nachgenannten Ausflugsvorschlägen noch nähere Angaben benötigen, bitten wir Sie, sich entweder an die jeweils angegebenen Kontaktadressen oder an die Geschäftsstelle des Verkehrsvereins Kempten e.V. im Städt. Verkehrsamt, Rathausplatz 14, 8960 Kempten (Allgäu), Tel. (0831) 25 25 - 237 zu wenden.

Öffnungszeiten:

Montag bis Freitag	8.00 bis 12.00 Uhr
Dienstag bis Donnerstag	13.30 bis 17.00 Uhr
Montag	13.30 bis 18.00 Uhr
Freitag	13.30 bis 16.00 Uhr

1. Freizeitpark »Illerparadies« bei Heising
2. Starzlachklamm bei Sonthofen
3. Breitachklamm bei Oberstdorf
4. Stellwagenfahrten in die Oberstdorfer Hochgebirgstäler
5. Oberstdorf
6. Fellhorn
7. Nebelhorn
8. Der Illerwinkel
9. Modelleisenbahn »Miniland« in Wengen
10. Argentobelbrücke und Wanderung durch den Eistobel
11. Besuch der ehemaligen freien Reichsstadt Isny
12. Ottobeuren
13. Forggensee-Schiffahrt
14. Automobil- und Bauernhof-Museum in Wolfegg
15. Besuch »Affenberg in Salem« (bei Uhldingen am Bodensee)
16. Pfänder-Bahn Bregenz am Bodensee
17. Insel Mainau und Lindau
18. Schwangau (mit Schlösser und Füssen
19. Wanderung um den Hopfensee
20. Tannheimer Tal und Vilsalpsee
21. Kleinwalsertal
22. Oberammergau, Ettal, Schloß Linderhof, Ammerwald, Plansee, Reutte
23. Ulm
24. Augsburg
25. München

Vorschlag 1)

Freizeitpark »Illerparadies« bei Heising

Der Spiel- und Freizeitpark bietet der ganzen Familie Erholung, Unterhaltung und Entspannung:

- – Restaurant und Wirtschaftsgarten
- – Wildgehege
- – Spiel- und Sporthalle
  (Tischtennis, Billard, Schießgeräte etc.)

KEMPTEN
Allgäu · Cambodunum

ULM
MEMMINGEN
OTTOBEUREN

AUGSBURG
MÜNCHEN

FÜSSEN
SCHONGAU
REUTTE

ISNY
LINDAU
BREGENZ

SONTHOFEN
OBERSTDORF

Ausflugsziele

Vorschlag 6)

Fellhorn

Bahn in Betrieb: täglich von 8.30 bis 17.00 Uhr

– **Käsereibesichtigung auf der Alpe Schlappold:**
jeden Dienstag, Freitag und Sonntag um 9.30 Uhr, von Anfang Juli
bis Anfang September (kostenlos). – Änderungen vorbehalten –

Treffpunkt:
direkt an der Alpe Schlappold
(ca. 20 Min. Fußweg von der Mittelstation)

– **Bergmesse am Fellhorn-Gipfelkreuz/Nebelhorn/Söllereck**
jeden Donnerstag bei guter Witterung um 11.00 Uhr
von Anfang Juli bis Ende September.

Auskünfte:
Wetter- und Wandertelefon: (08322) 30.35
Kurverwaltung Oberstdorf: (08322) 700-0
Söllereckbahn: (08322) 2855 + 3891

Vorschlag 7)

Nebelhorn

Bahn in Betrieb: täglich von 8.30 Uhr bis 17.00 Uhr

Auskünfte:
Nebelhornbahn, Oberstdorf (08322) 1092

Vorschlag 8)

Der Illerwinkel

1. **Bauernhofmuseum in Illerbeuren:**
Öffnungszeiten täglich:
vom 15. 4. bis 14. 10.
von 9.00 bis 12.00 + 13.30 bis 17.00
vom 15. 10. bis 14. 4.
von 10.00 bis 12.00 + 14.00 bis 16.00

2. **Schloß Kronburg**

3. **Wallfahrtskirche Maria Steinbach**

Auskünfte: Tel.: (08394) 282

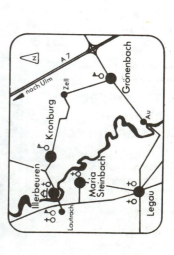

Vorschlag 9)

Modelleisenbahn »Miniland« in Wengen

Miniaturlandschaft mit H0-Modelleisenbahn
auf einem Riesentisch von 303 qm (67,5 × 4,5 m). Herrliche natur-
getreue Modell-Landschaft vom Meer bis zu den Alpen.
Öffnungszeiten:
Im Sommer täglich von 9.30 bis 18.00 Uhr (außer dienstags);
im Winter: Öffnungstage bitte telefonisch erfragen.

Auskünfte:
Tel. (08375) 8622

Vorschlag 10)

Argentobelbrücke und Wanderung durch den Eistobel

Täglich geöffnet.

In Richtung Isny hinter Maierhöfen liegt die Argentobelbrücke, unter
der in abenteuerlicher Tiefe der Eistobel liegt (Naturschutzgebiet mit
fast alpinem Charakter).

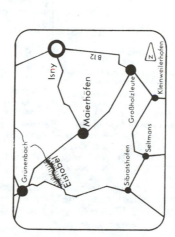

Vorschlag 11)

Besuch der ehemaligen freien Reichsstadt Isny

Sehenswürdigkeiten:
Stadtmauer, Museen, spätgotische Nikolaikirche, St.-Georgskirche
in Barock, historische Baudenkmale, Heimatmuseum, Prädikanten-
bibliothek etc.

Stadtführungen:
je nach Vereinbarung für Gruppen.

Auskünfte:
Verkehrsamt Isny
7972 Isny
Tel. (07562) 701-10

Vorschlag 12)

Ottobeuren

– **Besichtigung der Barock-Basilika und des Klostermuseums:**
täglich geöffnet von 10.00 bis 12.00 + 14.00 bis 17.00 Uhr
– **Konzerte in der Basilika Ottobeuren:**
Termine bitte telefonisch erfragen

Auskünfte: Kurverwaltung Ottobeuren
8942 Ottobeuren, Tel. (08332) 6817

Vorschlag 13)

Forggensee-Schiffahrt (vom 15. Juni bis Ende September)

Kleine Rundfahrt

Ca. 50 Min., Anlegen in Waltenhofen und Osterreinen
(bei genügender Beteiligung, ab Füssen)

ab	10.45	14.00	16.00	Füssen (Weidach Bootshafen)	11.35	14.50	16.50	an
	10.55	14.10	16.10	Waltenhofen, Schwangau, Hohenschwangau, Brunnen	11.25	14.40	16.40	
an	11.15	14.30	16.30	Osterreinen, Rieden, Café Maria	11.15	14.30	16.30	ab

Für Gesellschaften werden Sonderfahrten durchgeführt (entspre-
chende Ermäßigungen!). Bitte vorher telefonisch anmelden.

Auskünfte: Städt. Forggensee-Schiffahrt
8958 Füssen, Tel. (08362) 6221

Vorschlag 14)

Automobil- und Bauernhof-Museum in Wolfegg

– **Automobilmuseum von Fritz B. Busch, am Schloß:**
vom 15. März bis Ende Oktober tägl. geöffnet von 9.00 bis 12.00 Uhr
und von 13.00 bis 18.00 Uhr; sonntags: 9.00 bis 17.00 Uhr.
Letzter Einlaß: jeweils eine 3/4 Stunde vor Schließung.
Bauernhofmuseum:
täglich geöffnet von 10.00 bis 12.00 + 14.00 bis 17.00 Uhr
(Montag Ruhetag; im Juli, August und September auch montags
geöffnet)
– **weitere Sehenswürdigkeiten:**   2. Barock-Schloßkirche
1. Renaissance-Schloß   3. Loreto-Kapelle

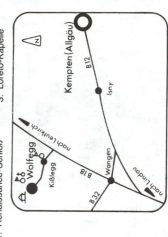

Prospekt   Tourist Brochure

aachen
sprudelnde vielfalt

Feste und Ausstellungen

Veranstaltungsübersicht 1986

Kinderkostümzug	9. 2.
Rosenmontagszug	10. 2.
Frühjahrsbend	29. 3. - 14. 4.
Flohmarkt	20. 4.
Int. Karlspreis	8. 5.
Markt der Künstler	17. 5. - 18. 5.
Studentischer Früh-schoppen auf dem Markt	1. 6.
Fest anl. des 150-jährigen Bestehens der Freiwilligen Feuerwehr	7. 6. - 8. 6.
Hist. Jahrmarkt Kornelim.	20. 6. - 22. 6.
Flohmarkt	29. 6.
Behindertenfest auf dem Katschhof	5. 7.
Weltmeisterschaft der Springreiter	9. 7. - 13. 7.
Sommerbend Europäischer Kunst-handwerkermarkt	8. 8. - 18. 8. 30. 8. - 31. 8.
Parkillumination	6. 9.
Heiligtumsfahrt	3. 9. - 15. 9.
89. Deutscher Katholikentag	10. 9. - 14. 9.
Musikfest	21. 9.
Stadtfest	10. 10. - 12. 10.
Flohmarkt	19. 10.
Weihnachtsmarkt	22. 11. - 22. 12.
Flohmarkt	14. 12.

Die Daten sind unverbindlich!

Aachen entdecken Angebote für jeden Geschmack

Sehr geehrter Aachen-Freund, sehr geehrter Aachen-Interessent,

auf den folgenden Seiten finden Sie - getreu unserem Motto: „Aachen — sprudelnde Vielfalt" — lohnende Angebote mit indivi-

duellem Zuschnitt. Sie sollen es Ihnen leichtmachen, Ihren Aufenthalt in Aachen gezielt zu planen und zu einem „runden" Erlebnis werden zu lassen.
Die einzelnen Angebote sind bis auf Widerruf gültig, die Preise verstehen sich je Person bei Unterbringung in einem Doppelzimmer.
Der Einzelzimmer-Mehrpreis beträgt bei allen Angeboten für Standard I und Standard II 20,- DM pro Tag, für First class 25,- DM pro Tag, für Luxus 30,- DM pro Tag.
Haben Sie Ihr Programm gefunden?

Verkehrsverein Bad Aachen e.V.
Bahnhofplatz 4
Telefon (02 41) 3 06 00
Telex 8 329 768 vva d

Kuren in Bad Aachen

Aachen ist auch Bad Aachen - seit 1974 staatlich anerkanntes Heilbad. Während der ganzjährigen Kursaison stehen Ihnen in Bad Aachen nach neuesten Erkenntnissen ausgestattete und arbeitende Kuranstalten und -hotels, Thermalbäder und Trinkbrunnen zur Verfügung. Sie bieten die beste Voraussetzung zur Rehabilitation und gezielten Prävention bei allen rheumatischen Erkrankungen und verschiedenen anderen Heilanzeigen.
Ein Verzeichnis der Kurkliniken und Sanatorien finden Sie in diesem Heft auf Seite 39.

Weitere Informationen gibt Ihnen unser Spezialprospekt baden und kuren, sowie die Kurgastbetreuung im Haus des Gastes,
Burtscheider Markt,
5100 Bad Aachen,
Tel. 02 41 / 60 19 27.

Aachen „life" erleben

Erleben Sie Aachen als Stadt der Vielfalt. Hier ist Altehrwürdiges und Modernes harmonisch vereint.
Ob zu Fuß oder per Bus, Aachen erleben kann man aus jeder Perspektive. Stets umgibt Sie Aachens 2000 Jahre alte lebendige Geschichte. Wenn Sie vom vielen Erobern hungrig und durstig geworden sind, finden Sie sicher in einer der vielen Pinten oder typischen Studentenlokale Stärkung. Und in den stilvollen Cafés können Sie die berühmten Aachener Printen versuchen.
Lassen Sie sich vom Charme dieser Stadt verführen.

Allgemeine Leistungen:
1 oder 2 Übernachtungen/ Frühstück

Rahmenprogramm:
Begrüßungsdrink im Hotel
Aachener Tageszeitung
Führung durch die historische Altstadt
Besuch der Neuen Galerie - Sammlung Ludwig
Besuch des Zeitungsmuseums
Besuch des Internationalen Spielcasinos Aachen

Historisches Aachen

Erleben Sie die Stadt der Vielfalt in ihrer Vielfalt. Nehmen Sie sich Zeit für den Besuch der Museen, des Doms und des größten Domschatzes nördlich der Alpen. Und entspannen Sie sich bei Aachener Spezialitäten im alten Aachener Kaffee-Haus. Lassen Sie sich vom Charme dieser Stadt verführen.

Allgemeine Leistungen:
1 oder 2 Übernachtungen/ Frühstück

Rahmenprogramm:
Begrüßungsdrink im Hotel
Aachener Tageszeitung
Führung durch die historische Altstadt
Führung durch den Aachener Dom und die Schatzkammer
Besuch des Aachener Rathauses
Besuch des Couven-Museums
Besuch des Suermondt-Ludwig-Museums
Besuch des Heimatmuseums Burg Frankenberg
Kaffee-Gedeck in einem historischen Aachener Kaffeehaus

Thermalbaden im Römerbad
Info-Mappe mit Aachen-Postkarten
Aachen-Souvenir

Preise pro Person in der Woche in DM

	1 Üb.	2 Üb.
Luxus	—	255,-
First class	129,-	208,-
Standard I	101,-	162,-
Standard II	98,-	157,-

Preise pro Person am Wochenende in DM:

	1 Üb.	2 Üb.
Luxus	—	235,-
First class	122,-	194,-
Standard I	95,-	150,-
Standard II	93,-	145,-

Thermalbaden im Römerbad
Ein Glas original Aachener Lagerbier
Info-Mappe mit Aachen-Postkarten
Aachen-Souvenir

Preise pro Person in der Woche in DM

	1 Üb.	2 Üb.
Luxus	—	245,-
First class	114,-	195,-
Standard I	85,-	147,-
Standard II	83,-	142,-

Preise pro Person am Wochenende in DM

	1 Üb.	2 Üb.
Luxus	—	225,-
First class	107,-	179,-
Standard I	80,-	135,-
Standard II	75,-	130,-

Ausflug Excursion

MÄRCHENHAFTE TROPFSTEIN-
FORMATIONEN

EINMALIGE FELSGEBILDE

UNTERIRDISCHE WASSERLÄUFE
UND SCHLUCHTEN

RIESENDOM

Steiermark
das grüne Herz Österreichs

DIE LURGROTTE SEMRIACH

Die ganzjährig geöffnete SEMRIACHER LURGROTTE, eine der größten Tropfsteinhöhlen Österreichs, liegt 30 km nördlich von Graz nahe (2 km) dem reizvollen Markt Semriach. Man erreicht Semriach auf einer sehr gut ausgebauten Straße. Die einmaligen Naturschönheiten der SEMRIACHER LURGROTTE können auf gut ausgebauten und mit elektrischer Beleuchtung versehenen Wegen bequem besucht werden. Während einer Führung, sie dauert rund 5/4 Stunden, erhält der Naturfreund einen nachhaltigen Eindruck von dieser zauberhaften Märchenwelt tief im Innern des Tannebenstocks. In der Grotte herrscht eine konstante Temperatur von +9°C bei ausgezeichneten Luftverhältnissen.

Führung: Der Eingang zur LURGROTTE befindet sich unter einer einer eindrucksvollen, 70 m hohen Felswand. Wir folgen kurz dem Wasserlauf des Lurbachs, steigen dann etwas höher und gelangen in den reich mit Tropfsteinen und kleinen Kolken ausgestatteten TROPFSTEINGANG. In diesem schönen, blaugrau marmorierten Grottenteil erregen insbesondere der STEIRISCHE KACHELOFEN und das MÄRCHENSCHLOSS allgemeine Bewunderung. Die anschließende BÄRENGROTTE – so benannt, weil hier fossile Bärenknochen gefunden wurden – ist geprägt durch den SILBERSCHLEIER, der die halbe Wand von oben herunter verhüllt und in herrlichsten Fransen und Falten endet. Durch einen schönen Tropfsteingang gelangen wir in einen der größten unterirdischen Hohlräume der Welt, in den GROSSEN DOM (Länge 120 m, Breite 80 m, Höhe 40 m). Vor uns liegt das TROPFSTEIN-PARADIES, ein Wunderwerk der Natur mit vielen Tropfsteingebilden. Der Weg führt nun hinunter zur RIESENGLOCKE, einem 10 m hohen Stalagmiten, und weiter in einen Raum, dessen Name ZAUBERGROTTE nur schwach das Gefühle wiedergibt, die der Besucher beim Betreten dieses Grottenteils empfindet. Wenn das Märchen auf dieser Welt noch ein Reich hat, so bestimmt hier. Die grandiosen Gesteinsformationen wie RIESENERKER, ZIGEUNERZELT, FITTERBURG und VESUV hinterlassen einen tiefen Eindruck. Zurückgekommen in den GROSSEN DOM, steigen wir hinauf in die BELVEDEREGROTTE, wo eines der schönsten Tropfsteingebilde, die PINIENGRUPPE, zu bewundern ist. Durch den KATAKOMBENGANG kommen wir zum größten freihängenden Tropfstein der Welt, den RIESEN (Länge 13 m, Umfang 9 m). Auf dem Rückweg bestaunen wir nochmals die Weiten des GROSSEN DOMS und besuchen die BRUDERGROTTE und den silberschimmernden OSTERLEUCHTER.

FÜHRUNGEN:

Ganzjährig zwischen 9 und 17 Uhr; auf Wunsch Sonderführungen.
Anmeldungen im Gasthof Schinnerl „Zur Lurgrotte".
Von dort führen eine Straße und ein Fußweg zum Höhleneingang. Ausgangspunkt der Führungen ist das Wartehaus vor dem Höhleneingang.
Getränke und Erfrischungen erhältlich.

Tropfsteinparadies

Die Riesentraube

Lurgrotte
SEMRIACH

Osterleuchter

STEIERMARK · ÖSTERREICH

Herausgeber: Gasthof Schinnerl – Lurgrotte Semriach. Fotos: Fischer, Graz. Druck: Steierm. Landesdruckerei, Graz. Repros: Schlick KG, Graz

Freizeit Hobby

NIEDERNSILL, Salzburger Land
Programm: Kerb- und Flachschnitzen
Kursleiter: Tischlermeister Thomas Waltl
Kursdauer: 2½ Tage, 9.00 bis 12.00 Uhr, 14.00 bis 17.00 Uhr
Kursgebühr: S 500,—
           S 50,— Übungsbrett
           S 50,— Schnitzmesser
Mindestteilnehmerzahl 10 Personen
Mitzubringen sind: Bleistift, Zirkel, Maßstab
Information und Anmeldung: Thomas Waltl, A-5722 Niedernsill

Basteln

PÖRTSCHACH AM WÖRTHER SEE, Kärnten
Programm: „Basteln Sie Ihr Souvenir selbst"
Kursleiter: Gertie Glaunach
Termin: ab 15. 6. , Lesesaal der Gemeinde
Kursdauer: einmal wöchentlich 2 Stunden
Kursgebühr: S 130,— inkl. Material
Information und Anmeldung: Kurverwaltung, A-9210 Pörtschach, Tel. (4272) 2354

Kochen

BLUDENZ, Vorarlberg
Kochen von „heimischen Spezialitäten"
Programm: Vorführung und Anleitung zum Kochen von Vorarlberger Spezialitäten
Kursleiter: Wolfgang Neyer
Kursdauer: viermal wöchentlich 2—3 Stunden nach Vereinbarung
Termin: Mai bis Oktober
Kursgebühr: Materialkosten S 350,—
Information und Anmeldung: Hotel Löwen, A-6700 Bludenz, Tel. (5552) 22 06, oder Verkehrsamt, Tel. (5552) 21 70

Pilze- und Beerensammeln

MILLSTATT, Kärnten
Programm: Fachkundige Führung zur Pilze- und Beerenzeit am unverbauten Südufer des Millstätter Sees oder auf der Millstätter Alpe
Leiter: Gärtnermeister Ferdinand Krampl
Kosten: S 50,— (Fähre und eventuelle Mitfahrten im Pkw werden gesondert verrechnet)
         S 45,— mit Kurkarte
Information und Anmeldung: Ferdinand Krampl, Haus Schmölzer, A-9872 Millstatt, Tel. (4766) 2156

Landschaft — Stilleben

Programm: Besonderes Augenmerk wird nicht nur auf die richtige Wiedergabe oder Umsetzung eines Gegenstandes gerichtet, sondern auch auf die spezifische Betrachtungsweise der Bildinhalte und ihre kompositionelle Ausformung
Kursleiter: Prof. Franz Luby
Termin: 2. 7.—14. 7.
Beginn am 1. Tag um 10.30 Uhr
Kursgebühr: S 1.700,— ohne Material
Programm: Praktikum der Maltechniken
Kursleiter: Prof. Fritz Itzinger
Termine: 19. 2.— 3. 3.
Beginn am 1. Tag um 10.00 Uhr
15. 10.—27.10.
Beginn am 1. Tag um 10.00 Uhr
Kursgebühr: S 1.750,— ohne Nebenkosten

GOLDEGG, Salzburger Land
Acht Tage Landschaftsmalen im Gebirge
Programm: Erfassen einer Gebirgslandschaft und Umsetzen in Farbe
Kursleiter: Prof. Fritz Itzinger
Termin: 7. 5.—12. 5.
Beginn am 1. Tag um 10.00 Uhr
Kursgebühr: S 1.200,— ohne Material
Auskunft und Anmeldung: Stift Geras, A-2093 Geras, Tel. (2912) 34 589

Malen auf Glas (Hohlglasmalerei), Bäuerliches Malen

Programm: Praktische Übungen, figurales Zeichnen und Malen, Motivwahl für die Glasbemalung, Materialkunde und Theorie
Kursleiter: Gitti Wascher
Termin: 14. 5.—19. 5.
Beginn am 1. Tag um 10.00 Uhr

Konservierung und Restaurierung von Bildern und Holzplastiken

Programm: Farbenlehre, Farbchemie, Konservierung und Restaurierung von Bildern auf Leinwandträgern, auf Holz und von Holzplastiken
Kursleiter: Akad. Maler Leo Beker
Termine: 5. 2.—17. 2.
11. 6.—23. 6.
15. 10. — 27.10.
Beginn jeweils am 1. Tag um 10.00 Uhr
Kursgebühr: ca. S 1.700,— ohne Material

---

austria information

Ernsthafte Familienväter steuern Dampfloks durch die Sommerlandschaft, berufstätige Frauen vergessen den Streß des Alltags, während sie rosig-runde Bauernblumen und knallrote Herzen malen. Abgeklärte Pensionisten und elegante Sekretärinnen schnitzen lustige Wurzelmännchen, andere Urlauber beugen sich über einen grauen Tonklumpen, der unter ihren Händen zum schön geschwungenen Topf wird.
Österreich ist das ganze Jahr über ein einziges Hobby-Zentrum, in dem Sie sich alle schöpferischen Wünsche erfüllen können. Vom Malen und Zeichnen bis zur Bildhauerei, zum Holzschnitzen, Klöppeln und Weben wird alles gelehrt, was ganz ohne Vorbildung mit geschickten Händen gemacht werden kann. Sportfexe lernen Bogenschießen, Jagen, Rennfahren, Wildwasserfahren, Abenteuerlustige spielen Lokführer auf Kleinbahnlinien, Fleißige sammeln Pilze und Beeren oder waschen Gold aus einem Gebirgsfluß.

Wer von der Fülle des Gebotenen erschöpft ist, entspannt sich bei einem Yogalehrgang, trinkt einen guten Tropfen beim Weinseminar oder lernt jodeln auf einer zünftigen Almhütte.
Das wird ein Urlaub!

Österreichische Fremdenverkehrswerbung
Austrian National Tourist Office
Office National Autrichien du Tourisme

Hohenstaufengasse 3
A-1010 Wien I
Austria – Österreich

Musik

FAAK AM SEE, Kärnten

Amateur-Blasmusiker haben die Möglichkeit, während ihres Urlaubs bei der örtlichen Trachtenkapelle mitzuspielen. Eigenes Instrument und Primavista-Spiel sind erwünscht.

Information und Anmeldung: Verkehrsverein, A-9583 Faak am See, Tel. (4254) 2110

PÖRTSCHACH AM WÖRTHER SEE, Kärnten

Chorgesang in einer Sängerrunde

Chorleiterin: Gretl Komposch vom Grenzlandchor Arnoldstein

Programm: Volks-, Kärntner- und Wanderlieder

Termin: einmal wöchentlich am Landspitz, bei Schlechtwetter im Lesesaal

Beginnzeiten werden auf den Wochenplakaten bekanntgegeben, Dauer ca. 2 Stunden

Kursgebühr: kostenlos

Information: Kurverwaltung, A-9210 Pörtschach, Tel. (4272) 2354

Wildwasserfahren

KLAUS AN DER STEYR, Oberösterreich

Kurse für Anfänger

Programm: Fahren auf ruhigem Wasser, Queren, Seilfähre, Fahren auf der Steyr

Kursleiter: Manfred Breiteneder

Kursdauer: 1 Woche, Montag bis Freitag, ca. 25 Stunden

Termine: Juli und August

Kursgebühr: S 1.300,— (mit kompletter Ausrüstung)

S 800,— (mit eigener Ausrüstung)

Information und Anmeldung: Wildwassersportschule, Manfred Breiteneder, A-4564 Klaus an der Steyr, Tel. (7585) 310

Jodeln

NEUSTIFT IM STUBAI, Tirol

„Stubaier Jodelakademie"

Programm: Erlernen von Volksliedern, Musikbegleitung zur Erlernung der Lieder mit Jodler, Erlernen von Volkstänzen; Urkunde zum Abschluß

Kursleiter: Dietmar Geiger

Termin: ganzjährig

Kursdauer: Dienstag bis Freitag, täglich von 17.00 bis 19.00 Uhr im „Weinstadel"

Kursgebühr: S 100,—

Information und Anmeldung: Fremdenverkehrsverein, A-6167 Neustift im Stubai, Tel. (5226) 228

Bau einer Armbrust

GERAS (nördlich von Horn), Niederösterreich

Programm: Bau einer barocken Scheibenarmbrust

Kursleiter: Günther Andorfer

Termin: 5. 3.—17. 3.

Beginn am 1. Tag um 10.00 Uhr

Kursgebühr: S 1.750,— ohne Nebenkosten

Auskunft und Anmeldung: Stift Geras, A-2093 Geras, Tel. (2912) 34 589

Heißluftballonfahren

PUCH BEI WEIZ, Steiermark

Programm: Theoretische Einweisung, Ballonausrüstung

Kursdauer: zweieinhalb Tage

Termine: 23. 2.—25. 2.

9. 3.—11. 3.

23. 3.—25. 3.

6. 4.— 8. 4.

Kursgebühr: S 460,— für Begleiter

S 2.450,— für Ballonfahrer im Preis inklusive: zwei Halbpensionen, Flug, Ballonkosten inkl. Gas, Ballontransport und -wartung, Verfolgungsfahrzeug für Rückfahrt, Versicherung, Taufurkunde, Bordbuch, Klubabzeichen

Information und Anmeldung: ÖAMTC-Reisebüro, Schubertring 1—3, A-1010 Wien, Tel. (222) 75 26 01

Jagd

OBERTAUERN, Salzburger Land

Programm: Revier- und Pirschgänge, theoretische Vorträge usw.

Kursdauer: 5½ Tage

Termin: 3. 9.—8. 9.

Kursgebühr: S 800,— pro Person

Gutes Schuhwerk und Kleidung in möglichst dunklem Farbton, Regenbekleidung, Jagdglas sind erforderlich

Vorbereitungskurse für Jagdprüfungsanwärter werden durchgeführt

Termin: 3. 9.—14. 9.

Kursgebühr S 1.800,— pro Person inkl. Beistellung des Lehrbehelfs

Information und Anmeldung: Hotel Kohlmayr, A-5562 Obertauern, Tel. (6456) 272 oder 282

Hobby-Lokführer

auf der Gurktalbahn: Für die Strecke Treibach—Zwischenwässern (3,2 km) steht eine Dampflok für Amateur-Lokführer zur Verfügung. Betrieb während der Sommermonate.

Kosten: S 500,— für eine Fahrt

Information und Anmeldung: Kärntner Museumsbahnen-V.K.E.F., Postfach 321, A-9011 Klagenfurt, Wendelin Eitzinger, Tel. (4222) 82 416, Hansgeorg Prix, Tel. (4222) 23 00 84, Peter Orasch, Tel. (4222) 33 90 14

RAMSAU AM DACHSTEIN, Steiermark

Wandern und fotografieren

Kursleiter: Hans Gsellmann

Kursdauer: 1 Woche

Termine: 28. 5.—2. 6.

24. 9.—6. 10.

Pauschalpreis: S 4.300,— bis S 5.000,— (Kurs, 1 Woche Halbpension, alle Nebenkosten wie Bus, Seilbahn usw.)

Information und Anmeldung: Verkehrsverein, Herr R. Lamm, A-8972 Ramsau am Dachstein, Tel. (3687) 2925

Stadtchronik   City History

BERLINER DATEN

30. Januar 1933 Mit der Berufung einer faschistischen Regierung, mit Hitler als Reichskanzler, beginnt die offene, terroristische Gewaltherrschaft der reaktionärsten, am meisten chauvinistischen, aggressivsten Kräfte des deutschen Finanzkapitals.

7. Februar 1933 Im Sporthaus Ziegenhals bei Berlin findet die erste illegale Tagung des Zentralkomitees der KPD statt. Ernst Thälmann umreißt vor etwa 40 leitenden Funktionären der Partei die veränderten Kampfbedingungen nach der Errichtung des faschistischen Regimes. Er orientiert die Kommunisten darauf, die Arbeiterklasse und alle Werktätigen zum Massenkampf gegen die Naziherrschaft und den faschistischen Terror zu mobilisieren.

27. Februar 1933 Die Faschisten inszenieren den Reichstagsbrand, bezichtigen die Kommunisten der Brandstiftung und eröffnen einen blutigen Terrorfeldzug gegen sie und die anderen Gegner des Naziregimes; allein in der Nacht vom 27. zum 28. Februar 1933 werden in Berlin 1 500 Antifaschisten, zumeist Kommunisten, verhaftet.

3. März 1933 Ernst Thälmann, Vorsitzender der KPD, fällt, durch Polizeispitzel verraten, den faschistischen Schergen in die Hände. Unter Leitung John Schehrs kämpft die KPD weiter. Auf der Parteikonferenz im Oktober 1935 wird Wilhelm Pieck für die Dauer der Einkerkerung Ernst Thälmanns zum Vorsitzenden der KPD gewählt.

21. Juni 1933 Beginn der Köpenicker Blutwoche, in der 91 Kommunisten, Sozialdemokraten und parteilose Arbeiter von den Nazibestien ermordet werden.

10. Mai 1933 Faschisten verbrennen auf dem Opernplatz (heute Bebelplatz) Schriften der Klassiker des Marxismus-Leninismus sowie bedeutende Werke der deutschen National- und der Weltliteratur.

1934/35 Trotz faschistischen Terrors setzen unter Führung der KPD die antifaschistischen Kräfte ihren Kampf gegen die Nazidiktatur fort; in Berlin erscheinen 78 illegale kommunistische Zeitungen.

Juni 1935 Die illegalen Bezirksvorstände Berlin-Brandenburg der Roten Hilfe und der SPD vereinbaren gemeinsame Maßnahmen gegen Spitzel und Provokateure und zur Unterstützung von Opfern des Naziterrors.

4. Dezember 1935 Erich Honecker, Mitglied des Zentralkomitees des Kommunistischen Jugendverbandes Deutschlands, wird in Berlin-Wedding von der Gestapo verhaftet und 1937 vom „Volksgerichtshof" zu zehn Jahren Zuchthaus, verurteilt.

1.–16. August 1936 Berliner Antifaschisten verbreiten unter Teilnehmern und Besuchern der XI. Olympischen Sommerspiele antifaschistische Flugblätter und Tarnschriften.

1939 Unter Führung der KPD ist Berlin zum Zentrum des antifaschistischen Widerstandskampfes geworden; illegale Parteiorganisationen bilden den Kern antifaschistischer Widerstandsgruppen. Der heldenhafte Kampf wird u. a. von den Genossen Bernhard Bästlein, Franz Jacob, Anton Saefkow und Robert Uhrig geleitet. Die Schulze-Boysen-Harnack-Organisation leistet wichtige Kundschaftertätigkeit für die Sowjetunion.

1. September 1939 Der faschistische deutsche Imperialismus entfesselt mit dem Überfall auf Polen den zweiten Weltkrieg.

November 1939 Berliner Antifaschisten rufen mit Flugblättern und Klebezetteln zum Widerstand gegen den Hitlerkrieg auf.

Frühjahr 1941 Der von Robert Uhrig geleiteten antifaschistischen Widerstandsorganisation gehören etwa 200 Mitglieder an; sie knüpft Verbindungen zu Widerstandsgruppen in vielen deutschen Städten.

22. Juni 1941 Mit dem wortbrüchigen räuberischen Überfall auf die Sowjetunion erreicht die faschistische Aggression ihren Höhepunkt. Die Sowjetunion trägt fortan die Hauptlast des Krieges gegen das faschistische Deutschland.

18. Mai 1942 Die von dem Jungkommunisten Herbert Baum geleitete Widerstandsgruppe setzt im Lustgarten eine antisowjetische Hetzausstellung in Brand.

Ende 1942/Anfang 1943 Die Gestapo verhaftet 130 antifaschistische Widerstandskämpfer der Schulze-Boysen-Harnack-Organisation; 18 Frauen und 31 Männer werden hingerichtet.

März 1943 In Berlin verhaftet die Gestapo weitere 2 663 Widerstandskämpfer, darunter 1 800 ausländische Zwangsarbeiter und Kriegsgefangene.

23./24. August 1943 Die Stadt erlebt den ersten schweren Luftangriff durch anglo-amerikanische Flugzeuge; Zehntausende Frauen und Kinder kommen im Bombenhagel und Flammenmeer um.

Herbst 1943 In Berlin entsteht wieder eine zentrale operative Leitung der KPD in Deutschland, die Verbindungen zu illegalen Widerstandsorganisationen in ganz Deutschland hat.

Sommer 1944 Die zentrale operative Leitung der KPD arbeitet mit dem Dokument „Wir Kommunisten und das Nationalkomitee ‚Freies Deutschland'" das Hauptziel des antifaschistischen Kampfes heraus; darin wird der Charakter der nach dem Sturz des Hitlerfaschismus zu errichtenden antifaschistisch-demokratischen Ordnung erläutert.

16. April 1945 Mit 2,5 Millionen Soldaten, 41 600 Geschützen und Granatwerfern, 6 250 Panzern und Sturmgeschützen und 7 500 Flugzeugen beginnt die Offensive der Sowjetarmee auf Berlin.

30. April 1945 Sowjetsoldaten hissen auf dem Reichstag die rote Siegesfahne.

14. Mai 1945 Die U-Bahn nimmt auf einigen Strecken den Betrieb wieder auf.

Geschichte   History

TRIER

Kurze Geschichte der ältesten Stadt Deutschlands

ANTE ROMAM TREVERIS STETIT ANNIS MILLE TRECENTIS. „Vor Rom stand Trier eintausend und dreihundert Jahre" behauptet die Inschrift am Roten Haus am Trierer Hauptmarkt. Das ist zwar eine mittelalterliche Erfindung, aber sie hat einen geschichtlichen Hintergrund. Im Trierer Tal gab es in der Tat schon im 3. Jahrtausend v. Chr. menschliche Siedlungen, und Trier war die erste Stadt, die diesen Namen nördlich der Alpen zu Recht trug.

AUGUSTA TREVERORUM, das spätere Trier, wurde um 16 vor Christus von den Römern unter Kaiser Augustus in der Nähe eines Stammesheiligtums der keltischen Treverer gegründet. Gegen Ende des 3. Jahrhunderts machte Kaiser Diokletian die jetzt TREVIRIS genannte Stadt zur römischen Kaiserresidenz und Hauptstadt des weströmischen Teilreiches. Etwa um die gleiche Zeit entwickelte sich hier ein Zentrum des frühen Christentums. Im 5. Jahrhundert von den Franken erobert, kam Trier bei der karolingischen Reichsteilung von 870 zum ostfränkisch-deutschen Reich.

958 entstand mit der Errichtung des Marktkreuzes der heutige Hauptmarkt als Zentrum der mittelalterlichen Stadt. Im 12. Jahrhundert wurden die Trierer Erzbischöfe Kurfürsten. Sie machten Trier zur Hauptstadt ihres Kurstaates, die bis zu dessen Auflösung an der Wende vom 18. zum 19. Jahrhundert Zeiten hoher Blüte und tiefen Niedergangs erlebte. Kurze Zeit in französischem Besitz, kam Trier 1815 zu Preußen und 1945 zum Bundesland Rheinland-Pfalz in der Bundesrepublik Deutschland.

Trier heute

Trier ist Bezirkshauptstadt des Regierungsbezirks Trier, Bischofssitz, Kultur-, Verkehrs- und Wirtschaftsmittelpunkt des Trierer Landes, Universitätsstadt, Hafenstadt am Moselschiffahrtsweg, Standort namhafter Industriebetriebe, Weinbau- und Weinhandelszentrum, Einkaufs-, Fremdenverkehrs- und Tagungsstadt. Es hat 100 000 Einwohner.

Baudenkmäler

Zwischen Porta Nigra und Amphitheater:

Porta Nigra, römisches Stadttor aus dem 2. Jahrh., Sandsteinquadern mit Eisenklammern verbunden; 11.–18. Jahrh. Doppelkirche St. Simeon, davon erhalten die romanische Apsis.

Simeonstift, 11. Jahrh., zweigeschossiger Kreuzgang um einen Innenhof (Brunnenhof).

Dreikönigenhaus, Simeonstr. 19, spätromanischer Wohnturm, 13. Jahrhundert.

Hauptmarkt mit **Marktkreuz,** 958, und **Petrusbrunnen,** 1595; gotische Marktkirche **St. Gangolf,** 14./15. Jahrh., Turm von 1507; Ratsweinhaus zur **Steipe,** 15. Jh., und **Rotes Haus,** 1684.

Frankenturm, Dietrichstraße 5, romanischer Wohnturm, 11. Jahrh.

Dom, Bischofskirche, römischer Kernbau: 4. Jahrh., romanischer Westbau: 11. Jahrh., Ostchor: 12. Jahrh., Domkreuzgang: 13. Jahrh., Domschatzkammer: 1716.

Liebfrauen, früheste gotische Kirche in Deutschland, 1235 bis 1260 an der Stelle einer römischen Basilika errichtet.

Palais Kesselstatt, Liebfrauenstr. 9, erbaut 1740–1745.

Römische Palastaula (Basilika), Anfang des 4. Jahrh., Thronsaal des Kaisers Constantin, später Burg der Trierer Kurfürsten, heute ev. Kirche.

Kurfürstliches Palais, Ost- und Nordflügel, Roter Turm und Petrusportal aus der Renaissance, 17. Jahrh., barocker Südflügel, erbaut 1757–1761 von Joh. Seiz; heute Sitz der Bezirksregierung.

Im **Palastgarten** Kopien von Barockfiguren; an der Ostseite des Parks Reste der mittelalterlichen Stadtmauer.

Kaiserthermen, Ruine eines römischen Bäderpalastes, Viertes Jahrh., mit Warmbad, Kaltbad und Sportplatz. Erhalten

ist das Mauerwerk des Warmbades und das weitläufige Kellergeschoß. (Bus 5, 7, 8, 16)

Amphitheater, 100 n. Chr., Oleewiger Str. 25, Ruine einer römischen Arena für Gladiatoren- und Tierkämpfe. Ränge für 25 000 Zuschauer. (Bus 6/16)

Vom Stadtkern zum Moselufer:

Jesuitenkirche, Jesuitenstr., 13. Jahrh., und **Alte Universität,** 1614 und 1775.

St.-Georgs-Brunnen, Kornmarkt, 1750. Entwurf von Joh. Seiz.

Barbarathermen, Südallee 48, römische Badeanlage, 2. Jahrh. (Bus 1)

Römerbrücke, Pfeiler aus römischer Zeit, 2. Jahrh., Brückenbogen von 1717/18. (Bus 1)

Am Moselufer zwei alte **Hafenkrane,** 1413 und 1774, und die ehem. Klöster **St. Irminen** (mit Resten der römischen Hafenspeicher), **St. Katharinen** und **St. Martin,** 17. und 18. Jahrh.; auf der Höhe jenseits der Mosel die **Mariensäule,** 1866; an der Brücke: **Zurlauben,** alte Häuserzeile, 18. Jahrh.

Vor den Toren der Römerstadt:

St. Matthias (Trier-Süd), romanische Abtei- u. Pfarrkirche 10./12. Jahrh., mit dem Grab des Apostels Matthias. Apsis und Einwölbung des Mittelschiffes um 1500, Portale und Turmkrönung 17. und 18. Jahrh., röm. Grabanlagen. (Bus 3, 4)

St. Paulin (Trier-Nord), Barockkirche, 1734–1751 nach Plänen Balthasar Neumanns errichtet, Hochaltar von Ferd. Tietz, Deckengemälde von Ch. Th. Scheffler. (Bus 3, 4)

Auf dem linken Moselufer:

Pfalzel, Sommerresidenz der römischen Kaiser und der Trierer Kurfürsten; Stiftskirche, Stadtmauer, Wohnhäuser.
(Bus 8. Bahn. In den Sommermonaten Motorbootverkehr ab Stadthafen)

Schloß Quint, erbaut um 1760 von Joh. Seiz. (Bahn u. Bus)

Museen

Landesmuseum

Ostallee 44: Kunst- und Kulturgut aus vorgeschichtlicher, römischer, frühchristlicher, mittelalterlicher Zeit.

Bischöfliches Museum

Banthusstr. 6: Funde aus frühchristlicher Zeit, kirchliche Kunst.

Domschatzkammer

Eingang durch den Dom. Domführungen: DomBüro-Anmeldung: Tel. 7 58 01

Städtisches Museum

Simeonstift: Dokumente zur Geschichte des Stadtbildes, Skulptur und Malerei vom Mittelalter bis zur Romantik und zum Realismus. Ausstellungen zeitgenössischer Kunst.

Stadtbibliothek

Weberbach 25: Im Ausstellungsraum Handschriften, Urkunden, Frühdrucke.

Karl-Marx-Haus

Brückenstraße 10: Karl-Marx-Museum im Geburtshaus des Begründers des modernen Sozialismus.

Öffnungszeiten siehe im Veranstaltungskalender „Der fröhliche Steuermann".

Aussichtspunkte

Weißhaus	(A 5),	15 Min.*
Kockelsberg	(A 5),	40 Min.*
Mariensäule	(C 5),	30 Min.*
Markusberg	(C 5),	40 Min.*
Petrisberg	(C 1),	20 Min.**

* = zu Fuß ab Kaiser-Wilhelm-Brücke.
** = zu Fuß ab Ostallee.

Zwischen dem Stadthafen Zurlauben und dem Weißhausterrasse verkehrt eine **Kabinenseilbahn,** zwischen Hauptmarkt und Kockelsberg ein Bus.

Eine ausführliche Beschreibung aller Sehenswürdigkeiten enthält der Trevirensia-Stadtführer „Ein Gang durch Trier".

DAS DMW MUSEUM IN MÜNCHEN

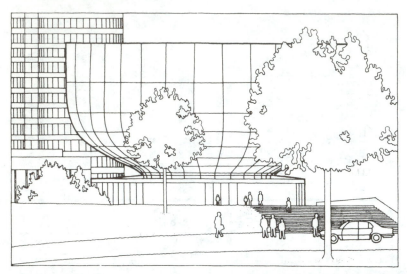

Das BMW Museum

entstand 1971 bis 1973 gleichzeitig mit dem BMW Hochhaus nach Plänen des Architekten Professor Karl Schwanzer (Wien) parallel zur Errichtung des Olympiaparks für die Olympischen Spiele 1972. Es zeigt seitdem, was ein Unternehmen mit seiner Zeit verbindet: in Politik und Wirtschaft, Kultur und Technik. 400 000 Gäste pro Jahr machen das BMW Museum München zum meistbesuchten Firmenmuseum in Deutschland und nach dem Deutschen Museum (Technik-Geschichte) sowie der Neuen Pinakothek (Gemäldegalerie) zum Museum mit der dritthöchsten Besucherzahl in München.

Die Museumsschale ist 19 m hoch und 41 m weit. Die technische Ausstattung im Inneren des Museums wurde 1984 komplett erneuert. Das Museum ist täglich, auch an Wochenenden, von 9.00–17.00 Uhr geöffnet; Einlaß bis 16.00 Uhr.

Ihr Weg durch das BMW Museum

wird in drei Stunden Rundgang den technischen Horizont von fünf Generationen ermessen lassen: von der Wende zum 20. Jahrhundert, als die ersten Motorkutschen noch nicht ahnen ließen, wie Automobile aussehen, bis weit in das 21. Jahrhundert hinein, so wie wir es heute erahnen können. Wie keine andere Technik haben Automobil, Motorrad und Flugzeug das Leben unseres Jahrhunderts bestimmt.

Die BMW AG hat im Laufe ihrer Geschichte Flugmotoren, Motorräder und Automobile gebaut. BMW Motoren waren überall zu Hause: in der Luft, zu Lande und zu Wasser. Von den Menschen, die sie gebaut haben, von ihren Lebensverhältnissen und ihren technischen Träumen ist in dieser Ausstellung die Rede. Von den Wandlungen, die die heutige Technik in unserer Zivilisation verursacht, und von Erwartungen, die wir an die Technik von morgen haben, werden Sie in dieser Ausstellung viel sehen. Sie spricht vier Sprachen gleichzeitig: deutsch, englisch, französisch, spanisch.

BMW 328 Mille Miglia. Der erfolgreichste deutsche Sportwagen der späten 30er Jahre ist der BMW 328. In Francorchamps, auf dem Nürburgring und auf der Avus sammelt dieser Sportwagen Erfolge. 1938 nehmen vier BMW 328 an dem berühmtesten Straßenrennen, der Mille Miglia, teil. Albert Fane bewältigt diese Strecke als Schnellster und wird nach 1610 Kilometern über Landstraßen, durch Ortschaften auf Kopfsteinpflaster in Brescia als Sieger gefeiert. Das 24-Stunden-Rennen von Le Mans, den Langstreckenklassiker, beendet 1939 ein 328 nicht nur als Klassensieger, sondern als Gesamtfünfter.
1940 kommt es zu einer Neuauflage der Mille Miglia. Diesmal ist es ein Dreieckskurs, 161 Kilometer lang, zehnmal zu durchfahren. Die Hauptrolle spielen fünf spezialkarossierte BMW 328. Drei offene und zwei geschlossene Versionen gehen an den Start. Die dünne Außenhaut aus Aluminium über einem Gitterrohrrahmen ermöglicht ein Gewicht von nur 650 Kilogramm. Nur einer der fünf BMW 328 fällt aus, die vier übrigen belegen die Plätze 1, 3, 5 und 6. Huschke von Hanstein fährt nicht nur die schnellste Runde, er beendet mit seinem Partner Walter Bäumer das Rennen auch als Gesamtsieger.

6 Zyl., 1971 ccm
135 PS (100 kW)
224 km/h
3 Exemplare
1938/40

BMW 500 ccm Maschine Schorsch Meier. Auf zwei Rädern kommt der erfolgreiche Durchbruch für BMW bereits in den 30er Jahren. Diese von BMW entwickelte Kompressormaschine ist schnell genug für Weltrekorde, aber auch zuverlässig genug, um bei der Internationalen Sechstagefahrt in den Alpen bestehen zu können. Als erster Ausländer auf einer ausländischen Maschine gewinnt Schorsch Meier mit ihr 1939 im Motorradland Großbritannien die „Senior Tourist Trophy" (Königsklasse) auf der Isle of Man.

2 Zyl., 494 ccm
Kompressor
55 PS (40 kW)
bei 8000/min.
140 kg
205 km/h
4 Exemplare
1937–1939

BMW 328 Roadster. Aus dem BMW Werk Eisenach, wo bis in den Zweiten Weltkrieg hinein alle BMW-Automobile gebaut werden, kommt 1936 dieser Sportwagen. Der mit Kastenträgern verstärkte Rohrrahmen trägt den leichten Aufbau mit zwei Sitzen und einem Gepäckraum. Der 2-Liter-Sechs-Zylindermotor macht dieses leichte Fahrzeug zu einem der schnellsten und erfolgreichsten serienmäßigen Sportwagen seiner Zeit.

6 Zyl., 1971 ccm
80 PS (59 kW)
bei 5000/min.
830 kg
150 km/h
464 Exemplare
1936–1940

BMW Futuro Experimentierfahrzeug. Als Zukunftsstudie wird die Futuro 1980 mit Hilfe des Frankfurter Spezialisten Buchmann gebaut. Geringes Gewicht, moderne Fahrwerkstechnik und Sicherheit zeichnen sie aus. Durch die günstige Aerodynamik ist eine hohe Spitzengeschwindigkeit ohne höhere Motorleistung möglich. Zum besseren Durchzug ist ein Turbolader eingebaut. Die Verkleidung aus kohlenstoffverstärktem Kunststoff verdeckt u. a. Vollscheibenräder und Bremsscheiben aus Alu. Im Cockpit microprozessorgesteuerte Digitalanzeigen.

2 Zyl., 800 ccm
75 PS (55 kW)
bei 7250/min.
180 kg
210 km/h
1 Exemplar
1980

BMW Motorrad K 100. Auch nach sechs Jahrzehnten hat das Boxer-Prinzip in seiner Leistungsklasse (bis 60 PS) nichts von seiner Gültigkeit verloren. Die Ziele der BMW Motorrad Gesellschaft in der „Big Bike"-Klasse, stärker und zugleich sparsamer und leiser zu fahren, sind mit dem Boxer jedoch nicht zu realisieren, wenn er seine bewährten Tugenden behalten soll, robust, einfach und dauerhaft zu sein.

An die Seite der Boxer tritt daher 1983 die K-Reihe mit ihrem patentierten Compact-drive-System. Der längsliegend eingebaute, wassergekühlte Vierzylinder-Reihenmotor besitzt eine elektronische Benzineinspritzung und Schubabschaltung. Die Kraftübertragung erfolgt wie beim Boxer über eine Kardanwelle zum einseitig gelagerten Hinterrad. Dieses Konzept ist so überzeugend, daß die K 100 schon in ihrem Einführungsjahr den Titel „Motorrad des Jahres" erhält.

4 Zyl., 987 ccm
66 kW (90 PS)
bei 8000/min.
239 kg betankt
215 km/h

Soziale Fragen   Social Issues

Video- und Diaprogramme

Die Dia- und Vídeoprogramme zu speziellen Themen der Ausstellung finden Sie im weiteren Verlauf dieser Broschüre erläutert.
Auf einzelnen Plattformen des Museums sind daneben Videoprogramme unter dem Leitthema „Science Fiction der Väter" zu sehen. Sie geben Ihnen einen Eindruck davon, wie die Zukunft in der Vergangenheit erwartet wurde.

Vier Collagen aus der BMW-Geschichte.

1916–1930: In den ersten Jahren ist BMW ein Flugmotorenhersteller. 1923 kommen Motorräder, 1928 Automobile dazu.

1930–1945: In den 20er Jahren wird die BMW AG ein Automobilhersteller mit sportlichem Ruf. Mit Motorrädern, Automobilen und Flugmotoren beteiligt sich BMW an der friedlichen Verkehrserschließung der Erde, der 2. Weltkrieg macht den Flugmotorenhersteller zu einem Rüstungskonzern und bei Kriegsende zu einem Trümmerhaufen.

1945–1960: Die BMW AG der Nachkriegszeit überlebt nur mühsam mit Motorrädern, der Isetta, dem BMW 600 und 700 und wenigen großen, teuren Limousinen. Ende der 50er Jahre gilt die Firma als nicht mehr lebensfähig; doch der Glaube an die Marke bleibt lebendig.

1960–heute: Seit BMW wieder kompakte, sportliche Tourenwagen baut (der BMW 1500 erscheint 1961), entsteht aus dem Münchner Unternehmen ein weltweit aktiver Konzern. BMW heute: 50 000 Menschen, 450 000 Automobile und 30 000 Motorräder jährlich, davon werden fast zwei Drittel in über einhundert Länder exportiert.

Videofilm (10:49 Min.)

Motorsport. Der erste Videofilm läuft in den blauen Kugeln. Hier, wie auch bei allen anderen Filmstationen, ist jeweils eine Monitorkugel im rechten Winkel angeordnet, damit auch Kinder und Behinderte in ihrem Rollstuhl die Filme gut verfolgen können.
Drücken Sie den Knopf für Ihre Sprache und schalten Sie sich mit Ihrem Kopfhörer in eine der Buchsen ein. Damit startet der Film neu. Er gibt in skizzenhaften Szenen das Erlebnis von Bewegung in verschiedenen Dimensionen und Empfindungen wieder.

Diaprogramm (5:44 Min.)

Der Motorsportler. Vor einigen Jahrzehnten war Motorsport ein Freizeitengagement des Fahrers, das er selbst finanzieren mußte. Heute steht der Champion an der Spitze eines Teams, mit dem er Meister wird.

Diaprogramm (6:06 Min.)

Der Ingenieur. Früher war der Weg von der Idee über die Entwicklung bis zur Realisierung lang. Der Ingenieur konstruierte damals wie heute die komplette Karosserie, nur wird ihm heute die Arbeit mit Rechnern, Plottern (Planzeichenmaschinen) und Computern erleichtert. Der Ingenieur wird also nicht ersetzt, sondern von Routinearbeiten befreit. Neue Berufsfelder entstehen: zum Beispiel der selbständige Informatik-Programmierer.

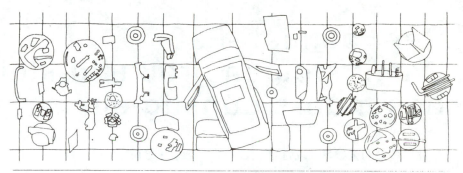

Videofilm (8:33 Min.)

Diaprogramm (5:37 Min.)

Der Arbeiter. Im Vergleich des Karosseriebaus von früher und heute werden die verbesserten Arbeits- und Lebensbedingungen des Arbeiters dargestellt. Sein Lebensstandard ist gewachsen. Roboter befreien ihn von schwerer und stupider Arbeit und helfen ihm, die Qualität seiner Arbeit zu verbessern. Roboter schaffen auch neue Arbeitsplätze, denn man braucht Menschen, um Roboter zu programmieren, zu kontrollieren und zu warten. Die Alternative heißt nicht: Arbeiter oder Roboter, sondern Arbeiter und Roboter.

Werkstatt der späten 20er Jahre. Vor Ihnen stehen Werkzeuge und Maschinen, wie sie zu der damaligen Zeit in Werkstätten üblich waren. Das Deutz 1-Zylinder-Aggregat, wie es zum Antrieb von Transmissionsriemen verwendet wurde, eine Ständerbohrmaschine, eine Werkbank. Der Eisele-Elektroprüfstand diente seit Anfang der 30er Jahre dazu, die Leistung von Anlassern und Lichtmaschine zu überprüfen. Die Leitspindel-Spitzendrehbank wurde bei der Bearbeitung der Achsen verwendet und war bis in die 80er Jahre am Tegernsee in Betrieb.

Technik. Der Film faßt alle wesentlichen Stationen der Technikgeschichte zusammen: von der Dampfmaschine über die Automatisierung bis hin zur elektronischen Revolution mit ihren Computern, die den Menschen durch Arbeitserleichterungen Freiraum für kreative Leistungen schaffen.

Der Eigentümer. Kapitalinvestitionen sind für die Zukunft eines Unternehmens von größter Bedeutung. BMW ist seit 1916 eine AG. Der Aktionär ist neben Aufsichtsrat, Vorstand und Geschäftsführung Mittelpunkt dieses Programms.
1959 gibt es auch bei BMW leere Kassen, aber die Kleinaktionäre bringen die geplante Fusion mir Daimler-Benz zu Fall. Herbert Quandt engagiert sich und wird Großaktionär. Die Erträge steigen; es kommt Geld für Investitionen in die Kassen: der Grundstein für eine positive Zukunft.

Fabrik der Zukunft. Die Veränderungen in der Fertigungstechnik sind in diesem Film zusammengefaßt. Früher waren viele Handgriffe nötig, heute arbeiten die Maschinen automatisch. In der Fabrik von morgen wird es eine Leitzentrale geben, in der eine Crew die vollautomatische Steuerung der Maschinen überwacht. Im Vordergrund steht die umweltfreundliche Fabrik der Zukunft.

Veränderungen. Der Film faßt noch einmal die Meilensteine zusammen, die die Ausstellung zum Thema Arbeitsplatz gestern, heute und morgen zeigt. Wie wurde früher geschraubt, geschweißt, konstruiert? Wie arbeitet man heute, rechnerunterstützt, und wie sieht der Arbeitsplatz der Zukunft aus?
Die Arbeitszeit wird sich zwar verkürzen, aber man wird permanent Neues erlernen müssen. Trotzdem wird mehr Zeit füreinande übrigbleiben. Dies alles wird im Film – als optisches Detail am Rande – mit Breakdance verbunden.

Jugend und Ausbildung. Früher bediente man Werkzeugmaschinen von Hand, die heute computergesteuert werden. Rechnerprogramme und Datenverarbeitung bestimmen die kaufmännischen Berufe. Neue, bessere Maschinen erfordern neue Berufe, wie zum Beispiel den Fertigungsmechaniker oder den Hybridtechniker. An einer guten Ausbildung ist auch das Unternehmen stark interessiert, denn die hohe Qualifikation der Mitarbeiter überträgt sich auf die Qualität des Produkts.

Frauen in der Industrie. Besteht für Frauen Chancengleichheit in Führungspositionen? Technik steht bei der Erziehung von Mädchen hinten an, was mit dazu beiträgt, daß Frauen in der Industrie schlechtere Chancen haben als Männer. Dazu kommt die Doppelbelastung Familie und Beruf. Aber durch neue Techniken und neue Medien werden immer mehr Arbeitsplätze nach Hause verlegt werden können.

Soziale Einrichtungen. Die BMW AG gibt im Jahr über 900 Millionen DM für soziale Aufwendungen aus. Eine sichere Altersversorgung, Weiterbildungsmaßnahmen, Familienheimfahrten, Erholungsaufenthalte, das Gesundheitswesen sind nur einige der Aufgaben, denen sich ein Unternehmen aus seiner sozialen Verantwortung heraus widmet. Sie wird in Zukunft noch an Bedeutung gewinnen.

Reisen: Einzelheiten   Travel: Details

Der Familien-Paß.
Damit steigen groß und klein besonders günstig ein.

Ein ganzes Jahr lang fahren und sparen.

Der Familien-Paß kostet 200 DM. Damit zahlen Sie bei jedem Fahrausweis für einfache Fahrt oder Hin- und Rückfahrt nur die Hälfte des normalen Fahrpreises, für den DB-Schienenverkehr sowie in den Bahnbussen, in den Bussen der Omnibus-Verkehrsgemeinschaft Bahn/Post, der Regionalverkehrsgesellschaften nach Maßgabe ihrer Tarife (Omnibusverkehrsbetrieb AUTOKRAFT GmbH, Kiel; Kraftverkehr GmbH [KVG], Stade; Regionalverkehr Hannover GmbH [RVH], Hannover; Regionalverkehr Köln GmbH [RKV], Köln und Regionalverkehr Oberbayern GmbH [RVO], München) und auf den Gemeinschaftslinien der DB bzw. der Deutschen Bundespost mit anderen Verkehrsunternehmen, soweit dies in den Linienbestimmungen der Gemeinschaftslinien festgelegt ist.

Was Sie bei S-Bahnen und Verkehrsverbünden beachten sollten.
Die ermäßigten Fahrausweise zum Familien-Paß gelten uneingeschränkt bei allen Fahrten, die über die „Grenzen" von S-Bahnen und Verkehrsverbünden hinwegführen. Also immer dann, wenn Ihre Reise z. B. in einen Verkehrsverbund hinein- oder aus einem Verkehrsverbund herausführt.
Für Fahrten innerhalb der Bereiche folgender S-Bahnen und Verkehrsverbünde gilt die Familien-Paß-Ermäßigung nicht:
S-Bahn Köln, Verkehrsverbund Rhein-Ruhr (VRR), Frankfurter Verkehrsverbund (FVV), Hamburger Verkehrsverbund (HVV), Großraumverkehr Hannover, Münchener Verkehrsverbund (MVV), Verkehrsverbund Stuttgart (VVS), Verkehrsgemeinschaft Deutsche Bundesbahn/Bremer Straßenbahn AG (DB/BSAG).

Im Bereich des VRR gibt es eine Ausnahme: In den Preiszonen R – R 4 des Regionaltarifs können Sie ermäßigte Fahrausweise zum Familien-Paß lösen. Sollten Sie innerhalb der Verkehrsverbünde Züge benutzen, für die Verbundfahrausweise nicht gelten, bekommen Sie auch hier die Familien-Paß-Ermäßigung.

Das Doppel zum Familien-Paß.

Zum Familien-Paß gibt es ohne Mehrpreis ein Doppel. Damit können die beiden Elternteile mit Kindern gleichzeitig zu verschiedenen Zielen reisen.

Wo und wie erhalten Sie den Familien-Paß und die ermäßigten Fahrausweise?

Den Familien-Paß und die ermäßigten Fahrausweise gibt es bei den Fahrkartenausgaben, DER-Reisebüros oder den anderen Verkaufsagenturen der Bahn. Sind Fahrausweisautomaten vorhanden und betriebsbereit, müssen Halbpreiskarten unter 51 km aus Automaten gelöst werden.

Zum Kauf des Passes bringen Sie bitte Ihren Personalausweis oder Ihr Familienstammbuch mit. Für Kinderausweise sind Lichtbilder erforderlich. Die ermäßigten Fahrausweise bekommen Sie gegen Vorlage des Familien-Passes, des Paß-Doppels oder des Kinderausweises. Fahrausweise unter 51 km für einfache Fahrt oder Hin- und Rückfahrt sind nur an dem Tag gültig, der auf den Fahrausweisen steht. Fahrausweise ab 51 km für einfache Fahrt gelten 4 Tage, für Hin- und Rückfahrt 2 Monate.

Wer fährt mit?

Familien, Ehepaare und Alleinstehende mit Kindern, d. h. eheliche und für ehelich erklärte Kinder. Adoptivkinder, nichteheliche Kinder und Stiefkinder, Pflegekinder nach dem Bundeskindergeldgesetz. Die Kinder dürfen noch keine 18 Jahre alt sein. Sie müssen unverheiratet sein und im gemeinsamen Haushalt leben. Es können also auch Ehepaare ohne Kinder sowie Elternteile mit mindestens 1 Kind bis zum vollendeten 18. Lebensjahr (hierzu zählen auch Kinder unter 4 Jahren) den Familien-Paß in Anspruch nehmen.

Bedingung ist, daß immer 2 Personen zusammen auf die Reise gehen. Kinder können auch alleine fahren. Dafür gibt's einen Kinderausweis zum Familien-Paß. Er gilt solange wie der Familien-Paß der Eltern.

Reisen mit dem Familien-Paß. Wo und wie nutzt man ihn?

Die ermäßigten Fahrausweise gelten in allen Personenzügen. Für Fahrten in zuschlagpflichtigen FD und Schnellzügen mit Fahrausweisen bis 50 km (einschl.) sowie in zuschlagpflichtigen IC werden zu den ermäßigten Fahrausweisen FD-, D- bzw. IC-Zuschläge zum halben Preis ausgegeben. Für TEE ist der volle tarifmäßige Zuschlag zu zahlen. Der Familien-Paß gilt nicht in Autoreisezügen und nicht bei Sonderfahrten. Alle mit dem Familien-Paß oder dem Doppel gemeinsam reisenden Familienmitglieder fahren in derselben Klasse. Sie können die Fahrt unterbrechen, Umwege fahren und sogar Rundreisen buchen.
Wenn Sie während Ihrer Reise von der 2. in die 1. Klasse umsteigen wollen, müssen Sie den Unterschied zwischen den ermäßigten Fahrpreisen beider Klassen zuzahlen.

Was kosten Ihre Reisen mit dem Familien-Paß?

Ihre Reisen mit dem Familien-Paß Der durch den Familien-Paß ermäßigte Fahrpreis beträgt:			pro Erwachsener (einfache Fahrt) DM		pro Kind unter 12. J. (einfache Fahrt) DM	
von	nach	km	2. Klasse	1. Klasse	2. Klasse	1. Klasse
1. Offenburg	– Freudenstadt	73	7,50	11,50	3,75	5,75
2. Hannover	– Lüneburg	129	12,50	19,00	6,25	9,50
3. Dortmund Hbf	– Bad Harzburg	291	28,00	42,00	14,00	21,00
4. Frankfurt (Main)	– Essen	300	28,00	42,00	14,00	21,00
5. Frankfurt (Main)	– München Hbf	423	40,00	60,00	20,00	30,00
6. Köln Hbf	– Regensburg Hbf	563	54,00	81,00	27,00	40,50
7. München Hbf	– Hannover	639	59,50	89,50	29,75	44,75
8. München Hbf	– Bremen Hbf	761	73,00	109,50	36,50	54,75
9. Hamburg	– Freiburg (Brsg)	814	75,50	113,50	37,75	56,75
10. Stuttgart	– Flensburg	903	83,50	125,50	41,75	62,75

Paßbesitzer zahlen für alle zuschlagpflichtigen FD-Züge, D-Züge und IC nur den halben Zuschlag einheitlich in 1. und 2. Klasse, also beim FD- und D-Zug jeweils 1,50 DM, beim IC 2,50 DM.
TEE-Zuschlag: 10,– DM

Tarifstand 1.1.19..